Lecture Notes in Computer Science 4729

Commenced Publication in 1973
Founding and Former Series Editors:
Gerhard Goos, Juris Hartmanis, and Jan van Leeu

Francesco Mele   Giuliana Ramella
Silvia Santillo   Francesco Ventriglia (Eds.)

Advances in Brain, Vision, and Artificial Intelligence

Second International Symposium, BVAI 2007
Naples, Italy, October 10-12, 2007
Proceedings

 Springer

Volume Editors

Francesco Mele
Giuliana Ramella
Silvia Santillo
Francesco Ventriglia
CNR, Istitute of Cybernetics "Eduardo Caianiello"
Pozzuoli (NA), Italy
E-mail: {f.mele, g.ramella, s.santillo}@cib.na.cnr.it
E-mail: franco@ulisse.cib.na.cnr.it

Library of Congress Control Number: 2007936295

CR Subject Classification (1998): I.2.10, I.4, I.5, J.3, F.1, F.2

LNCS Sublibrary: SL 6 – Image Processing, Computer Vision, Pattern Recognition, and Graphics

ISSN   0302-9743
ISBN-10   3-540-75554-3 Springer Berlin Heidelberg New York
ISBN-13   978-3-540-75554-8 Springer Berlin Heidelberg New York

Springer is a part of Springer Science+Business Media

springer.com

© Springer-Verlag Berlin Heidelberg 2007

Typesetting: Camera-ready by author, data conversion by Scientific Publishing Services, Chennai, India
Printed on acid-free paper   SPIN: 12172504   06/3180   5 4 3 2 1 0

Preface

Understanding the mechanisms involved in vision and intelligent behavior of the brain, both from a natural and artificial point of view, demands more and more multidisciplinary and integrated approaches of different disciplines: biophysics and neurobiology, visual and cognitive sciences and theoretical neuroscience being only a small sample.

The Brain, Vision and Artificial Intelligence Symposium 2007 (BVAI 2007, Naples, Italy, October 10-12, 2007) was the second edition of a multidisciplinary symposium that aims at gathering scientists involved in the study of basic brain, natural vision, artificial vision, and artificial intelligence to promote discussion, exchange of ideas, and integration.

BVAI 2007 was organized by researchers of the Institute of Cybernetics "E. Caianiello" of the Italian National Research Council, Pozzuoli, Italy (ICIB-CNR), with the support of the Italian Institute for Philosophical Studies (IISF). It was sponsored by EBSA (European Biophysics Societies Association), GIRPR (Italian Group of Researchers in Pattern Recognition), MARS (Microgravity Advanced Research Support) Center, NEATEK SpA, PAN (Palazzo delle Arti Napoli), SINS (Italian Society for Neurosciences), and Regione Campania. Travel grants were provided for deserving young participants by EBSA, SINS and GIRPR. The symposium was held under the auspices of the AI*IA (Italian Association of Artificial Intelligence), Comune di Napoli - Assessorato alla Cultura and SIBPA (Italian Society of Pure and Applied Biophysics), and with the help of the MQC^2 (Macroscopic Quantum Coherence and Computing) Association.

The scientific program included the participation of eight invited speakers, selected among international leading scientists in the above-mentioned fields: Michael Arbib, University of Southern California (USA), Matteo Carandini, The Smith-Kettlewell Eye Research Institute (USA), Karl Gegenfurtner, Justus-Liebig University (Germany), Petr Lansky, Academy of Sciences (Czech Republic), José del R. Millán, IDIAP Research Institute (Switzerland), Oliviero Stock, IRST and Fondazione Bruno Kessler (Italy), Massimo Tistarelli, University of Sassari (Italy), John K. Tsotsos, York University (Canada). Furthermore, the program included 50 contributions from worldwide participants, presented in plenary oral and poster sessions. The peer-reviewing process for the papers was performed by the Scientific Committee, including distinguished members of the scientific community, together with a number of additional reviewers, appointed by the Scientific Commitee members. The accepted contributions were selected among about 80 papers submitted to BVAI 2007.

In this volume, all contributions to the symposium have been gathered according to an increasing degree of abstraction, going from the most elemental aspects of the visual processes to the most complex cognitive ones. The material has been structured into the following parts: Basic Models in Visual Sciences, Cortical Mechanism of Vision, Color Processing in Natural Vision, Action-Oriented Vision, Visual Recognition and Attentive Modulation, Biometric Recognition, Image Segmentation and Recognition, Disparity Calculation and Noise Analysis, Signal Identification in Neural

Models, Natural and Artificial Representation Issues in Artificial Intelligence, Meaning-Interaction-Emotion, Robot Navigation and Control. In our opinion, these topics can be considered the flagstones paving the road to the ongoing integration among research in brain, vision and intelligence. We hope that this volume provides new insights and is the basis of constructive discussions.

We would like to thank the invited speakers and all the contributors, the members of the Scientific Committees, including the additional reviewers and all the participants. Acknowledgements are due to all our sponsors (ICIB-CNR, IISF, EBSA, GIRPR, MARS Center, NEATEK SpA, PAN, SINS, Regione Campania) for their financial contribution. We would like to acknowledge the Steering Committee members for their advice and support. A special thanks goes to the Local Committee and Secretariat members, who provided us with helpful assistance.

July 2007

Francesco Mele
Giuliana Raella
Silvia Santillo
Francesco Ventriglia

Organization

BVAI 2007 was organized by researchers of the Institute of Cybernetics "E. Caianiello" of the Italian National Research Council (ICIB-CNR), Pozzuoli, Italy.

Conference Chairs

General Chairs

Francesco Mele and Francesco Ventriglia
ICIB-CNR, Pozzuoli (Naples), Italy

Program Chairs

Giuliana Ramella and Silvia Santillo
ICIB-CNR, Pozzuoli (Naples), Italy

Steering Committee

Massimo De Gregorio (ICIB-CNR)
Vito Di Maio (ICIB-CNR)
Maria Frucci (ICIB-CNR)
Carlo Musio (ICIB-CNR)
Gabriella Sanniti di Baja (ICIB-CNR)

Scientific Committee

Moshe Abeles (Israel)
Igor Aleksander (UK)
Shun-ichi Amari (Japan)
Carlo Arcelli (Italy)
Michele Barbi (Italy)
Nicoletta Berardi (Italy)
Josef Bigun (Sweden)
Giuseppe Boccignone (Italy)
Roman Borisyuk (UK)
Alfred Bruckstein (Israel)
Ernesto Burattini (Italy)
Antonio Calabrese (Italy)
Leo Chalupa (USA)
Gustavo Deco (Spain)
Péter Érdi (USA)

Anna Esposito (Italy)
Stefano Fusi (Switzerland)
Josef Kittler (UK)
Zoe Kourtzi (UK)
R. Beau Lotto (UK)
Brian Lovell (Australia)
Gerard Medioni (USA)
Michele Migliore (Italy)
Takako Nishi (Japan)
Nicolai Petkov (The Netherlands)
John Rinzel (USA)
Laura Sacerdote (Italy)
Carles Sierra (Spain)
Kostas Stathis (UK)
Mriganka Sur (USA)
Cloe Taddei-Ferretti (Italy)
Giancarlo Tassinari (Italy)
Settimo Termini (Italy)
Francesca Toni (UK)
Giuseppe Trautteur (Italy)
Shimon Ullman (Israel)
Vincent Walsh (UK)
Barbara Webb (UK)

Additional Referees

Michael Arbib (USA)
Manuel Atencia (Spain)
Andrew Bagshaw (UK)
Anthony N. Burkitt (USA)
Rich Clarke (UK)
Simon Colton (UK)
Paolo Coraggio (Italy)
Francesco Cutugno (Italy)
Massimo De Gregorio (Italy)
Sergio De Nicola (Italy)
Pilar Dellunde (Spain)
Salvatore Di Gregorio (Italy)
Vito Di Maio (Italy)
Brent Doiron (USA)
Alessandro Farini (Italy)
Ernst Gebetsroither (Spain)
Sindhu Joseph (Spain)
Rajesh Krishnan (UK)
Priscila M.V. Lima (Brazil)
Paul-Amaury Matt (UK)

Francesco Mele (Italy)
Giovanni Minei (Italy)
Carlo Musio (Italy)
Paolo Napoletano (Italy)
Alfredo Petrosino (Italy)
Roberto Prevete (Italy)
Giuliana Ramella (Italy)
Gabriella Sanniti di Baja (Italy)
Carlo Sansone (Italy)
Samuel D. Schwarzkopf (UK)
Oliviero Stock (Italy)
Jamie Theobald (UK)
Francesco Ventriglia (Italy)

Local Committee

Antonio Cotugno (ICIB-CNR)
Salvatore Piantedosi (ICIB-CNR)

Secretariat

Paolo Coraggio (University of Naples "Federico II")
Luigia Cristino (ICIB-CNR)
Silvia Rossi (University of Naples "Federico II")

Sponsoring and Endorsing Institutions

BVAI 2007 was organized with the support of the Italian Institute for Philosophical Studies (IISF).

It was sponsored by EBSA (European Biophysics Societies Association), GIRPR (Italian Group of Researchers in Pattern Recognition), MARS (Microgravity Advanced Research Support) Center, NEATEK SpA, PAN (Palazzo delle Arti Napoli), SINS (Italian Society for Neurosciences), and Regione Campania.

The symposium was held under the auspices of the AI*IA (Italian Association of Artificial Intelligence), Comune di Napoli - Assessorato alla Cultura and SIBPA (Italian Society of Pure and Applied Biophysics), and with the help of the MQC^2 (Macroscopic Quantum Coherence and Computing) Association.

Francesco Maio (Italy)
Giovanni Miele (Italy)
Carlo Mario (Italy)
Paolo Napoletano (Italy)
Alfredo Petrosino (Italy)
Roberto Prevete (Italy)
Giuliana Ramella (Italy)
Gabriele Schenk di Bros (Italy)
Carlo Sansone (Italy)
Samuel O. Schwarzkopf (UK)
Oliver Shea (Italy)
Isaac Theobald (UK)
Francesco Ventriglia (Italy)

Local Committee

Antonio Origlia (IIT-CNR)
Salvatore Piantadosi (IIT-CNR)

Secretariat

Pablo Cassaggio (University of Naples Federico II)
Luigia Cristino (ICB-CNR)
Silvia Rossi (University of Naples Federico II)

Sponsoring and Endorsing Institutions

BVAI 2007 was organised with the support of the Italian Institute for Philosophical Studies (IISF).

It was sponsored by IBRA, European Biophysics Societies Association (EBSA), Italian Group of Researchers in Pattern Recognition, MARS srl, FEI, Leica Microsystems, SpringerLink, Camera of MATTM SpA, EANN, Olympus Italia, Naples Neuroscience Society for Neurosciences, and Regione Campania.

The symposium also had under the auspices of the AIIA (Italian Association of Artificial Intelligence), Cyber Club Biomedica, Associazione Cotrau and SIBPA (Italian Society of Pure and Applied Biophysics), and with the help of the MVC (Microscopic Quantitative Cytochrome and Computing) Association.

Table of Contents

Action Oriented Vision

Visual Recognition and Attentive Modulation

Biometric Recognition

Image Segmentation and Recognition

Disparity Calculation and Noise Analysis

Signal Identification in Neural Models

Natural and Artificial Representation Issues in Artificial Intelligence

Meaning, Interaction and Emotion

Robot Navigation and Control

Physiology of Simple Photoreceptors in the Abdominal Ganglion of *Onchidium*

Takako Nishi [1], Kyoko Shimotsu[2], and Tsukasa Gotow[2]

[1] Laboratory of Physiology, Institute of Natural Sciences,
Senshu University, 2-1-1 Higashimita Kawasaki 214-8580, Japan
nishi@isc.senshu-u.ac.jp

[2] Laboratory for Neuroanatomy, Department of Neurology, Kagoshima University Graduate School of Medical and Dental Sciences, 8-35-1 Sakuragaoka Kagoshima 890-8520, Japan
tsukasa@m.kufm.kagoshima-u.ac.jp

Abstract. Simple photoreceptors without microvilli or cilia, the photoresponsive neurons, designated as A-P-1, Es-1, Ip-2, and Ip-1, exist in the abdominal ganglion of sea slug *Onchidium*. Of these, A-P-1 and Es-1 respond to light with a depolarizing receptor potential, caused by the closing of light-dependent, cGMP-gated K^+ channels, whereas Ip-2 and Ip-1 are hyperpolarized by light, owing to the opening of the same K^+ channels. Studies show the first demonstration of a new type of cGMP cascade, in which Ip-2 and Ip-1 cells are hyperpolarized when light activates GC through a Go-type G-protein. This new cascade thus contrasts with the well-known phototransduction cGMP cascade mediated by a Gt-type G-protein, seen in rods and cones as well as A-P-1 and Es-1 cells. Studies also suggest that the *Onchidium* simple photoreceptors and vertebrate simple photoreceptors, called ipRGCs, might be different from the conventional eye photoreceptors, which function as the pattern vision system and that they may be involved in a new sensory modality, the non-visual photoreceptive system, which functions as encoding of ambient light intensities, instead of spatial and temporal resolution. Finally, it is suggested that the *Onchidium* simple photoreceptors operate in the general regulation by light and dark of synaptic transmission of sensory inputs and subsequent behavioral responses.

Keywords: Molluscan photoresponsive neurons; Non-specialized photoreceptors; Non-visual photoreceptive modality; Non-visual function, facilitation/depression.

1 Introduction

There are intrinsically photoresponsive neurons in the abdominal ganglion of marine mollusk, *Onchidium verruculatum* [7], [16]. We refer to these neurons as 'simple' photoreceptors, due to their lack of any specialized structures, such as the microvilli or cilia characteristic of eye photoreceptors. Recently, similar simple photoreceptors, the intrinsically photosensitive retinal ganglion cells (ipRGCs), were discovered in rat and mouse retinas [3], [15].

The simple photoreceptors examined in this work, designated as A-P-1, Es-1, Ip-2, and Ip-1, are located on the abdominal ganglion of the *Onchidium* (Fig. 1A). We have

F. Mele et al. (Eds.): BVAI 2007, LNCS 4729, pp. 1–10, 2007.
© Springer-Verlag Berlin Heidelberg 2007

previously shown that the depolarizing photoreceptor potential of the A-P-1 and Es-1 cells results from the closing of a light-dependent, cGMP-gated K^+ channel [8], [10], [11], (Fig. 1B). We also found that the hyperpolarizing of the other simple photo-receptors, Ip-2 and Ip-1 cells is produced by the opening of the same type of light-dependent, cGMP-gated K^+ channel that becomes closed in A-P-1 or Es-1 cells [11], (Fig. 1C). On the other hand, it has been shown that these simple photoreceptors are not only first-order photosensory cells, but are also second-order interneurons, relaying several kinds of sensory input [6], [12], [13], similar to those of the above ipRGCs (for review, see [4]). A considerable amount of information has been obtained about the intracellular mechanisms of photoresponse of these simple photo-receptors (e.g., [8], [9], [11], [14], [20], [22]). However, almost nothing has yet been established about how these act as the interneurons *in vivo*.

The present study examines their light-sensing and physiological role (the non-visual function) as an interneuron of the simple photoreceptors, which differs from the pattern vision function of conventional (specialized) eye photoreceptors. This result also is of general interest in the field of ipRGCs.

2 Material and Methods

Experimental animals, the opisthobranch (or pulmonate) mollusc *Onchidium verruculatum* weighting 10-15 g, were collected from the intertidal zone of Sakura-jima, Kagoshima, Japan. The circumesophageal ganglia were isolated by dissecting through the mid-dorsal surface of the animal and were isolated after overlying connective tissue had been removed. The procedure for preparing and conditioning of the photoresponsive neurons in the abdominal ganglion of this animal were similar to that described previously [13]. In some experiments, a whole animal, the semi-intact preparation was used to examine the possible electrophysiological correlates of the behavioral phenomena observed.

The normal solution, artificial seawater (ASW) used for continuous perfusion of each preparation, had the following composition (mM): NaCl, 450; KCl, 10; $CaCl_2$, 10; $MgCl_2$ 50; Tris buffer, 10. The pH was 7.8.

For electrophysiology, an individual, identified neuron was inserted with up to four microelectrodes for the recording of membrane potential or current, passing current under visual control. The general techniques of voltage-, current-, and patch-clamp recordings have been fully described in detail elsewhere [8], [10], [11], [14], [21]. For stimulation from nerves, small glass tubes were used for suction electrodes. For intracellular staining, 100 mM $NiCl_2$ was injected into neurons through microelectro-des by means of microinjector manually.

3   Results and Discussion

3.1   Characterization of the Phototransduction of the Simple Photoreceptors A-P-1, Es-1, Ip-2, and Ip-1 in the *Onchidium* Ganglion

As shown in the Introduction and Fig. 1, A-P-1 or Es-1 cells respond to light by becoming depolarized, following the closing of a particular type of light-dependent, cGMP-gated K^+ channel, whereas Ip-2 or Ip-1 cells become hyperpolarized by light, owing to the opening of the same type of channel. The present study suggested a new type of cGMP cascade, in which Ip-2 and Ip-1 cells (Ip-2/Ip-1) are hyperpolarized when light activates guanylate cyclase (GC) through a Go-type G-protein, leading to an increase in the level of second messenger cGMP, thereby leading to the opening of the light-dependent, cGMP-gated K^+ channels [11], [14], [22]. We have also shown that A-P-1 and Es-1 cells (A-P-1/Es-1) are depolarized when light activates phosphodiesterase (PDE) through a Gt-type G-protein, leading to a decrease in the level of the same cGMP, thereby leading to the closing of the same K^+ channels, [8], [10], [11], [21], as in the phototransduction of eye photoreceptors, rods or cones (for review, see [27]). A mechanism similar to that of the above new phototransduction in Ip-2 and Ip-1 cells, in which a G-protein is involved in the activation of GC to increase internal cGMP levels, has been already shown in the scallop ciliary hyperpolarizing eye photoreceptors [5]. However, they have provided no evidence that identifies whether the G-protein involved in the mechanism is Gi or Go. Unfortunately, a light-absorbing photopigment, such as a melanopsin ([25], see also Table1), has not yet been found in the *Onchidium* simple photoreceptors.

Table 1. Comparison of simple photoreceptors and eye photoreceptors

	Refs.	Phoresponse (Receptor potential)	Visual pigments	Morphology	Characteristics of photoresponse	Function
Simple photoreceptors						
Onchidium A-P-1/ Es-1	This	Depolarization		Non-specialized, simple structures	Slow kinetics (Several tens of second)	
Onchidium Ip-2 / Ip-1	text	Hyperpolarization	Rhodopsin-like?	and	and	Non-visual photorooeptive modality
Mammals ipRGCs	Berson et al. (2002) Hatter et al. (2002) Qiu et al. (2005)	Depolarization	Melanopsin	Second-order neurons (In addition to first-order photosensory cells)	Little adaptation	
Eye photoreceptors						
Pecten Proximal cells	McReynolds & Gorman (1970)	Depolarization	Rhodopsin	Specialized-microvilli	Fast kinetics (A few ms)	Pattern vision system
Distal cells	Kojima et al (1997)	Hyperpolarization		Specialized-cilia	and	
Vertebrates Rod/Cone	Berson (2003)	Hyperpolarization	Rhodopsin	Specialized-cilia	Adaptation	

On the other hand, a remarkable characteristic of these photoresponses of simple A-P-1/Es-1 and Ip-2/Ip-1 is their slow kinetics, as seen in Fig. 1 (B, C). These photoreceptors reach their peak responses 20 to 30 s after the stimulus onset, contrasting with the fast and adaptive response of a few milliseconds in well-known eye photoreceptors (e.g., *Pecten* proximal and distal cells; [19]). Furthermore, as described in the Introduction, these simple photoreceptors are not only first-order photosensory cells, but are also second-order interneurons. Similar characteristics are also shown by a comparison with vertebrate eye photoreceptors, rods and cones. Such a comparison of the simple photoreceptors and specialized eye photoreceptors is

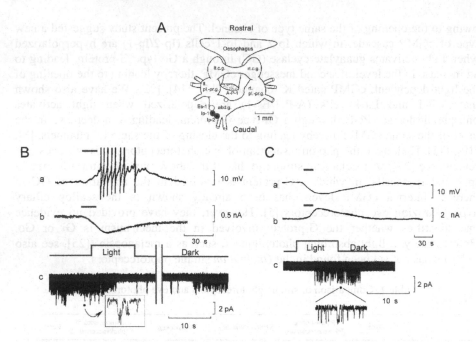

Fig. 1. Non-specialized simple photoreceptors, photoresponsive neurons and their macroscopic and microscopic photoresponses in *Onchidium* ganglia. A: A diagram of the dorsal aspect of central ganglia, showing the approximate positions of the somata of Ip-2 and Ip-1 neurons (filled circles), and A-P-1 and Es-1 neurons (open circles) neurons, which are located on the abdominal ganglion (abd. g.). lt. c. g. and rt. c. g. are the left and right cerebral ganglia, respectively, and lt. pl-pr. g. and rt. pl-pr. g. are the left and right pleuro-parietal ganglia, respectively. B, C: Macroscopic (a, b) and microscopic (c) photoresponses of depolarizing A-P-1 (B) and hyperpolarizing Ip-2 (C) cells. Horizontal short bars above each trace in a and b, and upward step marks above each trace in c show the timings of identical white light. B-a; a depolarizing receptor potential at -50 mV. The top parts of spikes superimposed on the receptor (generator) potential are cut. C-a; a hyperpolarizing receptor potential at -40 mV. B-b, C-b; depolarizing inward K^+ photocurrent responses and hyperpolarizing outward when both cell types are voltage-clamped at -40 mV. B-c; a light-dependent K^+ single-channel current recording from a cell-attached patch of A-P-1. The inward channel current trace at the point mark is shown on the expanded time scale. C-c; the same K^+ single-channel current recording of Ip-2 (modified from ref. 14).

summarized in Table 1. From this Table, it is suggested that the *Onchidium* simple photoreceptors and ipRGCs may be different from the conventional eye photoreceptors, which function as the image-forming visual system (or the pattern vision system), and that they may be involved in a new sensory modality, the non-visual photoreceptive system, which functions as encoding of ambient light intensity levels. In addition, this table also suggests that the ipRGCs may be homologous to (evolved from) the *Onchidium* simple photoreceptors.

3.2 Output Organization of A-P-1, Es-1, Ip-2, and Ip-1

As shown in Fig. 2A, the cell bodies and axonal branches (running of axons) of A-P-1 and Es-1 were simultaneously stained and visualized by the intracellular injection of

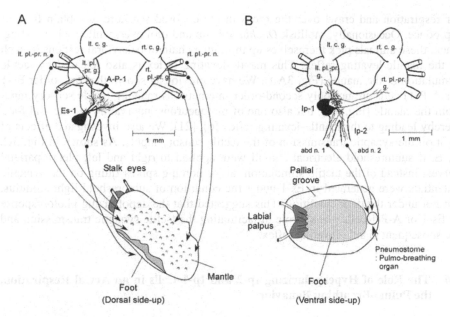

Fig. 2. A: sketch of the dorsal surface of central ganglia showing A-P-1 and Es-1 stained simultaneously with Lucifer Yellow and their nervous (axonal) innervation sending toward the animal body. B: sketch showing Ip-2 and Ip-1 stained simultaneously with Ni^{2+}-rubeanic acid complex and their axonal innervation.

Lucifer Yellow [21]. The initial segment of axon of Es-1 typically branches into three main axons: An axon branch running toward the left side further branches and enters three left pleuro-parietal nerves leaving the left pleuro-parietal ganglion; The second justify at the right side of the line; The rest sent out one branch as the abdominal nerve 1 (abd. n. 1). These axonal branchings were electrophysiologically confirmed by the simultaneous recording of the evoked somatic spike and the subsequent axonal spike in the concerned nerves (data not shown). Further, an anatomical analysis showed that the left and right three pleuro-parietal nerves and the abdominal nerve terminate the whole area of mantle and foot, respectively. Fig. 2B shows the cell bodies and axonal branches of Ip-2 and Ip-1 which were simultaneously stained and visualized by the intracellular injection of Ni^{2+} - rubeanic acid complex. The Ip-2 and Ip-1 cells each send their axonal branches into the abd. n. 1 and abd. n. 2, in the same way. These two axonal branches arising from the cell bodies of Ip-2 and Ip-1 were confirmed by simultaneous recordings of the orthodromic conduction of spike on their branches and its triggered somatic spike (data not shown). The abd. n. 1 and abd. n. 2 sending out their axonal branches were anatomically suggested to terminate around pulmonary sac, connected to pneumostome, and partly to terminate on the visceral organs containing pericardium.

3.3 The Role of Depolarizing Es-1 or A-P-1 Cells

Onchidium is an intertidal and amphibian mollusk. Thus, the animals which submerge at high tide, use gill-trees, but at low tide they interchange with lung (pulmonary sac) for respiration and crawl over the rocks in the exposed seashore, to obtain food or reproduce. Occasionally, mollusk *Onchidium* slip and turn over, while rock-crawling. Then, these animals pick themselves up through a chain of behavioral responses, such as the mantle-levating reflex. This mantle-levating reflex is also released by tactile stimulation of the mantle (Fig. 3A-I). We have previously shown that first-order Es-1 (or A-P-1) cells are not only second-order interneurons relaying tactile sensory input from the mantle (Fig. 3B), but also one of motoneurons innervating mantle and foot, thereby leading to the mantle-levating reflex [6], [21]. We also investigated effects of light on the synaptic transmission of the tactile sensory inputs. As shown in Fig. 3C, D, E, if subthreshold electrical stimuli were applied to right and left pleuro-parietal nerves, instead of the tactile stimulation, all or nothing spikes riding on the synaptic potentials were generated in Es-1 under the condition of subthreshold light stimulus, but not under the dark condition. This suggested that the depolarizing photoresponse of Es-1 or A-P-1 cells plays a role in facilitating the tactile synaptic transmission and the subsequent mantle-levating reflex.

3.4   The Role of Hyperpolarizing Ip-2 and Ip-1 Cells in an Aerial Respiration, the Pulmo-Breathing Behavior

At low tide, amphibian mollusks *Onchidium* open a pneumostome, the orifice of pulmonary sac, to begin an aerial respiration, although they close the pneumostome at high tide. This breathing behavior is also constantly observed at an experimental seawater-aquarium in the room. The present study has suggested that the above opening and closing of pneumostome for respiration depend on at least two kinds of nervous network of the right and left pleuro-parietal nerves relaying sensory inputs of water pressure from the surface of mantle, and the hyperpolarizing Ip-2 and Ip-1 cells sending out motor outputs toward the pneumostome (Fig. 2B). We have already shown that Ip-2 and Ip-1 are connected by low-pass filtering electrical synapses, thereby enabling their cells to establish either synchronous beating or bursting firing [13]. We further investigated the input and output organization of Ip-2 and Ip-1 cells electrophysiologically, with the aid of a recording technique of neural activity from the semi-intact animal preparation [23]. For example, a train of electrical stimuli to abd. n. 1 and/or abd. n. 2 sending out the axonal branches from Ip-2 and Ip-1 cells produced a contraction (the opening) of pneumostome (data not shown). Simultaneous intracellular recordings of membrane potentials from Ip-2 and Ip-1 cells showed that synchronous bursting discharges are depressed by the presynaptic nerve- and/or light-stimulation (Fig. 4). Taken together, these results suggested that the hyperpolarizing photoresponse of simple photoreceptors Ip-2 and Ip-1 plays a role in depressing the synaptic transmission and the subsequent breathing behavior.

3.5   Concluding Remarks and Non-visual Function of Simple Photoreceptors

Simple photoreceptors similar to those of *Onchidium* have long been known in the central ganglion of crayfish [17], [24] and *Aplysia* [1], [2]. However, details of their phototransduction mechanism and function remain unclear. The present study

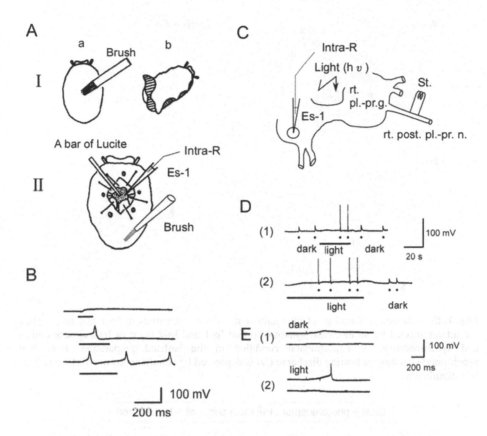

Fig. 3. A-I: the mantle-levating reflex of *Onchidium*. A-II: a semi-intact animal preparation for Es-1. B: firing of spike riding on synaptic potentials induced by tactile stimuli to animal. C: sketch showing the experimental condition in the isolated preparation. D: facilitation of electrical nerve stimulation by light. E: the expanded trace in dark (1) and light (2).

suggested that the *Onchidium* simple photoreceptors as well as ipRGCs function as a new sensory modality, the non-visual system, which is different from the pattern vision system of well-known eye photoreceptors, encoding spatial and temporal resolution. As the non-visual function of ipRGCs, it is known that they contribute to pupillar light reflex and circadian clocks. However, nothing is known about their function as interneurons (Fig. 5).

The present study showed that *Onchidium* simple photoreceptors may modulate the general synaptic transmission and behavioral responses, such as the mantle-levating reflex and aerial respiration. Fig. 5 shows a scheme to explain such a non-visual function of the interneurons. The depolarizing (excitatory) responses of simple photoreceptors may facilitate the timing and frequency of spike generation. Conversely, the hyperpolarizing (inhibitory) photoresponses may depress those same timing and frequency. On the other hand, another respiratory behavior of the pond snail *Lymnaea* is well-known [26]. However, there is no participation of photoreceptive neurons in its respiration.

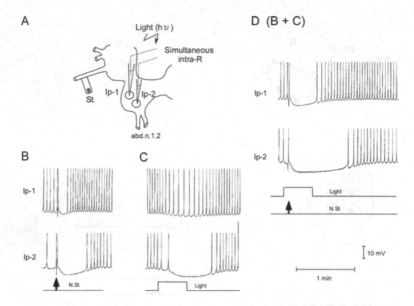

Fig. 4. Simultaneous recordings of intracellular membrane potentials of Ip-1 and Ip-2. They are interconnected by an electrical synapse, so that Ip-1 and Ip-2 burst or beat spontaneously and synchronously. A: experimental condition in the isolated preparation. Note that synchronous bursting or beating discharge (D) is depressed by simultaneous nerve (B) and light (C) stimulation.

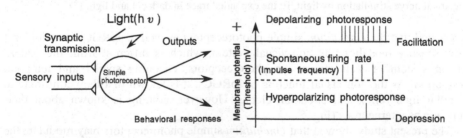

Fig. 5. Non - image - forming visual (Non-visual) function of *Onchidium* simple photoreceptors

Finally, the present results might be useful in understanding the phototransduction mechanism and function as interneurons of ipRGCs.

Acknowledgments. This study was supported in part by a 2007 Senshu University research grant for the study of *Onchidium* nervous systems.

References

1. Andresen, M.C., Brown, A.M.: Photoresponses of a Sensitive Extraretinal Photoreceptor in Aplysia. J. Physiol. 287, 267–282 (1979)
2. Arvanitaki, A., Chalazonitis, N.: Nervous Inhibition. In: Florey, E. (ed.) Excitatory and Inhibitory Processes Initiated by Light and Infra-red Radiations in Single Identifiable Nerve Cells (Giant Ganglion cells of Aplysia), pp. 194–231. Pergamon, Oxford (1961)
3. Berson, D.M., Dunn, F.A., Takao, M.: Phototransduction by Retinal Ganglion Cells that Set the Circadian Clock. Science 295, 1070–1073 (2002)
4. Berson, D.M.: Strange Vision: Ganglion Cells as Circadian Photoreceptors. Trends Neurosci. 26, 314–320 (2003)
5. Gomez, M., Nasi, E.: Light Transduction in Invertebrate Hyperpolarizing Photoreceptors: Possible Involvement of a Go-regulated Guanylate Cyclase. J. Neurosci. 20, 5254–5263 (2000)
6. Gotow, T., Tateda, H., Kuwabara, M.: The Function of Photoexcitive Neurones in the Central Ganglia for Behavioral Activity of the Marine Mollusc Onchidium verruculatum. J. Comp. Physiol. 83, 361–376 (1973)
7. Gotow, T.: Decrease of K^+ Conductance Underlying a Depolarizing Photoresponse of a Molluscan Extraocular Photoreceptor. Experientia 42, 52–54 (1986
8. Gotow, T.: Photoresponses of an Extraocular Photoreceptor Associated with a Decrease in Membrane Conductance in an Opisthobranch Mollusc. Brain Res. 479, 120–129 (1989)
9. Gotow, T., Nishi, T.: Roles of Cyclic GMP and Inositol Trisphosphate in Phototransduction of the Molluscan Extraocular Photoreceptor. Brain Res. 557, 121–128 (1991)
10. Gotow, T., Nishi, T., Kijima, H.: Single K^+ Channels Closed by Light and Opened by Cyclic GMP in Molluscan Extra-ocular Photoreceptor Cells. Brain Res. 662, 268–272 (1994)
11. Gotow, T., Nishi, T.: Light-dependent K^+ Channels in the Mollusc Onchidium Simple Photoreceptors arc Opened by cGMP. J. Gen. Physiol. 120, 581–597 (2002)
12. Gotow, T., Nishi, T., Nakagawa, S.: Membrane Properties as Interneurons of the Extraocular Photoreceptors in the Onchidium Ganglia. Neurosci. Res. 50, S190 (2004)
13. Gotow, T., Shimotsu, K., Nishi, T.: Non-image Forming Function of the Extraocular Photoreceptors in the Ganglion of the Sea Slug Onchidium. In: De Gregorio, M., Di Maio, V., Frucci, M., Musio, C. (eds.) BVAI 2005. LNCS, vol. 3704, pp. 136–145. Springer, Heidelberg (2005)
14. Gotow, T., Nishi, T.: Involvement of a Go-type G-protein Coupled to Guanylate Cyclase in the Phototransduction cGMP Cascade of Molluscan Simple Photoreceptors. Brain Res. 1144, 42–51 (2007)
15. Hattar, S., Liao, H.-W., Takao, M., Berson, D.M., Yau, K.-W.: Melanopsin-Containing Retinal Ganglion Cells: Architecture, Projections, and Intrinsic Photosensitivity. Science 295, 1065–1070 (2002)
16. Hisano, N., Tateda, H., Kuwabara, M.: Photosensitive Neurones in the Marine Pulmonate Mollusc Onchidium verruculatum. J. Exp. Biol. 57, 651–660 (1972)
17. Kennedy, D.: Physiology of Photoreceptor Neurons in the Abdominal Nerve Cord of the Crayfish. J. Gen. Physiol. 46, 551–572 (1963)
18. Kojima, D., Terakita, A., Ishikawa, T., Tsukahara, Y., Maeda, A., Shichida, Y.: A Novel Go-mediated Phototransduction Cascade in Scallop Visual Cells. J. Biol. Chem. 272, 22979–22982 (1997)
19. McReynolds, J.S., Gorman, A.L.: Photoreceptor Potentials of Opposite Polarity in the Eye of the Scallop, Pecten irradians. J. Gen. Physiol. 56, 376–391 (1970)

20. Nishi, T., Gotow, T.: A light-induced Decrease of Cyclic GMP is Involved in the Photoresponse of Molluscan Extraocular Photoreceptors. Brain Res. 485, 185–188 (1989)
21. Nishi, T., Gotow, T.: A Neural Mechanism for Processing Colour Information in Molluscan Extra-ocular Photoreceptors. J. Exp. Biol. 168, 77–91 (1992)
22. Nishi, T., Gotow, T.: Light-increased cGMP and K^+ Conductance in the Hyperpolarizing Receptor Potential of Onchidium Extra-ocular Photoreceptors. Brain Res. 809, 325–336 (1998)
23. Nishi, T., Gotow, T., Nakagawa, S.: Non-image-forming Visual Function of the Simple Photoreceptors in the Sea Slug Onchidium Ganglion. Neurosci. Res. 55, S176 (2006)
24. Prosser, C.L.: Responses to Illumination of the Eyes and Caudal Ganglion. J. Cell Comp. Physiol. 4, 363–378 (1934)
25. Qiu, X., Kumbalasiri, T., Carlson, S.M., Wong, K.Y., Krishna, V., Provencio, I., Berson, D.M.: Induction of Photosensitivity by Heterologous Expression of Melanopsin. Nature 433, 745–749 (2005)
26. Syed, N.I., Harrison, D., Winlow, W.: Respiratory behavior in the Pond Snail Lynmaea stagnalis I. Behavioral Analysis and the Identification of Motor Neurons. J. Comp. Physiol A 169, 541–555 (1991)
27. Yau, K.-W., Baylor, D.A.: Cyclic GMP-activated Conductance of Retinal Photoreceptor Cells. Annu. Rev. Neurosci. 12, 289–327 (1989)

Diffuse Nerve Net of *Hydra* Revealed by NADPH-Diaphorase Histochemical Labeling

Luigia Cristino, Vittorio Guglielmotti, Carlo Musio, and Silvia Santillo[CA]

Istituto di Cibernetica "Eduardo Caianiello" del CNR,
Via Campi Flegrei 34, I-80078 Pozzuoli (Napoli), Italy
{l.cristino,v.guglielmotti,c. musio,[CA]s.santillo}@cib.na.cnr.it

Abstract. The processing of the information coming from the external environment, including the interactions between molecular and cellular key-players involved in, is perhaps the "hard problem" in the cybernetic approach to the nervous system. As a whole, this information shapes the behavioral activity of an organism. The problem is faced considering the information processing flow in action from the lower organisms' nervous elements to the higher cognitive levels of man. The cnidarian *Hydra* is the first organism of the zoological scale in which a nervous system is encountered. It is composed by isolated nerve cells scattered throughout the animal body constituting a diffuse nerve net for the input-output activity. In this paper is reported, for the first time in *Hydra* nerve net, the histochemical indication of a NADPH-diaphorase (NADPH-d) activity as putative marker of nitric oxide synthase (NOS) activity. The identification and the tentative localization of nitric oxide (NO) in *Hydra* is discussed in the light of the emerging role that such a signaling molecule exerts in sensory (visual particularly) and motor neural systems.

1 Introduction

Comparative Neurobiology's main goal regards the solving of cutting-edge queries on the evolution of the nervous system. In particular, how does a simple nervous system, without centralization and with a rough isotropic distribution of its elements, generate and modulate a periodic behavior according to the environmental issues and demands? Also, are the key-elements of neurotransmission and signaling pathways already expressed and localized, at different cellular levels, in so-called simple animal model and hence phylogenetically conserved in higher organisms?

Local circuits, or networks, in the central nervous system are responsible for considerable information processing and integration in which sensory information is transformed into appropriate motor outputs. The output of a network depends not only on its inputs, but also on various modulatory mechanisms that modify the neural signal at any level within the network [1].

The neural net of the diploblastic fresh-water coelenterate *Hydra* (Cnidaria, Hydrozoa), with a great economy of specialized structures, enables *Hydra* to produce its periodic shortening-elongation behavior, which has a high biological significance for its survival, being linked to osmoregulation and locomotion related to feeding.

F. Mele et al. (Eds.): BVAI 2007, LNCS 4729, pp. 11–20, 2007.

Hydra is the first known metazoan among animal phyla having a nervous system; it belongs to Cnidaria, an early-diverging metazoan phylum [2]. Since a couple of century *Hydra* has been a suitable model for experimental studies on the evolution of developmental mechanisms [3].

Cnidaria (and *Hydra* among them) nerve nets share with the nervous systems of organisms at higher levels in the zoological phylogenetic scale many basic synaptic features, including transmission and conduction mechanisms, and neurotransmitter types [4]. A major difference with bilaterian nervous systems is that *Hydra* nerve net seems to be strongly peptidergic [5]. In fact cnidarians produce large amount of neuropeptides that may function as neurotransmitters, neuromodulators and also as neurohormones in the control of developmental processes. Although *Hydra* nervous system is primitive, many neurons co-express more than one neuropeptide for signaling like in higher animals [6]. Nevertheless, data collected by multidisciplinary approaches indicate that several neurotransmitters like glycine, endocannabinoids, and glutamate (AMPA and NMDA receptors) have early evolved in *Hydra* as part of phylogenetically old behavioral control systems [7].

On the contrary, a minor body of evidence is available about the existence and the role of nitric oxide (NO) in cnidarian nervous systems. The free radical nitric oxide (NO), although it is not reported as classical neurotransmitter, is an important intracellular and intercellular signaling molecule involved in various physiological processes in vertebrates and invertebrates [8-9]. In particular it is involved as neural messenger modulating the processing of sensory signals [10]. Several studies have provided strong indications that NO signaling pathway is widespread throughout the phylogenetic scale from invertebrates, including few species of cnidarian (see section 3), to higher vertebrates and mammals. NO appears to modulate the response to "olfactory" stimuli in *Hydra* [11], but initial studies on different cnidarians, including *Hydra* itself [12-13], have failed to confirm the presence of nitric oxide synthase (NOS, the enzyme responsible for synthesising NO) in any of their neurons. Evidence for the nNOS expression in cnidarians is an essential element to prove NO as an ancestral neurotransmitter.

Here, we apply, for the first time to the *Hydra* nerve net, the NADPH-diaphorase (NADPH-d) staining method to verify the presence and the distribution of putative nitric oxide synthase (NOS) assessing the location of nitric oxide (NO) activity.

2 *Hydra*'s Nerve Net and Neurobehavioral Issues

Hydra is a sessile diblastic organism with radial symmetry. It has a coelenteron and, at the distal end, a mouth (hypostome) surrounded by tentacles. It is characterized by a simple neural net (46), by limited types of sensory input channels and output effectors and by a behavior showing periodically repetitive phases of body shortenings and elongations. Two cell-layers (ectoderm and endoderm) constitute the animal. They are separated by an acellular supporting mesoglea, and are composed by epitheliomuscular cells, *i.e.* epithelial cells containing myofibrils on the face near the mesoglea [2]. Due to the myofibril arrangement, the ectoderm and the endoderm act like an agonist/antagonist system, running respectively the animal shortening and elongation. The ectoderm plays also an ionic active transport in order to balance the ion loss while the endoderm has also the digestive function.

The *Hydra* nerve net triggers, maintains and modulates the animal's behavior, in particular its periodicity [14]. At first glance, the nervous system has the configuration of a simple bidimensional isotropic network, which lies between the ectoderm and the endoderm [15], and does not have a concentration of neuron bodies in ganglia, nor arrangement of neuronal processes in specific pathways (Fig. 1i).

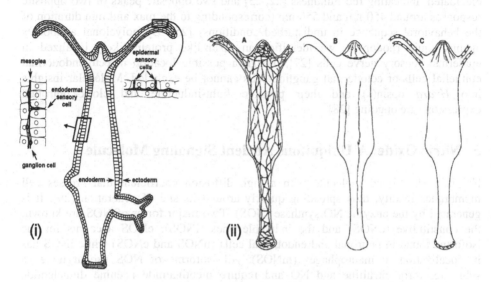

Fig. 1. Location and distribution sketches of nerve cells in *Hydra*. (i) Longitudinal section showing the ectodermal and the endodermal layers, and the arrangement of the nerve net (modified from ref. 20). (ii) Topography of ectodermal nerve cells: A - Ganglion cells, B - Nerve ring and distinctive neurons, C – Sensory cells (modified from ref. 19).

The nervous elements are made of ganglion and sensory neurons with different distribution and concentration (70% of the net neurons lie at the ectodermal side of the mesoglea) [16-17]. Several distinct neuronal subtypes, with different functional properties and with constant and specific location in the animal, can be recognized morphologically and immunochemically [18-19]. A thin nerve ring (consisting of four different subsets of neurons) connected to the nervous net has been observed between the hypostome and the tentacle zone [19]. In the ectoderm the sensory neurons are found in the tentacles and around the mouth, while in the endoderm they are along the body column; they have a putative receptive function [19-20] (Fig. 1ii). Ganglion cells have a more regular distribution pattern spread over the whole animal and are converted to sensory cells when the neurons move from the body column to the hypostome. However, both the ganglion and the sensory neurons may be multifunctional neurons, having from one to four distinct features of a sensory-inter-moto-neurosecretory neuron [19].

The periodic (shortening/elongation) behavior of *Hydra* is exhibited even under absolutely constant environmental conditions and it involves two neuromuscular pacemaker groups that are in a mutual inhibitory interaction [21]. The behavior is completely absent in nerve-free preparations where neurons are experimentally lost.

Hydra responds to light by body contractions and tactic movements [22], showing extraocular photoreception [23-24] since it does not have conventional visual structures; single or clustered photosensitive cells have not yet been identified as well [25]. Our previous studies proved a photo-modulation of the bioelectric correlates of the animal's behavior [25-26]. *Hydra*'s behavioral action spectrum has been elucidated, indicating red blindness [22, 25] and two opposite peaks of two opposite responses around 450 nm and 550 nm (corresponding to the max and min duration of the behavioral sequence in undisturbed conditions) [25]. By polyclonal antibodies against squid rhodopsin, we identified an opsin-like protein likely localized in epidermal sensory nerve cells [27], though a possible location in ecto/endodermal epithelial cells or ectodermal ganglion cells cannot be excluded. Molecular insights into *Hydra* opsin(s) and their possible light-inducible and clock-controlled expressions are ongoing [28].

3 Nitric Oxide: A Ubiquitous Ancient Signaling Molecule

NO is a short-lived molecule with a high diffusion coefficient that crosses cell membranes readily, thus spreading quickly around its site of generation [29]. It is generated by the enzyme NO synthase (NOS). Two major forms of NOS are known: the constitutive (cNOS) and the inducible ones (iNOS). cNOS accounts for the isoforms found in neuronal and endothelial cells (nNOS and eNOS) while iNOS has its localization in macrophages (mNOS). All isoforms of NOS use arginine as substrate, form citrulline and NO and require nicotinamide adenine dinucleotide phosphate (NADPH) as electron donor. The primary structure of brain NOS [30] reveled binding consensus sequences for calmodulin (CaM), FMN, FAD and NADPH displaying a close homology only with cytochrome P-450 reductase (CPR). NOS and CPR are unique in possessing all these binding sites in the same polypeptide to constitute an electron transport chain. The activity of cNOS is regulated by Ca^{2+}/CaM signal. The CaM-complex bent to the enzyme aligns the domini allowing the electrons flux from the reductase domain to the oxygenase one. The iNOS is always active due to its permanent link to the Ca^{2+}/CaM complex, having for it a high affinity. Inside its target cells, NO can activate soluble guanylate cyclase (sGC) and thereby increase the level of the second messenger guanosine 3',5'-cyclic monophosphate (cGMP) [30].

Due to the low homology between known invertebrate and mammalian NOS isoforms, the use of mammalian anti-NOS antisera in invertebrate preparations can provide contradictory results [31]. On the contrary, NADPH-d activity has been widely used as a marker for nNOS activity in vertebrate and invertebrate preparations: this technique remains one of the most suitable procedures to screen for NOS-containing cells. The use of NADPH-d histochemical technique (that catalyzes the NADPH-dependent conversion of a soluble salt in an insoluble visible one) as a marker for nNOS in paraformaldehyde fixed tissues is definitely accepted [32] and is producing a large data collection indicating various signaling function for NO in central nervous and peripheral tissues of the major bilaterian invertebrate groups [33].

Nitric oxide (NO) is thought to play essential roles in signaling from the early stages of the evolution of life [33]. It has been largely identified in mammals in which it supports important functions as neurotransmitter and neuromodulator [34], as well as in major invertebrate *phyla* such as mollusks, annelids, arthropods and cnidarians [7, 12, 33], and in basal eukaryotes such as fungi and plants [35].

Various functions for NO-cGMP pathway have been proved in learning and memory [36], feeding [11, 37], olfaction [38], and regulation of smooth muscle tone [39]. Unexpectedly, NO supplies both sensory and motor modalities for the same behavior but exerted with different strategies. In gastropod feeding, NADPH-d labeling was reported in peripheral putative sensory cells in the herbivorous *Aplysia* and in central motoneurons in the predatory *Pleurobranchaea californica* [40].

Among sensory systems [10], NO plays a crucial control at every level of vision processing [41]. In the vertebrate retina NO/cGMP signaling modulates ion channel functions of photoreceptors [42]. In lower vertebrates NO provides signals in the earliest stages of retinal development [43]. In invertebrates, NADPH staining of the visual structures of insects indicates that NO is generally implicated in visual development and processing [10, 44] while it is a necessary key-player in visual learning tasks in *Octopus* [36]. Recently, it was reported that the NOS/cGMP pathway mediates the entrainment of light responses of the circadian clock in mammals [45].

4 Materials and Methods

About fifty specimens of *Hydra vulgaris* were used for all experiments. Stock cultures were maintained in a medium containing $CaCl_2$ 1 x 10-3 M and EDTA 1.25 x 10-5 M at constant 17±1 °C under a 600 lx 12:12 h light/dark cycle. Animals were fed twice a week with *Artemia salina* nauplii and washed 4 h after the meal. Experimental animals were starved three weeks before the fixative procedure. To move the specimens during each step, before of xylene, a plastic cell strainer was used (BD Falcon). Whole animals were relaxed in a medium solution of 2% ethyluretane (Carlo Erba Reagents) for two minutes and fixed in 4% paraformaldehyde in 0.1 M phosphate buffer (Sigma), pH 7.4 for two hours at 4°C. After, were rinsed thoroughly in phosphate buffer at pH 7.4 (PB) for one hour at room temperature and the last five min. in 0.3% Triton-X 100 in PB. Subsequently, were incubated at 37°C for one hour in the dark in a solution of 1 mg/ml ß-NADPH (Sigma), 0.4 mg/ml (2-2'-benzothiazolyl)-5-styryl-3-(4'-phthalhydrazidyl)-tetrazolium chloride (BSPT) (Sigma) as substrate in 200 μl of N,N-dimethylformamide (ICN Biomedicals), 0.3% Triton-X100 in PB. After incubation, the (whole) animals were rinsed consecutively in PB, in H2O, each for half hour at room temperature, dehydrated in ascending alcohol and finally transferred in xilene for half hour and collected on a coverglass. When the excess of xylene was evaporated the specimens were covered with dense DPX (Aldrich). For the observation at the microscope, the specimens protruding the coverglass were inserted in the hole (ø 12 mm) of a plastic slide, in order to protect them by damage and to leave the free surface of the coverglass to the observation. The slides were observed with a Zeiss Axioskop 2 brightfield microscope and the images were photographed by using a digital camera (Leica DFC 320). Contrast and brightness were adjusted using Adobe PhotoShop 7.0 software (Adobe System).

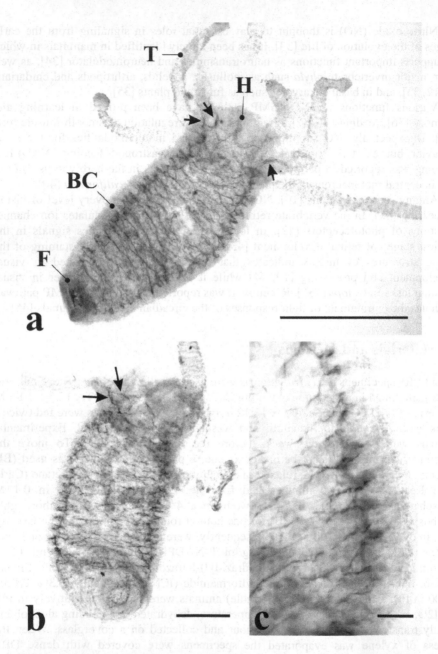

Fig. 2. Nerve net of *Hydra* visualized by NADPH-d labeling in three different whole-mounts preparations. (**a, b**) General views. BC, body column; F, foot; H, head; T, tentacles. Note the NADPH-d reactivity distribution (dark staining) with a network-like arrangement. Arrows point to NADPH-d reactivity near the base of tentacles. (**c**) High magnification of the body column region. Note the marked labelling of nerve fibres. Bars, a) 100 μm, b) 50 μm, c) 20 μm.

5 Results and Discussion

As stated before, the enzyme NOS can be localized by NADPH-d histochemistry. Here we have applied this technique to whole-mount preparations of *Hydra* and revealed a possible NO distribution within the nerve net. The salt substrate BSPT employed in this study enabled to reveal a more precise localization of the diaphorase reaction, because yields a formazan precipitate with osmiophilic and solvent resistant properties which are different from the classic nitroblue tetrazolium salt (NBT) [46]. This substrate is frequently used in the histological procedures for ultrastructural studies of the nervous system [47]. We used hydra whole-mounts because histological sections were less suitable for our purpose due to the thin animal's thickness.

Widespread distribution of NADPH-d is associated with diffuse nerve fibers but not with identified cell body groups (Fig. 2). Consistent staining patterns are regularly diffused along the body column (Fig 2c) while no marked zones are showed in the tentacles with few exceptions represented at the base of tentacles closer to the head (Fig 2a, b). Similarly, no remarkable labeling was observed in the head (nerve ring neurons included) and foot (peduncle and pedal disk included) regions.

In a first instance, the identification of a sharp cellular localization to NADPH-d labeling becomes hazy. This kind of uncertainty is already known for whole-mount preparations of *Hydra*. In fact, Arg-vasopressin-like immunoreactive peptides have been identified in nerve cell subsets throughout the *Hydra* body but with no clear identification of the cell and tissue layer types [48].

Therefore, the attribution of the reactivity pattern to the ectoderm or the endoderm is rather difficult. Our results could fit the distribution pattern and the fiber arrangement of the ectodermal ganglion cells showed in Fig 1ii, although in our experiments no striking labeling is present along the tentacles. According to the latter, it is difficult to report a localization of ectodermal sensory cells for NOS activity because that type of nerve cells is mostly present in tentacles. On the contrary, due to the higher percentage of sensory cells in the endoderm of the body column, the localization of NO activity in such cells cannot be excluded at all. Notably, the distribution pattern found by us has some similarities with the spatial pattern of the CC04$^+$ neurons reported as ectoderm ganglion cells in *H. viridissima* [49].

Nevertheless, our data prove that the distribution of NADPH-d activity in *Hydra*, being restricted to the nerve net only, is certainly indicative of the NO presence at neural level.

Accordingly, the identification of NO-sensitive neural elements is needed to delineate the function of NO in *Hydra* nerve net and its possible involvement in signal processing of motor and/or sensory information. So far, in Cnidaria NO has the following multifunctional roles in effector systems [7]: 1) control of the tentacles' movements in the GSH feeding response of *Hydra* [11]; 2) activation of the slow swimming in *Aglantha* [50]; 3) modulation of the peristaltic muscle contractions in *Renilla* [51]; and 4) triggering of the nematocyst discharge in *Aiptasia* [13]. Only items 2 and 3 reported histochemical evidence for NO.

A role of NO in sensory signals should be deepened also in *Hydra*. The already proposed olfactive task [11] would need further evidences and, presently, cannot be entirely confirmed by our data as tentacles are barely stained. Moreover, an involvement in photosensitive issues seems fascinating. We noted that the distribution of NADPH-d showed here resembles to some extent the fluorescence pattern of the opsin-like protein identified by us [27]. As part of our research on *Hydra* phototransductive processes, searching for putative second messengers of the signal cascade we have obtained by immunohistochemistry early results on the presence of cGMP (unpublished data). By comparison with data showed here, it could be interesting verify if putative photosensitive cells, being likely multifunctional, use cGMP as effector belonging - or not - to the cGMP/NO signal transduction pathway.

A role of NO in the developmental dynamics of neurons and in the mechanisms controlling nerve net formation could be hypothesized too. As known in *Hydra*, neurons are continuously renewed and differentiated from interstitial undifferentiated cells [19]. As a result of a steady state of production/loss, neurons are continuously displaced changing their location (with the exception of nerve ring neurons) [20]. The displacement provides metastable cell phenotypes as many neurons switch their typology, undergoing morphological and immunochemical transformations [19-20]. So NO as small highly flowing molecule could intervene to modulate the complex signaling belonging to those dynamics. This role occurs in lower vertebrates where nNOS expression is indicative of neuroprotective potential effects after neuronal damage [52] and during development of the nervous system [53].

Finally, our data set in a primitive nervous system (likely the oldest one) the histochemical presence of NO acting as ancestral neural messenger with yet unknown physiological tasks. Next investigations and experimental approaches will be hopefully addressed to reveal and clarify the role of that intriguing signaling system.

Acknowledgements

We are grateful to Antonio Cotugno for his skilful work with hydra cultures.

References

1. Katz, P.S.: Evolution and development of neural circuits in invertebrates. Curr. Opin. Neurobiol. 17, 59–64 (2007)
2. Lentz, T.L.: The cell biology of hydra. John Wiley, New York (1966)
3. Steele, R.E.: Developmental signaling in Hydra. Dev. Biol. 248, 199–219 (2002)
4. Mackie, G.O.: The elementary nervous system revisited. Amer. Zool. 30, 907–920 (1990)
5. Grimmelikhuijzen, C., et al.: Neuropeptides in cnidarians. Can. J. Zool. 80, 1690–1702 (2002)
6. Hansen, G.N., Williamson, M., Grimmelikhuijzen, C.J.: A new case of neuropeptide coexpression (RGamide and LWamides) in Hydra, found by whole-mount, two-color double-labeling in situ hybridization. Cell Tissue Res. 308, 157–165 (2002)
7. Kass-Simon, G., Pierobon, P.: Cnidarian chemical neurotransmission, an updated overview. Comp. Biochem. Physiol. A 146, 9–25 (2007)
8. Moncada, S., Palmer, R.M., Higgs, E.A.: Nitric oxide: physiology, pathophysiology, and pharmacology. Pharmacol. Rev. 43, 109–142 (1991)
9. Palumbo, A.: Nitric oxide in marine invertebrates: a comparative perspective. Comp. Biochem. Physiol. A 142, 241–248 (2005)
10. Ott, S., Burrows, M., Elphick, M.E.: The neuroanatomy of nitric oxide-cGMP signaling in the locust: functional implications for sensory systems. Amer. Zool. 41, 321–331 (2001)

11. Colasanti, M., Venturini, G., Merante, A., et al.: Nitric oxide involvement in Hydra vulgaris very primitive olfactorylike system. J. Neurosci. 17, 493–499 (1997)
12. Elofsson, R., Carlberg, M., Moroz, L., et al.: Is nitric oxide (NO) produced by invertebrate neurones? Neuroreport 4, 279–282 (1993)
13. Salleo, A., Giovanni, M., Barra, P., Calabrese, L.: The discharge mechanism of acomitial nematocytes involves the release of nitric oxide. J. Exp. Biol. 199, 1261–1267 (1996)
14. Taddei-Ferretti, C., Musio, C.: The neural net of Hydra and the modulation of its periodic activity. In: Mira, J.M. (ed.) IWANN 1999. LNCS, vol. 1606, pp. 123–137. Springer, Heidelberg (1999)
15. Burnett, A.L., Diehl, N.A.: The nervous system of Hydra. I. Types, distribution and origin of nerve elements. J. Exp. Zool. 157, 217–226 (1964)
16. Tardent, P., Weber, C.: A qualitative and quantitative inventory of nervous cells in Hydra. In: Mackie, G. (ed.) Coelenterate ecology & behaviour, pp. 501–512. Plenum, New York (1976)
17. Epp, L., Tardent, P.: The distribution of nerve cells in Hydra attenuata Pall. Wilhelm Roux's Arch. 185, 185–193 (1978)
18. Grimmelikhuijzen, C.J.P., Westfall, J.A.: The nervous systems of Cnidarians. In: Breidbach, O., Kutsch, W. (eds.) The nervous systems of invertebrates, pp. 7–24. Birkhäuser, Basel (1995)
19. Koizumi, O.: Developmental neurobiology of hydra. Can. J. Zool. 80, 1678–1689 (2002)
20. Bode, H.R.: Continuous conversion of neuron phenotype in hydra. Trends Genetics 8, 279–284 (1992)
21. Passano, L.M., McCullough, C.B.: Pacemaker hierarchies controlling the behaviour of hydras. Nature 199, 1174–1175 (1963)
22. Passano, L.M., McCullough, C.B.: The light response and the rhythmic potentials in Hydra. Proc. Natl. Acad. Sci. USA 48, 1376–1382 (1962)
23. Musio, C.: Extraocular photosensitivity in invertebrates. In: Taddei-Ferretti, C. (ed.) Biophysics of Photoreception, pp. 245–262. World Scientific, Singapore (1997)
24. Martin, V.J.: Photoreceptors of cnidarians. Can. J. Zool. 80, 1703–1722 (2002)
25. Taddei-Ferretti, C., Musio, C.: Photobehaviour of Hydra and correlated mechanisms: a case of extraocular photosensitivity. J. Photochem. Photobiol. B: Biol. 55, 88–101 (2000)
26. Taddei-Ferretti, C., Musio, C., Santillo, S., Cotugno, A.: The photobiology of Hydra's periodic activity. Hydrobiologia 530/531, 129–134 (2004)
27. Musio, C., Santillo, S., Taddei-Ferretti, C., Robles, L.J., et al.: First identification and localization of a visual pigment in Hydra. J. Comp. Physiol. 187A, 79–81 (2001)
28. Santillo, S., Orlando, P., De Petrocellis, L., Cristino, L., Guglielmotti, V., Musio, C.: Evolving visual pigments: Hints from the opsin-based proteins in a phylogenetically old eyeless invertebrate. BioSystems 86, 3–17 (2006)
29. Palmer, R.M., Ferrige, A.G., Moncada, S.: Nitric oxide release accounts for the biological activity of endothelium-derived relaxing factor. Nature 327, 524–526 (1987)
30. Bredt, D.S., Snyder, S.H.: Nitric oxide, a novel neuronal messenger. Neuron 8, 3–11 (1992)
31. Moroz, L.L., Winlow, W., Turner, R.W., et al.: Nitric oxide synthase-immunoreactive cells in the CNS and periphery of Lymnaea. Neuroreport 5, 1277–1280 (1994)
32. Hope, B.T., Michael, G.J., Knigge, K.M., Vincent, S.R.: Neuronal NADPH-diaphorase is a nitric oxide synthase. Proc. Natl Acad. Sci. USA 88, 2811–2814 (1991)
33. Moroz, L.L.: Gaseous transmission across time and species. Am. Zool. 41, 304–320 (2001)
34. Garthwaite, J., Boulton, C.L.: Nitric oxide signaling in the central nervous system. Annu. Rev. Physiol. 57, 683–706 (1995)

35. Ninnemann, H., Maier, J.: Indications for the occurrence of nitric oxide synthases in fungi and plants and the involvement in photoconidiation of Neurospora crassa. Photochem. Photobiol. 64, 393–398 (1996)
36. Robertson, J.D., Bonaventura, J., Kohm, A., Hiscat, M.: Nitric oxide is necessary for visual learning in Octopus vulgaris. Proc. R. Soc. Lond., B Biol. Sci. 263, 1739–1743 (1996)
37. Elphick, M.R., Kemenes, G., Staras, K., O'Shea, M.: Behavioural role for nitric oxide in chemosensory activation of feeding in a mollusc. J. Neurosci. 15, 7653–7664 (1995)
38. Gelperin, A.: Nitric oxide mediates network oscillations of olfactory interneurons in a terrestrial mollusc. Nature 369, 61–63 (1994)
39. Bult, H., Boeckxstaens, G.E., Pelckmans, P.A., et al.: Nitric oxide as an inhibitory non-adrenergic non-cholinergic neurotransmitter. Nature 345, 346–347 (1990)
40. Moroz, L.L., Gillette, R.: NADPH-d localization in the CNS and peripheral tissues of the predatory sea-slug Pleurobranchaea californica. J. Comp. Neurol. 367, 607–622 (1996)
41. Cudeiro, J., Rivadulla, C.: Sight and insight - on the physiological role of nitric oxide in the visual system. Trends Neurosci. 22, 109–116 (1999)
42. Kurenny, D.E., Moroz, L.L., Turner, R.W., et al.: Modulation of ion channels in rod photoreceptors by nitric oxide. Neuron 13, 315–324 (1994)
43. Florenzano, F., Guglielmotti, V.: Selective NADPH-diaphorase histochemical labeling of Müller radial processes and photoreceptors in the earliest stages of retinal development in the tadpole. Neurosci. Lett. 292, 187–190 (2000)
44. Gibbs, S.M.: Regulation of Drosophila visual system development by nitric oxide and cGMP. Amer. Zool. 41, 268–281 (2001)
45. Golombek, D.A., Agostino, P.V., Plano, S.A., Ferreyra, G.A.: Signaling in the mammalian circadian clock: the NO/cGMP pathway. Neurochem. Internat. 45, 929–936 (2004)
46. Kalina, M., Plapinger, R.E., Hoshino, Y., Seligman, A.M.: Nonosmiophilic tetrazolium salts that yield osmiophilic, lipophobic formazans for ultrastructural localization of dehydrogenase activity. J. Histochem. Cytochem. 20, 685–695 (1972)
47. Altman, F.P.: Tetrazolium salts and formazans. Prog. Histochem. Cytochem. 9, 1–56 (1976)
48. Morishita, F., Nitagai, Y., Furukawa, Y., Matsushima, O., Takahashi, T., et al.: Identification of a vasopressin-like immunoreactive substance in hydra. Peptides 24, 17–26 (2003)
49. Sakaguchi, M., Mizusina, A., Kobayakawa, Y.: Structure, development, and maintenance of the nerve net of the body column in Hydra. J. Comp. Neurol. 373, 41–54 (1996)
50. Moroz, L.L., Meech, R.W., Sweedler, J.V., Mackie, G.O.: Nitric oxide regulates swimming in the jellyfish Aglantha digitale. J. Comp. Neurol. 471, 26–36 (2004)
51. Anctil, M., Poulain, I., Pelletier, C.: NO modulates peristaltic muscle activity associated with fluid circulation in the sea pansy Renilla koellikeri. J. Exp. Biol. 208, 2005–2017 (2005)
52. Cristino, L., Pica, A., Della Corte, F., Bentivoglio, M.: Plastic changes and nitric oxide synthase induction in neurons which innervate the regenerated tail of the lizard Gekko gecko: I. The response of spinal motoneurons to tail amputation and regeneration. J. Comp. Neurol. 417, 60–72 (2000)
53. Cristino, L., Florenzano, F., Bentivoglio, M., Guglielmotti, V.: Nitric oxide synthase expression and cell changes in dorsal root ganglia and spinal dorsal horn of developing and adult Rana esculenta indicate a role of nitric oxide in limb metamorphosis. J. Comp. Neurol. 472, 423–436 (2004)

On Global Geometry of Image on Eye's Back

Paolo d 'Alessandro

Paolo d 'Alessandro, Department of Mathematics
Third University of Rome
dalex@mat.uniroma3.it

Abstract. We investigate the geometric properties of the global image that forms on the hemispheric back of the eye.

Keywords: Natural Vision, Visual Perception, Visual Cognition.

1 Introduction

Historically, the study of visual perception has overemphasized planar analysis. Art and then Science and Technology have embraced the standpoint of representing visual world on a plane. Paraxial image theory has been considered the golden standard to which optics have to conform. An ideal optical system must track paraxial performance, and the measure of aberration is "the amount by which rays miss the paraxial image point " [1]. Explicit in this round of ideas is the continuous reference to a similitude between the eye and a camera. We question these beliefs and provide evidence of smooth but substantial depart from paraxial behavior.

The back of human eye has the approximate form of an hemisphere which is completely covered by an "aerial image " (humoral is more exact, but there is no harm in using a more euphonic name). Instead of concentrating attention on foveal image (and ignoring the curvature of the back), our purpose is to move toward the study of the geometry of the whole image, thus including peripheral vision. Here, for brevity, we deal with the single eye, whereas the additional functionality of stereoscopic vision, in terms of spherical geometry, will be the subject of a subsequent study.

In so doing we should be careful in specifying the scheme of the interconnected blocks system that realizes human vision (which has even feedback links). We must disaggregate precisely, individuating each block and its input and output. So we distinguish the optical system, whose output is the aerial image, from the downstream sensor system whose input is such an image. Our effort is to obtain insight on the geometric features of the map defined by the optical system, and then to argue on how the downstream blocks will follow through. In this way we clarify the ensuing framework and we give an orientation for further research, which will necessarily involve nonlinear differential equations.

Given that the back is spherical what is the appropriate representation of the external world? It seems most logical to partition it in hemispheres centered on the eye, instead of insisting on planes. It is not only a common sense idea, there

F. Mele et al. (Eds.): BVAI 2007, LNCS 4729, pp. 21–29, 2007.

is also a no way around mathematical barrier that make it unavoidable. In fact it is impossible to specify an isometry (i.e., preserve distances) mapping a plane to a sphere. This fact (actually much more than that) was discovered rigorously by Gauss in 1827 (an excellent account is e.g. in [3]). Gauss was so enthusiast of his discovery, that called it *Egregium Theorem* (meaning *outstanding* in Latin and not "*totally awesome*" as said in [3]).

There is a huge literature on the image quality of the human eye, which not only deals with foveal image but also leans toward medical issues. An account goes beyond our purpose and space. We just give a taste with a couple of examples [10], [7]. Medical issues also fall outside our scope and competence.

The optical system of the eye is one of extreme sophistication (the crystalline is altogether an aspherical, variable geometry and GRIN lens) and of peculiar structure. It is even believed that it uses "pixel shifting technology", by means of saccades, to increase resolution. Nevertheless, our starting point is again paraxial analysis,.not finalized, this time, to determine an ideal performance to which the system must abide, but rather, to start gathering clues of how external hemispheres are mapped on the internal hemispherical back.

In what follows reference to Nature has no other meaning than a way to streamline exposition.

2   The Second Nodal Point

Paraxial optics is a classical topic, covered e.g. in [2].The method amounts to linear functions (obtained linearizing Snell's law) on R^2, that is, matrices. The vectors represents distance from center and angles. It is natural to adopt once and for all the lexicographic convention of having the rays traveling left to right, and hence also defining transformation of vectors in the same orientation (right vector as a function of left one).

Now, what should we look for in paraxial optics? In our work (implemented in MatLab) we do calculate the right focus point, but just for validation and debugging purposes. It is instead much more interesting for us to look at nodal points.

Because eye's back is hemispherical, we can use as coordinates two angles: latitude (actually colatitude - north pole, along the optical axis, at zero latitude, but we stick with the term latitude for simplicity) and longitude. ¿From these coordinates there are well-known formulas to compute the metric i.e., given any two points, their distance along a great circle (which is a geodesic).

Back to the optical mapping, the external longitude is mapped isometrically, given the rotational symmetry (downstream the sensors' layout is almost rotationally symmetric as well) . Thus we focus on the other angle, i.e. latitude.

There are only two special positions for the second nodal point, that realize the first a proportionality by a factor 1/2 and the second an identity, of latitude ϕ on visual field as a function of latitude x on eye's back. These positions are the intersection with the sphere (the approximate ball shape of the eye - near the cornea) and the center of the sphere. One might hope that computation produce one of this two favorable cases. If that were so, of course the question would be: which one? If instead it were not so, how about the other positions?

A priori both these two vantage position realize a substantial isometry, but they are far from indifferent. We explain this in detail below and examine as well what happens in all other positions.

1 - If Nature had chosen the first position, it would have got a low latitude external angles amplification that accompanies the superior foveal sensor system resolution. But at the same time Nature would have to alter substantially, in peripheral areas, the optical map to accommodate, by means of lower amplification, external angles that reach largely 90 degrees, passing the 45 degree limit of this paraxial functionality, and to accommodate the need of maintaining normal incidence of rays on sensors. In foveal vision a linear transformation on angles (internal as a function of external) given by a diagonal 2×2 matrix with a 1 and a 2 on diagonal would hold. It is still reconducible to an isometry on our angular coordinates, but we are at the same time we are certain that such transformation cannot hold over the whole field. However, the ensuing degrading amplification for large external angles can still be expected to yield an invertible function, so that we may presume that brain's downstream image processing system can invert such function and obtain an isometry for latitude angles as well. On the other hand, we can claim that brain has certainly this sort of capacity because the radial density of the sensors ' pattern is not uniform and the brain must compensate for such disuniformity. We may as well expect that the brain is able to calculate geodesic distance on eye's back.

2 - If Nature had chosen the second position, it would have got an identity transformation of internal angular coordinates as a function of external ones. Mathematically it would be paradise, and the brain would only have the burden of compensating for sensor densities. The 90 degrees angle is accommodated automatically, and an ideal vision based on a geodesics would result (more on this later).

3 - If Nature had chosen neither of the above, the latitude on the eye's back would be non-linearly mapped as explained below

We stress that condition 1 implies that non-paraxial optics is substantially different from peripheral optics and that it will be *much as if the second nodal point should travel from the first to the second position as latitude increases* and, hence, its distance from center of the eye would be a decreasing function of latitude..

To make explicit the above arguments let c is the distance from the center of the nodal point (normalized to radius). Then the expression of ϕ (exterior latitude) as a function of x (latitude on eye's back) is readily seen to be

$$\phi(c, x) = tan^{-1}(\frac{sinx}{c + cosx})$$

If $c = 1$, a trigonometry exercise shows that $\phi = x/2$, and, of course, if $c = 0$ then $\phi = x$. These are the two vantage points. For other values the law retain its complexity. There is a very important observation in this respect though. Let's look at the partial derivatives.. A little computation shows that

$$\frac{\partial \phi}{\partial c} = -\frac{sinx}{1 + c^2 + 2 \times c \times cosx}$$

$$\frac{\partial \phi}{\partial x} = \frac{1 + c \times cosx}{1 + c^2 + 2 \times c \times cosx}$$

Thus we have a continuous smooth function which is *monotone increasing* with respect to decreasing c and *increasing* with respect to x. If, as we must presume (sticking to the nodal point concept), c were a decreasing function of x then ϕ would become an increasing function of x. Thus this function can be inverted. For example let $c(x) = 1 - sinx$. Then we obtain $\phi(0) = 0$, $\phi(\pi/2) = \pi/2$ and

$$\frac{d\phi}{dx} = \frac{1 + cox}{[1 - sinx + cosx]^2 + sin^2x}$$

so that $\phi(x)$ is monotone increasing. Thus invertible.

In the next Section we will show that case 1 holds. In view of the above discussion, we may reasonably argue that, although traces of these disuniformities might be present in the brain image, *the brain is capable of reconstructing, from eye's back image and the consequent sensors' output, the aerial image defined by case 2.*

3   Paraxial Computations

We need a dozen parameters to carry out this exercise. We noticed that no two authors agree on averages, and reported values have an extended range. We have experimented just a little, using the focus point as validation check.

At each optical surface and each translation it corresponds a transformation. Overall we have 7 transformations. More precisely:

First Transition: Air to Cornea Surface (Tac)

Second Transition: Translation inside cornea (Ttc)

Third Transition: Cornea to Humor Surface (Tch)

Fourth Transition: Translation in Humor (Tth)

Fifth Transition: Humor to lens Surface (Thl)

Sixth Transition: Translation in lens (Ttl)

Seventh transition: Lens to vitreous Humor Surface (Tlv)

At each surface the transition is given by (quantities with index 1 on the left, index 2 on the right).

$$\begin{pmatrix} y_2 \\ \alpha_2 \end{pmatrix} = \begin{pmatrix} 1 & 0 \\ \frac{n_2 - n_1}{n_2 R} & \frac{n_1}{n_2} \end{pmatrix} \begin{pmatrix} y_1 \\ \alpha_1 \end{pmatrix}$$

where it is an all positive except that R is negative when the ray meets a concave surface and positive if it meets a convex surface. Translation by a distance D correspond instead to the matrix

$$\begin{pmatrix} 1 & D \\ 0 & 1 \end{pmatrix}$$

Therefore the matrix of the whole optical system is given by

$$T = Tlv * Ttl * Thl * Tth * Tch * Ttc * Tac$$

Once the 2×2 matrix of the optical system $T = [t_{ij}]$ has been computed we place a translation D_1 on the left and a translation D_2 on the right. Multiplying the three matrices it is obtained the transformation S that depends on the parameters D_1 and D_2

$$S(D_1, D_2) = \begin{pmatrix} t_{11} + D_2 t_{21} & D_1 t_{11} + t_{12} + D_2(D_1 t_{21} + t_{22}) \\ t_{21} & D_1 t_{21} + t_{22} \end{pmatrix}$$

$$\begin{pmatrix} y_2 \\ \alpha_2 \end{pmatrix} = S(D_1, D_2) \begin{pmatrix} y_1 \\ \alpha_1 \end{pmatrix}$$

We may look for special solutions that provide constraints on D_1 and D_2. Assuming invariance of the second coordinate subspace

$$\begin{pmatrix} 0 \\ \alpha_2 \end{pmatrix} = S(D_1, D_2) \begin{pmatrix} 0 \\ \alpha_1 \end{pmatrix}$$

will impose $s(1, 2) = 0$. If we ask also proportionality $\alpha_2 = \gamma.\alpha_1$, and set, for example, $\gamma = 1$, then we have the other constraint

$$D_1 t_{21} + t_{22} = 1$$

$$D_1 = \frac{1 - t_{22}}{t_{21}}$$

which yields the first nodal point. Substituting in S, the identity $D_1 t_{21} + t_{22} = 1$:

$$S = \begin{pmatrix} t_{11} + D_2 t_{21} & D_1 t_{11} + t_{12} + D_2 \\ t_{21} & 1 \end{pmatrix}$$

and hence imposing $s(1, 2) = 0$

$$D_2 = -(D_1 t_{11} + t_{12})$$

which yields the second nodal point. We do not repeat the exercise for right focus point fp, because can be found in textbooks and it turns out that

$$fp = -t(1, 1)/t(2, 1)$$

Our MatLab code gave the following answers. Distance from cornea of focus point is $16, 6$ mm, an acceptable validation. Distance of second nodal point from cornea is $0, 71789$ mm (inside lens). Thus Nature very nearly chose the first vantage points, bearing in mind that the cornea protrudes a little from the spherical shape.. So this is what happens in reality and here computations hold good, there is nothing conjectural. Similarly, the compression of latitude moving toward peripheral vision is now an assessed fact, and *so is a radical depart from paraxial behavior.*

4   The Approximate Pinhole Abstraction

Our arguments motivate a closer look to case 2 of Sec.2, which is equivalent to pinhole camera with an hemispherical instead of planar back and the hole in the center on the limiting plane of the hemisphere. It projects isometrically on eye's back each external hemisphere centered on our eye. Therefore this image functionality provides an exact measure of angles (latitude and longitude and by symmetries of the sphere, any other angle with vertex on the pinhole as well).

This means that at a given distance from the eye, thus on a hemisphere in front of it, objects have an apparent size proportional to their angular dimension and given the size of an object its apparent size is inversely proportional to the distance from the eye over the whole visual field, approximately 90 degrees in each direction. Gauss theorem prevents this to be true for any device that collect the image on a plane.

A geodesic of a sphere is a great circle. Geodesics are the equivalent of straight lines in Euclidean world. A geodesic segment joining two points is the shortest path between the two points. However, there is no more the familiar Euclidean parallelism concept. To visualize this fact think of meridians, and notice that their distance varies and that, eventually, they intersect.

Not only geodesic segments of hemispheres in front of the eye, but also straight segments are transformed into segments of geodesic in the aerial image. The proof is obvious. It suffices to say that in our pinhole model the three points given by the extreme of a segment and the pinhole itself define a plane that intersect the spherical back in a geodesic line. This is true for any segment, there are no constraints for its endpoints (unless, of course, the segment lies on a ray emanating from the pinhole).

So can we distinguish a external segment from a geodesic with the same extremes? Ideally not, but in practice it suffices a minimal additional landmark. Suppose now we graduate both the geodesic and the segment in equal parts. Then because angles are measured exactly, and because the function $arcsin$ is not linear we will see the two graduations differ from each other. This can give us cues of what is straight and what is not.

But this is by no means the only cue. Just to give an example let's add some illumination by direct light with parallel rays (e.g. sunlight) . It goes alone that the intensity of reflected light is uniform in the case of a linear stick but not in the case of a curved one. And we can also judge about orientation in the space looking at the way the two objects reflect the light. Actually, when the endpoint of a segment are not on the same hemisphere, length depends both on angular coordinates and distance of endpoints, and hence it is more difficult for the brain.to estimate it.

To illustrate another significant property of our spherical vision, suppose we look at a building in front of us, at certain distance with a regular rectangular face. Because each of the sides defines an external segment, it follows that in the aerial image we obtain a geodesic trapezoid. Incidentally, this shows that *perspective*, of which artists, architects and photographers are so fond of, *is to a large extent an esthetic abstraction, without a rigorous foundation.*

5 Sensors' Pattern

It is all well-known that there is an approximate rotational symmetry in the layout of the sensors ([9], [8]), with density degrading with latitude (almost independently from longitude, but not exactly so) and there are cones at the fovea, cones and roads outside. Also Nature has adopted essentially an hexagonal tessellation to position the sensors. All this is very much in contrast with current digital technology.

In this respect two observations are natural. The first regards density of packing of the sensor. This relates to the issue of kissing spheres in geometry. The tip of the cones in two dimension is roughly circular. From the point of view of efficient packing on a plane Gauss proved that the density of the hexagonal layout is $\pi/\sqrt{12}$ which corresponds to 90,6899682% whereas the Cartesian packing has density $\pi/4$ which corresponds to 78,539163%. In 1940 László Fejes Tóth proved that this pattern achieves the maximum of possible densities. So Nature maximized sensor's density.

Certainly this 12% plus was appealing, but is it the only explanation and and is it possible to realize the hexagonal packing on a spherical surface? A simple computation shows that hexagonal kissing spheres pattern is disrupted on the surface of a sphere: one of the six spheres has to pop out. This suggests the form of a cone to make the pattern consistent with the spherical layout constraint. In the image of [8] the cones are so tightly packed that the contours adapt to each other and actually resemble a hexagonal tiling.

Next, if look at directions of maximal resolution, we see that we have a direction of maximum resolution each 60 degrees in the hexagonal layout. By contrast we have a direction of maximal resolution each 90 degrees in the square layout. There are no other regular tessellations available and a different choice would have inflicted a serious damage to the species. Again Nature optimized and gave us the maximum number of directions for best recognizing details. This is another fundamental explanation of the hexagonal tessellation.

Outside the fovea the cones are more distantiated and the gap is filled with rods. That pattern is more disordered but still legible in terms of hexagons with the contours of the rods even more deformed to adapt to the pattern. The different form and structure (rods vs cones) is known to be connected to the different physiology of the two sensors in terms wavelength and sensitivity.

6 Concluding Remarks

First we try to summarize some crucial points.

There is no way to circumvent Gauss Egregium Theorem. Nature abided to it and banned planes.

Nature chose a variable metric on latitude (along with variable sensor density), but still leaving plenty of room for the brain to derive an isometry of external hemispheres to the internal hemispherical back. Incidentally, this means that we are able instantly to guess how far is an already known object over the whole visual field without the need of turning the eyes or the head. This is very favorable capability for our species.

We hope that our discussion shows that the time is ripe to start thinking to spheres instead of planes when we deal with visual world. There is indeed sure evidence that bars any possibility of reasoning in terms of planes and of Euclidean geometry.

Regarding technology we have first to ask ourselves if the idea of spherical vision have already occurred and in what sense. Here we have to cite [5], who has developed and implemented full surround display technology. Although this line of research is highly appreciated it does not match what we proposed here.

To avoid that Gauss Egregium Theorem undermine a simulation of a spherical visual world with a consequent impression of unrealism by our brain, it is necessary *comply to the isometry* of Sec.4, in each and every block of the implementation, from the taking picture phase all the way to the display phase.

The digital revolution may help in this respect. A curved sensor device, almost unthinkable with film, might be a conceivable design goal in digital technology. Similarly, the development of curved digital displays is needed. We believe that it not as crucial to surround the viewer with a display (as in [5]), but rather, to give to our visual system an image true to actual spherical external world. From this standpoint ,we think of a common shape for the sensor and the display given by a spherical rectangle, (intersection of orthogonal lunes - of course radiuses are different, but angular dimensions are the same in sensors and displays). This kind of display device requires a certain more restricted optimal viewing distance, because the viewer must be approximately at the center of curvature of the device. However, and even better, we may also conceive the display as a projector which transduces the image from a panel (or three in colors separation) of the above spherical form to a screen of the same form. This may give more freedom on the size of the screen yielding more near-optimal viewing positions. As to the taking and projecting lenses, they must be designed to have the matching focus field curvature imposed by the adopted spherical rectangle. What is today an optical aberration, will become a design goal of tomorrow technology!

As two the layout of sensor, it is obvious that the optimum way to go is to adopt the hexagonal pattern (again both in taking picture devices and in screens). It looks like that this too has never been considered so far by technology (most sensor have a rectangular layout with an exception of the strange octagonal layout of a certain well-known brand).

We cannot conclude without a brief mention of Cinerama. Its inventor Fred Waller was convinced that we have in some sense a spherical vision and, consequently, of the importance of peripheral vision. He developed a three cameras movie picture system (three taking cameras and three projectors with accompanying five channels audio). Thus the surface was made up by three angled plane rectangles so that the horizontal covering angle was 146 degrees. This surface is isomorphic to the plane. The same is true even for a portion of cylinder. Thus neither of this solutions goes in the direction indicated here. They do not pass the barrier of Gauss Egregium Theorem.

And yet the visual experience was pleasant because it gratified peripheral vision at an approximately constant distance from the viewer. Marketing almost immediately killed Cinerama substituting it with the dreadful anamorphic technology, arguing that the public would not have noticed the difference. Personally I noticed and I was very disappointed (I was a child at the time of these events). Incidentally, Waller also invented other devices like the Vitarama gunnery trainer that used eleven 16mm cameras and projected on the surface of a quarter of sphere (half dome).

A final comment on oil painting, that, albeit actuated by an human hand, is actually a sort of technology. Up to the nineteenth century artists refined the study of image and visual perception, and in that century they paid a more careful attention to peripheral vision, widening angles of view. An example is Jaques Tissot who was a master in illuding the spectator to be part of the scene. Also it might be little known that the idea of multiple directions of view was pioneered by a forgotten impressionist Gustave Caillebotte. It has been established (see [6]) that he used to combine multiple directions of view, in today's terms, multiple cameras in panoramic vision. About a century before Waller, but, unfortunately, still on a planar canvas.

References

1. Smith, W.R.: Modern Optical Engineering. Mc Graw Hill, New York (2000)
2. Born, M., Wolf, E.: Principles of Optics, 7th edn. Cambridge University Press, Cambridge (1999)
3. Lee, J.M.: Riemannian Manifolds. Springer, Heidelberg (1997)
4. Hecht, Eugene: Optics, 2nd edn. Addison Wesley, Reading (1987)
5. Iwata, H.: Full surround image display technology. Internetional Journal of Computer Vision 58(3), 227–235
6. Galassi, P.: Caillebotte Method. In: Varnedoe, K. (ed.) Gustave Caillebotte, Yale University Press, New Haven (2000)
7. Marcos, S., Moreno, E., Navarro, R.: The depth-of-field of the human eye with polychromatic light from objective and subjective measurements. Vision Research 39, 2039–2049 (1999)
8. Curcio, C.A., Sloan, K.R., Kalina, R.E., Hendrickson, A.E.: Human photoreceptor topography. Journal of Comparative Neurology 292, 497–523 (1990)
9. Roorda, A., Williams, D.R.: The Arrangement of the Three Cone Classes in the Living Human Eye. Nature 397, 520–522 (1999)
10. Thibos, L.N., Hong, X., Bradley, A., Applegate, R.E.: Metrics of Optical Quality of the Eye. In: ARVO 2003 Annual Meeting, ISSN 1534-7362

Independent Encoding of Position and Orientation by Population Responses in Primary Visual Cortex

Robert A. Frazor, Andrea Benucci, and Matteo Carandini

Smith-Kettlewell Eye Research Institute, 2318 Fillmore Street, San Francisco, CA 94115
USA
{robby,andrea,matteo}@ski.org

Abstract. The primary visual cortex (area V1) encodes visual attributes such as direction of motion, orientation, and position through the activity of populations of neurons. We asked how this activity is affected by different combinations of these attributes. We measured population responses by imaging voltage-sensitive dye fluorescence in area V1 of anesthetized cats with dye RH-1692 in response to stimuli that are both oriented and localized in space. We tested whether the resulting activation could be explained by a simple rule of combination that assumes the activation is a point-by-point multiplication of the map of orientation preference with a blurred prediction of the stimulus' footprint in cortex derived from a map of retinotopy. This simple rule of combination provided good fits of the responses and implies that the effects of stimulus orientation and position on population responses are independent.

Keywords: Visual Cortex, Retinotopy, Orientation.

1 Introduction

The visual cortex represents stimuli through the activity of neuronal populations, and is organized according to maps of selectivity. These maps of selectivity concern stimulus attributes such as position, orientation, and direction. It is of interest to know how these maps combine to determine the overall population response.

This question has been recently investigated for the maps of orientation preference and direction preference. Basole et al. [1] showed that the population response to a moving, oriented stimulus can not be simply predicted based on selectivity for stimulus orientation and stimulus direction measured independently. Specifically, they showed that the population response to a set of drifting oriented bars was not simply the product of a map of orientation preference and a map of direction preference.

This result could be explained, by a simple energy model of neuronal responses [2]. According to this model, neurons in visual cortex derive their selectivity from a receptive field that operates in space and time. The responses of such a receptive field depend jointly on stimulus orientation, direction, and speed, and thus the population response to stimuli that simultaneously vary in these stimulus properties will be a conflation of these joint dependencies.

The energy model, however, makes a different prediction for the effects of changing stimulus position; in this case the energy model predicts that the population

F. Mele et al. (Eds.): BVAI 2007, LNCS 4729, pp. 30–41, 2007.
© Springer-Verlag Berlin Heidelberg 2007

response can be determined from independent combinations of a map of retinotopy and a map of orientation preference. Neurons in the primary visual cortex have relatively small receptive fields, so they perform computations over a finite, localized region. Thus the model would predict that the response at a single location in the cortex to a localized, oriented stimulus should be predictable from independent measures of the retinotopic preference and orientation selectivity of that location. Specifically, it predicts that the response is the product of a function of orientation (determined by the map of orientation preference) and a function of position (determined by the map of retinotopy). We sought to evaluate this prediction of the model by measuring the population response of primary visual cortex to stimuli that are both oriented and localized in space.

We imaged population responses in area V1 by staining the cortex with a voltage-sensitive dye (VSD). VSD imaging delivers parallel recording from tens of square millimeters [3] with a resolution of ~100 μm in space (limited by light scatter in tissue) and few ms in time (limited by photon noise). This method targets the superficial layers , which provide the main output to the rest of the cortex [4]. The dye fluoresces in proportion to membrane potential and thus provides a measure of neural activity elicited by the stimulus in a population of cortical neurons.

Stimuli that are both oriented and localized in space, such as oriented bars or gratings windowed by elongated apertures, will activate regions of cortex that are both broad and patchy [5]. The center of the activity will depend upon the retinotopic position of the stimulus and the patchiness of the activity will depend upon the stimulus orientation. The width of the activated region, in turn, will depend upon the point spread function of the cortex. That is, the width of the activated region depends on what the cortical representation of a single retinotopic location is. Microelectrode studies suggest that the point spread function of cat primary visual cortex is approximately 2.6 mm [6].

We consider whether it is possible to describe the broad but patchy activation of the cortex with a simple rule that combination. The rule posits that, for any point on the cortex, the activation resulting from a localized, oriented stimulus should be simply predictable from maps of retinotopic and orientation preference, taking into account the point spread function of the cortex.

2 Methods

2.1 Physiology

The methods described here are similar to those described in Benucci et al. . Young adult cats (2-4 Kg) were anesthetized first with Ketamine (22 mg/kg i/m) and Xylazine (1.1 mg/kg i/m) and then with Sodium Penthotal (0.5-2 mg/kg/hr i/v) and Fentanyl (typically 10 μg/kg/hr i/v), supplemented with inhalation of N2O (typically 70:30 with O2). A 1 cm craniotomy was performed over area V1 (usually area 18, occasionally area 17), centered on the midline. The eyes were treated with topical atropine and phenylephrine, and protected with contact lenses. A neuromuscular blocker was given to prevent eye movements (pancuronium bromide, 0.15 mg/kg/hr, i.v.). The animal was artificially respirated, and received periodic doses of an antibiotic (Cephazolin, 20 mg/kg IM, twice daily), of an anti-edematic steroid (Dexamethasone, 0.4 mg/kg daily), and of an anticholinergic agent (atropine sulfate, 0.05 mg/kg, i/m, daily). Fluid balance was maintained by intravenous infusion. The level of anesthesia was monitored through the EEG. Additional physiological parameters that were monitored include temperature, heart rate, end-tidal CO2, and lung pressure. Experiments typically lasted 48-72 hours. Procedures were approved by the Institutional Animal Care and Use Committee.

2.2 Stimuli

Stimuli were square gratings, presented monocularly on a CRT monitor (Sony Trinitron 500PS, refresh rate 125 Hz, mean luminance 32 cd/m^2), modulating sinusoidally in contrast. The dominant spatial frequency was 0.2-0.4 cpd, depending on the area imaged, and contrast was 50%. The windows were square (40x40 deg) for orientation experiments, and rectangular (typically 6X40 deg) for retinotopy experiments. Stimuli were preceded by ~2 s of uniform gray, typically lasted 1-2 s, and were presented in random order in blocks that were typically presented 10-20 times.

To examine the effects of context on the response to localized stimuli we also presented small patches (2 degree square) of square wave grating whose contrast was reversed according to a binary m-sequence. In one condition only a single patch was presented. In a second condition the same patch (modulating with the same temporal sequence) was surrounded by other patches whose contrast reversed in a temporally uncorrelated fashion (specifically by using a time shifted version of the same m-sequence [7]). The response of the cortex was defined as the average VSD response following a contrast reversal in the center patch (regardless of whether it was presented alone or in the context of other patches).

2.3 Imaging Method

Methods for VSD imaging were described by Grinvald and collaborators [3, 8, 9]. We stained the cortex with the VSD RH-1692 and imaged its fluorescence in 15-30 mm^2 of V1. The dye was circulated in a chamber over the cortex for 3 hours, and washed out with saline. We acquired images with a CMOS digital camera (1M60 Dalsa, Waterloo, Ontario), as part of the Imager 3001 setup (Optical Imaging Inc, Rehovot, Israel). Images were acquired at a frame rate of 110 Hz, with spatial resolution of 28 μm per pixel. Additional spatial filtering was performed offline (bandpass, 0.2-2.2 cycles/mm). Frame acquisition was synchronized with the respirator. Illumination from a 100 W halogen light was delivered through two optic fibers. The excitation filter was bandpass at 630 ± 10 nm, and the emission filter was highpass, with cutoff at 665 nm.

2.4 Fourier Analysis

The amplitude spectrum of each pixel was computed from their temporal traces. To compute a single Fourier component (for the current study the 2nd harmonic of the stimulating frequency) we usually multiplied the traces by the appropriate complex exponential. Maps of the amplitude of the complex response, as a function of stimulus and position and orientation, were used to evaluate the performance the model of retinotopy.

2.5 Predictive Model

The four parameters of the mapping function, and the one parameter of the point spread function (the standard deviation σ), were found by carrying out a forward prediction of the data and minimizing the deviation between prediction and measurement.

The predictive model of responses was defined as follows. Consider a localized, oriented stimulus (Fig. 2A). Let θ be the stimulus orientation, and let the position and shape of the stimulus be defined by the distribution of contrast C(w), which is 1 inside the rectangle and 0 outside. Step 1 is to compute the cortical representation of the stimulus locations (Fig. 2B,D): $r_1(z) = C(f^{-1}(z))$, where f is the retinotopy mapping. The result of the computation (Fig. 2E) is the "footprint" of the stimulus on cortex, assuming a point-to-point mapping between the stimulus and the cortical representation. Step 2 is to blur by convolving with the point spread function (Fig. 2F), $r_2(z) = [r_1 * G_\sigma](z)$, with G_σ a Gaussian with standard deviation σ. The result of this computation (Fig. 2G) is a blurred "footprint" that takes into account that a single point on the stimulus is processed by a population of neurons. Step 3 is to multiply pointwise the result by the map of orientation preference (Fig. 2H) $r_3(z) = r_2(z)r_\theta(z)$, where $r_\theta(z)$ is the response of pixel z to a full-field stimulus with orientation θ. The result of this computation (Fig. 2I) is the model's prediction of the cortical response to the stimulus.

3 Results

We have shown previously that VSD imaging in area V1 reflects the responses of complex cells, as opposed to simple cells, and that high-resolution functional maps can be obtained with stimuli that reverse in contrast sinusoidally . Complex cells respond to such a stimulus with an oscillation at twice the frequency of the reversal. These 2nd harmonic responses stand clear of the noise, and result in functional maps with high signal/noise ratios. Based upon these findings we used contrast reversing gratings, modulating sinusoidally at 5 Hz (and thus giving strong stimulus responses at 10 Hz), to obtain functional maps of orientation preference and retinotopy.

To measure maps of orientation preference, we imaged the 2nd harmonic responses to large, oriented square-wave gratings (Fig. 1A-D, inset). Stimuli of different orientations elicited the profiles of activity typical of cat V1 , with orthogonal orientations yielding complementary maps (Fig. 1A-D). These profiles of activity could be combined to produce a map of orientation preference (Fig. 1E).

To measure maps of retinotopy, we imaged the 2nd harmonic responses to square-wave gratings windowed in narrow rectangular apertures, whose orientation was parallel to the orientation of the aperture (**Fig. 1F-I**, inset). Changing the stimulus elevation from high to low caused the resulting activity to move from posterior to anterior (**Fig. 1F-I**). These profiles of activity could be combined (in conjunction with those obtained using stimuli at various horizontal positions, not shown) to produce a map of retinotopic preference (**Fig. 1J**).

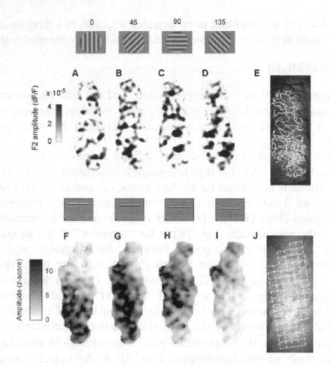

Fig. 1. Maps of orientation and position preference obtained from 2nd harmonic responses (**A-D**) Amplitude of the 2nd harmonic responses to standing gratings with different orientations, whose contrast reversed at 5 Hz. For graphical purposes, these maps were corrected by subtracting the average response to 8 orientations ("cocktail correction"), and ignoring negative responses. Experiment 50-2-3. (**E**) Map of orientation selectivity obtained from these responses (plus other 4 that are not shown). Each line is an iso-orientation contour. (**F-I**) For stimulus position, stimuli were gratings windowed in narrow rectangles. Cortical responses to stimuli of different position are shown. As the stimulus moves downward on the CRT monitor the cortical response moves more anterior. (**J**) Map of retinotopic preference. Each solid line shows an iso-elevation contour and each dotted line shows an iso-azimuth contour. Experiments 67-2-1 and 67-2-2.

The function underlying our maps of retinotopy is very simple. This mapping function relates a point in visual space to a point in cortex. It is linear and is specified by only 4 parameters: the two Cartesian coordinates of the area centralis in cortex, the angle of rotation, and the magnification factor. The function can be described most succinctly in the complex domain. It maps a point $w = u+iv$ in the visual field to a point $z = x+iy$ in cortex. This point is given by

$$z = f(w) = \rho \exp(i\,\phi)\,w + z_0, \tag{1}$$

where ρ is the magnification factor (in mm/deg), ϕ in the rotation angle (in radians), and $z_0 = x_0+iy_0$ are the cortical coordinates of the area centralis (the point $w = 0$).

This simple mapping function has a number of limitations, but it suffices for the job at hand. The first limitation is that, because the mapping function is one-to-one, it is only appropriate when our window on the cortex views a single visual area (i.e., area 17 or area 18, but not a region that spans the two). This limitation is of minor concern, because our images mostly centered on one area. A second limitation of our mapping function is that it is linear, which is only appropriate for local regions of cortex over the full extent of V1 the magnification factor shows great variation [10, 11]. A more realistic logarithmic mapping function , however, was not found to improve our fits despite the additional parameters.

We can use the model described above to test the prediction that the population response to a localized, oriented stimulus is determinable from independent measures (maps) of orientation and retinotopic preference. If the population response is a conflation of stimulus orientation and position (i.e., the response depends on the specific combination of position and orientation), then the model will be a poor characterization of the population responses. This is because the model assumes that the population response can be determined from independent measures of position and orientation preference.

A key factor influencing the response of the cortex to a focal stimulus is the point spread function of the cortex. This function describes the extent of cortex that is activated by a pointwise visual stimulus, and can be calculated from arguments based on the cortical magnification factor and receptive field size [12]. In cat V1, the width of the point spread function averages 2.6 mm, regardless of eccentricity [6].

The structure of orientation preference maps is finer than the scale of the point spread function and thus a small oriented stimulus activates a region of cortex that is extended (because of the point spread function), but not uniform (because of the map of orientation preference, [5].

Therefore the pattern of activity elicited by a localized, oriented stimulus must depend on the interplay of at least three factors, (1) the map of retinotopy; (2) the point spread function; and (3) the map of orientation preference. We investigated the rules of combination for these three factors. Because our stimuli are both localized in space (they are framed by narrow windows) and oriented (the gratings are parallel to the window) they are well suited for addressing this interplay. We found that these stimuli activate regions that are patchy (Fig. 1C,D). The patchiness results from the functional organization of orientation preference. When the combined responses to horizontal bars are subtracted from the combined responses to vertical bars, the result is a clear map of (horizontal vs. vertical) orientation preference (Fig. 2H).

We tested a simple rule of combination. First, we predicted the representation of the envelope of our stimulus in cortex based on the map of retinotopy (Fig. 1J). The result is a tight region of activation with sharp borders (Fig. 2E). Second, we blurred this region of activation by convolving it with the point spread function that was modeled as a 2-dimensional Gaussian profile (Fig. 2F). The result is a broad region of activation with blurred borders (Fig. 2G). Finally, we multiplied this region of activation point by point with the map of preferred orientation, i.e. with the profile of activation expected for a large oriented stimulus (Fig. 2H). The final result is a broad but patchy activation (Fig. 2I).

This rule of combination provided good fits of the responses. The maps of activation predicted by the model (**Fig. 3C**) resemble the actual responses (**Fig. 3B**). The model explained 78 % of the variance for the data in our example experiment, and 74 ± 8 % of the variance on average (s.d., n = 7). From the model fit we can estimate the point spread function of area V1. The standard deviation of the

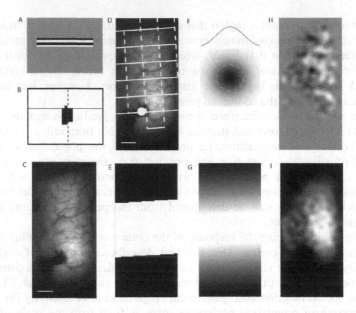

Fig. 2. Model of retinotopy (**A**) The gray square depicts the CRT monitor on which is presented a grating stimulus viewed through an elongated aperture. (**B**) The black region represents the projection of the imaged region of cortex on the CRT monitor. (**C**) A picture of the region of cortex being imaged using the voltage sensitive dye method. (**D**) The solid lines overlaid on the picture of imaged cortex correspond to iso-elevation contours and dotted lines correspond to iso-asimuth contours. The white dot represents the Area Centralis. (**E**) The white region is the point-to-point mapping (or "footprint") of the stimulus on the CRT monitor to the corresponding part of cortex. (**F**) the point spread function of the cortex (the region of cortex activated by a pointwise stimulus) is modeled as a two dimensional Gaussian. (**G**) The result of convolving the point-spread function with the "footprint" of the stimulus shown in Figure 1E. (**H**) A map of the difference between the responses to vertical stimuli and horizontal stimuli (vertical preferring regions shown in white, horizontal preferring regions shown in black). (**I**) The prediction of the response to an oriented, localized stimulus is given by multiplying, point-by-point, the map shown in G with the map of activation to a horizontal stimulus.

2-dimensional Gaussian was 0.7 mm for the example experiment, and 1.1 ± 0.4 mm across experiments (s.d., n = 7). The overall width of the estimated point spread function (~2.2 mm at two standard deviations) is consistent with the value of ~2.6 mm estimated with electrodes [6].

We further validated the model, by testing its performance on a new data set. This data set was not used to obtain the model's parameters, but also consists of localized, oriented stimuli. We first obtained the model parameters from an experiment like the one described above (Fig. 1). We then fixed the parameters at those values and asked whether the model could predict responses to a second experiment. In this second experiment, we measured cortical responses to flashed elongated grating patches of various orientations and positions (**Fig. 4A,D**). Responses to the new stimulus were patchy and extended (measured at the peak of the associated response), similar to

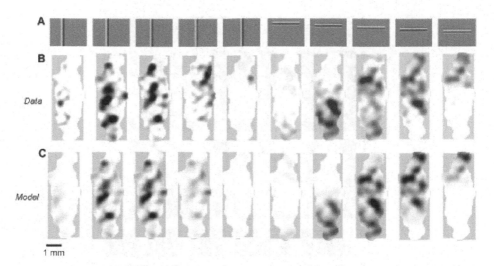

Fig. 3. (A) Stimuli are the same as Fig. 1, varying in vertical and horizontal position. **(B)** Amplitude of 2nd harmonic responses (similar to the data shown in Fig. 1**F-I**). Experiments 67-2-1 and 67-2-2. **(C)** Predictions of the model for the amplitude of 2nd harmonic responses. Gray scale as in **B** .

those observed in Figure 3 (**Fig. 4B,C**) This experiment included gratings presented not only in horizontal and vertical windows (**Fig. 4A**), but also in diagonal windows (**Fig. 4B**). Reassuringly, the predictions of the model resembled the actual data in all stimulus conditions (Figure 4c,f), including diagonal stimulus conditions that were not used to determine the parameters of model that describe the mapping function.

4 Discussion

It has long been clear that the profile of activation elicited in V1 by a stimulus that is localized and oriented depends on the map of retinotopy, on the point spread function, and on the map of orientation preference [6, 12]. It was not known, however, how these factors interact to yield the response to a given visual stimulus.

We described a simple rule of interaction that we found to be highly effective (Fig. 2). This rule involves three steps, each of which can be interpreted in terms of anatomical connections and physiological mechanisms. We can think of the map of retinotopy as a map of projections from the visual field (through the lateral geniculate nucleus) to the cortex. The projection, however, is not from one point to another point, but rather from one point to a whole cloud of points: the center of the cloud is specified by the mapping function (step 1, Fig. 2D), and the width of the cloud is specified by the point spread function (step 2, Fig. 2F). A stimulus of a given orientation, in turn, will not excite all points in cortex, but only those whose preferred orientation matches the stimulus (step 3, Fig. 2H). This could be because the cloud of connections is patchy [13], or because V1 neurons do not integrate inputs from regions of the visual field that are inconsistent with their orientation selectivity [14].

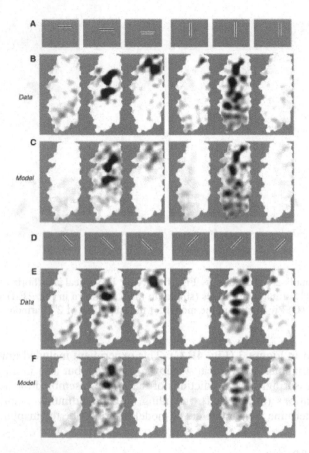

Fig. 4. Application of the retinotopy model to a novel stimulus. (**A**) Horizontal and vertical gratings were flashed on the CRT monitor (**B**). The responses to the flashed grating (measured at the peak of the flash response). (**C**) The prediction of the model, whose parameters were determined from a separate experiment like the one shown in Fig. 1. (**D**) Oblique gratings were also flashed on the CRT monitor. (**E**) The responses to the oblique gratings (also measured at the peak of the flash response). (**F**) The prediction of the model to the oblique stimuli. Note that oblique stimuli are novel for the model. Experiment 70-3-8.

The success of pointwise multiplication indicates that, for each pixel, the selectivity for stimulus position was independent of stimulus orientation and the selectivity for stimulus orientation was independent of stimulus position.

This independence in the effects of two stimulus attributes may seem to contradict the conflation of maps that has been recently reported [1]. The two results, however, are complementary, and both follow from the widely accepted model of V1 selectivity based on local spatiotemporal receptive fields. Basole et al. [1] imaged the responses to an oriented stimulus that was also moving, and found that they could not simply predict those responses by multiplying the relevant maps: the one of orientation preference and the one of direction selectivity. This is precisely the result that would be expected if the selectivity of V1 neurons were due to a local spatiotemporal receptive field, as in such a mechanism the effects of orientation and direction are not independent [2]. We, in turn, imaged responses to an oriented stimulus that was also localized in space, and found that we could indeed predict those responses by multiplying the relevant maps: the one of orientation preference and the one of retinotopy. Again, this is the result that might arguably be expected if selectivity of V1 neurons were due to a local spatiotemporal receptive field: changing stimulus position would scale the responses of the receptive field with little effect on its selectivity for orientation.

One open question concerns the degree to which the maps of orientation preference and retinotopy might influence or distort the other, perhaps in the interest of coverage [12, 15, 16]. An early study reported a strong dependence between the two maps [17], but later studies argued otherwise [5, 18], and recent anatomical results suggest that the map of retinotopy is in fact remarkably free from local distortions [19, 20]. Our methods lack the spatial resolution to address this question; we hope it will be put to rest through two-photon microscopy .

4.1 Limitations of the Model

We have demonstrated that a simple model that assumes that the orientation and retinotopic preferences of a single location on the cortex are independent does a good job of describing the VSD response of the cortex to a localized, oriented stimulus. The model has limitations in its current form. The model assumes a linear transformation from degrees of visual angle to millimeters of cortex. As we have noted above, such a transformation is inconsistent with the wealth of anatomical and physiological data that shows that the transformation is nonlinear. A more realistic model would take into account this approximately logarithmic transformation. Under the conditions of the current study, however, the logarithmic version of the model did not notably improve the quality of the fits despite having an extra parameter. Presumably if our window on the cortex were larger, the logarithmic version of the model would outperform the linear version.

In this experiment we did not systematically vary the contrast of the stimulus. Varying the contrast of the stimulus changes the magnitude of the VSD responses, but it might also change the extent of cortex that is activated. Examination of single units has provided evidence that higher contrast stimuli result in smaller receptive field sizes ([21]). Consequently, we might expect that higher contrast stimuli might activate smaller regions of the cortex or, in the terms of our model, reduce the point spread function. Alternatively, higher contrast stimuli might make the apparent region of activated cortex larger, as a larger portion of the cortex is activated above some baseline noise threshold. Further investigation will be necessary to determine the effect of stimulus contrast on these measurements.

Finally, we note that our localized, oriented stimuli are extremely simplified, and the model should be tested with more complex spatial configurations. There is a great deal of physiological evidence to suggest that spatial context can impact the cortical response to an oriented stimulus [for a review see 22]. In fact, we have observed this impact using a white noise stimulus. In **Fig. 5A** we show a focal patch of squarewave grating whose contrast polarity is reversed according to a pseudorandom sequence.

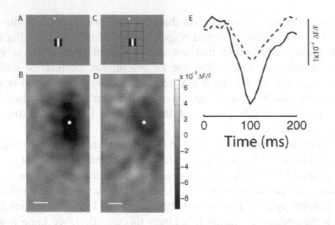

Fig. 5. The effect of spatial context on responses to a localized stimulus (**A**) The gray rectangle depicts the CRT monitor. The stimulus is 2 deg square patch of oriented square wave grating whose contrast reverses in time according to an m-sequence. The white dot represents the location of the Area Centralis. (**B**) The response of the cortex 100 ms after a contrast reversal of the patch. Scale bar is 1 mm (**C**) As in **A** except that the patch is surrounded by other contrast reversing patches whose locations are given by the grid of dotted lines. (**D**) The response of the cortex 100 ms after a contrast reversal of the center patch. (**E**) The time course of the response following a contrast reversal. Thesolid line is the response (in the neighborhood of the pixel shown in **B** with the white dot) to the patch presented in isolation. The dotted line is the response to the same patch presented in the context of additional patches.

We measured the 1st order response of the cortex to that patch using standard event related methods. The response 100 ms after a contrast reversal is shown in **Fig. 5B**. If we now present exactly the same patch, but while it is surrounded by spatiotemporally uncorrelated contrast modulating patches (**Fig. 5C**), we note that the response 100 ms after a contrast reversal (of the center patch) is greatly reduced (**Fig. 5D**). The time course of the 1st order response (following a contrast reversal) is shown in **Fig. 5E**; the solid curve shows the response when the patch is presented in isolation and the dotted curve shows the response when the patch is presented in the context of the surrounding patches.

This suppression of the response we observe when the patch is presented in context may be related to the suppression observed with single unit methods [e.g, 22, 23]. In any case, the simple local model we have presented would fail to account for it. Additional studies that examine the effect of spatial configuration on the responses to localized, oriented stimuli may be able to address how and whether the principles of combining orientation and retinotopic preference depend on the spatial context in which stimuli are shown.

Acknowledgements

Supported by an NRSA postdoctoral award (to RAF), by NEI grants R21-EY016441 and R01-EY017396, and by a Scholar Award from the McKnight Endowment Fund for Neuroscience.

References

1. Basole, A., White, L.E., Fitzpatrick, D.: Mapping multiple features in the population response of visual cortex. Nature 423, 986–990 (2003)
2. Mante, V., Carandini, M.: Mapping of stimulus energy in primary visual cortex. J. Neurophysiol. 94, 788–798 (2005)
3. Grinvald, A., Hildesheim, R.: VSDI: a new era in functional imaging of cortical dynamics. Nat. Rev. Neurosci. 5, 874–885 (2004)
4. Gilbert, C.D., Kelly, J.P.: The projections of cells in different layers of the cat's visual cortex. J. Comp. Neurol. 163, 81–106 (1975)
5. Bosking, W.H., Crowley, J.C., Fitzpatrick, D.: Spatial coding of position and orientation in primary visual cortex. Nat. Neurosci. 5, 874–882 (2002)
6. Albus, K.: A quantitative study of the projection area of the central and the paracentral visual field in area 17 of the cat. I. The precision of the topography. Exp. Brain Res. 24, 159–179 (1975)
7. Reid, R.C., Victor, J.D., Shapley, R.M.: The use of m-sequences in the analysis of visual neurons: linear receptive field properties. Vis. Neurosci. 14, 1015–1027 (1997)
8. Shoham, D., et al.: Imaging cortical dynamics at high spatial and temporal resolution with novel blue voltage-sensitive dyes. Neuron 24, 791–802 (1999)
9. Sharon, D., Grinvald, A.: Dynamics and constancy in cortical spatiotemporal patterns of orientation processing. Science 295, 512–515 (2002)
10. Tusa, R.J., Palmer, L.A., Rosenquist, A.C.: The retinotopic organization of area 17 (striate cortex) in the cat. J. Comp. Neurol. 177, 213–236 (1978)
11. Tusa, R.J., Rosenquist, A.C., Palmer, L.A.: Retinotopic organization of areas 18 and 19 in the cat. J. Comp. Neurol. 185, 657–678 (1979)
12. Hubel, D.H., Wiesel, T.N.: Uniformity of monkey striate cortex: a parallel relationship between field size, scatter, and magnification factor. J. Comp. Neurol. 158, 295–305 (1974)
13. Mooser, F., Bosking, W.H., Fitzpatrick, D.: A morphological basis for orientation tuning in primary visual cortex. Nat. Neurosci. 7, 872–879 (2004)
14. Alonso, J.M., Usrey, W.M., Reid, R.C.: Rules of connectivity between geniculate cells and simple cells in cat primary visual cortex. J. Neurosci. 21, 4002–4015 (2001)
15. Swindale, N.V., et al.: Visual cortex maps are optimized for uniform coverage. Nat. Neurosci. 3, 822–826 (2000)
16. Blasdel, G., Campbell, D.: Functional retinotopy of monkey visual cortex. J. Neurosci. 21, 8286–8301 (2001)
17. Das, A., Gilbert, C.D.: Distortions of visuotopic map match orientation singularities in primary visual cortex. Nature 387, 594–598 (1997)
18. Buzas, P., et al.: Independence of visuotopic representation and orientation map in the visual cortex of the cat. Eur. J. Neurosci. 18, 957–968 (2003)
19. Adams, D.L., Horton, J.C.: A precise retinotopic map of primate striate cortex generated from the representation of angioscotomas. J. Neurosci. 23, 3771–3789 (2003)
20. Adams, D.L., Horton, J.C.: The representation of retinal blood vessels in primate striate cortex. J. Neurosci. 23, 5984–5997 (2003)
21. Sceniak, M.P., et al.: Contrast's effect on spatial summation by macaque V1 neurons. Nat. Neurosci. 2, 733–739 (1999)
22. Sengpiel, F., Sen, A., Blakemore, C.: Characteristics of surround inhibition in cat area 17. Exp. Brain Res. 116, 216–228 (1997)
23. DeAngelis, G.C., Freeman, R.D., Ohzawa, I.: Length and width tuning of neurons in the cat's primary visual cortex. J. Neurophysiol. 71, 347–374 (1994)

A Neural Model for Attentional Modulation of Lateral Interactions in the Visual Cortex

Mia Šetić and Dražen Domijan

Department of Psychology, Faculty of Philosophy, University of Rijeka
Ivana Klobučarića 1, 51000 Rijeka, Croatia
{ddomijan,mia-setic}@ffri.hr

Abstract. Neurophysiological investigations showed that attention influences neural responses in the visual cortex by modulating the amount of contextual interactions between cells. Attention acts as a gate that protects cells from lateral excitatory and inhibitory influences. A recurrent neural network based on dendritic inhibition is proposed to account for these findings. In the model, two types of inhibition are distinguished: dendritic and lateral inhibition. Dendritic inhibition regulates the amount of impact that surrounding cells may exert on a target cell via dendrites of excitatory neurons and dendrites of subpopulation of inhibitory neurons mediating lateral inhibition. Attention increases the amount of dendritic inhibition and prevents contextual interactions, while it has no effect on the target cell when there is no contextual input. Computer simulations showed that the proposed model reproduces the results of several studies about interaction between attention and horizontal connections in the visual cortex.

Keywords: Attention; Contrast; Contour Integration; Visual Cortex; Dendritic Inhibition.

1 Introduction

Directing attention to an object in a receptive field of a cell in a visual cortex significantly alters its response. Earlier studies showed that cells in V4 and IT reduce firing rate if attention is shifted away from the preferred stimulus despite the fact that it is still present in a receptive field (reviewed in [13, 17]). The primary visual cortex can also be influenced by attention. Ito *et al.* [6,7] investigated how attention modulates excitatory contextual interactions in V1. They showed that attention operates as a gate that prevents excitatory influence from surrounding cells with collinear receptive fields. The cell's activity reduces to the level where there are no contextual stimuli present in the visual field. Furthermore, perceptual learning has similar effect on firing rates as attention. That is, prolonged exposure to the same stimuli reduces the impact of collinear stimuli.

Similar results have been obtained with inhibitory interactions in a V2 and V4. Reynolds *et al.* [14] measured and compared neural activity of the target cell in a case when there are no competing stimuli present in the visual field and when they are present. Activity is measured in two conditions: when attention is directed toward the target stimulus and when the attention is diverted away from the target stimulus.

F. Mele et al. (Eds.): BVAI 2007, LNCS 4729, pp. 42–51, 2007.

When attention is diverted away from the preferred object of the target cell, its activity is reduced if competing stimulus is present. This effect is attributed to the inhibitory interactions between cells responsive to different stimuli. When attention is focused on a preferred object of the target cell, its activity increases to the level as if the preferred object is presented alone in the visual field. Therefore, attention isolates cells from surrounding inhibition [14].

How attention interacts with horizontal (or lateral) connections in a visual cortex has been explicated in several neural models [4,9]. Grossberg and Raizada [4] proposed that attention influences the feedforward visual processing via top-down on-centre off-surround pathway which enables enhancement of attended stimulus and suppression of unattended stimuli. Attention enters the processing stream at the stage before excitatory horizontal interactions take place and can not directly influence contour integration. Grossberg and Raizada [4] demonstrated that their model correctly simulates data of Reynolds et. al. [14]. Modulation is achieved by the attentional off-surround signals which reduce the feedforward inhibitory influences from the surrounding cells. However, their model is not able to simulate data of Ito, et al. [6,7] because the size of the attentional influence is restricted to the size of a receptive field. Therefore, attention could not reach contextual input that is outside of the receptive field and could not reduce its impact on the target cell. In a model of contour integration proposed by Li [9] excitatory and inhibitory pathways are combined in the same network. She suggested that attention could directly influence the stage at which lateral interactions occur, either through pyramidal cells or inhibitory interneurons. However, if attention directly influences the excitatory cells then its effects should be observed even in the case when there are no surrounding stimuli present in the stimuli. On the other hand, empirical data shows that attentional influence on the single stimulus presented alone is negligible [6,7]. If attention influences inhibitory cells, the amount of influence should be precisely balanced with lateral excitation in order to achieve proper reduction in contour integration.

The aim of the present paper is to show how dendritic inhibition might contribute to the contour integration and how attentional signals delivered by dendritic inhibition prevent excitatory contextual interactions. The model also needs to be consistent with biased competition account of the role of attention in modulating the inhibitory contextual interactions in the striate and the extrastriate visual cortex.

2 Model Description

In order to provide a unified account of attentional modulations in excitatory and inhibitory interactions, we consider a simple recurrent network of linear-threshold neurons with dendrites as special computational units. In the model, two types of inhibitory interneurons are distinguished (Fig 1). One type receives excitation from non-collinear neighbouring pyramidal cells and delivers lateral inhibition to the target pyramidal cell. This is equivalent to the classical lateral inhibition used in other models of cortical computation [4,9]. The second type of inhibitory interneuron mediates dendritic inhibition from the target cell to its dendrites. In this way dendritic inhibition controls the amount of excitation which the target cell receives from the neighbouring cells with collinear receptive fields (Fig 1a). Such control allows excitatory cells to mutually reinforce each other but prevents unbounded growth of their activity. The same interneuron also delivers inhibition to inhibitory pathway from non-collinear pyramidal cells to lateral inhibitory interneuron (Fig 1b). We assume that attention or top-down signals exert their influence on recurrent activity by contacting the inhibitory interneuron that mediates dendritic inhibition. Therefore, the attentional signal directly enters into recurrent communication between cortical cells. This is in contrast with Reynolds' and Desimone's [14] implementation of the biased competition model where attention influences feedforward signals from the previous network layer. Also, the present approach differs from Spratling's and Johnson's [16] feedback model of attention based on dendritic computation. Here, attention excites a specific subset of inhibitory interneurons which controls the amount of recurrent communication between cells. Spratling and Johnson [16] do not distinguish between these inhibitory subpopulations which prevents their model to simulate attentional influence on contour integration.

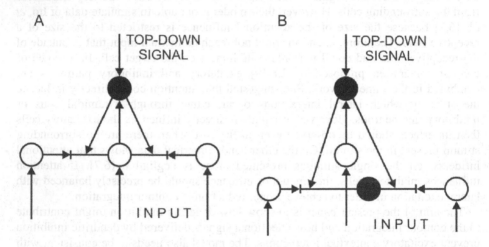

Fig. 1. A model of a cortical circuit for attentional modulations of the excitatory and the inhibitory contextual interactions. Open circles are the excitatory cells and filled circles are the inhibitory. Lines with T endings are dendrites which independently integrate input signals. A) Excitatory components of the model. B) Inhibitory components of the model.

The basic architecture of the network is depicted in Figure 1. Formally, the model is described with a set of nonlinear differential equations. The activity level of the excitatory target cell, $x_{i\theta}$, at spatial position i; with preferred orientation θ; and its corresponding inhibitory interneuron, $y_{i\theta}$, is given by

$$\frac{dx_{i\theta}}{dt} = -Ax_{i\theta} + \sum_{j}\left[w_{ji\theta}f_j\left(x_{j\theta}\right)-y_{i\theta}\right]^+ +$$

$$I_{i\theta} - x_{i\theta}\sum_{k}\left[w_{ki\theta}f_k\left(x_{k\theta}\right)-y_{i\theta}\right]^+$$

(1)

$$\frac{dy_{i\theta}}{dt} = -Ay_{i\theta} + z_i f_i(x_{i\theta}) + TD_{i\theta},$$ (2)

where

$$[x]^+ = \max(x,0).$$ (3)

The terms $-Ax_{i\theta}$ and $-Ay_{i\theta}$ denote passive activity decay which forces cell's activity to a resting state if there is no external input. It is assumed that the resting potential is zero. Eqn (3) describes rectification, which is necessary in a biologically plausible model, because it prevents excitatory connection from becoming inhibitory and the vice versa. $I_{i\theta}$, is an input which represents a classical receptive field of the cell with preferred orientation, θ. It influences the target cell separately from recurrent signals as in the model of Spratling and Johnson [16]. In order to simplify the model, the inhibitory interneuron that mediates lateral inhibition is not explicitly represented by a separate differential equation; rather, it is included in the inhibitory term of eqn (1). We did not model a detailed structure of contextual connections between cells in the primary visual cortex [4,9]. We simplify the model by assuming that the neighbouring cells with similar orientation selectivity will excite each other. On the other hand, the neighbouring cells responsive to perpendicular line orientation, θ', will inhibit each other. Only the nearest neighbours are used, so j=i+1 or j=i-1 for excitatory and inhibitory interactions. Function f() represent the output signal from the target cell to the inhibitory interneuron, and the recurrent excitatory and the inhibitory output from neighbouring cells, respectively. Function f() is assumed to be linear above the threshold. The inhibitory interneuron, $y_{i\theta}$, receives input from the corresponding excitatory cell, $x_{i\theta}$, and projects axons to the dendrites of the excitatory cells and dendrites of the inhibitory interneurons which mediates lateral inhibition. It also receives an excitatory projection from higher visual centres which serves as a source of attentional signals, $TD_{i\theta}$. Term, z_i, describes the strength of synaptic contact between the excitatory cell and the inhibitory cell mediating dendritic inhibition. Synaptic weights for connections between excitatory cells, $w_{ji\theta}$, and synaptic weights for lateral inhibition, $w_{ki\theta}$, are assumed to be of unit strength. However, this simplification does not reduce the generality of the model because parametric simulations reveal that the model behaviour is not altered by changes in the strength of excitatory connections. The same is also true for inhibitory weights.

3 Computer Simulations

Model behaviour is assessed through numerical integration of differential equations using the Runge-Kutta method. Model parameters were set to: A=1, z_i=.5, and $I_{i\theta}$=1 if stimulus is present in the cell's receptive field or $I_{i\theta}$=0 if stimulus is absent. First, we showed that attention prevents collinear contextual facilitation. Therefore, we set $w_{ji\theta}$=1 and $w_{ki\theta}$=0 in order to focus on excitatory lateral connections and ignore the lateral inibition. Figure 2 shows how excitatory horizontal connections enhance the activity of the target cell in the absence of the top-down attentional signal. Adding the collinear line segment induces mutual excitation among cortical cells tuned to appropriate line orientation. Without dendritic inhibition recurrent excitation will drive the cells to saturation. Dendritic inhibition allows excitatory cells to remain sensitive to the amplitude of the input or to achieve analogue sensitivity. Therefore, dendritic inhibition has a functional role in controlling the recurrent excitation and it was not introduced in the model just to simulate attentional influences per se.

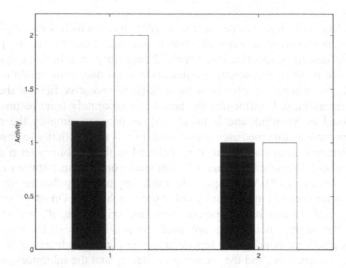

Fig. 2. Modelling the influence of attention on the recurrent excitatory interactions. 1 - attention is directed away from the target cell. 2 – attention is directed on the target cell. Black bars – target stimulus is presented alone. White bars – collinear contour segment is present. Adding collinear contextual input increases the target cell's response but only if the attention is distributed or diverted away from the location of the target cell. When attention is directed to the location of the target cell, collinear stimuli are not able to influence its activity.

Here, it is assumed that the distributed attention can be represented by very weak signals that are equally distributed to all cells in a network. Therefore, they do not contribute much to the operation of the model and these signals were ignored (i.e., $TD_{i\theta}=0$). When attention is distributed or when attention is directed away from collinear contour segments, contour integration occurs (Fig 2, left white bar). When attention is focused on a target cell, the top-down signal is delivered to its inhibitory interneuron, $TD_{i\theta}=2$. Top-down or attentional signal distributes inhibition to all dendrites to which the inhibitory interneuron is connected. In this way, the top-down signal closes the gates between the target cell and its collinear neighbours (Fig 2, right white bar). Effectively, the target cell is isolated from lateral influences and only the feedforward signal can reach it because the inhibitory interneuron does not have connection with the input pathway. Therefore, the cell's activity will converge to the activity value as is the case when the contour segment is presented alone (Fig 2, black bars).

The model is also tested with inhibitory interactions (Fig 3). In this case, model parameters were set as follows: A=1, z_i=1, $w_{ji\theta}$=0 and $w_{ki\theta}$=1. When the target stimulus is placed near non-collinear stimulus, mutual inhibition results in reduction of activity for the corresponding cells if attention is directed elsewhere ($TD_{i\theta}$=0). But when attention is focused on the target stimulus ($TD_{i\theta}$=.3), dendritic inhibition prevents lateral inhibition from neighbouring cells and the target cells' activity is restored to the value where there is no contextual input present. The model is also consistent with psychophysical study of the role of attention with regard to contrast detection when inhibitory surrounding stimuli are present. Zenger *et al.* [18] showed that attention exerts its influence only when the target stimulus has a lower contrast compared to the surrounding stimuli. In that case, the detection threshold is significantly reduced. When the target stimulus has a higher contrast compared to the surrounding, attention has no influence on the threshold for target detection. In the model this is the consequence of the protective role of dendritic inhibition. If target stimulus has a higher contrast than surrounding stimuli, the corresponding cell will protect itself from the surrounding inhibition even if attention is not directed to it. It will simply override recurrent inhibition arriving from the surrounding. When target stimulus has a low contrast, attention will help in reducing the inhibitory impact from the surrounding. Here, we simply assumed that the threshold for target detection is inversely proportional to the strength of the neural activity. Therefore, the cell with stronger activity level will be easier to detect.

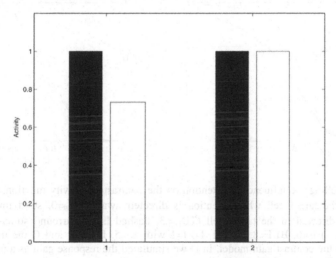

Fig. 3. Modelling the influence of attention on the recurrent inhibitory interactions. 1- attention is directed away from the target cell. 2 – attention is directed on the target cell. Black bars – target stimulus is presented alone. White bars – competing surround stimulus is present. Surround stimulus may exert its inhibitory influence only if attention is directed away from the target stimulus.

Furthermore, we checked how attention changes the contrast sensitivity function (CSF) of the simulated cells (Fig 4). In the empirical studies two types of attentional influences were observed. In the study of McAdams and Maunsell [12], attention multiplicatively increases the cell's response by a constant gain factor. Therefore, the cell's saturation point is effectively increased. On the other hand, in the studies of Reynolds *et al.* [15] it was shown that attention shifts the contrast response function leftward. This means that attention increases the stimulus' effective contrast. Attention exerts the strongest effect on the mid-level contrast. On the other hand, when low and high, the contrast effect of attention is minimal. This is indicated by the fact that the cell's saturation point remains on the same level with or without attention [17].

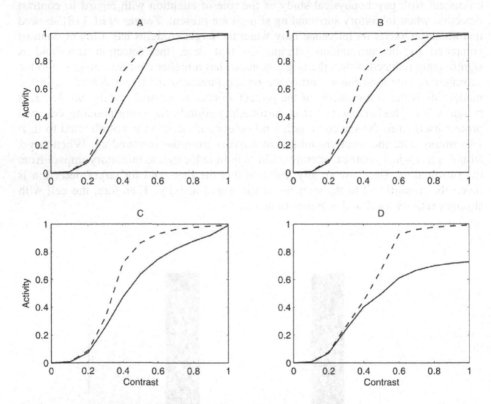

Fig. 4. Modelling the influence of attention on the contrast sensitivity function. Graphs show activity of the target cell when attention is directed away ($TD_{i\theta}=0$, solid line) and when attention is directed to the target cell ($TD_{i\theta}=.3$, dashed line). Surround stimulus had fixed intensity at: A) $I=.6$, B) $I=.8$, C) $I=1$, D) $I=1$ with $z_i=.5$. In A, B and C the model behaves according to the contrast gain model. In D we simulated the response gain as a mechanism for attentional influence on CSF.

We simulated the contrast response function by the systematic variation in input amplitude from 0 to 1 in steps of .1. In order to approximate the contrast response of real neurons better, we applied the sigmoid function of the form $c(I) = I^n / (.01+I^n)$ where $n=4$. Sigmoid nonlinearity is applied to the input signal prior to reaching the target excitatory cell. In this way we simulate nonlinearity present in the visual system. The input amplitude of the surround cell was kept constant at $I=.6$ or $I=.8$ or $I=1$ during systematic changes of the input amplitude for the target cell. As can be seen from the Fig 4, both type of attentional influence can be observed in the proposed model with a small change in a single network parameter. When, $z_i=.5$ model behaves consistently with the observation of McAdams and Maunsell [12] (Fig 4d). On the other hand, when $z_i=1$ the model behaves according to the contrast gain response (Fig 4abc). Reynolds et al. [15] argued that discrepant results between these studies may be the consequence of the difference in methodology because McAdams and Maunsell [12] may have not utilised the full range of stimulus contrast. Our results show that the same network may exhibit the response gain or the contrast gain depending on the strength of synaptic connection between the excitatory cell and its corresponding inhibitory interneuron which mediates dendritic inhibition. Therefore, it may not be justified to make such a strong distinction between the response gain and the contrast gain when discussing potential mechanisms for attentional modulation [17].

4 Discussion

Empirical studies using single-unit recordings from the primate visual cortex provide a rich set of data for modelling attentional influences on neural activity [13,17]. An important observation was that attention does not influence the cell's activity directly because there is small or even non existent change in the neural activity when the cell's preferred stimulus is the only object in the visual field. Stronger attentional modulation is observed when there are more competing stimuli present in the input pattern. The introduction of a new pattern in the surround space reduces the cell's response to its preferred stimulus. Reduction is possibly due to the lateral inhibition from the neighbouring cells. However, directing the attention to the cell's preferred stimulus increases its response close to the value as when the preferred stimulus is presented alone. Therefore, focused attention has a protective effect for the cell which is responsive to the attended object. Attention simply prevents inhibitory influences from the surrounding patterns.

Similar results were obtained with excitatory interactions [6,7]. It is known that in the primary visual cortex cells are particularly sensitive to the oriented edge or line elements. When several such segments are aligned to form an extended contour, the cells with preferred orientation show a strong increase in activity [3,8,9]. Therefore, placing a collinear contour segment in a cell's surrounding, facilitates the cell's response. Facilitation occurs despite the fact that surrounding segment can not activate that cell in isolation because the surrounding segment is outside of the cell's classical receptive field. The collinear contour segment also decreases the threshold for detecting the target stimulus in psychophysical investigation. These effects are assumed to occur due to the long-range horizontal excitatory connections [6-9]. When attention is drawn to one oriented segment, the influence of surrounding segments is almost completely abolished. Later studies confirmed that such effect could not be attributed to the feedback from higher visual centres but it is a consequence of the modulation of horizontal excitatory connections.

The common pattern emerging from these studies is that attention acts on horizontal (or recurrent) connections between the cells tuned to different stimuli and modulates the amount of interaction between them. Several models explain how attention modulates inhibitory interactions [1,14,16] but it is not clear how they can be generalized to modulation of the excitatory connections as observed in the studies of Ito et al. [6,7]. Grossberg and Raizada [4] were the first to provide a comprehensive account of interaction between attention and spatial integration. However, their model is not able to accommodate the important result of Ito *et al.* [6,7], which shows that attention prevents collinear contour integration in a similar manner as it biases competitive interactions. The reason for this failure is the fact that attention in its model acts on a different network layer and it has no direct access to the stage where collinear contour integration occurs. Indirect modulation is also difficult to achieve because it would require complete removal of the collinear stimulus. We suggest that attention exerts its influence by contacting a special group of inhibitory interneurons which make contacts with dendrites of the excitatory and the inhibitory cells.

An important feature of the new model is the hypothesis that dendrites are independent, active elements of cortical information processing [5,11]. Dendrites are incorporated in the model as a set of independent linear threshold units whose output is integrated by a target cell. Recently, several empirical studies demonstrated an active role of dendrites in the signal transmission between the cortical cells [5,11]. For instance, Liu [10] showed that inhibitory synapse has an effect on the excitatory synaptic input only if it is localised on the same dendritic branch as the excitatory synapse and if they are activated simultaneously. Dendritic inhibition was previously used in a feedback model of attention proposed by Spratling and Johnson [16]. Their model was able to simulate a wide variety of attentional influences on competitive neural activity. However, it could not be extended to the modelling of contour integration because the same problem emerges as in the model of Grossberg and Raizada [4]. That is, attention does not influence the excitatory cells responsible for contour integration directly and the only way to reduce the impact of collinear contextual input is to completely remove it from the neural representation. In conclusion, dendritic inhibition is a plausible neurophysiological mechanism that may subserve attentional modulation of contextual interactions in the visual cortex. We showed that a model based on dendritic computation provides a unified account of how attention may influence excitatory and inhibitory horizontal connections in the visual cortex. However, it should be mentioned that a recent single-unit study suggests that attention might influence the oscillatory neural activity by increasing or decreasing the amount of synchronization or desynchronization among cells [2]. It is not clear whether the synchronization of neural activity is a cause of firing rate modulations described in previous studies or is it a consequence of some other mechanism. Further investigations are needed to clarify this issue. Nevertheless, synchronization of neural activity is also governed by recurrent connections and it is possible that dendritic inhibition might modulate it depending on the attentional signals.

Acknowledgments. This work is supported by EBSA travel grant and by Bial Foundation research grant No. 80/06.

References

1. Bundasen, C., Habekost, T., Kyllingsbaek, S.: A neural theory of visual attention: Bridging cognition and neurophysiology. Psych. Rev. 112, 291–328 (2005)
2. Fries, P., Reynolds, J.H., Rorie, A.E., Desimone, R.: Modulation of oscillatory neuronal synchronization by selective visual attention. Science 291, 1560–1563 (2001)
3. Gilbert, C.D., Ito, M., Kapadia, M.K., Westheimer, G.: Interactions between attention, context and learning in the primary visual cortex. Vis. Res. 40, 1217–1226 (2000)

4. Grossberg, S., Raizada, R.D.S.: Contrast-sensitive perceptual grouping and object-based attention in the laminar circuits of primary visual cortex. Vis. Res. 40, 1413–1432 (2000)
5. Häusser, M., Mel, B.W.: Dendrites: bug or feature? Curr. Opin. Neurobiol. 13, 372–383 (2003)
6. Ito, M., Westheimer, G., Gilbert, C.D.: Attention and perceptual learning modulate contextual influences on the visual perception. Neuron 20, 1191–1197 (1998)
7. Ito, M., Gilbert, C.D.: Attention modulates contextual influences in the primary visual cortex of alert monkeys. Neuron 22, 593–604 (1999)
8. Kapadia, M.K., Ito, M., Gilbert, C.D., Westheimer, G.: Improvement in visual sensitivity by changes in the local context: parallel studies in human observers and in V1 of alert monkeys. Neuron 15, 843–856 (1995)
9. Li, Z.: A neural model of contour integration in the primary visual cortex. Neural Comput. 10, 903–940 (1998)
10. Liu, G.: Local structural balance and functional interaction of excitatory and inhibitory synapses in hippocampal dendrites. Nat. Neurosci. 7, 373–379 (2004)
11. London, M., Häusser, M.: Dendritic computation. Annu. Rev. Neurosci. 28, 503–532 (2005)
12. McAdams, C.J., Maunsell, J.H.R.: Effects of attention on orientation-tuning functions of single neurons in macaque cortical area V4. J. Neurosci. 19, 431–441 (1999)
13. Reynolds, J.H., Chelazzi, L.: Attentional modulation of visual processing. Annu. Rev. Neurosci. 27, 611–647 (2004)
14. Reynolds, J.H., Chelazzi, L., Desimone, R.: Competitive mechanisms subserve attention in macaque area V2 and V4. J. Neurosci. 19, 1736–1753 (1999)
15. Reynolds, J.H., Pasternak, T., Desimone, R.: Attention increases sensitivity of V4 neurons. Neuron 26, 703–714 (2000)
16. Spratling, M.W., Johnson, M.H.: A feedback model of visual attention. J. Cogn. Neurosci. 16, 219–237 (2004)
17. Treue, S.: Neural correlates of attention in primate visual cortex. Trends Neurosci. 24, 295–300 (2001)
18. Zenger, B., Braun, J., Koch, C.: Attention effects on contrast detection in the presence of surround masks. Vis. Res. 40, 3717–3724 (2000)

Testing Viewpoint Invariance in the Neural Representation of Faces: An MEG Study

Michael P. Ewbank[1], William A.P. Smith[2], Edwin R. Hancock[2], and Timothy J. Andrews[1]

[1] Department of Psychology, The University of York, UK
{m.ewbank,t.andrews}@psych.york.ac.uk
[2] Department of Computer Science, The University of York, UK
{wsmith,erh}@cs.york.ac.uk

Abstract. The aim of this study was to determine the extent to which the neural representation of faces in the visual cortex is viewpoint invariant. MEG was used to measure evoked responses to faces during an adaptation paradigm. Using familiar and unfamiliar faces, we compared the amplitude of the M170 response to repeated images of the same face compared to images of different faces. We found a reduction in the M170 amplitude to repeated presentations of the same face image compared to images of different faces when shown from the same viewpoint. To establish if this adaptation to the identity of a face was invariant to changes in viewpoint, we varied the viewing angle of the face within a block. In order to exert strict control over the viewpoint from which the face was viewed, we used 3D models recovered from single images using shape-from-shading. This makes the study unique in its use of techniques from machine vision in order to test human visual processes. We found a reduction in response was no longer evident when images of the same face were shown from different viewpoints. These results imply that the face-selective M170 response either reflects an early stage of face processing or that the computations underlying face recognition depend on a viewpoint-dependent neuronal representation.

1 Introduction

Recognising faces in a visual scene is a simple, effortless process for most human observers. However, the face of any individual can generate countless different retinal images depending on the viewing conditions. The visual system must take into account sources of variation caused by changes in viewpoint, but at the same time be able to detect differences between faces. Models of face processing propose that the earliest level of processing involves computing a view-dependent representation. Information from this early stage of processing is compared to view-invariant representations of familiar faces for recognition [1].

Functional imaging studies have also revealed a network of face-selective regions in the occipital and temporal lobe that are thought to underlie our ability to perceive and recognise faces [2]. Processing of facial identity is associated with inferior

F. Mele et al. (Eds.): BVAI 2007, LNCS 4729, pp. 52–61, 2007.

temporal lobe regions, such as the fusiform face area (FFA) [3]. These inferior temporal lobe structures project to anterior temporal regions that contain semantic information associated with a particular facial identity [4]. A region posterior to this, known as the inferior occipital cortex, or occipital face area (OFA) [5] is thought to be implicated in an earlier structural encoding stage of face processing [6].

Event related potential (ERP) and Magnetoencephalography (MEG) studies have also shown that faces and other objects can be distinguished by the pattern of electrical activity across the occipitotemporal lobe [7]. For example, ERP studies have shown a face-selective potential occurring between 140 and 200ms after stimulus onset which appears twice as large for face stimuli compared to a variety of other stimuli [8]. MEG studies have also revealed an early face-selective potential, known as the M170, which has been shown to correlate with the successful recognition of a face [8].

The aim of this study is to use the technique of adaptation to ask whether the M170 potential reflects an underlying representation of facial identity, and whether this representation is invariant to changeable aspects of faces. The principle underlying adaptation is that repetitive presentation of a stimulus results in a decrease in the response of a neuronal population that is selective for that stimulus [9]. The nature of the neural representation can be determined by varying the stimulus. If the underlying neural representation is insensitive to a change then the neural response will remain the same. Alternatively, if the neurons are sensitive to this manipulation, the response will return to the initial level. Although little is know about the effect of stimulus repetition on the M170 response, a recent study has shown a reduction in the amplitude of the M170 following repetition of different face images when using rapid presentation rates [10]. Recently, we reported that adaptation of the N170 potential to facial identity was sensitive to changes in the viewpoint of the image [11]. However, the changes in viewpoint used in these studies were quite large (variations in subject pose were of the order of 45) and only unfamiliar faces were used. It is possible, therefore, that viewpoint-invariant responses may be found when presenting smaller changes in viewing angle (for example, variations of ¡10), or when showing faces that are familiar to the observer. Our hypothesis is that, if the neural representation underlying the M170 response is selective for the identity of a face, we would predict a reduced response to repeated images of the same face. We would also predict that this adaptation should be invariant to changes in the viewpoint of the face and that this invariance should be found over a greater degree of viewpoint change for familiar compared to unfamiliar faces. In contrast, any recovery from adaptation when images of the same face are presented over different viewpoints would suggest that the M170 reflects a viewpoint-specific stage in face processing.

2   Methods

Eighteen subjects (9 females; mean age 23) participated in the study. All observers had normal or corrected-to-normal visual acuity. Fifteen subjects were right-handed. Written consent was obtained from all subjects. All imaging took place at the York Neuroimaging Centre (YNiC).

2.1 Localiser Scan

In order to identify sensors that responded preferentially to images of faces, subjects viewed greyscale images from different object categories: (1) unfamiliar faces; (2) familiar faces; (3) inanimate objects; (4) places (buildings, indoor and natural landscapes) and (5) textures. Photographs of unfamiliar faces were taken from a database of the Psychological Image Collection at Stirling (PICS: http://pics.psych.stir.ac.uk), images of familiar faces were taken from the World Wide Web. Images of inanimate objects, places and textures were obtained from various sources including commercial clip-art collections (CorelDraw, Microsoft). All images were projected onto a screen at a viewing distance of approximately 80cm and subtended a viewing angle of $9° \times 9°$. Images were presented in a series of stimulus blocks, with each block containing 25 images. Each image was presented for a period of 400ms, and was followed by a blank screen containing a fixation cross for 1100ms. In each stimulus block, five images from each object category were randomly interleaved. A total of eight stimulus blocks were presented. Subjects were required to perform a target detection task, by pressing a response button when they saw an image containing a small red dot. Target trials were removed from the subsequent analysis. A resting period was inserted in between each block, during which an equiluminant grey screen was presented for 8 seconds.

2.2 Adaptation Scans

There were two adaptation scans, one consisting of unfamiliar faces (Fig. 1) and another containing familiar faces (Fig. 2). The experimental procedure was identical for both scans. In each scan, stimulus blocks contained either 12 images of the same face (same-identity) or 12 images of different faces (different-identity). Stimulus blocks also varied in the degree of viewpoint change about the vertical axis between images. Four different viewpoint change conditions were used: (1) 0° same viewpoint; (2) 2° change; (3) 4° change; (4) 8° change. Thus, there were 8 different stimulus conditions in each scan. Images in the same viewpoint condition were shown from a frontal viewpoint throughout the block. In the viewpoint change conditions, the first face image in each block was always a frontal view; this was followed by subsequent images rotation to the left or right of the preceding image (see Figs 1 and 2). Faces were rotated 3 increments to the left and the right. For example, in the 2° change condition faces were shown over a range of 12° (0°, 2°, 4°, 6°, 4°, 2°, 0°, −2°, −4°, −6°, −4°, −2°).

2.3 Synthesising Stimulus Images

Acquiring images of faces under strict variations in viewpoint is very difficult to achieve with accuracy and repeatability. In the case of famous subjects, it is infeasible. Hence, to generate the images of unfamiliar and familiar faces at

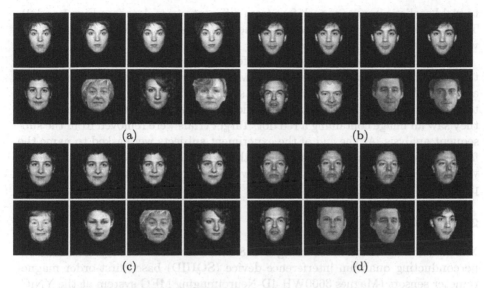

Fig. 1. Examples of unfamiliar face images

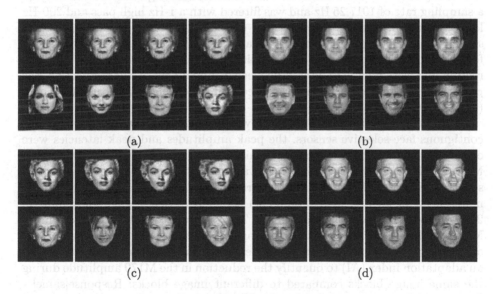

Fig. 2. Examples of familiar face images

different viewpoints, we instead turn to a technique developed within the machine vision community and recover a 3-dimensional model of each face from a single, frontal view using shape-from-shading. This technique exploits a statistical model of facial shape to render the shape-from-shading problem tractable [12]. By restricting the algorithm to a certain class of objects (namely faces), the model provides a sufficiently powerful constraint to allow accurate reconstructions from a single image. The estimated 3-dimensional models can be rotated to yield realistic images of each face from different viewpoints (see Figs 1 and 2). This makes our study particularly unique in its use of techniques from machine vision to test human visual processes.

Each image was presented for 400ms followed by a 1100ms blank screen containing a fixation cross. Each condition was repeated four times in a counterbalanced block-design, making a total of 32 stimulus blocks. Subjects were required to perform a target detection task in which they were required to respond when they saw an image containing a red dot. Target trials were removed from the subsequent analysis. At the end of the experiment subjects were asked to name the familiar faces that had been shown in the experimental scan. Stimulus blocks were separated by periods of fixation when an equiluminant grey screen was presented for 8 seconds.

2.4   MEG Analysis

MEG recordings were made using a 248-channel whole head system with superconducting quantum interference device (SQUID) based first-order magnetometer sensors (Magnes 3600WH 4D-Neuroimaging MEG system at the YNiC, University of York, UK). Magnetic brain activity was digitized continuously at a sampling rate of 1017.25 Hz and was filtered with a 1-Hz high pass and 200-Hz low pass cut-off. Average waveforms for each subject were computed using a 1 second epoch (200 ms before and 800 ms after stimulus onset). The average waveforms were further processed off-line using a 200ms pre-stimulus baseline correction and were high-pass filtered between 3- and 30-Hz. Artifact rejection was performed to remove epochs that exceeded a predetermined amplitude threshold (alpha $= 0.05$).

In the localiser scan, a contour plot was then used to locate the 10 largest contiguous face-selective sensors. the peak amplitudes and peak latencies were calculated for each condition in each hemisphere for each subject. Analysis of the MEG amplitude in the viewpoint scans was then restricted to these face-selective sensors of interest (SOIs). A multi-factorial ANOVA was used to determine the main effects of identity (same, different) hemisphere (left, right), viewpoint (0, 2, 4, 8) and fame (familiar, unfamiliar). To assess whether the reduction in the M170 amplitude was statistically significant in different conditions, we performed a two-sample t-test on the peak amplitudes across subjects. Finally, we calculated an adaptation index (AI) to quantify the reduction in the M170 amplitude during the same image blocks compared to different image blocks: Response[same] - Response[different].

3   Results - Localiser Scan

First, we determined which sensors showed selective responses to images of faces compared to other categories of stimuli (Fig. 4). We located SOIs in occipitotemporal regions that had a significantly higher response to images of unfamiliar and familiar faces than to non-face stimuli in each subject.

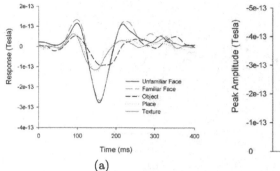

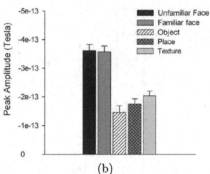

(a)   (b)

Fig. 3. (a) Average MEG waveform recorded for each category of object in the localiser scan. Waveforms are shown in face-selective sensors in right hemisphere averaged across all subjects. (b) Bar graph representing amplitude of the average peak M170 response to each category across subjects. Error bars represent ±1 standard error.

18 subjects showed face-selective M170 responses in right hemisphere sensors, with 12 showing an additional left-hemisphere face-selective M170. We then measured the peak amplitude of the M170 in response to each of the five categories shown in the localiser scan (Figs 3(a) and 3(b)). A 2 way ANOVA (Hemisphere × Category) revealed a highly significant effect of category ($F(4, 48) = 51.63, P < 10^{-17}$), no effect of hemisphere ($F(1, 12) = 1.65, P = 0.22$), and no interaction between hemisphere and category ($F(4, 48) = 0.73, P = 0.57$). The mean amplitude response to unfamiliar faces in both the right and left hemisphere was signifi-

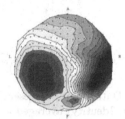

Fig. 4. MEG shaded contour map of one representative subject, showing distribution of response to images of unfamiliar faces, approximately 163 msecs after stimulus onset. Anterior regions are to the top of the image.

cantly greater than objects RH: ($t(17) = 8.79, P < 10^{-8}$); LH: ($t(12) = 6.29, P < 0.0001$); places RH: ($t(17) = 10.44, P < 10^{-9}$); LH: ($t(12)11.82, P < 10^{-7}$), and textures RH: ($t(17) = 7.68, P < 10^{-7}$); LH: ($t(12) = 7.73, P < 0.0001$). There was no significant difference between the response to unfamiliar faces and familiar faces in either the right ($t(17) = 0.25, P = 0.80$), or left hemisphere ($t(12) = -0.06, P = 0.95$). The mean amplitude to familiar faces in both hemispheres was also significantly larger than objects RH: ($t(17) = 9.30, P < 10^{-8}$); LH: ($t(12) = 11.29, P = 10^{-7}$), places RH: ($t(17) = 11.58, P < 10^{-9}$); LH: ($t(12) = 7.99, P < 10^{-6}$), and textures RH: ($t(17) = 8.72, P < 10^{-7}$); LH: ($t(12) = 5.53, P < 0.0001$). The mean latency of the face-selective M170 was 155.6 ms in right hemisphere and 166.7 ms in left hemisphere. A 2 way ANOVA of latency (Hemisphere × Category) revealed a significant effect of hemisphere ($F(4, 48) = 27.0, P > 0.001$) with all categories showing a significantly earlier potential in right hemisphere sensors than left hemisphere sensors. Response

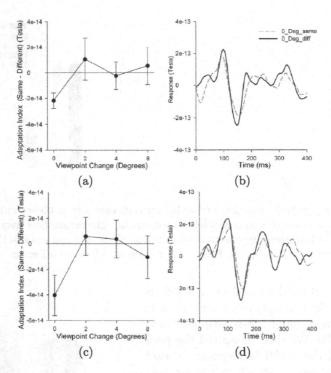

Fig. 5. Data points represent adaptation-index of M170 response (Same Identity - Different Identity) averaged across all subjects in right hemisphere sensors of interest for (a) unfamiliar faces and (c) familiar faces. Error bars represent ±1 standard error. MEG waveforms of one representative subject showing responses to the same and different identity images in the 0° (same viewpoint) condition for (b) unfamiliar and (d) familiar faces.

data indicated no difference in the response times across different categories in the target detection task ($F(4, 68) = 0.65, P = 0.84$).

4   Results - Adaptation Scans

A 4 way ANOVA 2×2×2×4 (Identity, Hemisphere, Familiarity, Viewpoint) found no effect of identity, fame, hemisphere or viewpoint. However, there was a significant interaction between Hemisphere × Identity × View ($F(3, 36) = 4.04, P < 0.05$). Fig. 5 shows the response of the M170 in the right hemisphere to thedifferent face conditions. A 3 way ANOVA ($2 \times 2 \times 4$) (Identity, Fame, Viewpoint) revealed a significant effect of viewpoint ($F(3, 51) = 4.33, P < 0.01$), and a significant interaction between viewpoint and identity ($F(3, 51) = 4.00, P < 0.05$), in the right hemisphere. In the 0° (same viewpoint) condition, we found that the peak M170 response to images of the same face was significantly lower than the response to different faces in face-selective sensors for both unfamiliar ($t(17) = 3.57, P < 0.01$) and familiar ($t(17) = 2.25, P < 0.05$) faces (see Fig. 5).

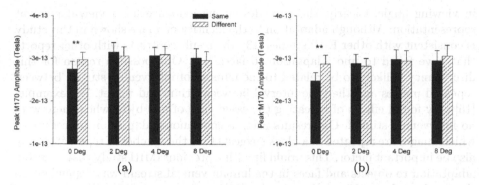

Fig. 6. Bar graphs representing the average peak M170 amplitude in the right hemisphere across all subjects to (a) unfamiliar and (b) familiar faces with the same or different identity. Error bars represent ±1 standard error.

We then measured the M170 response to the same and different unfamiliar faces during the 2°, 4° and 8° angle change conditions. The results showed no difference in the M170 response to images of the same face compared to different faces at a rotation of 2° (unfamiliar, $t(17) = -0.60, P = 0.53$; familiar, $t(17) = -0.40, P = 0.69$), 4° (unfamiliar, $t(17) = -0.22, P = 0.82$; familiar, $t(17) = -0.25, P = 0.80$) or 8° (unfamiliar, $t(17) = 0.35, P = 0.72$; familiar, $t(17) = 0.62, P = 0.54$) for either the unfamiliar or familiar conditions (Fig. fig:fig5). We found no difference in the latencies of the target response across the same and different conditions. No significant effects were found in the left hemisphere.

5 Conclusions

The aim of this experiment was to determine the role of the M170 response in face recognition. Specifically, we asked whether the M170 response: (1) is involved in representing facial identity; (2) reflects a viewpoint-dependent or a viewpoint-invariant representation of faces and (3) differs in its response to familiar and unfamiliar faces. Using an adaptation paradigm, we found that the M170 amplitude in the right hemisphere is significantly reduced during the presentation of identical face images shown at the same viewpoint compared to different face images shown at the same viewpoint. To determine whether the neural representation underlying the M170 response was invariant to changes in the face image, we varied the viewpoint of the images. We found that there was no difference in the magnitude of the M170 response between the same or different conditions when the viewpoint was varied. Furthermore, we found no significant difference in the M170 response to familiar and unfamiliar faces.

These results are consistent with a recent ERP study, in which we showed that a similar N170 response was elicited to the same and different faces when they varied in viewing angle [11]. The present study goes beyond this by showing that this viewpoint-dependent response is still evident for quite small changes in viewing angle. Clearly, this provides strong evidence for a view-dependent representation. Although adaptation to the identity of a face shown in this study is consistent with other ERP studies [13], the result contrasts with other reports that have failed to find adaptation to faces [14]. One possible reason for this discrepancy is likely to be related to the number of intervening stimuli between repeated images and the time interval between prime and target. For example, [15] only found effects of repeating the same view of an object when there were no intervening stimuli. Our results using a continuous adaptation procedure in which images are repeated in a block suggests that the number of repetitions may also be important factor. This would fit with a previous fMRI study that reported adaptation to objects and faces in the human ventral stream was dependent on the number of repetitions of a stimulus [16].

We found no significant effect of familiarity in the M170 response to faces. This is consistent with fMRI studies that have shown familiarity has little effect on the response of face-selective regions [17]. However, these neuroimaging results contrast with the fact that human subjects are very good at identifying familiar faces (even from very low quality images), whereas performance in recognition or matching of unfamiliar faces is poor [18].

A central question in the visual recognition of objects is whether this process depends on a viewpoint-dependent or viewpoint-invariant neuronal representation. Models of face processing suggest that the initial stage of processing is based on a view dependent structural representation and that further recognition of facial identity is based on matching to a viewpoint invariant representation [1]. It would appear, therefore, that the view-dependent nature of the M170 response for familiar and unfamiliar faces could be taken as an indication of an early stage in face processing. On the other hand, a number of behavioural studies provide evidence that faces and other objects could be represented by a view-dependent neural representation. In a previous fMRI study, we found that face-selective regions within the inferior temporal lobe showed a reduced response to repeated face images and that this adaptation was invariant to changes in the size of the face, but was sensitive to changes in expression and viewpoint [19]. These findings provide some support for the idea that faces may be represented in a view-dependent representation [20]. However, it remains to be established if a view-invariant representation exists for familiar faces. The results from this study suggest that this type of process must happen at a later stage of processing.

In conclusion, we found that the M170 potential adapts to faces with the same identity if they are shown from an identical viewpoint. However, there was a recovery from adaptation when the viewpoint of the images was varied. The view-dependent nature of the M170 response did not differ according to the familiarity of a face. These results do not rule out the possibility that a view-invariant neural representation may exist within the visual system analogous to face recognition units [1].

References

1. Bruce, V., Young, A.W.: Understanding face recognition. Br. J. Psychol. 77, 305–327 (1986)
2. Haxby, J.V., Hoffman, E.A., Gobbini, M.I.: The distributed human neural system for face perception. Trends in Cognitive Science 4, 223–233 (2000)
3. Grill-Spector, K., Knouf, N., Kanwisher, K.: The fusiform face area subserves face perception, not generic within-category identification. Nature Neuroscience 7, 555–562 (2004)
4. Rotshtein, P., Henson, R.N., Treves, A., Driver, J., Dolan, R.J.: Morphing marilyn into maggie dissociates physical and identity face representations in the brain. Nat. Neurosci. 8, 107–113 (2005)
5. Gauthier, I., Tarr, M.J., Moylan, J., Skudlarski, P., Gore, J.C., Anderson, J.W.: The fusiform face area is part of a network that processes faces at the individual level. J. Cogn. Neurosci. (2000)
6. Hoffman, E.A., Haxby, J.V.: Distinct representations of eye gaze and identity in the distributed human neural system for face perception. Nat. Neurosci. 3, 80–84 (2000)
7. Allison, T., Puce, A., Spencer, D., McCarthy, G.: Electrophysiological studies of human face perception: I. potentials generated in occipitotemporal cortex by face and non-face stimuli. Cerebral Cortex 9, 415–430 (1999)
8. Liu, J., Harris, A., Kanwisher, N.: Stage of processing in face perception: an meg study. Nat. Neurosci. 5, 910–916 (2002)
9. Grill-Spector, K., Henson, R., Martin, A.: Repetition and the brain: neural models of stimulus-specific effects. Trends in Cognitive Science 10, 14–23 (2006)
10. Harris, A., Nakayama, K.: Rapid face-selective adaptation of an early extrastriate component in meg. Cerebral Cortex 17, 63–70 (2007)
11. Ewbank, M.P., Andrews, T.J.: Size-invariant, but viewpoint-specific adaptation of the n170 potential to faces. In: Proc. 12th Annual Meeting of the Organisation for Human Brain Mapping (2006)
12. Smith, W.A.P., Hancock, E.R.: Recovering facial shape using a statistical model of surface normal direction. IEEE Trans. PAMI 28, 1914–1930 (2006)
13. Kovacs, G., Zimmer, M., Banko, E., Harza, I., Antal, A., Vidnyanszky, Z.: Electrophysiological correlates of visual adaptation to faces and body parts in humans. Cereb. Cortex 16, 742–753 (2006)
14. Schweinberger, S.R., Huddy, V., Burton, A.M.: N250r: A face-selective brain response to stimulus repetitions. NeuroReport 15, 1501–1505 (2004)
15. Henson, R.N., Rylands, A., Ross, E., Vuilleumeir, P., Rugg, M.D.: The effect of repetition lag on electrophysiological and haemodynamic correlates of visual object priming. Neuroimage 21, 1674–1689 (2004)
16. Grill-Spector, K., Kushnir, T., Hendler, T., Edelman, S., Itzchak, Y., Malach, R.: Differential processing of objects under various viewing conditions in human lateral occipital complex. Neuron 24, 187–203 (1999)
17. Eger, E., Schweinberger, S.R., Dolan, R.J., Henson, R.N.: Familiarity enhances invariance of face-representations in human ventral visual cortex: fmri evidence. NeuroImage 26, 1128–1139 (2005)
18. Hancock, P.J.B., Bruce, V., Burton, A.M.: Recognition of unfamiliar faces. Trends in Cognitive Sciences 4, 330–337 (2000)
19. Andrews, T.J., Ewbank, M.P.: Distinct representations for facial identity and changeable aspects of faces in the human temporal lobe. NeuroImage 23, 905–913 (2004)
20. Wallis, G., Bulthoff, H.: Learning to recognize objects. Trends in Cognitive Sciences 3, 22–31 (1999)

Modeling Visual Information Processing in Brain:
A Computer Vision Point of View and Approach

Emanuel Diamant

VIDIA-mant, P.O. Box 933, 55100 Kiriat Ono, Israel
emanl@012.net.il

Abstract. Image understanding and image semantics processing have recently become an issue of critical importance in computer vision R&D. Biological vision has always considered them as an enigmatic mixture of perceptual and cognitive processing faculties. In its impetuous and rash development, computer vision without any hesitations has adopted this stance. I will argue that such a segregation of image processing faculties is wrong, both for the biological and the computer vision. My conjecture is that images contain only one sort of information – the perceptual (physical) information, which can be discovered in an image and elicited for further processing. Cognitive (semantic) information is not a part of image-conveyed information. It belongs to a human observer that acquires and interprets the image. Relying on a new definition of "information", which can be derived from Kolmogorov's complexity theory and Chaitin's notion of algorithmic information, I propose a unifying framework for visual information processing, which explicitly accounts for perceptual and cognitive image processing peculiarities. I believe, it would provide better scaffolding for modeling visual information processing in human brain.

1 Introduction

This paper is a continuation of a discussion that I tried to initiate at the first BVAI 2005 Symposium [1].

The explosive growth of visual information in our surroundings has raised an urgent demand for effective means for organizing and handling these immense volumes of information. Because humans are known to be very efficient in such tasks, it is not surprising that computer vision designers are trying again and again to get answers for their worrying problems among the solutions that Human Visual System has developed in course of millions of years of natural evolution. Near a half of our cerebral cortex is busy with processing visual information [2], but how it is actually done remains a puzzle and an enigma for many generations of thinkers, philosophers, and contemporary scientific researchers.

Nevertheless, a working theory of human visual information processing has been established about twenty five years ago by the seminal works of David Marr [3], Anne Treisman [4], Irving Biederman [5], and a large group of their associates and followers. Since then it has become a classical theory, which dominates today in all farther developments in the field. The theory considers human visual information

F. Mele et al. (Eds.): BVAI 2007, LNCS 4729, pp. 62–71, 2007.

processing as an interplay of two inversely directed processing streams. One is an unsupervised, bottom-up directed process of initial image information pieces discovery and localization. The other is a supervised, top-down directed process, which conveys the rules and the knowledge that guide the linking and binding of these disjoint information pieces into perceptually meaningful image objects.

In modern biological vision research this duality is referred to as perceptual and cognitive faculties of vision. In computer vision terminology, these are the low-level and high-level paths of visual information processing. Although Treisman's theory [4] definitely positions itself as "A Feature-Integration Theory", the difficulties in defining proper rules for this feature integration have impelled a growing divergence between perceptive and cognitive fields of image processing [6]. Obviously, that was a wrong and a counter-productive development, and human vision researchers were always aware of its harmful consequence [7]. For this reason, the so-called "binding problem" has been announced as a critical exploration goal, and massive research efforts have been directed to its resolution, [8]. Unfortunately, without any discernable success.

In computer vision, the situation is even more bizarre. In fact, computer vision community is so busy with its everyday problems that there is no time to raise basic research ventures. Principal ideas (and their possible solutions) are usually borrowed from biological vision research. Therefore, following the trends in biological vision, the computer vision R&D for decades has been deeply involved in bottom-up pixel-oriented image processing. Low-level image computations have become its prime and persistent goal, while the complicated issues of high-level processing were just neglected and disregarded.

However, it is impossible to ignore them completely. It is generally acknowledged that any kind of image processing is unfeasible without incorporation into it the high-level knowledge ingredients. For this reason, the whole history of computer-based image processing is an endless saga on attempts to seize the needed knowledge in any possible way. The oldest and the most common ploy is to capitalize on the expert domain knowledge and adapt it to each and every application case. It is not surprising, therefore, that the whole realm of image processing has been (and continues to be) fragmented (segmented) according to high-level knowledge competence of the experts in the corresponding domains. That is why we have today: medical imaging, aerospace imaging, infrared, biologic, underwater, geophysics, remote sensing, microscopy, radar, biomedical, X-ray, and so on "imagings".

The advent of the Internet, with huge volumes of visual information scattered over the web, has demolished the long-lasting custom of capitalizing on the expert knowledge. Image information content on the Web is unpredictable and diversified. It is useless to apply specific expert knowledge to a random set of distant images. To meet the challenge, the computer vision community has undertaken an enterprise to develop appropriate (so-called) Content-Based Image Retrieval (CBIR) technologies, [9], [10]. However, deprived of any reasonable sources of the desired high-level information, computer vision designers were forced to proceed in only one possible direction of trying to derive the high-level knowledge from the available low-level information pieces, [11], [12].

In doing so, computer vision designers have once again demonstrated their reliance on biological vision trends and fashions. In biological vision, a rank of theoretical and experimental work has been done in order to support and to justify this above-mentioned tendency. Two ways of thinking could be distinguished in this regard: chaotic attractors modeling [13], [14], and saliency attention map modeling [15], [16]. We will not review these approaches in details. We will only note that both of them presume low-level bottom-up processing as the most proper way for high-level information recovery. Both are computationally expensive. Both definitely violate the basic assumption about the leading role of high-level knowledge in the low-level information processing.

It will be a mistake to say that computer vision people are not aware of these discrepancies. On the contrary, they are well informed about what is going on in the field. However, they are trying to justify their attempts by promoting a concept of a "semantic gap", an imaginary gap between low- and high-level image features. They sincerely believe that they would be able to bridge it again some day, [17].

It is worth to mention that all these developments (feature binding in biological vision and semantic gap bridging in computer vision) are evolving in atmosphere of total indifference to prior claims about high-level information superiority in the general course of visual information processing. Such indifference seems to stem from a very loose understanding about what is the concept of "information", what is the right way to use it properly, and what information treatment options could arise from this understanding.

2   Re-examining the Basic Assumptions

Everyone, who is not deaf, knows that we live today in the Information Age, where information is an indispensable ingredient of our life. We consume it, create it, seek for it, transfer, exchange, hide, reveal, accumulate, and disseminate it – in one word: information is a remarkably important component of our life. But can someone explain me what we have in mind when the word "information" is uttered? My attempts (undertaken several years ago) to get my own answer for this question were so desperate that I was almost ready to accept the stance that information is an indefinable entity (like "space" and "time" in classical physics, e.g.). Fortunately, at the end, I have hit on an information definition fitting my visual information handling aims. It turns out that this definition can be derived from Solomonoff's theory of Inference [18], Chaitin's Algorithmic Information theory [19], and Kolmogorov's Complexity theory [20]. Recently, I have learned that Kolmogorov's Complexity and Chaitin's Algorithmic Information theory are referred as respected items of a list of seven possible contestants suitable to define what actually information is [21]. In this regard, I was very proud of myself that I was lucky to avoid the traps of Shannon's Information Theory, which is known to be useful in communication applications, but it is absolutely inappropriate for visual information explorations that I am trying to conduct. The reason for this is that Shannon's information properly describes the integrated properties of an information message, while Kolmogorov's definition is suitable for evaluation of information content of separate isolated subparts of a message (separate message objects). This is, indeed, much closer to the way in which humans perceive and grasp their visual information.

The results of my investigation have been already published on several occasions, [1], [22], [23], [24], and interested readers can easily get them from a number of freely accessible repositories (e.g., arXiv, CiteSeer (the former Research Index), Eprintweb, etc.). Therefore, I will only repeat here some important points of these early publications, which properly reflect my current understanding of the matters.

The main point is that **information is a description**, a certain alphabet-based or language-based description, which Kolmogorov's theory regards as a program that (when executed) trustworthy reproduces the original object [25]. In an image, such objects are visible data structures from which an image consists of. So, a set of reproducible descriptions of image data structures is the information contained in an image.

The Kolmogorov's theory prescribes the way in which such descriptions must be created: at first, the most simplified and generalized structure must be described. Then, as the level of generalization is gradually decreased, more and more fine-grained image details (structures) are become revealed and depicted. This is the second important point, which follows from the theory's pure mathematical considerations: image **information is a hierarchy of recursive decreasing level descriptions** of information details, which unfolds in a coarse-to-fine top-down manner. (Attention, please: any bottom-up processing is not mentioned here. There is no low-level feature gathering and no feature binding. The only proper way for image information elicitation is a top-down coarse-to-fine way of image processing.)

The third prominent point, which immediately pops-up from the two just mentioned above, is that the top-down manner of image **information elicitation does not require incorporation of any high-level knowledge** for its successful accomplishment. It is totally free from any high-level guiding rules and inspirations. What immediately follows from this, is that high-level image semantics is not an integrated part of image information content (as it is traditionally assumed). It can not be seen more as a natural property of an image. Image semantics must be seen as a property of a human observer that watches and scrutinizes an image. That is why we can say now: **semantics is assigned to an image by a human observer**. That is strongly at variance with the contemporary views on the concept of semantic information. Following the new information elicitation rules, it is impossible to continue to pretend that semantics can be **extracted from an image**, (as in [26]), or should be **derived from low-level information features** via the semantic gap bridging, (as in [27], [28], and many others). That simply does not hold any more.

3 Computer Vision Implications

This new definition of information has forced us to reconsider our former approach to image information processing. The validity of our new assumptions and the inevitable changes in design philosophy that acceptance of these assumptions imply, have motivated us to test the issues in a framework of a visual robot design enterprise. The enterprise is aimed to creating an artificial vision system with some human-like cognitive capabilities. It is generally agreed that the first stage of such a system has to be an image segmentation stage at which the whole bulk of image pixels (image raw data) has to be decomposed into a finite set of image patches. The latter are submitted afterwards to a process of image content analysis and interpretation.

A practical algorithm based on the announced above principles has been developed and subjected to some systematic evaluations. The results were published, and can be found in [1], [23], [24]. There is no need to repeat again and again that excellent, previously unattainable segmentation results have been attained in these tests, undoubtedly corroborating the new information processing principles. Not only an unsupervised segmentation of image content has been achieved, (in a top-down coarse-to-fine processing manner, without any involvement of high-level knowledge). A hierarchy of descriptions for each and every segmented lot (segmented object) has been achieved as well. It contains the center of mass coordinates, the direction of object's main axeses, object's contour and shape depiction rules (in a system of these axeses), and other object related parameters (object related **information**), which enable subsequent object reconstruction. That is exactly what we have previously defined as information. That is the reason why we specify this information as "physical information", because that is the only information present in an image, and therefore **the only information that can be extracted from an image**. For that reason it must be dissociated from the semantic information, which (as we understand now) is a property of an external observer. Therefore it must be treated (or modeled) in accordance with specific his/her cognitive information processing rules.

What are these rules? A consensus view on this topic does not exist as yet in the biological vision theories and in the computer vision practice. So, we have to blaze our own trails. We decided, thus, to meet this challenge by suggesting a new approach based on our previously declared information elicitation principles. The preliminary results of our first attempt were published recently in [29]. As in the case of physical information, we will not repeat here all the details of this publication. We will proceed with only a brief reproduction of some critical points needed to follow up our discussion.

Human's cognitive abilities (including the aptness for image interpretation and the capacity to assign semantics to an image) are empowered by the existence of a huge knowledge base about the things in the surrounding world kept in human brain/head. This knowledge base is permanently upgraded and updated during the human's life span. So, if we intend to endow our visual robot with some cognitive capabilities we have to provide it with something equivalent to this (human) knowledge base.

It goes without saying that this knowledge base will never be as large and developed as its human prototype. But we are not sure that the requirement to be large and huge is valid in our case. After all, humans are also not equal in their cognitive capacity, and the magnitude, the content of their knowledge bases is very diversified too. (The knowledge base of aerial photographs interpreter is certainly different from the knowledge base of roentgen images interpreter, or IVUS images, or PET images). The knowledge base of our visual robot has to be small enough to be effective and manageable, but sufficiently ample to ensure robot's acceptable performance. Certainly, for our feasibility study we can be satisfied even with a relatively small, specific-task-oriented knowledge base.

The next crucial point is the knowledge (base) representation issue. To deal with it, we first of all must arrive at a common agreement about what is the meaning of the term "knowledge". (A question that usually has not a commonly accepted answer.)

We state that in our case a suitable and a sufficient definition of it would be: "Knowledge is a memorized information". Consequently, we can say that knowledge (like information) must be a hierarchy of descriptive items, with the grade of description details growing in a top-down manner at the descending levels of the hierarchy.

What else must be mentioned here, is that these descriptions have to be implemented in some alphabet (as it is in the case of physical information) or in a description language (which better fits the semantic information case). Any farther argument being put aside, we will declare that the most suitable language in our case is a natural human language. After all, the real knowledge bases that we are familiar with are implemented on a natural human language basis.

The next step, then, is predetermined: if natural language is a suitable description implement, the suitable form of this implementation is a narrative, a story tale [30]. If the description hierarchy can be seen as an inverted tree, then the branches of this tree are the stories that encapsulate human's experience with the surrounding world. And the leaves of these branches are single words from which the stories are composed of. In computer vision terminology these single words are defined as nodes.

The descent into description details, however, does not stop here, and each single word can be farther decomposed into its attributes and rules that describe the relations between the attributes. At this stage the notion of physical information comes back to the game. Because the words are usually associated with physical objects in the real world, words' attributes must be seen as memorized physical information descriptions. Once derived (by a visual system) from the observable world and learned to be associated with a particular word, these physical information descriptions are soldered in into the knowledge base. Object recognition, thus, turns out to be a comparison and similarity test between currently acquired physical information and the one already retained in the memory. If the similarity test is successful, starting from this point in the hierarchy and climbing back on the knowledge base ladder we will obtain: first, the linguistic label for a recognized object, and second, the position of this label (word) in the context of the whole story. In this way, object's meaningful categorization can be acquired, a first stage of image annotation can be successfully accomplished, paving the way for farther meaningful (semantic) image interpretation.

One question has remained untouched in our discourse: How this artificial knowledge base has to be initially created and brought into the robot's disposal? The vigilant reader certainly remembers the fierce debates about learning capabilities of neural networks and other machine learning technologies. We are aware of these debates. But in our case they are irrelevant for a simple reason: the top-down fashion of the knowledge base development pre-determines that all responsibilities for knowledge base creation have to be placed on the shoulders of the robot designer.

Such an unexpected twist in design philosophy will be less surprising if we recall that human cognitive memory is also often defined as a "declarative memory". And the prime mode of human learning is the declarative learning mode, when the new knowledge is explicitly transferred to a developing human from his external surrounding: From a father to a child, from a teacher to a student, from an instructor to a trainee. There is evidence that this is not an especially human prerogative. Even ants are transferring knowledge in a similar way, [31]. So, our proposal that robot's knowledge base has to be designed and created by the robot supervisor is sufficiently correct and is fitting our general concept of information use and management.

4 Brain Vision Implications

The main idea of my BVAI 2005 paper [1] was the following: Despite the striking differences between biological and computer vision philosophy, there must be a more general and comprehensive basis that underpins and reconciles these usually detached and divergent fields of vision. It is not clear how successful were my efforts. However, the challenge is tempting, and paving the way for better computer vision understanding it is always right to see how biological vision research can benefit from the proposed new ideas, which are really general enough to reconcile the current divergence.

While the mainstream of biological vision research continues to approach visual information processing in a bottom-up fashion [32], it turns out that the idea of primary top-down processing was never extraneous to biological vision. The first publications addressing this issue are dated by the early eighties of the last century, (David Navon at 1977 [33], and Lin Chen at 1982 [34]). The prominent authors were persistent in their views, and farther research reports were published regularly until the recent time, [35], [36]. However, it looks like they have been overlooked, both in biological and in computer vision as well. Only in the last years, a tide of new evidence has become visible and is pervasively discussed now. Although the spirit of these discussions is still different from ours, the trend is certainly in favor of the foremost top-down visual information processing [37], [38].

The field of cognitive vision is not ready yet to leave the traditional information processing dogmas. However, supporting evidence for a "declarative" interpretation of physical information can be already found in [39], where it is convincingly shown how a color is "assigned" to a given object. Evidence for knowledge transfer from the outside we have already mentioned earlier (the case of ants that are learning in tandem [31]). The so-called Horizontal Gene Transfer phenomenon responsible for antibiotic resistance development of bacteria [40] can also be seen as a supporting evidence for this hypothesis.

However, the most surprising insights are still awaiting their farther clarification and confirmation. If our definition of information as a description is correct, then the current belief that a spiking neuron burst is a valid form of information exchange and representation [41] does not hold any more. The variance in spikes' heights or duty times is an inadequate alphabet to implement information descriptions of a desired complexity. We can boldly speculate that a biomolecular alphabet would be a much better and appropriate solution in such a case. Support for this kind of speculations can be definitely derived from the recent advances in molecular biology research [42], [43], and the spikes that we observe and investigate today could be seen as a reflection of charges that are carried by ionized parts of the molecular information messages.

This molecular description hypothesis also fits very well our new brain memory organization theory, which pretty well resembles the paradigm of computer memory organization. Dendrite spines can be seen as a proper accommodation for the molecular descriptions, and hypotheses about "object files" [44] and "event files" [45] are repeatedly emerging in biological vision literature during the last decades. It would be interesting to notice that event file concept fits very well also the narrative knowledge transfer and representation hypothesis proposed earlier in Section 3. Recall that our memories first of all evolve as stories and almost never as single static objects or scenes.

Farther support for the idea that a complex information description can be stored in a single memory cell can be seen in [46]. In this case as well, reactivation and retrieval of a memorized description fits very well the paradigm of a computer memory store/fetch access, a single_write/multiple_read memory handling mode.

I am definitely excited by the options that brain vision research can gain from such a back projection of a computer vision theory (about the essence of information) on the issues of modeling visual information processing in human brain.

5 Some Concluding Remarks

In this paper, we propose a new definition of information suitable for our computer vision peculiarities studies. We afford an exploration of benefits that a skilled use of this definition can provide both in computer and biological vision research. We hope that this would pave a way for an anticipated machine-based image understanding.

The present proposal is incomplete and tentative since this is just a first step, and further research remains to be done. We are aware that our approach is very different from those that are extensively explored and developed in frame of other research programs [47]. However, the enterprise that we are aimed at, is not a task for a single person or a small group of developers. It requires consolidated efforts of many interesting parties. We hope that the time for this is not far away.

References

1. Diamant, E.: Does a plane imitate a bird? Does computer vision have to follow biological paradigms? In: De Gregorio, M., Di Maio, V., Frucci, M., Musio, C. (eds.) BVAI 2005. LNCS, vol. 3704, pp. 108–115. Springer, Heidelberg (2005), http://www.vidiamant.info
2. Milner, D., Goodale, M.: The Visual Brain in Action. Oxford Psychology Series, vol. 27. Oxford University Press, Oxford (1998)
3. Marr, D.: A Computational Investigation into the Human Representation and Processing of Visual Information. Freeman, San Francisco (1982)
4. Treisman, A., Gelade, G.: A feature-integration theory of attention. Cognitive Psychology 12, 97–136 (1980)
5. Biederman, I.: Recognition-by-Components: A Theory of Human Image Understanding. Psychological Review 94(2), 115–147 (1987)
6. Barsalou, L.W.: Perceptual symbol systems. Behavioral and Brain Sciences 22, 577–660 (1999)
7. Palmeri, T., Gauthier, I.: Visual Object Understanding. Nature Reviews: Neuroscience 5, 291–304 (2004)
8. Treisman, A.: The binding problem. Current Opinion in Neurobiology 6, 171–178 (1996)
9. Khefri, M.L., Ziou, D., Bernardi, A.: Image Retrieval From the World Wide Web: Issues, Techniques, and Systems. ACM Computing Surveys 36(1), 35–67 (2004)

10. Lew, M.S., Sebe, N., Djeraba, C., Jain, R.: Content-based Multimedia Information Retrieval: State of the Art and Challenges. In: ACM Transactions on Multimedia Computing, Communications, and Applications, ACM Press, New York (February 2006)
11. Mojsilovic, A., Rogowitz, B.: Capturing image semantics with low-level descriptors. In: ICIP-01. Proceedings of the International Conference on Image Processing, Thessaloniki, Greece, pp. 18–21 (October 2001)
12. Zhang, C., Chen, T.: From Low Level Features to High Level Semantics. In: Furht, B., Marques, O. (eds.) Handbook of Video Databases: Design and Applications, CRC Press, Boca Raton, USA (October 2003)
13. McRae, K.: Semantic Memory: Some insights from Feature-based Connectionist Attractor Networks. In: Ross, B.H. (ed.) The Psychology of Learning and Motivation, vol. 45 (2004), http://amdrae.ssc.uwo.ca/
14. Johansson, C., Lansner, A.: Attractor Memory with Self-organizing Input. In: Ijspeert, A.J., Masuzawa, T., Kusumoto, S. (eds.) BioADIT 2006. LNCS, vol. 3853, pp. 265–280. Springer, Heidelberg (2006)
15. Treue, S.: Visual attention: the where, what, how and why of saliency. Current Opinion in Neurobiology 13, 428–432 (2003)
16. Itti, L.: Models of Bottom-Up Attention and Saliency. In: Itti, L., Rees, G., Tsotsos, J. (eds.) Neurobiology of Attention, pp. 576–582. Elsevier, San Diego, CA (2005)
17. Hare, J., Lewis, P., Enser, P., Sandom, C.: Mind the Gap: Another look at the problem of the semantic gap in image retrival. In: SPIE. Proceedings of Multimedia Content Analysis, Management and Retrieval Conference, vol. 6073 (2006), http:// www. ecs. soton. ac.uk/ people/
18. Solomonoff, R.J.: The Discovery of Algorithmic Probability. Journal of Computer and System Science 55(1), 73–88 (1997)
19. Chaitin, G.J.: Algorithmic Information Theory. IBM Journal of Research and Development 21, 350–359 (1977)
20. Kolmogorov, A.: Three approaches to the quantitative definition of information. Problems of Information and Transmission 1(1), 1–7 (1965)
21. Floridi, L.: Trends in the Philosophy of Information. In: Adriaans, P., van Benthem, J. (eds.) Handbook of Philosophy of Information, Elsevier, Amsterdam (forthcoming), http:// www.philosophyofinformation.net
22. Diamant, E.: Image information content estimation and elicitation. WSEAS Transaction on Computers 2(2), 443–448 (2003), http://www.worldses.org/journals/
23. Diamant, E.: Top-Down Unsupervised Image Segmentation (it sounds like an oxymoron, but actually it isn't). In: PRRS'04. Proceedings of the 3rd Pattern Recognition in Remote Sensing Workshop, Kingston University, UK (August 2004)
24. Diamant, E.: Searching for image information content, its discovery, extraction, and representation. Journal of Electronic Imaging 14(1) (January-March 2005)
25. Vitanyi, P.: Meaningful Information. IEEE Transactions on Information Theory 52(10), 4617–4624 (2006), http://www.cwi.nl/ paulv/papers
26. Naphade, M., Huang, T.S.: Extracting Semantics From Audiovisual Content: The Final Frontier in Multimedia Retrieval. IEEE Transactions on Neural Networks 13(4), 793–810 (2002)
27. Zhou, X.S., Huang, T.S.: CBIR: From low-Level Features to High-Level Semantics. In: Proceedings SPIE, San Jose, CA, January 24-28, 2000, vol. 3974, pp. 426–431 (2000), http://www.ifp.uiuc.edu/ xzhou2/
28. Petridis, K., Kompatsiaris, I., Strintzis, M., Bloehdorn, S., Handschuh, S., Staab, S.,Simou, N., Tzouvars, V., Avrithis, Y.: Knowledge Representation for Semantic Multimedia

Content Analysis and Reasoning. IEEE Transactions on CSVT 15(10), 1210–1244 (2005), http://www.iti.gr/db.php/publications

29. Diamant, E.: In Quest of Image Semantics: Are We Looking for It Under the Right Lamppost? http://arxiv.org/abs/cs.CV/0609003

30. Tuffield, M., Shadbolt, N., Millard, D.: Narratives as a Form of Knowledge Transfer: Narrative Theory and Semantics. In: Proceedings of the 1st AKT (Advance Knowledge Technologies) Symposium, Milton Keynes, UK (June 2005)

31. Franks, N., Richardson, T.: Teaching in tandem-running ants. Nature 439, 153 (2006)

32. Serre, T., Kouh, M., Cadieu, C., Knoblich, U., Kreiman, G., Poggio, T.: A theory of object recognition: computations and circuits in the feedforward path of the ventral stream in primate visual cortex, CBCL MIT paper (November 2005), http://web.mit.edu/serre/...

33. Navon, D.: Forest Before Trees: The Precedence of Global Features in Visual Perception. Cognitive Psychology 9, 353–383 (1977)

34. Chen, L.: Topological structure in visual perception. Science 218, 699–700 (1982)

35. Navon, D.: What does a compound letter tell the psychologist's mind? Acta Psychologica 114, 273–309 (2003)

36. Chen, L.: The topological approach to perceptual organization. Visual Cognition 12(4), 553–637 (2005)

37. Ahissar, M., Hochstein, S.: The reverse hierarchy theory of visual perceptual learning. Trends in Cognitive Science 8(10), 457–464 (2004)

38. Juan, C-H., Campana, G., Walsh, V.: Cortical interactions in vision and awareness: hierarchies in reverse. Progress in Brain Research 144, 117–130 (2004)

39. Hansen, T., Olkkonen, M., Walter, S., Gegenfurtner, K.: Memory modulates color appearance. Nature Neuroscience 9(11), 1367–1368 (2006)

40. Lawrence, J., Hendrickson, H.: Lateral gene transfer: when will adolescence end? Molecular Microbiology 50(3), 739–749 (2003)

41. Diba, K., Koch, C., Segev, I.: Spike propagation in dendrites with stochastic ion channels. Journal of Computational Neuroscience 20, 77–84 (2006)

42. Kandel, E.: The Molecular Biology of Memory Storage: A Dialogue Between Genes and Synapses. Science 294, 1030–1038 (2001)

43. Routtenberg, A., Rekart, J.: Post-translational protein modification as the substrate for long-lasting memory. TRENDS in Neurosciences 28(1), 12–19 (2005)

44. Kahneman, D., Treisman, A., Gibbs, B.: The reviewing of object files: Object-specific integration of information. Cognitive Psychology 24, 175–219 (1992)

45. Hommel, B.: Event files: Feature binding in and across perception and action. TRENDS in Cognitive Sciences 8(11), 494–500 (2004)

46. Waydo, S., Kraskov, A., Quiroga, R., Freid, I., Koch, C.: Sparse Representation in the Human Medial Temporal Lobe. The Journal of Neuroscience 26(40), 10232–10234 (2006)

47. European IST Research: Building on Assets, Seizing Opportunities (2005-2006),available: http://europa.eu.int/information_society/

Higher Order Color Mechanisms
for Image Segmentation

Thorsten Hansen and Karl R. Gegenfurtner

Justus-Liebig University Giessen, 35394 Giessen, Germany
Thorsten.Hansen@psychol.uni-giessen.de
http://www.allpsych.uni-giessen.de/hansen

Abstract. Recent physiological evidence has shown that neurons at the early visual stages are selective for a combination of color, luminance and orientation. Neurons with a linear response tuning, resulting in broad tuning curves, are found at all stages, but the proportion of nonlinear neurons, narrowly tuned for color, increases along the visual pathway. We ran psychophysical experiments to characterize the number and tuning widths of the mechanisms underlying image segmentation. We used a noise masking paradigm with different types of noise to disentangle mechanisms with narrow and broad tuning characteristics. The data were best described by a chromatic detection model with multiple, broadly tuned mechanisms, where narrow tuning curves emerge due to off-axis looking. We then analyzed a set of calibrated natural images and determined the joint statistics of color and luminance edges. The majority of edges in natural scenes was characterized by a contrast in both color and luminance, while some prominent object boundaries were signalled only in the chromatic plane. Based on the converging evidence from different disciplines we conclude that multiple linear, broadly tuned mechanisms which are selective for a combination of chromatic contrast, luminance contrasts and orientations play a central role for contour extraction and robust image segmentation.

1 Introduction

Color vision starts with the transduction of electromagnetic radiation by three types of photoreceptors in the retina. Based on their peak sensitivities at short, medium and long wavelength the photoreceptors are commonly denoted S, M, and L. Already at the level of retinal ganglion cells the signals of these three types of photoreceptors are combined to form three color-opponent channels: an achromatic channel from pooled L and M cone input (L+M), and two chromatic channels, one channel that signals differences of L and M cone responses (L−M), and another channel that signals differences between S cone responses and summed L+M cone responses (S−(L+M)). The properties of these early stages have been studied in great detail and are well understood [1,2,3]. However, the properties of subsequent "higher order" stages of cortical processing are less clear and a subject of intense research.

F. Mele et al. (Eds.): BVAI 2007, LNCS 4729, pp. 72–83, 2007.
© Springer-Verlag Berlin Heidelberg 2007

Here we present recent findings from different disciplines addressing the properties of these higher order stages. Overall, a coherent picture emerges, where multiple linear, broadly tuned mechanisms which are selective for a combination of chromatic contrast, luminance contrasts and orientations play a central role for contour extraction and robust image segmentation. The article is organized as follows: First we summarize findings from neurophysiology. Second, we present results from a psychophysical experiment where we have studied the number and tuning width of higher order mechanisms. Third, we present findings from scene statistics of natural images.

2   Neurophysiological Findings

At the very first stage of color processing, electromagnetic radiation between 400–700 nm is absorbed by three different types of cone photoreceptors with peak sensitivities at short (S, 430 nm), medium (M, 530 nm) and long (L, 560 nm) wavelengths [4]. The S cone photoreceptor absorbs light from 400-600 nm, while the L and M cones have even broader absorption spectrum, that cover almost the entire visible spectrum (Fig. 1, a). At the second stage retinal ganglion cells combine the cone signals into three cone-opponent channels, one achromatic channel (L+M) and two chromatic channels, L−M and S−(L+M). The DKL color space [5,6] is a spherical color space spanned by these three cone-opponent axes, which are often termed "cardinal" directions (Fig. 1, b). Note that the cone-opponent channels are different from the color-opponent axis black-white, red-green, and blue-yellow: Colors along the L−M channel vary between a pinkish-red and a bluish-green, and color along the S−(L+M) channel vary between a yellowish green and purple. The unique hues red, green, blue and yellow are clearly different form the colors at the cardinal directions (Fig. 1, c).

Chromatic mechanisms are typically characterized by their number, tuning peak direction, and tuning width. Subcortical neurons in the retina and the LGN have peak sensitivities that cluster along the cardinal directions (Fig. 2, a).

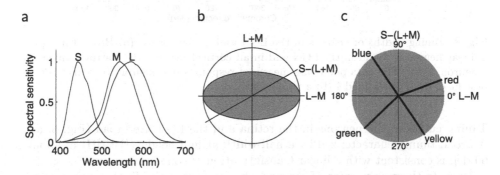

Fig. 1. (a) Cone absorption spectra. (b) DKL color space with the isoluminant plane shown in gray. (c) The isoluminant plane of the DKL color space. The unique hues do not coincide with the cardinal axes of the DKL color space.

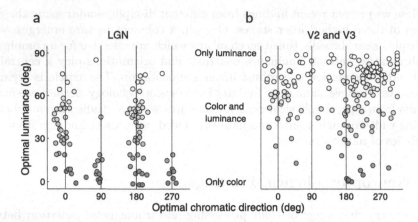

Fig. 2. Color and luminance preferences of neurons (a) in the LGN and (b) in the cortex (V2 and V3). The x-axis denotes the optimal chromatic direction as azimuth in the isoluminant plane, the y-axis denotes the preferred luminance as elevation above the isoluminant plane. (a) Neurons in the LGN cluster around the cardinal directions, (b) neurons in the cortex do not. Most neurons in the LGN and the cortex respond to luminance and color.

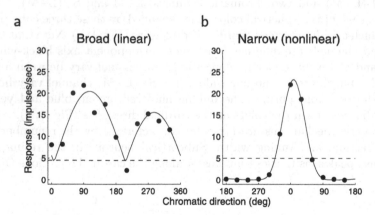

Fig. 3. Tuning widths of neurons in the LGN and in the cortex. (a) Broad tuning of a linear neuron is found in the LGN and in all cortical regions. (b) Narrow tuning of a neuron in V2. The data points are measured responses of a neuron, the curve is the best fit of (a) a linear model (b) a nonlinear model.

Tuning curves of the neurons in the retina and the LGN are broad (Fig. 3, a). A broad tuning characterized by a half-width at half height (HWHH) of about 60 deg is consistent with a linear transformation of cone inputs.

How do these properties of neurons change during the further processing? First peak sensitivities of cortical neurons do not cluster, but have a continuous distribution (Fig. 2, b).Second, neurons with narrow tuning curves are found (Fig. 3, b). Broad tuning curves still occur at all level of the further processing,

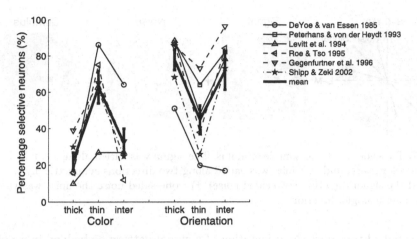

Fig. 4. Segregation and integration in V2. The graph shows the proportions of cells selective for color and orientation in different compartments of area V2 (thick stripes, thin stripes and interstripes). The data are from six studies. The heavy black lines represent the means across all six studies. The proportion varies in the different compartments, but not clear segregation is evident.

but the proportion of neurons with a narrow tuning width increases as the processing proceeds along the hierarchy of visual areas [7]. For example, in V1 of macaque monkey, tuning widths with HWHHs ranging from 10 deg to 90 deg have been found [8]. Narrow tuning widths below 60 deg indicate a nonlinear transformation of cone inputs. One of the most fundamental questions of cortical processing is whether visual attributes such as form, color and luminance are processing in segregated streams or together. Early hypothesis have favored the idea of a neatly segregated processing. In the domain of color and form, the coloring book theory is an example of such a segregated processing [9]. It assumes that first a sketch of achromatic edges of the scene is extracted, which is subsequently colored by chromatic surface information. Recent physiological findings consistently has drawn a different picture. A meta analysis of six studies investigating color and luminance preference in different compartments of macaque monkey V2 reveals that no clear segregation exists (Fig. 4). Further it has been shown that many neurons in the primary visual cortex cells respond best to oriented chromatic contrast [10], and that the vast majority of color-selective neurons in V1 and V2 are also selective for orientation [11]. Recent physiological findings consistently show that in the early cortical processing color, luminance and orientation are processed together by the same neurons.

3   Psychophysical Findings from a Masking Experiment

In the psychophysical experiments we investigated the properties of post-receptoral chromatic mechanisms for image segmentation, in particular their number and tuning characteristics [12]. We used a noise masking paradigm where

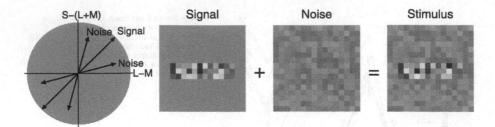

Fig. 5. Two-side noise and sample stimulus. The signal was varied along a single direction in color space, and the noise was varied along two directions symmetrically spaced around the signal direction (two-sided noise). For one-sided noise the noise was varied only a long a single direction.

observers had to report the orientation of a signal pattern embedded in a noisy background texture (Fig. 5). The signal consisted of dynamic squares whose colors were drawn from a uniform distribution along a single direction in color space. Colors of the noise pattern were uniformly distributed either along a single direction in color space ("one-sided noise") or along two directions equally spaced around the direction of the signal color ("two-sided noise"). The chromatic directions of the signal and the noise were independently varied, and the signal contrast was measured at which the observer could reliably indicate the orientation of the signal.

We found that masking was generally highest when signal and noise were modulated along the same direction, and minimal for orthogonal noise. No differences were found for signals modulated along cardinal directions or intermediate direction. However, measured tuning widths critically depend on the type of noise: one-sided noise resulted in narrow tuning, while two-sided noise resulted in broad tuning. We developed a chromatic detection model and tested various combinations of tuning widths k and number of mechanisms N. We found that a chromatic detection model with multiple broadly tuned mechanisms ($N = 16$, $k = 1$) successfully accounts for the experimental findings. With this single parameter setting both narrow and broad tuning curves emerged, depending on the type of noise used. Other tested models failed to reproduce the data, in particular Models with four broadly tuned cardinal mechanisms ($N = 4$, $k = 1$) or multiple narrowly tuned mechanisms ($N = 16$, $k = 10$). Our results suggest that multiple chromatic mechanisms play a central role in image segmentation. In the following we will present the chromatic detection model in more detail.

3.1   Chromatic Detection Model

We developed a chromatic detection model for a better understanding of the data obtained in the psychophysical experiment. In particular, we want to investigate whether the different tuning curves measured for the two types of noise could be

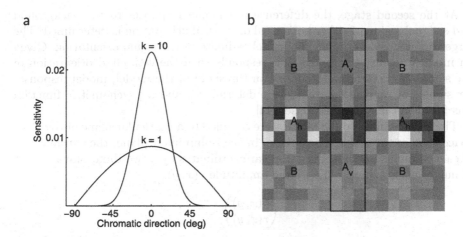

Fig. 6. (a) Sensitivity profiles of the chromatic mechanisms for different values of the exponential k. The sensitivity functions are normalized such that they integrate to unity. (b) Partitioning of a sample input stimulus into background B and two putative signal regions A_h and A_v. In this example, the ΔR value for A_h would be much larger than the value for A_v, and the model would correctly detect the horizontal signal.

accounted for by a single underlying circuit and, if so, to determine the number and tuning widths of the underlying detection mechanisms.

The chromatic line-element model comprises two main processing stages. At the first stage, color signals are processed by multiple channels each tuned to a particular direction in color space. The number of channels N and their tuning width k are the basic model parameters. The N mechanisms are defined in a single plane of the cone-opponent DKL color space. Each mechanism has the same raised cosine shaped tuning profile but different chromatic preferences or peak sensitivities μ. Formally, the sensitivity of the ith of N mechanisms to different chromatic directions θ is given by the sensitivity profile $S_i(\theta)$

$$S_i(\theta) = [\cos^k(\theta - \mu)]^+ \quad \mu = 360 \deg \frac{i}{N} + \eta, \quad i = 1, \dots, N \ .$$

The operator $[\,\cdot\,]^+$ denotes half-wave rectification. The parameter k determines the tuning width of the sensitivity profile [13]. A value of $k = 1$ results in the standard cosine profile, consistent with a linear combination of the color opponent signal. Increasing k sharpens the profile. A value of $k = 10$ results in narrowly tuned sensitivity functions of the same width as observed in the psychophysical experiments with one-sided noise (Fig. 6, a).

The parameter μ determines the peak sensitivity of the N chromatic channels, which are equally spaced in the chromatic plane. For example, $N = 4$ mechanisms would result in a spacing of 360 deg/4 = 90 deg. sensitivities are allowed to vary at each stimulus position by a normally distributed noise process η with a standard deviation of 10 deg, to model the variability of the preferred hue in individual LGN neurons as observed experimentally [5].

At the second stage, the difference in channel responses to the background and a signal region of either horizontal or vertical orientation is determined. The larger difference determines the model estimate of the signal orientation. Given an input stimulus, the model thus responds with the estimated orientation of the signal. To determine the detection threshold of the model, model responses for signals of varying contrasts were determined, and a psychometric function was fitted to the model responses [14].

The input stimuli to the model were confined to a particular plane of the DKL space such as the isoluminant plane. In the isoluminant plane, the chromaticity of each stimulus patch is given in polar coordinates by a two-dimensional vector of hue or color azimuth $\theta(x, y)$ and amplitude $r(x, y)$:

$$\begin{pmatrix} \theta(x, y) \\ r(x, y) \end{pmatrix} .$$

Each channel i integrates color signals within a particular region A of the stimulus, resulting in an average response $R_{A,i}$ of ith channel to all patches in the stimulus within region A:

$$R_{A,i} = \frac{1}{\|A\|} \sum_{(x,y) \in A} r(x, y) S_i(\theta(x, y)) ,$$

where r is the chromatic contrast and θ is the chromatic direction of the square at the particular position (x, y), and $\|A\|$ denotes the magnitude of the set A, i.e., the number of elements in A. The overall difference ΔR_A between a signal region A and the background region B is computed by taking the norm of the contrast between signal and background responses for each channel:

$$\Delta R_A = \begin{vmatrix} c(R_{A,1}, R_{B,1}) \\ c(R_{A,2}, R_{B,2}) \\ \vdots \\ c(R_{A,N}, R_{B,N}) \end{vmatrix} .$$

We use the Michelson contrast to compute the contrast function c, which is defined as $c(x, y) = (x - y)/(x + y)$. For the norm we use the standard vector norm (L2 norm, Euclidean distance), which approximates probability summation across channels [15]. Two values ΔR are computed for two putative signal regions A_h and A_v to test for either horizontal or vertical signal orientation (Fig. 6, b). The larger of the two values then determines the orientation as estimated by the model.

3.2   Simulation Results

First we verified that the model faithfully replicates the basic properties of noise masking. In particular, we verified that the model shows a linear increase in threshold with noise contrast when the noise is modulated along the same direction, as well as virtually no increase in threshold when the noise is modulated

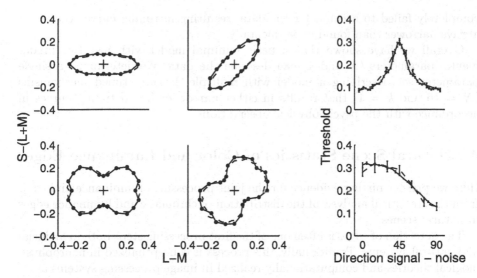

Fig. 7. Experimental results (solid) and model simulations (dashed) for a model with multiple, broadly-tuned mechanisms ($N = 16$, $k = 1$). The model accounts both for narrow tuning curves measured for one-sided noise (top row) and for broad tuning curves measured for two-sided noise (bottom row). The columns, from left to right, show the tuning curves for a signal modulated along a cardinal direction (0 deg), along an intermediate direction (45 deg), and the mean tuning curve averaged across four signal directions.

along directions orthogonal to the signal. We then investigated the model responses when probed with the masking stimuli used in our experiments, having either one-sided or two-sided noise.

As stated above, the number of the detection mechanisms N and their tuning width k are basic model parameters. Three different regimes are of particular interest: a basic quasi-linear model with four broadly tuned mechanisms at the cardinal directions ($N = 4$, $k = 1$); a model with multiple narrowly tuned mechanisms with a tuning width similar to the experimentally observed tuning for one-sided noise ($N = 16$, $k = 10$); and a model with multiple, broadly tuned mechanisms ($N = 16$, $k = 1$). Simulation results for a model with multiple, broadly-tuned mechanisms ($N = 16$, $k = 1$) are shown in Fig. 7. The simulations show that a model with multiple, broadly tuned mechanisms ($N = 16$, $k = 1$) can account for the experimentally observed tuning curves, both for one-sided and two-sided noise. In particular, a model with a single parameter set can result in different tuning widths, depending on the type of noise. Other model variants, such as a quasi-linear model ($N = 4$, $k = 1$), or a model with multiple narrowly tuned channels ($N = 16$, $k = 10$) failed to reproduce the empirical findings. A quasi-linear model with four linear mechanisms showed a large variability in tuning curves depending on the chromatic direction of the signal, contrary to the empirical data. A model with multiple narrowly tuned mechanisms ($N = 16$, $k = 10$)

completely failed to account for the data, resulting in tuning curves that were always narrower than found experimentally.

Overall we have shown that a basic minimal model with just two fundamental parameters (N and k) can describe the data. We determined a single parameter set describing a model with multiple, broadly tuned mechanisms ($N = 16$ and $k = 1$) that results in either narrow or broad tuning curves in accordance with the psychophysical observations.

4   Natural Scene Statistics of Color and Luminance Edges

Here we present further evidence for the joint processing of luminance and color from the statistical analysis of the distribution of chromatic and luminance edges in natural scenes.

The detection of edges is often one of the first processing steps both in artificial and natural systems. Traditionally, this process is conceptualized in neurophysiological theories and computationally realized in image processing systems as an *achromatic* process. However, important information about object boundaries is sometimes represented only in chromatic channels. Consider the image of a red fruit on green foliage (Fig. 8): In the luminance image, the edges of the fruit are hardly detectable, because the luminance of the fruit is almost the same as the luminance of the background foliage. Any image processing system which tries to detect objects based on luminance information alone would probably miss the fruit. Adding chromatic information changes the situation completely. In the L−M channel, which represents reddish-greenish signal variations, the object boundaries of the fruit is almost perfectly represented. An image processing system which can use this chromatic information will probably detect the fruit.

Here we analyzed the co-occurrence of achromatic and color edges in natural scenes to assess the possible contributions of chromatic information to visual

input image   L−M edges   luminance edges

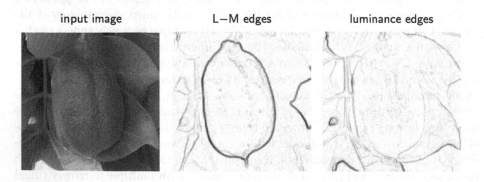

Fig. 8. Image of a fruit and the edges detected in the luminance plane and the L−M plane which signals reddish-greenish variations. While the object contour is faintly if at all represented by the luminance edges, a strong response occurs in the L−M plane which almost perfectly delineates the object. Chromatic information helps to separate objects from their background.

Fig. 9. McGill data base of color calibrated images. Each row shows sample images from the nine categories of the image data base (animals, flowers, foliage, fruits, land and water, man-made, shadows, snow, and textures).

form and edge detection. The analysis is based on 764 images from a publically available data base of calibrated color images [16]. The images are grouped into nine categories (Fig. 9). to analyze the co-occurrence of chromatic and luminance edges, the calibrated images are first transformed into LMS cone space, modeling responses of the L, M and S cones of a human observer. Next, LMS responses are transformed into a cone-opponent space spanned by three cardinal axes, one achromatic axis (L+M), and two chromatic axes, L−M and S−(L+M). These axes resemble the chromatic preferences of retinal ganglion cells and LGN cells (Sec. 2). Edges are detected in these three color-opponent planes and the joint histogram of edge strengths is computed (Fig. 10). The joint histogram of luminance and L−M edges has a high excursion along the luminance axis and also strong isoluminant L−M edges (Fig. 10, a). The large majority of edges do not fall on either axes, and is defined by a combination of both luminance and chromatic contrast. The joint histogram is not symmetric but slightly skewed and compressed along the main diagonal, indicating that bright green/dark red edges are of on average of higher contrast than bright red/dark green edges. For the co-occurrence of luminance edges and S−(L+M) edges a similar joint histogram occurs (Fig. 10, b).

Inspection of edge maps in individual images reveals that some prominent object boundaries that are weak or missing in the luminance edge map are clearly delineated in the L−M plane (e.g., Fig. 8). For example, red fruits or

a   b

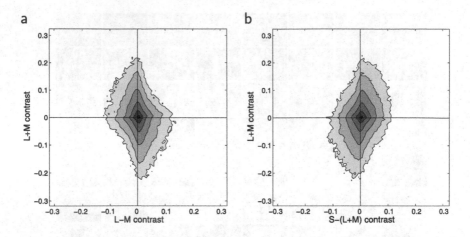

Fig. 10. Joint edge histograms for luminance edges and (a) L−M edges or (b) S−(L+M) edges. The gray levels in the contour plot code the frequency of occurrences. Edges are rare events, so most of the pixels have a contrast close to zero (black). Strong edges of high contrast (white) are less frequent.—Co-occurrence maps of luminance and chromatic edges do not peak at the cardinal axes, showing that the vast majority of edges combine luminance and chromatic information.

flowers against green foliage, that are hardly visible in the luminance plane, give rise to strong object boundaries in the L−M plane.

Object boundaries are not always characterized by pure luminance variations. Instead, most edges are characterized by a co-occurrence of chromatic and luminance contrast. Further, some prominent object boundaries are signalled robustly only in the chromatic L−M plane. Chromatic edges are also robust against luminance variations cause by, e.g., cast shadows. Overall, this suggests an important role for color in the detection of object boundaries. The neural networks in early visual areas seems to be perfectly adapted to the joint occurrence of luminance and chromatic edges in natural scenes.

In computer vision, edge detection algorithms were mostly designed for the processing of achromatic images. However, despite tremendous effort, the multi-purpose edge detector which faithfully detects the relevant edges in an image has not been found yet. This failure may point to the importance of other visual modalities apart from luminance that play an important role in edge detection. Our results suggest that color is one modality which makes edge detection more robust.

Acknowledgements

The work has been supported in part by the German Science Foundation grant Ge 879/5.

References

1. Boynton, R.M., Ikeda, M., Stiles, W.S.: Interactions among chromatic mechanisms as inferred from positive and negative increment thresholds. Vision Research 4(1), 87–117 (1964)
2. Hurvich, L.M., Jameson, D.: An opponent-process theory of color vision. Psychological Reviews 64(6), 384–404 (1957)
3. Thornton, J.E., Pugh, E.N.: Red/Green color opponency at detection threshold. Science 219(4581), 191–193 (1983)
4. Stockman, A., Sharpe, L.T.: Cone spectral sensitivities and color matching. In: Gegenfurtner, K.R., Sharpe, L.T. (eds.) Color Vision – From Genes to perception, pp. 3–51. Cambridge University Press, New York (1999)
5. Derrington, A.M., Krauskopf, J., Lennie, P.: Chromatic mechanisms in lateral geniculate nucleus of macaque. Journal of Physiology 357, 241–265 (1984)
6. Lee, B.B.: Receptive field structure in the primate retina. Vision Research 36(5), 631–644 (1996)
7. Gegenfurtner, K.R.: Cortical mechanisms of colour vision. Nature Reviews Neuroscience 4(7), 563–572 (2003)
8. Wachtler, T., Sejnowski, T.J., Albright, T.D.: Representation of color stimuli in awake macaque primary visual cortex. Neuron 37(4), 681–691 (2003)
9. Marr, D.: Vision. W. H. Freeman & Co., San Francisco (1982)
10. Johnson, E.N., Hawken, M.J., Shapley, R.: The spatial transformation of color in the primary visual cortex of the macaque monkey. Nature Neuroscience 4(4), 409–416 (2001)
11. Friedman, H.S., Zhou, H., von der Heydt, R.: The coding of uniform colour figures in monkey visual cortex. Journal of Physiology 548, 593–613 (2003)
12. Hansen, T., Gegenfurtner, K.R.: Higher level chromatic mechanisms for image segmentation. Journal of Vision 6(3), 239–259 (2006)
13. D'Zmura, M., Knoblauch, K.: Spectral bandwidths for the detection of color. Vision Research 38(20), 3117–3128 (1998)
14. Wichmann, F.A., Hill, N.J.: The psychometric function: I. Fitting, sampling, and goodness of fit. Perception & Psychophysics 63(8), 1293–1313 (2001)
15. Goda, N., Fujii, M.: Sensitivity to modulation of color distribution in multicolored textures. Vision Research 41(19), 2475–2485 (2001)
16. Olmos, A., Kingdom, F.A.: McGill calibrated color image database (2004), http://tabby.vision.mcgill.ca

How Does the Brain Arrive at a Color Constant Descriptor?

Marc Ebner

Universität Würzburg, Lehrstuhl für Informatik II
Am Hubland, 97074 Würzburg, Germany
ebner@informatik.uni-wuerzburg.de
http://wwwi2.informatik.uni-wuerzburg.de/staff/ebner/welcome.html

Abstract. Color is not a physical quantity which can be measured. Yet we attach it to the objects around us. Colors appear to be approximately constant to a human observer. They are an important cue in everyday life. Today, it is known that the corpus callosum plays an important role in color perception. Area V4 contains cells which seem to respond to the reflectance of an object irrespective of the wavelength composition of the light reflected by the object. What is not known is how the brain arrives at a color constant or approximately color constant descriptor. A number of theories about color perception have been put forward. Most theories are phenomenological descriptions of color vision. However, what is needed in order to understand how the visual system works is a computational theory. With this contribution we describe a computational theory for color perception which is much simpler in comparison to previously published theories yet effective at computing a color constant descriptor.

1 Motivation

The measured color varies with the type of illuminant used. The energy Q measured by a sensor is proportional to the reflectance R at the corresponding object point and is also proportional to the irradiance E at the corresponding object point, i.e. we have

$$Q(\lambda) \propto R(\lambda)E(\lambda)$$

for wavelength λ. The fact that the measured color varies with the type of illuminant is observed by many amateur photographers all around the world. One simply has to compare a photograph of the same scene once using incandescent light and once using sunlight. Professional photographers are well aware of this and can use filters to change the color balance [1,2]. Digital cameras apply post-processing algorithms which can change the color balance such that the resulting photograph looks more natural. In contrast, the color observed by a human observer stays remarkably constant [3]. This phenomenon has been investigated in detail by Land [4,5]. Obviously, it is of great interest to learn what algorithm is actually used by the human visual system in order to arrive at a color constant descriptor which remains constant (or at least approximately

F. Mele et al. (Eds.): BVAI 2007, LNCS 4729, pp. 84–93, 2007.

constant) irrespective of the illuminant used. Several psychophysical models of color perception have been put forward. However, such models do not explain how or why the color perceived by an observer could depend on either average apparent reflectance or the average luminance. Such models are phenomenological descriptions of color vision. What is needed is a computational theory of color vision [6].

Quite a large number of color constancy algorithms have been developed, from Land and McCann's Retinex theory [7] and its many variants [8,9,10,11,12], Buchsbaum's gray world hypothesis [13], gamut constraint methods [14,15,16], color cluster rotation [17] to comprehensive normalization [18] and computation of intrinsic images [18]. Most color constancy algorithms assume that the illuminant is constant within the image. A notable exception is Land and McCanns Retinex algorithm together with the variants of Horn [8], Blake [11] and Rahman et al. [12].

2   Iterative Computation of Local Space Average Color

Land's alternative formulation of the Retinex algorithm [9] as well as the algorithm of Rahman et al. [12] require that some form of averaging of image pixel be carried out. Land [9] assumes that input from several receptors is averaged. The algorithm of Rahman et al. [12] computes the blurred image using a convolution. Local space average color may also be computed iteratively as Ebner has shown [19,20,21].

The algorithm of Ebner assumes that a grid of processing elements exists with one processing element per image pixel. Each processing element is connected only to its nearest neighbors. Let $N(x, y)$ be the neighboring processing elements of the element located at position (x, y) of the image, i.e.

$$N(x, y) = \{(x', y') | (x', y') \text{ is neighbor of element } (x, y)\}.$$

Each processing element computes local space average color $\mathbf{a}(x, y)$

$$\mathbf{a}(x, y) = [a_r(x, y), a_g(x, y), a_b(x, y)].$$

Let us assume that we already have some average stored at each processing element. The following update equations are then iterated

$$\mathbf{a}'(x, y) = \frac{1}{|N(x, y)|} \sum_{(x', y') \in N(x, y)} \mathbf{a}(x', y')$$

$$\mathbf{a}(x, y) = \mathbf{c}(x, y) \cdot p + \mathbf{a}'(x, y) \cdot (1 - p)$$

where p is a small percentage. The first operation simply takes the local space average color which is available from neighboring elements and averages this data. In other words, we get a new average based on the data stored at neighboring elements. The color which is available at the current element is then slowly faded into the average using the second operation. If these two operations are iterated indefinitely, the data simply diffuses between neighboring elements. This process converges to local space average color irrespective of the data stored initially inside the processing elements.

The extent over which local space average color is computed, is determined by the parameter p. For a small value of p, local space average color is computed over an extensive area whereas for a large value of p, local space average color is computed over a small area. The iterative computation of local space average color is very similar though not identical to the convolution of the input image with an exponential kernel.

$$\mathbf{a}(x,y) = \int \int \mathbf{c}(x',y') e^{-\frac{|x-x'|+|y-y'|}{\sigma}} \, dx' dy'$$

The correspondence between the parameter σ and the parameter p is given by

$$\sigma = \sqrt{\frac{1-p}{4p}}.$$

Instead of using a grid of processing elements in order to compute local space average color, a resistive grid may also be used. With a resistive grid, adjacent points are simply connected through a resistor.

3   The Gray World Assumption

Local space average color may then be used to compute a color constant descriptor using the gray world assumption. The gray world assumption was originally proposed by Buchsbaum [13]. It is based on the assumption that on average, the world is gray. Buchsbaum assumed overlapping response characteristics of the sensors. We will derive the gray world assumption using non-overlapping response characteristics. Let $c_i(x,y)$ be the measured intensity of color channel i at position (x,y) of the image. The measured intensity is proportional to the reflectance and the irradiance.

$$c_i(x,y) = R_i(x,y)L_i(x,y).$$

Buchsbaum assumed that the illuminant is constant over the entire image, i.e. we have $L_i(x,y) = L_i$. This gives us

$$c_i(x,y) = R_i(x,y)L_i.$$

Thus, the illuminant scales the reflectances. A color constant descriptor can be computed once an estimate of the illuminant is available.

Let us now compute space average color over all image pixels. Space average color $\mathbf{a} = [a_r(x,y), a_g(x,y), a_b(x,y)]$ of an image with n pixels is given by

$$a_i = \frac{1}{n} \sum_{x,y} c_i(x,y) = \frac{1}{n} \sum_{x,y} R_i(x,y)L_i = L_i \frac{1}{n} \sum_{x,y} R_i(x,y).$$

We now assume that several differently colored objects are located inside the image. Since we don't know anything about the colors of the objects we simply assume that all colors are equally likely, i.e. we assume that the reflectances are uniformly distributed over the range $[0, 1]$. If we have a sufficiently large number of different colors inside the image, then we obtain for the expected value of the sum

$$\frac{1}{n} \sum_{x,y} R_i(x, y) = \frac{1}{2}.$$

We now see that the color of the illuminant can be estimated by computing global space average color.

$$L_i \approx 2a_i$$

We use the gray world assumption locally in order to estimate the color of the illuminant at each image pixel (x, y)

$$L_i(x, y) \approx 2a_i(x, y)$$

where local space average color **a** is computed iteratively as described above. Note that because the illuminant is estimated for each image pixel, the algorithm also works for a spatially varying illuminant, i.e. multiple light sources, provided that the environment is sufficiently diverse.

We then compute a color constant descriptor o_i by dividing each image pixel by twice local space average color.

$$o_i(x, y) = \frac{c_i(x, y)}{2a_i(x, y)} \approx \frac{c_i(x, y)}{L_i(x, y)} \approx \frac{R_i(x, y)L_i(x, y)}{L_i(x, y)} = R_i(x, y)$$

Figure 1 shows the results of this algorithm for a sample image. The image was taken with a Canon 10D. The white balance was set to 6500K and a yellowish illuminant was used. The image shown on the left is the input image and the image on the right is the output image. The color cast is removed nicely as can be seen in the output image.

Fig. 1. The input image is shown on the left. Local space average color is computed using an exponential kernel. The output image is shown on the right.

4 Usage of Color Shifts

Experiments done by Helson [22] indicate that human subjects appear to use color shifts in order to estimate the color of achromatic samples illuminated by colored light. The perceived color of the sample depends on the color of the illuminant as well as on the color of the background. He found that a bright patch located on a gray background will have the color of the illuminant. A dark patch will have the complementary color of the illuminant. Patches which have an intermediate reflectance will appear achromatic. The algorithms of Land [9], Horn [8,23], Moore et al. [24] and Rahman et al. [12] do not reproduce this behavior. This is because the ratio between the color of the pixel and local space average color is computed. If one computes this ratio, the color of the illuminant falls out of the equation. The stimuli will always appear to be achromatic for all settings that Helson investigated. A more extensive discussion is given in [25].

Ebner [19] has developed a computational algorithm for color constancy based on the use of color shifts. As we have seen above, we need to divide each image pixel by twice the space average color in order to obtain a color constant descriptor. However, we may also obtain a color constant descriptor if we shift local space average color onto the gray vector. The gray vector runs through the color space from black through gray and onto white. According to the gray world hypothesis, the average color of image pixels should be located on the gray vector. If the average color is not located on the gray vector it has to be corrected such that the gray world assumption is fulfilled. Let $\mathbf{w} = \frac{1}{\sqrt{3}}[1,1,1]^T$ be the normalized gray vector and let $\mathbf{c} = [c_r, c_g, c_b]^T$ be the color of the current pixel. Let $\mathbf{a} = [a_r, a_g, a_b]^T$ be local space average color computed for the same pixel. We first compute the component $\mathbf{a}_\perp$ of local space average color which is perpendicular to the gray vector. The vector $\mathbf{a}$ is projected onto the white vector $\mathbf{w}$ and the projection is then subtracted from $\mathbf{a}$. This gives us $\mathbf{a}_\perp$.

$$\mathbf{a}_\perp = \mathbf{a} - (\mathbf{a} \cdot \mathbf{w})\mathbf{w}$$

This vector points from the gray vector to the local space average color. We then subtract this vector from the color of the current pixel, i.e. we compute

$$\mathbf{o} = \mathbf{c} - \mathbf{a}_\perp.$$

Figure 2 illustrates how the shift is applied for two vectors $\mathbf{c}$ and $\mathbf{a}$. If we look at the individual components, i.e. color channels, we obtain

$$o_i = c_i - a_i + \frac{1}{3}(a_r + a_g + a_b).$$

Let $\bar{a} = \frac{1}{3}(a_r + a_g + a_b)$, then we have

$$o_i = c_i - a_i + \bar{a}.$$

The result of this operation is that the local space average color is shifted onto the gray vector and a color cast is removed. Since the shift is performed perpendicular to the gray axis the average intensity of the image pixels is not changed. This algorithm shows the same behavior as described by Helson.

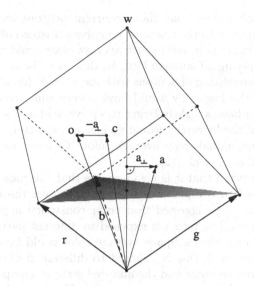

Fig. 2. The component $\mathbf{a}_\perp$ of local space average color $\mathbf{a}$ which is perpendicular to the gray vector $\mathbf{w}$ is subtracted from $\mathbf{c}$. The result is a color corrected image.

5   A Computational Theory of Color Perception

Theoretical models for color perception have been developed by Judd [26] and by Richards and Parks [27] among others. These are psychophysical models of color perception. They do not explain how or why the color could depend on either average apparent reflectance or the average luminance. They are phenomenological descriptions of color vision. What is needed is a computational theory of color vision [6]. The algorithms which would lend themselves to a biological realization are the parallel algorithms of Land and McCann [7], Land [9], Horn [8], Blake [11] and Ebner [19,20,21].

Of course, as of today, it is not yet known how the human visual system actually computes color constant descriptors. We do know that color constant cells have been found inside visual area V4 [3,28]. Area V4 may be subdivided into two subareas V4 and V4α [29]. V4 has a retinotopic organization whereas area V4α does not have a retinotopic organization. Cells found inside visual area V4 have very large receptive fields. These may be the cells which respond to either local or global space average color. They respond to the color of objects irrespective of the wavelength composition of the light reflected by the object. Area V4 also has callosal connections. The corpus callosum connects both hemispheres of the brain. Land et al. [30] have shown that an intact corpus callosum is required for accurate color perception.

Currently, we do not know how the processing of color information is actually done in V4. The computation of local space average color could either be done in space or in time [10]. Algorithms which perform an integration over time include the algorithms of Horn [8], Blake [11] and Ebner [19,20,21]. If the human visual system uses integration over time, then recurrent neurons are required which only have to be connected to their nearest neighbors. Instead of computing local space average color iteratively, local space average color could also be computed by consecutively applying a Gaussian blur. In this case, the neurons would have to form a hierarchy consisting of neurons with receptive fields of increasing sizes. The first neuron of the hierarchy would have a very small receptive field. The second neuron would have a sightly larger receptive field and so on. The neuron located at the top of the hierarchy would receive a completely blurred image as input, in other words, global space average color. This method would resemble the algorithm of Rahman et al. [12].

Hurlbert [10] suggested that it is also possible that the rods in the periphery of the retina are used to compute a spatial average over the image boundary. D'Zmura and Lennie [31] suggested that color constancy might be due to an adaptation mechanism. The retina is exposed to different parts of the scene as the eye, head and body moves. Space average color could be computed in the course of time, i.e. as the retina is exposed to different parts of the scene, by averaging the data per receptor and the adapted state at any point of the retina would be a function of this space average color. However, the experiments of Land and McCann [7] who have also experimented using short exposure times suggest that color constancy is an ability which exists even if the image is only perceived for a fraction of a second. The ability to perceive colors as constant is not dependent on long exposure times.

The first visual area where color constant cells have been found is V4. Assuming only local connections, i.e. that a highly parallel algorithm is employed, either the algorithm of Land [9], Horn [8] or Ebner [19,20] could be used by the visual system. A hierarchy of neurons, which is just used to compute a blurred image, would require an unnecessarily large neural architecture. Why should evolution favor this type of architecture if the same can be achieved using much simpler means? If the algorithm of Horn [8] is realized by the visual system, we would first need to construct a Laplacian operator. Local differencing could be used to implement a Laplacian operator. The output of the Laplacian operator would already be a color constant descriptor because the response of the photoreceptors is logarithmic (or nearly logarithmic) [32]. In order to implement the algorithm of Horn, we would now need a thresholding operation and an integration step. The integration would most likely be done in V4. Livingstone and Hubel [33] assume that such an algorithm is used by the visual system. Instead of operating on the cone channels red, green, and blue the Retinex algorithm is assumed to operate either in a longitude-latitude spherical polar coordinate system or inside a rotated coordinate system. In the spherical coordinate system of Livingstone and Hubel, radius denotes the dark-light scale, longitude the red-green axis and latitude the blue-yellow axis. That the Retinex algorithm can also be applied inside a rotated coordinate system was also noted by Land [9].

It may also be that the actual color signals inside the rotated coordinate system are averaged instead of averaging the thresholded output of the Laplacian. This would be essentially be the algorithm described by Ebner [19,20].

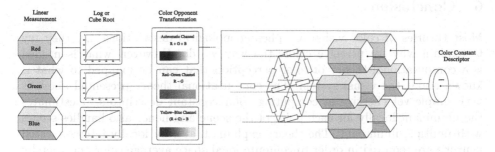

Fig. 3. Proposal of how the human visual system may arrive at a color constant descriptor

The advantage of this algorithm is that no threshold has to be set. In practice it is usually very difficult to properly choose a threshold. For this algorithm, local space average color would be subtracted from the color of the given pixel. Figure 3 shows the resulting architecture.

Livingstone and Hubel suggest that cells found inside the blobs of V1 act as building blocks which contribute to long-range interactions occurring in V4. It should be noted that in both models, the model of Horn [8] and the model of Ebner [19,20] no long range interactions are necessary. Only local connections between cells are required. The reason why distant areas may influence the color of a given point is most likely due to iterative propagation of data from one cell to the next.

We now dicuss our model in full. First, the cones of the retina measure the incident light for the three different color bands red, green, and blue. There is some dispute about whether the relationship between lightness and reflectance is logarithmic or follows a cube root or square root relationship. A logarithmic relationship was proposed by Faugeras [34]. See Hunt [35] for a discussion on why the relationship may either be a cube root or square root relationship. The reader should take note of the fact that the perceptually uniform CIE $L^*a^*b^*$ color space (see [36,37]) also uses a cube root transformation. With a suitable scaling factor and offset, all three functions are a possible approximation. Let us assume for simplicity that the first step is the application of a logarithmic or other closely related function. Then a coordinate transform follows. This coordinate transform is most likely carried out by the color opponent cells. The color space is now described by the three axes red-green, blue-yellow and black-white. Local space average color is then computed using interconnected neurons. We only require that the neurons be connected to their nearest neighbors. The smoothing step could be carried out through resistive coupling of neurons. It is known that gap junctions behave mainly as pure resistors [32]. Such gap junctions could be used to diffuse color information to adjacent neurons. Once local space average color has been computed, it is subtracted from the color of the current pixel. The result is a color constant descriptor.

6   Conclusions

Most theories of color vision are phenomenological descriptions, i.e. they try to explain why we perceive colors the way we do. However, what is needed is a computational theory of color perception that can be mapped to what is known about the visual system. The computational theory presented above is very simple yet effective at computing color constant descriptors. It estimates the illuminant locally for each point of the scene and hence also handles scenes with multiple illuminant. The theory explains that only locally interconnected neurons are required in order to compute local space average color and thereby a color constant descriptor. Local space average color can be computed by a set of interconnected neurons each receiving input from a particular point of the retina. Only resistive coupling between such neurons is required. According to this theory, the long range connections through the corpus callosum simply connect adjacent neurons of the left and right hemispheres of the brain. Due to the logarithmic response of the receptors one needs to subtract the computed local space average color from the input signal, i.e. a negative coupling between the output from local space average color and the input signal is all that is required. The result is a color constant descriptor.

References

1. Hedgecoe, J.: Fotografieren: die neue große Fotoschule. Dorling Kindersley Verlag GmbH, Starnberg (2004)
2. Jacobsen, R.E., Ray, S.F., Attridge, G.G., Axford, N.R.: The Manual of Photography. Photographic and Digital Imaging. Focal Press, Oxford (2000)
3. Zeki, S.: A Vision of the Brain. Blackwell Science, Oxford (1993)
4. Land, E.H.: The retinex. American Scientist 52, 247–264 (1964)
5. Land, E.H.: The retinex theory of colour vision. Proc. Royal Inst. Great Britain 47, 23–58 (1974)
6. Marr, D.: Vision. W. H. Freeman and Company, New York (1982)
7. Land, E.H., McCann, J.J.: Lightness and retinex theory. Journal of the Optical Society of America 61(1), 1–11 (1974)
8. Horn, B.K.P.: Determining lightness from an image. Computer Graphics and Image Processing 3, 277–299 (1974)
9. Land, E.H.: An alternative technique for the computation of the designator in the retinex theory of color vision. Proc. Natl. Acad. Sci. USA 83, 3078–3080 (1986)
10. Hurlbert, A.: Formal connections between lightness algorithms. J. Opt. Soc. Am. A 3(10), 1684–1693 (1986)
11. Blake, A.: Boundary conditions for lightness computation in mondrian world. Computer Vision, Graphics, and Image Processing 32, 314–327 (1985)
12. Rahman, Z., Jobson, D.J., Woodell, G.A.: Method of improving a digital image. United States Patent No. 5,991,456 (1999)
13. Buchsbaum, G.: A spatial processor model for object colour perception. Journal of the Franklin Institute 310(1), 337–350 (1980)
14. Forsyth, D.A.: A novel approach to colour constancy. In: Second International Conference on Computer Vision, Tampa, FL, December 5-8, 1988, pp. 9–18. IEEE Press, Los Alamitos (1988)

15. Finlayson, G.D.: Color in perspective. IEEE Transactions on Pattern Analysis and Machine Intelligence 18(10), 1034–1038 (1996)
16. Barnard, K., Finlayson, G., Funt, B.: Color constancy for scenes with varying illumination. Computer Vision and Image Understanding 65(2), 311–321 (1997)
17. Paulus, D., Csink, L., Niemann, H.: Color cluster rotation. In: ICIP. Proc. of the Int. Conf. on Image Processing, pp. 161–165. IEEE Computer Society Press, Los Alamitos (1998)
18. Finlayson, G.D., Schiele, B., Crowley, J.L.: Comprehensive colour image normalization. In: Burkhardt, H., Neumann, B. (eds.) ECCV 1998. LNCS, vol. 1407, pp. 475–490. Springer, Heidelberg (1998)
19. Ebner, M.: Color constancy using local color shifts. In: Pajdla, T., Matas, J.(G.) (eds.) ECCV 2004. LNCS, vol. 3023, pp. 276–287. Springer, Heidelberg (2004)
20. Ebner, M.: A parallel algorithm for color constancy. Journal of Parallel and Distributed Computing 64(1), 79–88 (2004)
21. Ebner, M.: Evolving color constancy. Special Issue on Evolutionary Computer Vision and Image Understanding of Pattern Recognition Letters 27(11), 1220–1229 (2006)
22. Helson, H.: Fundamental problems in color vision. I. the principle governing changes in hue, saturation, and lightness of non-selective samples in chromatic illumination. Journal of Experimental Psychology 23(5), 439–476 (1938)
23. Horn, B.K.P.: Robot Vision. MIT Press, Cambridge, Massachusetts (1986)
24. Moore, A., Allman, J., Goodman, R.M.: A real-time neural system for color constancy. IEEE Transactions on Neural Networks 2(2), 237–247 (1991)
25. Ebner, M.: Color Constancy. John Wiley & Sons, England (2007)
26. Judd, D.B.: Hue saturation and lightness of surface colors with chromatic illumination. Journal of the Optical Society of America 30, 2–32 (1940)
27. Richards, W., Parks, E.A.: Model for color conversion. Journal of the Optical Society of America 61(7), 971–976 (1971)
28. Zeki, S., Marini, L.: Three cortical stages of colour processing in the human brain. Brain 121, 1669–1685 (1998)
29. Zeki, S., Bartels, A.: The clinical and functional measurement of cortical (in)activity in the visual brain, with special reference to the two subdivisions (V4 and V4α) of the human colour centre. Proc. R. Soc. Lond. B 354, 1371–1382 (1999)
30. Land, E.H., Hubel, D.H., Livingstone, M.S., Perry, S.H., Burns, M.M.: Colour-generating interactions across the corpus callosum. Nature 303, 616–618 (1983)
31. D'Zmura, M., Lennie, P.: Mechanisms of color constancy. In: Healey, G.E., Shafer, S.A., Wolff, L.B. (eds.) Color, pp. 224–234. Jones and Bartlett Publishers, Boston (1992)
32. Herault, J.: A model of colour processing in the retina of vertebrates: From photoreceptors to colour opposition and colour constancy phenomena. Neurocomputing 12, 113–129 (1996)
33. Livingstone, M.S., Hubel, D.H.: Anatomy and physiology of a color system in the primate visual cortex. The Journal of Neuroscience 4(1), 309–356 (1984)
34. Faugeras, O.D.: Digital color image processing within the framework of a human visual model. IEEE Transactions on Acoustics, Speech, and Signal Processing ASSP-27(4), 380–393 (1979)
35. Hunt, R.W.G.: Light energy and brightness sensation. Nature 179, 1026–1027 (1957)
36. Glasser, L.G., McKinney, A.H., Reilly, C.D., Schnelle, P.D.: Cube-root color coordinate system. Journal of the Optical Society of America 48(10), 736–740 (1958)
37. International Commission on Illumination: Colorimetry, 2nd edn., corrected reprint. Technical Report 15.2, International Commission on Illumination (1996)

Temporal Characteristics of Artificial Retina Based on Bacteriorhodopsin and Its Variants

Teemu Tukiainen[1], Lasse Lensu[1], and Jussi Parkkinen[2]

[1] Dept. of Information Tech., Lappeenranta University of Technology, Finland
[2] Dept. of Computer Science, University of Joensuu, Finland

Abstract. Bacteriorhodopsin is the light-sensitive protein found in the archaean *Halobacterium salinarum*. Because of its versatile properties and possibilities to modify its characteristics, it has been proposed for a wide range of technical applications including the artificial retina. Here, a simulation model and tool for studying the characteristics of artifical retina based on biomolecules is introduced. Three types of bacteriorhodopsin with different light absorption and relaxation characteristics are used in a case study. The results show that the simulator is a versatile tool to study the temporal characteristics of bacteriorhodopsin variants and to support the design of artificial sensors.

1 Introduction

Microelectronics still dominates the design and construction of artificial vision systems. In contrast, nature has evolved highly different architectures for processing visual information. Consequently, there is an abundance of proposals where motivation and ideas are transferred from biology and physiology to artificial and technical systems. In molecular computing, for example, silicon circuits can be replaced by functional biomolecules such as bacteriorhodopsin.

Bacteriorhodopsin (BR) is a light-sensitive protein found in the purple membrane of the archaean *Halobacterium salinarum* [21]. BR resembles vertebrate and invertebrate photoreceptor rhodopsins both structurally and functionally. As with all rhodopsins, BR consists of seven transmembrane alpha-helices of aminoacids, and a functional retinal chromophore, a derivative of vitamin A. The purpose of BR is to take part in the energy balancing mechanism of the archaean. Under anaerobic conditions, BR produces a proton gradient across the cell membrane by the light-induced photocycle [4], which together with an electric potential difference between the cytoplasm and the outside enables the ATPases in the cell to convert ADP to ATP [1].

BR retains the photocycle even when isolated from the purple membrane and incorporated into an artificial membrane [22], or a thin polymer-based film [5]. Such films react to light with differential reponsivity common in motion detection, and when spatially arranged following the receptive field structure in the vertebrate eye, they can perform edge enhancement [6]. BR has properties that make it well suited for optical and photoelectric applications. Films produced

F. Mele et al. (Eds.): BVAI 2007, LNCS 4729, pp. 94–103, 2007.

by immobilizing wild-type BR in gelatin or polyvinylalcohol (PVA) are highly stable. A film of BR molecules produces a photoelectric response (PER) when illuminated, caused by the translocation of protons in the film. The most studied application area of BR is the optical memory, but it can be used to implement photodetectors [18], and suggestions to use BR films for real-time pattern recognition and colour-sensitive artificial retina have been made [10,17].

In natural vision, only a subset of rhodopsin's functionality can be explained based on characteristics related to perception of static stimuli. This is because in most cases, the vision system operates on continuous visual stimulus dependent on time. The same applies to artificial vision systems when they are designed for a similar purpose: their temporal characteristics are significant for the functionality. BR has a light-induced reversible photocycle consisting of several intermediates with different relaxation times. These intermediates and their relaxation times cause a significant impact to the temporal characteristics of artificial retina based on BR.

In our earlier studies [16,9], we have been able to determine the wavelength dependencies of BR films with different absorption properties, their PERs, and to compare the modeled PERs with the measurements for the elements containing wild-type BR and its two retinal analogs. We have also initially studied the temporal characteristics of BR [19], but the results were inconclusive because of improper interfacing to the electronics and response registration device. Here, we introduce a simulation model and tool for studying the characteristics of artifical retina based on biomolecules. Three types of bacteriorhodopsin and their temporal characteristics in continuous operation are used as examples.

2 Bacteriorhodopsin Sensors and Their Simulation

2.1 Bacteriorhodopsin Sensors

From the BR photocycle shown in Fig. 1, it can be seen that the relaxation times support the idea of real-time operation in an imaging application with continuous visual input. To study the photoelectric properties of BR, we have prepared dry BR thick films by using PVA as the matrix. The purple membrane patches of BR were isolated from *Halobacterium salinarum* wild type (S9). Two variants of the wild type BR were prepared by reconstituting bleached BR with synthetic 3,4-didehydro and 4-keto retinal analogues. The BR-PVA elements together with their photoelectric and optical properties are described in detail in [16].

The three types of BR have dissimilar relaxation times of the photocycle intermediates. The times depend on the chemical environment of the BR molecules. In aqueous solution, there are more than one M intermediates in the photocycles of all of the before-mentioned types [8]. Therefore, multiple populations having different relaxation time to the ground state coexist in the solution. In the aqueous solution, the ratios of the M-state relaxation times of the two analogs relative to the wild type are 25:1 and 60 000:1, whereas a polymer matrix changes the ratios to 2.5:1 and 155:1 [2]). The large difference in the relaxation times significantly affects the design and characteristics of an application making use of all three types.

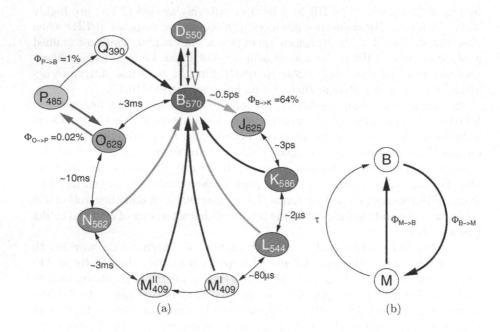

Fig. 1. (a) Wild-type bacteriorhodopsin photocycle consisting of the ground state B and other intermediate states. Thin arrows denote thermal transitions, whereas thick arrows denote light-induced photochemical transitions. The numbers represent wavelengths of absorption maxima, approximate transition times in neutral aqueous solution at ambient temperature, and quantum efficiencies Φ for known transitions (data from [3,7,11,12]). (b) Generic and simplified photocycle where τ represents the thermal transition time.

2.2 Sensor Simulation

To simulate the temporal characteristics of the BR sensors or any light-induced biomolecule, a model was developed for the photocycle. The initial model consists only of two states, but this can be justified with the fact that most of the photoelectric response amplitude within the time window of real-time visual input arises from the B-to-M transition. Matlab with Simulink was chosen for the actual implementation because this combination enables interactive experimentation with and demonstration of the model. Simulink is an ideal tool for simulating time-varying systems, such as photocycles, which interface with electronics.

The simulation model for the BR sensors has two blocks: one for the light source and another for the BR sensor. The light source used in the earlier physical measurements was a pulsed xenon flashlamp, Oriel series Q with the bulb 6426. The light source has a configurable discharge energy and pulsing frequency. For the Simulink model, the controls for the discharge energy and pulsing frequency were implemented. The time dependence and spectral content of the light output was modelled based on the manufacturer data shown in Fig. 2. The light source block includes also models for 16 narrow band Oriel interference filters, each having 20 nm window within the visible range of the electromagnetic spectrum. The filters are used to control the spectral content of light in accordance with the physical measurements.

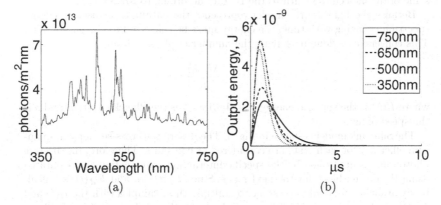

Fig. 2. (a) Spectral energy distribution, and (b) time-dependence of the light source based on manufacturer data

The initial BR sensor model consists of two intermediate states. Its purpose is to simulate the BR molecule photocycles between the states B and M. The model takes into account the total number of molecules in the sensor to enable future comparison of the results with the physical measurements. As the base for building the two-state model representing the BR states during the photocycle, the following rate-equation was used [13]:

$$\frac{\partial B(t)}{\partial t} = -(F(t)s_B B(t) - F(t)s_M M(t)) + \frac{1}{\tau}M(t) \tag{1}$$

where $B(t)$ and $M(t)$ are the number of molecules in the particular states at time t, $F(t)$ is the photon flux, and s_B and s_M are the interaction cross sections of molecules, where $s_B = \sigma_M \Phi_B$. τ defines the thermal transition time for the relaxation from the M to B state. The interaction cross section defines a set of molecules which transit from the B state to the M state, σ is the absorption cross section and Φ is the quantum efficiency for a particular transition. The data in the form of molar absorption coeffient ϵ $[Mol^{-1}cm^{-1}]$ can be converted to the absorption cross-section as follows:

$$\sigma_B = \frac{\varepsilon}{N_A}0.1ln10 \tag{2}$$

where N_A is the Avogadro constant. With discrete time used in Simulink models, the number of molecules in M and B states at time t can be derived based on Eq. 1 as follows:

$$M_t = N_0 - B_t \tag{3}$$

$$B_t = B_{t-1} - B_{t-1}s_B F_{t-1} + M_{t-1}s_M F_{t-1} + M_{t-1}\frac{T}{\tau} \tag{4}$$

where N_0 is the total number of molecules in the sensor, and T is the fixed time step. When the sensor is illuminated by the photon flux F, the number of molecules moving from the B state to M state is defined by $B_{t-1}s_BF_{t-1}$ in the Eq. 4. If there is no light, the molecules return back to the B state by thermal relaxation, according to $M_{t-1}\frac{T}{\tau}$ in the Eq. 4. In the case where there is light, some of the molecules return to the B state according to $M_{t-1}s_MF_{t-1}$.

Because the light source model represents the output as a discrete energy spectrum changing with time, the energy must be converted to the photon flux. This conversion is done by solving the number of photons from

$$N(\lambda, t) = \frac{\lambda E(\lambda)}{hc}, \tag{5}$$

where $E(\lambda)$ is the spectral energy distribution, h is the Planck constant and c is the speed of light.

The Simulink model is shown in Fig. 3. The absorption cross-section and quantum efficiency for each state are considered as constants. Therefore, the discrete photon flux is multiplied by the specific interaction cross-section and separated using the demux-block for the next stage. Since $F_B(t) \cdot s_B$ and $F_M(t) \cdot s_M$ is already available, it is only necessary to multiply these samples with the $B(t)$ and $M(t)$, which is done in Simulink simply by using the product-of-elements block.

From the amount of active molecules in the sensor, the number of molecules in the M state is subtracted, and the number of molecules returning from the M state is added. Now, the number of molecules in the B state is known, which is multiplied by the $F_B(t)s_B$ producing the number of molecules excited from the B state to the M state at time t. The number of molecules excited to the M state is added to the number of molecules already in that state. From the previous sum, the number of molecules which is returned to the B state by thermal relaxation and the number of molecules returned to the B state by the photon absorption are subtracted. Thermal relaxation is simulated in Matlab so that the number of molecules in the M state is multiplied with the $\frac{1}{\tau}T$, where T is the simulation timestep and τ the thermal relaxation time.

3   Experiments and Results

3.1   Simulation

The temporal characteristics of the three types of BR sensors were simulated. The parameters for the experiment were derived from the proposed microscale imaging device consisting of 1 μm^2 elements of the three BR types [15]. The parameters for the light source model were 160 mJ (discharge energy) and 100 Hz (pulsing frequency). The discharge energy was not varied in these simulations because, within a reasonable intensity range, the photoelectric response amplitude of BR has been shown to be linearly dependent on the light intensity [18].

For the BR sensors, most of the parameters were selected based on literature: the quantum efficiencies used were $\Phi_B = 0.64$ [23], the relaxation times of the M

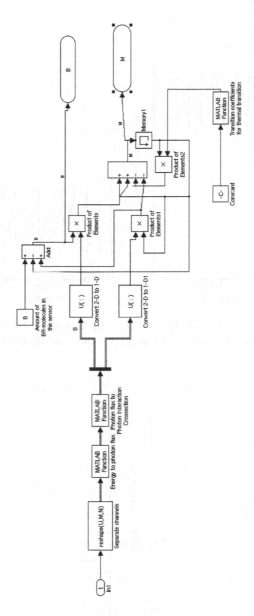

Fig. 3. Implementation of the two-state model with the Simulink

state were 10 ms, 250 ms, and 620 s for the wild-type, 3,4-didehydro, and 4-keto BR respectively [2], and the molar absorption coefficients were according to [11]. The initial value for the quantum efficiency of the M state was $\Phi_M = 0.64$. The fixed time step for the simulations was 77.6699 ns which was more than accurate for the two-state model with the used parameters.

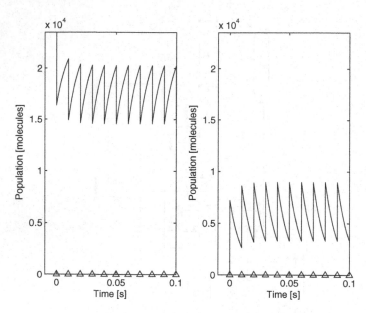

Fig. 4. Simulated populations of the B (left) and M (right) states of the wild-type bacteriorhodopsin sensor element. The triangles denote the times of the light pulses.

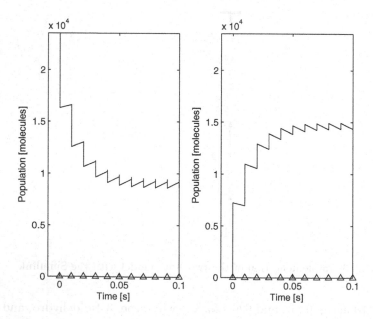

Fig. 5. Simulated populations of the B (left) and M (right) states of the 3,4-didehydro bacteriorhodopsin sensor element. The triangles denote the times of the light pulses.

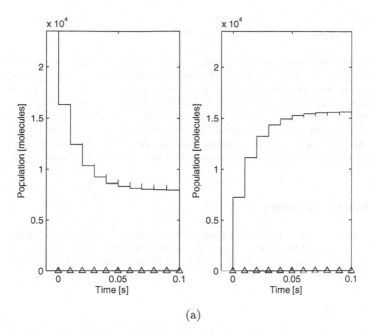

(a)

Fig. 6. Simulated populations of the B (left) and M (right) states of the 4-keto bacteriorhodopsin sensor element. The triangles denote the times of the light pulses.

The simulation results shown in Figures 4-6 show the differences between the three types of BR. The relaxation times cause different population trends for the three cases, but none of them fully saturate to the M state. This is because the return to the ground state B occurs due to thermal relaxation and also because of photostimulation [20]. The effect of relaxation time differences can be clearly seen when comparing the simulations: the short relaxation time of the wild-type BR causes the M state population to decay considerably before the arrival of the next light pulse. On the other hand, the 4-keto BR does not saturate fully to the M state only because of photostimulation.

4   Discussion and Future Work

Based on the simulation results, it is clear that the model is suitable for experimental design of artificial retina based on a biomolecule. The model can be used to study and demonstrate the effect of changes in the sensor, and in the light excitation used. The simulation model can also be used to study interfacing to the electronics. Currently, the adjustable parameters include BR concentration, sensor size, relaxation times of the photocycle intermediates, light source discharge energy, pulsing frequency, output time-dependent spectrum, and spectral filtering.

As the future work, the model will be improved by including the state-of-the-art photocycles for the three BR types, an orientation coefficient for the BR molecules within the sensor, and a separate model to convert the molecule populations into electric signals [14]. The model will be validated by comparing the simulation results to physical measurement data with rebuilt electronics to register the photoelectric responses. A streamlined version of the model will be also developed to enable real-time demonstration of the functionality, and additional Simulink blocks will be developed for other measurement devices when needed.

Acknowledgements

The research project has been supported by the Finnish Funding Agency for Technology and Innovation, Tekes, and the Academy of Finland. We wish to thank Ph.D. Michael Frydrych, Ph.D. Sinikka Parkkinen and prof. Timo Jaaskelainen for their efforts in the project.

References

1. Bickel-Sandkötter, S., Gärtner, W., Danc, M.: Conversion of energy in halobacteria: ATP synthesis and phototaxis. Archives of Microbiology 166, 1–11 (1996)
2. Birge, R.: Protein-based optical computing and memories. Computer 25(11), 56–67 (1992)
3. Birge, R., Gillespie, N., Izaguirre, E., Kusnetzow, A., Lawrence, A., Singh, D., Song, Q.W., Schmidt, E., Stuart, J., Seetharaman, S., Wise, K.: Biomolecular electronics: protein-based associative processors and volumetric memories. Journal of Physical Chemistry B 103, 10746–10766 (1999)
4. Bräuchle, C., Hampp, N., Drabent, R.: Optical applications of bacteriorhodopsin and its mutated variants. Advanced Materials 3, 420–428 (1991)
5. Bryl, K., Váró, G., Drabent, R.: The photocycle of bacteriorhodopsin immobilized in poly(vinyl alcohol) film. FEBS Letters 285(1), 66–70 (1991)
6. Chen, Z., Birge, R.: Protein-based artificial retinas. TIBTECH 11, 292–300 (1993)
7. Chen, Z., Takei, H., Lewis, A.: Optical implementation of neural networks with wavelength-encoded bipolar weight using bacteriorhodopsin. In: Proceedings, International Joint Conference on Neural Networks, San Diego, California, vol. 2, pp. 803–807 (1990)
8. Druzhko, A., Chamorovsky, S.: The cycle of photochromic reactions of a bacteriorhodopsin analog with 4-keto-retinal. Biosystems 35(2-3), 133–136 (1995)
9. Frydrych, M., Lensu, L., Parkkinen, S., Parkkinen, J., Jaaskelainen, T.: Photoelectric response of bacteriorhodopsin in thin PVA films and its model. In: De Gregorio, M., Di Maio, V., Frucci, M., Musio, C. (eds.) BVAI 2005. LNCS, vol. 3704, pp. 126–135. Springer, Heidelberg (2005)
10. Frydrych, M., Silfsten, P., Parkkinen, S., Parkkinen, J., Jaaskelainen, T.: Color sensitive retina based on bacteriorhodopsin. Biosystems 54(3), 131–140 (2000)
11. Gergely, C., Zimányi, L., Váró, G.: Bacteriorhodopsin intermediate spectra determined over a wide pH range. Journal of Physical Chemistry B 101, 9390–9395 (1997)

12. Hampp, N.: Bacteriorhodopsin as a photochromic retinal protein for optical memories. Chemical Reviews 100, 1755–1776 (2000)
13. Jaaskelainen, T., Leppanen, V.-P., Parkkinen, S., Parkkinen, J., Khodonov, A.: The photochromic properties of 4-keto bacteriorhodopsin. Optical Materials 6, 339–345 (1996)
14. Keszthelyi, L., Ormos, P.: Electric signals associated with the photocycle of bacteriorhodopsin. FEBS Letters 109(2), 189–193 (1980)
15. Lensu, L.: Photoelectric properties of bacteriorhodopsin films for photosensing and information processing. Doctoral thesis, number 141 in Acta Universitatis Lappeenrantaensis, Lappeenranta University of Technology (2002)
16. Lensu, L., Frydrych, M., Parkkinen, J., Parkkinen, S., Jaaskelainen, T.: Photoelectric properties of bacteriorhodopsin analogs for color-sensitive optoelectronic devices. Optical Materials 27(1), 57–62 (2004)
17. Lensu, L., Frydrych, M., Parkkinen, S., Jaaskelainen, T., Parkkinen, J.: Color-sensitive biosensors for imaging applications. In: Knopf, G.K., Bassi, A.S. (eds.) Smart Biosensor Technology. Optical Science and Engineering Series, ch. 16, vol. 118, pp. 437–460. CRC Press, Boca Raton, FL, USA (2007)
18. Lensu, L., Parkkinen, J., Parkkinen, S., Frydrych, M., Jaaskelainen, T.: Photoelectrical properties of protein-based optoelectronic sensor. Optical Materials 21(4), 783–788 (2003)
19. Lensu, L., Parkkinen, J., Parkkinen, S., Jaaskelainen, T.: Grabbing video sequences using protein based artificial retina. In: Proceedings of SPIE: Sensors and Camera Systems for Scientific, Industrial, and Digital Photography Applications III, San Jose, California, USA, January 21-23, 2002, vol. 4669, pp. 52–62 (2002)
20. Ludmann, K., Gergely, C., Dér, A., Váró, G.: Electrical signals during the bacteriorhodopsin photocycle, determined over a wide pH range. Biophysical Journal 75, 3120–3126 (1998)
21. Oesterhelt, D., Stoeckenius, W.: Rhodopsin-like protein from the purple membrane of Halobacterium Halobium. Nature New Biol. 233(39), 149–152 (1971)
22. Rigaud, J.-L., Paternostre, M.-T., Bluzat, A.: Mechanisms of membrane protein insertion into liposomes during reconstution procedures involving the use of detergents. 2. incorporation of the light-driven proton pump bacteriorhodopsin. Biochemistry 27, 2677–2688 (1988)
23. Tittor, J., Oesterhelt, D.: The quantum yield of bacteriorhodopsin. FEBS Letters 263(2), 269–273 (1990)

Vision and Action in the Language-Ready Brain: From Mirror Neurons to SemRep

Michael A. Arbib[1,2,3] and JinYong Lee[1]

[1] Computer Science
[2] Neuroscience
[3] USC Brain Project
University of Southern California, Los Angeles, CA 90089-2520, USA
{arbib,jinyongl}@usc.edu

Abstract. The general setting for our work is to locate language perception and production within the broader context of brain mechanisms for action and perception in general, modeling brain function in terms of the competition and cooperation of schemas. Particular emphasis is placed on mirror neurons – neurons active both for execution of a certain class of actions and for recognition of a (possibly broader) class of similar actions. We build on the early VISIONS model of schema-based computer analysis of static scenes to present SemRep, a graphical representation of dynamic visual scenes designed to support the generation of varied descriptions of episodes. Mechanisms for parsing and production of sentences are currently being implemented within Template Construction Grammar (TCG), a new form of construction grammar distinguished by its use of SemRep to express semantics.

Keywords: action, action recognition, brain mechanisms, competition and cooperation, construction grammar, dynamic visual scenes, language perception, language production, mirror neurons, visual perception, scene descriptions, schema theory, SemRep, vision.

1 Introduction

The present section provides the background for the novel material of this paper: Section 2, which presents SemRep, a graphical representation of dynamic visual scenes designed to support the generation of varied descriptions of episodes; and Section 3, which presents Template Construction Grammar (TCG), the version of construction grammar in which we locate our current efforts to implement mechanisms for the parsing and production of sentences. We also summarize the Mirror System Hypothesis, an evolutionary framework for analyzing brain mechanisms of language perception and production which places particular emphasis on the role of mirror neurons. We briefly note that the brain may be modeled in terms of the competition and cooperation of schemas. Finally, we recall key features of the early VISIONS model of schema-based computer analysis of static scenes to provide background for the design of SemRep.

F. Mele et al. (Eds.): BVAI 2007, LNCS 4729, pp. 104–123, 2007.

1.1 Schemas Which Compete and Cooperate

Vision is often seen as a process that classifies visual input, e.g., recognizing faces from photographs, or segmenting a scene and labeling the regions, or detecting characteristic patterns of motion in a videoclip. However, our approach to vision is concerned with its relevance to the ongoing behavior of an embodied agent be it frog, rat, monkey, human or robot [1, 2] – we view vision under the general rubric of *action-oriented perception*, as the "active organism" seeks from the world the information it needs to pursue its chosen course of action. A *perceptual schema* not only determines whether a given "domain of interaction" (an action-oriented generalization of the notion of object) is present in the environment but can also provide parameters concerning the current relationship of the organism with that domain. *Motor schemas* provide the control systems which can be coordinated to effect the wide variety of movement.

A *coordinated control program* is a schema assemblage which processes input via perceptual schemas and delivers its output via motor schemas, interweaving the activations of these schemas in accordance with the current task and sensory environment to mediate more complex behaviors [3]. A given action may be invoked in a wide variety of circumstances; a given perception may precede many courses of action. There is no one grand "apple schema" which links all "apple perception strategies" to "every action that involves an apple". Moreover, in the schema-theoretic approach, "apple perception" is not mere categorization – "this is an apple" – but may provide access to a range of parameters relevant to interaction with the apple at hand.

1.2 The VISIONS System

An early example of schema-based interpretation for visual scene analysis in the VISIONS system [4]. However, it is *not* an action-oriented system, but rather deploys a set of perceptual schemas to label objects in a static visual scene. In VISIONS, there is no extraction of gist – rather, the gist is prespecified so that only those schemas are deployed relevant to recognizing a certain kind of scene (e.g., an outdoor scene with houses, trees, lawn, etc.). Low-level processes take an image of such an outdoor visual scene and extract and builds a representation in the *intermediate database* – including contours and surfaces tagged with features such as color, texture, shape, size and location. An important point is that the segmentation of the scene in the intermediate database is based not only on bottom-up input (data-driven) but also on top-down hypotheses (e.g., that a large region may correspond to two objects, and thus should be resegmented).

VISIONS applies perceptual schemas across the whole intermediate representation to form confidence values for the presence of objects like houses, walls and trees. The schemas are stored in LTM (long-term memory), while the state of interpretation of the particular scene unfolds in STM (short-term or working memory) as a network of schema instances which link parameterized copies of schemas to specific portions of the image to represent aspects of the scene of continuing relevance.

Interpretation of a novel scene starts with the data-driven instantiation of several schemas (e.g., a certain range of color and texture might cue an instance of the foliage schema for a certain region of the image). When a schema instance is activated, it is linked with an associated area of the image and an associated set of local variables. Each schema instance in STM has an associated confidence level which changes on the basis of interactions with other units in STM. The STM network makes context explicit: each object represents a context for further processing. Thus, once several schema instances are active, they may instantiate others in a "hypothesis-driven" way (e.g., recognizing what appears to be a roof will activate an instance of the house schema to seek confirming evidence in the region below that of the putative roof). Ensuing computation is based on the competition and cooperation of concurrently active schema instances. Once a number of schema instances have been activated, the schema network is invoked to formulate hypotheses, set goals, and then iterate the process of adjusting the activity level of schemas linked to the image until a coherent interpretation of (part of) the scene is obtained. VISIONS uses *activation values* so that schema instances may compete and cooperate to determine which ones enter into the equilibrium schema analysis of a visual scene. (The HEARSAY speech understanding system [5] extends this into the time domain. In HEARSAY, entities at different levels – phonemes, words, phrases and sentences compete and cooperate to cover certain time periods of the auditory input in a consistent fashion. But in the end, what emerges is that single coherent symbolic representation.) Cooperation yields a pattern of "strengthened alliances" between mutually consistent schema instances that allows them to achieve high activity levels to constitute the overall solution of a problem. As a result of competition, instances which do not meet the evolving consensus lose activity, and thus are not part of this solution (though their continuing subthreshold activity may well affect later behavior). Successful instances of perceptual schemas become part of the current short-term model of the environment.

The classic VISIONS system had only a small number of schemas at its disposal, and so could afford to be lax about scheduling their application. However, for visual systems operating in a complex world, many schemas are potentially applicable, and many features of the environment are interpretable. In this case, "attention" – the scheduling of resources to process specific parts of the image in particular ways – becomes crucial. How this may be accomplished is described elsewhere [6], as is the way in which VISIONS may be extended to mediate action-oriented perception by an agent in continuous interaction with its environment [2].

1.3 From Visual Control of Grasping to Mirror Neurons

The minimal neuroanatomy of the brain of the macaque monkey and the human (or of mammals generally) that we need here is that the cerebral cortex can be divided into four lobes: the *occipital lobe* at the back (which includes primary visual cortex); the *parietal* lobe (moving up and forward from the occipital lobe); the *frontal lobe* and then moving back beneath frontal and parietal cortex, the *temporal lobe*. *Prefrontal cortex* is *at* the front of the frontal lobe, not *in* front of the frontal lobe. For the moment, we are particularly interested in three areas:

- Parietal area AIP, which is the anterior region within a fold of parietal cortex called the intra-parietal sulcus,
- A ventral region of premotor area called F5, and
- Inferotemporal cortex (IT), a region of the temporal lobe particularly associated with object recognition.

AIP and F5 anchor the cortical circuit in macaque which transforms visual information on intrinsic properties of an object into hand movements for grasping it. Discharge in most grasp-related F5 neurons correlates with an action rather than with the
individual movements that form it so that one may relate F5 neurons to various *motor
schemas* corresponding to the action associated with their discharge:

The FARS (Fagg-Arbib-Rizzolatti-Sakata) model [7] addresses key data on F5 and
AIP from the labs of Giacomo Rizzolatti in Parma and Hideo Sakata in Tokyo, respectively. In the FARS model, area cIPS (another parietal area – the details do not
matter for this exposition) provides visual input to parietal area AIP concerning the
position and orientation of the object's surfaces. AIP then extracts the *affordances* the
object offers for grasping (i.e., the visually grounded encoding of "motor opportunities" for grasping the object, rather than its classification [8]). The basic pathway AIP
→ F5 → F1 (primary motor cortex) of the FARS model then transforms the (neural
code for) the affordance into the coding for the appropriate motor schema in F5 and
thence to the appropriate detailed descending motor control signals (F1).

Going beyond the empirical data then available, FARS [7] stressed that there may
be several ways to grasp an object and thus hypothesized (a) that object recognition
(mediated by IT) can affect the computation of working memory, task constraints and
instruction stimuli in various parts of prefrontal cortex (PFC), and (b) that strong
connections from PFC can bias the selection in the AIP → F5 pathway of which grasp
to execute. The two major paths from visual cortex via parietal cortex (e.g., AIP) and
inferotemporal cortex (e.g., IT) are labeled as the *dorsal* and *ventral* paths, respectively. The dorsal path is concerned with the "how" or parameterization of action,
while the ventral path encodes the "what" or knowledge of action, appropriate to
planning a course of action rather than the fine details of its execution.

To proceed, we must note the discovery of a very significant subset of the F5 neurons related to grasping – the *mirror neurons*. These neurons are active not only when
the monkey executes a specific hand action but also when it observes a human or
other monkey carrying out a similar action. These neurons constitute the "mirror system for grasping" in the monkey and we say that these neurons provide the neural
code for matching execution and observation of hand movements. (By contrast, the
canonical neurons – which are the F5 neurons that actually get modeled in FARS –
are active for execution but not for observation.) A mirror *system* for a class X of
actions is a region of the brain that, compared with other situations, becomes more
active both when actions from class X are observed and when actions from class X
are executed. Mirror neurons exist for a range of actions in the macaque monkey, and
brain imaging experiments have demonstrated a mirror system for grasping in the
human, but we have no single neuron studies proving the reasonable hypothesis that
the human mirror *system* for grasping contains mirror neurons for specific grasps. In
work not reported here, we are extending our models of the mirror system [9, 10]
from hand movements to action recognition more generally. Our prior models are
based on neural networks for recognition of trajectory of the hand relative to an object. They use an object-centered coordinate system to recognize whether the hand is
on track to perform a particular action upon the object, which may explain data in
[11].

1.4   From Mirror Neurons to the Mirror System Hypothesis

Area F5 in the macaque is homologous to area 44 in the human, part of Broca's area, an area notmally associated with speech production. Yet this area in humans contains a mirror system to grasping. Tese data led Arbib & Rizzolatti [12] to develop the *Mirror-System Hypothesis* – Language evolved from a basic mechanism *not* originally related to communication: the *mirror system for grasping* with its capacity to generate *and* recognize a set of actions. More specifically, human Broca's area contains a mirror system for grasping which is homologous to the F5 mirror system of macaque, and this provides the evolutionary basis for *language parity* – namely that an utterance means roughly the same for both speaker and hearer.

This provides a neurobiological "missing link" for the hypothesis that communication based on manual gesture preceded speech in language evolution.

Arbib [13] has amplified the original account of Rizzolatti and Arbib to hypothesize seven stages in the evolution of language. Rather than offer details here, we simply note the synthesis of ideas on the dorsal and ventral pathways with the concept of mirror neurons and schema assemblages provided by [14].

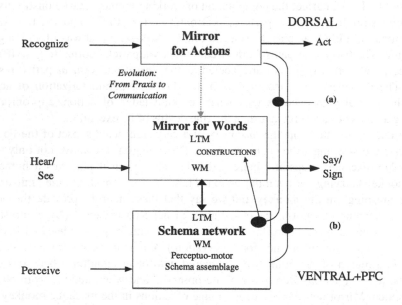

Fig. 1. Words link to schemas, not directly to the dorsal path for actions (from [14])

Saussure [15] distinguishes the *Signifier* from the *Signified* (or words from concepts), but then highlights the "Sign" as combining these with the linkage between them. Our action-oriented view is that the basic concepts are realized as the perceptual and motor schemas of an organism acting in its world, and that that there is no direct labeling of one word for one concept. Rather, the linkage is many-to-one, competitive and contextual, so that appropriate words to express a schema may vary from occasion to occasion, both because of the assemblage in which the schema instance is currently embedded, and because of the state of the current discourse. Let us diagram this in a way which makes contact with all that has gone before. The lower 2 boxes of Figure 1 correspond to words and concepts, but we now make explicit, following the Mirror System Hypothesis, that we postulate that a mirror system for phonological expression ("words") evolved atop the mirror system for grasping to serve communication integrating hand, face and voice. We also postulate that the concepts – for diverse actions, objects, attributes and abstractions – are represented by a network of concepts stored in LTM, with our current "conceptual content" formed as an assemblage of schema instances in Working Memory (WM – compare the STM of VISIONS). Analogously, the Mirror for Words contains a network of word forms in LTM and keeps track of the current utterance in its own working memory.

The perhaps surprising aspect of the conceptual model shown here is that the arrow linking the "Mirror for Actions" to the "Mirror for Words" expresses an evolutionary relationship, not a flow of data. Rather than directly linking the dorsal action representation to the dorsal representation of phonological form, we have two relationships between the dorsal pathway for the Mirror for Actions and the schema networks and assemblages of the ventral pathway and prefrontal cortex (PFC). The rightmost path in Figure 1 corresponds to the paths in FARS whereby IT and PFC can affect the pattern of dorsal control of action. The path just to the left of this shows that the dorsal representation of actions can only be linked to verbs via schemas.

Rather than pursuing the study of brain mechanisms further, we work within the framework provided by [6] to ask the following: "If we extend our interest in vision from the recognition of the disposition of objects in static scenes to the relations between agents, objects and actions dynamic visual scenes, what sort of representations are appropriate to interface the visual and language systems?"

2 SemRep: A Semantic Representation for Dynamic Visual Scenes

SemRep is a hierarchical graph-like representation of a visual scene, whether static or dynamically extended over time (an episode). A SemRep graph structure represents the semantics of *some* of the cognitively salient elements of the scene. We see SemRep as an extension of the schema assemblages generated by the VISIONS system, but with the crucial addition of actions and of extension in time. Only cognitively important events are encoded into SemRep while others are simply discarded or absorbed into other entities. The same scene can have many different SemReps, depending on the current task and on the history of attention. A prime motivation is to ensure that this representation be usable to produce sentences that describe the scene, allowing SemRep to bridge between vision and language.

The structure of SemRep does not have to follow the actual changes of an event of interest, but may focus on "conceptually significant changes" – a crucial difference from a sensorimotor representation, where motor control requires continual tracking of task-related parameters. For example, an event describable by the sentence "Jack kicks a ball into the net" actually covers several time periods: [Jack's foot swings] → [Jack's foot hits a ball] → [the ball flies] → [the ball gets into the net]. Note that

[Jack's foot swings] and [Jack's foot hits a ball] are combined into [Jack kicks a ball], and [the ball flies] is omitted. This taps into a schema network, which can use stored knowledge to "unpack" items of SemRep when necessary. On the other hand, a Gricean convention makes it unlikely that SemRep will include details that can be retrieved in this way, or details that are already known to speaker and hearer.

The same principle is applied to the topology of SemRep entities. The arrangement of conceptual entities and their connections might or might not follow that of the actual images and objects. A description "a man without an arm", for example, does not exactly match an actual object setting since it encodes the conceptual entity of an arm which is missing in the actual image. This relates to the previous point: one may need to include what is not in the image to block standard inferences in cases where they are inappropriate. This is akin the notion of inheritance in semantic networks.

Similarly, an event or entity with higher cognitive importance – or "discourse importance", what the speaker wishes to emphasize for the hearer – will be assigned to a higher level in the hierarchy independently of the methodology by which the entity is specified. For instance, even if the vision system had specified MAN first and this led to the zooming in on the face, FACE might be ranked higher in SemRep than MAN if the former is currently of greater interest.

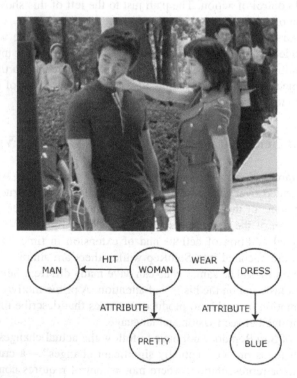

Fig. 2. Top: A picture of a woman hitting a man (original image from "Invisible Man Jangsu Choi", Korean Broadcasting System). Bottom: A SemRep graph that could be generated for the picture. This might yiels the sentence "A pretty woman in blue hits a man."

In order to encode the various conceptual entities and their relationships, SemRep structure takes the form of a graph structure. The two major elements of a SemRep graph are 'node' and 'relation (directed edge)'. Agents and various types of objects are usually represented as nodes, but we also use nodes to represent attributes. Relationships between nodes include actions linking agent and patient, spatial configuration, possessive relationship, movement direction or pointer which indicates the semantically identical node are represented as relations, as well as the relation between a node and its attributes. As mentioned above, a vision system can be one of the systems that create SemRep structure by imposing nodes and relations upon a visual image (or "videoclip"). An area interesting enough to capture attention is linked to a node (or a relation if an action is happening in that area) and then relations are specified among the found nodes, presumably by shifting attention. While most types of node and some types of relation – such as spatial, possessive, attributive relations – are established by static (spatial) analysis, action relations require dynamic (spatio-temporal) analysis.

Both nodes and relations may be attached to more detailed semantic descriptions defined as "conceptual structures". The properties of a recognized object are attached to a node for the object, and the semantics of an action are attached to an action relation. The attached concepts will later be translated into words by the language system. A relation includes the sets it relates and so a verb is not just a label for an action but incorporates restrictions on its slot fillers. However, the SemRep graph is not labeled with words but with more abstract descriptors, allowing the same graph to be expressed in multiple ways within a given language. Thus the concept YOUNG FEMALE could be translated into 'girl', 'woman' or even 'kid' and the action concept HITTING WITH HAND could be translated into 'hit', 'punch' or 'slap'. Again, the configuration where object A is placed vertically higher than B can be expressed as "A is above B", "B is below A", "A is on B", etc.

The action concept HIT may involve properties such as VIOLENT MOTION, BODY CONTACT, and CAUSING PAIN, and these properties implicitly show that the encoded concept describes an action. However, some of these processes may be directly perceptual (i.e., generated directly by the visual system) while others may be more inferential. It might be claimed [16] that mirror neurons will link action recognition to our own experience, so CAUSING PAIN might be perceived "directly", while the woman's ANGER might either be perceived directly or be more inferential.

Thus we view SemRep as providing a graphical structure which encompasses one analysis which captures a subset of the agents, objects, actions and relationships that may be present in a given (temporally extended) visual scene. Nodes in SemRep may also be given a *significance* value which expresses the importance of a particular aspect of the scene. Thus the same scene may be described by "John loves Mary" or "Mary is loved by John" depending on whether the focus (higher significance value) is given to John or Mary, respectively.

3   Template Construction Grammar (TCG)

Where many linguists operate within the framework of generative grammar (e.g., [17]), we work within the framework of *construction grammar* (e.g., [18, 19]).

Constructions are form-meaning pairings which serve as basic building blocks for grammatical structure – each provides a detailed account of the pairing of a particular syntactic pattern with a particular semantic pattern, including phrase structures, idioms, words and even morphemes. By contrast, in generative grammar, meaning is claimed to be derived from the systematic combination of lexical items and the functional differences between the patterns that constructions capture are largely ignored.

Generative grammar distinguishes the lexicon from the grammar, which is seen as having three separate components – phonological, syntactic and semantic – with linking rules to map information from one component onto another. The rules of grammar are said to operate autonomously within each component, and any "rule breaking" within a particular language is restricted to idiosyncrasies captured within the lexicon. But what of idiomatic expressions like *kick the bucket, shoot the breeze, take the bull by the horns* or *climb the wall*? Should we consider their meanings as a supplement to the general rules of the syntactic and semantic components and their linking rules? Instead of this, Fillmore, Kay & O'Connor [20] suggested that the tools they used in analyzing idioms could form the basis for *construction grammar* as a new model of grammatical organization, with constructions ranging from lexical items to idioms to rules of quite general applicability [18]. Many linguists have teased out the rule-governed and productive linguistic behaviors specific to each family of constructions. Constructions, like items in the lexicon, cut across the separate components of generative grammar to combine syntactic, semantic and even in some cases phonological information. The idea of construction grammar is thus to abandon the search for separate rule systems within syntactic, semantic and phonological components and instead base the whole of grammar on the "cross-cutting" properties of constructions.

Going beyond this "intra-linguistic" analysis, we suggest that "vision constructions" may synergize with "grammar constructions" in structuring the analysis of a scene in relation to the demands of scene description [6] in a way which ties naturally to our discussion of VISIONS. We argue that the approach to language via a large but finite inventory of constructions coheres well with the notion of a large but finite inventory of "scene schemas" for visual analysis. Each constituent which expands a "slot" within a scene schema or verbal construction may be seen as a hierarchical structure in which extended attention to a given component of the scene extends the complexity of the constituents in the corresponding part of parse tree of a sentence. This enforces the view that visual scene analysis must encompass a wide variety of basic "schema networks" – more or less abstract SemReps in the conceptualization of the previous sentence – in the system of high-level vision, akin to those relating *sky* and *roof*, or *roof, house* and *wall* in the VISIONS system. Of course, we do not claim that all sentences are limited to descriptions of, or questions about, visual scenes, but we do suggest that understanding such descriptions and questions can ground an understanding of a wide range of language phenomena.

We are currently implementing parsing and production systems for our own version of construction grammar, Template Construction Grammar (TCG). TCG adopts two major policies of conventional construction grammar (CG): each construction specifies the mapping between form and meaning, and the systematic combination of constructions yields the whole grammatical structure. However, in TCG, the meaning of an utterance is given as a SemRep graph (with suitable extensions to be provided in further work). A SemRep may correspond to one or more sentences, basically by covering the relevant portion of the given SemRep with a set of "small" subgraphs, where each is chosen such that a construction is available which expresses that subgraph in the given language. Figure 3 shows a construction defined in TCG, exemplifying the links that indicate which part of a "SemRep template" connect to which slot in a text form. Each construction encodes the specification of what can be mapped to which text/slot, and the mapping is assumed to be bidirectional – it can be used in production of a sentence as well as for comprehension. Most other computational approaches to CG, such as Fluid Construction Grammar (FCG) [21], are based on the use of predicate logic rather than graphs as the basis for constructions.

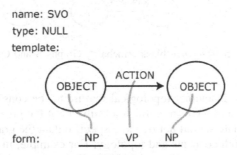

Fig. 3. An example '[subject] [verb] [object]' construction (a very general construction) in TCG. The template is an "abstract" SemRep, i.e., a graph like a SemRep but with either generic or (not in this case) specific labels on the edges and nodes, with each linked to a text or an empty slot for which there may be restrictions as to what can serve as slot fillers.

In production mode, the template acts to match constraints for selecting proper constructions by being superimposed on the SemRep graph that is going to be expressed in words. The semantic constraint of each construction is considered to be encoded in the template since the template also contains concepts as well as the topology of a SemRep graph. In comprehension mode, the template provides a frame where the interpreted meaning builds up as parsing progresses. The details of the interpreted SemRep graph are filled with the meaning of the constructions found by matching with the currently processed text (or word) one by one. Originally, form of each construction has to be a series of phonemes that would be combined into words, but it is assumed that these phonemes are already properly perceived and processed, and the correct words are given in a text form.

As mentioned above, the template is an (abstract) SemRep graph. The matching process in production mode is done by comparing the template of a construction to the given SemRep graph. The contents (given as the attached concepts) of nodes and relations and the connective structure of nodes and relations is considered in the process. The construction with the most 'similar' template will be chosen over other constructions, though provision must be made for backtracking. Note, too, that the similarity might be to a subgraph bottom up or a set of high-level nodes top-down – choices compete and cooperate till a spanning structure is formed. "Similarity" for the attached concepts is decided, for example, by how many common attributes they share – SemRep includes (though we have omitted the details from this paper) the ability to capture concepts by the superimposed distributed representation of attributes. Again, similarity for the structure of the template is decided by how close the topology of the template is to the given SemRep graph – the number of nodes and relations has to be matched as well as the connections between them.

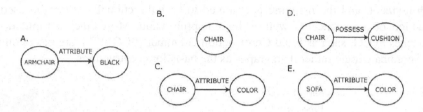

Fig. 4. SemRep graph A represents a 'black armchair'. Graphs B and C are "similar" to graph A but D and E are not.

Embedded structure is another topological feature to be considered. Matching requires that the template of a construction is a "subset" of the given SemRep graph. In other words, the template should not be more specific than the graph being compared. This rule applies to both concepts and topology. For example, in Figure 4 graph C is an appropriate match to graph A since ARMCHAIR is a kind of CHAIR and BLACK is a kind of COLOR and the topology is the same as that of graph A. Graph B is also appropriate because the topology is less specific. Graph D is inappropriate since the relations (ATTRIBUTE and POSSESSION) do not match each other; and Graph E is inappropriate since SOFA is a more detailed concept than ARMCHAIR. Among the appropriate graphs B and C, graph C will win over the competition because it is more similar to graph A than is B. If there were a graph identical to graph C except that it had BLACK node instead of COLOR, then this graph would have been the winner.

In the current version of TCG, the input text is assumed to be preprocessed and segmented into morphemes at a level that corresponds to the construction repertoire. Matching text can be somewhat simpler than matching templates since in matching text there is no need to perform complex comparison of graph structures. This is not to minimize the various obstacles to comprehending a sentence offered by anaphor, ellipsis, and ambiguity in interpretation, etc. And consider idiomatic expressions. For example, the idiom "a piece of cake" might be processed with a single construction which has the whole text in its form and the semantic meaning of "being easy". But it also can be processed with one or more general constructions. Allowing constructions with more specific information to be selected provides one possible default (in this case, idiomatic constructions would win over general constructions) but the eventual system must provide mechanisms for broader context to settle the issue: in parsing "Would you like a piece of cake?", the idiomatic construction is inappropriate.

In order to apply constructions hierarchically, each construction is assigned a *type* which specifies a sort of grammatical category for the construction, but such a type is not the highly abstract syntactic category of generative grammar, but is more like an emergent categorization rule generated by the relationship between constructions in the repertoire. Each empty slot in the form of a construction indicates the type of the construction that should fill the slot.

When translating the given SemRep graph into a sentence, the graph would activate a number of constructions with matching templates. In TCG, the construction with the best-matching template will be selected and its form will be output as the translated text, but if the form has any empty slot, it should be filled first. An empty slot specifies not only the type of construction that is expected, but also indicates the area of SemRep that is going to be considered for comparison; each slot is linked to a pre-specified area in the template, and only an area of SemRep corresponding to that area is considered for finding matching constructions for the slot. The link between the template and form provides the form-meaning pairing of a construction in TCG.

Since constructions are bidirectional, the same set of constructions used in production of sentence are also used in comprehension. All of the matching (or activated) constructions are eligible for translation until further processing reveals ineligibility. As input text is read, it is compared to the forms of activated constructions and the constructions with unmatched forms are ruled out. Ambiguity may also be resolved based on contextual information, which is in this case is the translated SemRep graph. However, top-down influences in sentence comprehension are beyond the scope of the current version of TCG.

The type of the activated construction is also treated as input to the system and the matching mechanism is very similar to that for the text case, except that it is matched with the slot in the form rather than the text. For example, if an input sentence is given as "A big dog barks" then the first word "a" would activate at least two constructions, "a [adjective] [noun]" and "a [noun]" (or "[determinant] [adjective] [noun]" and "[determinant] [noun]" with "a" activating a construction of type [determinant]). Other configurations are possible, depending on the construction repertoire.

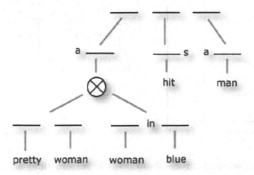

Fig. 5. The sentence "A pretty woman in blue hits a man" and the corresponding construction architecture. The language system would translate the SemRep graph in Figure 2 into the above sentence. During the process, constructions will be built into the hierarchical structure shown in the figure.

Given the activated constructions "a [adjective] [noun]" and "a [noun]", the next word "big" would activate a construction whose type is [adjective], ruling out the second construction due to mismatch of the construction type required in the slot.

Figure 5 shows one of the sentences that can be generated from the SemRep graph shown in Figure 2 and the resulted hierarchical build-up of constructions. Note that because of the multiple embedded structures in the WOMAN node, constructions for both "pretty woman" and "woman in blue" are present at the lowest level. These constructions are then combined into one expression "pretty woman in blue". The set of constructions might differ from those of other speakers to some extent. In that case, the constructions could be organized in a different structure and the hierarchy among constructions might change.

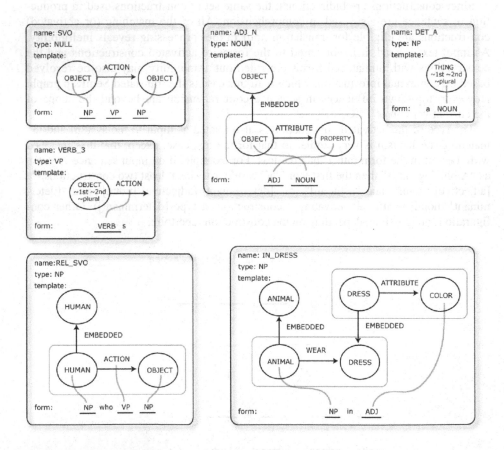

Fig. 6. Abstract constructions used for translation. These constructions are assumed to encode grammatical information.

Figure 6 and Figure 7 provide detailed description for all the constructions used in this example. Some auxiliary information such as activation values, the tense or number is not shown but is assumed to be encoded in the templates (more precisely in the concept attached to the corresponding node or relation) of the constructions. Although activation value is not considered here, it is – as we noted earlier – important in determining the sentence structure – whether it is active or passive. For some constructions, such as SVO or REL_SVO, it is assumed that the activation value for the node corresponding to the agent of an action is higher than that of the patient node and this would lead to produce an active voice. Furthermore, construction VERB_3 is an example of the negation of attributes. Only a single third object is eligible for the conjugation specified in the construction and this grammatical constraint is set by adding negation attributes. Relatively abstract constructions with complex templates and slots in the form are shown in Figure 6 and constructions corresponding to single words are shown in Figure 7. We leave it to the reader to "simulate" the processes of parsing/comprehension and production whereby TCG finds the constructions which convert the SemRep of Figure 2 into the sentence considered here, and vice versa.

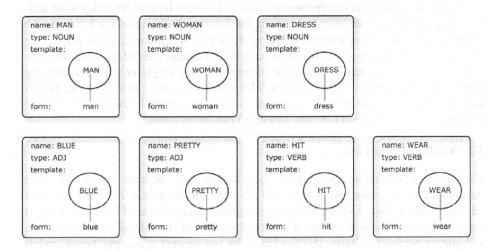

Fig. 7. This figure illustrates the sort of simple construction that corresponds to an element in the lexicon. These constructions are assumed to encode semantic information and can be directly translated into words.

4 Conclusions

4.1 How SemRep Reshapes Construction Grammar

Template Construction Grammar (TCG) shares basic principles with other construction grammar approaches but is explcitly designed to link the semantics of sentences to the representation of visual scenes. However, the use SemRep involves a sufficiently general graphical structure that we are confident of its extensibility to ther meanings. SemRep simplifies production and comprehension. Since the task semantics are given as SemRep graphs, the sentence production process is reduced to a general task of matching graphs and the interpreted meaning of a sentence can be directly built by the combination of templates of the activated constructions in the comprehension process.

In addition to template and form pairings, constructions in TCG also encode auxiliary information such as type which specifies the grammatical role that the construction plays. With this information at hand, the language system can build and parse various kinds of grammatical structures appropriate to the task. In any case, the detailed resulting structure is largely dependent on the construction repertoire of the system. The repertoire is maintained in a very dynamic and flexible way, well representing the grammatical constitution and usage pattern that language shows.

Moreover, the concept attached to a node and relation in SemRep graph in TCG formalism exploits the combination of attributes or properties, providing a key comparison mechanism among conceptual entities. During production of sentences, a given graph activates a number of constructions and is compared with a number of constructions for similarity. Only the winner is to be chosen to produce sentences.

On the other hand, in comprehension mode, a textual form is basically what activates constructions by an inverse matching mechanism. In this case, the form, not the template, is what is being compared against the input. When proper constructions are chosen, a new SemRep graph would be built from the templates of the constructions. When multiple constructions are to be combined into a single node or relation, the attributes of the concept of that entity will be added up, getting more specific. In this way, the transformation between different kind of hierarchical structures (back and forth between SemRep and sentence structure) can be executed.

4.2 Another Perspective

The literature on brain mechanisms of vision, and on forms of representation of visual information is, of course vast, and beyond the scope of this article. A subfield of great relevance here is that of vision in embodied agents, with an interest in linking explicit computational analysis of vision in robots to studies of the role of vision in animal and human behavior. Clearly, this field includes our interest in computational models of the control of action and of mirror systems which are involved in both the self's control of action and its vision-based recognition of actions conducted by others. In particular, then, we need to situate our work within the set of studies which unite the study of vision in embodied agents with studies of communication (especially using language) between such agents concerning their visual perceptions (e.g., [22-24]. Another area of concern is discussion of the extent to which construction grammar can be linked to implementations based on neural networks or brain mechanisms (e.g., [25, 26]). However, in this paper, we restrict our discussion to one paper, [27], from the group of Luc Steels, a group which has not only been a leader in linking the study of vision in embodied agents with studies of communication, but has done so within the framework of simulated evolution (though not linked to neurobiology), and has developed its own version of construction grammar, Fluid Construction Grammar (FCG).

Steels and Loetzsch [27] use interactions between robots to study the effect of perspective alignment on the emergence of spatial language. Although the authors state that their "experiments rest on the Fluid Construction Grammar framework [21], which is highly complex software for language processing", there is no syntax in the language studied in their paper – rather, visual scenes are described simply by a list of words which are associated with one or more categories applicable to the observed scene. We postpone a comparison (and, perhaps integration) of TCG and FCG for another occasion, and instead focus on scene representation in [27] and then compare it with SemRep to help clarify directions for future work.

[27] employs an actual vision system to generate scene descriptions from visual input provided by cameras mounted on 2 or more AIBO robots. In a typical episode, two robots are placed in a cluttered room and move about till each has both the other robot and a ball in their visual field; they then stay still while a human uses a stick to move the ball from one position to the other. Each robot generates a description of the ball's trajectory using Cartesian coordinates for the ground plane, with the robot at the origin and its direction of gaze determining the vertical axis. The descriptors given are

(1) x of start point, distance to start point, x of end point, y of end point, distance to end point, angle to end point, angle of movement, length of trajectory, change in x, change in y, change in angle, and change in distance.

The key property of language addressed in [27] is that of *perspective alignment* – different observers may describe the same scene in deifferent terms – does "on the left", for example, mean "on the speaker's left" or "on the hearer's left"? To address this challenge, each robot is programmed to use its vision to judge the position and orientation of the other robot and then estimate the above coordinates (1) as seen from the other robot's viewpoint. This *perspective transformation* is a simple translation and rotation in Euclidean space, but the result is an estimate because the robot's assessment of the relevant coordinates may contain errors and these are unlikely to correlate with errors of the other robot.

Neither words nor categories for describing the scene are provided in advance. Rather, simple discriminant trees are used to create categories: every feature in (1) has a discrimination tree which divides the range of possible values into equally sized regions, and every region carves out a single category. Letter strings can be randomly generated to provide "words", and weighted, many-to-many links between words and categories can be stored in a bidirectional associative memory [28]. However, from this random initial state, interactions between 2 or more robots allow them to end up with a set of categories, and a set of words associated with those categories, that allow any 2 robots to communicate effectively about a scene, adopting either their own perspective or that of the other robot. As noted, each "utterance" consists of a small set of words; these activate certain categories. A robot will strengthen its current "knowledge" if it can match the word string it "hears" to the scene it "sees" or to its estimated perspective for the other. If neither match is possible, it will change its categories and/or vocabulary and/or bidirectional association between words and concepts to better match one perspective with the utterance.

More specifically, learning extends over thousands of episodes. After a successful exchange, the score of the lexical entries that were used for production or parsing is increased by 0.05. At the same time, the scores of competing lexical entries with the same form but different meanings are decreased by 0.05 (lateral inhibition). In case of a failure, the score of the involved items is decreased by 0.05. This adjustment acts as a *reinforcement learning* mechanism and also as *priming* mechanism so that agents gradually align their lexicons in consecutive games. Similar mechanisms apply to the updating – and eventual alignment – of categories in each robot on the basis of success or failure in each exchange.

With this, we use our understanding of [27] to sharpen our understanding of SemRep and to pose challenges for future research:

Rather than use a very limited type of description –how the same object, the ball, moves in each episode – we are concerned with a flexible description of an episode, or small number of contiguous episodes, that labels the visual field with concepts related to agents, objects and actions and their attributes, and links them in hierarchical ways. In other words, where [27] focuses on a single intransitive movement (the ball rolls), we have a special concern with transitive actions, based on evaluating the movement of an agent with respect to an object or other agent.

We have not implemented a vision front-end, but note that in fact the language-related work in [27] does not make essential use of the vision front-end, since the "real processing" starts with the Cartesian coordinates provided in (1) both from the robot's own perspective and as estimated for the other robot's perspective. In terms of the VISIONS system [4], this would correspond to the converged state of the intermediate database, but rather than giving coordinates of a single trajectory in the ground plane, an extension of VISIONS would label shapes and edges and their relative position and motion in the three-dimensional visual field of the observer. Just as [27] uses this description as the basis for extracting a small set of categories, so we would use the intermediate database as the basis for constructing a SemRep, while noting that the choice of SemRep may depend on attentional factors and task relevance [6, 29], including the state of discourse.

Concepts and words are emergent in [27] through attempts to share descriptions of observed scenes. SemRep uses hand-crafted concepts, words and constructions.

Perspective-taking is almost obligatory in [27] – in all but one experiment (see below) each robot must compute the description (1) as seen by the other robot. In SemRep, we do not use any such global transformations, but rather rely on a set of appropriate "subscene schemas", so that a portion of the same SemRep could be described by "the man to the left of the woman" or, if we take into account the orientation of the woman's body, "the man in front of the woman." We note the further challenge of deciding when two SemReps could apply to the same scene as viewed from different perspectives (perhaps with different foci of attention) or, more subtly, could describe two different time slices" of a spatially extended scene.

"Cognitive effort" is defined in [27] as the average number of perspective transformations that the hearer has to perform. Their Figure 12 reports an experiment which shows (perhaps unsurprisingly) a marked reduction in cognitive effort when perspective is marked, i.e., when one of the categories that must be expressed is whether the trajectory descriptors in (1) are based on the perspective of the "speaker" or the "hearer". In this experiment, separate words emerged for perspective in addition to words where perspective is part of the lexicalization of the predicate. Steels and Loetzsch [27] comment that "This is similar to natural language where in *the ball to my left*, *my* is a general indicator of perspective, whereas in [...] *come* and *go*, perspective is integrated in the individual word" and assert that "this experiment explains why perspective marking occurs in human languages and why sometimes we find specific words for it." However, the experiment does not explain this directly, since the choice of perspective is added by the authors as an explicit category – thus making it likely that words will emerge to express or incorporate this category. However, an important evolutionary point is made: if the perspective category or word is available (whether through biological or cultural evolution) then processing is more efficient, thus giving creatures with access to such items a selective advantage. When we turn from robot routines to human development, the question is how the child comes to recognize its similarity and difference from others so that terms like "my left hand" versus "your left hand" become understood, and then how such spatial terms extend from the body to peripersonal space and then to space generally. It is not surprising that – just as in the language games described here – different languages will describe this extension in different ways.

We close by a (perhaps surprising) link from the present discussion back to our earlier concern with models of the mirror system. Figure 10 of [27] summarizes an experiment in which the agents perceive the scene through their own camera but they "do not take perspective into account." In this case, the agents do not manage to agree on a shared set of spatial terms. Steels and Loetzsch concludes that this proves that "grounded spatial language without perspective does not lead to the bootstrapping of a successful communication system." However, this does not take account of the extent to which the results depend on what is built into the system. Other approaches are possible. Suppose the room had several distinctive landmarks. Then instead of locating the ball in one of the two prespecified Cartesian coordinate systems, one could locate the ball in terms of descriptions like "It started close to landmark-3 and moved halfway to landmark-7." (In neural terms, such a description might build on the activity of place cells in the hippocampus [30].) Here no perspective transformation is involved. The latter approach is more like that taken in the MNS models [9,10]. Instead of describing the movement of the hand in, e.g., retinal coordinates, we there described it in object-centered coordinates, thus eliminating the issue of perspective-taking. Of course, this does not guarantee that our assumption is justified. However, one argument in favor of (but not proving) the assumption is that the need for visual feedback for dexterity would provide selection pressure for a system that could translate retinal input into such an object-centered (or affordance-based) view of the hand.

References

[1] Arbib, M.A.: Rana computatrix to human language: towards a computational neuroethology of language evolution. Philos. Transact. A Math. Phys. Eng. Sci. 361, 2345–2379 (2003)
[2] Arbib, M.A., Liaw, J.-S.: Sensorimotor Transformations in the Worlds of Frogs and Robots. Artificial Intelligence 72, 53–79 (1995)
[3] Arbib, M.A.: Perceptual structures and distributed motor control. In: Brooks, V.B. (ed.) Handbook of Physiology — The Nervous System II. Motor Control, pp. 1449–1480. American Physiological Society, Bethesda, MD (1981)

[4] Draper, B.A., Collins, R.T., Brolio, J., Hanson, A.R., Riseman, E.M.: The schema system. International Journal of Computer Vision 2, 209–250 (1989)

[5] Erman, L.D., Hayes-Roth, F., Lesser, V.R., Reddy, D.R.: The HEARSAY-II speech understanding system: Integrating knowledge to resolve uncertainty. Computing Surveys 12, 213–253 (1980)

[6] Itti, L., Arbib, M.A.: Attention and the minimal subscene. In: Arbib, M.A. (ed.) Action to language via the mirror neuron system, pp. 289–346. Cambridge University Press, Cambridge (2006)

[7] Fagg, A.H., Arbib, M.A.: Modeling parietal-premotor interactions in primate control of grasping. Neural Netw. 11, 1277–1303 (1998)

[8] Gibson, J.J.: The ecological approach to visual perception. Houghton Mifflin, Boston (1979)

[9] Bonaiuto, J., Rosta, E., Arbib, M.: Extending the mirror neuron system model, I: Audible actions and invisible grasps. Biol. Cybern. 96, 9–38 (2007)

[10] Oztop, E., Arbib, M.A.: Schema design and implementation of the grasp-related mirror neuron system. Biol. Cybern. 87, 116–140 (2002)

[11] Gershkoff-Stowe, L., Goldin-Meadow, S.: Is there a natural order for expressing semantic relations? Cognitive Psychology 45, 375–412 (2002)

[12] Arbib, M.A., Rizzolatti, G.: Neural expectations: a possible evolutionary path from manual skills to language. Communication and Cognition 29, 393–424 (1997)

[13] Arbib, M.A.: From Monkey-like Action Recognition to Human Language: An Evolutionary Framework for Neurolinguistics (with commentaries and author's response). Behavioral and Brain Sciences 28, 105–167 (2005)

[14] Arbib, M.A.: Broca's Area in System Perspective: Language in the Context of Action-Oriented Perception. In: Grodzinsky, Y., Amunts, K. (eds.) Broca's Region, pp. 153–168. Oxford University Press, Oxford (2006)

[15] Saussure, F.: Cours de linguistique générale. In: Bally, C., Sechehaye, A., Riedlinger, A. (eds.) Payot Lausanne and Paris (1916) (English translation by W. Baskin, Course in General Linguistics, Fontana/Collins, Glasgow (1977))

[16] Gallese, V., Goldman, A.: Mirror neurons and the simulation theory of mind-reading. Trends Cognit. Sci. 2, 493–501 (1998)

[17] Chomsky, N.: Lectures on Government and Binding. Foris, Dordrecht (1981)

[18] Croft, W., Cruse, D.A.: Cognitive Linguistics. Cambridge University Press, Cambridge (2005)

[19] Goldberg, A.E.: Constructions: A new theoretical approach to language. Trends in Cognitive Science 7, 219–224 (2003)

[20] Fillmore, C.J., Kay, P., O'Connor, M.K.: Regularity and idiomaticity in grammatical constructions: the case of let alone. Language & Cognitive Processes 64, 501–538 (1988)

[21] De Beule, J., Steels, L.: Hierarchy in Fluid Construction Grammar. In: Furbach, U. (ed.) KI 2005. LNCS (LNAI), vol. 3698, pp. 1–15. Springer, Heidelberg (2005)

[22] Roy, D.: Semiotic schemas: A framework for grounding language in action and perception. Artificial Intelligence 167, 170–205 (2005)

[23] Steels, L.: Evolving grounded communication for robots. Trends in Cognitive Sciences 7, 308–312 (2003)

[24] Cangelosi, A., Riga, T.: An Embodied Model for Sensorimotor Grounding and Grounding Transfer: Experiments With Epigenetic Robots. Cognitive Science 30, 673–689 (2006)

[25] Dominey, P.F., Hoen, M.: Structure mapping and semantic integration in a construction-based neurolinguistic model of sentence processing. Cortex 42, 476–479 (2006)

[26] Feldman, J., Narayanan, S.: Embodied meaning in a neural theory of language. Brain Lang. 89, 385–392 (2004)

[27] Steels, L., Loetzsch, M.: Perspective Alignment in Spatial Language. In: Coventry, K.R., Tenbrink, T., Bateman, J.A. (eds.) Spatial Language and Dialogue, Oxford University Press, Oxford (2007)

[28] Kosko, B.: Bidirectional associative memories. IEEE Transactions on Systems, Man and Cybernetics 18, 49–60 (1988)

[29] Navalpakkam, V., Itti, I.: Modeling the influence of task on attention. Vision Research 45, 205–231 (2005)

[30] Guazzelli, A., Corbacho, F.J., Bota, M., Arbib, M.A.: Affordances, Motivation, and the World Graph Theory. Adaptive Behavior 6, 435–471 (1998)

A Neural Network Model for a View Independent Extraction of Reach-to-Grasp Action Features

Roberto Prevete, Matteo Santoro, Ezio Catanzariti, and Giovanni Tessitore

Department of Physical Sciences
University of Naples Federico II
80126, Naples, Italy

Abstract. The aim of this paper is to introduce a novel, biologically inspired approach to extract visual features relevant for controlling and understanding reach-to-grasp actions. One of the most relevant of such features has been found to be the grip-size defined as the index finger-tip - thumb-tip distance. For this reason, in this paper we focus on this feature. The human visual system is naturally able to recognize many hand configurations – e.g. gestures or different types of grasps – without being affected substantially by the (observer) viewpoint. The proposed computational model preserves this nice ability.

It is very likely that this ability may play a crucial role in action understanding within primates (and thus human beings). More specifically, a family of neurons in macaque's ventral premotor area F5 have been discovered which are highly active in correlation with a series of grasp–like movements. This findings triggered a fierce debate about imitation and learning, and inspired several computational models among which the most detailed is due to Oztop and Arbib (MNS model). As a variant of the MNS model, in a previous paper, we proposed the MEP model which relies on an *expected perception* mechanism. However, both models assume the existence of a mechanism to extract visual features in a *viewpoint independent* way but neither of them faces the problem of how this mechanism can be achieved in a biologically plausible way. In this paper we propose a neural network model for the extraction of visual features in a viewpoint independent manner, which is based on the work by Poggio and Riesenhuber.

1 Introduction

Over the last few years researchers have been taking a keen interest in developing computational models for *action recognition*. From a pragmatic point of view, action recognition can be considered a (very interesting) sub-topic of pattern recognition and computer vision. Indeed, to recognize correctly actions is a challenging task because it requires to detect and recognize not only static/dynamic objects and (parts of) human beings present in the scene, but also the interaction among them.

One can easily distinguish between two main impulses of the research work undertaken in this area. The first one comes mainly from basic and applied reseach in computer science, where efficient algorithms for action recognition are developed to be used for applications in many technological contexts such as, e.g., robotics or intelligent surveillance systems. It is worth pointing out that, due to the great variability of input

F. Mele et al. (Eds.): BVAI 2007, LNCS 4729, pp. 124–133, 2007.

patterns, prospective algorithmics for such systems must show a large invariance under changes in image acquisition conditions, such as the viewpoint.

On the opposite side, a second impulse comes from computational neuroscience. Our everyday experience shows that our brain is terrifically good at understanding other people's actions (and intentions). In order to study these high level brain functions one needs to develop a suitable model of action recognition. Possible neural candidates responsible for such key ability have been discovered in the ventral premotor area F5 in macaques. The activity of this specific population of neurons seems correlated with grasp–like actions. A subpopulation of these neurons are called mirror neurons (MNs) because they exhibit multi–modal properties by responding congruently to the observation of different types of grasps performed either by another monkey or by the observer himself – that is to say that mirror neurons are involved in both sensor and motor activity. Many functional interpetrations speculate about high level functions of mirror neurons, such as action understanding, imitation, and language but relatively few computational models of mirror neuron behaviour have been proposed. As it will be clear after Section 1.1, some of them definitely need a system for extracting visual features invariant (to some extent) to changes of the viewpoint.

The rest of the paper is organized as follows. SubSection 1.1 briefly summarises the current scientific/experimental knowledge about the mirror system. In Section 1.2 the basics of the proposed approach are presented, while all the details are described in Sections 2 and 3. The effectiveness of the method and the invariance properties are tested and evaluated experimentally in Section 4. Finally, in Section 5 we summarize the results obtained and discuss possible future directions of this work.

1.1 Background

In this Section we recall the basic findings about mirror neurons, and refer to two computational models proposed over the last few years in order to make it clear why they would considerably benefit from the results described in this paper.

Some of the macaque's cortical circuits (e.g., PF, AIP–F5 circuit) have been found to be strongly involved in a series of prehension movements that relate body parts (effectors like hand or mouth) of the subject to a three-dimensional target-object (e.g., to grasp a food piece by a precision grip). More specifically, these findings have been found in relation to actions which require arm and hand movements in order to reach and manipulate target-objects [1]. Moreover, these findings assume a special importance because their functional interpretations have been related to such concepts as *action understanding and representation* [2], *language evolution* [3], and *evolution of mind-reading abilities* [4]. On the basis of the above mentioned findings several computational models for controlling and understanding reach-to-grasp actions have been proposed [5,6]. One of the more interesting and detailed models to date is the Oztop and Arbib model (MNS model)[5]. As a variant of the MNS model, in a previous paper [7] we proposed a model (MEP) based on an *expected perception* mechanism.

Both the above mentioned models rely on viewpoint independent measures of high-level visual features such as, for example, index finger-tip and thumb-tip distance, the angle between the target-object axis and the *(index finger-tip thumb-tip)* vector, the distance to target and so on. However, neither of them faces the problem of how these features can be computed in a biologically plausible way.

This problem is tackled in this paper, where we propose a biologically inspired neural network architecture for the extraction of visual features in a viewpoint independent manner, based on the recognition system described in [8], which is a model of the visual stream from area V1, V2, V4 to area IT .

Before going further, it is important to define more clearly the range of actions on which we focused, and correspondingly the range of input images from which we are going to extract the features.

Throughout this paper, we refer to the specific class of actions known as reach-to-grasp actions, where the expression *reach-to-grasp actions* denotes a series of agent's hand/arm movements which are executed in order to grasp $3D$ objects of various shapes and dimensions. Figure 1 represents a prototypical reach-to-grasp action and provide an example of the kind of the input images we used.

Fig. 1. An example of *reach-to-grasp action* used in this paper

1.2 The Approach

Our goal is to define a viewpoint independent measure of high-level visual features relevant for recognizing reach-to-grasp actions. Such high-level features can be related to the hand of the agent performing the reach-to-grasp action, to the target-object and/or to the hand-target association [5,9]. In this paper we focus on just one high-level feature. This feature is the grip-size, defined as the index finger-tip thumb-tip distance [10]. The use of only the grip-size in order to recognize a reach-to-grasp action could not be a strong limitation because very few features are sufficient for determining the hand shape [11] and, according to Jeannerod [10], the grip-size is the most informative feature for assessing the progression of a reach-to-grasp action.

These considerations led us to focus on just one high-level visual feature which represents a measure of the grip-size of the hand present in the image. In our approach, we assume that for a given observer (viewpoint) the grip-size can be measured as the superposition of three basic hand shapes corresponding to three predefined grip-size,i.e., *fully opened grip-size* (BS_1), *middle grip-size* (BS_2) and *fully closed grip-size* (BS_3) (Fig. 2). Note that BS_1, BS_2 and BS_3 are fixed values of the grip-size which are not dependent of the specific action.

Therefore, it is possible to restate our goal in terms of computing a measure of the grip-size by a viewpoint idependent similarity measure between the current shape and the three basic ones described above.

In order to achieve this task we propose a feedforward neural network logically comprising two layers of computation. In the first layer the similarity of the image to the three basic hand shapes is computed, in a viewpoint independent way, on the basis of

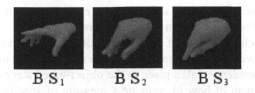

$$B\,S_1 \qquad\qquad B\,S_2 \qquad\qquad B\,S_3$$

Fig. 2. Basic hand shapes for a given viewpoint: From left to right *fully opened grip–size*, *middle grip–size* and *fully closed grip–size*

a large set of low-level features extracted from the image. In the second layer, the grip size measure is obtained as the superposition of the previously computed values. In the next two Sections we provide the details of the *NE*ural network architecture for computing a *G*rip-size measure which is *O*bserver *I*ndependent. We called this computational model *NeGOI*.

2 The First Step: Low–Level, Viewpoint–Based Features

Poggio and colleagues [8] proposed a quantitative theory of the feed-forward computation in the ventral stream of the visual cortex. The theory is based on a set of visual features which exhibit a fairly good trade-off between invariance and selectivity, and are also "consistent" with several properties of neurons in the cortical areas $V1$, $V2$, $V4$, and IT. From a computational point of view, such features are obtained by combining the response of local edge–detectors, which are slightly position– and scale–tolerant, over neighboring positions and multiple orientations[1]. The resulting feature representation is dense and redundant, and one can try to use it to discriminate between similar images by exploiting somehow such information overload. It has been shown [12] that such a system exhibits excellent recognition performance, and outperforms several state–of–the–art systems on a variety of image datasets including many different object categories. Moreover, the system is able to learn from very few examples even in the case of cluttered scenes.

In short, the computation is sequentially performed through a two layer ($S1$ and $C1$, respectively) architecture. The former (the simple cells $S1$) are selectively tuned to different preferred stimuli[2], and weight locally the information contained in the neighborhood of each pixel of the input image. The latter (the complex cells $C1$) pool the information of different $S1$ layers with the same orientation but different position and scale.

The role of visual experience in the perception of the world is accounted for by a further layer called $S2$, whose units are exposed to a large amount of different natural images (e.g. car, faces, landscapes, hand gestures, etc.) becoming tuned to a specific pattern of activity. This sort of *imprinting* process makes each group of $S2$ cells specifically sensitive (or tuned) to a particular input stimulus. Hence, when the input matches exactly the learned patterns, the $S2$ unit gives the maximum response. A final layer, $C2$,

---

[1] The approach closely mimics the behavior of simple and complex cells in primary visual cortex
[2] $S1$ layers are implemented as a battery of Gabor filters over the input image.

computes the max over all positions and scales for each $S2$ map. It is easy to see that the resulting feature vector is position– and scale–invariant.

In this model the classical task of object recognition in a 3D rotation independent way (which is what we refer as *independence from the viewpoint* or, in an equivalent way, *viewpoint independence*) takes place in the object-tuned stage of the recognition process, but the problem of how to compute a measure of specific features, such as *hand grip-size* or *hand-target distance*, in a viewpoint independent way is not explicitly tackled.

In the present work, we have implemented a version of such system where the scale and position independent features as computed by $C2$ layer appear in the form of a visual feature vector which we call F.

3 Towards the Independence from the Viewpoint: NeGOI Architecure

NeGOI architecture is made up of three layers (Figure 3). The first layer is composed of three ordered groups of units receiving as input the scale and position independent vector F. Each group is composed of N ordered units. Let GV_{ij} be the j-th unit belonging to i-th group, with $i = 1, 2, 3$ and $j = 1, 2, ...N$. Each GV_{ij} unit is therefore scale and position independent but is selective to both the basic hand shape BS_i and the viewpoint j. The second layer is composed of three viewpoint independent units selective to the three basic hand shapes. Let GS_i be the i-th unit of the second layer, with $i = 1, 2, 3$. The unit GS_i receives only connections from units belonging to i-th group of the first layer. Each unit GS_i is selective to the basic hand shape BS_i but is viewpoint independent. The third layer is composed of just one unit. Let us call it GS. GS unit receives connections from all GS_i. The output of GS is a scale, position and viewpoint independent value belonging to the interval $[0, 1]$. In the pratical implementation, the units of the first layer are the output neurons of a Radial Basis Function neural network (RBF)[13] receiving the F vector as input. We have only nine output neuron, i.e., three neurons for each selected basic hand shape: GV_{1j} selective to both fully opened grip-size and viewpoint $view_j$, GV_{2j} selective to both middle grip-size and viewpoint $view_j$, GV_{3j} selective to both fully closed grip size and viewpoint $view_j$, with $j = 1, 2, 3$. The viewpoints $view_1$, $view_2$ and $view_3$ are selected viewpoint separated by about 22 degree between each other (Figure 4), i.e., correspond to rotations of a camera around an axis Z (perpendicular to the surface of a table and centered on the target object) of about 22 degree.

In the second layer the GS_i neurons ($i = 1, 2, 3$) compute the linear combination of the outputs of GV_{ij}, with $j = 1, 2, 3$. Therefore, the GS_1,GS_2 and GS_3 neurons, once trained, are selective to fully opened, middle and fully closed grip-size, respectively (Figure 3-b). In the last layer, the unit GS is obtained as output node of an another RBF network.

We have trained both GV_{ij} and GS_i neurons using three different training sets. Each set, composed of 450 frames of hand shapes recorded from the viewpoint $view_j$, comprises 150 frames representing fully opened grip-size, 150 frames representing middle grip-size and 150 frames representing fully closed grip-size.

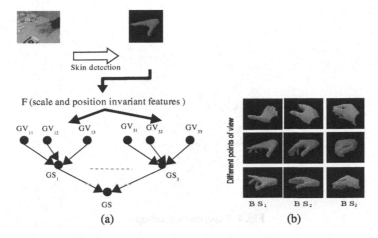

Fig. 3. (a) NeGOI architecture. (b) Basic grip-size.

The GS neuron has been trained under the hypothesis that the output of the GS_1, GS_2 and GS_3 neurons are Gaussians centered on fully opened grip-size, middle grip-size and fully closed grip-size, respectively.

4   Experimental Results

A subject was asked to perform a number of reach-to-grasp actions. The actions were executed with the subject seated at a table with two marks (m_1 and m_2) at a distance of roughly 40cm from each other: each reach-to-grasp action starts at m_1 and ends at m_2 (Figure 4). For each target-object, the subject was asked to position the hand on starting position m_1 and to reach and grasp the target object located on mark m_2. Each action was recorded using a camera placed at a fixed distance from the target (roughly 70 cm) and at a fixed height from the surface of the table (roughly 50 cm). As above said, it is possible to rotate the camera around the axis Z perpendicular to the surface of the table and centered on the target object. Each action is therefore represented as a sequence of frames (160×160 pixels). A skin model is computed from an histogram color model in RGB color space. A simple non-parametric model is therefore used to transform each frame into gray-level image where each pixel value represents the probability of that pixel to be skin. The image thus obtained is further post-processed by morphological filtering to eliminate the effect of image noise on the segmented image. The final result is a gray-level image in which the hand is shown as a gray region on a black background (Figure 3). From this gray-level image the vector F is extracted and given as input to the NeGOI system described previously for the subsequent feature extraction step. The process of feature extraction is performed for all recorded reach-to-grasp actions.

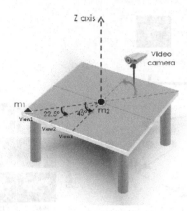

Fig. 4. Experimental set-up

4.1   Grip Size Measure

In order to test the capability of NeGOI to measure the grip-size we recorded, from the same viewpoint, 8 grasp actions using 8 targets (cubes) of different sizes (cm 2,3, ...,9). It is known [10] that during a grasp action the hand grip-size temporal profile has a standard form (Figure 5(a)). A good evidence for the soundess of NeGOI approach is to compare the grip-size measure (computed as output by our system) with the expected profile of Figure 5(a), albeit this can not be used as a quantitative evaluation criterion. Moreover, the value of the maximum grip size occurs at roughly $70-80\%$ of the action duration and it has a linear relation with the dimension of the target. It follows that the correctness of NeGOI approach to measure grip-size can be proved if the values thus obtained exhibit the above mentioned properties.

Results. For all grasp actions the temporal profile of grip-size (Figure 5(b)) as measured by NeGOI has *similar* shape as the one measured by Jeannerod . The maximum grip size value shows a clear linear relation with the dimension of the target (Figure 6). In fact, by performing a linear regression between the maximum grip size values and the target dimensions, we obtain an average determination index $\overline{r_2} \simeq 0.90$. The values of the maximum grip size occur, on the average, at roughly 80% of the action duration.

4.2   Viewpoint Independence

In order to test the viewpoint independence capibility of the NeGOI architecture, we asked the subject to assume specifc hand configurations corresponding to grip-size values equal to roughly 2,4,6,8 cm. For each hand configuration we recorded the hand while rotating the camera from the viewpoint $view_1$ to the viewpoint $view_3$ and viceversa. Therefore, for each hand configuration we obtained a sequence of about 120 images (as an example see Figure 7). Each image was processed by NeGOI, so obtaining for each hand configuration a sequence of about 120 grip-size values. The capability of NeGOI to obtain a viewpoint independent measure can be proved if each sequence of

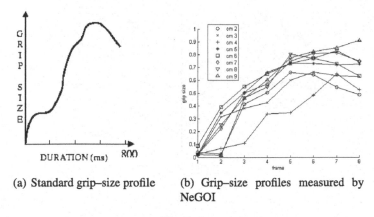

(a) Standard grip–size profile

(b) Grip–size profiles measured by NeGOI

Fig. 5.

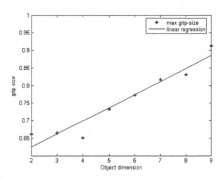

Fig. 6. Linear relation between maximum grip-size and dimension of the target-object

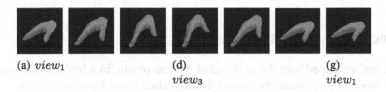

(a) $view_1$　　　(d)　　　　　(g)
　　　　　　　　$view_3$　　　$view_1$

Fig. 7. An example of a sequence of images from $view_1$ to $view_3$ and viceversa.

grip-size values is "almost stable". This stability can be measured verifying if the difference between the means of two consecutive sequences of grip-size values is greater than the sum of the corresponding standard deviations.

Results. We obtained the sequences of grip-size values showed in Figure 8(a). In Figure 8(b) are shown mean and standard deviation for each sequence. It can be seen that for each hand configuration the grip size measures assume a value independent of the corresponding viewpoint in the range $view_1$-$view_3$. In fact, the difference between the means of two consecutive sequences of grip-size values is greater than the sum of the corresponding standard deviations.

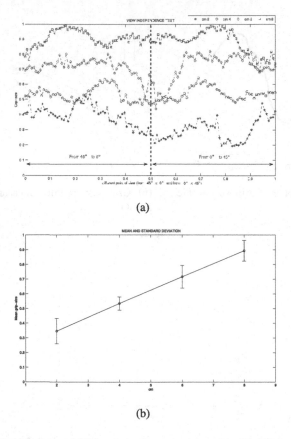

(a)

(b)

Fig. 8. Viewpoint Independence:(a)Grip-size values as measured by NeGoI for four different actual grip sizes versus different viewpoints.(b) Mean and Standar Deviation for each sequence.

5 Conclusions and Discussions

In this paper, we coped with the problem of how to obtain, in a biologically plausible way, a viewpoint independent measure of distinguished visual features of reach-to-grasp actions. To this purpose, we identified a critical visual feature of such actions, the grip-size, and we proposed a biologically inspired neural network architecture for a viewpoint indepepenent measure of it, based on a recognition system which is a model of the visual stream from area V1, V2, V4 to area IT. We have verified the validity of the proposed architecture in a limited subset of grasp actions. Preliminary results are encouraging. We believe that this approach can be augmented to include further distinguished visual features of reach-to-grasp actions.

At the moment of writing we are performing experiments without the skin detection, as we believe that the system is robust enough to do well without this preprocessing step.

Even though modeling in computational neuroscience has been the main motivation of our work, we think the proposed approach can be useful in itself as a non-trivial pattern recognition system. Indeed, starting from the classification of specific hand configurations taken under different viewpoints, it allows the measure of high-level visual features such as grip-size in a view independent way.

References

1. Rizzolatti, G., Luppino, G., Matelli, M.: The organization of the cortical motor system: new concepts. Electroencephalogr. Clin. Neurophysiol. 106, 283–296 (1998)
2. Gallese, V.: A neuroscientific grasp of concepts: from control to representation. Phil. Trans. Royal Soc. London (2003)
3. Arbib, M.: From monkey-like action recognition to human language: An evolutionary framework for neurolinguistics. Behavioral and Brain Sciences 28(2), 105–124 (2005)
4. Umilta', M., Kohler, E., Gallese, V., Fogassi, L., Fadiga, L., Keysers, C., Rizzolatti, G.: I know what you are doing: A neurophysiological study. Neuron 31, 155–165 (2001)
5. Oztop, E., Arbib, M.: Schema design and implementation of the grasp-related mirror neuron system. Biological Cybernetics 87(2), 116–140 (2002)
6. Demiris, Y., Johnson, M.: Distributed, predictive perception of actions: a biologically inspired robotics architecture for imitation and learning. Connection Science 15, 231–243 (2003)
7. Prevete, R., Santoro, R., Mariotti, F.: Biologically inspired visuo-motor control model based on a deflationary interpretation of mirror neurons. In: CogSci2005 - XXVII Annual Conference of the Cognitive Science Society, pp. 1779–1784 (2005)
8. Riesenhuber, M., Poggio, T.: Neural mechanisms of object recognition. Current Opinion in Neurobiology 12, 162–168 (2002)
9. Santello, M., Soechting, J.: Gradual molding of the hand to object contours. J. Neurophysiol. 79, 1307–1320 (1998)
10. Jeannerod, M.: Intersegmental coordination during reaching at natural visual objects. In: Attention and Performance. Hillsdale, pp. 153–168 (1981)
11. Santello, M., Flanders, M., Soechting, J.: Patterns of hand motion during grasping and the influence of sensory guidance. J. Neurophysiol. 22(4), 1426–1435 (2002)
12. Serre, T., Wolf, L., Poggio, T.: Object recognition with features inspired by visual cortex. In: CVPR (2), pp. 994–1000 (2005)
13. Bishop, C.: Neural Networks for Pattern Recognition. Hinton (1996)

Neuromimetic Indicators for Visual Perception of Motion

Claudio Castellanos-Sánchez

Laboratory of Information Technologies of Centre for Research and Advanced Studies
LTI Cinvestav - Tamaulipas, Ciudad Victoria, Tamaulipas, México
castellanos@cinvestav.mx

Abstract. This paper presents three neuromimetic indicators for the visual perception of motion. They estimate the motion, the speed and the direction. All of them emerge from the first two stages in the Castellanos model [1], where a causal spatio-temporal filtering of Gabor-like type captures the oriented contrast and an antagonist inhibition mechanism estimates the motion. These neuromimetic indicators have been evaluated on sequences of natural and synthetic images.

1 Introduction

The visual system of human being has been getting optimised since millions of years by natural selection and this visual perception of motion helps us to detect the pattern of 3D moving objects, its depth, speed and direction estimation, etc.

The research in connectionism is inspired by complexity of neural interactions and their organisation in the brain that can help us to propose a feasible neuromimetic model. Visual perception of motion has been an active research field for the scientific community since motion is of fundamental relevance for most machine perception tasks [2].

Recent research on computational neuroscience has provided an improved understanding of human brain functionality and bio-inspired models have been proposed to mimic the computational abilities of the brain for motion perception and understanding [1].

Several bio-inspired models exist for visual perception of motion some of them are inspired from the primary visual cortex (V1) with a strong neural cooperative-competitive interactions that converge to a local, distributed and oriented auto-organisation [3,4,5]. The others are inspired by the middle temporal area (MT) with the cooperative-competitive interactions between V1 and MT and an influence range [6,7]. And some others are inspired by the middle superior area (MST) for the coherent motion and ego-motion [8,9]. For more details see [1].

All these works are specialised in each cortical area. In this paper I present three neuromimetic indicators for visual perception of motion that emerged from [1,10] to identify : null motion, motion, ego-motion, and their speed and direction. To the begin with, I show the main characteristics of the first two stages

F. Mele et al. (Eds.): BVAI 2007, LNCS 4729, pp. 134–143, 2007.
© Springer-Verlag Berlin Heidelberg 2007

of Castellanos model [1,10]. Next, I continue with the manipulation of the several parameters issued by the antagonist inhibition mechanism and I show three neuromimetic indicators for motion estimation. I carried out some experiments on real images and end with propositions for future work.

2   Neuromimetic Connectionist Architecture

This section broadly describes the mathematical and biological foundations of the proposed bio-inspired model for visual perception of motion based on the neuromimetic connectionist model reported in [1,10].

The first stage of this neuromimetic model is mainly based on the causal spatiotemporal Gabor-like filtering and the second stage is a local and massively distributed processing defined in [10], where they have proposed a retinotopically organised model of the following perception principle : local motion information of a retinal image is extracted by neurons in the primary visual cortex, V1, with local receptive fields restricted to small areas of spatial interactions (first stage : causal spatio-temporal filtering, CSTF); these neurons are densely interconnected for excitatory-inhibitory interactions (second stage : antagonist inhibition mechanism, AIM).

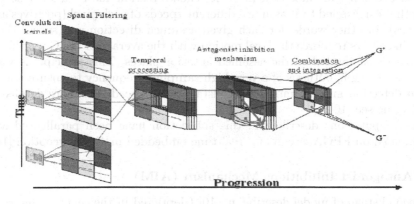

Fig. 1. Architecture of neuromimetic connectionist model adapted of [10]

I will describe in this section these stages : the spatial processing for modelling orientation selective neurons of V1, temporal processing for modelling the speed selectiveness of neurons in the medium temporal area, MT, and connectionist processing to mimic the excitatory-inhibitory local interactions in the cerebral cortex of human beings and self-organising mechanisms for coherent motion estimation. The biological foundations and the mathematical details will not be discussed in this paper (for reference see [10]). The neuromimetic indicators will be presented in section 3.

2.1 Causal Spatio-Temporal Filtering (CSTF)

The first stage of the model depicted in the first three parts of figure 1 (convolution kernels, spatial filtering and temporal processing) performs a causal spatio-temporal filtering. It models the magnocellular cells seen as motion sensors that depend on the gradient of image intensity and on its temporal derivatives [11,12,13]. This filtering is performed in two steps : a spatial filtering and a causal temporal processing [10,14].

The equation 1 show this filtering.

$$H_{t,\theta_i,v}(x,y) = \int S_{\theta_i}(x - \hat{v}_1, y - \hat{v}_2)dt \qquad (1)$$

$$\hat{v}_1 = \frac{\hat{t}}{\tau - 1}v_1 cos\theta_i, \quad \hat{v}_2 = \frac{\hat{t}}{\tau - 1}v_2 sin\theta_i \qquad (2)$$

where $S_{\theta_i}(\cdot, \cdot)$ is the spatial Gabor-like filtering, $v = (v_1, v_2)$ the speed vector, τ the number of subsequence images, and $0 \leq \hat{t}, t < \tau$.

For the spatial filtering, Gabor-like filters are implemented as image convolution kernels in Θ different directions. I usually work with $\Theta = 8$, then $0 \leq i < \Theta$ and $\theta_i = \frac{2\pi i}{\Theta}$.

On the other hand, the causal temporal processing involves the computation of a temporal average of Gabor-like filters for each direction and for a set of search places that correspond to V assumed different speeds of each pixel (positives and negatives). In other words, for each given assumed direction and speed, these Gabor-like filters reinforce the local motion with the average of the Gabor filters applied to past images on the assumed anterior places. This principle is valid under the strong hypothesis of a very high sampling frequency to ensure a local motion detection and an immediate constant local speed. For more details on this filtering see [10].

The computations described in this subsection have been parallelised and implemented on FPGA circuits for real-time embedded motion perception [14].

2.2 Antagonist Inhibitions Mechanism (AIM)

The second stage of model describe in [10] (depticted in the centre of figure 1) emulates an antagonist inhibition mechanism by means of excitatory-inhibitory local interactions in the different oriented cortical columns of V1.

In this mechanism each neuron receives both excitation and inhibition signals from neurons in a neighbourhood or influence range to regulate its activity. The figure 1 shows the excitatory and inhibitory local interactions where neurons interact with their close neighbours in this mechanism that change the internal state of neurons and, consequently, their influence range, which generate a dynamic adaptive process.

Usually in excitatory-inhibitory neural models, the weighted connections to and from neurons have modulated strength according to the distance from one another. Nevertheless, I call it an antagonist inhibition mechanism because the inhibitory connections among neurons regulate downwards the activity of opposing or antagonist neurons, i.e. neurons that do not share a common or similar orientation and speed. On the other hand, excitatory connections increase the neuron activity towards the emergence of coherent responses, i.e. grouping neuron responses to similar orientations and speeds through an interactive process.

Then the updating of the internal state of a neuron is

$$\eta \frac{\partial H(x,y,T)}{\partial T} = -A \cdot H(x,y,T)$$
$$+(B - H(x,y,T)) \cdot Exc(x,y,T) \qquad (3)$$
$$-(C + H(x,y,T)) \cdot Inh(x,y,T)$$

where $-A \cdot H(\cdot)$ is the passive decay, $(B - H(\cdot)) \cdot Exc(\cdot)$ the feedback excitation and, $(C + H(\cdot)) \cdot Inh(\cdot)$ the feedback inhibition. Each feedback term includes a state-dependent nonlinear signal ($Exc(x,y,T)$ and $Inh(x,y,T)$) and an automatic gain control term ($B - H(\cdot)$ and $C + H(\cdot)$, respectively). $H(x,y,T)$ is the internal state of the neuron localised in (x,y) at time T, $Exc(x,y,T)$ is the activity due to the contribution of excitatory interactions in the neighbourhood $\Omega_{(x,y)}^{\Omega_E}$ and $Inh(x,y,T)$ is the activity due to the contribution of inhibitory interactions in the neighbourhood $\Omega_{(x,y)}^{\Omega_I}$. Both neighbourhoods depend on the activity level of the chosen neuron in each direction. A, B and C are the real constant values and η is the learning rate. For more details on the excitation and inhibition areas see [1,10].

Let ρ be the influence range of neuron (x,y) in this stage. This neuron receives at most ρ^2 excitatory connections from neurons with the same direction and speed and at most $(V \cdot \Theta - 1) \cdot \rho^2$ inhibitory connections from other close neurons.

At this level, each pixel correspond to $\Theta \cdot V$ different neurons that encode informations of directions and speeds.

The computations described in this subsection analysing its neural and synaptic parallelism have been implemented on FPGA circuits [15].

3   Neuromimetic Indicators

The visual perception of motion is not totally determined in the local responses of the V1 neurons. They are processed to obtain the speed after being collected and combined from V1 and being integrated in MT. It is this combination of signals that resolve the local ambiguity of responses of neurons in V1 [1]. This activity is the inspiration of the last part of figure 1 (directions and speeds combination and integration).

3.1   Controlled Generation of Sequences of Real Images

The model described here has several parameters to be fixed. The results shown are the product of several experiments. To begin with, I analysed the active neurons in each direction and speed, the frequencies of active neurons after updating (ANaU) and the negative updating increase (NUI) through m different sequences of real images about 384×288 pixels per image.

Next, to analyse egomotion, I selected n images of each sequence of real images and for each selected image I generated $\Theta \times V$ controlled subsequences ($\Theta=$ different directions and $V=$ different speeds) indicated in the figure 2.

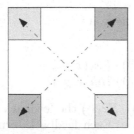 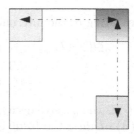

Fig. 2. Different directions of controlled subsequences of real images generated for each supposed speed

Finally for motion classification, I took a subsequence of each sequence of real images too where : a) the motion does not exist, b) one object moves, c) two or more objects move simultaneously.

The interpretation of the different obtained values are shown in the next subsections.

3.2 Motion Type

The equation 3 shows the actualisation rule in the AIM for the active neurons. Let S be a real image sequence and let $R \subset S$ be a subsequence with $Card(R) = \tau$ the subsequence size and let p be the percentage of the neurons to update.

The AIM mechamism updates $p\%$ of active neurons and I obtain in it two frequency percentages : the active neurons after updating ($ANaU$) and negative updating increase (NUI, see the right side in the equation 3).

The frequencies of the products between $ANaU$ and NUI indicators in all the different controlled subsequences (see section 3.1) inspire us to propose our first neuromimetic indicator : *neuromimetic motion indicator*, $NMI = ANaU*NUI$. The experimented ranges of NMI obtained are shown in table 1.

3.3 Speed and Direction

MT neurons sum the responses of V1 neurons with receptive field positions inside a local spatial neighbourhood that is defined through time and generates a response according to the speed of the visual stimulus [1]. This locality of the AIM mechanism on all the several considered motion directions in V1 bring an emerging answer corresponding to the global direction [1,10].

On the other hand, neuro physiological studies roughly indicate that neurons in MT of the visual cortex of primate brains are selective to speed of visual stimuli; which implies that neurons respond strongly in a preferred direction and with a preferred speed [6].

Table 1. Experimental ranges for neuromimetic motion indicator (NMI)

Condition	Description
$NMI < 0.10$	Null motion
$NMI < 1.00$	Small moving objects or bruit
$NMI < 5.00$	One or two moving objetcs
$NMI < 10.00$	Three to five moving objects
$NMI < 40.00$	Six or more moving objects, or ego-motion
$NMI < 250.00$	Ego-motion or big moving objects
$NMI < 400.00$	Ego-motion
$NMI \geq 400.00$	No processed

For each real subsequence R and for the filtering images generated in the equation 1 I define

$$sat^+ = max_{t,\theta,v}(H_{t,\theta,v}(x,y)), \quad sat^- = min_{t,\theta,v}(H_{t,\theta,v}(x,y)) \qquad (4)$$

where sat^+ and sat^- are the positive and negative saturation, respectively.

For each direction and speed of each neuron, I count the neurons with a response greater than at. This parameter is the average of positive and negative saturations. The equation 6 shows its behaviour and the equation 5 computes this frequency in direction θ with speed v.

$$C(\theta, v) = \sum_{(x,y)} D(at, H_{t,\theta,v}(x,y))) \qquad (5)$$

with

$$D(at, H_{t,\theta,v}(x,y)) = \begin{cases} 1 \text{ if } H_{t,\theta,v}(x,y) > at \\ 0 \text{ otherwise} \end{cases} \qquad (6)$$

where $D(\cdot, \cdot)$ is the threshold of the CSTF filtering.

The collection and combination in MT for direction estimation is computed by :

$$E(\theta, v) = 3 \cdot C(\theta, v) + 2 \cdot (C(\theta - \phi, v) + C(\theta + \phi, v)) + C(\theta - 2\phi, v) + C(\theta + 2\phi, v) \quad (7)$$

where $\phi = \frac{2\pi}{\theta}$ is the separation in degrees between each oriented column and $E(\cdot, \cdot)$ is the sum of several oriented responses of V1 that activate a neuron in MT. Finally, I computed the frequencies for negative and positive supposed speeds by the equations :

$$G^+ = \sum_{v>0,\theta} C(\theta, v), \quad G^- = \sum_{v<0,\theta} C(\theta, v) \qquad (8)$$

Then I arranged $E(\theta, v)$ in a direction according to each speed and arranged G^+ and G^- too for processing them to obtain speed and direction indicators. These indicators will be describe in the next two paragraphs.

Table 2. Experimental ranges for neuromimetic speed indicator (NSI)

Type	Condition Relative speed	Prototype speed
	$NSI > 70.0 \; rs = (100.0 - NSI)/29.0$	0
Weak if $v1 > v2$	$NSI > 12.0 \; rs = (71 - NSI)/59 + 1$	1
	otherwise $\;\; rs = (12 - NSI) * 0.3529/12 + 2$	2
	$NSI > 22.0 \; rs = (NSI * 0.6470)/22 + 2.3530$	3
Strong if $v1 < v2$	$NSI > 39.0 \; rs = (NSI - 22)/10 + 3$	4
	otherwise Speed not processed	≥ 5

Speed. To obtain the winner speed, I propose the *neuromimetic speed indicator (NSI)* defined by equation 9 :

$$NSI = \frac{100 \cdot min(G^+, G^-)}{max(G^+, G^-)} \tag{9}$$

With this indicator I compute the relative speed (rs) that compares the different speed frequencies and their proportion. The table 2 shows my experimental values for $V = 5$. Then $v_i = \{-2, -1, 0, 1, 2\}$, with $v1$ is the frequency of $|v_i| = 1$ and $v2$ is the frequency of $|v_i| = 2$.

Direction. Finally, for an interpretation of integration of directions for each neuron in MT, I compute $E(\theta, v)$ of the equation 7 for each direction and speed.

Next, I arrange their values from major to minor and I take the first three. If these candidates are contiguous in direction, the winner will be at the centre of the three candidates' directions. This is my *neuromimetic direction indicator NDI.*

Finally, if the maximum of the two computed speeds in the equation 8 is the negative one, the winner direction will be its antagonist, ei, $\theta = \theta - 180°$.

4   Experimental Results

The free parameters of my model were set according to the suggestions in [1]. I chose only three sequences of images among $m = 50$ analysed sequences : the Yosemite Fly-Through (sequence of synthetic images), the Hamburg Taxi and the BrowseB issue of video surveillance. They include various numbers of RGB images (15, 42 and 875 images, respectively) and of sizes of : 316×252, 256×191, 384×288, respectively, and they are first gray-scaled.

The figure 3 shows four images of these sequences and their graph of the proposed neuromimetic indicators. The values of NMI are between 0 (null motion) and 1000 (ego-motion), of NSI between 0 and 6, and NDI is in $\{1, 2, 3, 4, 5, 6, 7, 8\}$ ($0°, 45°, ..., 315°$).

The synthetic Yosemite Fly-Through sequence shows an aeroplane flying on the mountains. This sequence presents an ego-motion with a speed of five pixels (down image) that diverge and two pixels for the moving clouds to the right

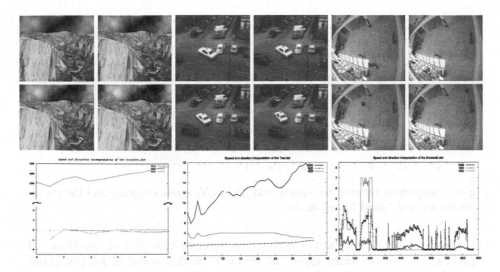

Fig. 3. Sequences of real and synthetic images used in this work: Yosemite, Taxi and BrowseB, in each two columns respectively and from top-left to down-left in clockwise direction, four images of each sequence and their neuromimetic indicators are shown below

(top image). The NMI is between 300 and 450, then according to the table 1 it proposes an ego-motion with 2 pixels per image moving at around 45 °.

In the figure 4, I show the average of direction and speed of optical real flow of Yosemite sequence and the experimental results obtained by my model. My model presents a conceptual error of around 22.5 °, despite which it is sufficient to describe the real movement towards the North-East. Finally, the speed is not numerically exact, but its behavior is very similar to the real one. Then, the global motion obtained here is very similar to the Yosemite Fly-Through data.

The real Hamburg Taxi sequence shows three moving cars and a pedestrian. The NMI is between 6 and 18, then according to the table 1 there are about three moving objects and the global speed is 2 pixels per image moving at approximatly 180 ° and end at around 135 °.

Finally, the BrowseB sequence issue of video surveillance in the hall of INRIA laboratory, Grenoble, France, may be split into three parts : (1) a person walks to the centre, stops and returns; (2) there is no motion; (3) another person walks in, stops and goes farther.

The last two columns of the figure 3 show the BrowseB sequence. The first part (images 0 to 220) may be split into three parts according to NMI : two parts with motion and the other part with null motion that correspond to the first person walking between 90 ° and 135 ° and with a speed of 4 to 2 pixels per image, stops and returns between 270 ° and 315 ° and with a speed of 2 to 4 pixels per image.

For the second part (images 221 to 325) there is null motion. The last part may be split too into three parts according to NMI : (1) motion, (2) generally

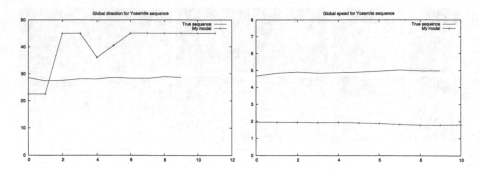

Fig. 4. Comparison between the optical real flow of Yosemite sequence and the experimental results obtained by my model

null motion and (3) motion, respectively to describe this part of the BrowseB sequence. The person walks approximatly at 0 ° with a speed of 1-2 pixels per image. Next, a period of null motion with very weak motions (see pics in the graph between image 550 and 750). Finally, the person moves to about 90 ° with a speed of about 2 pixels per image.

5   Conclusions

This work is based on the Castellanos model [10] : a neuromimetic connectionist model for visual perception of motion. A model fully inspired by the visual cortex system, the superior areas and their relations.

In this paper I took advantage of the low-level analysis to detect local motions to obtain the global speed and direction. They are determined by the neuromimetic motion indicator issued by AIM mechanism.

Our first experiments show that this model is capable of estimating the null motion, simple motion and ego-motion with an estimation of global speed and direction in an environment where other persons or objects move. The estimation of motion is robust in quite complex scenes without any predefined information. Nevertheless, the estimation of NMI is fastidious. The experimental values are correct for the sequence of real images of ±33% the size of 384 × 288.

My current work includes experimenting on the other sizes the images for the generalisation of the NMI and studying the same neuromimetic indicators for the moving fields only.

Acknowledgments

This research was partially funded by project number 51623 from "Fondo Mixto Conacyt-Gobierno del Estado de Tamaulipas".

References

1. Castellanos-Sánchez, C.: Neuromimetic connectionist model for embedded visual perception of motion. PhD thesis, Université Henri Poincaré (Nancy I), Nancy, France, Bibliothèque des Sciences et Techniques (October 2005)
2. McCane, B., Novins, K., Grannitch, D., Galvin, B.: On benchmarking optical flow. Computer Vision and Image Undestanding, 126–143 (2001)
3. Fellez, W.A., Taylor, J.G.: Establishing retinotopy by lateral-inhibition type homogeneous neural fields. Neurocomputing 48, 313–322 (2002)
4. Latham, P.E., Nirenberg, S.: Computing and stability in cortical networks. Neural Computation, 1385–1412 (2004)
5. Moga, S.: Apprendre par imitation: une nouvelle voie d'apprentissage pour les robots autonomes. PhD thesis, Université de Cergy-Pontoise, Cergy-Pontoise, France (September 2000)
6. Simoncelli, E.P., Heeger, D.J.: A model of neural responses in visual area mt. Visual Research 38(5), 743–761 (1998)
7. Mingolla, E.: Neural models of motion integration and segmentation. Neural Networks 16, 939–945 (2003)
8. Pack, C., Grossberg, S., Mingolla, E.: A neural model of smooth pursuit control and motion perception by cortical area mst. Technical Report CAS/CNR-TR-99-023, Department of Cognitive and Neural Systems and Center for Adaptive Systems, Boston University, 677 Beacon St, Boston, MA 02215 (September 2000)
9. Zemel, R.S., Sejnowski, T.J.: A model for encoding multiple object motions and self-motion in area mst of primate visual cortex. The Journal of Neurosciences 18(1), 531–547 (1998)
10. Castellanos-Sánchez, C., Girau, B., Alexandre, F.: A connectionist approach for visual perception of motion. In: Smith, L., Hussain, A., Aleksander, I. (eds.) BICS 2004. Brain Inspired Cognitive Systems, September 2004, vol. BIS3-1, pp. 1–7 (2004)
11. Pollen, D., Ronner, S.: Phase relationships between adjacent simple cells in the visual cortex. Science 212, 1409–1411 (1981)
12. Newsome, W.T., Gizzi, M.S., Movshon, J.A.: Spatial and temporal properties of neurons in macaque mt. Investigative Ophtalmology and Visual Science Supplement 24, 106 (1983)
13. Hammond, P., Reck, J.: Influence of velocity on directional tuning of complex cells in cat striate cortex for texture motion. Neuroscience Letters 19, 309–314 (1981)
14. Torres-Huitzil, C., Girau, B., Castellanos-Sánchez, C.: On-chip visual perception of motion: A bio-inspired connectionist model on fpga. Neural Networks 18(5-6), 557–565 (2005)
15. Torres-Huitzil, C., Girau, B.: Fpga implementation of an excitatory and inhibitory connectionist model for motion perception. In: Brebner, G.J., Chakraborty, S., Wong, W.F. (eds.) FPT 2005. IEEE International Conference on Field-Programmable Technology, December 2005, pp. 259–266. IEEE Computer Society Press, Los Alamitos (2005)

Reversal of "Cubic" and "Cylindric" Figures

Jirina Radilova[1], Cloe Taddei-Ferretti[2,3], Carlo Musio[2], Silvia Santillo[2],
Edoardo Cibelli[3], Antonio Cotugno[2], and Tomáš Radil[1]

[1] Institute of Physiology, CAS, Prague, Czech Republic
[2] Istituto di Cibernetica "Eduardo Caianiello", CNR, Pozzuoli, Italy
[3] Istituto di Filosofia, PFTIM-SL, Napoli, Italy

Abstract. Spontaneous figure reversal of ambiguous patterns was analyzed in
humans by presenting "Necker-cube"-like, or "drum"-like figures having square
or round shaped "front" and "rear" surfaces, and either large or small "depth".
The figures were perceived alternately according to one or the other of two
possible mental orientation-interpretations. The subjects signalled the instant of
subjective pattern-reversals. Results: perceptual intervals corresponding to both
interpretations of "drum" were longer than those of "cube"; the perceived
"depth" of the figures was less relevant for reversal timing ("deeper" figures
reversed only slightly more slowly and the corresponding intervals were
somewhat longer). Although the shape of "front" and "rear" surfaces was not a
crucial geometrical feature for representing the three-dimensional nature of the
patterns on the two-dimensional stimulus plane, it markedly influenced the
timing of figure reversals. More, or longer information processing steps should
needed for perceptual-cognitive representations of curvilinear patterns in
comparison with rectangular ones.

Keywords: Ambiguous pattern reversal, Necker cube, Information processing
steps, Object recognition, Mental interpretation.

1 Introduction

It is known, and accepted, that there is an automatic tendency toward spontaneous
subjective alternation of possible perceptual-cognitive interpretations, when
ambiguous figures are being presented to human subjects [9], [10]. This fact is
probably due to the incomplete geometrical representation of the real three-
dimensional objects in question in the two-dimensional stimulus plane, usually.
Speaking in general terms, the lack of information concerning the patterns seems to
be compensated by alternation of the possible cognitive interpretations concerning
their geometry [17].

Thus the assumption was natural, that the amount of information concerning
essential geometrical features, related to dimensionality of the real objects represented
on the two dimensional plane, could be an important factor determining the rate of
figure reversal. On the basis of this reasoning we incresed in previous experiments the
amount of information contained in a "double reversible figure" (capable of reversing

F. Mele et al. (Eds.): BVAI 2007, LNCS 4729, pp. 144–149, 2007.
© Springer-Verlag Berlin Heidelberg 2007

either in two-, or in three-dimensional mental space, depending on the cognitive instruction given to the subjects) by drawing further graphical details concerning the three-dimensional interpretation of the figure [11], [13], [14], [16]. We have found, that this caused a proportional decrease of the figure reversal rate both in two-, and three-dimensional mental space. A possible explanation was, that more information contained in the pattern reqired more sequential data processing steps in any interpretation interval, and therefore also more time.

It was, however, demonstrated in further experiments, that, in contrary, reduction of the information content in the stimulus pattern, by drawing it in an incomplete way, was also combined with a proportional decrease of the reversal rate [12]. Higher requirements for processing time could have been caused by the need for some sort of "mental reconstruction" of the patterns by means of the perceptual cognitive mechanisms involved.

On the basis of the above experiments the conclusion, that information content was in general terms a relevant factor in timing of figure reversal, seemed to be plausible. However, it had to be also assumed, that the above factor did not act in a single, and simply monotonous way (as it followed from the similar effect of both an increase, and a decrease of information content). Moreover, in the experiments mentioned, manipulation with the amount of information in the patterns was combined with parallel changes in the graphical representation of the patterns, and in some cases also in the amount of semantic information involved.

Therefore the next question to be analyzed was, whether additional factors, not related in a direct way to the geometrical features crucial for figure reversal, might also influence spontaneous reversal rate.

We intended therefore to perform experiments with reversible patterns in which their principal geometrical features, and the specific information (or the lack of it) on which figure reversal was being based upon, remained equal, but the geometry of their graphical representation was different. The question was whether the latter factor would influence the speed of figure reversal too.

2 Methods and Procedures

Two types of reversible figures were designed, and generated by means of a computer for the above purpose: rectangular Necker "cubes" (C) patterns, and "drum"-like (D) cylindric patterns differing from the former ones only in the shape of the "front", and "rear" side of the structure, which ware round instead of square. The area of the squares, and circles representing the sides of both structures, was equal. Two variants of both patterns were used, differing in subjective "depth", depending on the length of the four oblique straight lines connecting the "front", and "rear" surfaces of the structures, and oriented under the angle of 45 degrees with respect to the vertical. The length of those oblique lines corresponded to 71% of the the sides of the squares for "small depth" (S), and to 47% for "large depth" (L). They were equal for the "squares" and the corresponding "drums" (Fig.1).

The subjects were ten healthy volonteers, 5 males, and 5 females, with normal visus. They were naïve as to the essence, and purpose of the experiments. However, they were pretrained to understand the principle of figure reversal, and to signal it in a skillful way. The patterns were generated on the display of a computer, and their size was 8 cm. The subjects sat on a comfortable chair, and viewed the dispay under day light condition from the dictance of about 80 cm. They were instructed to watch the center of the pattern on the display during each experiment. A computer mouse, on which the subjects had to tap synchronously with subjective reversals of the pattern, was used as imput for measuring the inter-reversal intervals.

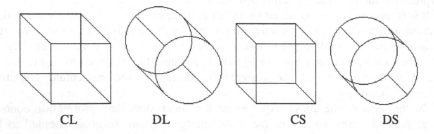

CL   DL   CS   DS

Fig. 1. Schematic representation of the stimulus patterns generated by means of a computer: cube-like (C), and drum-like (D) patterns, with large (L), or small (S) perceived "depth".

Each experiment with a subject consisted of different experimental sessions. In each session, two of the four patterns were presented, each one for 2 minutes. The possible pairs of two different patterns were six, and thus the total duration of the whole of the six possible sessions was 24 minutes. During the whole of the six sessions, each of the four patterns resulted to be presented three times, and thus the total presentation time for each pattern was 6 minutes. The sequence of pattern presentation was random. As we have found, that the values of average inter-reversal intervals were similar for each single pattern in different sessions, such values could be combined. The statistical evaluation was performed.

3 Results

After preliminary results [15], [23], present experimental results (Fig. 2) indicate, that perceptual intervals corresponding to both ("small depth", and "large depth") interpretations of the "drum" were longer than those for the "cube" (1-way ANOVA: $F = 7.14$, $p = 0.0086$). The perceived "depth" of the figures (subjective size of the patterns, corresponding to the subjective distance of "front" and "rear" surfaces, for "small depth" and "large depth" patterns) was less relevant for reversal timing than the shape difference of "front" and "rear" surfaces; however, the intervals corresponding to "deeper" figures tended to be slightly longer (2-way ANOVA: $F = 4.31$, $p = 0.0402$).

It followed, that, although the shape of the "front" and "rear" surface of the patterns was not a crucial geometrical feature for representing (in an ambiguous way) the three-dimensional nature of the patterns on the two-dimensional stimulus plane, it did markedly influence the timing of figure reversals.

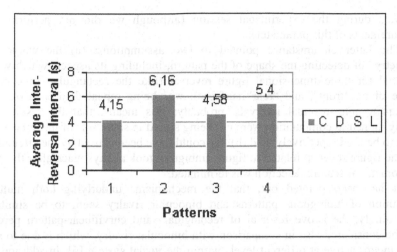

Fig. 2. Average inter-reversal intervals given in seconds for "cube"-like (C), and "drum"-like (D) shape patterns, as well es for small (S), and large (L) perceived "depth" of the patterns (respectively pattern 1, 2, 3, and 4).

4 Discussion

Longer inter-reversal intervals could be interpreted in the sense, that more, or longer information processing steps in the brain were probably needed for the perceptual-cognitive representation of the patterns curvilinear along the stimulus plane in comparison with the rectangular ones.

It is probable, that the underlying neural mechanisms are located at a relatively peripheral level in the visual system. The efficiency of the analysis required for edge detection during early visual processing depends also on edge structure (sharp or smooth) [27]. During late visual processing, a representation related to fine metric specifications such as segment length or curvature degree should be performed too slowly for object recognition, while the recognition of simple primitive volumes requires "only" categorical activation of edge characteristics [2]. Considering the geometrical features involved, the Necker "cube" patterns have 6 external "arrow" and 2 internal "Y"-shaped vertices, all relevant for edge identification; whereas the "drum"-like patterns are characterized by only 4 external "tangent Y"-like vertices, relevant for edge identification, as well as by 2 external "w", and 2 internal "curved Y"-like unimportant vertices (definitions from [1], modified). However, the approach adopted in the present experiments did not allow to judge on the essence of the neural algorithms for the processing of the described geometrical information by the brain.

Two aspects seemed to be relevant in this connection. The first one was, that "curvilinearity" concerned only the two-dimensional "front" and "rear" surfaces of the three-dimensional "real object" represented by the stimulation patterns. Those "front" and "rear" surfaces did not seem *a priori* to play a crucial role in the figure reversal taking place in three-dimensional mental space. Nevertheless, their curvilinear shape did markedly increase inter-reversal intervals. The second aspect was, that we did not witness any clear tendency toward shortening of inter-reversal intervals during the experimenal session (although we did not perform formal measurements of this parameter).

The latter circumstance pointed to two assumptions: (a) the whole "brain geometry" of detecting the shape of the pattern, including its aspects which were not essential for three-dimensional figure reversal (like the rectangular, or curvilinear nature of its "front", and "rear" surfaces), was being repeated in each one of the subsequent inter-reversal intervals, probably; this means, that the results of the undelying neural computation were not being stored in some sort of memory buffer in order to be used repetitively; and (b) this could have been caused by the circumstance, that the figure reversal related to figure ambiguity took always place after the process of geometrical-feature detection was terminated.

It has been pointed out, that the mechanisms underlying both multistable perception of ambiguous patterns and binocular rivalry seem to be similar [5]. Accordingly, the above reversal of rectangular- and curvilinear-pattern perception may be considered also in comparison with binocular rivalry, which is due to several mechanisms active at different levels within the visual system [6]. In addition, while the information on the above curvilinear and rectangular petterns may be processed at relatively early levels of the visual system, the voluntary control of perception reversal, which has been ascertained with the same rectangular pattern (Necker cube) [18], [19], [20], [21], [22], as well as other results obtained with different experimental settings [3], [4], [7], [8], [24], [25], [26], point towards an intentional high-level top-down processing intervening toghether with an automatic low-level bottom-up processing.

References

1. Biederman, J.: Recognition-by-Components: A Theory of Human Image Understanding. Psychol. Rev. 94, 115–147 (1987)
2. Biederman, J.: Visual Oobject Recognition. In: Kosslyn, S.M., Osherson, D.N. (eds.) An Invitation to Cognitive Science, 2nd edn. Visual Cognition, vol. 2, pp. 121–165. MIT Press, Cambridge, MA (1995)
3. Isoglu-Alkac, Ü., Strüber, D.: Necker Cube Reversals during Long-Term EEG Recordings: Sub-bands of Alpha Activity. Int. J. Psychophysiol. 59/2, 179–189 (2006)
4. Leopold, D.A.: Visual Perception: Shaping What We See. Current Biol. 13, R10-R12 (2003)
5. Logothetis, N.K.: Single Units and Conscious Vision. Phil. Trans. Roy. Soc. Lond. Ser. B 353, 1801–1818 (1998)
6. Logothetis, N.K., Blake, R.: Visual Competition. Nature Rev. Neurosci. 3, 13–23 (2002)
7. Long, G.M., Toppino, T.C.: Enduring Interest in Perceptual Ambiguity: Alternating Views of Reversible Figures. Psychol. Bull. 130, 748–768 (2004)
8. Meng, M., Tong, F.: Can Attention Selectively Bias Bistable Perception? Differences between Binocular Rivalry and Ambiguous Figures. J. Vision $/7, 539–551 (2004)
9. Radilova, J.: Reversible Figures. Academia Publishing House, Prague (1983)
10. Radilova, J.: Temporal Aspects in Visual Perception and Cognition. In: Taddei-Ferretti, C. (ed.) Biocybernetics of Vision: Integrative Mechanisms and Cognitive Processes, pp. 239–250. World Scientific, Singapore (1997)

11. Radilova, J., Radil-Weiss, T.: Subjective Figure Reversal in Two and Three Dimensional Perceptual Space. Internat. J. Psychophysiol. 2, 59–62 (1984)
12. Radilova, J., Radil, T., Virsu, V.: Incomplete Geometrical Representation of the Double-Reversible Figure. In: Taddei-Ferretti, C., Musio, C. (eds.) Downward Processes in the Perception Representation Mechanisms, pp. 298–310. World Scientific, Singapore (1997)
13. Radilova, J., Radil-Weiss, T., Riani, M., Tuccio, M.T.: Subjective Reversal of Figures of Increasing Complexity in Three- and Two-Dimensial Perceptual Space. In: Atti 5 Congresso Nazionale di Cibernetica e Biofisica, Pisa, Italy, pp. 299–306 (1979)
14. Radilova, J., Radil-Weiss, T., Spunda, J., Indra, J.: Visual Pattern Interpretable as Reversible or Figure Background. Activitas Nervosa Superior 17, 54–55 (1975)
15. Radilova, J., Taddei-Ferretti, C., Musio, C., Santillo, S., Colucci, R., Cotugno, A., Radil, T.: The Perception of Cylindric and Cubic Ambiguous Patterns. In: Taddei-Ferretti, C., Musio, C. (eds.) Neuronal Bases and Psychological Aspects of Consciousness, pp. 357–360. World Scientific, Singapore (1999)
16. Riani, M., Tuccio, M.T., Borsellino, A., Radilova, J., Radil, T.: Perceptual Ambiguity and Stability of Reversible Figures. Percept. Motor Skills 63, 191–205 (1986)
17. Robinson, O.J.: The Psychology of Visual Illusion. Hutchison University Library, London (1972)
18. Taddei-Ferretti, C., Musio, C., Colucci, R.F.: Top-Down Interference in Visual Perception. In: Marinaro, M., Morasso, P.G. (eds.) ICANN '94, vol. 1, part 1, pp. 30–33. Springer, Heidelberg (1994)
19. Taddei-Ferretti, C., Musio, C., Santillo, S., Colucci, R.F., Cotugno, A.: The Top-Down Contribution of Will to the Modulation of Bottom-Up Inputs in the Reversible Perception Phenomenon. In: Moreno-Diaz, R., Mira-Mira, J. (eds.) Brain Processes, Theories and Models, pp. 446–455. MIT Press, Cambridge, MA (1996)
20. Taddei-Ferretti, C., Musio, C., Santillo, S., Colucci, R.F., Cotugno, A.: A Quantitative Approach to the Problem of Will. Internat. Conf. "Toward a Science of Consciousness" (Tucson III), Tucson, AZ, USA. Consciousness Res. Abstr. of J. Consc. Stud. 224, 110 (1998)
21. Taddei-Ferretti, C., Musio, C., Santillo, S., Cotugno, A.: Conscious and Intentional Access to Uncnscious Decision-Making Module in Ambiguous Visual Perception. In: Mira, J.M. (ed.) IWANN 1999. LNCS, vol. 1606, pp. 765–775. Springer, Heidelberg (1999)
22. Taddei-Ferretti, C., Musio, C., Santillo, S., Cotugno, A.: Will: a Vague Idea or a Testable Event? In: Yasue, K., Jibu, M., Della Senta, T. (eds.) No Matter, Never Mind. Series Advances in Consciousness Research, vol. 33, pp. 155–165. John Benjamins, Amsterdam, Philadelphia (2002)
23. Taddei-Ferretti, C., Radilova, J., Musio, C., Santillo, S., Cibelli, E., Cotugno, A., Radil, T.: Mental Manipulations Related to Figure Reversal of Rectangular and Curvilinear Ambiguous Patterns. In: Proc. Sixth Internat, IBRO World Congress of Neuroscience. Prague, Czeck Republic, p. 450 (2003)
24. Toppino, T.C.: Reversible Figure Perception: Mechanisms of Intentional Control. Percpt. Psychophys. 65, 1285–1298 (2003)
25. van EE, R., van Dam, L.C.J., Brouwer, G.J.: Voluntary Control and the Dynamics of Perceptual Bi-stability. Vision Res. 45, 41–55 (2005)
26. Windmann, S., Wehrmann, M., Calabrese, P., Gunturkun, O.: Role of the Prefrontal Cortex in Attentional Control over Bistable Vision. J. Cognit. Neurosci. 18, 456–471 (2006)
27. Yuille, A.L., Ullman, S.: Computational Theories of Low-Level Vision. In: Osherson, D.N., Kosslyn, S.M., Hollerbach, J.M. (eds.) An Invitation to Cognitive Science. Visual Cognition and Action, vol. 2, pp. 5–39. MIT Press, Cambridge, MA (1990)

Different Binding Strategies for the Different Stages of Visual Recognition

John K. Tsotsos[1], Antonio Jose Rodriguez-Sanchez,
Albert L. Rothenstein, and Eugene Simine

Dept. of Computer Science and Engineering, and Centre for Vision Research
York University, Toronto, Ontario Canada

Abstract. Many think attention needs an executive to allocate resources. Although the cortex exhibits substantial plasticity, dynamic allocation of neurons seems outside its capability. Suppose instead that the processing structure is fixed, but can be 'tuned' to task needs. The only resource that can be allocated is time. How can this fixed structure be used over periods of time longer than one feed-forward pass? Can the Selective Tuning model provide the answer? This short paper has one goal, that of explaining a single figure (Fig.1), that puts forward the proposal that by using multiple passes of the visual processing hierarchy, both bottom-up and top-down, and using task information to tune the processing prior to each pass, we can explain the different recognition behaviors that human vision exhibits. To accomplish this, four different kinds of binding processes are introduced and are tied directly to specific recognition tasks and their time course.

1 Introduction

Topics like visual attention, recognition, or binding command a large, conflicting literature. For example, the nature of the attentional influence has been debated for a long time. Among the more interesting observations are those of James (1980) "everyone knows what attention is..." juxtaposed with that of Pillsbury (1908) "attention is in disarray" and Sutherland's (1998) "after many thousands of experiments, we know only marginally more about attention than about the interior of a black hole". Even Marr, basically discounted the importance of attention by not considering the time intervals of perception where attentive effects appear. When describing grouping processes and the full primal sketch, he says, "our approach requires that the discrimination be made quickly - to be safe, in less than 160ms - and that a clear psychophysical boundary be present" (Marr 1982, p.96). Not only is the number of experimental investigations enormous, but also the number of different models, theories and perspectives is large. Attention has been viewed as early selection (Broadbent 1958), using attenuator theory (Treisman 1964), as a late selection process (Norman 1968, Deutsch & Deutsch 1963), as a result of neural

---

[1] JKT is also with the Depts. of Computer Science and of Ophthalmology at the University of Toronto, and holds the Canada Research Chair in Computational Vision.

F. Mele et al. (Eds.): BVAI 2007, LNCS 4729, pp. 150–160, 2007.
© Springer-Verlag Berlin Heidelberg 2007

synchrony (Milner 1974), using the metaphor of a spotlight (Shulman et al. 1979), within the feature integration theory (Treisman & Gelade, 1980), as an object-based phenomenon (Duncan 1984), using the zoom lens metaphor (Eriksen & St. James 1986), as a pre-motor theory subserving eye movements (Rizzollati et al. 1987), as biased competition (Duncan & Desimone 1995), as feature similarity gain (Treue & Martinez-Trujillo 1999), and more.

Within all of these different viewpoints, the only real constant seems to be that attentional phenomena seem to be due to inherent limits in processing capacity in the brain (Tsotsos 1990). But even this does not constrain a solution. Even if we all agree that there is a processing limit, what is its nature? How does it lead to the mechanisms in the brain that produce the phenomena observed experimentally?

We suggest that the terms attention, recognition and binding have become so loaded that they mask the true problems; each may be decomposed into smaller, easier problems. For example, consider the observations that different recognition tasks require different processing times. Detection and categorization seem to take about 150ms, identification takes about 65ms longer, localization of a stimulus so that detection can be expressed through a saccade or pointing action takes 200ms or more, and harder tasks such as detection in clutter, transparent motion or difficult conjunctions take even longer.

We propose that the process of binding visual features to objects in each of these tasks differs and that different sorts of binding actions take different amounts of processing time. Some require attention, others do not. We introduce a novel set of four binding processes: convergence, partial and full recurrence, and iterative binding. These are tied to different recognition tasks: detection or categorization, identification, localization and hard detection. The Selective Tuning model (Tsotsos 1990; Tsotsos et al. 1995), through its execution time course and due to its inherent tuning functionality, provides much of the computational substrate for these types of binding, recognition and attentive modulation.

2 The Stages of Recognition

Which knife can one use to carve 'recognition' into manageable slices? There are many possibilities. Should those slices be different brain areas, each responsible for different sub-tasks? Should those slices be different tasks? What about varying feature, object or scene complexity? The argument made by this paper is that the same neural machinery of the visual cortex is used for any of these dimensions (admittedly, some areas perhaps more involved than others) and that the most effective way of carving up the problem is to cut along the dimension of time. That is, different tasks are known to take different amounts of processing time even though they require the same neural machinery for that processing.

Much past experimental research has already provided what is needed. Consider the time course of events during a typical visual search experiment. An abstraction of this appears in the next paragraph. For each step, it is the same pair of eyes, the same retinal cells, the same, LGN, V1, V2 and so forth, that process the incoming stimuli. Each step in the processing pathway requires processing time; no step is instantaneous or can be assumed so. In such experiments, the timings for each of the input arrays is manipulated presumably in order to investigate different phenomena.

Consider the following characterization of the typical course of activities for an experiment investigating attention or recognition behavior:

1. provide the subject with task information, including
   - what are the cues if any
   - what is the task and what criteria are used to judge a successful trial
   - what sequence of events will the subject see
2. attend fixation stimulus
3. onset of stimulus array
4. process stimulus array, perhaps including
   - detect items in array
   - attend to one or more items, re-applying or modifying task guidance in order to solve the task
   - interpret item's characteristics as required for the task
5. respond to stimulus array using one of the following
   - key press while continuing to fixate
   - saccade to perceived location
6. subject feedback on response
7. onset of next stimulus array, using one or more of
   - mask
   - blank
   - new stimuli to relate to previous

There are many, many variations on this basic theme and this is where the ingenuity of the best experimentalists can shine. However, for those wishing to explain the experimental observations the sequence of actual events plays a more important role than has been acknowledged. A modeler cannot simply take the conclusion of the experiment as the basis of a model without also including the spatial and temporal environment of the experiment into account. This would only lead to models that do not reflect the reality of the experiment or do not generalize and thus produce useful predictions.

3 Different Stages of Recognition

If models are to be sensibly compared to results from human experimentation, the models must consider the same sequence of events as in the experiment and examples of such a sequence appeared in the previous section.

Most models assume that a hierarchical sequence of computations defines the selectivity of a neuron. A feed-forward pass through the hierarchy would yield the strongest responding neurons if stimuli match existing neurons, or the strongest responding component neurons if stimuli are novel.

But, the first set of computations to be performed, following the sequence presented in the previous section, is related to priming of the hierarchy of processing areas. Task knowledge, such as fixation point, target/cue location, task success criteria, is applied to 'tune' the hierarchy (Posner et al. 1978). In experiments, it has been shown that such task guidance must be applied 300 to 100ms before stimulus onset to be effective (Müller & Rabbitt 1989). This informs us that significant processing time is required for this step alone. It is a sufficient amount of time to complete a top-down traversal of the full processing hierarchy. Figure 1 shows a proposed sequence of processing stages in visual recognition tasks. The first stage, the leftmost element of the figure, shows the priming stage. Once complete, the stimulus can be presented (the second element of the figure from the left).

The third element of Fig. 1 represents the *Detection/Categorization Task*. Detecting whether or not a particular object is present in an image seems to take about 150ms (Thorpe et al. 1996). This kind of 'yes-no' response can be called 'pop-out' in visual search with the added condition that the speed of response is the same regardless of number of distractors (Treisman & Gelade 1980). To name the object, or to categorize, also seems to take the same amount of time (Grill-Spector & Kanwisher 2005; Evans & Treisman 2005). Interestingly, the median time required for a single feed-forward pass through the visual system is about 150ms (Bullier 2001). Thus, many conclude that a single feed-forward pass suffices for this visual task. This first feed-forward pass is shown in the figure emphasizing the feed-forward divergence of neural connections and thus stimulus elements are 'blurred' progressively more in higher areas of the hierarchy. This task does not include location or location judgments, the need to manipulate, point, or other motor commands specific to the object and usually, all objects can be easily segmented. These are the kinds of stimuli Marr had in mind for his work as mentioned previously.

To provide details about an object, such as identity (within-category identification) or type, requires additional processing time, 65ms or so (Grill-Spector & Kanwisher 2005; Evans & Treisman 2005); this is the *Identification Task* and is represented by the fourth from the left element of Figure 1. If the highest levels of the hierarchy can provide the basic category of the stimulus, such as 'bird', where are the details that allow one to determine the type of bird? The sort of detail required would be size, color, shape, and so forth. These are clearly lower level visual features and thus they can only be found in earlier levels of the visual hierarchy. They can be accessed by looking at which feature neurons feed into those neurons that provided the category information. One way to achieve this is to traverse the hierarchy downwards, beginning with the category neuron and moving downwards through the needed feature maps. This downwards traversal is what requires the additional time observed. The extent of downward traversal is determined by the task, that is, the aspects of identification that are required. It is interesting to consider an additional impact of a partial downwards traversal. This traversal may be partial not only because of the task definition but also because the full traversal is interrupted and not allowed to complete either because new stimuli enter the system before there is enough time for completion or because not enough time is permitted due to other tasks. The result is that there is the potential for errors in localization and these may lead to the well-known illusory conjunction phenomenon (Treisman & Schmidt 1982).

If additional localization is required for description or a motor task, (pointing, saccade, etc..), then the top-down traversal process must be allowed to complete and

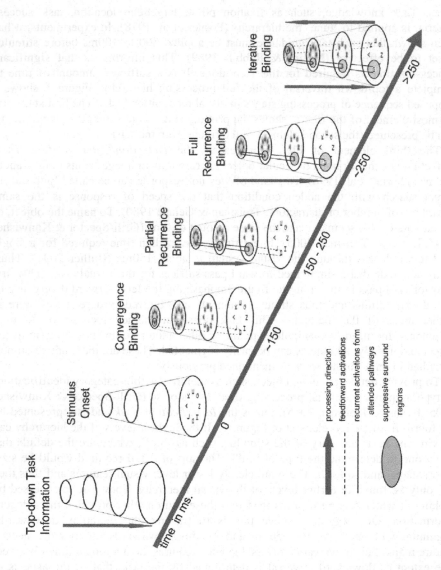

Fig. 1. The time course of visual recognition stages with types of visual binding required for each

thus additional time is required. This is called the *Localization Task*. How much time? A single saccade seems to require 200ms (with a range of 100-300ms) of processing time (Becker 1991). A lever press response seems to need 250-450ms in monkey (Mehta et al. 2000). During this task, the temporal pattern of attentional modulation shows a distinct top-down pattern over a period of 35 - 350ms post-stimulus. The 'attentional dwell time' needed for relevant objects to become available to influence behavior seems to be about 250ms (Duncan et al. 1994). Pointing to a target in humans seems to need anywhere from 230 to 360ms (Gueye et al. 2002; Lünenburger & Hoffman 2003). Still, none of these experiments cleanly separate visual processing time from motor processing time; as a result, these results can only provide an encouraging guide for the basic claim of our model and further experimental work is needed.

Behavior, i.e., an action relevant to the stimulus, requires localization. The location details are available only in the earliest layers of the visual processing hierarchy because that is where the finest spatial resolution of neural representation can be found. As a result, the top-down traversal initiated for the Identification Task must complete so that is reaches these earliest layers as shown in the figural element second from the right in Fig. 1.

All of the above tasks as described can be characterized by stimuli that are well separated, can be easily segregated from the background, and are in an important sense, simple. In most real world scenes and many more complex experimental displays, even more time is needed. The *Hard Recognition Task* includes difficult conjunction searches, resolving illusory conjunctions, determining transparency, recognizing objects in cluttered scenes, and more (Treisman & Gelade 1980; Treisman & Schmidt 1982; Wolfe 1998; Schoenfeld et al. 2003). The final element of the figure, the rightmost element, depicts the start of a second feed-forward pass to illustrate this. The idea is that it is likely that several iterations of the entire process, feed-forward and feedback, may be required to solve difficult tasks.

4 The Visual Feature Binding Problem

Following Roskies (1999), the canonical example of binding is the one suggested by Rosenblatt in which one sort of visual feature, such as an object's shape, must be correctly associated with another feature, such as its location, to provide a unified representation of that object. Such explicit association ("binding") is particularly important when more than one visual object is present, in order to avoid incorrect combinations of features belonging to different objects, otherwise known as "illusory conjunctions" (Treisman & Schmidt 1982). Binding is a broad problem: visual binding, auditory binding, binding across time, cross-modal binding, cognitive binding of a percept to a concept, cross-modal identification and memory reconstruction.

Classical demonstrations of binding seem to rely on two things: the existence of representations in the brain that have no location information, and, representations of pure location for all stimuli. However, there is no evidence for a representation of location independent of any other information. Similarly, there is no evidence for a representation of feature without a receptive field. Nevertheless, location is *partially* abstracted away within a hierarchical representation as part of the solution to complexity (Tsotsos 1990). A single neuron receives converging inputs from many receptors and each receptor provides input for many neurons. Precise location is lost in such a network of diverging feed-forward paths yet increasingly larger convergence onto single neurons. How can location be recovered and connected to the right features and objects as binding seems to require?

We might begin by developing requirements for the solution of the binding problem. Define the binding task as requiring the solution of three sub-problems: Detection (is a given object/event present in the display?), Localization (location and spatial extent of detected object/event) and Attachment (explicit object/event links to its constituent components). We will be able to recognize a solution when an algorithm can correctly provide correct answers to the above, and this occurs in images that: a) contain more than one copy of a given feature each at different locations; b) contain more than one object/event each at different locations; and, c) contain objects/events that are composed of multiple features and share at least one feature type.   These constraints provide us with a way of designing solutions and testing them with well-defined success criteria. They also provide constraints on what kinds of stimuli and tasks actually require binding in the first place. They will be used in the next section to suggest solutions to the kinds of binding that the different stages of recognition require. Previous proposals for the binding problem (see Roskies 1999) have not dealt with such constraints on the definition of the problem and this points to the uniqueness of the present proposal.

5   The Kinds of Binding Needed for the Stages of Recognition

A novel set of four different binding processes are introduced that are claimed to suffice for solving the recognition tasks described above.

Convergence Binding achieves the *Detection/Categorization Task* via hierarchical neural convergence, layer by layer, in order to determine the strongest responding neural representations at the highest layers of the processing hierarchy. This feed-forward traversal follows the task-modulated neural pathways through the 'tuned' visual processing hierarchy. This is consistent with previous views on this problem (Treisman 1999; Reynolds & Desimone 1999). This type of binding will suffice only when the abstraction achieved as a result of neural convergence does not obscure location or feature information that may be needed, and if stimulus elements do not lead to ambiguity at the higher levels due to the large receptive fields. That is, stimulus elements that fall within the larger receptive fields must not be too similar or otherwise interfere with the response of the neuron to its ideal tuning properties. Such interference may be thought of as 'noise' with the target stimulus being 'signal'. Convergence binding provides neither method for reducing this noise nor a method for recovering precise location. According to the requirements for a binding solution, this is not strictly an example of binding; it is named so here for continuity with past literature.

Full Recurrence Binding achieves the *Localization Task*. If Convergence Binding is followed by a complete top-down traversal, attended stimuli in each feature map of the hierarchical representation can be localized. Recurrent (or feedback) traversals through the visual processing hierarchy 'trace' the pathways of neural activity that lead to the strongest responding neurons at the top of the hierarchy resulting from the feed-forward traversal. Even for the strongest responding neurons with very large receptive fields where a number of stimulus elements fall within that receptive field, the reason why that response is strong lies within that receptive field and can be found.

There is one more critical component of the top-down traversal, appearing on the figures as gray regions indicating areas of neural suppression or inhibition in the area surrounding the attended stimulus. This area is defined by the projection of the receptive field of the neuron that best describes the stimulus through the processing hierarchy. That is, it is the set of neural pathways that feed that neuron. The reason for this particular definition stems from the previous discussion on signal versus noise in the input scene. Inputs corresponding to the stimulus most closely matching the tuning characteristics of the neuron form the signal while the remainder of the inputs is the noise. Any lateral connections are also considered as noise for this purpose. Thus, if it can be determined what those signal elements are, the remainder of the receptive field is suppressed, enhancing the overall signal-to-noise ratio of processing for that neuron. The method for achieving this was first described in (Tsotsos 1993) and fully detailed together with proofs of convergence and other properties in (Tsotsos et al. 1995). It is based on the assumption that the signal is defined by the strongest responses in each layer and within the receptive field of the neuron or neurons selected at the top of the hierarchy (again by strongest response).

However, the top-down process is complicated by the fact that each neuron within any layer may receive input from more than one feature representation. How do the different representations contribute to the selection? Different features may have different roles. For example, there are differing representations for many different values of object velocity however an object can only exhibit one velocity. These different representations can be considered as mutually exclusive, so the top-down search process must select one, the strongest. On the other hand, there are features that cooperate, such as the features that make up a face (nose, eyes, etc.). These contribute to the neuron in a weighted sum manner and the top-down search process much select appropriate elements from each. There may be other roles as well. The key here is that each neuron may have a complex set of inputs, specific to its tuning properties, and the top-down traversal must be specific to each. This is accomplished by allowing the choices to be made locally, at each level, as if there were a localized saliency representation for each neuron (Tsotsos et al. 2005). There is no global representation of saliency in this model.

If the full recurrence binding process does not complete for any reason, this is called *Partial Recurrence Binding*. Partial recurrence binding can find the additional information needed to solve the *Identification Task* if it is represented in intermediate layers of the processing hierarchy. If this is not deployed directly due to task needs but is due to interruption, then this results in illusory conjunctions. A variety of different effects may be observed depending on when during the top-down traversal the process is interrupted.

Iterative Binding is needed for the *Hard Detection Task*, i.e., discrimination, description, search, etc. Iterative Binding is defined as one of more Convergence Binding-Full Recurrence Binding cycles. The processing hierarchy may be tuned for the task before each traversal as appropriate. The iteration terminates when the task is satisfied. This iterative feed-forward-feedback cycle was first described in Tsotsos 1990.

Simulations of this strategy show strong agreement with a variety of psychophysical and neurophysiologic experiments such as static visual searches of varying difficulties, segregation of transparent dot pattern motions, surround inhibition, and more (Rothenstein & Tsotsos 2006; Rodriguez-Sanchez et al. 2006; Tsotsos et al. 2005; Tsotsos et al. 1995). In particular the surround inhibition prediction seems well supported by a variety of experimental studies (Cutzu & Tsotsos 2003: Hopf et al. 2005: Tombu & Tsotsos 2007). The top-down attentional modulation hypothesis also proposed by Selective Tuning has strong support (Mehta et al. 2000; O'Connor et al. 2002).

6 Conclusion

A novel view of how attention, visual feature binding, and recognition are inter-related has been presented. It differs from any of those presented previously (Roskies 1999). The greatest point of departure is that it provides a way to integrate binding by convergence with binding depending on attention. The visual binding problem is decomposed into four kinds of processes each being tied to one of the classes of recognition behaviors that have been investigated experimentally over the past decades that are defined by task and time course. This view differs from conventional wisdom that considers both binding and recognition as monolithic tasks. The decomposition has the promise of dividing and conquering these problems, and the Selective Tuning strategy previously presented is proposed as the computational substrate for their solution. There are three basic ideas behind this solution:

- top-down task directed priming before processing;
- feed-forward traversal through the 'tuned' visual processing hierarchy
   following the task-modulated neural pathways;
- recurrent (or feedback) traversals through the visual processing hierarchy that
   'trace' the pathways of neural activity that lead to the strongest responding
   neurons at the top of the hierarchy that result form the feed-forward traversal.

These three basic steps are used in combination, and repeated, as needed to solve the given visual task. The details of how exactly these processes may be accomplished are detailed elsewhere (Tsotsos 1990; Tsotsos et al. 1995; Tsotsos et al. 2005). In simulation with artificial as well as real images as input, the model exhibits good agreement with a wide variety of experimental observations.

The model has a number of important characteristics: a particular time course of events during the recognition process covering the simplest to complex stimuli that can be directly compared with experimental time courses; an iterative use of the same visual processing hierarchy in order to deal with the most complex stimuli; iterative tuning of the same visual processing hierarchy specific to task requirements; suppressive surrounds due to attention that assist with difficult segmentations; a particular time course of events for recognition ranging from simple to complex recognition tasks; a top-down localization process for attended stimuli based on tracing feed-forward activations guided by localized saliency computations. Each of these may be considered a prediction for human or non-human primate vision. It would be very interesting to explore each.

Acknowledgments

Research support was gratefully received from NSERC, CFI/OIT and the Canada Research Chairs Program.

References

Becker, W.: Saccades. In: Carpenter, R.H.S. (ed.) Eye Movements, pp. 95–137. CRC Press, Boca Raton, USA (1991)

Broadbent, D.: Perception and communication. Pergamon Press, NY (1958)

Bullier, J.: Integrated Model of Visual Processing. Brain Research Reviews 36, 96–107 (2001)

Cutzu, F., Tsotsos, J.K.: The selective tuning model of visual attention: Testing the predictions arising from the inhibitory surround mechanism. Vision Research 43, 205–219 (2003)

Deutsch, J., Deutsch, D.: Attention: Some theoretical considerations. Psych. Review 70, 80–90 (1963)

Desimone, R., Duncan, J.: Neural mechanisms of selective visual attention. Ann. Rev. of Neuroscience 18, 193–222 (1995)

Duncan, J.: Selective attention and the organization of visual information. J. Exp. Psychol. Gen. 113(4), 501–517 (1984)

Duncan, J., Ward, J., Shapiro, K.: Direct measurement of attentional dwell time in human vision. Nature 369, 313–315 (1994)

Eriksen, C., James, J.S.: Visual attention within and around the field of focal attention: a zoom lens model. Percept. Psychophys. (4), 225–240 (1986)

Evans, K., Treisman, A.: Perception of Objects in Natural Scenes: Is It Really Attention Free? J. Experimental Psychology: Human Perception and Performance 31(6), 1476–1492 (2005)

Grill-Spector, K., Kanwisher, N.: Visual recognition: As soon as you know it is there, you know what it is. Psychological Science 16, 152–160 (2005)

Gueye, L., Legalett, E., Viallet, F., Trouche, E., Farnarier, G.: Spatial Orienting of Attention: a study of reaction time during pointing movement. Neurophysiologie Clinique 32, 361–368 (2002)

Hopf, J.-M., Boehler, C.N., Luck, S.J., Tsotsos, J.K., Heinze, H.-J., Schoenfeld, M.A.: Direct neurophysiological evidence for spatial suppression surrounding the focus of attention in vision. PNAS 103(4), 1053–1058 (2006)

James, W.: The Principles of Psychology, H. Holt (1890)

Lünenburger, L., Hoffman, K.-P.: Arm movement and gap as factors influencing the reaction time of the second saccade in a double-step task. European J. Neuroscience 17, 2481–2491 (2003)

Marr, D.: Vision: A Computational Investigation into the Human Representation and Processing of Visual Information. Henry Holt and Co., New York (1982)

Treue, S., Martinez-Trujillo, J.: Feature-based attention influences motion processing gain in macaque visual cortex. Nature 399(6736), 575–579 (1999)

Mehta, A., Ulbert, I., Schroeder, C.: Intermodal selective attention in monkeys. I: distribution and timing of effects across visual areas. Cerebral Cortex 10(4), 343–358 (2000)

Milner, P.: A model for visual shape recognition. Psych. Rev. 81, 521–535 (1974)

Müller, H., Rabbitt, P.: Reflexive and Voluntary Orienting of Visual Attention: Time course of activation and resistance to interruption. J. Exp. Psychology: Human Perception and Performance 15, 315–330 (1989)

Norman, D.: Toward a theory of memory and attention. Psych. Review 75, 522–536 (1968)

O'Connor, D., Fukui, M., Pinsk, M., Kastner, S.: Attention modulates responses in the human lateral geniculate nucleus. Nature Neuroscience 5(11), 1203–1209 (2002)

Posner, M.I., Nissen, M., Ogden, W.: Attended and unattended processing modes: The role of set for spatial locations. In: Pick, Saltzmann (eds.) Modes of Perceiving and Processing Information, pp. 137–158. Erlbaum, Hillsdale, NJ (1978)

Reynolds, J., Desimone, R.: The Role of Neural Mechanisms of Attention in Solving the Binding Problem. Neuron 24, 19–29 (1999)

Rizzolatti, G., Riggio, L., Dascola, I., Umilta, C.: Reorienting attention across the horizontal and vertical meridians - evidence in favor of a premotor theory of attention. Neuropsychologia 25, 31–40 (1987)

Rodriguez Sanchez, A., Simine, E., Tsotsos, J.K.: Feature Conjunctions in Serial Visual Search. In: Int. Conf. Artificial Neural Networks, Athens, Greece (September 10-14, 2006)

Roskies, A.: The Binding Problem - Introduction. Neuron 24, 7–9 (1999, 1999b)

Rothenstein, A., Tsotsos, J.K.: Selective Tuning: Feature Binding Through Selective Attention. In: Int. Conf. Artificial Neural Networks, Athens, Greece (September 10-14, 2006)

Schoenfeld, M., Tempelmann, C., Martinez, A., Hopf, J.-M., Sattler, C., Heinze, H.-J., Hillyard, S.: Dynamics of feature binding during object-selective attention. Proc. National Academy of Sciences 100(20), 11806–11811 (2003)

Shulman, G., Remington, R., McLean, J.: Moving Attention through Visual Space. J. Experimental Psychology 92, 428–431 (1979)

Sutherland, S.: Feature Selection. Nature 392, 350 (1998)

Thorpe, S., Fize, D., Marlot, C.: Speed of processing in the human visual system. Nature 381, 520–522 (1996)

Tombu, M., Tsotsos, J.K.: Attending to orientation results in an inhibitory surround in orientation space. Perception & Psychophysics (to appear, 2007)

Treisman, A.: The effect of irrelevant material on the efficiency of selective listening. American J. Psychology 77, 533–546 (1964)

Treisman, A.M., Gelade, G.: A feature-integration theory of attention. Cognitive Psychology 12(1), 97–136 (1980)

Treisman, A., Schmidt, H.: Illusory conjunctions in the perception of objects. Cognitive Psychology 14, 107–141 (1982)

Treisman, A.: Solutions to the Binding Problem: Progress through Controversy and Convergence. Neuron 24(1), 105–125 (1999)

Tsotsos, J.K.: A Complexity Level Analysis of Vision. Behavioral and Brain Sciences 13, 423–455 (1990)

Tsotsos, J.K.: An Inhibitory Beam for Attentional Selection. In: Harris, L., Jenkin, M. (eds.) Spatial Vision in Humans and Robots, pp. 313–331. Cambridge University Press, Cambridge (1993)

Tsotsos, J.K., Culhane, S., Wai, W., Lai, Y., Davis, N., Nuflo, F.: Modeling visual attention via selective tuning. Artificial Intelligence 78(1-2), 507–547 (1995)

Tsotsos, J.K., Liu, Y., Martinez-Trujillo, J., Pomplun, M., Simine, E., Zhou, K.: Attending to Motion. Computer Vision and Image Understanding 100(1-2), 3–40 (2005)

Wolfe, J.M.: Visual Search. In: Pashler, H. (ed.) Attention, pp. 13–74. Psychology Press Ltd., Hove, UK (1998)

The Bayesian Draughtsman: A Model for Visuomotor Coordination in Drawing

Ruben Coen Cagli[1], Paolo Coraggio[1],
Paolo Napoletano[2], and Giuseppe Boccignone[2]

[1] DSF, Robot Nursery Laboratory - Università di Napoli Federico II
via Cintia, Napoli, Italy
{coen,pcoraggio}@na.infn.it
[2] Natural Computation Lab
DIIIE - Università di Salerno
via Ponte Don Melillo, 1 Fisciano (SA), Italy
{pnapoletano,boccig}@unisa.it

Abstract. In this article we present a model of realistic drawing accounting for visuomotor coordination, namely the strategies adopted to coordinate the processes of eye and hand movement generation, during the drawing task. Starting from some background assumptions suggested by eye-tracking human subjects, we formulate a Bayesian model of drawing activity. The resulting graphical model is shaped in the form of a Dynamic Bayesian Network that combines features of both the Input–Output Hidden Markov Model and the Coupled Hidden Markov Model, and provides an interesting insight on mechanisms for dynamic integration of visual and proprioceptive information.

1 Introduction

It has been argued that the function of art and the function of the visual brain are one and the same, and that the aims of art constitute an extension of the functions of the brain [1]. In this article we address a broader picture: that of art making as an extension of visuomotor coordination.

We consider realistic drawing, that is the activity of representing an *original scene* by means of visible traces on a surface (the *canvas*), trying to render the contours defining objects/regions within the scene as faithfully as possible on the canvas. Subjects involved with this task clearly adopt a visuomotor strategy; further, even though strategies can vary significantly among individuals, interesting regularities can be observed.

In a more general view, the issue we address here is at the crossing edge of most current research in neuroscience, Active Vision, and Artificial Intelligence: the understanding and the modeling of strategies adopted by any agent situated in the world to coordinate vision and action in order to succeed in a performing a given task.

Sensorimotor coordination has been treated in the framework of either *motor control* (with or without feedback) or *active perception*. Sensorimotor models

F. Mele et al. (Eds.): BVAI 2007, LNCS 4729, pp. 161–170, 2007.

usually reflect the functional architecture of the primate cortico-cerebellar system [4]. Most successful ones cast the issue of movement planning and execution as an optimization problem [5]. In such framework the sensory apparatus is always considered as passive.

On the other hand, in the case of active vision, the object of study is the overt attentional process, namely how sensory resources are allocated, e.g. via eye movements (*saccades*). Models have been proposed that reflect the functional organization of the primate visual system, and generate saccades on the basis of image properties alone [7] or combined with top–down cognitive influences [8].

As opposed to motor control research, eye tracking research [9,10] has shown that most fixations are targeted to extract information that is relevant to the motor execution of the task. Further, most recent results suggest that spatial attention is the consequence of motor preparation (premotor theory of attention [12]). Yet, we lack a well defined framework for integrating active vision models with feedback motor control strategies.

In this article we present a computational model of realistic drawing accounting for visuomotor coordination, namely strategies adopted to coordinate the processes of eye and hand movement generation, during the drawing task. The model extends a previous one [3], whose aim was to simulate the scanpath of the draughtsman, and is formulated in terms of a Bayesian generative model and its corresponding graphical model, a novel kind of Dynamic Bayesian Network (DBN).

The rationale behind the adoption of a probabilistic framework grounds in the fact that signals in sensory and motor systems are corrupted by variability and noise, and the nervous system needs to estimate these states [6].

Background assumptions of the model rely upon eye-tracking experiments with human subjects, some of which are presented in the following Section.

2   Basic Assumptions and Behavioral Analysis

Eye tracking experiments on draughtsmen at work [2] provide evidence of two nested execution cycles: the longer, external cycle is an oscillation between periods when the hand is not drawing and globally distributed eye movements can be observed, and periods when the hand is *tracing*; within the tracing period a shorter nested cycle can be noticed, with eye movements localized alternately in small parts of the scene and the canvas.

Further analysis [3] indicates that four main subtasks should be distinguished: 1) Segmentation of the original scene; 2) Evaluation of the emerging result; 3) Feature extraction for motion planning; 4) Visual feedback for motion control.

The oscillation between local and global scanpaths may be understood by recalling that gaze–shifts can be considered as the motor realization of overt shifts of attention. Visual attention arises from the activation of those same circuits that process sensory and motor data [12]. In particular, selective attention for spatial locations is related to the dorsal visual stream that has been named *action pathway* after Goodale and Humprey [11], and is mainly devoted to trigger prompt actions in response to environmental varying conditions (*Vision for Action*). On the contrary, selective attention for objects derives from activation of ventral cortical areas involved in the *perception pathway*, responsible for object recognition, with tight integration to high–level, cognitive tasks of frontal areas (*Vision for Perception*,[11]). Clearly, the two pathways are not segregated but cooperate/compete to provide a coherent picture of the world and gaze control is the ultimate product of such integration.

In this framework behaviors 1 and 2, that require globally distributed eye movements, could be associated to the Vision for Perception stream, while 3 and 4 produce localized eye movements related to the Vision for Action stream. Thus, the oscillation can be seen as a part of a high level strategy, which takes advantage of the functional architecture of the human visual system to keep separate two classes of visual behaviors, the first of which is global in nature and perceptual in purpose, while the second is local and pragmatic, sub-serving a precise hand movement.

In this article we will focus exclusively on subtasks 3 and 4, since tightly coupling vision (eye movements) and action (hand drawing). Thus, in the following we take for granted that the viewed scene has been already segmented in a finite set of objects (cf. [3])

Three assumptions can be introduced to capture the essential features that distinguish drawing from other tasks [3].

1. *All fixations on an object are executed within a time interval in which no fixations occur on other objects.*
2. *Fixations are distributed among the original objects according to the number of salient points on each object, and on each single object following the distribution of most salient points.*
3. *The sequence of fixations on the original scene is constrained to maximize continuity of tracing hand movements.*

The first assumption states that a peculiar feature of the drawing behavior is that the gaze does not move back and forth among different objects, but proceeds sequentially. Gaze is directed to an object only when it becomes relevant to the task, i.e. during the time that it is being copied.

Salient points can be defined as those with local orientation contrast [7] above a given threshold and the second assumption requires the draughtsman to move the gaze towards all salient points. This implies a segmentation which is finer than the initial object-based segmentation and is directly related to pragmatic sensorimotor control.

Third assumption implies that feedback information on hand motion plays an important role in determining the actual scanpath. One possible implication is that the scanpath on the original scene should resemble a coarse–grained edge following along the contours of the objects, which has never been observed in the eye–tracking literature up to the best of our knowledge.

2.1 Experiments with Eye-Tracked Subjects

We performed eye tracking experiments on three subjects who were given the instruction to make realistic drawings of simple bidimensional shapes. Fig. 1 illustrates the experimental set-up (cf., Appendix A, for details).

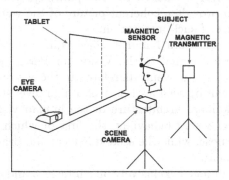

Fig. 1. Experimental setup for eye tracking recordings during the drawing task. The Subject sits in front of a vertical Tablet. In the left half of the Tablet hand–drawn images are displayed, while the Subject is instructed to copy the images the right half. The eye tracker integrates data from the Eye Camera and the Magnetic Sensor and Transmitter; eye position is then superimposed on the Scene Camera video stream, which takes the approximate subjective point of view.

Due to space constraints, here we do not present the complete data analysis, but focus on those aspects directly related to the hypotheses.

In one of the trials the image displayed was composed by two closed contours that are spatially separated (Fig. 2(a)). From qualitative analysis it resulted that all the subjects started drawing the second object only after completion of the first one. Thus we defined, for each subject, two time intervals, T_1 and T_2, corresponding to the two drawing phases, and two Regions Of Interest (ROI), R_1 and R_2, each one containing one object. Fig. 3 shows, for each subject, the distribution of the number of fixations on the original image (F), over the three regions OFF, R_1, R_2. In accordance with assumption 1, the maximum of the distribution is always in the region corresponding to the time interval considered, and the percentage of F in the *wrong* region is always below 13%.

Analysis of the same trial shows also agreement with hypothesis 2, as appears from the comparison, for each subject, of the saliency map (Fig. 2(e)) of the original image with the x–y plot (Fig. 2(b), 2(c), 2(d)) of the fixations for the complete trial, and the fixation map (Fig. 2(f), 2(g), 2(h)).

Finally, the temporal sequence of fixations is addressed in Fig. 4. It shows for each subject, the cumulative x–y plot of fixations at increasing times after the beginning of a trial with curve shape, which provides evidence that the scanpath on the original image can be well described as a coarse grained edge following.

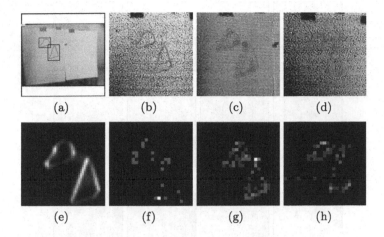

Fig. 2. Figures 2(a) and 2(e) show respectively the Regions Of Interest and the saliency map in the two objects trial. For each subject (columns 2–4) we show the x–y plot (2(b), 2(c), 2(d)) of the fixations (circles) and the fixation map (2(f), 2(g), 2(h)).

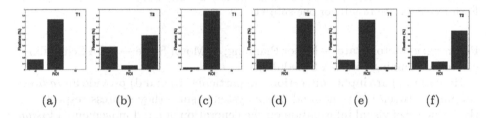

Fig. 3. Distribution of the number of fixations over three regions (outside, R1 or R2). Each couple of plots refer to time intervals T1 and T2 for one subject.

3   The Model

The model accounts for the sensorimotor coupling between the Vision for Action stream and the motor system and is based on four core modules and their interactions.

Top-down FOA scheduling produces appropriate plans for generating gaze-shifts, while *Motor Planning* drives hand movement planning. The *Action* and *Motor State* modules play the role of generating suitable sensory inputs to the planning modules, respectively providing information extracted from the visual input along the visual dorsal stream, and information about the state of the hand on the basis of proprioception. Here we are not concerned with how such inputs are generated, but only with how they contribute to the joint planning of eye and hand movements.

The tight interplay between saccades and hand movements is provided by the following cross-connections: a) Action → FOA Scheduling; b) Action → Motor

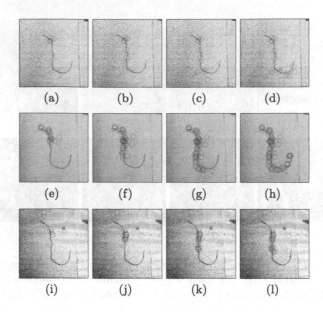

Fig. 4. Cumulative x–y plot of fixations (circles) at increasing times (left to right). Each rowshows the results for one subject.

Planning; c) Motor State → Motor Planning; d) Motor State → FOA Scheduling; e) Motor Planning ↔ FOA Scheduling.

Here a) to d) are input connections: in particular b) and d) provide an *indirect* coupling between the visual and motor systems, since they express respectively the influence of visual information on the generation of hand movements (*Vision For Action*), and the influence of proprioceptive information on the state of the hand in generating a saccade (*Proprioceptive Feedback*).

The bidirectional connection e) represents the *direct* reciprocal influence of eye and hand motor plans, which must unfold in time appropriately to preserve a task–specific causal relation between eye and hand movements. We call the two directions of such connection *Eye To Hand* (E2H) – i.e. the process of generating a saccade on the basis of the previous hand plan –, and *Hand To Eye* (H2E) – the generation of a hand movement on the basis of previous saccades.

Figure 5 outlines the functional model at a glance. In the same figure, the information flow between modules is represented via dotted lines. Inputs and outputs are formally identified in terms of the following variables:

- u: the input for eye and hand movement planning processes; it concerns information regarding the perceived current position of the hand (fusing visual and proprioceptive data) and features extracted from the portion of the original image corresponding to the previous fixation;
- x^e: the state of the eye movement process, encoding the planned eye movement as a displacement vector relative to the current fixation point;
- y^e: the eye–movement output, encoding the performed displacement;

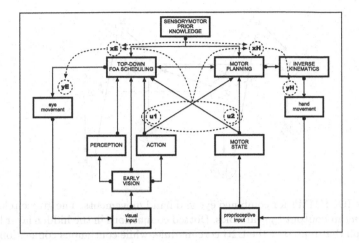

Fig. 5. The functional architecture: each module (box) can be seen as an implementation of a specific process. Overlaid (dotted lines), the underlying graphical model, which will be explicitly represented in Fig. 6.

- $\mathbf{x^h}, \mathbf{y^h}$; the state and output of the hand–movement process, analogous to eye state and output variables;

Indeed, the computational problem we want to solve is the joint evaluation of eye and hand movement state at a given time.

To this end, we resort to a probabilistic Bayesian framework and consider the values of such variables as realizations of corresponding random variables. This way we can map the functional model outlined in Fig. 5 into the graphical model shown in Fig.6, where nodes denote the random variables, and arrows, conditional dependencies. Note that, since we are dealing with a process unfolding in time, the network is in the form of a Dynamical Bayesian Network (DBN [13]) and the graph depicted in Fig 6 pictures two temporal slices.

Notice that, within each time slice, we assume a causal relation (directed edge) from eye movement to hand movement; this reflects the behavior we observed in the experiments on the drawing task, where most fixations could be classified as *look–ahead* [9], i.e. with the gaze moving to a location where the hand will move shortly after.

In such framework, the input streams a) to d) can be treated as conditioning both planning processes by a single variable (the arrows out of the upper circle in figure 6).

This way, the H2E process, which accounts for the probability of the current fixation conditional on previous fixation and hand movement, can be formally modeled as the probability distribution $p(x^e_{t+1}|u_{t+1}, x^e_t, x^h_t)$. Similarly, we can write E2H, which considers the probability of the current hand movement given the current fixation and the previous hand movement, as $p(x^h_{t+1}|u_{t+1}, x^e_{t+1}, x^h_t)$.

Both terms denote *state–transition* probabilities, and represent the core modules H2E and E2H respectively, enriched with the input.

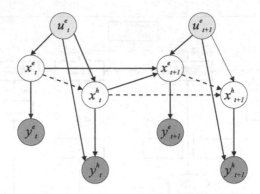

Fig. 6. The IOCHMM's for combined eye and hand movements. The gray circles denote the input (u) and output (y) variables. Dotted connections in the hidden layer highlight the subgraph that represent the E2H core module, while continuous connections denote H2E.

By considering again the dependencies in the graphical model, we can write the statistical dependence of the eye output signal on the corresponding state variable as the distribution $p(y_{t+1}^e | x_{t+1}^e)$; similarly for the output hand movement, we can write the density $p(y_{t+1}^h | u_{t+1}, x_{t+1}^h)$ which also depends on the input value. Both represent the *emission* probability distributions.

Eventually, by generalizing the time slice snapshot of Fig. to a time interval $[1, T]$ we can write the joint distribution of the state and output variables, conditioned on the input variables as:

$$p(\bar{x}_{1:T}, \bar{y}_{1:T} | \bar{u}_{1:T}) = p(x_1^e | u_1)p(y_1^e | x_1^e)p(x_1^h | u_1, x_1^e)p(y_1^h | u_1, x_1^h)$$

$$\cdot \prod_{t=1}^{T-1} \Big[p(x_{t+1}^e | u_{t+1}, x_t^e, x_t^h)p(y_{t+1}^e | x_{t+1}^e)$$

$$\cdot p(x_{t+1}^h | u_{t+1}, x_{t+1}^e, x_t^h)p(y_{t+1}^h | u_{t+1}, x_{t+1}^h) \Big] \quad , \quad (1)$$

where $\bar{u}_{1:T}$ denotes the input sequence from $t = 1$ to T, $\bar{x}_{1:T}$ denotes the pair of state sequences $(x_{1:T}^e, x_{1:T}^h)$, and similarly for $\bar{y}_{1:T}$.

4 Discussion and Final Remarks

The formalization provided in the previous Section, seems to suggest that visuomotor coordination requires a regular switching in time between the two modalities E2H and H2E, which depends on input and outputs; this results in a DBN graphical model that unifies two kinds of DBNs known in the literature, the Input–Output Hidden Markov Model and the Coupled Hidden Markov Model [13]. We call the DBN represented in Fig. 6) an *Input–Output Coupled Hidden Markov Model* (IOCHMM).

It is worth noting, though beyond the scope of this article, that the joint probability distribution in Eq. (1) can be further simplified in terms of mean field approximation [13]) by defining suitable potential functions, that express local dependencies among the hidden and input variables; then, standard algorithms for network learning and inference can be easily exploited [13].

Here, due to space limitation, we prefer focusing on the modeling part of our current research work, and the main result is that a Bayesian approach can be suitably adopted for sensorimotor integration in the drawing task. To the best of our knowledge this is the first attempt in this direction.

On the one hand the adoption of a Bayesian framework, allows to formalize a computational model in a principled way, by incorporating constraints and prior knowledge as derived by experimental observations of human subjects and theoretical findings in the current literature of visual spatial attention and sensorimotor coordination.

On the other hand, the model reconciles the *active vision* and the *feedback motor control* approaches and we believe that understanding how such formal model may be linked to the underlying activity in the visual and motor areas of the human brain could shed new light on the problem of visuomotor coordination in general.

Interestingly enough, the anatomical correlates for the input stream that we related to Vision For Action is the existence of several frontoparietal circuits, by means of which the outputs of the visual dorsal stream are projected from IP to oculomotor and premotor areas [12]. Conversely, we suggest that the pathway related to Proprioceptive Feedback could correspond to the portion of the cortico–cerebellar loop in which the cerebellum returns projections to cortical areas of the frontal lobe via the thalamus [4]. Further, the core connections we called E2H and H2E could find a biological justification in the existence of cortico–cortical connections among premotor and oculomotor areas.

Eventually, current research work concentrates on performing more experiments with human drawers in order to compare with preliminary results of simulations obtained via the IOCHMM prototype and its integration with the segmentation module developed in previous work.

Acknowledgments

The authors wish to express their gratitude to prof. A. Marcelli for providing eye–tracking resources, and prof. G. Trautteur for enlightening discussions.

References

1. Zeki, S.: Inner Vision. An Exploration of Art and the Brain. Oxford University Press, Oxford, UK (1999)
2. Tchalenko, J., Dempere-Marco, R., Hu, X.P., Yang, G.Z.: Eye Movement and Voluntary Control in Portrait Drawing. In: The Mind's Eye: Cognitive and Applied Aspects of Eye Movement Research, ch. 33, Elsevier, Amsterdam (2003)
3. Coen Cagli, R., Coraggio, P., Napoletano, P.: DrawBot – A Bio–Inspired Robotic Portraitist. Digital Creativity Journal (in press, 2007)

4. Ramnani, N.: The primate cortico–cerebellar system: anatomy and function. Nature Review Neuroscience 7 (2006)
5. Todorov, E., Jordan, M.: Optimal feedback control as a theory of motor coordination. Nat. Neurosci. 5, 1226–1235 (2002)
6. Kording, K.P., Wolpert, D.M.: Bayesian decision theory in sensorimotor control. Trends in Cognitive Sciences 10(7) (2006)
7. Itti, L., Koch, C.: Computational modelling of visual attention. Nature Reviews Neuroscience 2(3), 194–203 (2001)
8. Pylyshyn, Z.W.: Situating vision in the world. Trends in Cognitive Sciences 4(5) (2000)
9. Land, M., Mennie, N., Rusted, J.: Eye movements and the roles of vision in activities of daily living: making a cup of tea. Perception 28, 1311–1328 (1999)
10. Hayhoe, M.M., Ballard, D.H.: Eye Movements in Natural Behavior. Trends in Cognitive Science 9(188) (2005)
11. Goodale, M.A., Humphrey, G.K.: The objects of action and perception. Cognition 67, 181–207 (1998)
12. Rizzolatti, G., Riggio, L., Sheliga, B.M.: Space and selective attention. In: Umiltà, C., Moscovitch, M. (eds.) Attention and Performance XV, MIT Press, Cambridge (1994)
13. Murphy, K.: Dynamic Bayesian Networks: Representation, Inference and Learning. PhD dissertation, Berkeley, University of California, Computer Science Division (2002)

A   Experimental Settings

Eye scan records were obtained from three right–handed individuals, one female ages 27-33. All had normal or corrected-to-normal vision.

The experimental setup is shown in figure 1. Subjects were presented with a horizontal tablet 40 cm × 30 cm, viewed binocularly from such a distance that they could comfortably draw. Slight head movements were allowed. In the left half of the tablet hand–drawn images were displayed, while a white sheet was on the right half. The original images represented simple contours drawn by hand with a black pencil on white paper. One image per trial was shown, and the subjects were instructed to copy its contours faithfully on the right hand. These instructions did not make specific mention of eye movements and did not give constraints on the execution time.

The subject's left eye movements were recorded with a remote eye tracker (ASL Model 504) with the aid of a magnetic head tracker, with the eye position sampled at the rate of 60 Hz. The instrument can integrate eye and head data in real time and can deliver a record with an accuracy of less than 1 deg.

Independent Component Analysis of Layer Optical Flow and Its Application

Naoya Ohnishi[1] and Atsushi Imiya[2]

[1] School of Science and Technology, Chiba University, Japan
Yayoi-cho 1-33, Inage-ku, Chiba, 263-8522, Japan
ohnishi@graduate.chiba-u.jp
[2] Institute of Media and Information Technology, Chiba University, Japan
Yayoi-cho 1-33, Inage-ku, Chiba, 263-8522, Japan
imiya@faculty.chiba-u.jp

Abstract. In this paper, we present an algorithm for detecting obstacles using independent components of optical flow fields for visual navigation of a mobile robot. For the computation of optical flow, the pyramid transform of an image sequence is used for the analysis of global motion and local motion. We detect obstacles from optical flow fields at each layer in the pyramid. Therefore, our algorithm allows us to achieve both global perception and local perception for the robot vision. We show experimental results for both test image sequences and real image sequences captured by a mobile robot.

1 Introduction

In this paper, for the concurrent detection of local and global motion, we use independent components of optical flow fields on pyramidal layers. It is known that animals, insects, and human beings use the independent component of optical flow fields for visual behavior [10,17,19]. In human object recognition, the hierarchical model is proposed [3]. Furthermore, for the computation of optical flow, the pyramid transform of an image sequence is used for the analysis of global motion and local motion [2,12]. The pyramid transform generates multiple-resolution images as layered images. These layered images are used for computation of optical flow in its original images from the image in the lowest layer. This idea based on the assertion that global motion is described as the collection of local motion. We introduce the application of hierarchical image expression for motion analysis. That is, we develop an algorithm for the detection layered optical flows from a multi resolution image sequence.

The optical flow [1,6,11] is the apparent motion of successive images and is independent of the features in images, unlike edges or corner points in images. Furthermore, optical flow is considered to be fundamental information for navigation and obstacle avoidance in the context of biological data processing [19]. Therefore, the use of optical flow is valid for ground-plane detection by a mobile robot in an environment. In autonomous robot navigation and autonomous car navigation in the unrestricted outdoor environments, the detection of global

F. Mele et al. (Eds.): BVAI 2007, LNCS 4729, pp. 171–180, 2007.

configuration is required for global navigation. We apply obstacle detection by optical flow to layered images derived by the pyramid transform. Therefore, we can detect obstacles as layered information. Then, our method allows the hierarchical detection of obstacles in navigation. We detect obstacles from optical flow fields at each layer in the pyramid. Therefore, our algorithm allows us to achieve global perception and local perception for the robot vision.

Independent component analysis(ICA) [8] extracts statistically independent features from signals and steel images. The optical flow field observed by a moving vision can be assumed to be a mixture of patterns in an environment [16]. In neuroscience, it is known that the medial superior temporal (MST) area performs visual motion processing. For motion cognition at the MST area in the field 7a of the brain [17,20], it is shown that independent components of optical flow are used. Therefore, ICA allows us to separate the blind source signals of optical flow into independent components. Furthermore, since the optical flow field on an image can be represented as a linear combination of independent components of optical flow[17], we can use ICA for detecting a ground plane by separating obstacles and a dominant part in an image.

The dominant planar part in an image is called the dominant plane [15]. The dominant plane corresponds to the largest planar region in an image. Using the dominant plane, the robot selects a possible region for the corridor path in a robot work space. In this paper, we assume the following constrains for robot navigation.

1. The ground plane, on which the robot moves, is the planar area.
2. The camera mounted on a mobile robot is downward-looking.
3. The robot observes the world using the camera mounted on itself for navigation.
4. The camera on the robot captures a sequence of images since the robot is moving.

These assumptions are illustrated in Fig. 1. The robot does not touch to the obstacles. Therefore, if there are no obstacles around the robot, the ground plane corresponds to the dominant plane in the image observed through the camera mounted on the mobile robot.

Statistical approaches to the optical-flow analysis have also been examined [4,18]. Fermüller et al. analyzed noise parameters of optical flow using the maximum likelihood [4]. Roth and Black developed a method for learning the spatial statistics of optical flow fields using a Markov random field model [18]. Therefore, it is appropriate to use the statistical properties of optical flow for mobile robot navigation in a real environment.

2   Optical-Flow Computation with Pyramid Transform

Setting $I(x, y, t)$ and $(\dot{x}, \dot{y})^\top$ to be the time-varying gray-scale-valued image at time t and optical flow, respectively, optical flow $(\dot{x}, \dot{y})^\top$ at each point $(x, y)^\top$ satisfies

$$I_x \dot{x} + I_y \dot{y} + I_t = 0. \tag{1}$$

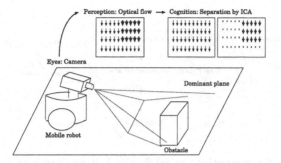

Fig. 1. Perception and cognition of motion and obstacles in the workspace by an autonomous mobile robot. The mobile robot has a camera, which corresponds to eyes. The robot perceives an optical flow field from ego-motion. By ICA, the optical flow field can be separated into the dominant plane and obstacles.

The computation of $(\dot{x}, \dot{y})^{\top}$ from $I(x, y, t)$ is an ill-posed problem. Therefore, additional constraints are required to compute $(\dot{x}, \dot{y})^{\top}$. The most commonly used constraints are those indicated by Horn and Schunck [6], Lucas and Kanade [11], and Nagel and Enkelmann [13].

Setting $I^{0}(x, y, t) = I(x, y, t)$ as the original image and $I^{l}(x, y, t)$ as the pyramid transformation of image $I(x, y, t)$ at the layer l, the pyramid representation is expressed as

$$I^{l+1}(x, y, t) = \sum_{\alpha, \beta \in N_l} a_{\alpha\beta} I^l(2x - \alpha, 2y - \beta, t), \tag{2}$$

where N_l is the neighborhood of point $(x, y)^{\top}$ at the layer l and $a_{\alpha\beta}$ is the weight parameter of the neighborhood pixel. We set N_l as a 3×3 neighborhood and

$$a_{\alpha\beta} = \begin{cases} \frac{1}{4}, & (\alpha = 0, \beta = 0) \\ \frac{1}{8}, & (\alpha = \pm 1, \beta = 0), (\alpha = 0, \beta = \pm 1) \\ \frac{1}{16}, & (\alpha = \pm 1, \beta = \pm 1) \end{cases}. \tag{3}$$

We use the Lucas-Kanade method with pyramids [2]. Therefore, Eq. (1) can be solved by assuming that the optical flow vectors of pixels are constant in the neighborhood of each pixel. We set the window size to be 5×5. Equation (1) is expressed as a system of linear equations,

$$I_{\alpha x}\dot{x} + I_{\beta y}\dot{y} + I_t = 0, \quad |\alpha| \leq 2, |\beta| \leq 2 \tag{4}$$

$$I_{\alpha\beta}(x, y, t) = I(x + \alpha, y + \beta, t + 1), \tag{5}$$

where $I_{\alpha\beta}(x, y)$ is the spatial neighborhood of a pixel. Optical flow $(\dot{x}, \dot{y})^{\top}$ is solved by the Lucas-Kanade method [11]. Setting this phase as the estimation of optical flow at the layer 0 of the pyramid representation of the image, we estimate optical flow at layers from 0 to L.

The optical flow is obtained by warping the optical flows of each layer of the pyramid representation. The procedure is illustrated in Fig. 2, which is taken

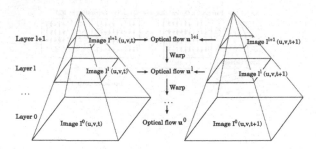

Fig. 2. Procedure for computing optical flow in L-K method with pyramids. Optical flow is obtained by integration of optical flows of each layers of pyramid representation

from to Bouguet [2]. We call $u(x, y, t)$, which is a set of optical flow $(\dot{x}, \dot{y})$ computed for all pixels in an image, the optical flow field at time t. Furthermore, we set $u^l(x, y, t)$ to be the optical flow field at the l-th layer in the pyramid transform, where $u^0(x, y, t) = u(x, y, t)$. The traditional optical flow analysis computes $u^0(x, y, t)$. We, however in this paper, use optical flow vectors in all layers in multi-resolution images. This method allow us to extract hierarchical information from optical flows.

3 Obstacle Detection Using ICA on Pyramid Layers

Our algorithm is processed at layers $l = 0, \cdots, L$ in the pyramid transform. Using the optical flow field $u^l(x, y, t)$ at the layer l, we detect obstacles in a image sequence. In this section, for the simplification, u means the optical flow field $u^l(x, y, t)$ at the layer l.

ICA is a statistical technique for separating linear combined signals into the original signals [8]. For a set of independent measures $\{x_i\}_{i=1}^n$, if $\{x_i\}_{i=1}^n$ is a linear combination of independent components $\{s_i\}_{i=1}^n$, we have the linear relation

$$X = AS, \quad \text{where } X = [x_1 \; x_2 \cdots x_n], S = [s_1 \; s_2 \cdots s_n]. \tag{6}$$

A is a matrix of the mixture coefficient. In ICA, setting W to be the inverse of A, W is estimated from $\{x_i\}_{i=1}^n$ and independent components $\{s_i\}_{i=1}^n$ are output.

$$S = WX \tag{7}$$

As previously introduced [17,20], we accept the assumption that optical flow fields observed by the moving camera are linear combinations of optical flow fields of the dominant plane and the obstacles. That is, setting u_{dominant} and u_{obstacle} to be optical flow fields of the dominant plane and the obstacles, respectively, the observed optical flow field u is approximately expressed by a linear combination of u_{dominant} and u_{obstacle} as

$$u = a_1 u_{\text{dominant}} + a_2 u_{\text{obstacle}}, \tag{8}$$

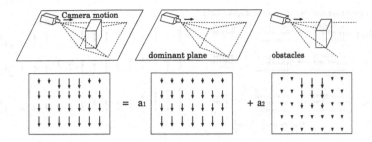

Fig. 3. Linear combination of optical flow field in the scene. The optical flow field (bottom right) is expressed as a linear combination of those shown at the bottom middle and the bottom right. a_1 and a_2 are mixture coefficients.

where a_1 and a_2 are the mixture coefficients, as shown in Fig. 3. This assumption is numerically and geometrically acceptable if motion displacement is small compared with the size of obstacles, as shown in the numerical experiment. Therefore, ICA is suitable for the separation of optical flow into the independent flow components. For each image in a sequence, we consider that optical flow vectors in the dominant plane correspond to independent components.

ICA requires at least two input signals for separation into two independent components. Then, we use optical flow field $u = \{(\dot{u}, \dot{v})_{ij}^{\top}\}_{i=1,j=1}^{h,w}$ and planar flow field $\hat{u} = \{(\hat{u}, \hat{v})_{ij}^{\top}\}_{i=1,j=1}^{h,w}$ as the input vectors of ICA for the detection of the dominant plane, where w and h are the width and the height of an image. The algorithm for estimating the planar flow field is described in [15]. Since planar flow is the motion of the dominant plane relative to the robot motion, the use of planar flow is suitable for separation into the dominant plane and obstacles.

Setting v_α and v_β to be the output optical flow fields of ICA, Eq. (6) corresponds to

$$\begin{cases} u = a_{11}v_\alpha + a_{12}v_\beta \\ \hat{u} = a_{21}v_\alpha + a_{22}v_\beta \end{cases}, \tag{9}$$

where a_{ij} is the mixture coefficient. ICA estimates independent optical flow fields v_α and v_β from optical flow fields u and planar flow fields $\hat{u}$.

The outputs v_α and v_β have ambiguity in the order of each component, since ICA has ambiguity in the order of the independent components [8]. We are required to determine whether components have optical flow of the dominant plane or of obstacle areas. We solve this problem using the difference between the variances of the norms of v_α and v_β.

Setting $l_{\alpha,\beta} = \{l_{ij}\}_{i=1,j=1}^{h,w}$ to be the norm of $v_{\alpha,\beta} = \{(\dot{u}, \dot{v})_{ij}\}_{i=1,j=1}^{h,w}$, as

$$l_{ij} = |(\dot{u}, \dot{v})_{ij}|, \tag{10}$$

and the variance σ^2 is computed as

$$\sigma^2 = \frac{1}{hw} \sum_{i=1,j=1}^{h,w} (l_{ij} - \bar{l})^2, \quad \text{where } \bar{l} = \frac{1}{hw} \sum_{i=1,j=1}^{h,w} l_{ij}. \tag{11}$$

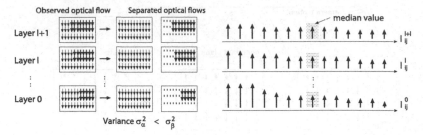

Fig. 4. Left: Difference in the motions of the dominant plane and obstacles. The dominant plane motion is smooth on the images compared with obstacle motion. Therefore,
the order of the components can be determined by using variances σ_α^2 and σ_β^2. Right:
Sorting using the norm l for determination of output order. l_{ij}^l means the norm l at
l-th layer. The area which has the median value of the component is detected as the
dominant plane, since the dominant plane occupies the largest domain in the image.

(a) I^3 (b) I^2 (c) I^1 (d) image I

Fig. 5. Pyramidal representation of the Marbled-Block images in a simulated environment

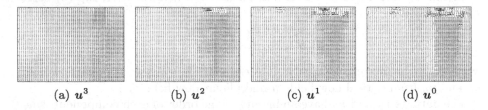

(a) $\boldsymbol{u}^3$ (b) $\boldsymbol{u}^2$ (c) $\boldsymbol{u}^1$ (d) $\boldsymbol{u}^0$

Fig. 6. The layer optical flow fields. $\boldsymbol{u}^i$ is the optical flow field from I^i in Fig. 5.

The motions of the dominant plane and obstacles in the images are different,
and the dominant-plane motion is smooth on the images compared with obstacle
motion, as shown in Fig. 4(Left). Consequently, the output signal of obstacle
motion has larger variance than the output signal of dominant-plane motion.
Therefore, if $\sigma_\alpha^1 > \sigma_\beta^2$, we use the norm l_α of output flow field $\boldsymbol{v}_\alpha$ for dominant-
plane detection; else we use the norm l_β of output flow field $\boldsymbol{v}_\beta$.

Since the planar flow field is subtracted from the optical flow field including
obstacle motion, l is constant on the dominant plane. However, the length of l
is ambiguous, because of the form of Eq. (9). Then, we use the median value

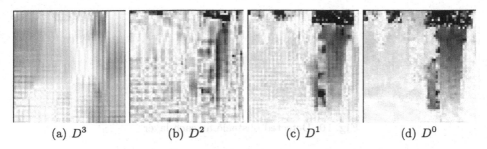

(a) D^3 (b) D^2 (c) D^1 (d) D^0

Fig. 7. Detected obstacle at each layer

(a) I^3 (b) I^2 (c) I^1 (d) Image I

Fig. 8. Pyramidal representation of captured images in a real environment

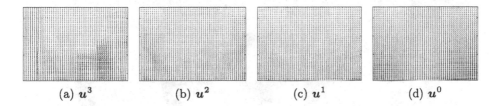

(a) $\boldsymbol{u}^3$ (b) $\boldsymbol{u}^2$ (c) $\boldsymbol{u}^1$ (d) $\boldsymbol{u}^0$

Fig. 9. The layer optical flow fields. $\boldsymbol{u}^i$ is the optical flow field from I^i in Fig. 8.

of l for the detection of the dominant plane. Since the dominant plane occupies the largest domain in the image, we compute the distance between l and the median of l, as shown in Fig. 4(Right). The area which has the median value of the component is detected as the dominant plane. Setting m to be the median value of the elements in l, the distance $\boldsymbol{d} = \{d_{ij}\}_{i=1,j=1}^{h,w}$ is

$$d_{ij} = |l_{ij} - m|. \tag{12}$$

We detect the area in which $d_{ij} \approx 0$ as the dominant plane.

4   Experimental Results

We show experimental results on the detection of obstacles in an image sequence at each layer. For the computation of optical flow, we use the Lucas-Kanade method with pyramids [2]. We set the maximum layer $L = 3$. For the visual

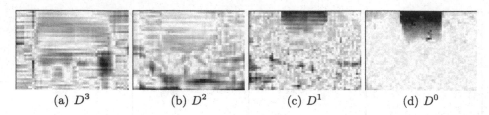

(a) D^3 (b) D^2 (c) D^1 (d) D^0

Fig. 10. Detected obstacle at each layer

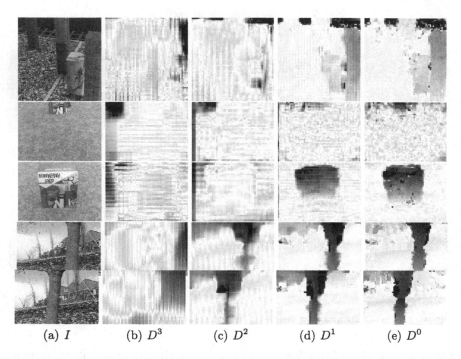

(a) I (b) D^3 (c) D^2 (d) D^1 (e) D^0

Fig. 11. Experimental results. (a) Original image. (b) (c) (d) and (e) are detected obstacles at the layers 3, 2, 1, and 0, respectively.

representation of the results of obstacle detection, the value of d_{ij} in Eq. (12) is normalized in the range from 0 to 255. The image of the detected obstacle $D^l(u, v)$ at the l-th layer is defined as

$$D^l(i, j) = \frac{d_{ij} \times 255}{\max(d_{ij}^l)}, \tag{13}$$

where d_{ij}^l is d_{ij} at the l-th layer.

The Marbled-Block image sequence and captured images in a real environment are used for the experiment. Fig. 5 shows the Marbled-Block images at each layer. The computed optical flow fields at each layer from each image are Fig. 6, respectively. Fig. 7 shows the detected obstacle at each layer. In this figure, the black and white region indicate the obstacle and dominant plane, respectively.

Fig. 8 shows the captured images in a real environment using a mobile robot. The mobile robot moved toward the obstacle in front of the robot. Figs. 9 and 10 are computed optical flow fields and detected obstacles at each layer, respectively. Another experimental results are shown in Fig. 11.

These examples show that in each layer the obstacle-regions are detected. Therefore, the algorithm detects the global configuration of obstacles from higher layer images, though the lower layer images allows us to detect the detailed configuration of obstacles. The hierarchical description of the layered obstacle-region [14] and the extraction of the navigation-direction from this hierarchical expression are future problems.

5   Conclusions

We developed an algorithm for detecting obstacles in an image sequence using independent components of optical flow fields. The optical flow fields are observed through a moving camera. The use of the ICA for the optical flow enables the robot to detect a feasible region in which robot can move without any preknowledge. The presented experimental results support the application of our method to the navigation and path planning of a mobile robot with a vision system. We processed the obstacle detection at each layer in pyramid transform. We conclude that the process emulates biological perception for visual behavior.

References

1. Barron, J.L., Fleet, D.J., Beauchemin, S.S.: Performance of optical flow techniques. International Journal of Computer Vision 12, 43–77 (1994)
2. Bouguet, J.-Y.: Pyramidal implementation of the Lucas Kanade feature tracker description of the algorithm. Intel Corporation, Microprocessor Research Labs, OpenCV Documents (1999)
3. Domenella, R.G., Plebe, A.: A neural model of human object recognition development. In: Proc. of 1st International Symposium on Brain, Vision and Artificial Intelligence, pp. 116–125 (2005)
4. Fermüller, C., Shulman, D., Aloimonos, Y.: The statistics of optical flow. Computer Vision and Image Understanding 82, 1–32 (2001)
5. van Hateren, J., van der Schaaf, A.: Independent component filters of natural images compared with simple cells in primary visual cortex. In: Proc. of the Royal Society of London. Series B, vol. 265, pp. 359–366 (1998)
6. Horn, B.K.P., Schunck, B.G.: Determining optical flow. Artificial Intelligence 17, 185–203 (1981)
7. Hurri, J., Gavert, H., Sarela, J., Hyvarinen, A.: The FastICA package for MATLAB, website: http://www.cis.hut.fi/projects/ica/fastica/
8. Hyvarinen, A., Oja, E.: Independent component analysis: algorithms and application. Neural Networks 13, 411–430 (2000)
9. Hyvarinen, A., Hoyer, P.: Topographic independent component analysis. Neural Computation 13, 1525–1558 (2001)

10. Jabri, M.A., Park, K.-Y., Lee, S.-Y., Sejnowski, T.J.: Properties of independent components of self-motion optical flow. In: Proc. of IEEE International Symposium on Multiple-Valued Logic, pp. 355–362. IEEE Computer Society Press, Los Alamitos (2000)
11. Lucas, B., Kanade, T.: An iterative image registration technique with an application to stereo vision. In: Proc. of 7th IJCAI, pp. 674–679 (1981)
12. Mahzoun, M.R., Kim, J., Sawazaki, S., Okazaki, K., Tamura, S.: A scaled multigrid optical flow algorithm based on the least RMS error between real and estimated second images. Pattern Recognition 32, 657–670 (1999)
13. Nagel, H.-H., Enkelmann, W.: An investigation of smoothness constraint for the estimation of displacement vector fields from image sequences. IEEE Transaction on PAMI 8, 565–593 (1986)
14. Ohnishi, N., Imiya, A.: Model-based plane-segmentation using optical flow and dominant plane. In: Proceedings of MIRAGE 2007. LNCS, vol. 4418, pp. 295–306. Springer, Heidelberg (2007)
15. Ohnishi, N., Imiya, A.: Dominant plane detection from optical flow for robot navigation. Pattern Recognition Letters 27, 1009–1021 (2006)
16. Ohnishi, N., Imiya, A.: Dominant plane detection using optical flow and independent component analysis. In: Proc. of 1st International Symposium on Brain, Vision and Artificial Intelligence, pp. 478–496 (2005)
17. Park, K.-Y., Jabri, M., Lee, S.-Y., Sejnowski, T.J.: Independent components of optical flows have MSTd-like receptive fields. In: Proc. of the 2nd International Workshop on ICA and Blind Signal Separation, pp. 597–601 (2000)
18. Roth, S., Black, M.J.: On the spatial statistics of optical flow. Proc. of IEEE International Conference on Computer Vision 1, 42–49 (2005)
19. Vaina, L.M., Beardsley, S.A., Rushton, S.K.: Optic flow and beyond. Kluwer Academic Publishers, Dordrecht (2004)
20. Zemel, R.S., Sejnowski, T.J.: A model for encoding multiple object motions and self-motion in area mst of primate visual cortex. Neuroscience 18, 531–547 (1998)

A Self-organizing Approach to Detection of Moving Patterns for Real-Time Applications

Lucia Maddalena[1] and Alfredo Petrosino[2]

[1] ICAR - National Research Council, Via P. Castellino 111, 80131 Naples, Italy
lucia.maddalena@na.icar.cnr.it
[2] DSA - University of Naples Parthenope, Via A. De Gasperi 5, 80133 Naples, Italy
alfredo.petrosino@uniparthenope.it

Abstract. Detection of moving objects in video streams is the first relevant step of information extraction in many computer vision applications. Aside from the intrinsic usefulness of being able to segment video streams into moving and background components, detecting moving objects provides a focus of attention for recognition, classification, and activity analysis, making these later steps more efficient. We propose an approach based on self organization through artificial neural networks, widely applied in human image processing systems and more generally in cognitive science. The proposed model allows to capture structural background variation due to periodic-like motion over a long period of time under limited memory. Our method can handle scenes containing moving backgrounds or illumination variations, and it achieves robust detection for different types of videos taken with stationary cameras. We compared our method with other modeling techniques. Experimental results, both in terms of detection accuracy and in terms of processing speed, are presented for color video sequences which represent typical situations critical for video surveillance systems.

Keywords: visual surveillance, motion detection, self organization, neural network.

1 Introduction

Visual surveillance has attracted much attention in the computer vision community due to its potential applications. The main problem in visual surveillance systems include motion detection, object classification, tracking, activity understanding, and semantic description. Motion segmentation, moving object classification, and tracking have been widely studied for many years [8,14]. Aside from the intrinsic usefulness of being able to segment video streams into moving and background components, detecting moving objects provides a focus of attention for recognition, classification, and activity analysis, making these later steps more efficient, since only moving pixels need be considered [5]. The problem is known to be significant and difficult [18]. Conventional approaches to moving object detection include temporal differencing [15], background subtraction [18], and optical flow [2].

F. Mele et al. (Eds.): BVAI 2007, LNCS 4729, pp. 181–190, 2007.
© Springer-Verlag Berlin Heidelberg 2007

Temporal differencing takes into account differences in consecutive sequence frames, which allow to discern static objects (having null differenccs) from moving objects (having non-null differences). This approach is very adaptive to dynamic environments, but it is strictly dependent on the velocity of moving objects in the scene and it is subject to the foreground aperture problem.

In contrast, optical flow techniques aim at computing an approximation to the 2D motion field (projection of the 3D velocities of surface points onto the imaging surface) from spatio-temporal patterns of image intensity [2]. They can be used to detect independently moving objects in the presence of camera motion, but most optical flow computation methods are computationally complex, and cannot be applied to full-frame video streams in real-time without specialized hardware.

Surely background subtraction is the most common and efficient method to tackle the problem for scenes from stationary cameras (e.g. [13]). It is based on the comparison of the current sequence frame with a reference background, including information on the scene without moving objects. It is independent on the velocity of moving objects and it is not subject to the foreground aperture problem, but it is extremely sensitive to dynamic scene changes due to lighting and extraneous events. Although these are usually detected, they leave behind holes where the newly exposed background imagery differs from the known background model (ghosts). While the background model eventually adapts to these holes, they generate false alarms for a short period of time.

Therefore, it is highly desirable to construct a general approach for motion detection based on the background model automatically generated by a self-organizing method without prior knowledge of the pattern classes. A possible approach consists in using biologically inspired problem-solving methods to solve motion detection tasks, typically based on visual attention mechanisms. The aim is to obtain the objects that keep the users attention in accordance with a set of predefined features, including gray level, motion and shape features. Some referenced selective attention models are reported in [1,3,9]. Following the conjecture of Backer *et al.* [1], our approach defines a method for the generation of an active attention focus on a dynamic scene to monitor a scene for surveillance purposes. We propose to adopt a self-organizing method for learning motion patterns represented by trajectories in the HSV space. By learning the trajectories and features of moving objects, the background model is built up. Based on the learned background model through a map of motion and stationary patterns, our algorithm can detect motion and update, when necessary, the background model. Specifically a novel neural network mapping method is proposed to use a whole trajectory incrementally fed as an input to the network. This makes the network structure much simpler and the learning process much more efficient. A similar model was reported in [10], where vector quantization is used to incrementally construct a codebook in order to generate a background/foreground model. Anyway, vector quantization does not take the neighborhood into consideration: when a neuron c best matches the input vector, only neuron c is excited, and all others are inhibited. According to the model reported here, the weight sensitivity is used to ensure that each neuron can be excited at some stage.

Indeed, when vector quantization is used to learn moving patterns, most neurons are not excited at the early stage of training and shift toward the center of samples just according to the weight sensitivity determined in the learning process. This slows down the speed of the network convergence and greatly affects the learning accuracy.

The paper is organized as follows. In Section 2 we describe the approach adopted for moving object detection. In Section 3 we present results obtained with the implementation of the proposed approach in terms of execution times and attained accuracy, while Section 4 includes conclusions and further research directions.

2   Modeling the Background by Self-organization

In the proposed approach the background model is based on a HSV representation of the images and a self organizing neural network, inspired by Kohonen [11]. The Kohonen self-organizing feature map usually consists of a 2-D flat grid of simple nodes. Each node j (called an output neuron) has a weight vector W_j where the i-th component of W_j is represented with $W_{i,j}$ which is the weight between the i-th component of the input vector and the j-th output neuron. The input feature vectors are presented sequentially to all of the neurons. For each input vector X, the best matching neuron c, compared with other neurons, holds the minimal Euclidean distance to X. The neighborhood is used to reflect the short range and side-feedback actions between neurons in the grid. The neurons in neighborhood NE_c of the best matching neuron c are all excited, while neurons outside neighborhood NE_c are inhibited.

In our approach, the background is encoded on a pixel-by-pixel basis. For each pixel, it builds a neuronal map consisting of nine weight vectors. Samples at each pixel are clustered into the set of weight vectors based on a HSV distance measure. Moving object detection involves testing the difference of the current image from the background model with respect to the adopted measure. If an incoming pixel is similar to the background according to such measure, it is classified as background; otherwise, it is classified as foreground. In order to allow for adaptivity of the background model and detection, the background model is updated according to running average with selectivity.

2.1   Initial Background Model

The initial background model is set to the first sequence frame; that is, each of the nine weight vectors corresponding to a pixel is initialized to the corresponding pixel of the first sequence frame.

In order to represent each weight vector, we choose the HSV colour space, which allows to specify colours in a way that is close to human experience of colours, relying on the hue, saturation and value properties of each colour. Let (r, g, b) be the RGB components (in $[0, 1]$) of the generic pixel (x, y) of the first sequence frame I_0, and let $C = (c_1, c_2, \ldots, c_9)$ be the codebook for pixel (x, y). Each weight vector $c_i, i = 1, \ldots, 9$, is a 3D vector initialized as $c_i = (h, s, v)$, i.e. the HSV components of pixel (x, y).

The complete set of weight vectors for all pixels of an image I with N rows and M columns is represented as a neuronal map A with $3N$ rows and $3M$ columns, where the weight vectors for the generic pixel (x, y) of I are at neuronal map positions (i, j), $i = 3x, \ldots, 3x + 2$ and $j = 3y, \ldots, 3y + 2$. An example of such neuronal map structure for a simple image I with $N = 2$ rows and $M = 2$ columns is given in Fig. 1. The upper left pixel a of I in Fig. 1-(a) has weight vectors $(a_1, \ldots, a_9)$ stored into the 3×3 elements of the upper left part of neuronal map A in Fig. 1-(b). Analogously, the lower right pixel f of I in Fig. 1-(a) has weight vectors $(f_1, \ldots, f_9)$ stored into the 3×3 elements of the lower right part of neuronal map A in Fig. 1-(b). This configuration allows to easily

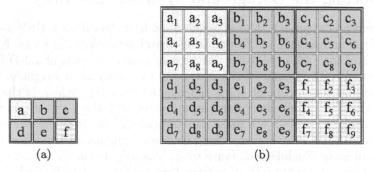

(a)   (b)

Fig. 1. A simple image (a) and the neuronal map structure (b)

take into account spatial relationship among pixels and corresponding weight vectors, and to adopt the neuronal map A as an enlarged background model for image I, as we shall see in the following subsection.

2.2   Subtraction and Update of the Background Model

By subtracting the current image from the background model, each pixel p_t of the t-th sequence frame I_t is compared to the current pixel weight vectors to determine if there exists a weight vector that best matches it. The best matching weight vector is used as the pixel's encoding approximation, and therefore p_t is detected as foreground if no acceptable matching weight vector exists; otherwise it is classified as background.

To determine which weight vector gives the best match, several metrics for detecting changes in color imagery, such as those reported in [7,16,17] and in references therein, could be adopted. Experiments drove us to employ the Euclidean distance of vectors in the HSV color hexcone adopted in [7], which gives the distance between two pixels $p_i = (h_i, s_i, v_i)$ and $p_j = (h_j, s_j, v_j)$ as:

$$d(p_i, p_j) = \|(v_i s_i \cos(h_i), v_i s_i \sin(h_i), v_i) - (v_j s_j \cos(h_j), v_j s_j \sin(h_j), v_j)\|_2.$$

Indeed, the representation of HSV values as vectors in the HSV color hexcone used in the distance measure allows to avoid problems with the periodicity of hue h and with the instability of h for small values of saturation s [7].

Weight vector c_m, for some m, gives the best match for the incoming pixel p_t if its distance from p_t is minimum in the neighborhood C of p_t and is no greater than a fixed threshold:

$$d(c_m, p_t) \min_{i=1,\ldots,9} d(c_i, p_t) \leq \epsilon. \tag{1}$$

The threshold ϵ allows to distinguish between foreground and background pixels, and suitable values range in $[0.005, 0.02]$.

In order to allow for adaptivity of the background model and detection, we update the best matching weight vector $c_m \in C$, together with all other weight vectors in a 3×3 neighborhood of the background model A, using running average with selectivity, weighted by a Gaussian filter. The updating eventually involves also weight vectors belonging to the 3×3 neighborhood of pixels adjacent to p_t, on the basis of the hypothesis that adjacent pixels move accordingly.

In details, given the incoming pixel $p_t(x, y)$ at spatial position (x, y) and time t, if there exist a best match c_m in its neighborhood C, and c_m is present in the background model as $A(\overline{x}, \overline{y})$, then weight vectors in the 3×3 neighborhood of pixel $(\overline{x}, \overline{y})$ of A are updated according to

$$A_{t+1}(i, j) = (1 - \alpha_{i,j})A_t(i, j) + \alpha_{i,j}p_t(x, y), \quad \begin{array}{l} i = \overline{x} - 1, \ldots, \overline{x} + 1, \\ j = \overline{y} - 1, \ldots, \overline{y} + 1, \end{array} \tag{2}$$

where $\alpha_{i,j} = \alpha w_{i,j}$. α represents the learning rate, whose typical value is 0.05, while $w_{i,j}$ is the Gaussian weight in the 3×3 neighborhood, that well corresponds to the lateral inhibition activity of neurons. If the best match c_m is not found, the background model A remains unchanged.

Selectivity allows to adapt the background model to scene modifications without introducing the contribution of pixels not belonging to the background scene. Moreover, weighting of neighborhood weight vectors allows to take into account spatial relationships among incoming pixel with its surrounding.

The background subtraction and update for an incoming pixel value p_t in sequence frame I_t allows to obtain the binary mask $B(x)$ defined as in the following algorithm:

HSV-SO background subtraction and update algorithm

```
Initialize codebook C for pixel p₀ and store it into A
for t=1, LastFrame
    Find best match cₘ in C to current sample pₜ as in eqn. (1)
    if (no match found) then
    B(pₜ) = foreground
    else
    B(pₜ) = background
    update A in the neighborhood of cₘ = A(x̄,ȳ) as in eqn. (2)
```

Filtering techniques (such as morphological operations) could still be needed in order to eliminate spurious pixels in the binary mask and enhance the successive phases of the video surveillance process. Moreover, shadow suppression algorithms, such as the one described in [6], can be readily inserted into HSV-SO background subtraction and update algorithm, having care of not updating the neuronal map for background pixels detected as shadows [12].

3   Experimental Results

Experimental results for moving object detection using the proposed approach have been produced for several image sequences. Here we report results obtained for two different sequences, which represent typical situations critical for video surveillance systems. Further results can be found in [12].

3.1   Data and Detection Results

The sequences adopted are named Msa and $Walk1$. The Msa sequence is an indoor sequence manually labeled, consisting of 555 frames of 320×240 spatial resolution, acquired at a frequency of 30 frames/sec. One representative frame together with obtained results is reported in Fig. 2. Here we report one of the sequence frames (Fig. 2-(a)) and the original frame with corresponding moving object detection mask computed by the HSV-SO algorithm (Fig. 2-(b)). The detection mask shows that the walking man is perfectly detected. Moreover the bag, which has been left by the man in previous frames, is still detected as an object extraneous to the background. A layering approach (not yet introduced in our system) could help the algorithm to signal the bag as a stopped object.

In Fig. 2 we also show the background model A computed by the HSV-SO algorithm (Fig. 2-(c)) and its change mask from previous frame (2-(d)). We would remark that the background model A is represented by a neuronal map whose size is 9 times greater than that of the original image I. In the reported figures they appear to have the same size only for space constraints and for an easier comparison. We can observe that the background model is a quite accurate (enlarged) representation of the real background. Small differences with the real background can be noticed only in few pixels near the column; these are due to a previous passage of the man in front of the column and the consequent only partial update of the corresponding background pixels.

The $Walk1$ sequence of the CAVIAR Project [4] is labeled and comprise 611 frames of 384×288 spatial resolution, captured at a frequency of 25 frames/sec. The sequence presents some critical factors, such as light change and mimetics. One representative frame is reported in Fig. 3-(a), while the frame with superimposed the corresponding moving object detection mask computed by the HSV-SO algorithm is reported in Fig. 3-(b). By looking at the detection mask we can observe that the man in the center of the room is perfectly detected, even though some parts of the man (such as the arm) tend to camouflage with the pavement and could have led to a partial detection. The group of persons lying close to the lower left side of the image (in the reflection on the pavement of the light coming through the windows) is partially detected. This is reasonable since such persons are barely distinguishable also for the human eye. Same observations hold for the person lying close to the plant in lower center side of the image.

(a)   (b)

(c)   (d)

Fig. 2. Results of HSV-SO algorithm on Msa sequence: (a) original frame; (b) original frame with moving object detection mask; (c) background model; (d) background model change mask from previous frame

In Fig. 3 we also show the background model A computed by the HSV-SO algorithm (Fig. 3-(c)) and its change mask from previous frame (3-(d)). We can observe that the background model is a quite accurate (enlarged) representation of the real background. The change mask of the background model shows clearly that wide areas of constant intense white (in the reflection on the pavement of the light coming through the windows) are not updated from previous frame.

3.2 Accuracy and Performance Results

In order to assess accuracy of the proposed approach and to compare it with other approaches, we adopted Recall and Precision functions computed over tp (true positives), fn (false negatives) and fp (false positives):

$$Recall = \frac{\sum tp}{\sum tp + \sum fn}; \quad Precision = \frac{\sum tp}{\sum tp + \sum fp},$$

where $(\sum tp + \sum fn)$ is the total number of objects in the *ground truth*, and $(\sum tp + \sum fp)$ is the total number of detected objects.

Results obtained with the proposed HSV-SO algorithm have been compared with those obtained with three other algorithms: *Pfinder*, *VSAM*, and *CB*. In the *Pfinder* algorithm the background model assumes that the intensity values of a pixel can be modeled by a Gaussian distribution $N(\mu, \sigma^2)$ [19]. The *VSAM* algorithm implements the approach proposed in [5], based on the integration of

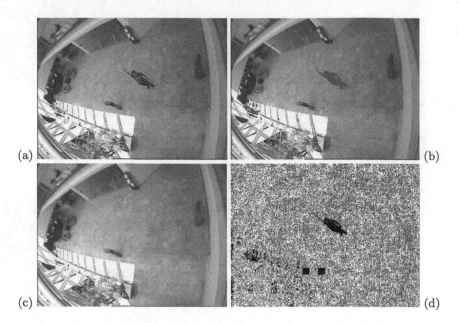

Fig. 3. Results of HSV-SO algorithm on $Walk1$ sequence: (a) original frame; (b) original frame with moving object detection mask; (c) background model; (d) background model change mask from previous frame

pixel analysis and region analysis modules to extract motion by a finite state machine; it is able to recognize when moving objects have stopped and to disambiguate overlapping objects. The CB algorithm reported in [10] has already been briefly sketched in §1. For all the considered algorithms we experimented with different settings of adjustable parameters until the results seemed optimal over the entire sequence.

From results reported in Table 1 we can observe that most of the considered algorithms perform quite well on the MSA sequence; only the Pfinder algorithm has low Recall, due to the fact that it readily incorporates into background moving objects that have stopped (the bag). From results obtained for the more challenging $Walk1$ sequence we can notice that HSV-SO performs much better than the Pfinder method, and slightly better than CB and VSAM methods.

To complete our analysis, in Table 2 we report mean execution times, in terms of msecs/frame, of the three considered algorithms on the video sequences Msa and $Walk1$ on a Pentium 4 with 2.40 GHz and 512 MB RAM, running Windows

Table 1. Precision and Recall for sequences Msa and $Walk1$

	Precision (Msa)	Recall (Msa)	Precision ($Walk1$)	Recall ($Walk1$)
HSV-SO	0.99	0.99	0.69	0.85
Pfinder	0.97	0.45	0.57	0.60
VSAM	0.98	0.99	0.82	0.68
CB	0.99	0.98	0.60	0.88

Table 2. Mean execution times (in msecs/frame) for sequences *Msa* and *Walk1*

	Mean execution times (*Msa*)	Mean execution times (*Walk1*)
HSV-SO	32.08	44.88
Pfinder	17.72	28.10
VSAM	20.47	32.42
CB	38.71	56.86

XP operating system. Execution times do not include I/O. The table shows that HSV-SO improves performance speed of CB, but is always slower than Pfinder and VSAM. Some optimization of HSV-SO could be, for instance, in terms of pruning of the not winning weight vectors, although experimental results in this direction have not yet reported appreciable improvements.

4   Conclusions and Ongoing Work

We have presented a new self-organizing method for modeling background by learning motion patterns and so allowing foreground/background separation for scenes from stationary cameras, strongly required in video surveillance systems. Unlike existing methods that use individual flow vectors as inputs, our method learns in a self organizing manner motion trajectories. This makes the neural network structure much simpler. Experimental results using two different sets of data and two different methods have demonstrated the effectiveness of the proposed algorithms.

In order to make our technique more practically useful in a visual surveillance system, we plan to improve the method by layered modeling/detection. The motivation of layered modeling and detection is to still be able to detect foreground objects against new backgrounds which were obtained during the detection phase. If we do not have those background layers, interesting foreground objects (e.g., people) will be detected mixed with other stationary object s (e.g., car). The scene can change after initial training, for example, by parked cars, displaced books, etc. These changes should be used to update the background model.

References

1. Backer, G., Mertsching, B., Bollmann, M.: Data- and Model-Driven Gaze Control for an Active-Vision System. IEEE Trans. on PAMI 23(12), 1415–1429 (2001)
2. Barron, J.L., Fleet, D.J., Beauchemin, S.S.: Performance of Optical Flow Techniques. IJCV 12(1), 42–77 (1994)
3. Cantoni, V., Marinaro, M., Petrosino, A. (eds.): Visual Attention Mechanisms. Kluwer Academic/Plenum Publishers, New York (2002)
4. CAVIAR Project: IST 2001 37540,
   http://homepages.inf.ed.ac.uk/rbf/CAVIAR/

5. Collins, R.T., Lipton, A.J., Kanade, T., Fujiyoshi, H., Duggins, D., Tsin, Y., Tolliver, D., Enomoto, N., Hasegawa, O., Burt, P., Wixson, L.: A System for Video Surveillance and Monitoring. The Robotics Institute, Carnegie Mellon University, CMU-RI-TR-00-12 (2000)

6. Cucchiara, R., Piccardi, M., Prati, A.: Detecting Moving Objects, Ghosts, and Shadows in Video Streams. IEEE Transactions on Pattern Analysis and Machine Intelligence 25(10), 1–6 (2003)

7. Fisher, R.B.: Change Detection in Color Images, 1999 (unpublished), available at http://homepages.inf.ed.ac.uk/rbf/PAPERS/iccv99.pdf

8. Haritaoglu, I., Harwood, D., David, L.S.: W4: Real-time Surveillance of People and their Activities. IEEE Trans. on PAMI 22(8), 809–830 (2000)

9. Itti, L., Koch, C., Niebur, E.: A Model of Saliency-Based Visual Attention for Rapid Scene Analysis. IEEE Trans. on PAMI 20(11), 1254–1259 (1998)

10. Kim, K., Chalidabhongse, T.H., Harwood, D., Davis, L.S.: Real-time Foreground-background Segmentation using Codebook Model. Real-Time Imaging 11, 172–185 (2005)

11. Kohonen, T.: Self-Organization and Associative Memory, 2nd edn. Springer, Heidelberg (1988)

12. Maddalena, L., Petrosino, A.: A Self-Organizing Approach to Detection of Moving Patterns for Real-Time Applications, web page containing results for this article http://www.na.icar.cnr.it/~maddalena.l/HSV-SO/HSV-SO2007.html

13. Piccardi, M.: Background Subtraction Techniques: a Review. In: Proc. of IEEE Int. Conf. on Systems, Man and Cybernetics, The Hague, The Netherlands, IEEE Computer Society Press, Los Alamitos (2004)

14. Regazzoni, C., Ramesh, V., Foresti, G.: Special Issue on Video Communications, Processing, and Understanding for Third Generation Surveillance Systems. Proc. of the IEEE 89(10), 1355–1539 (2001)

15. Rosin, P.L., Ellis, T.: Image Difference Threshold Strategies and Shadow Detection. In: Proc. British Machine Vision Conference, pp. 347–356 (1995)

16. Sarifuddin, M., Missaoui, R.: A New Perceptually Uniform Color Space with Associated Color Similarity Measure for Content-based Image and Video Retrieval. In: Multimedia Information Retrieval Workshop, Salvador Brazil (2005)

17. Smith, J.R., Chang, S.-F.: VisualSEEk: a Fully Automated Content-based Image Query System. In: ACM Multimedia, Boston, MA, ACM Press, New York (1996)

18. Toyama, K., Krumm, J., Brumitt, B., Meyers, B.: Wallflower: Principles and Practice of Background Maintenance. In: Proc. of the Seventh IEEE Conference on Computer Vision, vol. 1, pp. 255–261. IEEE Computer Society Press, Los Alamitos (1999)

19. Wren, C., Azarbayejani, A., Darrell, T., Pentland, A.: Pfinder: Real-Time Tracking of the Human Body. IEEE Trans. on PAMI 19(7), 780–785 (1997)

Recognition of Human Faces:
From Biological to Artificial Vision

Massimo Tistarelli[1], Linda Brodo[2], Andrea Lagorio[3], and Manuele Bicego[3]

[1] DAP - University of Sassari, piazza Duomo 6 - 07041 Alghero (SS) - Italy
tista@uniss.it
[2] DSL - University of Sassari, piazza Università 21 - 07100 Sassari - Italy
brodo@uniss.it
[3] DEIR - University of Sassari, via Torre Tonda 34 - 07100 Sassari - Italy
{lagorio,bicego}@uniss.it

Abstract. Face recognition is among the most challenging techniques for personal identity verification. Even though it is so natural for humans, there are still many hidden mechanisms which are still to be discovered. According to the most recent neurophysiological studies, the use of dynamic information is extremely important for humans in visual perception of biological forms and motion. Moreover, motion processing is also involved in the selection of the most informative areas of the face and consequently directing the attention. This paper provides an overview and some new insights on the use of dynamic visual information for face recognition, both for exploiting the temporal information and to define the most relevant areas to be analyzed on the face. In this context, both physical and behavioral features emerge in the face representation.

1 Introduction

Biometric recognition has attracted the attention of scientists, investors, government agencies as well as the media for the great potential in many application domains. It turns out that there are still a number of intrinsic drawbacks in all biometric techniques. In this talk we postulate the need for a proper data representation which may simplify and augment the discrimination among different instances or biometric samples of different subjects. In fact, considering the design of many natural systems, it turns out that spiral (circular) topologies are the best suited to economically store and process data. Among the many developed techniques for biometric recognition, face analysis seems to be the most promising and interesting modality. The ability of the human visual system of analyzing unknown faces, is an example of the amount of information which can be extracted from face images. This is not limited to the space or spectral domain, but heavily involves the time evolution of the visual signal. Nonetheless, there are still many open problems which need to be faced as well. This not only requires to devise new algorithms but to determine the real potential and limitations of existing techniques, also exploiting the time dimensionality to boost recognition performances.

F. Mele et al. (Eds.): BVAI 2007, LNCS 4729, pp. 191–213, 2007.

This paper highlights some basic principles underlying the perceptual mechanisms of living systems, specially related to dynamic information processing, to gather insights on sensory data acquisition and processing for recognition [1].

Recently, the analysis of video streams of face images has received an increasing attention in biometric recognition [2,3,4,5,6,7,8,9]. Not surprisingly, the human visual system also implements a very sophisticated neural architecture to detect and process visual motion [10].

A first advantage in using dynamic video information is the possibility of employing redundancy present in the video sequence to improve still images recognition systems. One example is the use of voting schemes to combine results obtained for all the faces in the video, or the choice of the faces best suited for the recognition process. Another advantage is the possibility is to use the frames in a video sequence to build a 3D representation or super-resolution images.

Besides these motivations, recent psychophysical and neural studies [1,11] have shown that dynamic information is very crucial in the human face recognition process. These findings inspired the development of true spatio-temporal video-based face recognition systems [2,3,4,5,6,7,8,9]. Last, but not least, the recognition of faces in the human visual system also involves attention mechanisms to detect and analyze the "most salient" features in the face. How these features are defined and detected is still not completely understood. Nonetheless, very distinctive information are used to characterize human faces. A computer implementation is introduced where salient regions are defined by analyzing several individuals. A set of multi-scale patches are extracted from each face image before projecting them into a common feature space. The degree of "distinctiveness" of any patch depends on its distance in feature space from patches mapped from other individuals. Both a perceptual experiment, involving 45 observers and a technological experiment were performed and compared. A further comparative analysis showed that the performance of the n-ary approach is as good as several contemporary unary, or binary, methods - whilst tapping a complementary source of information.

2   Human Vision and Information Processing

Neural systems that mediate face recognition appear to exist very early in life. In normal infancy, the face holds particular significance and provides nonverbal information important for communication and survival [12].

The ability to recognize human faces is present during the first 6 months of life, while a visual preference for faces and the capacity for very rapid face recognition are present at birth [13,14]. By 4 months, infants recognize upright faces better than upside down faces, and at 6 months, infants show differential event-related brain potentials to familiar versus unfamiliar faces [15,16]. Apart from speech, face analysis is certainly the first and major biometric cue used by humans and therefore very important to be accurately studied.

Early studies on face recognition in primates revealed a consistent neural activity in well identified areas of the brain, mainly involving the temporal sensory

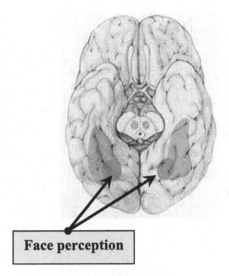

Face perception

Fig. 1. Picture of the human brain as seen from below. The highlighted areas are those initially devoted to the perception of faces and object's form.

area. More recent research revealed that this is not the case, but many different brain areas are taken into play at different stages of face analysis and recognition. This also recalls the need for a very complex representation including both photometric and dynamic information on the facial characteristics.

2.1   Space-Variant Image Representations

To achieve any visual task, including face recognition, humans are able to purposively control the flow of input data limiting the amount of information gathered from the sensory system [17,18,19]. This is needed to reduce the space and computation time required to process the incoming information. The anatomy of the early stages of the human visual system is a clear example: despite the formidable acuity in the fovea centralis (1 minute of arc) and the wide field of view (about 140x200 degrees of solid angle), the optic nerve is composed of only 10^6 nerve fibres. The space-variant distribution of the ganglion cells in the retina allows a formidable data flow reduction. In fact, the same resolution would result in a space-invariant sensor of about $6x10^8$ pixels, thus resulting in a compression ratio of 1:600 [20]. The probability density of the spatial distribution of the ganglion cells, which convey the signal from the retinal layers to the optic nerve and is responsible for the data compression, follows a logarithmic-polar law. The number of cells decreases from the center of the retina toward the periphery, with the maximal resolution in the fovea [21]. The same data compression can be obtained on electronic images, either by using a specially designed space-variant sensor [22], or re-sampling a standard image according to the log-polar transform [19,20]. The analytical formulation of the log-polar mapping describes

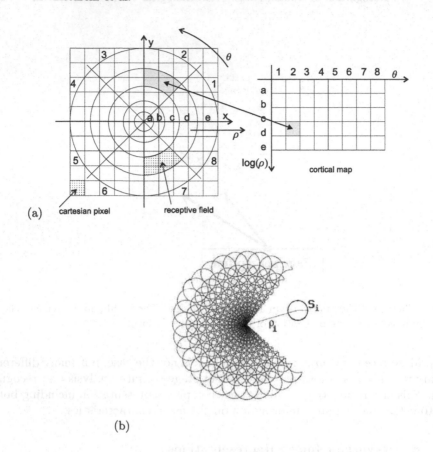

(a) cartesian pixel   receptive field

(b)

Fig. 2. (a) Log-polar sampling for Cartesian image remapping and (b) discrete log-polar model

the mapping that occurs between the retina (retinal plane (ρ, θ)) and the visual cortex (log-polar or cortical plane (ξ, η)). The derived logarithmic-polar law, taking into account the linear increment in size of the receptive fields, from the central region (fovea) towards the periphery, is given by:

$$\begin{cases} x = \rho \cos \theta \\ y = \rho \sin \theta \end{cases} \qquad \begin{cases} \eta = q \, \theta \\ \xi = \ln_a \frac{\rho}{\rho_0} \end{cases} \qquad (1)$$

where a defines the amount of overlap among neighboring receptive fields, ρ_0 is the radius of the innermost circle, $\frac{1}{q}$ is the minimum angular resolution of the log-polar layout, and (ρ, θ) are the polar coordinates of an image point.

Other models for space-variant image geometries have been proposed, like the truncated pyramid [23], the reciprocal wedge transform (RWT) [24] and the complex logarithmic mapping (CLM) [25]. Several implementations of space-variant imaging have been developed: space-variant sensors [22], custom designed image re-sampling hardware [26], and special software routines [19,27]. Given the high processing power of current computing hardware, image re-mapping can be performed at frame rate without the need of special computing hardware, and also allows the use of conventional, low cost, cameras.

3   Visual Attention and Selective Processing

A very general and yet very important perceptual mechanism in humans is visual attention [28]. This mechanism is exploited by the human perceptual system to parse the input signal in various dimensions: "signal space" (low or high frequency data), depth (image areas corresponding to objects close or far from the observer), motion (static or moving objects) etc. The selection is controlled through ad-hoc band-limiting or focusing processes, which determine the areas of interest in the scene to which direct the gaze [29].

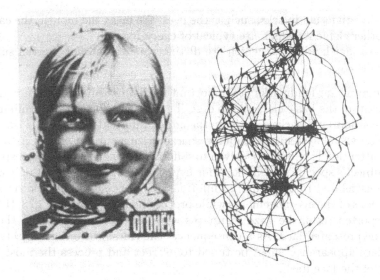

Fig. 3. Schema of the saccades performed by the human visual system analyzing an unfamiliar face (reprinted from [28])

In the case of face perception, both space-variant image re-sampling and the adoption of a selective attention mechanism can greatly improve the performance of any recognition/authentication algorithm. While the log-polar mapping allows to adaptively reduce the frequency content of the input signal, more sophisticated processes are needed to discard low information areas in the image. Visual attention in humans is also devoted to detect the most informative areas in the face to produce a compact representation for higher level cognitive processes.

Behavioral studies suggest that, in general, the most salient parts for face recognition are, in order of importance, eyes, mouth, and nose [30]. Eye-scanning studies in humans and monkeys show that eyes and hair/forehead are scanned more frequently than the nose [28,31], while human infants focus on the eyes rather than the mouth [32]. Using eye-tracking technology to measure visual fixations, Klin [33] recently reported that adults with autism show abnormal patterns of attention when viewing naturalistic social scenes. These patterns include reduced attention to the eyes and increased attention to mouths, bodies, and objects. The high specialization of specific brain areas for face analysis and recognition motivates the relevance of faces for social relations. On the other hand, this further demonstrates that face understanding is not a low level process but involves higher level functional areas in the brain.

Even though visual attention is generally focused on almost fixed facial landmarks, this does not imply that these are the only areas processed for face perception. Facial features are not simply distinctive points on the segmented face, but rather a collection of image features representing specific (and anatomically stable) areas of the face such as the eyes, eyebrows, ears, mouth, nostrils etc. Two different kind of landmarks can be defined:

- face-invariant landmarks, such as the eyes, the nose, the mouth, the ears and all other elements which are typical of every face;
- face-variant landmarks, which are distinctive elements for a given subject's face [34,35].

The face-invariant landmarks are important to distinguish faces from non-faces, and constitute the basic elements to describe both familiar and unfamiliar faces. All face-variant landmarks constitute the added information, which is learned by the human visual system, to uniquely characterize a subject's face. As a consequence, attention is selectively driven to different areas of the face corresponding to the subject's specific landmarks. This hypothesis is grounded, not only on considerations related to the required information processing, but also on several observations of the eye movements while processing human faces [13,28,31,32,33]. In all reported tests, the gaze scanpaths were different according to the identity of the presented face. As a consequence, the classification of subjects based on the face appearance, must be tuned to extract and process the most salient features of the face itself.

3.1   A Computational Model for Selective Face Processing

In order to define distinctive or salient areas of an individual's face a comparative analysis is made. All the areas of an individual's face, that appear distinct when compared to other faces from the population, are selected.

Because the appearance of different subjects is compared, this approach is conceptually different from most of the existing feature extraction methods that rely on the detection and analysis of specific face areas for authentication or recognition purposes—e.g. the Elastic Bunch Graph Matching technique [36]. It differs also from more elaborate techniques that identify the most "salient" parts within the face according to a pre-specified criterion. Among these [37,38,39,40], the system described by [41] that detects "key points" from a set of lines extracted from the face image and that in [42] which selects "characteristic points"

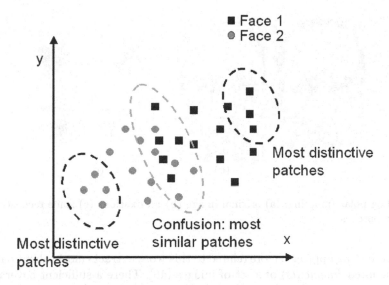

Fig. 4. Schema describing the pair-wise differences algorithm. The x and y axes represent two hypothetical coordinates in the feature space.

in a generic image by means of a local optimization process applied to the difference of Gaussians image, filtered at different scales and orientations. Though they all vary in implementation, robustness, computational requirements and accuracy, each of the above approaches is essentially a *unary* technique: salient regions are defined by analyzing *only one* instance of the face class, namely only images of the *same* individual. On the contrary, we identify local patches within an individual's face that are *different* from other individuals by performing a pair-wise, or binary, analysis. This avoids issues that may arise when invoking a single average face, or canonical model, against which each face would then be distinguished. In particular, differences between faces are determined by directly extracting from one individual's face image the most distinguishing or dissimilar patches with respect to another's. Image patches from the same individual tend to cluster together when projected in a multi-dimensional space and the distance, in that space, of that patch from clusters formed by other faces can be used as a measure of "distinctiveness"—as sketched, in just 2-D, in Fig. 8.

It is worth noting that the concept of comparative face analysis is also inherent in the work by Penev and Atik [43] (Local Feature Analysis), as well as by Li *et al.* [44] (Local Nonnegative Matrix Factorization), and by Kim *et al.* [45] (Locally Salient Independent Component Analysis). These are locally salient versions of dimensionality reduction techniques, applied to a database of images so to obtain a local representation (as a set of basis) of the training set. Even if not explicitly developed to extract salient parts of a face, all these techniques find utility in characterizing a face by performing a comparative local analysis.

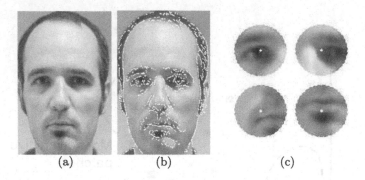

(a)   (b)   (c)

Fig. 5. Log polar sampling: (a) original image (b) all fixations (c) some reconstructed log-polar patches

An interesting approach more related to this work extracts most salient patches (there denoted *fragments*) of a set of images [46]. There a sufficient coverage of patches are extracted from a set of "client" images, before each patch is weighted in terms of its mutual information with respect to a selected set of classes. However, the optimality criterion there used to select the most relevant patches differs from ours. We use a *deterministic* criterion computing the distance from the "impostor" set, while they adopt a *probabilistic* criterion based on empirical estimation of probability function. In order to obtain a reliable estimate, their approach thus requires a considerably large training set.

Multi-scale patches extraction. From each face-image, candidate patches are extracted. These patches must be spatially distributed in a way to cover most of the face area. This methodology is similar to the one adopted in patch-based image classification [47,48,49,50] and image characterization [51]. Since face recognition requires to process information at different spatial resolutions, there may be an advantage in extracting candidate patches at multiple scales. In agreement with the analysis presented in a previous section, a space-variant, multi-scale image sampling is adopted. This allows to avoid two notable pitfalls: (a) blind analysis - whereby information revealed at one scale is not usefully available at other scales, and (b) repeated image processing - which would add to the overall computational expense. Each face-image is sampled using patches derived from a log-polar mapping [27], considering the resulting sampled vectors as our features.

As an example, Figure 5(b) shows the sampling points (corresponding to fovea fixations) of one face.

In particular, the face-image is re-sampled at each point following a log-polar scheme so that the resulting set of patches represents a local space-variant remapping of the original image, centered at that point.

Finding differences between face-pairs. Without loss of generality, we start by considering the two-face case, i.e. when client set and impostor set contain

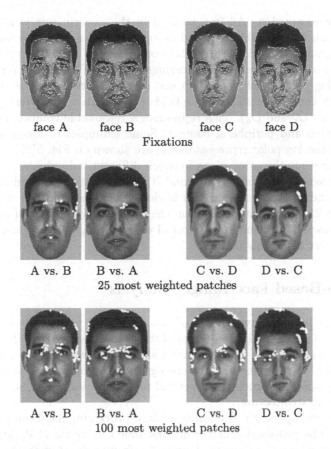

face A   face B   face C   face D
Fixations

A vs. B   B vs. A   C vs. D   D vs. C
25 most weighted patches

A vs. B   B vs. A   C vs. D   D vs. C
100 most weighted patches

Fig. 6. Two examples of differences extracted from pairs of images of different persons: (A,B) and (C,D)

only one face each. Later we examine how this process can be expanded to the multi-face case.

The main idea is that the patches from one face-image will tend to form their own cluster in the feature space, while those of the other face-image ought to form a different cluster—e.g. see Fig. 8. The "distinctiveness" of each patch can be related to its locus in feature space with respect to other faces. Any patches of the first face, found near loci of a second face can be considered less distinctive since they may easily be confused with the patches of that second face, and thus may lead to algorithmic misclassification. Conversely, a patch lying on the limb of its own cluster, that is most distant from any other cluster, should turn out to be usefully representative, and may thus be profitably employed by a classifier.

We formalize the degree of distinctiveness of each face patch by weighting it according to its distance from the projection of the other data-cluster. Patches with the highest weights are then interpreted as encoding the most important differences between the two face-images.

Qualitative examples. All images used in the experiments were gray-level, with resolution 320 × 200 pixels, and cropped in order to reduce the influence of the background. Fixations, or centers of the patch sampling process (edge-points), were computed using zero-crossings of a LoG filter. After a preliminary evaluation, log-polar patch resolution was set to 15 eccentricity steps (N_r), at each of which there were 35 receptive fields (N_a), with a 70% overlap along the two directions (O_r and O_a). This represents a reasonable compromise between fovea resolution and peripheral context. Some examples of log-polar patches, rebuilt from the log-polar representations, are shown on Fig. 5(c).

Fig. 6 represents the comparison between different individuals.

The first two columns (subjects A and B) reveal that the main differences are in the ears and in the eyebrows: this is clearly evidenced in row 3 that shows that the first 25 patches are located on the ear in the right part of the face and on the eyebrows. This result is re-enforced when adding patches (last row): note how the left ear is now highlighted.

4   Video-Based Face Image Analysis

Conversely to previous hypotheses of human neural activity, face perception rarely involve a single, well defined area of the brain. It seems that the traditional "face area" is responsible for the general shape analysis but it is not sufficient for recognition. In the same way, face recognition by computers can not be seen as a single, monolithic process, but several representations must be devised into a multi-layered architecture.

An interesting approach to multi-layer face processing has been proposed by Haxby [52]. The proposed architecture (sketched in figure 7) divides the face perception process into two main layers: the former devoted to the extraction of basic facial features and the latter processing more changeable facial features such as lip movements and expressions. It is worth noting that the encoding of changeable features of the face also captures some behavioral features of the subject, i.e. how the facial traits are changed according to a specific task or emotion.

4.1   Relevance of the Time Dimension

As shown by Vaina et al. [10], the visual task strongly influences the areas activated during visual processing. This is specially true for face perception, where not only face-specific areas are involved, but a consistent neural activity is registered in brain areas devoted to motion perception and gaze control.

The time dimension is involved also when unexpected stimuli are presented [1,11]. Humans can easily recognize faces which are rotated and distorted up to a limited extent. The increase in time reported for recognition of rotated and distorted faces implies: the expectation on the geometric arrangement of facial features, and a specific process to organize the features (analogous to image registration and warping) before the actual recognition process can take place.

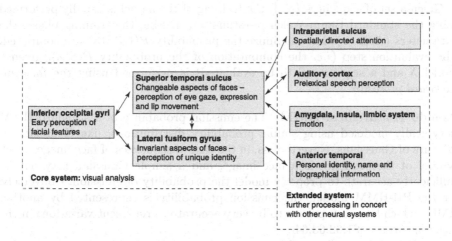

Fig. 7. A model of the distributed neural system for face perception (reproduced from [52])

On the other hand, it has been shown that the recognition error for an upside-down face decreases when the face is shown in motion [1].

From the basic element related to the face shape and color, subduing a multi-area neural activity, cognitive processes are started not only to determine the subject's identity, but also to understand more abstract elements (even uncorrelated to the subject's identity) which characterize the observed person (age, race, gender, emotion etc.) [10,53,54,55,56,57,58]. As a consequence, non-rigid and idiosyncratic facial motions constitute a very powerful "dynamic template" which augments the information stored for familiar faces and may also improve the memory recall of structured information for identity determination [11].

4.2   A Computational Model for Computing Face Shape and Motion

The double layered architecture proposed by Haxby [52] can be represented by two distinct but similar processing units devoted to two distinct tasks. The system proposed in the remainder of the paper proposes the use of the Hidden Markov Models as elementary units to build a double layer architecture to extract shape and motion information from face sequences. The architecture is based on a multi-dimensional HMM which is capable of both capturing the shape information and the change in appearance of the face. This multi-layer architecture was termed *Pseudo Hierarchical Hidden Markov Model* to emphasize the hierarchical nature of the process involved [59].

A discrete-time Hidden Markov Model λ can be viewed as a Markov model whose states cannot be explicitly observed: a probability distribution function is associated to each state, modelling the probability of emitting symbols from that state [60].

Given a set of sequences $\{S^k\}$, the training of the model is usually performed using the standard Baum-Welch re-estimation. During the training phase, the parameters $(\mathbf{A}, \mathbf{B}, \boldsymbol{\pi})$ that maximize the probability $P(\{S^k\}|\lambda)$ are computed. The evaluation step (*i.e.* the computation of the probability $P(S|\lambda)$, given a model λ and a sequence S to be evaluated) is performed using the *forward-backward procedure*.

Pseudo Hierarchical-HMM. The emission probability of a standard HMM is typically modeled using simple probability distributions, like Gaussians or Mixture of Gaussians. Nevertheless, in the case of sequences of face images, each symbol of the sequence is a face image, and a simple Gaussian may not be sufficiently accurate to properly model the probability of emission. Conversely, for the PH-HMM model, the emission probability is represented by another HMM, which has been proven to be very accurate to represent variations in the face appearance [61,62,63,64].

The PH-HMM can be useful when the data have a double sequential profile. This is when the data is composed of a set of sequences of symbols $\{S^k\}$, $S^k = s_1^k, s_2^k, \cdots, s_T^k$, where each symbol s_i^k is a sequence itself: $s_i^k = o_{i1}^k, o_{i2}^k, \cdots, o_{iT_i}^k$. Let us call S^k the first-level sequences, whereas s_i^k denotes second-level sequences.

Fixed the number of states K of the PH-HMM, for each class C the training is performed in two sequential steps:

1. *Training of emission.* The first level sequence $S^k = s_1^k, s_2^k, \cdots, s_T^k$ is "unrolled", i.e. the $\{s_i^k\}$ are considered to form an unordered set U (no matter the order in which they appear in the first level sequence). This set is subsequently split in K clusters, grouping together similar $\{s_i^k\}$. For each cluster j, a standard HMM λ_j is trained, using the second-level sequences contained in that cluster. These HMMs λ_j represents the emission HMMs.

   This process is similar to the standard Gaussian HMM initialization procedure, where the sequence is unrolled and a Mixture of K Gaussians is fitted to the unordered set. The Gaussians of the mixture are then used to roughly estimate the emission probability of each state (with a one to one correspondence with the states).

2. *Training of transition and initial states matrices.* Considering that the emission probability functions are determined by the emission HMMs, the transition and the initial states probability matrices of the PH-HMM are estimated using the first level sequences. In other words, the standard Baum Welch procedure is used, recalling that

$$b(o|H_j) = \lambda_j \tag{2}$$

The number of clusters determines the number of the PH-HMM states. This value could be fixed a priori or could be directly determined from the data (using for example the Bayesian Inference Criterion [66]). In this phase, only the transition matrix and the initial state probability are estimated, since the emission has been already determined in the previous step.

Because of the sequential estimation of the PH-HMM components (firstly emission and then transition and initial state probabilities), the resulting HMM is a "pseudo" hierarchical HMM. In a truly hierarchical model, the parameters **A**, π and **B** should be jointly estimated, because they could influence each other (see for example [67]).

Verification of face sequences. Given few video sequences captured from the subject's face, the enrollment or modelling phase aims at determining the best PH-HMM modeling the subject's face appearance. This model encompasses both the invariant aspects of the face and its changeable features. Identity verification is performed by projecting a captured face video sequence on the PH-HMM model belonging to the claimed identity.

The enrollment process consists on a series of sequential steps (for simplicity we assume only one video sequence $S = s_1, s_2, \cdots, s_T$, but the generalization to more than one sequence is straightforward):

1. The video sequence S is analyzed to detect all faces sharing similar expression, i.e. to find clusters of expressions. Firstly, each face image s_i of the video sequence is reduced to a raster scan sequence of pixels, used to train a standard spatial HMM [61,64]. The resulting face HMM models are clustered in different groups based on their similarities [68,69]. Faces in the sequence with similar expression are grouped together, independently from their appearance in time. The number of different expressions are automatically determined from the data using the Bayesian Inference Criterion [66].
2. For each expression cluster, a **spatial** face HMM is trained. In this phase *all the sequences* of the cluster are used to train the HMM. At the end of the process, K HMMs are trained. Each spatial HMM models a particular expression of the face in the video sequence. These models represents the emission probabilities functions of the PH-HMM.
3. The transition matrix and the initial state probability of the PH-HMM are estimated from the sequence $S = s_1, s_2, \cdots, s_T$, using the Baum-Welch procedure and the emission probabilities found in the previous step (see Sect. 4.2). This process aims at determining the temporal evolution of facial expressions over time. The number of states is fixed to the number of discovered clusters, this representing a sort of model selection criterion.

In summary, the main objective of the PH-HMM representation scheme is to determine the facial expressions in the video sequence, modelling each of them with a spatial HMM. The expressions change during time is then modelled by the transition matrix of the PH-HMM, which constitutes the "temporal" model (as sketched in Fig. 8).

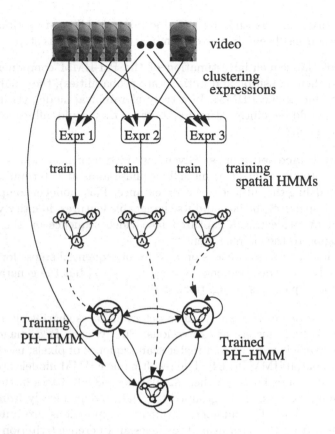

Fig. 8. Sketch of the enrollment phase of the proposed approach

4.3 Clustering Facial Expressions

The goal of this step is to group together all face images in the video sequence with the same appearance, namely the same facial expression. It is worth noting that this process does not imply a segmentation of the sequence into homogeneous, contiguous fragments. The result is rather to label each face of the sequence corresponding to its facial expression, independently from their position in the sequence. Since each face is described with an HMM sequence, the expression clustering process is casted into the problem of clustering sequences represented by HMMs [68,69,70,71]. Considering the unrolled set of faces $s_1, s_2, \cdots, s_T$, where each face s_i is a sequence $s_i = o_{i1}, o_{i2}, \cdots, o_{iT_i}$, the clustering algorithm is based on the following steps:

1. Train one standard HMM λ_i for each sequence s_i.
2. Compute the distance matrix $D = \{D(s_i, s_j)\}$, where $D(s_i, s_j)$ is defined as:

$$D(s_i, s_j) = \frac{P(s_j|\lambda_i) + P(s_i|\lambda_j)}{2} \tag{3}$$

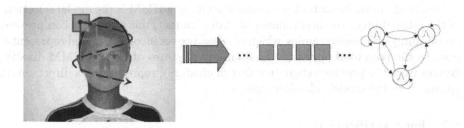

Fig. 9. Sampling scheme applied to generate the sequence of sub-images and the HMM model of the sampled sequence, representing a single face image

This is a natural way for devising a measure of similarity between stochastic sequences. Since λ_i is trained using the sequence s_i, the closer is s_j to s_i, the higher is the probability $P(s_j|\lambda_i)$. Please note that this is not a quantitative but rather a qualitative measure of similarity [68,69].

3. Given the similarity matrix D, a pairwise distance-matrix-based method (*e.g.* an agglomerative method) is applied to perform the clustering. In particular, the agglomerative complete link approach [72] has been used.

In typical clustering applications the number of clusters is defined a priori. In this application, it is practically impossible (or not viable in many real cases) to arbitrarily establish the number of facial expressions which may appear in a sequence of facial images. Therefore, the number of clusters has been estimated from the data, using the standard Bayesian Inference Criterion (BIC) [66]. This is a penalized likelihood criterion which is able to find the best number of clusters as the compromise between the model fitting (HMM likelihood) and the model complexity (number of parameters). It is defined as:

$$BIC(M_k) = \log P(X|\hat{M}_k) - \frac{1}{2}|\hat{M}_k|\log(N) \qquad (4)$$

where X is the data set (of cardinality N) to be modeled, $\{M_k\}$ ($k_{min} \leq k \leq k_{max}$) are the candidate models, $\hat{M}_k$ is the Maximum Likelihood estimate of the model M_k, and $|\hat{M}_k|$ is the number of free parameters of the model M_k.

4.4 PH-HMM Modeling: Analysis of Temporal Evolution

From the extracted set of facial expressions, the PH-HMM is trained. The different PH-HMM emission probability functions (spatial HMMs) model the facial expressions, while the temporal evolution of the facial expressions in the video sequence is modelled by the PH-HMM transition matrix. In particular, for each facial expression cluster, one spatial HMM is trained, using all faces belonging to the cluster. The transition and the initial state matrices are estimated using the procedure described in section 4.2.

One of the most important issues when training a HMM is the model selection, or the estimation of the best number of states. In fact, this operation can prevent overtraining and undertraining which may lead to an incorrect model representation. In the presented approach, The number of states of the PH-HMM directly derives from the previous stage (number of clusters), representing a direct smart approach to the model selection issue.

4.5 Face Verification

The verification of a subject's identity is straightforward. Captured a sequence of face images from an unknown subject, and a claimed identity, the sequence is fed to the corresponding PH-HMM, which returns a probability value. The claimed identity is verified if the computed probability value is over a predetermined threshold. This comparison corresponds to verifying if the captured face sequence is well modeled by the given PH-HMM.

The system has been tested using a database composed of 21 subjects. During the video acquisition, each subject was requested to vocalize ten digits, from one to ten. A minimum of five sequences for each subject have been acquired, in two different sessions. Each sampled video is composed of 95 to 195 color images, with several changes in facial expression and scale (see fig. 10). The images have a resolution of 640x480 pixels. For the face classification experiments the images have been reduced to gray level with 8 bits per pixel. It is worth noting that there is no need for an explicit normalization for the different length of the sequences. The normalization in the time domain is obtained by self transitions of temporal HMM's states. In other words, if the subject takes 10 frames to change expression, it is likely that the system remains in the same expression state for 10 iterations before moving to the next state (self transitions).

The proposed approach has been tested against three other HMM-based methods, which do not fully exploit the spatio-temporal information. The first method, called "1 HMM for all", applies one spatial HMM to model all images in the video sequence. In the authentication phase, given an unknown video sequence, all the composing images are fed into the HMM, and the sum of their likelihoods represents the matching score. In the second method, called "1 HMM for cluster", one spatial HMM is trained for each expression cluster, using all the sequences belonging to that cluster. Given an unknown video, all images are fed into the different HMMs (and summed as before): the final matching score is the maximum among the different HMMs' scores. The last method, called "1 HMM for image", is based on training one HMM for each image in the video sequence. As in the "1 HMM for cluster" method, the matching score is computed as the maximum between the different HMMs' scores.

In all experiments only one video sequence for each subject has been used for the enrollment phase. Full client and impostor tests have been performed computing a ROC (Receiving Operating Characteristic) curve. Testing and training sets were always disjoint, allowing a more reliable estimation of the error rate. In table 1 the Equal Error Rates (error when false positive and false negatives are equal) for the four methods are reported.

Fig. 10. (Top) Example frames of one subject extracted from the collected video database. (Bottom) One sample frame of five subjects, extracted from the first acquisition session.

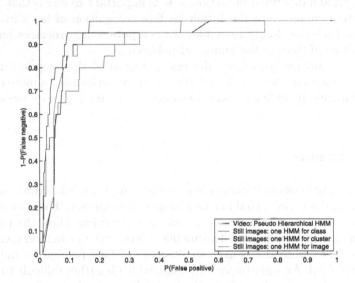

Fig. 11. The computed ROC curve for the verification experiment from video sequences of faces for the 4 methods reported

The analysis of the video sequences with the hierarchical, spatio-temporal HMM model produced a variable number of clusters, varying from 2 to 10, depending on the coding produced by the spatial HMMs. To choose the HMM that best fits the data, the Bayesian Inference Criterion (BIC) [66].

It is worth noting that when incorporating temporal information into the analysis a remarkable advantage is obtained, thus confirming the importance of explicitly modeling the face motion for identification and authentication.

The adopted test database is very limited and clearly too small to give a statistically reliable estimate of the performances of the method. Nonetheless, the results obtained on this limited data set already show the applicability and the

Table 1. Verification results for the reported HMM-based, face modeling methods

Method	EER
Still Image: 1 HMM for all	20.24%
Still Image: 1 HMM for cluster	10.60%
Still Image: 1 HMM for image	13.81%
Video: PH-HMM	6.07%

potential of the method in a real application scenario. On the other hand, the tests performed on this limited dataset allowed to compare different modeling schemes where the face dynamics was loosely integrated into the computational model. The proposed PH-HMM model outperforms all other modeling schemes based on the HMMs, at the same time it represents a very interesting computational implementation of the human model of face recognition, as proposed by Haxby in [52] and described in section 4. It is important to stress that, far from being the best computational solution for face recognition of faces from video, the proposed scheme closely resembles the computational processes underlying the recognition of faces in the human visual system.

In order to further investigate the real potential of the proposed modeling scheme, the results obtained will be further verified performing a more extensive test on a database including at least 50 subjects and 10 image sequences for each subject.

5 Conclusions

The human visual system encompasses several complex mechanisms for parsing and analyzing the visual signal in space, time and frequency. These mechanisms, which include scale-space analysis and selective attention, allow the perception and recognition of complex and deformable objects, such as human faces. There is much to learn from the neural architecture of face perception and on the processes involved. Another important issue, which is rather difficult to address, is how human faces are "coded" in the brain. It seems that a complex mechanism exists which is adaptive to the nature of the perceived faces, i.e. if they are familiar or unfamiliar. Within this context, a crucial role is plaid by the concept of "model face", which is the reference for face detection and recognition. While a standard face model is required for distinguishing faces from non-faces, a personalized, user-dependent model is required for recognition. This concept can be stretched up to the definition of a subject-dependent face model, which is linked not only on the identification of standard facial landmarks, such as the eyes and the mouth (which indeed are demonstrated to be actively scanned by the gaze during face fixations) but rather on distinguishing face landmarks. These must correspond to very distinctive patterns on the face.

In this paper, a method to automatically extract the most distinguishing patterns in the subject's face has been proposed. The system, which has been tested on a standard face database, demonstrated to be able to select the face areas which are the most distinguishing for a given subject. The algorithm is based on the analysis of a number of randomly sampled matches on the face image. The results obtained show a remarkable similarity with the most prominent facial features perceived by human subjects. This method will be very important to devise facial templates which are not related to a general face model nor to a general template model, but rather the resulting template is fully adaptable to the subject's appearance.

Despite of the simple neural architectures for face perception hypothesized in early neurological studies, the perception of human faces is a very complex task which involves several areas of the brain. The neural activation pattern depends on the specific task required rather than on the nature of the stimulus. This task-driven model may be represented by a dual layer architecture where static and dynamic features are analyzed separately to devise a unique face model. The dual nature of the neural architecture, subduing face perception, allows to capture both static and dynamic data. As a consequence, not only physiological features are processed, but also behavioral features, which are related to the way the face traits are changing over time. This last property is characteristic of each individual and implicitly represents the changeable features of the face.

A statistical model of the face appearance, which reflects the described dual-layered neural architecture, has been presented. In order to capture both static and dynamic features, the model is based on the analysis of face video sequences using a multi-dimensional extension of Hidden Markov Models, called Pseudo Hierarchical HMM. In the PH-HMM model, the emission probability of each state is represented by another HMM, while the number of states is determined from the data by unsupervised clustering of facial expressions in the video. The resulting architecture is then capable of modeling both physiological and behavioral features, represented in the face image sequence and well represents the dual neural architecture described by Haxby in [52]. It is worth noting that the proposed approach far from being the best performing computational solution for face recognition from video, has been explicitly devised to copy the neural processes subduing face recognition in the human visual system.

Even though the experiments performed are very preliminary, already demonstrate the potential of the algorithm in coupling photometric appearance of the face and the temporal evolution of facial expressions. The proposed approach can be very effective in face identification or verification to exploit the subject's cooperation in order to enforce the required behavioral features and strengthen the discrimination power of a biometric system.

Acknowledgments

This work has been supported by grants of the Italian Ministry of Scientific Research and by the IST European Network of Excellence Biosecure.

References

1. Knight, B., Johnston, A.: The role of movement in face recognition. Visual Cognition 4, 265–274 (1997)
2. Yamaguchi, O., Fukui, K., Maeda, K.: Face recognition using temporal image sequence. In: Proc. Int. Conf. on Automatic Face and Gesture Recognition (1998)
3. Biuk, Z., Loncaric, S.: Face recognition from multi-pose image sequence. In: Proc. of Int. Symp. on Image and Signal Processing and Analysis (2001)
4. Li, Y.: Dynamic face models: construction and applications. PhD thesis, Queen Mary, University of London (2001)
5. Shakhnarovich, G., Fisher, J.W., Darrell, T.: Face recognition from long-term observations. In: Proc. of European Conf. on Computer Vision (2002)
6. Zhou, S., Krueger, V., Chellappa, R.: Probabilistic recognition of human faces from video. Computer Vision and Image Understanding 91, 214–245 (2003)
7. Liu, X., Chen, T.: Video-based face recognition using adaptive hidden markov models. In: Proc. Int. Conf. on Computer Vision and Pattern Recognition (2003)
8. Lee, K.C., Ho, J., Yang, M.H., Kriegman, D.: Video-based face recognition using probabilistic appearance manifolds. In: Proc. Int. Conf. on Computer Vision and Pattern Recognition (2003)
9. Hadid, A., Pietikäinen, M.: An experimental investigation about the integration of facial dynamics in video-based face recognition. Electronic Letters on Computer Vision and Image Analysis 5(1), 1–13 (2005)
10. Vaina, L.M., Solomon, J., Chowdhury, S., Sinha, P., Belliveau, J.W.: Functional Neuroanatomy of Biological Motion Perception in Humans. Proc. of the National Academy of Sciences of the United States of America 98(20), 11656–11661 (2001)
11. OToole, A.J., Roark, D.A., Abdi, H.: Recognizing moving faces: A psychological and neural synthesis. Trends in Cognitive Science 6, 261–266 (2002)
12. Darwin, C.: The expression of the emotions in man and animals. John Murray, London, UK (1965) (original work published 1872)
13. Goren, C., Sarty, M., Wu, P.: Visual following and pattern discrimination of face-like stimuli by newborn infants. Pediatrics 56, 544–549 (1975)
14. Walton, G.E., Bower, T.G.R.: Newborns form "prototypes" in less than 1 minute. Psychological Science 4, 203–205 (1993)
15. Fagan, J.: Infants' recognition memory for face. Journal of Experimental Child Psychology 14, 453–476 (1972)
16. de Haan, M., Nelson, C.A.: Recognition of the mother's face by 6-month-old infants: A neurobehavioral study. Child Development 68, 187–210 (1997)
17. Ballard, D.H.: Animate vision. Artificial Intelligence 48, 57–86 (1991)
18. Aloimonos, Y.: Purposize, qualitative, active vision. CVGIP: Image Understanding 56(special issue on qualitative, active vision), 3–129 (1992)
19. Tistarelli, M.: Active/space-variant object recognition. Image and Vision Computing 13(3), 215–226 (1995)
20. Schwartz, E.L., Greve, D.N., Bonmassar, G.: Space-variant active vision: definition, overview and examples. Neural Networks 8(7/8), 1297–1308 (1995)
21. Curcio, C.A., Sloan, K.R., Kalina, R.E., Hendrickson, A.E.: Human photoreceptor topography. Journal of Computational Neurology 292(4), 497–523 (1990)
22. Sandini, G., Metta, G.: Retina- like sensors: motivations, technology and applications. In: Secomb, T.W., Barth, F., Humphrey, P. (eds.) Sensors and Sensing in Biology and Engineering, Springer, Heidelberg (2002)

23. Burt, P.J.: Smart sensing in machine vision. In: Machine Vision: Algorithms, Architectures, and Systems, Academic Press, London (1988)
24. Tong, F., Li, Z.N.: The reciprocal-wedge transform for space-variant sensing. In: 4th IEEE Intl. Conference on Computer Vision, Berlin, pp. 330–334. IEEE Computer Society Press, Los Alamitos (1993)
25. Schwartz, E.L.: Spatial mapping in the primate sensory projection: Analytic structure and relevance to perception. Biological Cybernetics (25), 181–194 (1977)
26. Fisher, T.E., Juday, R.D.: A programmable video image remapper. In: Proceedings of SPIE, vol. 938, pp. 122–128 (1988)
27. Grosso, E., Tistarelli, M.: Log-polar Stereo for Anthropomorphic Robots. In: Vernon, D. (ed.) ECCV 2000. LNCS, vol. 1842, pp. 299–313. Springer, Heidelberg (2000)
28. Yarbus, A.L.: Eye Movements and Vision. Plenum Press, New York (1967)
29. Yeshurun, Y., Schwartz, E.L.: Shape description with a space-variant sensor: Algorithms for scan-path, fusion and convergence over multiple scans. IEEE Trans. on PAMI PAMI-11, 1217–1222 (1993)
30. Shepherd, J.: Social factors in face recognition. In: Davies, G., Ellis, H., Shepherd, J. (eds.) Perceiving and remembering face, pp. 55–79. Academic Press, London (1981)
31. Nahm, F.K.D., Perret, A., Amaral, D., Albright, T.D.: How do monkeys look at faces? Journal of Cognitive Neuroscience 9, 611–623 (1997)
32. Haith, M.M., Bergman, T., Moore, M.J.: Eye contact and face scanning in early infancy. Science 198, 853–854 (1979)
33. Klin, A.: Eye-tracking of social stimuli in adults with autism. In: NICHD Collaborative Program of Excellence in Autism, May 2001, Yale University, New Haven, CT (2001)
34. Tistarelli, M., Grosso, E.: Active vision-based face authentication. Image and Vision Computing: Special issue on Facial Image Analysis 18(4), 299–314 (2000)
35. Bicego, M., Grosso, E., Tistarelli, M.: On finding differences between faces. In: Kanade, T., Jain, A., Ratha, N.K. (eds.) AVBPA 2005. LNCS, vol. 3546, pp. 329–338. Springer, Heidelberg (2005)
36. Wiskott, L., Fellous, J.M., der Malsburg, C.V.: Face recognition by elastic bunch graph matching. IEEE Trans. on Pattern Analysis and Machine Intelligence 19, 775–779 (1997)
37. Tsotsos, J., Culhane, S., Wai, W., Lai, Y., Davis, N., Nuflo, F.: Modelling visual attention via selective tuning. Artificial Intelligence 78, 507–545 (1995)
38. Lindeberg, T.: Detecting salient blob-like image structures and their scales with a scale-space primal sketch: A method for focus-of-attention. Int. Journal of Computer Vision 11(3), 283–318 (1993)
39. Koch, C., Ullman, S.: Shifts in selective visual-attention - towards the underlying neural circuitry. Human Neurobiology 4, 219–227 (1985)
40. Salah, A., Alpaydın, E., Akarun, L.: A selective attention-based method for visual pattern recognition with application to handwritten digit recognition and face recognition. IEEE Trans. on Pattern Analysis and Machine Intelligence 24(3), 420–425 (2002)
41. González-Jiménez, D., Alba-Castro, J.: Biometrics discriminative face recognition through Gabor responses and sketch distortion. In: Marques, J.S., Pérez de la Blanca, N., Pina, P. (eds.) IbPRIA 2005. LNCS, vol. 3523, pp. 513–520. Springer, Heidelberg (2005)
42. Lowe, D.: Distinctive image features from scale-invariant keypoints. Int. Journal of Computer Vision 60(2), 91–110 (2004)

43. Penev, P., Atick, J.: Local feature analysis: a general statistical theory for object representation. Network: computation in Neural Systems 7(3), 477–500 (1996)
44. Li, S., Hou, X., Zhang, H.: Learning spatially localized, parts-based representation. Computer Vision and Image Understanding 1, 207–212 (2001)
45. Kim, J., Choi, J., Yi, J., Turk, M.: Effective representation using ica for face recognition robust to local distortion and partial occlusion. IEEE Trans. on Pattern Analysis and Machine Intelligence 27(12), 1977–1981 (2005)
46. Ullman, S., Vidal-Naquet, M., Sali, E.: Visual features of intermediate complexity and their use in classification. Nature Neuroscience 5, 682–687 (2002)
47. Agarwal, S., Roth, D.: Learning a sparse representation for object detection. In: Heyden, A., Sparr, G., Nielsen, M., Johansen, P. (eds.) ECCV 2002. LNCS, vol. 2353, pp. 113–130. Springer, Heidelberg (2002)
48. Fergus, R., Perona, P., Zisserman, A.: Object class recognition by unsupervised scale-invariant learning. In: Proc. Int. Conf. on Computer Vision and Pattern Recognition, vol. 2, p. 264 (2003)
49. Dorko, G., Schmid, C.: Selection of scale-invariant parts for object class recognition. In: Proc. Int. Conf. on Computer Vision, vol. 2, pp. 634–640 (2003)
50. Csurka, G., Dance, C., Bray, C., Fan, L., Willamowski, J.: Visual categorization with bags of keypoints. In: Proc. Workshop Pattern Recognition and Machine Learning in Computer Vision (2004)
51. Jojic, N., Frey, B., Kannan, A.: Epitomic analysis of appearance and shape. In: Proc. Int. Conf. on Computer Vision, vol. 2, pp. 34–41 (2003)
52. Haxby, J.V., Hoffman, E.A., Gobbini, M.I.: The distributed human neural system for face perception. Trends in Cognitive Sciences 4(6), 223–233 (2000)
53. Wiskott, L., Fellous, J.M., Kruger, N., von der Malsburg, C.: Face recognition and gender determination. In: Proceedings Int.l Workshop on Automatic Face and Gesture Recognition, Zurich, Switzerland, pp. 92–97 (1995)
54. Wechsler, H., Phillips, P., Bruce, V., Soulie, F., Huang, T. (eds.): Face Recognition. From Theory to Applications. NATO ASI Series F, vol. 163. Springer, Heidelberg
55. Cottrell, G., Metcalfe, J.: Face, gender and emotion recognition using holons. In: Touretzky, D. (ed.) Advances in Neural Information Processing Systems, San Mateo, CA, vol. 3, pp. 564–571. Morgan Kaufmann, San Francisco (1991)
56. Braathen, B., Bartlett, M.S., Littlewort, G., Movellan, J.R.: First Steps Towards Automatic Recognition of Spontaneous Facial Action Units. In: ACM Workshop on Perceptive User Interfaces, Orlando, FL, November 15-16, 2001, ACM Press, New York (2001)
57. Picard, R.W.: Toward computers that recognize and respond to user emotion. IBM System (39), 3/4 (2000)
58. Picard, R.W.: Building HAL: Computers that sense, recognize, and respond to human emotion. MIT Media-Lab TR-532, also in Society of Photo-Optical Instrumentation Engineers. Human Vision and Electronic Imaging VI, part of SPIE9s Photonics West (2001)
59. Bicego, M., Grosso, E., Tistarelli, M.: Person authentication from video of faces: a behavioral and physiological approach using Pseudo Hierarchical Hidden Markov Models. In: Zhang, D., Jain, A.K. (eds.) Advances in Biometrics. LNCS, vol. 3832, pp. 113–120. Springer, Heidelberg (2005)
60. Rabiner, L.: A tutorial on Hidden Markov Models and selected applications in speech recognition. Proc. of IEEE 77(2), 257–286 (1989)
61. Kohir, V.V., Desai, U.B.: Face recognition using DCT-HMM approach. In: AFI-ART. Proc. Workshop on Advances in Facial Image Analysis and Recogniti Technology, Freiburg, Germany (1998)

62. Samaria, F.: Face recognition using Hidden Markov Models. PhD thesis, Engineering Department, Cambridge University (October 1994)
63. Nefian, A.V., Hayes, M.H.: Hidden Markov models for face recognition. In: ICASSP. Proc. Int. Conf. on Acoustics, Speech and Signal Processing, Seattle, pp. 2721–2724 (1998)
64. Bicego, M., Castellani, U., Murino, V.: Using Hidden Markov Models and wavelets for face recognition. In: IEEE. Proc. of Int. Conf on Image Analysis and Processing, pp. 52–56. IEEE Computer Society Press, Los Alamitos (2003)
65. Bicego, M., Grosso, E., Tistarelli, M.: Probabilistic face authentication using hidden markov models. In: Proc. of SPIE Int. Workshop on Biometric Technology for Human Identification (2005)
66. Schwarz, G.: Estimating the dimension of a model. The Annals of Statistics 6(2), 461–464 (1978)
67. Fine, S., Singer, Y., Tishby, N.: The hierarchical hidden markov model: Analysis and applications. Machine Learning 32, 41–62 (1998)
68. Smyth, P.: Clustering sequences with hidden Markov models. In: Mozer, M., Jordan, M., Petsche, T. (eds.) Advances in Neural Information Processing Systems, vol. 9, p. 648. MIT Press, Cambridge (1997)
69. Panuccio, A., Bicego, M., Murino, V.: A Hidden Markov model-based approach to sequential data clustering. In: Caelli, T.M., Amin, A., Duin, R.P.W., Kamel, M.S., de Ridder, D. (eds.) SPR 2002 and SSPR 2002. LNCS, vol. 2396, pp. 734–742. Springer, Heidelberg (2002)
70. Rabiner, L., Lee, C., Juang, B., Wilpon, J.: HMM clustering for connected word recognition. In: ICASSP. Proc. Int. Conf. on Acoustics, Speech and Signal Processing, pp. 405–408 (1989)
71. Li, C.: A Bayesian Approach to Temporal Data Clustering using Hidden Markov Model Methodology. PhD thesis, Vanderbilt University (2000)
72. Jain, A.K., Dubes, R.: Algorithms for clustering data. Prentice-Hall, Englewood Cliffs (1988)

Incremental Subspace Learning for Cognitive Visual Processes

Bogdan Raducanu[1] and Jordi Vitrià[1,2]

[1] Computer Vision Center, Building "O" - Campus UAB
[2] Computer Science Dept., Autonomous University of Barcelona (UAB)
08193 Bellaterra, Barcelona
Spain
{bogdan,jordi}@cvc.uab.es

Abstract. In real life, visual learning is supposed to be a continuous process. Humans have an innate facility to recognize objects even under less-than-ideal conditions and to build robust representations of them. These representations can be altered with the arrival of new information and thus the model of the world is continuously updated. Inspired by the biological paradigm, we propose in this paper an incremental subspace representation for cognitive vision processes. The proposed approach has been applied to the problem of face recognition. The experiments performed on a custom database show that at the end of incremental learning process the recognition performance achieved converges towards the result obtained using an off-line learning strategy.

1 Introduction

The human visual cognitive system is very robust among a large range of variations in environmental conditions. Opposite to this, a similar robustness of visual cognition is still far to be achieved with artificial systems. Despite of the progresses reported in areas like vision sensors, statistical pattern recognition and machine learning, what for humans represents a natural process, for machines is still a far-fetched dream. One of the factors that limit these performances is the learning strategy that has been used. Most of the nowadays approaches, require the intervention of the human operator to collect, store and segment hand-picked images and train pattern classifiers with them.[1]. It is unlikely that such a manual operation could meet the demands of many challenging cognition tasks that are critical for generating intelligent behavior, such as object recognition, in general, and face recognition, in particular. The desired goal is to enable machines to learn directly from sensory input streams while interacting with the environment, including humans. During the interaction, the human is not allowed to interfere in the internal state of the system [2].

The cognitive approach in generating intelligent behavior consists of an integrated, recursive process that aims at building a model of the 'world' and a continuous adaptation of this model [8]. In consequence, it is the system itself which

---

[1] In real world scenarios, it is unlikely to know beforehand the number of total classes or the exact number of instances per class.

F. Mele et al. (Eds.): BVAI 2007, LNCS 4729, pp. 214–223, 2007.

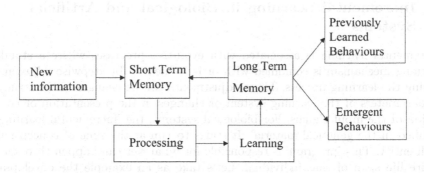

Fig. 1. The structure of cognitive processes

is responsible of how to analyze, interpret and represent the information. The system will learn new concepts (develop new competencies) based on previous data and the experience acquired over time. When a new piece of information becomes available, it is responsible to analyze it and in case it is relevant, should be added to the existing representation (at times, might be necessary a change of representation structure). This way, the system could present two classes of behaviors: one class, consisting of specifically learned behaviors and another one, corresponding to emergent behaviors. This cognitive strategy is depicted in figure 1.

A very important characteristic of cognitive processes is represented by information management. We have to distinguish between two types of memory: a short-term and a long-term memory. The short-term memory is responsible for maintaining the information for a very brief period of time (acting like a buffer), after which it is discarded. On the other hand, the long-term memory represents the knowledge database built over time. If the information passed from short-term memory is relevant, than the knowledge content of long-term memory is updated. The long-term memory is responsible for guaranteeing the system viability over large period of times (weeks, maybe months or years). A phenomenon that can affect the long-term memory is the 'forgetting' or 'degradation' (partial or total loss of some data). Sometimes, this process can be irreversible. These are also characteristics of human mind.

In the current paper we will focus on the long-term memory, i.e. how the knowledge database can be built incrementally. We introduce an online version of the non-parametric discriminant analysis (NDA)[6]. The proposed solution is applied to the problem of face recognition and is presented as an application for social robotics. The paper is structured as follows: in the next section, we will present a comparative between incremental learning in biological and artificial systems. Section 3 is dedicated to the introduction of the novel incremental non-parametric discriminant analysis (from now on referred as IncNDA). In section 4 we discuss the application of our approach to the problem of face recognition. We will show that at the end of the learning process, the recognition performance achieved converges towards the result obtained using an off-line version of the NDA (from now on referred as BatchNDA). Finally, section 5 contains our conclusions and the guidelines for future work.

2   Incremental Learning in Biological and Artificial Systems

Incremental learning is associated with evolutive processes where a standard learning mechanism is combined with or is influenced by stepwise adjustments during the learning process. These adjustments can be changes in the structure or parameters of the learning system or changes in the presentation or constitution of the input signals. For biological systems, the 'incremental learning' is codified in the genetical material. It starts to run at the time of conception of each entity. This 'program' is responsible for whatever can happen through the entire life span of that individual. Let's take as an example the development of human visual learning system. In [5], the authors claim that the newborn babies arrive to this world pre-wired with the ability to recognize face-like patterns. It looks like that they are attracted by moving stimuli which resemble human faces. Later on, and according with the evolution of our cognitive abilities, we learn to distinguish different subclasses within face class: males/females, young/mature/old, familiar/unfamiliar, etc. [7].

In its most general sense (by analogy with their biological counterpart), the 'incremental learning' for an artificial system should start to manifest at its 'birth'. This process enables the machine to develop skills through direct interactions with its environment through its perceptual mechanisms. For machines to truly understand the world, the environment must be the physical world, including humans and the machine itself. It must enable the machine with ability to learn new tasks that a human creator cannot foresee in the design phase. This implies that the representation of any task that the machine learns must be generated by the machine itself.

In the context of the current paper, we will refer to 'incremental learning' with the acceptance of 'online pattern training'. In this case, the initial representation of the knowledge is continuously updated, as new patterns become available. Visual learning in the case of artificial systems is often approached by the appearance based modelling of objects. Object modelling is often followed by a feature selection and extraction step. The outcome of this process consists of obtaining either an efficient data representation (through dimensionality reduction, when class labels are ignored) or an effective data discrimination (when besides the dimensionality reduction, we are focused also on class labels) [10]. For the latter, parametric and non-parametric forms have been proposed [4].

So far, several online knowledge representations have been proposed. In [3,9,1] the Incremental Principal Component Analysis (IPCA) is presented. The update of the covariance matrix is achieved through a residual procedure. They keep only the learned coefficients of the eigenspace representation and discard the original data. In the same context of IPCA, in [15] it is demonstrated that is possible to build incrementally an eigenspace representation without the need to compute the covariance matrix at all. On the other hand, some incremental versions of Linear Discriminant Analysis (ILDA) are proposed in [13] and [12]. In the next section we present a brief review of the classical NDA and introduce its online version. Our choice for NDA is motivated by the fact that being a non-parametric method, its application is not limited to gaussian distributions of data. Another advantage provided by this method is that it extracts those features which work well with the nearest-neighbor classifier [11].

3   Non-parametric Discriminant Analysis

As introduced in [6], the within-class scatter matrix S_w and between-class scatter matrix S_b are used as a measure of inter-class separability. One of the most used criteria is the one that maximize the following expression:

$$\zeta = tr(S_b S_w) \tag{1}$$

It has been shown that the $M \times D$ linear transform that satisfies the equation 2 optimizes also the separability measure ζ:

$$\hat{W} = \arg \max_{W^T S_w W = I} tr(W^T S_b W) \tag{2}$$

This problem has an analytical solution and is mathematically equivalent to the eigenvectors of the matrix $S_w^{-1} S_b$.

3.1   BatchNDA

Let's assume that the data samples we have belong to N classes $C_i, i = 1, 2, ..., N$. Each class C_i is formed by n_i samples $C_i = \{x_1^i, x_2^i, ..., x_{n_{C_i}}^i\}$. By $\bar{x}^{C_i}$ we will refer to the mean vector of class C_i. According to [6], the S_w and S_b scatter matrices are defined as follows:

$$S_w = \sum_{i=1}^{C_N} \sum_{j \in C_i} (x_j - \bar{x}^{C_i})(x_j - \bar{x}^{C_i})^T \tag{3}$$

$$S_b = \sum_{i=1}^{C_N} \sum_{j=1, j \neq i}^{C_N} \sum_{t=1}^{n_{C_i}} W(C_i, C_j, t)(x_t^i - \mu_{C_j}(x_t^i))(x_t^i - \mu_{C_j}(x_t^i))^T \tag{4}$$

where $\mu_{C_j}(x_t^i)$ is the local $K-$NN mean, defined by:

$$\mu_{C_j}(x_t^i) = \frac{1}{k} \sum_{p=1}^{k} NN_p(x_t^i, C_j) \tag{5}$$

where $NN_p(x_t^i, C_j)$ is the $p-$th nearest neighbor from vector (x_t^i) to the class C_j. The term $W(C_i, C_j, t)$ which appears in equation 4 is a weighting function whose role is to emphasize the boundary class information. It is defined by the following relation:

$$W(C_i, C_j, t) = \frac{min\{d^\alpha(x_t^i, NN_k(x_t^i, C_i)), (x_t^i, NN_k(x_t^i, C_j))\}}{d^\alpha(x_t^i, NN_k(x_t^i, C_i)) + d^\alpha(x_t^i, NN_k(x_t^i, C_j))} \tag{6}$$

Here α is a control parameter that can be selected between zero and infinity. The sample weights take values close to 0.5 on class boundaries and drop to zero as we move away. The parameter α adjusts how fast this happens.

3.2 IncNDA

The shortcoming of the BatchNDA described in the previous section, is that assumes that all the data are available at the classification. This is not the case for real applications, when the data is coming over time, at random time intervals, and the representation of the data must be updated. Computing from the beginning the scatter matrices, each time a new sample arrives, is not computationally feasible, especially when the number of classes is very high and the number of samples per class increases significantly. For this reason, we propose the IncNDA technique, that can process sequentially later-on added samples, without the need for recalculating entirely the scatter matrices. In order to describe the proposed algorithm, we assume that we have computed the S_w and S_b scatter matrix from at least 2 classes. Let's now consider that a new training pattern y is presented to the algorithm. We distinguish between two situations.

The new training pattern belongs to an existing class. Let's assume, for instance, that y belongs to one of the existing classes C_L (i.e. y^{C_L}, where $1 < L < N$). In this case, the equation that updates S_b is given by:

$$S_b' = S_b - S_b^{in}(C_L) + S_b^{in}(C_{L\prime}) + S_b^{out}(y^{C_L}) \tag{7}$$

where $C_{L\prime} = C_L \bigcup \{y^{C_L}\}$, $S_b^{in}(C_L)$ represents the covariance matrix between the existing classes and the class that is about to be changed, $S_b^{in}(C_{L\prime})$ represents the covariance matrix between existing classes and the updated class $C_{L\prime}$ and by $S_b^{out}(y^{C_L})$ we denote the covariance matrix between the vector y^{C_L} and the other classes:

$$S_b^{in}(C_L) = \sum_{j=1, j \neq L}^{C_N} \sum_{i=1}^{n_{C_j}} W(C_j, C_L, i)(x_i^j - \mu_{C_L}(x_i^j))(x_i^j - \mu_{C_L}(x_i^j))^T \tag{8}$$

$$S_b^{out}(y^{C_L}) = \sum_{j=1, j \neq L}^{C_N} (y^{C_L} - \mu_{C_j}(y^{C_L}))(y^{C_L} - \mu_{C_j}(y^{C_L}))^T \tag{9}$$

In the case of S_w' the update equation is the following:

$$S_w' = \sum_{j=1, j \neq L}^{C_N} S_w(C_j) + S_w(C_{L\prime}) \tag{10}$$

where

$$S_w(C_{L\prime}) = S_w(C_L) + \frac{n_{C_L}}{n_{C_L} + 1}(y - \bar{x}^{C_L})(y - \bar{x}^{C_L})^T \tag{11}$$

The new training pattern belongs to a new class. Let's assume that y belongs to a new class C_{N+1} (i.e. $y^{C_{N+1}}$).

For this case, the updated equations for the scatter matrices are given by:

$$S'_b = S_b + S_b^{out}(C_{N+1}) + S_b^{in}(C_{N+1}) \tag{12}$$

where $S_b^{out}(C_{N+1})$ and $S_b^{in}(C_{N+1})$ are defined as follows:

$$S_b^{out}(C_{N+1}) = \sum_{j=1}^{C_N}(y^{C_{N+1}} - \mu_{C_j}(y^{C_{N+1}}))(y^{C_{N+1}} - \mu_{C_j}(y^{C_{N+1}}))^T \tag{13}$$

$$S_b^{in}(C_{N+1}) = \sum_{j=1}^{C_N}\sum_{i=1}^{n_{C_j}} W(C_j, C_{N+1}, i)(x_i^j - \mu_{C_{N+1}}(x_i^j))(x_i^j - \mu_{C_{N+1}}(x_i^j))^T \tag{14}$$

Regarding, the new S'_w matrix, this one remains unchanged, i.e:

$$S'_w = S_w \tag{15}$$

4   Face Recognition: A Case Study

The incremental learning approach introduced in the previous section has been tested on a face recognition problem using a custom face database. The image acquisition phase was extended over several weeks and was performed in an automatic manner. For this purpose, we put the camera in an open space and snapshots were taken each time a person was passing in front of it. The face was automatically extracted from the image using the face detector based on [14]. We didn't impose any restrictions regarding ambient conditions.

Overall, our database consists of 6882 images of 51 people (both male and female)[2]. Since no arrangements were previously made, some classes contain only a handful of images (as much as 20), meanwhile, the largest of them contains over 400. Segmented faces were normalized at a standard size of 48x48 pixels. Because of the particularity of the acquisition process, face images reflect the changes in appearance suffered by subjects over time. Furthermore, since our application was thought to run in real-time (and to give it a more ad-hoc impression), we didn't perform any pre-processing step to face images before passing them to the classifier. That's why the faces used in the experiment show a certain degree of variation in pose and size and are not constrained to be exactly frontal. For the same reason, face images used to be a little wider than the face region itself. Some samples of these face images are presented in figure 2.

To test the IncNDA technique, we used 90% of the images (i.e. about 6000) as training set and the remaining ones as test set. ¿From the training set, we used 15% of the images (belonging to 5 classes and representing 900 samples) to build

---

[2] In the current study we put the accent in having a reasonable number of classes with a lot of instances rather having an excessive number of classes with very few instances

Fig. 2. Samples of face images from CVC custom database showing a certain degree of variation in illumination, pose and size

the initial IncNDA eigenspace. In order to overcome the singularity problem, a PCA step was performed beforehand[3]. This way, data dimensionality was downsized from 2304 to 60. The remaining samples (5100) from the training set were added later on in a sequential manner (the samples were drawn randomly) and this way the NDA-eigenspace was updated.

In figure 3 (left) we depicted the evolution of the learning process after each update (a new sample added) of the initial IncNDA eigenspace. In the early stages, there are a lot of new classes presented at very short intervals. It can be appreciated that, with almost 50% of the remaining training samples introduced, all classes have been represented. In figure 3 (right), we depicted the percentage of incremental training samples introduced so far (the stars represent the moment when a new class has been added). This graphic should be read in concordance with the above one.

As a final proof of accuracy, we compared IncNDA with the BatchNDA. In figure 4, we show that indeed the IncNDA is converging (at the end of the learning process) towards BatchNDA. The common recognition rate achieved is around 95%, which in our opinion is a very good result, taking into account the difficulty of the database. Both graphics were plotted after averaging the results obtained from a ten-fold cross-validation procedure (the training samples

---

[3] Because the dimensionality of a typical image (i.e. the number of pixels in it) is usually much larger than the number of available samples, the scatter matrices might be singular. In order to avoid this phenomenon, a dimension reduction procedure (PCA) is applied previously.

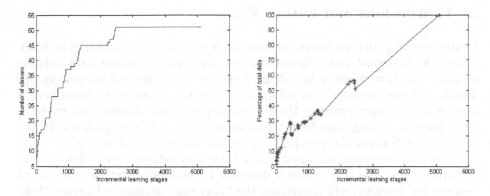

Fig. 3. Learning process: evolution of the number of classes function of learning stages (left) and the percentage of the training data function of learning stages (right)

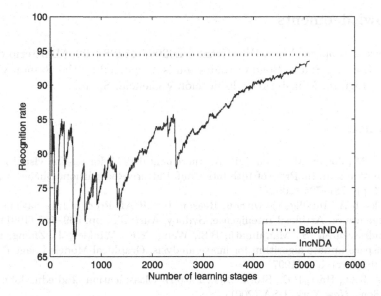

Fig. 4. IncNDA vs. BatchNDA curves. IncNDA converges towards BatchNDA at the end of the learning process

were chosen in a random manner in each run). We repeated the experiments considering different number of neighbors (1, 3, 5, 7) in computing the equation 4, but the best results obtained correspond to a number of neighbors equal to 3. The figure 4 corresponds to this case. The oscillation of the IncNDA in its early stages corresponds to the situation when a significant number of new classes have been added at very short intervals and only a very few samples of those classes were available. After some learning stages, when enough samples for each class became available, we can appreciate that the evolution curve regulates its tendency and becomes constantly ascending.

5   Conclusions and Future Work

In the current paper we presented some aspects regarding the cognitive development in biological and artificial systems. By using an incremental learning strategy, we showed how a knowledge representation can be continuously updated, with the arrival of new information. For this purpose, we introduced a novel approach represented by the online non-parametric discriminant analysis. This learning strategy has been tested on a face recognition problem. In the future, we will study the possibility to replace the sequential way of updating the knowledge representation by a parallel one, in which we present data chunks of variable size. Another research direction is represented by the analysis of decremental learning, which emulates the 'forgetting' process in humans: those patterns which became irrelevant are removed from the knowledge representation after a certain period of time.

Acknowledgements

This work is supported by MEC Grant TIN2006-15308-C02, Ministerio de Educacin y Ciencia, Spain. Bogdan Raducanu is supported by the Ramon y Cajal research program, Ministerio de Educación y Ciencia, Spain.

References

1. Artač, M., Jogan, M., Leonardis, A.: Incremental PCA for on-line visual learning and recognition. In: Proc. of 16th Intl. Conf. Pattern Recognition, Québec, Canada, vol. 3, pp. 781–784 (2002)
2. Brooks, R.A.: Intelligence without Reason. In: IJCAI. Proc. of International Joint Conference on Artificial Intelligence, Sydney, Australia, pp. 569–595 (1991)
3. Chandrasekaran, S., Manjumath, B.S., Wang, Y.F., Winkler, J., Zhang, H.: An eigenspace update algorithm for image analysis. Graphical Models Image Processing 59(5), 321–332 (1997)
4. Duda, R.O., Hart, P.E., Stork, D.G.: Pattern Classification, 2nd edn. John Wiley and Sons, New York, USA (2001)
5. Fischler, M.A., Elschlager, R.A.: The Representation and Matching of Pictorial Structures. IEEE Transactions on Computers COM-22, 67–92 (1973)
6. Fukunaga, K.: Introduction to Statistical Pattern Recognition, 2nd edn. Academic Press, Boston, USA (1990)
7. de Gelder, B., Rouw, R.: Beyond Localisation: A Dynamical Dual Route Account of Face Recognition. Acta Psychologica 107, 183–207 (2001)
8. Grow, G.O.: A Cognitive Model of Learning. Part of the paper: Serving the Strategic Reader: Cognitive Reading Theory and Its Implications for the Teaching of Writing, Original paper available as Eric Documentation Reproduction Service No. ED 406 644 (1996), available on-line at: http://www.longleaf.net/ggrow
9. Hall, P., Marshall, D., Martin, R.: Incremental Eigenanalysis for Classification. In: Proc. of British Machine Vision Conference, Southampton, UK, vol. 1, pp. 286–295 (1998)

10. Martinez, A.M., Kak, A.C.: PCA versus LDA. IEEE Trans. on Pattern Analysis and Machine Intelligence 23(2), 228–233 (2001)
11. Masip, D., Kuncheva, L.I., Vitrià, J.: An Ensemble-based Method for Linear Feature Extraction for two-class problems. Patterns Analysis and Applications 8, 227–237 (2005)
12. Pang, S., Ozawa, S., Kasabov, N.: Chunk Incremental LDA Computing on Data Streams. In: Wang, J., Liao, X.-F., Yi, Z. (eds.) ISNN 2005. LNCS, vol. 3497, pp. 51–56. Springer, Heidelberg (2005)
13. Skočaj, D., Uray, M., Leonardis, A., Bischof, H.: Why to Combine Reconstructive and Discriminative Information for Incremental Subspace Learning. In: Chum, et al. (eds.) Proc. of Computer Vision Winter Workshop, Telč, Czech Republic, pp. N/A (2006)
14. Viola, P., Jones, M.J.: Robust Real-Time Face Detection. International Journal of Computer Vision 57, 137–154 (2004)
15. Weng, J., Zhang, Y., Hwang, W.-S.: Candid covariance-free incremental principal component analysis. IEEE Trans. on Pattern Analysis and Machine Intelligence 25(8), 1034–1040 (2003)

Real–Time Robot Manipulation Using Mouth Gestures in Facial Video Sequences

Juan B. Gómez[1], Jorge E. Hernández[1], Flavio Prieto[1], and Tanneguy Redarce[2]

[1] Universidad Nacional de Colombia Sede Manizales,
Manizales, Colombia
{jbgomezm,jehernandezl,faprietoo}@unal.edu.co
[2] Laboratoire Ampère, INSA de Lyon,
Lyon, France
tanneguy.redarce@insa-lyon.fr

Abstract. In this paper a novel method for the automatic command of three degrees of freedom of a robot using mouth gestures is presented. The method uses a set of different pixel–based segmentation algorithms and morphological restrictions in order to extract the mouth area from the frames. A fuzzy inference system is then used in order to produce a small subset of discriminante features for gesture classification. A state machine was designed in order to stabilize the robot command task by using a temporal sliding mean on the detected gestures. Experimental results show that the method is both robust and reliable when operated by different people, and fast enough to keep the detection's rate in real–time.

Keywords: Human-machine interface, gesture-driven systems, lip segmentation.

1 Introduction

Traditional surgery in laparoscopy requires the aid of a person to manipulate the endoscope according to the instructions of the surgeon. This technique of operation is not optimal because the laparoscope moves constantly, due to the tremors of the hand of the operator. The orders of the surgeon can be interpreted badly by the operator and, therefore, badly executed. This problem can be solved by developing a Laparoscopy Positioning System for a Robot Arm (LPSRA). That is a robot arm controlled directly by the surgeon who manipulates the laparoscope [1].

The LPSRA that use an interface based on joystick or pedal, require using the hand or the foot of the surgeon. These types of interface are not of easy use, because the surgeon has already occupied his hands and feet. Some works tried to use the voice to develop a LPSRA [2], these systems have as disadvantage the background noise, which can be interpreted by the robot like orders. Therefore, it seems that the best way to control a LPSRA is by using face gestures. Face gestures have also been used in virtual character animation and control, automatic speech recognition from video [3] and subject recognition [4].

F. Mele et al. (Eds.): BVAI 2007, LNCS 4729, pp. 224–233, 2007.

One of the newest and more precise assisted surgery systems, the DaVinci^{TM}, has enough medical instuments to keep the legs and the arms bussy during its command. The operation console of the Surgical System DaVinci (see [5]) is usually located to 3 meters far from the patient. In this console the surgeon does not require mouth covers and therefore he can use his lips to control the laparoscope camera. This control is made by a camera that follows the movement of the surgeon lips. So, the laparoscope movement could be modeled by a state machine, whose inputs are defined by the lips position.

We propose in this paper a system able to manipulate, in real time, a robot by making an analysis of lips video images. After lips movement segmentation and features extraction, a state machine is activated and controlled by the face gestures, the output of the state machine allows the control of three degrees of freedom that command a robot.

The paper is organized as follows. Section 2 gives a brief introduction in lip segmentation and feature extraction from facial video sequences. Section 3 describes our method for segmentation, feature extraction and the proposed state machine. Section 4 shows the results of the operation of the whole system when connected to an industrial robot. Conclusions are presented in Section 5.

2 Related Work

The FAce MOUSe system [6], is an interface based on the movements of the face, in which a normal camera observes the head of the surgeon, who controls the laparoscope position and direction with intentional head movements. This way, the surgeon can control a LPSRA by head movements, without a special device. Nevertheless, it seems to be more natural to control the laparoscope with mouth gestures rather than voice commands and/or head movements.

One major issue in mouth gesture identification lies in the mouth segmentation process. For real–time lip segmentation several pixel–based techniques have been used. In [7] it is presented a new set of complex non-linear transformations in the YCbCr color space. They show that the non-linear transformation is able to improve significantly the contrast between the mouth area and the rest of the face. In [8] the authors define a new transformation based on RGB color space, that transformation enhances the difference between lips and skin, and allows robust lip detection under non uniform lighting conditions. In [9] a system for segment the lips area in video sequence is present, they use an logarithmic HSV color space transformation and a spatiotemporal neighborhood analysis. For accurate lip detection, some region–based techniques have been developed. In [10], the authors proposed a new method of fuzzy lip segmentation based in a multi-background and one object scheme. In [4] a FCM segmentator based in a representation in CIELAB and CIELUV color spaces is used. In [11] a new region-based lip contour extraction algorithm that combines the merits of the point-based model and the parametric model is presented.

In the Human-Robot Interface, Hasanuzzaman et al. [12] presented a vision-based face and gesture recognition system. They used the face and hands information (finger movements) as inputs in a decision rule. The skin segmentation was made using YIQ color representation. These gesture commands were sent to robot through TCP/IP network for human-robot interaction. Zelinsky [13] and Heinzmann [14] proposed a robotic system that is safely able work with a human operator. The human-robot interface is vision-based to achieve a natural interaction between the operator and the robot. The vision system is able to find and track the operators face, to recognize facial gestures and to determine the users gaze point. In both works, the real time is not really important.

3   Gesture Classification in Video Sequences

In order to obtain an appropriate real–time gesture detection and classification, a set of different steps must be carefully chosen and/or designed. That set is composed by a lip and mouth segmentation stage, a feature extraction stage and a classification and robot command stage. In this section each stage in the process is explained.

3.1   Mouth Segmentation

Video segmentation can be done in a spatial–based scheme (over each frame), a temporal–based scheme, or a mixture of them. In this work we use a spatial–based scheme, aimed to produce a fast and accurate result. Since fast segmentation methods rejects the use of elaborated techniques, such as fuzzy connectiveness, we used a pixel–based approach in which several color space transformations are involved. Each color component presents specific advantages in lips segmentation, and therefore complements the others.

Most of the relevant information in lip detection lies in the green and blue color distribution [15]. In fact, green and blue based color transforms are commonly used in facial recognition and segmentation [15,7]. In this approach we propose the use

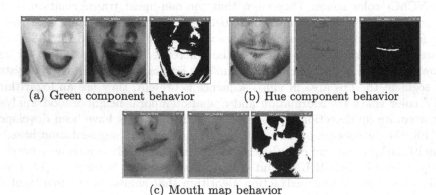

(a) Green component behavior   (b) Hue component behavior

(c) Mouth map behavior

Fig. 1. Behavior of the three components used in the proposed algorithm

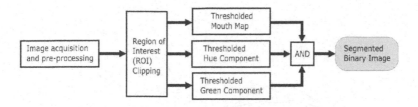

Fig. 2. Mouth Segmentation Process

of the green component of the RGB color space, the hue component of the hue–saturation based transforms, and the mouth map color space (based in the YCbCr color transformation) presented in [7]. The figure 1 shows the behavior of these three components in facial images. The green component is quite discriminant by itself when the image is almost shadow–free. Otherwise it is very permissive, making it hard to determine whether the region belongs to mouth areas or to dark areas (like the nostrils). The Hue component enhances the difference between the lips area and the rest of the face, but is very sensitive to noise and to the dark areas in the image. The mouth map is a complex non–linear transformation, in which the mouth tends to be well delimited, but not in all cases. We use this three sources of information in three different thresholding processes.

The figure 2 shows the workflow of the algorithm. First of all we perform the necesary color transformations in order to obtain the green information, the Hue and the mouth map. The green channel thresholding is intended to be dynamic, in order to compensate illumination changes [16]. The values of the mouth map transformation and those of the Hue component are thresholded using the ones given by [7] and [17], respectively. The three binary images are then blended using the conjunction operator AND. In that way, only those pixels that are white in the three binary images remain white in the output image. An elliptical clipping of the Region Of Interest (ROI) is performed, assuming that the whole mouth area will be contained in the next frame of the sequence using the same ellipse. The elliptical clipping has been used in similar applications like [10], helping to avoid the inclussion of the nostrils and other small regions in the resulting binary segmentation. The ellipse parameters are updated using the features found on each video frame.

3.2 Feature Extraction and Initial Classification

Once the mouth area has been segmented, the next step is to extract some discriminant features that help in the later gesture classification. One possible set o features are the rotation angle of the mouth (θ) and the two main axis of the mouth (d_1 and d_2), as shown in figure 3. This features are computed by using four landmarks that are searched in each frame. The landmarks are the horizontal and vertical corners of the mouth (p_1, p_2, p_3 and p_4), as shown in figure 3(a). The landmarks are searched by performing horizontal and vertical accumulations of white pixels inside the ROI–clipped segmented image. Since the

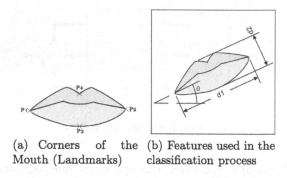

(a) Corners of the   (b) Features used in the
Mouth (Landmarks)   classification process

Fig. 3. Mouth landmarks and selected features

first image does not have an initial ellipse, the first four landmarks are searched in the whole image.

An important measure is the opening degree of the mouth (called γ), which can be expressed by the relation $\gamma = d_2/(d_1 + d_2)$. The value of γ remains in the range $[0, 0.7]$. Experimental results shows that in most of cases, for values that are smaller than 0.2, the face shows a thin mouth gesture, while when the value is greater than 0.4, the face shows an open mouth. However, optimal boundaries are subject of analysis, and are particular for each person.

In order to increase the robustness and confidence of the gesture detection, a Takagi-Sugeno-Kang Fuzzy Inference System (TSK FIS) is used. The input variable of the FIS is the opening degree of the mouth (γ), and the outputs are the inferred degrees of opening and thiness (i_{op} and i_{th}, respectively). The input variable has two associated fuzzy sets, called "open" (μ_{op}) and "thin" (μ_{th}); both of them are biquadratic–sigmoidal shaped, as shown in figure 4.

In both membership functions, the values of a and b determines the falling or rising interval of the function; Γ_{th} and Γ_{op} are the inflection points of $\mu_{th}(\gamma)$ and $\mu_{op}(\gamma)$, respectively. The FIS behavior can be described solely in terms of the computed values of $\mu_{th}(\gamma)$ and $\mu_{op}(\gamma)$, as shown in the following expression:

Fuzzy Inference Rules

if γ is μ_{op} then $i_{op} = 1$ and $i_{th} = 0$
if γ is μ_{th} then $i_{op} = 0$ and $i_{th} = 1$

Resulting Expressions for i_{th} and i_{op}

$$i_{th}(\gamma) = \frac{\mu_{th}(\gamma)}{\mu_{th}(\gamma) + \mu_{op}(\gamma)}$$

$$i_{op}(\gamma) = \frac{\mu_{op}(\gamma)}{\mu_{th}(\gamma) + \mu_{op}(\gamma)}$$

$$(1)$$

Since all the terms in the equation are known for each frame, the FIS can be solved just by evaluating the expression. The membership functions of the input variable γ can be adjusted in an adaptive way using several different techniques, providing a powerful tool in algorithm set-up and tuning. If properly tuned, the FIS produces $i_{th} = 0$ and $i_{op} = 1$ if the mouth is wide open, and $i_{th} = 1$ and $i_{op} = 0$ if the mouth is performing a thin gesture. The tuning process can be done by performing a statistical analysis over a set of measures taken from different frames of thin mouths and open mouths. That measures serve to adjust

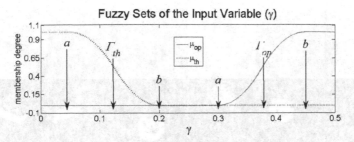

Fig. 4. Fuzzy sets of the input variable of the FIS

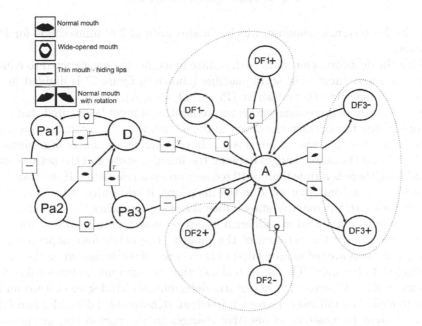

Fig. 5. State machine flow chart

the values of the biquadratic–sigmoidal function's parameters of the membership functions $\mu_{th}(\gamma)$ and $\mu_{op}(\gamma)$.

3.3   Gesture Stabilization and Robot Command

In order to control the robot movements we designed a state machine, in which the inputs are the inferred opening and "thinness" fuzzy indexes, and the rotation of the mouth. Those inputs are stabilized using the detected value during an eight video frames interval. The information of the eight frames is taken into account to conform an inertial factor that doesn't let the system change quickly from one detected gesture to another. However, this inertial factor introduces a

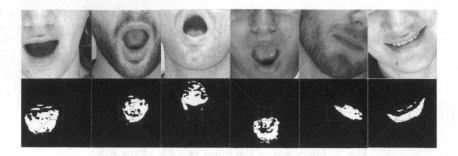

Fig. 6. Mouth gesture detection

delay in the system's response, which remains around 330 miliseconds for PAL systems.

With the decision being stabilized, a state machine was constructed to control the robot's movement. The state machine (shown in figure 5) is divided in two main parts: inactive (D) and active (Pa1, Pa2, Pa3, A).

With the aim of increasing the system reliability, it must be ensured that there will not be any involuntary movement of the mouth which can cause a movement of the robot. For that reason, we chose to have different sequences of movements which indicate the state changes between the inactive state and the active states. In addition, there is a time limit of 10 seconds on each transition. If the transition reaches the time limit (named T in the diagram), it will automatically send the system back into the inactive state. Once the system reaches the "A" state, the user is able to command six different types of movements to the robot. Two movements involve the rotation of the mouth. The other four depend on the location of the center of mass related to the center of the image when the mouth is detected to be open. The figure 6 shows the six different gestures taken into account in the "A" state. Those gestures determine which degree of freedom has to be moved. The different degrees of freedom, denoted by DF1, DF2 and DF3, can be moved by positive or negative changes in the parameter, as shown in figure 6.

4   Tests and Results

The system was conformed by a PC with a 3.2 GHz Intel Pentium IV processor with 1 GB of RAM memory, a SONY teleconference video camera with automatic brightness compensation, and a Staübli RX90 robot with its command console. Two 20 W hallogen spotlights were also used in order to minimize the efect of the shadows in the face under different ambient illumination conditions. A NI IMAQ 1411 card was attached for video acquisition; the video system setup is PAL compliant, with a maximum resolution of 640x480 pixels at 25 fps. The algorithms were implemented in C++. A subset of the NI IMAQ Vision library were also used to link the video acquisition and visualization into the C++ code.

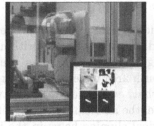

Fig. 7. Sample sequence of the rotation command

Table 1. Detection performance in the initial classification process

(a) Gesture detection rates

Detected Gesture / Ground Truth	Open	Thin	Other	Total
Open	**87.64%**	0.48%	11.88%	**100%**
Thin	22.12%	**46.08%**	31.8%	**100%**
Other	7.95%	8.98%	**83.07%**	**100%**

(b) Rotation detection rates

Detected Rotation / Ground Truth	Normal	Rotated	Total
Normal	**95.13%**	4.87%	**100%**
Rotated	10.05%	**89.95%**	**100%**

Prior to the segmentation stage, four third–order low–pass filters were applied in each frame in order to reduce the effects of noise. The ROI is initialized to cover the whole 300x300 pixels acquisition frame. After the first detection the landmarks are used to compute the elliptical ROI. The hue thresholds were taken from [17].

By performing a statistical analysis the parameters of the FIS membership functions were set up. The inflection point of $\mu_{th}(\gamma)$ (named Γ_{th}, see figure 4) was set in 0.1, and its falling limits (a and b) were set in 0.09 and 0.11, respectively. Also, the inflection point of $\mu_{op}(\gamma)$ (named Γ_{op}) was set in 0.38, and the curve's rising limits (a and b) were set in 0.37 and 0.39, respectively. In order to measure the FIS performance in gesture detection we tested five video sequences (with more than 5000 frames in total), with four different subjects. The subjects were instructed to perform different sequences in front of the camera, but they were not able to see the current state nor the robot's movement. The results of the detection process are shown in table 1.

In both tables, the values in the diagonal (bold numbers) are the correct detection rate for each gesture. Notice that the correct detection rate for the thin mouth gesture is quite low (below 50%); however, the temporal stabilization raised the detection rate for the "thin" mouth up to 70%, and generated an overall detection improvement in the other gestures. The figure 7 shows an example of the robot command. In this case, the detected rotation of the mouth causes a rotation in the robot's tool. The system operated at the same frame rate of the PAL acquisition standard in both segmentation and initial classification. For pre–recorded sequences the system kept its performance between 32 and 60 frames per second.

5 Conclusions

We designed a method which is able to detect properly the mouth in video sequences for different individuals. The set of algorithms have a good performance compared with most of algorithms presented in the literature. The system is capable to segment the mouth area under variable lighting conditions. This can be stated due to the fact that, even when we used two focal lights to compensate the shadows in the face, the ambient light was different among the acquired video sequences. The elliptical clipping helps in the ROI selection and the nostrils's discarding. However, it can be unstable when the mouth becomes very thin compared to the normal mouth state.

We propose the use of the on–line estimation of the membership function parameters in the input variable, using the values presented in this paper as a starting point. An incremental calculation of the detected thin and open mouth in the running video sequence can adapt the system to improve its performance for each different user.

Acknowledgement

This work has been supported by ECOS Franco-Colombian program (ECOS-Nord/COLCIENCIAS/ICFES/ICETEX).

References

1. Sackier, J.M., Wang, Y.: Robotically assisted laparoscopic surgery from concept to development. Surgical Endoscopy 8(1), 63–66 (1994)
2. Murioz, V.F., Thorbeck, C.V., DeGabriel, J.G., Lozano, J.F., Sanchez-Badajoz, E., Garcia-Cerezoand, A., Toscano, R., Jimenez-Garrido, A.: A medical robotic assistant for minimally invasive surgery. In: IEEE Int. Conf. Robotics and Automation, San Francisco, CA, USA, pp. 2901–2906. IEEE Computer Society Press, Los Alamitos (2000)
3. Hong, X., Yao, H., Wan, Y., Chen, R.: A pca based visual dct feature extraction method for lip-reading. In: IIH-MSP, pp. 321–326 (2006)
4. Arsic, I., Vilagut, R., Thiran, J.P.: Automatic extraction of geometric lip features with application to multi-modal speaker identification. In: ICME. IEEE International Conference on Multimedia and Expo, Toronto, ON, Canada, pp. 161–164. IEEE Computer Society Press, Los Alamitos (2006)
5. WEB: www.intuitivesurgical.com/index.aspx
6. Nishikawa, A., Hosoi, T., Koara, K., Negoro, D., Hikita, A., Asano, S., Kakutani, H., Miyazaki, F., Sekimoto, M., Yasui, M., Miyake, Y., Takiguchi, S., Monden, M.: Face mouse: A novel human-machine interface for controlling the position of a laparoscope. IEEE Trans. on Robotics and Automation 19(5), 825–841 (2003)
7. Hsu, R., Abdel-Mottaleb, M., Jain, A.: Face detection in color images. IEEE Trans. on Pattern Analysis and Machine Intelligence 24(5), 696–706 (2002)
8. Eveno, N., Caplier, A., Coulon, P.: A new color transformation for lips segmentation. In: IEEE Fourth Workshop on Multimedia Signal Processing, Cannes, France, pp. 3–8. IEEE Computer Society Press, Los Alamitos (2001)

9. Liévin, M., Delmas, P., Coulon, P., Luthon, F., Fristot, V.: Automatic lip tracking: Bayesian segmentation and active contours in a cooperative scheme. In: ICMCS (1999)
10. Wang, S., Lau, W., Leung, S., Liew, A.: Lip segmentation with the presence of beards. In: IEEE International Conference on Acoustics, Speech and Signal Processing, vol. 3, pp. 529–532. IEEE Computer Society Press, Los Alamitos (2004)
11. Wang, S., Lau, W., Leung, S.: Automatic lip contour extraction from color images. Pattern Recongnition 37(12), 2375–2387 (2004)
12. Hasanuzzaman, M., Zhang, T., Ampornaramveth, V., Ueno, H.: Gesture-based human-robot interaction using a knowledge-based software platform. Industrial Robot: An International Journal 33(1), 37–49 (2006)
13. Zelinsky, A., Heinzmann, J.: Human-robot interaction using facial gesture recognition. In: Proceedings of the International Workshop on Robot and Human Communication, pp. 256–261 (November 1996)
14. Heinzmann, J.: Real-time human face tracking and gesture recognition. Master's thesis, Universität Karlsruhe, Fakultät für Informatik (1996)
15. Lewis, L., Powers, D.: Lip feature extraction using red exclusion. In: Trent, W. (ed.) Pan-Sydney Workshop on Visual Information Processing (2001)
16. Gómez, J., Prieto, F., Redarce, T.: Lips movement segmentation and features extraction in real time. In: CISSE'06. International Joint Conferences on Computer, Information and Systems Sciences and Engineering (2006)
17. Eckert, M.: Compensación de movimiento avanzada para codificación de vídeo. PhD thesis, Universidad Politécnica de Madrid (2003)

A Variational Bayes Approach to Image Segmentation

Giuseppe Boccignone[1], Mario Ferraro[2], and Paolo Napoletano[1]

[1] Natural Computation Lab
DIIIE - Università di Salerno
via Ponte Don Melillo, 1 Fisciano (SA), Italy
{boccig,pnapoletano}@unisa.it
[2] DFS - Università di Torino
via Pietro Giuria 1, Torino, Italy
ferraro@ph.unito.it

Abstract. In this note we will discuss how image segmentation can be handled by using Bayesian learning and inference. In particular variational techniques relying on free energy minimization will be introduced. It will be shown how to embed a spatial diffusion process on segmentation labels within the Variational Bayes learning procedure so to enforce spatial constraints among labels.

1 Introduction

Survival of organisms depends critically on their ability to represent and estimate the most likely state of the world; however representations must be constructed through sensory information, and hence the problem organism's brain has to contend with is to find a function of the sensed input, the data Y, allowing to actively recover the hidden states, say X, of external resources and hazards.

In vision, world's hidden state X can be for instance the partitioning of the meaningful parts/objects within the scene (segmentation), or a function indicating if a prey or a predator is present (detection and recognition). Assume that an image or a set of images Y is generated by a mapping $X \xrightarrow{\mathcal{T}_\Theta} Y$ where Θ are the parameters of the mapping $\mathcal{T}_\Theta$. Such mapping represents a generative or forward model. The key point here is that such model $\mathcal{T}_\Theta$ may not be easily invertible and that the estimation of world states from input, $X \xleftarrow{\mathcal{T}_\Theta^{-1}} Y$ may be fundamentally ill posed and there exists an infinite number of state configurations generating image Y. Actually, the forward mapping involves a loss of information, and the task of recovering X from Y by the visual system has been decribed as a process of unconscious inference [1], which means ascertaining the probability of each potential cause given an observation.

The recourse to probability is not an expedient or a matter of subjective choice, but stems from the fact that signals in sensory and motor systems are corrupted by variability and plagued noise, and the nervous system needs to estimate these states [2]. This overall uncertainty places the problem of estimating

F. Mele et al. (Eds.): BVAI 2007, LNCS 4729, pp. 234–243, 2007.
© Springer-Verlag Berlin Heidelberg 2007

the state of the world and the control of the motor system within a statistical framework, in which he Bayesian approach has gained wide popularity in most recent research (see [3], [4] for an overview). The adoption of Bayesian methods is further motivated by the need of learning the parameters Θ of the generative model $\mathcal{T}_\Theta$; indeed, the goal of learning is more generally to acquire a recognition model for inference that is effectively the inverse of a generative model [5].

In this paper we will discuss how the problem of perceptual Bayesian learning and inference can be suitably managed by using variational techniques relying on free energy minimization [5], [6], and to this purpose we will address segmentation, a difficult problem for which a reasonable solution is crucial for many vision tasks [7]. The use of Variational Bayes (VB) techniques is fairly recent in computer vision (see Frey [4] for an in-depth discussion), and to the best of our knowledge there is only one attempt to exploit it for segmentation [8], but with some important limitations (loss of spatial constraints). Here we will show how such limitation can be overcome by embedding a spatial diffusion process on segmentation labels within the VB learning procedure.

2   Bayesian Learning and Inference for Segmentation

Segmentation, in a probabilistic view, can rather naturally be considered as a missing data problem requiring both learning and inference [9]. The complete data space is represented by a pair of random fields: $Y = \{y_n\}_{n=1}^N$ is the observed random field whose configuration (image) consists of the measurements at each random variable y_n (pixel), which may be either a scalar or D dimensional vector-valued; $X = \{x_n\}_{n=1}^N$ represents a configuration of unobservable, hidden variables, where the value (label) of each random variable x_n indicates to which region or object $k \in K$ each pixel belongs. Here n indexes the set of sites $S = \{1, 2, \cdots, N\}$, the square lattice domain of the image.

A segmentation process, starting from the observed data Y, uses the inverse mapping $\mathcal{T}_\Theta^{-1} : Y \to X$ to estimate for each pixel the object/class it belongs to. This implies *learning* the model, using the model to *infer* the partitioning probability and *deciding* the most reliable partitioning.

In a Bayesian setting, the generative model $\mathcal{T}_\Theta$ indexed by $m \in \mathcal{M}$ within the set of models $\mathcal{M}$ is specified in terms of both a prior distribution over the causes (X, Θ), namely $P(X, \Theta|m)$, and the likelihood function $P(Y|X, \Theta, m)$: $P(Y, X, \Theta, m) = P(Y|X, \Theta, m)P(X, \Theta|m)$. Thus, hidden and observable data are coupled by the generative model specified through the joint probability distribution $P(Y, X, \Theta|m)$.

Learning a generative model corresponds to making the probabilistic distribution of input data, implied by a generative model of parameters Θ, as close as possible to those actually observed. To this end, it is possible to derive the marginal distribution of the data generated under the model m (evidence) that has to be matched to the input distribution $P(Y)$

$$P(Y|m) = \int_{X,\Theta} P(Y|X, \Theta, m)P(X, \Theta|m)dXd\Theta, \qquad (1)$$

Once the parameters of the generative model have been learned, the recognition model is defined in terms of inverse probability [5], and *inference* of hidden variables X defining the partitioning of the image, is performed via Bayes' rule:

$$P(X|Y,\Theta,m) = \frac{P(Y|X,\Theta,m)P(X,\Theta|m)}{P(Y|m)} \tag{2}$$

Finally for a given pixel configuration Y, the best segmentation estimate $\hat{X}$ can be recovered under some suitable extremum principle (e,g., minimum mean squared error, MMSE or maximum a posteriori, MAP) related to the posterior probability $P(X|Y,\Theta,m)$. However, marginalization in Eq. 1 is often difficult because, in principle, all parameters of the model can be coupled; furthermore, the estimate $\hat{X}$ can be difficult to compute without approximations. Thus, in general, the generative model can not be easily inverted and it may not be possible to parameterise the posterior distribution.

A variational solution is to posit a simpler approximate distribution $Q(X,\Theta)$ that is consistent (same support) with the generative model $P(X,\Theta,Y)$ (in the following we drop model index m for notational simplicity). Any such distribution can be used to provide a lower bound to the evidence $P(Y)$, or equivalently to the log-likelihood $\mathcal{L}(Y) = \log P(Y)$, which can be rewritten as:

$$\mathcal{L}(Y) = \overbrace{\int_{X,\Theta} Q(X,\Theta) \log \frac{P(X,\Theta,Y)}{Q(X,\Theta)} dXd\Theta}^{F(Q)} + \overbrace{\int_{X,\Theta} Q(X,\Theta) \log \frac{Q(X,\Theta)}{P(X,\Theta|Y)} dXd\Theta}^{KL(Q||P)}, \tag{3}$$

where $KL(Q||P)$ is the *Kullback-Leibler* divergence between the approximating distribution and the true posterior distribution. By definition $KL(Q||P) \geq 0$, being equal to 0 when $Q(X,\Theta) = P(X,\Theta|Y)$. This implies that $\mathcal{L}(Y) \geq F(Q)$.

The "best" approximating distribution $Q(X,\Theta)$ is then the one that maximixes F, or equivalently minimizes the Kullback-Leibler divergence between Q and the joint posterior over hidden states and parameters; when KL = 0 then $\mathcal{L}(Y) = F$.

It is a common practice to restrict the family of Q so that they comprise only tractable distributions, and consider a factorization of the variational distribution between the hidden variables and the parameters, $Q(X,\Theta) = Q(X)Q(\Theta)$.

These can be further factorized in terms of mean field approximation [5], $Q(\Theta) = \prod_{i=1}^{N_p} Q(\Theta_i)$ and $Q(X) = \prod_{n=1}^{N} Q(x_n)$, with N_p being the number of parameters. For notational simplicity, define the latent variables $Z = \{X,\Theta\}$ so that $Q(Z) = \prod_{i=1}^{M} Q_i(Z_i)$ with $M = N_p + N$.

It has been shown that the free-form variational optimization of $F(Q)$ with respect to the distributions Q_i provides the optimal solution [6]:

$$Q_j^*(Z_j) = \frac{\exp[I(Z_j)]}{\int \exp[I(Z_i)]dZ_i} \tag{4}$$

with $I(Z_j) = \int \log P(Z,Y) \prod_{i \neq j} Q_i(Z_i) dZ_i$ The variational approximation thus maximises $F(Q)$ as a functional of the distribution $Q(X,\Theta)$, by iteratively maximizing F, with respect to each Q_j, $\frac{\partial F(Q)}{\partial Q_j} = 0, j = 1 \cdots M$.

Note that the set of equations used to recover $Q_j^*(Z_j)$ is a set of coupled fixed point equations ($Q_j^*(Z_j)$ is computed in terms of $Q_i(Z_i) dZ_i$), that require an iterative solution. Along iterations, the step performing the computation of hidden variables distribution $Q(X)$ by consideringr fixed $Q(\Theta)$, is defined the Variational Bayes E step (VBE), while the computation of $Q(\Theta)$ for given $Q(X)$ performs a Variational Bayes M step (VBM). These steps represent a Bayesian generalizazion of the E and M steps of the classic Expectation-Maximization (EM) algorithm [5] and in the following this method will be called the VBEM algorithm.

3 Learning an Image Model with Spatial Constraints

Clearly the core of the VB procedures is the generative model $P(Z,Y)$ that must be learned; in probabilistic image segmentation Finite Gaussian Mixtures (FGM, see Appendix 6 for a formal description) are widely used [9], [10], [8] . Unfortunately, the FGM model relies upon the assumption of independence of pixel data and class labels , which is inadequate for images where some form of spatial constraints should be introduced.

Spatial constrains can be introduced explicitly but this makes usually very complex the underlying graphical model and the learning/inference procedures [10], [11]. Here, to keep the model structure simple we introduce spatial constraints while performing the VB learning algorithm.

It is convenient to define the following quantities in analogy with statistical physics, that allow a deeper insight of the physical meaning of the bounding functional F: the Helmholtz free energy $F_H = -\mathcal{L}(Y)$; the Gibbs' variational free energy $F_G = -F$; the average energy (internal energy) $U(Q) = -\int Q(X,\Theta|Y) \log P(X,Y,\Theta|m) dX d\Theta$; the entropy

$$S((Q(X,\Theta)) = -\int_{X,\Theta} Q(X,\Theta|Y) \log Q(X,\Theta|Y) dX d\Theta. \tag{5}$$

By taking into account Eq. 3, then $F_G = F_H + KL(Q||P) = U(Q) - S(Q)$, which shows that the Kullback-Leibler distance will be zero, when the variational Gibbs free energy F_G achieves the Helmholtz free energy F_H. From this point of view, the problem of learning is the problem of minimizing the Gibbs free energy with respect to the distribution $Q(X,\Theta)$, which is exactly what is obtained by VBE and VBM steps.

Assume that after a VBE step the new distribution $Q(X)$ has been obtained. Then, before minimizing Gibbs free energy F_G with respect $Q(\Theta)$ (the VBM step), spatial constraints can be enforced by suitably modifying the distribution of segmentation labels $Q(X)$. Suitably means that we apply any trasformation $\mathcal{G}(Q) \rightarrow \tilde{Q}$ provided that the negative free energy increases or the Gibbs free energy F_G increases.

For instance, since $F_G = U(Q) - S(Q)$, one can choose a mapping $\mathcal{G}(Q)$ such that the entropy $S(Q)$ (Eq. 5) increases.

By using latent variable factorization $Q(X, \Theta) = Q(X)Q(\Theta)$, the normalization constraints $\int Q(X)dX = 1$ and $\int Q(\Theta)d\Theta = 1$, and assuming Θ fixed, Eq. 5 can be rewritten as:

$$S(Q(X, \Theta)) = - \int_X Q(X) \log Q(X)dX - \int_\Theta Q(\Theta) \log Q(\Theta)d\Theta = S(Q(X)) + const$$

(6)

At this point we need to specify a transformation $\mathcal{G}(\cdot)$ that increases the entropy of the hidden variables, namely $S(Q(X)) = - \int Q(X) \log Q(X)dX$, while taking into account the spatial correlations among labels.

Distribution $Q(X)$ on segmentation labels can be represented through a multinomial distribution $Q(X) = \prod_{n=1}^{N} \prod_{k=1}^{K} q_{nk}^{x_{nk}}$ (see Eq. 17, Appendix 6), where $q_{nk} \simeq P(k|y_n, \mu_k, \Lambda_k^{-1})$, i.e. are labels that represent an approximation to the posterior probability of classifying pixel y_n in the k-th class. The set $\{q_{nk}\}_{n=1}^{N}$ is a spatial layer representing label assignments of the image to class k.

Then, $S(Q(X)) = - \sum_{k=1}^{K} \sum_{n=1}^{N} q_{nk} \log q_{nk} = \sum_{k=1}^{K} S_k(Q(X))$ where $S_k(Q(X)) = \sum_{n=1}^{N} q_{nk} \log q_{nk}$ is a spatial entropy on label probabilities.

Define a scale-space transformation $q_{nk} \rightarrow \mathcal{G}_t(q_{nk})$, $t \geq 0$. It is well known that trasformations from fine to rough scales of resolution increase spatial entropy, and the simplest, and more widely used, one is the linear isotropic transformation generated via the diffusion equation $\frac{\partial q_{nk}}{\partial t} = g\nabla^2 q_{nk}$, where g is a constant. Isotropic, linear diffusion leads to a maximum spatial entropy, since the asymptotic q_{nk}^* are uniform distribution on the random field lattice $\mathbf{S}$, however this very fact makes it impossible to select select an optimal label, in that all probability assignements are equal.

Note that, instead, neighboring pixels should have the same probability to be assigned a given label k and labels at boundaries between regions should be characterized by an abrupt change of probability values. Thus, at each q_{nk} the field should be a piecewise constant function across the image and this result can be achieved [12] by a system of k anisotropic diffusion equations

$$\frac{\partial q_{nk}(t)}{\partial t} = \nabla \cdot (g(\|\nabla q_{nk}\|)\nabla q_{nk}(t))$$

(7)

one for each label probability plane; $g(\cdot)$ is a suitable conductance function, monotonically decreasing. Hence small differences of q_{nk} among pixels close to each other are smoothed out, since diffusion is allowed, whereas large variations are preserved.

Second, it has been shown that [12] for either isotropic or anisotropic $\mathcal{G}_t$, the functional $-S_k = \sum_{n=1}^{N} q_{nk} \log q_{nk}$ is a Lyapunov functional, decreasing under the transformation for $t \rightarrow \infty$. Equivalently, $S_k(\mathcal{G}_t(Q(X)))$ increases for $t \rightarrow \infty$. For each component k, Eq. 7 maximizes the k-th entropy $S_k(Q(X))$, thus increasing the total entropy $\sum_{k=1}^{K} S_k(Q(X))$ and consequently the total entropy in Eq. 6.

Once $Q(X)$ has been modified to account for spatial constraints through a diffusion step (VBD step), it can be used in the VBM step to maximize free energy with respect to the parameters.

We name this procedure the Variational Bayes Diffused EM (VBDEM). A graphical interpretation of the method is reported in Fig. 1.

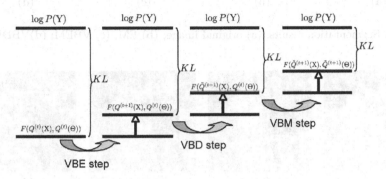

Fig. 1. The VBDEM algorithm. In the VBE step the variational posterior $Q(X)$ is set. In the VBD step diffusion is performed obtaining the diffused posterior $\tilde{Q}(X)$. In the VBM $\tilde{Q}(\Theta)$ is obtained. Each step is guaranteed to increase or leave unchanged the lower bound F on the fixed marginal likelihood.

4   Segmentation Via Spatially Constrained FGM Image Model

The FGM model is adopted (Appendix 6) where each pixel y_n is generated by one among K Gaussian distributions $\mathcal{N}(y_n; \mu_k, \Lambda^{-1}{}_k)$, with μ_k, Λ_k the means and the precision matrix (inverse covariance) of the k-th Gaussian and likelihood

$$P(y_n|\Theta) = \sum_{k=1}^{K} \pi_k \mathcal{N}(y_n; \mu_k, \Lambda^{-1}{}_k) \qquad (8)$$

Here $\{\pi_k\}_{k=1}^{K}$ are the mixing coefficients, with $\sum_{k=1}^{K} \pi_k = 1$ and $\pi_k \geq 0$ for all k.

Standard VB learning of the FGM model [6], [13] amounts to an iterative update of hidden variables and parameters distributions (Eqs. 17, 18, 19, Appendix 6). This entails an iterative solution in which the computation of the approximating posteriors q_{nk} (VBE step)

$$q_{nk} = e^{\left(-\frac{D}{2}\log 2\pi\right)} \tilde{\pi}_k \tilde{\Lambda}_k^{1/2} e^{\left(-\frac{1}{2}\nu_k (y_n - m_k)^T W_k (y_n - m_k)\right)} e^{\left(-\frac{D}{2\beta_k}\right)} \qquad (9)$$

and of hyperparameters (VBM step)

$$\alpha_k = \alpha_0 + \overline{N}_k, \quad \beta_k = \beta_0 + \overline{N}_k, \quad m_k = \frac{\beta_0 m_0 + \overline{N}_k \overline{\mu}_k}{\beta_k},$$

$$W_k^{-1} = \overline{N}_k \overline{\Sigma}_k + \frac{\overline{N}_k \beta_0}{\beta_k} (\overline{\mu}_k - m_0)(\overline{\mu}_k - m_0)^T + W_0^{-1}, \quad \nu_k = \nu_0 + \overline{N}_k, \qquad (10)$$

is repeated until convergence [6], [13].

(a)   (b)   (c)   (d)

Fig. 2. Segmentation results. (a) original image; (b) EM; (c) VBEM; (d)VBDEM.

(a)   (b)   (c)   (d)

Fig. 3. Segmentation results. (a) original image; (b) EM; (c) VBEM; (d)VBDEM.

To compute the hyperparameters update the following statistics of the observed data with respect to the q_{nk} need to be calculated [6], [13]: $\overline{\pi}_k = \frac{1}{N}\sum_{n=1}^{N} q_{nk}$, $\overline{N}_k = N\overline{\pi}_k$, $\overline{\mu}_k = \frac{1}{\overline{N}_k}\sum_{n=1}^{N} q_{nk}\mathrm{y}_n$, $\overline{\Sigma}_k = \frac{1}{\overline{N}_k}\sum_{n=1}^{N} q_{nk}(\mathrm{y}_n - \overline{\mu}_k)(\mathrm{y}_n - \overline{\mu}_k)^T$

Spatial constraints on the segmentation label distribution $Q(\mathrm{X})$ are applied through the discretized version of diffusion equation 7:

$$q_{nk}(\tau + 1) = q_{nk}(\tau) + \lambda(\nabla \cdot (g(\nabla q_{nk})\nabla q_{nk}(\tau))) \qquad (11)$$

Summing up, the VBDEM segmentation algorithm consists in the following steps: 1) Model *learning* by iteratively computing posteriors $q_{nk}(t)$ via Eq. 9, diffusing to impose spatial constraints (Eq. 11) and computing hyperparameters (Eqs. 10); 2) *Inference* by setting $P(k|\mathrm{y}_n, \boldsymbol{\mu}_k, \Lambda_k^{-1}) \simeq q_{nk}$; 3) *Classification* by setting $\mathrm{y}_n = \boldsymbol{\mu}_{k^*}$ where $k^* = \arg\max_k P(k|\mathrm{y}_n, \boldsymbol{\mu}_k, \Lambda_k^{-1})$.

5   Simulation

We have experimented the method on different kinds of natural and sports images. Here we present two examples, obtained using the *lighthouse* and the *players* images, and shown in Figs.2(a) and 3(a), respectively.

For all the experiments, the input is an RGB image $[\mathrm{y}^R, \mathrm{y}^G, \mathrm{y}^B]$ which is converted to $[\mathrm{y}^Y, \mathrm{y}^{Cr}, \mathrm{y}^{Cb}]$ in the YCrCb color space. For the proposed method and the VBEM one, hyperparameters $\alpha_0, W_0, \nu_0, \beta_0, \mathrm{m}_0$, are initialized as in [13]; approximate posteriors q_{nk} are initialized by using few iterations (5) of the 'k-means' algorithm [5]. On this basis we can initialize sufficient statistics $\overline{N}_k$,

$\overline{\Sigma}_k$, $\overline{\mu}_k$ and π_k and then hyperparameters $\alpha_k, W_k, \nu_k, \beta_k, \mathrm{m}_k$ as in Eqs. 10. At this point we iterate the VBE (Eq. 9), VBD (Eq: 7), and VBM (Eqs. 10) steps until convergence, $|F^{(p+1)} - F^{(p)}| < \epsilon$, where p indexes the iteration steps and $\epsilon = 10^{-4}$.

For what concerns the VBD step, the conductance function g can have a quite general form, but must be such that label boundaries are preserved, numerical stability guaranteed. In our experiments we set $g(\nabla q_{nk}) = |\nabla q_{nk}|^{-9/5}$, $\lambda = 0.01$ and a number of $\tau = 10$ iterations was used. The functions $q_{nk}(\tau)$ are renormalized so that their sum is one after each iteration.

We have used the same initialization for VBEM and VBDEM, and few iterations of the k-means algorithm for the EM initialization. Otherwise, different number of classes are used for each image, specifically, a number $K = 10$ was used for the *lighthouse* and $K = 6$ for the *players* image. For all the methods, the same convergence criterion was used.

Most important, it can be noted that, by using the mean vector μ_k as the color to represent the region of class k, the segmented result is chromatically coherent with the original image, as shown by comparing the results obtained by standard EM (Fig. 2(b), 3(b)), VBEM method (Fig. 2(c), 3(c)), and VBDEM method (Fig. 2(d), 3(d)) with the original image (Fig. 2(a), 3(a)). In fact, it is apparent the higher perceptual significance and the reliability of the VBDEM results, (Fig. 2(d), 3(d), as regards region classification for both the images.

6   Concluding Remarks

This paper contributes a novel approach to image segmentation where a VB technique is spatially constrained in order to overcome drawbacks due to independent pixel labelling [8]. The VB algorithm proposed is somehow related to attempts performed in the classic Maximum Likelihood (ML) setting, that have tried to incorporate within the EM algorithm a prior term in order to maximize a log posterior probability instead of log-likelihood e.g., [11], [10]. However here, different from ML, we are working in a full Bayesian framework where parameters are treated as random variables and a distribution is derived for each of them, with the advantages of avoiding the overfitting problem and achieving regularized solution.

Interestingly enough in [8] the unconstrained VBEM algorithm can be considered a learning procedure for a Gaussian neural network. From this point of view it can be seen, at each pixel, as a competitive process among the k different labels. In the algorithm we propose here, competition is integrated with a cooperation in terms of a diffusion step within sites on the same labelling plane.

Eventually, the problem of model selection (in the FGM, the number K of Gaussians) has not been discussed here, due to space limitations . However it should be noted that model selection is naturally handled in the Bayesian framework [5], [6], and is matter of ongoing research.

Acknowledgments

We gratefully acknowledge the Italian Group of Italian Researchers in Pattern Recognition (GIRPR) for financial support to Dr. Paolo Napoletano.

References

1. Helmholtz, H.: Physiological Optics: The Perception of Vision, Optical Society of America, Rochester, NY, vol. III (1925)
2. Kording, K., Wolpert, D.: Bayesian decision theory in sensorimotor control. Trends in Cognitive Sciences 10(7) (July 2006)
3. Chater, N., Tenenbaum, J., Yuille, A.: Probabilistic models of cognition: Conceptual foundations. Trends in Cognitive Sciences 10(7), 287–291 (2006)
4. Frey, B., Jojic, N.: A comparison of algorithms for inference and learning in probabilistic graphical models. IEEE Trans. on Pattern Analysis and Machine Intelligence 27, 1392–1416 (2005)
5. MacKay, D.J.C.: Information Theory, Inference & Learning Algorithms. Cambridge University Press, Cambridge, UK (2002)
6. Bishop, C.M.: Pattern Recognition and Machine Learning. Springer, Heidelberg (2006)
7. Lucchese, L., Mitra, S.K.: Color image segmentation: A state-of-the-art survey. In: INSA-A. Proc. Indian National Science Academy, vol. 67, pp. 207–221 (March 2001)
8. Nasios, N., Bors, A.G.: Variational learning for gaussian mixture models. IEEE Trans. on System, Man, and Cybernetics-B 36(4), 849–862 (2006)
9. Forsyth, D., Ponce, J.: Computer Vision: A Modern Approach. Prentice Hall International, Englewood Cliffs (2002)
10. Zhang, Y., Brady, M., Smith, S.: Segmentation of Brain MR Images Through a Hidden Markov Random Field Model and the Expectation-Maximization Algorithm. IEEE Trans. on Medical Imaging 20, 45–57 (2001)
11. Gopal, S.S., Hebert, T.: Bayesian pixel classification using spatially variant finite mixtures and the Generalized EM algorithm. IEEE Trans. on Image Processing 7, 1014–1028 (1998)
12. Weickert, J.: Applications of nonlinear diffusion in image processing and computer vision. Acta Math. Univ. Comenianae 70, 33–50 (2001)
13. Penny, W.: Variational bayes for d-dimensional gaussian mixture models. Technical report, Wellcome Department of Cognitive Neurology, University College, London, UK (2001)

Appendix: Unconstrained Finite Gaussian Mixture Model

Denote $\Theta = \{\pi, \mu, \Lambda\}$ the vector of parameters (random variables), with $\pi = \{\pi_k\}_{k=1}^{K}$, $\mu = \{\mu_k\}_{k=1}^{K}$, $\Lambda = \{\Lambda_k\}_{k=1}^{K}$. The set of hidden variables is $X = \{x_n\}_{n=1}^{N}$ where each hidden variable x_n related to observation y_n, is a 1-of-K binary vector of components $\{x_{nk}\}_{k=1}^{K}$, in which a particular element x_{nk} is equal to 1 and all other elements are equal to 0, that is $x_{nk} \in \{0, 1\}$ and $\sum_k x_{nk} = 1$. In other terms, x_n indicates which Gaussian component is responsible for generating pixel y_n, $P(y_n|x_{nk} = 1, \Theta) = \mathcal{N}(y_n; \boldsymbol{\mu}_k, \Sigma_k)$. The FGM generative model (joint probability $P(Y, X, \Theta)$) is defined as follows:

$$P(Y, X, \boldsymbol{\pi}, \boldsymbol{\mu}, \Lambda) = P(Y|X, \boldsymbol{\mu}, \Lambda)P(X|\boldsymbol{\pi})P(\boldsymbol{\pi})P(\boldsymbol{\mu}, \Lambda). \tag{12}$$

where:

$$P(Y|X, \boldsymbol{\mu}, \Lambda) = \prod_{n=1}^{N} P(y_n|x_n, \boldsymbol{\mu}, \Lambda) = \prod_{n=1}^{N} \prod_{k=1}^{K} \mathcal{N}(y_n, \boldsymbol{\mu}_k, \Lambda_k^{-1})^{x_{nk}}, \tag{13}$$

$$P(X|\boldsymbol{\pi}) = \prod_{n=1}^{N} P(x_n|\boldsymbol{\pi}) = \prod_{n=1}^{N} \prod_{k=1}^{K} \pi_k^{x_{nk}}, \tag{14}$$

$$P(\boldsymbol{\pi}) = \mathbf{Dir}(\boldsymbol{\pi}|\alpha) = \frac{\Gamma(\sum_{k=1}^{K} \alpha_k)}{\prod_{k=1}^{K} \Gamma(\alpha_k)} \prod_{k=1}^{K} \pi_k^{\alpha_k - 1} = C(\alpha) \prod_{k=1}^{K} \pi_k^{\alpha_0 - 1}, \tag{15}$$

$$P(\boldsymbol{\mu}, \Lambda) = \prod_{k=1}^{K} \mathcal{N}(\boldsymbol{\mu}_k; \mathbf{m}_0, (\beta_0 \Lambda_k)^{-1}) \mathcal{W}(\Lambda_k; W_0, \nu_0). \tag{16}$$

$\mathcal{N}(\boldsymbol{\mu}_k; \mathbf{m}_0, (\beta_0 \Lambda_k)^{-1})$ and $\mathcal{W}(\Lambda_k; W_0, \nu_0)$ are the Gaussian and Wishart distributions respectively.

In a Bayesian setting, parameters are treated as random variables governed by conjugate prior distributions $P(\boldsymbol{\pi})$, $P(\boldsymbol{\mu}, \Lambda)$ shaped as Dirichlet and Gaussian-Wishart distributions, respectively. Here, $\alpha_0, W_0, \nu_0, \beta_0, \mathbf{m}_0$ are the *hyperparameters* of the model. The approximating distribution $Q(X, \boldsymbol{\pi}, \boldsymbol{\mu}, \Lambda)$ is factorized as $Q(X)Q(\boldsymbol{\pi}, \boldsymbol{\mu}, \Lambda) = Q(X)Q(\boldsymbol{\pi})Q(\boldsymbol{\mu}, \Lambda)$, and the lower bound F(Q),is maximized by applying Eq. 4. The factors of the variational posterior can be calculated as [6], [13]:

$$Q(X) = \prod_{n=1}^{N} \prod_{k=1}^{K} q_{nk}^{x_{nk}} \tag{17}$$

$$Q(\boldsymbol{\pi}) = C(\alpha) \prod_{k=1}^{K} \pi_k^{(\overline{N}_k + \alpha_0 - 1)}, \tag{18}$$

$$Q(\boldsymbol{\mu}, \Lambda) = \prod_{k=1}^{K} \mathcal{N}(\boldsymbol{\mu}_k; \mathbf{m}_k, (\beta_k \Lambda_k)^{-1}) \mathcal{W}(\Lambda_k; W_k, \nu_k). \tag{19}$$

where $q_{nk} \simeq P(k|y_n, \boldsymbol{\mu}_k, \Lambda_k^{-1})$, represent an approximation to the posterior probability of labelling pixel y_n as belonging to the k-th class.

Watershed Segmentation Via Case-Based Reasoning

Maria Frucci[1], Petra Perner[2], and Gabriella Sanniti di Baja[1]

[1] Institute of Cybernetics "E.Caianiello", CNR, Pozzuoli, Italy
m.frucci@cib.na.cnr.it, g.sannitidibaja@cib.na.cnr.it
[2] Institute of Computer Vision and Applied Computer Science, Leipzig, Germany
p.perner@ibai-institut.de

Abstract. This paper proposes a novel grey-level image segmentation scheme employing case-based reasoning. Segmentation is accomplished by using the watershed transformation, which provides a partition of the image into regions whose contours closely fit those perceived by human users. Case-based reasoning is used to select the segmentation parameters involved in the segmentation algorithm by taking into account the features characterizing the current image. Preliminarily, a number of images are analyzed and the parameters producing the best segmentation for each image, found empirically, are recorded. These images are grouped to form relevant cases, where each case includes all images having similar image features, under the assumption that the same segmentation parameters will produce similarly good segmentation results for all images in the case.

1 Introduction

Image segmentation is a necessary preliminary step for any image analysis task. This process partitions an image into a number of constituting regions. Each partition region is homogeneous with respect to a given property, while the set including any two adjacent regions is not homogeneous. Segmentation has been widely studied, as it is witnessed by the large relative literature (see, e.g., [1-5]). Different homogeneity criteria can be used, e.g., based on grey-level distribution, texture, color, and so on. In this paper we will consider grey-level distribution.

Watershed transformation (WT) is a basic tool for image segmentation exploiting both region-based and edge-detection-based methodologies (see, e.g., [6,7]). The basic idea of this segmentation scheme is to identify in the gradient image of a grey-level image a suitable set of seeds from which to perform a growing process. The growing process determines the region associated to each seed, by gathering into the region all pixels that are closer to the corresponding seed more than to any other seed, provided that a certain homogeneity in grey-level is satisfied.

Watershed segmentation is not severely affected by the drawbacks characterizing region-based and edge-detection-based segmentation methods. In fact, the seeds from which region growing is performed are detected in the gradient image of the input grey-level image as the sets of pixels with locally minimal grey-level (called *regional minima*). In turn, the problem of identifying closed edges surrounding the regions of interest is solved, since the regions (and, hence, their boundaries) are determined by the growing process.

F. Mele et al. (Eds.): BVAI 2007, LNCS 4729, pp. 244–253, 2007.

Watershed segmentation has been used in different image domains, generally producing satisfactory results, since the obtained image partition is into regions whose boundaries closely fit those perceived by human users.

One of the main problems in using the WT is the excessive fragmentation of the image into a large number of partition regions, not all perceptually meaningful. Thus, watershed segmentation generally includes a merging phase aimed at suitably reducing the number of partition regions. To this purpose, a number of measures of properties of the partition regions have to be taken into account to distinguish meaningful and non-meaningful regions, and suitable thresholds on the values of these measures have to be set. The same region properties can be adequate in different image domains, but they do not always equally contribute to obtain the best segmentation results. In some cases, the computed measures of certain properties should be weighted more than the remaining measures. To automatically identify the proper weights for the measures, it can be useful to resort to case-based reasoning (CBR).

The use of CBR for image segmentation has been already attempted successfully in the past for segmentation methods different from those based on the use of the WT. In [8], CBR has been introduced in the framework of histogram-based segmentation. In [9], CBR has been used to optimize image segmentation at the low-level stage of the process, i.e., by taking into account image acquisition conditions and image quality. In [10], CBR and dissimilarity classification methods have been considered and in [11], improving system performance by controlling the image similarity measure has been described.

This work proposes a novel image watershed segmentation scheme employing case-based reasoning. In our approach, CBR is used to select the proper weights to be assigned to the measures of the region properties according to the current image characteristics. We assume that for images with similar image characteristics, similarly good segmentation results will be obtained by using the same weights.

This paper is organized as follows. In Section 2, we briefly discuss the general case-based approach to image segmentation. In Section 3, the watershed segmentation method proposed in [12] is sketched. In Section 4, we show how to improve the segmentation results of the algorithm [12] by using CBR. Some discussions and conclusions are given in Section 5.

2   The Case-Based Image Segmentation Approach

The segmentation problem can be seen as a classification problem, where the image at hand is compared to the images in a data-base to identify the best matching and, hence, select the segmentation criteria for the image at hand. The classifier needs a learning phase. In particular, the classifier needs to learn the mapping function between the image features and the segmentation parameters involved in the selected algorithm. Our basic idea is that there is a strong correlation between the features of an image and the obtained segmentation results. Using the same segmentation parameters for images with similar features should produce similarly good results.

The learning of the classifier should be accomplished on a large set of data, in order to build a general model for the segmentation problem. This is generally not the case, and the segmentation model should be adjusted to fit new data by means of a suitable case-base maintenance process. Though, case-base maintenance is an important topic, we will not discuss it in this communication. We remark that a general model does not always guarantee the best segmentation for each image. It guarantees an average best fit over the data-base.

Case-based reasoning can be used as basic methodology for image segmentation. The relative CBR process is shown in Fig.1.

The characteristics of an image can be, for example, some statistical features extracted from the grey-level image (mean, variance, skewness, kurtosis, variation coefficients, energy, entropy, centroid). These features are used for indexing the case-base and for retrieval of a set of cases that include images close to the current image, based on a proper image similarity measure. A case consists of the statistical features as well as the values assigned to the segmentation parameters. Among the close cases, the one maximizing image similarity with the current image is selected and the segmentation parameters adopted for this case are given to the image segmentation unit to process the current image. The output is the segmented image.

The result of the segmentation process is evaluated by the user. If the user considers the obtained result as non correct, the current image has to be added to the case-base as a new case. This means that the correct segmentation parameters have to be empirically identified.

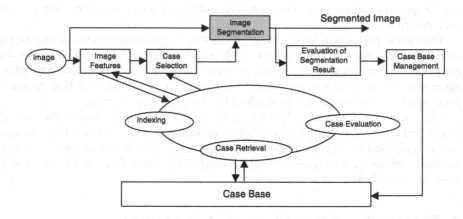

Fig. 1. Scheme of the CBR process

3   The Watershed Segmentation

The segmentation method we use in this work is based on the watershed transformation, [6]. This technique exploits both the region-based approach and edge detection. The seeds from which to perform region growing are detected as the regional minima in the gradient image of the input grey-level image. The partition regions are determined by the growing process. This is based on the distance of any pixel from the seeds, as well as on the grey-level so generating a partition of the image into regions characterized by homogeneity in grey-level.

The mechanism according to which the watershed partition is obtained can be understood by referring to the landscape paradigm. The gradient image can be interpreted as a 3D landscape, where the grey-level of a pixel in position (x,y) is interpreted as its height. Thus, high grey-levels are mapped into mountains and low grey-levels into valleys. Pixels with locally higher grey-level identify peaks, and pixels with locally lower grey-level correspond to pits in the landscape. If the pits are pierced and the landscape is immersed in water, the landscape will start to be flooded as soon as the water level will reach the pits. The valleys that will be flooded first are those whose pits are the lowest ones, since they are reached first by the increasing level of the water. A dam is built to prevent water to spread from a catchment's basin into the close ones, wherever waters from different basins are going to meet. When the whole landscape has been covered by water, the top lines of the dams constitute the watershed lines, i.e., the boundaries of the partition regions of the input grey-level image.

Watershed segmentation can be used for a wide repertory of images and the watershed lines generally border in a satisfactory way the regions into which the image is partitioned. However, if all the regional minima detected in the gradient image are used as seeds for the growing process, the image is fragmented into a too large number of homogeneous regions, not all perceptually significant. This problem, known as over-segmentation, can be solved by selecting only a reduced, significant, set of regional minima, or by merging the obtained partition regions. In general, both seed selection and region merging are taken into account. Once the final partition is available, its regions have to be classified as belonging to either the foreground or the background [13]. This task depends on problem domain.

3.1 Seed Selection Based on Region Significance

To reduce over-segmentation, only seeds corresponding to significant regions should be detected and used during the growing process. Seed reduction can be achieved by using a filter to remove irrelevant minima, but a priori knowledge on the class of images would be necessary to design the proper filter. We use a fully automatic way to reduce the number of seeds performing well on different image domains. The method is based on the notion of significance of the regions of the watershed partition and is accomplished by means of techniques that, by using the landscape paradigm, can be called *flooding* and *digging*.

The general scheme is the following. The notion of significance is used to discriminate the significant and the non-significant regions in the initial watershed partition of the grey-level image. Flooding and digging are then used to cause disappearance of the regional minima corresponding to the non-significant regions. The watershed transform is computed again, starting from the seeds surviving flooding and digging, so that a less fragmented partition of the image is obtained. The process is iterated until no seed can be removed by flooding and digging, meaning that all surviving seeds are relevant.

The definition of significant region is crucial to obtain a meaningful partition. In [12], a new criterion was introduced to evaluate region significance in watershed partitioned images and to filter out the irrelevant seeds by flooding and digging. In particular, flooding and digging reduce the seeds in such a way to cause merging of non-significant regions during the region growing process only with selected adjacent regions.

The significance of a catchment basin was defined by taking into account the portion of the landscape where the basin is placed, i.e., was evaluated with respect to the adjacent basins. Let us consider the basin X and let Y be one of the basins adjacent to X. The pixel p at the minimal height along the ridge separating X from Y is called the *relative local overflow* of X with respect to Y and its grey-level is denoted by LO_{XY}. The local overflow pixel is the one where the dam separating X from Y should start to be built to prevent overflow from X to Y. See Fig.2.

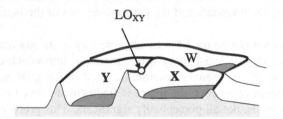

Fig. 2. Local overflow pixel for the basin X with respect to the basin Y

For a basin X, the set of pixels of X having grey-levels less than the relative local overflow LO_{XY} was considered. This set of pixels is the lake formed when the water reaches the relative local overflow pixel and is denoted by L_{XY}. Let us denote by R_X the grey-level of the pit of the basin X. With reference to Fig. 2 we can define the *depth* D_{XY} of X with respect to Y as follows:

$$D_{XY} = \max_{p \in L_{XY}} \{LO_{XY} - p\} = LO_{XY} - R_X$$

A relative *region similarity measure* SM_{XY} was also introduced, as the absolute value of the difference in altitude between the pits of X and the adjacent basin Y:

$$SM_{XY} = |R_X - R_Y|$$

The relative depth D_{XY} and the region similarity measure SM_{XY} were, then, used to evaluate the relative significance of X with respect to Y. Precisely, a basin X was termed significant with respect to Y if the following holds:

$$SM_{XY} > St \quad \text{OR} \quad D_{XY} > Dt \qquad (1)$$

where St and Dt are threshold values, computed automatically by using statistics on the initial watershed partition of the grey-level image.

In Fig. 3, the watershed partition of an image is shown as an example of the performance of flooding and digging to reduce over-segmentation, With respect to the initially detected 1213 basins, only 79 basins are found in the final image.

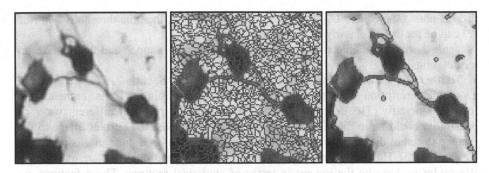

Fig. 3. Input image, left, partition of the image obtained by WT in 1213 regions, middle, segmentation by the algorithm [12] in 79 regions, right

4 Improving Watershed Segmentation by CBR

To improve the performance of the segmentation algorithm [12], we should not use a crisp test to decide about merging. In fact, according to rule (1) it is enough that one of the two measures overcomes the relative threshold, in order a region be classified as significant with respect to an adjacent region. We think that better results could be achieved if we require that both measures SM_{XY} and D_{XY} are taken into account, possibly giving different weights to their contributions. We also think that the weights should be determined by analyzing the image characteristics. Thus, we here use image characteristics and CBR to weight the influence of the two measures SM_{XY} and D_{XY}. Depending on image characteristics, we weight the influence of region similarity and of depth by means of two weights a and b, and introduce a threshold T as in the following:

$$\frac{1}{2}(a \cdot \frac{SM_{XY}}{St} + b \cdot \frac{D_{XY}}{Dt}) > T \tag{2}$$

If at least one of the values SM_{XY}/St and D_{XY}/Dt is larger than 1, then rule (1) would classify the region X as significant with respect to the adjacent region Y. If $a=b=1$ and the threshold T is set to 0.5, rule (2) would also classify X as significant with respect

Table 1. Possible combinations of the values a, b and T

a	b	T	Interpretation
1.5	0,5	1	Region similarity is weighted more than depth.
1	1	0,5	Region similarity and depth are equally weighted.
0,75	1,25	0,7	Depth is weighted more than region similarity.
0,75	1,25	1,35	Region similarity is weighted less than depth, and SM_{XY} and D_{XY} are quite larger than the relative thresholds St and Dt.
1	1	0,95	Region similarity and depth are equally weighted, and SM_{XY} and D_{XY} can be smaller than the relative thresholds St and Dt.

to Y. If both SM_{XY}/St and D_{XY}/Dt have value larger than 1, then the threshold T in rule (2) can be set to 1 to classify X as by rule (1).

Table 1 shows possible combinations of values for a, b and T and the relative interpretations.

To use CBR we need to build our case-base. As said in Section 2, a case consists of a suitable description of an image, coupled with the best solution to its segmentation, found empirically. The description of the image can be given in different ways. A possibility could be to directly store the image and compare the current image to the images stored in the cases, pixel to pixel. Some work has been done in this direction, e.g., in [14,15]. However, memory occupation and computational cost are quite large. We prefer to describe the images in terms of statistical features. These features are statistical measures of the grey levels, like mean, variance, skewness, kurtosis, variation coefficient, energy, entropy, and centroid, as suggested in [16]. These features are shown in Table 2, where the first order histogram $H(g)$ is equal to $N(g)/S$, being g the grey-level, $N(g)$ the number of pixels with grey-level g and S the total number of pixels. The image similarity is calculated on the basis of these features.

Table 2. Image Features

Feature Name	Calculation	Feature Name	Calculation
Mean	$\bar{g} = \sum_g g \cdot H(g)$	Variance	$\delta_g^2 = \sum_g (g-\bar{g})^2 H(g)$
Skewness	$g_s = \dfrac{1}{\delta_g^3} \sum_g (g-\bar{g})^3 H(g)$	Kurtosis	$g_k = \dfrac{1}{\delta_g^4} \sum_g (g-\bar{g})^4 H(g) - 3$
Variation Coefficient	$v = \dfrac{\delta}{\bar{g}}$	Entropy	$g_E = -\sum_g H(g) \log_2 [H(g)]$
Centroid_x	$\bar{x} = \dfrac{\sum_x \sum_y x f(x,y)}{\bar{g}S}$	Centroid_y	$\bar{y} = \dfrac{\sum_x \sum_y y f(x,y)}{\bar{g}S}$

We compute the image similarity SIM between two images A and B in the data-base of images as the complement to 1 of the distance between A and B. The distance between A and B is computed as follows:

$$dist_{AB} = \frac{1}{k} \sum_{i=1}^{K} w_i \left| \frac{C_{iA} - C_{i\min}}{C_{i\max} - C_{i\min}} - \frac{C_{iB} - C_{i\min}}{C_{i\max} - C_{i\min}} \right|$$

where C_{iA} and C_{iB} are the values of the i-th feature of A and B, respectively, $C_{i\min}$ and $C_{i\max}$ are the minimum and maximum value respectively of the i-th feature of all images in the data-base, and w_i is the weight for the i-th feature with $w_1 + w_2 + ... + w_i + ... + w_k = 1$. In our case, we assign the same value to all weights.

5 Discussion and Conclusion

Our case-base includes images mainly of biological nature, like different kinds of cells. The results we have achieved are generally satisfactory. The evaluation of the results has been done by comparing the segmentation obtained by our method with the segmentation manually performed by an expert. With respect to the algorithm [12], the new method based on CBR generally performs better. The two algorithms perform mostly the same, when the case retrieved from the case-base for the image at hand suggests that the best solution is for $a=1$, $b=1$ and $T=0,5$, i.e., when region similarity and depth have the same influence and at least one out of SM_{XY}/St and D_{XY}/Dt is larger than 1. This occurs for the input image shown in the example of Fig.3. The two segmentations obtained for this image by the algorithm [12] and the new algorithm are shown in Fig. 4. In turn, the new method performs significantly better whenever image similarity suggests that the best solution for the current image is obtained with a different choice for a, b and T. See for example the images shown in Fig. 5. In Fig.5 top, the image is segmented into 286 regions by the algorithm [12], while a significantly less over-segmented partition in 54 regions is obtained by using the solution $a=1.5$, $b=0.5$ and $T=1$ as suggested by taking into account the image similarity between the current image and those stored in the case-base. Analogously, for the image in Fig.5 bottom, a segmentation in 126 regions is obtained by using the solution with $a=1$, $b=1$ and $T=0.95$, while 200 regions were obtained by the algorithm [12].

We have tried to use our method for a general image domain, including for example faces, animals and natural scenes. Some of these images, though appearing to the user as clearly different from the biological images in the case-base, where characterized by similar statistical features. Thus, these images would be expected to be well segmented by using the same values for a, b and T adopted for the correspondingly similar biological images. Unfortunately, the values empirically found as those producing the best segmentation results for the non biological images did not coincide with those found via CBR. This means that to extend the validity of our method to a general image domain, further work related to image description is necessary. The alternatives we are currently considering are the use of other statistical features, or a combination of statistical features with an image description directly based on the images, or by considering also non-image information (such as the position of the camera, the relative movement of the camera, and the object category).

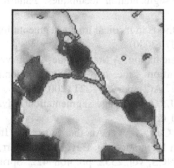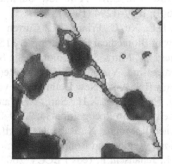

Fig. 4. Two very similar results, obtained by using the algorithm in [12], left, and the new method, right

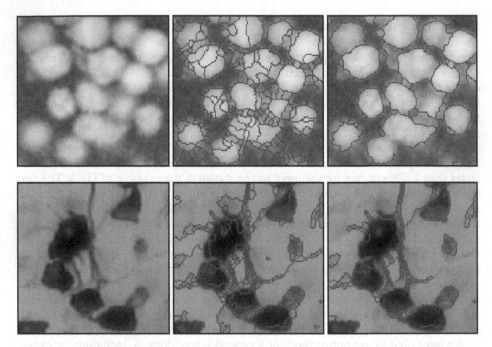

Fig. 5. Input image, left, segmentation with the algorithm [12], middle, and segmentation with the new method, right. In both top and bottom examples, a better segmentation is obtained by the new method.

Acknowledgements

This work has been partially supported by the Italian National Research Council, CNR, in the framework of the Short Term Mobility Program 2006.

References

1. Pal, N.R., Pal, S.K.: A review on image segmentation techniques. Pattern Recognition 26(9), 1277–1294 (1993)
2. Pham, D.L., Xu, C., Prince, J.L.: Current methods in medical image segmentation. Annual Review of Biomedical Engineering 2, 315–337 (2000)
3. Lucchese, L., Mitra, S.K.: Color Image Segmentation: A State-of-the-Art Survey. In: Image Processing, Vision, and Pattern Recognition. Proc. of the Indian National Science Academy (INSA-A), New Delhi, India, vol. 67 A(2), pp. 207–221 (2001)
4. Cheng, H.D., Jiang, X.H., Sun, Y., Wang, J.: Color image segmentation: advances and prospects. Pattern Recognition 34, 2259–2281 (2001)
5. Freixenet, J., Muñoz, X., Raba, D., Martí, J., Cufí, X.: Yet Another Survey on Image Segmentation: Region and Boundary Information Integration. In: Heyden, A., Sparr, G., Nielsen, M., Johansen, P. (eds.) ECCV 2002. LNCS, vol. 2352, pp. 408–422. Springer, Heidelberg (2002)

6. Beucher, S., Lantuejoul, C.: Use of watersheds in contour detection. In: Proc. Int. Workshop on Image Processing, Real-Time Edge and Motion Detection/Estimation, Rennes, France (1979)
7. Beucher, S., Meyer, F.: The morphological approach of segmentation: the watershed transformation. In: Dougherty, E. (ed.) Mathematical Morphology in Image Processing, Marcel Dekker, New York, pp. 433–481 (1993)
8. Perner, P.: An Architecture for a CBR Image Segmentation System. Journal on Engineering Application in Artificial Intelligence 12(6), 749–759 (1999)
9. Perner, P.: CBR Ultra Sonic Image Interpretation. In: Blanzieri, E., Portinale, L. (eds.) EWCBR 2000. LNCS (LNAI), vol. 1898, pp. 479–481. Springer, Heidelberg (2000)
10. Perner, P.: Are case-based reasoning and dissimilarity-based classification two sides of the same coin? Journal Engineering Applications of Artificial Intelligence 15(3), 205–216 (2002)
11. Perner, P., Perner, H., Müller, B.: Similarity Guided Learning of the Case Description and Improvement of the System Performance in an Image Classification System. In: Craw, S., Preece, A.D. (eds.) ECCBR 2002. LNCS (LNAI), vol. 2416, pp. 604–612. Springer, Heidelberg (2002)
12. Frucci, M.: Oversegmentation Reduction by Flooding Regions and Digging Watershed Lines. International Journal of Pattern Recognition and Artificial Intelligence 20(1), 15–38 (2006)
13. Frucci, M., Arcelli, C., Sanniti di Baja, G.: Detecting and ranking foreground regions in gray-level images. In: De Gregorio, M., Di Maio, V., Frucci, M., Musio, C. (eds.) BVAI 2005. LNCS, vol. 3704, pp. 406–415. Springer, Heidelberg (2005)
14. Zamperoni, P., Starovoitov, V.: How dissimilar are two gray-scale images. In: Proceedings of the 17th DAGM Symposium, pp. 448–455. Springer, Heidelberg (1995)
15. Wilson, D.L., Baddeley, A.J., Owens, R.A.: A new metric for grey-scale image comparison. International Journal of Computer Vision 24(1), 1–29 (1997)
16. Dreyer, H., Sauer, W.: Prozeßanalyse. Verlag Technik, Berlin (1982)

Digital Removal of Blotches with Variable Semi-transparency Using Visibility Laws

Vittoria Bruni[1], Andrew Crawford[1,2], Anil Kokaram[3], and Domenico Vitulano[1]

[1] Istituto per le Applicazioni del Calcolo "M.Picone" - C.N.R.
Viale del Policlinico 137, 00161 Rome, Italy
{bruni,vitulano}@iac.rm.cnr.it
[2] Dip. di Modelli e Metodi Matematici per le Scienze Applicate
Universitá di Roma "La Sapienza"
Via A. Scarpa 16, 00161 Rome, Italy
ajcrawford@gmail.com
[3] Electronic and Electrical Engineering Department
University of Dublin, Trinity College, Ireland
akocaram@tcd.ie

Abstract. This paper presents an automatic technique that removes blotches from archived photographs. In particular, we focus on blotches caused by water and dirt that cause a variable semi-transparency in the degraded region. The proposed digital removal consists of an automatic shrinking of the blotch that preserves the original image details. This operation is based on visibility laws in the wavelet domain. Preliminary experimental results show that the proposed model is also effective on critical blotches produced by dust and dirt.

Keywords: Wavelet transform, visibility laws, Bayes minimization, blotch removal.

1 Introduction

The huge amount of ancient documents and photos held in archives represents a great treasure from a cultural heritage point of view. However, they are subjected to various kinds of degradation [1] among which the most frequent is probably the semitransparent blotch [2,3]. It is caused by a water drop falling on the document support — usually paper. The spreading and the penetration of the water causes a darker region on the document with variable shape, color and intensity. The artifact becomes also more complicated if dirt and dust are present. Despite an immediate detection by most human observers, both digital detection and restoration are very difficult. Detection is difficult as the semi-transparency nature of the blotch leaves almost all high frequency information unchanged — see for instance [2,4]. Restoration is not trivial. In fact, the objective is to recover the document information as much as possible and then methods that synthesize information as in [5,6] can not be applied. An automatic model for the detection of blotches in the HSV color space [7] has been proposed in [8]. It defines a new visibility based distortion measure (alternative to [9,10,11,12]), whose behaviour

F. Mele et al. (Eds.): BVAI 2007, LNCS 4729, pp. 254–263, 2007.

is similar to a rate distortion curve [13]. This approach provides a quite accurate mask of the blotches on the document under study.

In this paper we propose a restoration approach based on visibility, that works on both classical (only water) and dirt-affected blotches. It firstly performs the detection for each blotch and then refines the results to the correct boundary. Hence, a different strategy is applied on the three color channels since the analysed images are sepia. As regards the luminance component, a suitable shrinking of the degraded region using a spline interpolated surface is performed. This phase is required for reshaping the blotch as a classical one — i.e. without dust and dirt. In practice, in this phase the darker region around boundary is reduced. The shrinking effect also reduces the contrast between the blotch and the surrounding information according to the Weber's law. But, a uniform shrinking for the whole blotch could create annoying artifacts because of the complicated structure of both the original (clean) information and the blotch. Hence, a Bayesian refinement oriented to give a local smooth shrinking is required. As regards the two chroma components, just the bayesian shrinkage is usually enough for giving a satisfactory result. Experimental results show

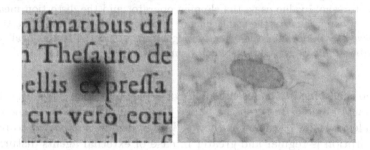

Fig. 1. (Left): Blotch on a paper. It does not contain a darker border. (**Right**) Blotch on photographs: it has a darker boundary due to the presence of dust and dirt.

the satisfactory performances in terms of subjective quality of the proposed approach on some selected images, where moisture causes a strongly variable semi-transparency of the defect.

The outline of the paper is the following. Section II shows some simple concepts about the physical formation of the considered type of blotch. A short review of the detection approach in [8] and a possible refinement of its results are then contained in Section III. Section IV presents the proposed restoration phase while some experimental results and conclusions are offered in Section V.

2   Physical Formation of a Water Blotch

From a physical point of view, the formation of a blotch on a paper such as photos, books, etc. can be described by the water spreading and the penetration into a porous medium [14,15]. In particular, when a drop of water falls on a paper, the wetting front advances till an equilibrium state is reached. The duration of contact between the pores and the water regulates the absorption. The central region of the blotch absorbs more than the external one [14], as shown in Fig. 1 (middle). The physical behavior is difficult to describe since it depends on casual external agents that can influence the absorption process as well as the topology of both the drop and the paper, etc.. A simplification is then required. The

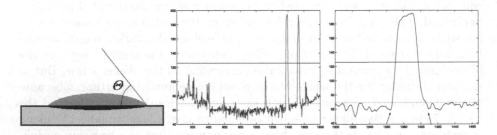

Fig. 2. (**Left**) Simplified behaviour of a water drop on a porous medium. (**Middle**) Section of an image containing a blotch and (**Right**) its zoom. The straight line indicates the threshold value using the clipping operator and the distortion measure $\overline{D}$ on saturation component of the whole image. The dotted line indicates the threshold value achieved by performing the detection algorithm, restricted to the locality of the blotch. Arrows indicate the correct blotch boundary.

water drop is assumed to be a semi sphere or a part of a sphere (see Fig. 2.Left). The (contact) angle Θ between the paper plane and the surface of the drop in correspondence to its boundary is then $\leq \frac{\pi}{2}$. This angle is expected to be small if the absorption is regular and greater in case of external agents disturbing it. In general, a blotch is dark in its central part and as lighter as one approaches the boundary. Nonetheless, this is not the case when dirt and dust (or paper irregularity) are present before the water damage. In this case the blotch appears darker at its edge too — see Fig. 1 (right). It is therefore evident that the contact angle provides important information about the absorption process. It can be estimated exploiting the radius and the height (in intensity) of the blotch.

3 A Short Review About the Detection Phase

In this section we give a short review of the visibility based detection phase in [8], as it is useful to understand the rest of the paper.

Even though water blotches contain most of the original information (due to their semi-transparency), they are usually visible at first glance. The detection phase exploits this feature via a visibility based model. Once digitized, archive photographs appear as sepia images and the blotches are colored (reddish or yellowish) regions. The HSV color space (Hue, Saturation, Value) is used for two reasons: *i)* it correlates well with the HVS (Human Visual System) behaviour [7]; *ii)* blotches are visible as bright areas in the saturation component.

The **first step** of the detection phase consists of achieving an automatic trade-off between blotch regularization and loss of redundant information — from a visibility point of view. This step consists of iteratively convolving the scaling function ϕ_j (of a wavelet basis) with the saturation component at various resolutions j. The best level of resolution J is the one measuring the minimum perceivable contrast between two successive blurred images as in [16], i.e.

$$J = argmin_{j \in \mathbf{N}} \{C(j) \leq 0.02\}, \tag{1}$$

where

$$C(j) = \frac{1}{|\Omega|} \sum_{(x,y) \in \Omega} \frac{|(S * \phi_j)(x,y) - (S * \phi_{j-1})(x,y)|}{(S * \phi_j)(x,y)}, \tag{2}$$

S is the saturation component, j is the scale level, Ω is the image domain and $|\Omega|$ is its size. The optimal point coincides with the maximum inflection of the contrast curve, providing the blurred saturation version S^J.

The **second step** consists of eliminating spurious bright regions in S^J. They coincide with black or white objects in the luminance component. We can build an adaptive non linear filter whose aim is to shrink saturation values $S^J(x,y)$ with respect to the corresponding ones in the luminance $V^J(x,y)$. The filter is

$$w(x,y) = \left(1 - \frac{|V^J(x,y) - MED|}{max_{x,y}|V^J(x,y) - MED|}\right), \quad (x,y) \in \Omega$$

where Ω is the image domain and MED is the median value of V^J. Hence, the new shrinked saturation is then

$$S_{sh}(x,y) = w(x,y)S^J(x,y). \tag{3}$$

Pixels whose luminance value is far from the median value are shrinked toward zero, while values approaching the median are left almost unchanged.

The **third step** aims to determine a threshold that splits S_{sh} into degradation and clean information. It is achieved by successive thresholding and a new distortion metric $\overline{D}$ — for alternative approaches see for instance [9,10,11,12,17]. $\overline{D}$ measures the change of perception of the thresholded S_{sh} and is defined as follows:

$$\overline{D}(\Omega_{T(t)}) = \frac{1}{|\Omega_{T(t)}|} \sum_{(x,y) \in \Omega_{T(t)}} D_1(x,y)D_2(x,y). \tag{4}$$

$D_1(x,y)$ is: $D_1(x,y) = \frac{I(x,y) - I_{T(t)}(x,y)}{M}$, $\forall (x,y) \in \Omega$, and it measures the change of perception of two different images I and $I_{T(t)}$ on a fixed background of intensity M. I is the original image while $I_{T(t)}$ is I clipped by the threshold value $T(t)$. The second distortion D_2 describes the contrast of the same object I over different backgrounds ($M_{T(t)}$ and M):

$$D_2(x,y) = \frac{I(x,y)(M_{T(t)} - M)}{M_{T(t)}M}, \quad \forall (x,y) \in \Omega, \tag{5}$$

and it can be seen as the product of two different components: $\frac{I}{M_{T(t)}}$ and $\frac{(M_{T(t)}-M)}{M}$. When $\overline{D}$ is calculated on S_{sh} using different thresholds $T(t)$, the corresponding curve $(|\Omega_{T(t)}|, \overline{D}(\Omega_{T(t)}))$ can be seen as a rate distortion curve and gives the optimal point of separation between the foreground and the background. Its maximum value corresponds to the maximum contrast that is able to separate different objects of the image without introducing artifacts [8].

3.1 A Proposal for Refining the Detection

Even if automatic, the detection model above gives a threshold value able to discriminate all blotches inside a scene. We then expect that this value will not be precise for a given blotch, especially in case of blotches caused by water and dirt — the topic of this paper. In this case the limit angle is high, providing a high gradient in correspondence of the blotch boundary $\partial\Omega$. The situation does not improve if we perform the detection in a smaller region containing the blotch. This is due to the high variability of the image (see Fig. 2) and the fact that the distortion $\overline{D}$ is a global measure. It is obvious that a wrong result in detection leads to an incorrect restoration that leaves a portion (around the boundary) of the damaged region. This is further emphasized by the fact that any restoration strategy would introduce a visible edge in correspondence to the boundary $\partial\Omega$. A refinement is then necessary for each blotch — both dirt and clean.

The aim of this operation is to give a new region $\tilde{\Omega}$ that exactly matches the degraded region and whose size will be greater than $|\Omega|$. The strategy then consists of looking for a new boundary $\partial\tilde{\Omega}$ circumscribing $\partial\Omega$ such that

$$\partial\tilde{\Omega} = \{x \in \tilde{\Omega}: \quad |\nabla S_{sh}(x)| \leq \tan(\overline{\theta}) \quad \wedge \quad d(x, \partial\Omega) \text{ is minimum}\} \quad (6)$$

where $d(.)$ is the euclidean distance. In other words, the new boundary includes all points whose gradient falls within the range $[0, \overline{\theta}]$ of admissible contact angle for a water blotch on a paper [14], i.e. $\overline{\theta} = 60°$. Even though more sophisticated techniques can be employed, $\tilde{\Omega}(x, y)$ can be simply calculated by computing the horizontal and vertical discrete differences and then selecting those points that satisfy (6) and that are closest to $\Omega(x, y)$.

4   The Proposed Restoration

The choice of the wavelet basis is fundamental for the restoration phase. In fact, the contact angle for classical blotches regulates the choice of the vanishing moments of wavelet basis to use. The most suitable bases are those which are less sensitive to both the curvature variation in correspondence to the boundary and to the inner part of a classical blotch, giving small wavelet coefficients. It has been empirically found that Daubechies wavelet [18] having four vanishing moments is suitable for most of the classical blotches.

4.1 Restoration of the Approximation Band

The first step consists of decomposing both the saturation component S and the luminance one V in a wavelet basis till the scale level J [18]. While the luminance decomposition is required for restoration, the saturation component S_{sh} is still useful in the restoration as follows. We can interpolate the blotch region in the approximation band of the saturation component at scale level J, by just considering the information outside Ω. The saturation component is the most suitable: it contains little image information because of its sepia nature but any blotch appears bright in it. A 2D spline interpolation is then performed achieving a new approximation band of the saturation component S_i^J. This will correspond to S^J outside $\tilde{\Omega}$ and to a smoothly interpolated surface inside. This new shape looks like a classical blotch — without any boundary. We then have to reshape the approximation band of the luminance component exploiting the new shape above. It can be achieved using the following attenuation:

$$V_a^J = \frac{V^J + \gamma V_i^J}{1 + \gamma} \tag{7}$$

where V^J is the original approximation band of V, V_a^J its attenuated version and V_i^J the interpolated approximation band of V. The shrinking parameter γ accounts for the different variance inside and outside the region $\tilde{\Omega}$. It is estimated on S_i^J and then used in (7) for V component. γ implicitly contains the Weber law, since just the (estimated) blotch shape is attenuated to reduce the contrast. However, this shrinking operation still gives a slightly visible region. The reason stems from the fact that a rigid shrinking is not suitable for complicated shape like that of blotches. Hence, the following bayesian refinement is applied. In agreement with the aforementioned semi-transparency hypothesis, V_a^J can be modeled as a multi-layer image similar to [19], where it can be seen as a mixture between the clean image layer and the blotch layer [20]. Our blotch can then be written as:

$$V_a^J(\mathbf{x}) = \alpha(\mathbf{x}) V_r^J(\mathbf{x}) + \epsilon(\mathbf{x}) \tag{8}$$

where V_a^J is the observed luminance approximation band at point $\mathbf{x}$, $\alpha(\mathbf{x})$ the distortion layer and $V_r^J(\mathbf{x})$ the clean luminance approximation band. Noise is represented by $\epsilon(\mathbf{x}) \sim N(0, \sigma_\epsilon^2)$.

We look for values of V_r^J and α that maximise

$$p(V_r^J, \alpha | V_a^J, \sigma_\epsilon^2) \propto p(V_a^J | V_r^J, \alpha, \sigma_\epsilon^2) p(\alpha | \overline{\alpha}) p(V_r^J | \overline{V_r^J}) \tag{9}$$

where $\overline{\alpha}$ and $\overline{V_r^J}$ are α and V in the neighbourhood of $\mathbf{x}$ respectively.

The three terms composing the rightmost member require smoothness of both α and $V_r^J(\mathbf{x})$ and their mixing. Rewriting these terms as follows:

$$p(V_a^J | V_r^J, \alpha, \sigma_\epsilon^2) \propto exp(\frac{-(V_a^J(\mathbf{x}) - \alpha(\mathbf{x}) V_r^J(\mathbf{x}))^2}{2\sigma_\epsilon^2})$$

$$p(\alpha | \overline{\alpha}) \propto exp(-\sum_{k=0}^{n} \lambda_k (\alpha(\mathbf{x}) - \alpha(\mathbf{x} + q_k))^2)$$

$$p(V_r^J | \overline{V_r^J}) \propto exp(-\sum_{k=0}^{n} \lambda_k (V_r^J(\mathbf{x}) - V_r^J(\mathbf{x} + q_k))^2)$$

where $\mathbf{x} + q_k$ is a neigbouring sample and λ_k is a weight depending on the distance to this sample. But to maximize $p(V_r^J, \alpha | V_a^J, \sigma_\epsilon^2)$ is equivalent to minimising the following energy:

$$E = W_1 \frac{(V_a^J(\mathbf{x}) - \alpha(\mathbf{x}) V_r^J(\mathbf{x}))^2}{2\sigma_\epsilon^2} + W_2 \sum_{k=0}^{n} \lambda_k (\alpha(\mathbf{x}) - \alpha(\mathbf{x} + q_k))^2 +$$

$$+ W_3 \sum_{k=0}^{n} \lambda_k (V_r^J(\mathbf{x}) - V_r^J(\mathbf{x} + q_k))^2. \quad (10)$$

Weights W_1, W_2 and W_3 regulate the emphasis on the different constraints modeled by the 3 terms of (10).

The energy (10) can be minimized in two steps. The first one provides a "first guess" to each pixel belonging to the blotch region. In other words, the pixel value is taken from clean pixels out of the blotch region, as in [20]. They lie on a circle, centered on the current pixel, whose radius is defined as: $log(d(\mathbf{x}) + 1) + S_{\psi_J}$, where $d(\mathbf{x})$ is the distance to the edge and S_{ψ_J} is the wavelet support at the considered scale level J. The second step of minimization uses ICM (Iterative Conditional Mode) algorithm [21] for minimizing (10) and the first guess in the first step as initial condition. Minimization consists of recursively and alternatively improving estimates for V_r^J and α. The blotch is processed from the outside-in on the premise that values drawn from closer neighbourhoods are more likely to be accurate. The blotch is divided into Onion-like orbital rings calculated using morphological operators.Minimization is performed on individual rings, firstly from the outside-in then inside-out, accounting for the update.

4.2 Blotch Removal from the Luminance Wavelet Details

We have seen that the Daubechies wavelet basis with 4 vanishing moments is the best empirical choice for regular blotches. This basis provides the minimum measured contact angle θ_{min} yielding a visible boundary. If n is the number of vanishing moments of the adopted wavelet, θ_{min} is simply tied to the minimum of the error of the $(n-1)^{th}$ Taylor expansion around the point $x = \overline{R}$ of the function $y(x) = \sqrt{R^2 - x^2}$, $|x| \leq \overline{R}$, with $\overline{R} = Rsin(2\theta)$. $y(x)$ is the arc that models of the blotch shape — i.e. its luminance intensity. With our basis, $n = 4$ and then

$$\theta_{min} = \frac{1}{2} arcsin(\frac{1}{\sqrt{6}}). \quad (11)$$

The contrast for making the blotch invisible is then the difference between the ideal contact angle θ_{min} and the measured angle $\theta = arctg\left(\frac{h}{\overline{R}}\right)$, where h and $\overline{R}$ respectively are the height and half of the width of the analyzed blotch. It is obvious that h and $\overline{R}$ can only describe the luminance of the measured blotch but not the real blotch that depends on various unknown physical parameters.

The strategy is very simple. If $\theta_{min} < \theta$, then the blotch is smooth enough and therefore invisible. No action is required.

Otherwise, for each row (column) of the considered detail band D_j, we can apply the following attenuation: $\tilde{D}_j(\mathbf{x}) = min(1, w_j(\mathbf{x})) \, D_j(\mathbf{x}), \quad \forall (\mathbf{x}) \in \Omega_j$, with $w_j(\mathbf{x}) = \dfrac{1}{\frac{|D_j(\mathbf{x})|}{c_1 \sigma_{ext}} \frac{|D_j(\mathbf{x})|}{c_2 H_{loc}} \frac{|D_j(\mathbf{x})|}{|D_j(\mathbf{x}) - D_j(N(\mathbf{x}))|}}$, where Ω_j is the region of the blotch boundary at scale level j ($|\Omega_j| = S_{\psi_j}$), σ_{ext} is the standard deviation of the external part of the blotch; $H_{loc} = \overline{R} \, tg(\theta_{min})$ is the minimum height measured by the adopted wavelet; $c_1 = 1.02$ and $c_2 = 0.98$ are the Weber coefficients; $\dfrac{|D_j(\mathbf{x})|}{|D_j(\mathbf{x}) - D_j(N(\mathbf{x}))|}$ is the local contrast computed using the Weber's law — $N(\mathbf{x})$ indicates the local neighborhood of the analysed pixel.

It is easy to see that the three contrasts in the aforementioned shrinking are the well known contrast masking, contrast sensitivity and the local contrast [22].

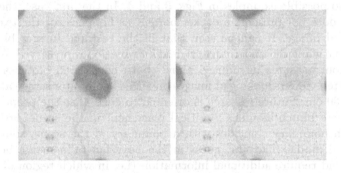

Fig. 3. Left) Image containing a blotch without darker border. **Right)** Restored image using the proposed algorithm.

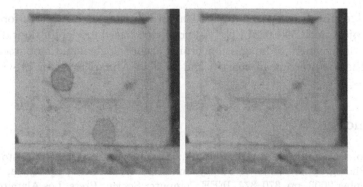

Fig. 4. Left) Image containing two blotches having darker borders. **Right)** Restored image using the proposed algorithm.

4.3 Restoration of Chroma Components

The considered digitized images are ancient photos and then they should be in gray levels. Nonetheless, as already outlined, they are sepia due to their age. Even if this color does not influence the scene description, it is important from an historical point of view and then chroma components have to be restored too. Anyway, since they are almost constant in color, the bayesian minimization described above can be directly applied on their original copy — without any wavelet decomposition.

5 Some Experimental Results and Conclusions

We have performed the proposed approach on various images from different historical archives. It is worth outlining that water blotches present very different behaviors and then it is difficult to select the most representative cases. However, we show two possible examples in Figs. 3 and 4. In the first case, the blotch is dark but it does not presents a darker border, as happens for the two blotches in the second image. It can be seen that in the restored images blotches are quite invisible while the underlying original information is preserved. Apart from the distortion measures introduced above, both considered blotches appeared invisible by ten viewers looking at images on a 15.4" computer screen at distances from 15 to 30 cm. Future research is oriented to generalize the proposed model to cases where blotch assumes a critical placement in the scene. For instance, when blotch boundary coincides with a boundary of the scene, some parts of the proposed model (like first guess in the bayesian refinement) become not automatic and require additional information (i.e. in which region of the scene to take information). A part of the future work will also be devoted to decrease the computational effort of some steps of the algorithm, like the determination of the first guess and the ICM algorithm.

Acknowledgments. Thanks to the Italian Ministry of Education for funding (FIRB project no.RBNE039LLC, "A knowledge-based model for digital restoration and enhancement of images concerning archaeological and monumental heritage of the Mediterranean coast") and to F.lli Alinari SpA for providing the images.

References

1. Stanco, F., Ramponi, G., De Polo, A.: Towards the Automated Restoration of Old Photographic Prints: A Survey. In: IEEE EUROCON, Ljubljana, Slovenia, September 2003, pp. 370–374. IEEE Computer Society Press, Los Alamitos (2003)
2. Bruni, V., Crawford, A., Stanco, F., Vitulano, D.: Visibility Based Detection and Removal of Semi-Transparent Blotches on Archived Documents. In: VISAPP. International Conference on Computer Vision Theory and Applications, Setubal, Portugal, pp. 64–71 (February 2006)

3. Stanco, F., Tenze, L., Ramponi, G.: Virtual restoration of vintage photographic prints affected by foxing and water blotches. Journal of Electronic Imaging 14(4) (Decemebr 2005)
4. Ramponi, G., Stanco, F., Dello Russo, W., Pelusi, S., Mauro, P.: Digital Automated Restoration of Manuscripts and Antique Printed Books. In: EVA 2005. Electronic Imaging and the Visual Arts, Florence, Italy, March 2005, pp. 186–191 (2005)
5. Bertalmio, M., Shapiro, G., Caselles, V., Bellester, B.: Image inpainting. In: Proc. of SIGGRAPH 2000, pp. 417–424 (2000)
6. Criminisi, A., Perez, P., Toyama, K.: Region filling and object removal by exemplar-based image inpainting. IEEE Transactions on Image Processing 13(9), 1200–1212 (2004)
7. Gonzalez, R.C., Woods, R.E.: Digital Image Processing, 2nd edn. Prentice-Hall, Englewood Cliffs (2002)
8. Bruni, V., Crawford, A.J., Vitulano, D.: Visibility Based Detection Of Complicated Objects: A Case Study. In: Proc. of CVMP 06, pp. 55–64 (November 2006)
9. Damera-Venkata, N., Kite, T.D., Evans, B.L., Bovik, A.C.: Image Quality Assessment Based on a Degradation Model. IEEE Transactions on Image Processing 9(4), 636–650 (2000)
10. Gutiérrez, J., Ferri, F.J., Malo, J.: Regularization Operators for Natural Images Based on Nonlinear Perception Models. IEEE Transactions on Image Processing 15(1), 189–200 (2006)
11. Carnec, M., Barba, D.: Simulating the human visual system: towards objective measurement of visual annoyance. IEEE Transactions on Systems, Man and Cybernetics 6 (October 2002)
12. Pappas, T.N., Safranek, R.J.: Perceptual criteria for image quality evaluation. In: Bovik, A.C. (ed.) Handbook of Image and Video Processing, pp. 669–684 (2000)
13. Salomon, D.: Data Compression: The complete reference. Springer, Heidelberg (2004)
14. Clarke, A., Blake, T.D., Carruthers, K., Woodward, A.: Spreading and Imbibition of Liquid Droplets on Porous Surfaces. Langmuir Letters 2002 American Chemical Society 18(8), 2980–2984 (2002)
15. Seveno, D., Ledauphine, V., Martic, G., Voué, M.: Spreading Drop Dynamics on Porous Surfaces. Langmuir 2002 American Chemical Society 18(20), 7496–7502 (2002)
16. Peli, E.: Contrast in complex images. Journal of the Optical Society of America 7(10), 2032–2040 (1990)
17. Nadenau, M.J., Reichel, J., Kunt, M.: Wavelet-Based Color Image Compression: Exploiting the Contrast Sensitivity Function. IEEE Transactions on Image Processing 12(1), 58–70 (2003)
18. Mallat, S.: A Wavelet Tour of Signal Processing. Academic Press, London (1998)
19. Wang, J.Y.A., Adelson, E.H.: Representing Moving Images With Layers. IEEE Trans. on Image Processing 3(5), 625–638 (1994)
20. White, P.R., Collis, W.B., Robinson, S., Kokaram, A.C.: Inference Matting. In: CVMP 2005. Proc. of Conference on Visual Media Production, pp. 168–172 (November 2005)
21. Besag, J.R.: On the statistical analysis of dirty pictures. Journal of the Royal Statistical Society B 48(3), 259–302 (1986)
22. Winkler, S.: Digital Video Quality - Vision Models and Metrics. John Wiley and Sons, Chichester (2005)

Classification with Positive and Negative Equivalence Constraints: Theory, Computation and Human Experiments

Rubi Hammer[1,2], Tomer Hertz[1,3], Shaul Hochstein[1,2], and Daphna Weinshall[1,3]

[1] Interdisciplinary Center for Neural Computation
[2] Neurobiology Department, Institute of Life Sciences
[3] School of Computer Sciences and Engineering
The Hebrew University of Jerusalem
Jerusalem, Israel 91904
rubih@alice.nc.huji.ac.il

Abstract. We tested the efficiency of category learning when participants are provided only with pairs of objects, known to belong either to the same class (Positive Equivalence Constraints or PECs) or to different classes (Negative Equivalence Constraints or NECs). Our results in a series of cognitive experiments show dramatic differences in the usability of these two information building blocks, even when they are chosen to contain the same amount of information. Specifically, PECs seem to be used intuitively and quite efficiently, while people are rarely able to gain much information from NECs (unless they are specifically directed for the best way of using them). Tests with a constrained EM clustering algorithm under similar conditions also show superior performance with PECs. We conclude with a theoretical analysis, showing (by analogy to graph cut problems) that the satisfaction of NECs is computationally intractable, whereas the satisfaction of PECs is straightforward. Furthermore, we show that PECs convey more information than NECs by relating their information content to the number of different graph colorings. These inherent differences between PECs and NECs may explain why people readily use PECs, while many of them need specific directions to be able to use NECs effectively.

Keywords: Categorization; Similarity; Rule learning; Expectation Maximization.

1 Introduction

In many supervised-learning scenarios, whether human or machine, a classifier is trained using a subset of labeled elements from a set of target categories (e.g. being presented with pictures of animals with their categorical identity such as "dogs" or "cats"). This training set can be used to learn a classification principle that can be generalized with regard to novel instances which were not encountered during the training stage. This problem has been studied extensively in the fields of machine [4, 6] and human [7, 5, 1] learning. We note that generally, labels indicate the relation

F. Mele et al. (Eds.): BVAI 2007, LNCS 4729, pp. 264–276, 2007.
© Springer-Verlag Berlin Heidelberg 2007

between the training instances, telling the classifier whether different instances are from the same or different categories: Elements with the same label provide Positive Equivalence Constraints (PECs), and elements with different labels provide Negative Equivalence Constraints (NECs). Nevertheless, equivalence constraints can be provided without the use of labels [9, 14]. In fact, it is not hard to think of many indirect contextual clues that may indicate the categorical relation between two or more exemplars. For example, seeing two animals playing together, one may assume that they are from the same species, while seeing one animal chasing another may indicate that the two are not the same. Examples of equivalence constraints, in the absence of labels, are shown in Figure 1.

There has been little effort to date to separate between the contributions of these two types of constraints. One way of separating them involves informing the classifier that pairs of elements belong to the same class (or to different classes), without providing class labels. In this paper, we study the separate contributions of PECs and NECs in the context of human behavior (Section 2) and machine learning (Section 3). We then provide a theoretical basis and explanatory description of the classification limitations when using PECs vs. NECs (Section 4).

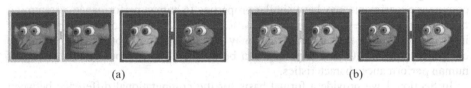

(a)   (b)

Fig. 1. Examples of Positive equivalence constraints (PECs – creatures paired by light-gray frames) and Negative equivalence constraints (NECs – creatures paired by dark-gray frames) using "alien creatures" created for the cognitive experiments. Note that no labels were used for specifying the categorical relations between creatures. In the current example, the pre-selected task-relevant dimensions are skin color and ear shape: (a) Two pairs showing one randomly selected PEC (left - the two creatures are from the same category despite differences in eye color and nose shape, since they share similar properties in the relevant dimensions) and one NEC (right, the two creatures differ in skin color, but also in some non relevant dimensions such as eye color and nose/chin shape). (b) Two pairs of highly informative constraints in which each pair differs in only one dimension, which is irrelevant in the case of PECs (left, eye color) and relevant in the case of NECs (right, face color).

The importance of investigating the separate contributions of PECs and NECs lies in the different ways that they are used and in their different basic properties. Though it would seem that the two types are equally important for category learning, actually they have very different characteristics, deriving both from how prevalent and how informative they are. The most obvious and intuitive underlying difference is that PECs may be compactly represented and efficiently satisfied, while simultaneous satisfaction of NECs is computationally difficult, usually requiring application of an approximation scheme.

In Section 2 we measure the differential use of PECs and NECs by humans. Our results suggest that people use PECs quite intuitively, but demonstrate a common difficulty in using the naturally less informative NECs. Even when we set up an experiment whereby NECs and PECs provide the same amount of information, many participants fail to use NECs efficiently. On the other hand, providing them with directions for the use of NECs dramatically improves performance, whereas the efficacy of using PECs is unchanged by the provision of similar directions. For further details concerning the experimental design and human findings reviewed here, see [9].

To gain further insight into the separate use of PECs and NECs, in Section 3 we analyze their separate contributions when incorporated into a clustering algorithm, using the constrained-EM algorithm suggested by Shental et al. [14]. The latter is an extension of the Expectation Maximization (EM) algorithm for estimating a Gaussian Mixture Model (GMM), which can make use of equivalence constraints of either type. While the constrained EM algorithm has been applied previously to several real-world datasets and shown to significantly enhance performance compared to its unconstrained counterpart [14], here we test this algorithm in a scenario which simulates the human experiments described above.

We stress that the computer experiments should not be considered as direct simulations of the cerebral events underlying the behavioral results. However, as shown below, comparison of the two results leads to interesting observations regarding the possible use of PECs and NECs. Specifically, the results of the computer experiments may have similar properties to human performance – stemming from the fact that they both perform classifications in the same context, using similar information. These shared properties may be understood more easily from the computer experiments, and hopefully can be used to improve our understanding of human performance characteristics.

In Section 4 we provide a formal basis for the computational difference between the use of PECs and NECs. Our analysis involves two distinct and complementary arguments: First of all, in Section 4.1 we use the language of complexity theory to argue that satisfying positive constraints can be done efficiently, while satisfying negative constraints is essentially intractable. Secondly, in Section 4.2 we define a measure of information for both types of constraints, and show that PEC information content is typically much larger than that of NECs.

2   Experiments and Results in Human Category Learning

In order to investigate how people use PECs and NECs, we conducted three category-learning experiments in which the two types of constraints were presented separately. In each experiment, participants performed a simple rule-based categorization of novel stimuli ("alien creatures faces") in which the relevant or irrelevant dimensions had to be identified by either the PECs or NECs provided. In each trial, participants reviewed three constrained object pairs and were then asked to identify which objects belong to the same category as a given standard. Thus, participants needed to learn from the constraints which dimensions are relevant for the current trial, and to compare the trial standard with the other objects solely on the basis of these dimensions. Note that in many trials the constrained objects belonged to different categories than that of the standard provided. In each experimental condition, participants performed 10 trials. Performance level is presented using the non-parametric sensitivity measure A' defined as

$$A' = 0.5 + \left[sign(H-F) \times \frac{(H-F)^2 + |H-F|}{4 \times max(H,F) - 4 \times H \times F} \right]$$

where H represents the normalized Hits and F represents the normalized False-Alarms. Score of 0.5 represents poor performance and score of 1 represents perfect performance. For further information concerning non-parametric signal analysis measures, see [8, 15].

2.1 Experiment 1: Randomly Selected Constraints

In order to evaluate the expected contribution of the two types of constraints in natural scenarios, when there is *no* deliberate selection of constraints to maximize the information provided to the classifier, in the first experiment we compared performance when using randomly selected PECs or NECs (see example in Fig. 1a) with a control condition where no equivalence constraints are provided (the "noEC" condition). The random constraints were preselected at the design stage (all participants were faced with the same constraints). Paired sample t-tests (see also Figure 2 left) showed that participants' performance with a random set of three PECs was better than with either three random NECs, $t(11) = 4.81$, $p < 0.001$, $d = 2.90$, or with no constraints at all, $t(11) = 4.33$, $p < 0.005$, $d = 2.61$. There was no significant difference between performance in the random NEC and noEC conditions $t(11) = 1.02$, $p = 0.33$.

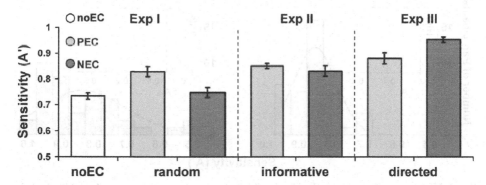

Fig. 2. Mean A′ scores with standard errors in all conditions. Exp 1: 12 participants, within-subject design: random PECs (0.83 ± 0.02), random NECs (0.75 ± 0.02), and no constraints (0.73 ± 0.01). Exp 2: 80 participants, between-subject design: highly informative highPECs (0.85±0.07) and highNECs (0.83 ± 0.13). Exp 3: 12 participants, within subject design: directed PECs (0.88 ± 0.07) and NECs (0.95 ± 0.04).

2.2 Experiment 2: Highly Informative Sets of Constraints

The results of Experiment 1 can simply derive from the fact that a small random set of PECs provide more information than a small random set of NECs, and not necessarily from the fact that classifying with NECs is more complex than with PECs (as will be shown in section 4). Thus, this result probably reflects inherent properties of the constraints and not participant proficiency in their use. Experiment 2 therefore tested the use of PECs and NECs when these were specifically chosen to provide all the information needed for perfect performance. Figure 1.b presents an example of such highly informative PECs and NECs.

Importantly, we found a difference here, too, in performance with PECs vs. NECs. Although independent sample t-test showed that the mean level of performance with highPECs was not different from that with highNECs, $t(78) = 0.85$ (see Fig. 2 middle), the Leven test for homogeneity of variances showed that the standard-deviation in the highPEC condition was significantly smaller than in the highNEC condition, $F(78) = 13.94$, $p < 0.001$. The Shapiro-Wilk test of normality further showed that although in the highPEC condition, sensitivity was normally distributed, $W(40) = 0.95$, $p = 0.11$, the sensitivity distribution in the highNEC condition differed significantly from normal, $W(40) = 0.89$, $p < 0.001$. Interestingly, we found that participants may be divided into two groups: those who are able to use informative NECs quite well (with above-median Hit and below-median FA rates in Fig. 3, right inset), and those who are unable to do so (with below-median Hit and above-median FA rates). This raises the possibility that using NECs is not only computationally difficult, but that it may be non-intuitive for some participants to derive the proper strategy for their use, perhaps due to their inexperience with informative NECs in most natural settings.

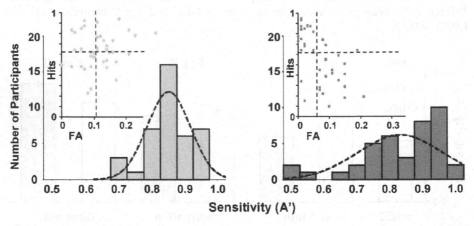

Fig. 3. Histograms of sensitivity showing its distribution across participants with highPECs (left) and highNECs (right). Dashed curves represent the expected normal distribution given the observed mean and standard deviation. Boxes represent the corresponding ROC (Receiver Operating Characteristic) diagrams, where dashed lines represent each group median FA (Vertical) and median Hit (horizontal).

2.3 Experiment 3: Highly Informative Constraints with Directions

Having found in Experiment 2 that some participants have difficulty using even informative NECs, we provided all participants in Experiment 3 with directions for the use of either highPECs or highNECs (identical to the constraints used in Exp. 2). We found that when provided with these directions all participants succeeded in using either type of constraint. Moreover, the bimodal pattern of performance with highNECs observed in Experiment 2 was replaced by a uniformly high success rate, and performance was higher than in the directed-highPEC condition, $t(11) = 3.29$, $p < 0.01$, $d = 1.98$; see Fig. 2 right. These findings further support the interpretation that it is the difference between PECs and NECs in natural circumstances that leads to the different proficiencies in their use.

2.4 Summary and Discussion

Evaluating baseline performance with randomly selected constraints in Experiment 1, we found a clear advantage for category learning from PECs compared to NECs. Moreover, random NECs were poorly informative, leading to categorization performance similar to that observed when participants merely performed associative categorization (in the control condition without constraints). Experiment 2 demonstrated that deliberately selected PECs, containing all the information needed for perfect performance, are in fact not more informative than randomly selected PECs. In contrast, informative NECs enabled much better performance than randomly selected NECs at least for some participants.

Taken as a group, participants in the highPEC and highNEC conditions had similar performance. However, further analysis revealed that in the highNEC condition, the performance distribution was bimodal with a relatively large standard-deviation. This highNEC condition bimodality was also apparent in the Hit and False-Alarm distributions, with about half of the participants in the highNEC condition performing almost perfectly and the other half performing very poorly, as though they had not received any informative constraints at all. In contrast, in the highPEC condition, performance was quite good for all participants, reaching only rarely the extremes of nearly-perfect or very poor performance.

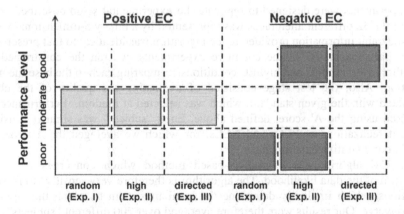

Fig. 4. Schematic summary of performance in the three experiments described above – with randomly chosen constraints (I) or highly informative constraints, without (II) or with (III) directions for their use

Providing directions for the use of the constraints in Experiment 3 revealed a number of surprising results. First of all, we found that the strategy for using highNECs could be readily learned via simple instructions, leading participants to nearly perfect performance. This result suggests that the failure of the poor performance subgroup in using highNECs was due to their inability to find the correct strategy, and not an inability to adopt new strategies. Still, it is surprising that a strategy for using highNECs was easily learned when instructions were provided, but many people (university students!) failed in intuitively implementing this strategy when performing the task without instruction. Secondly, we found that giving similar instructions for the best strategy for using PECs did not improve performance and participants remained at quite good, but not perfect performance levels. These differences between the benefit of instructions for using PECs and NECs were rather unexpected, and support our main claim that people use PECs, but not NECs, intuitively. Figure 4 summarizes participant performance in the three experiments.

3   Experiments Using the Constrained-EM Algorithm

In this section we analyze the contribution of PECs and NECs when separately incorporated into the constrained-EM clustering algorithm [14]. Recently, equivalence constraints have been used for learning distance functions and for clustering [2, 3, 10, 17]. A number of clustering algorithms have been adapted to incorporate equivalence constraints, including K-means [16], complete-linkage [12] and an EM of a Gaussian Mixture Model (GMM) [14]. While most of these algorithms can easily incorporate positive constraints, incorporating negative constraints into these algorithms is usually much harder computationally and requires the application of various heuristics, or approximations.

3.1   Experimental Setup

Our experiments were designed to replicate the experimental setup described above: Each of the 32 different alien faces was represented by a binary 5-dimensional vector. The constraint information provided to the algorithm was identical to that presented to human participants. As in the cognitive experiments, we ran the constrained EM algorithm in the randEC and highEC conditions, comparing each to the baseline noEC condition. Also, the test stage consisted of evaluating the quality of the cluster associated with the given standard, which was selected at random. Performance was measured using the A' score, defined above. Each "subject" was simulated using 5 different realizations of PECs and NECs, for which we averaged the A' scores, as done in our cognitive experiments.

The EM algorithm is a gradient-based method which converges to a local maximum of the data likelihood. The algorithm is therefore very sensitive to its initial conditions, which implicitly determine the local maximum to which the algorithm will converge. Our results were therefore averaged over 200 different "subjects", each performed five different categorization tasks.

3.2   Experimental Results

Figure 5 displays performance (A') histograms for the constrained EM algorithm when trained using NECs and PECs, respectively. Results for the 2 conditions (averages and standard deviations) are also summarized in Table 1.

Based on the results reported in Shental et al. [14], in which the constrained EM algorithm was tested on real world datasets, it came as no surprise to see that (on average) the constrained EM which used PECs achieved better A' scores than the same algorithm using only NECs. This is the case with both the random and the informative sets of constraints. There is no significant difference between performance using PECs in the two conditions, and no significant difference between average performance without constraints (noECs) compared to using NECs. This is in agreement with the human psychophysical findings above. When highNECs are provided, average performance is significantly higher than in the noEC condition, but still significantly lower than with highPECs. Unlike the results with human participants, the distribution of the highNEC scores is unimodal. This may suggest that the constrained-EM does not make optimal use of highNECs, similar to the "poorly-performing" human participants.

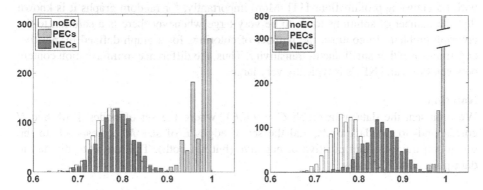

Fig. 5. Histograms of A' scores of the GMM simulations using the constrained EM algorithm. Left: Results of the random equivalence constraints (randEC) condition. Right: Results of the highly informative constraints (highEC) condition.

Performance in the unsupervised noEC condition is above chance similar to our findings in the cognitive experiments. This is due to use of proximity relations which rule out many impossible groupings. As in our cognitive experiments, performance in the randNEC condition is not significantly better than in the noEC condition, since these constraints are usually non-informative. However, when informative constraints are provided, the algorithm seeks a solution which also complies with the constraints, and this additional information can, in many cases, direct the algorithm towards better solutions both in terms of refining the cluster centers (easily done with PECs) and the deviation from the cluster centers (NECs and PECs).

Table 1. Average sensitivity scores of the constrained EM algorithm for the noEC, randEC and highEC conditions

Condition:	noEC	NECs	PECs
randEC	0.77 ± 0.04	0.78 ± 0.04	0.97 ± 0.02
highEC	0.77 ± 0.04	0.85 ± 0.04	0.99 ± 0.01

4 The Underlying Difference Between PECs and NECs

In order to provide a formal basis for the computational difference between negative and positive constraints, we analyze the problem in two ways. First, in Section 4.1 we show that clustering with NECs is related to the problem of finding the maximal cut in a graph, which is known to be very hard (NP-complete). In contrast, clustering with PECs is related to the analogous problem of finding the minimal cut in a graph, for which efficient polynomial algorithms are known.

Secondly, in Section 4.2 we define the notion of information for both types of constraints, and obtain a lower bound on the difference in information content between positive and negative constraints. Specifically, the information content of NECs is inversely related to the number of different graph colorings for the graph defined by the negative constraints. Computing this number is very hard (again, an NP-hard problem), with no known approximations [11]. More importantly, for random graphs it is known that the number of solutions tends to be very large whenever there is a solution to the coloring problem. In contrast, the number of colorings for a graph defined by positive constraints is rather small due to transitivity. Thus, the difference in information content between PECs and NECs is typically very large.

Notation
We represent the data as a graph $G = \{V,E\}$, where the set of nodes V of size N corresponds to the datapoints, and the set of edges E of size M corresponds to the given constraints, either positive or negative (but not both). The task is to divide the data-points into K classes.

4.1 The Complexity of Satisfying Positive or Negative Constraints

Assume $K = 2$, and the task is therefore to partition the data into two clusters. Each partition is represented by C – the set of all edges from E which connect nodes assigned to different clusters; the set C is called the *cut* of graph G. Each cut is assigned a cost – the number of edges in C.

Enforcing positive constraints is manageable
Given positive constraints, we seek a partition in which as few positive constraints as possible are violated. Finding this partition is equivalent to finding the minimal cut in the above graph. There are known efficient algorithms to solve this problem. Thus, in the complexity hierarchy of computer science, this problem is considered *tractable*.

Enforcing negative constraints is hard
Given negative constraints, we seek a partition in which as few negative constraints as possible are violated. Finding this partition is equivalent to finding the maximal cut in the graph defined above. There are **no** known efficient algorithms to solve this problem. Therefore, in the complexity hierarchy of computer science, this problem is almost certainly *intractable*.

4.2   The Information Content of Positive or Negative Constraints

We define the *information* of a set of constraints E to be the difference between the entropy H of all the partitions of the set of nodes V to K clusters,[1] and the entropy H_G of all such partitions consistent with E. Assuming that each allowed partition is assigned equal probability, the entropy H_G is equal to the log of the number of allowed partitions. We are interested in the difference between the information of positive and negative constraints, namely in

$$I = (H - H_G^+) - (H - H_G^-) = H_G^- - H_G^+ = \log \frac{\#_G^-}{\#_G^+} \tag{1}$$

where the entropy superscript $+$ or $-$ denotes respectively whether the set of constraints is positive or negative, $\#_G^-$ denotes the number of partitions consistent with E if the constraints are negative, and $\#_G^+$ is similarly defined if the constraints are positive.

To compute $\#_G^+$ we note that all the nodes in every connected component of the graph G should be assigned to the same cluster in each allowed partition[2]. We can therefore treat every connected component as a single meta-node, and the number of different partitions is

$$\#_G^+ = K^{N_c} \tag{2}$$

where N_C denotes the number of connected components of G. In particular, if the graph G has no loops, $N_C = N - M$ and therefore

$$\#_G^+ = K^{N-M} \tag{3}$$

where M is the number of edges in E.

It is quite hard to compute $\#_G^-$ in the general case: it represents the different number of colorings of graph G, a number whose computation is known to be NP-hard. We start with the simple case where graph G has no loops, for which we can show that

$$\#_G^- = K^{N-M}(K-1)^M \tag{4}$$

This result can be readily proven by induction on the number of constraints M.

We can now state the first result of this section:

Result 4.1
When the graph of constraints has no loops, as in the experiments described above, the information gain of positive over negative constraints is

---

[1] We allow partitions that assign no node to one or more clusters. However, it can be readily shown that the number of such partitions is negligible when $N \gg K$.

[2] A connected component is a subset of nodes that are connected to each other by edges from E.

$$I = M \log(K - 1)$$

The result follows from substituting (3) and (4) into (1).

For a general graph with N_C connected components, we note that each connected component in G has at least one legal coloring (by assumption). We immediately get the following bound

$$\#_G^- \geq \prod_{i=1}^{N_C} \frac{K!}{(K-q_i)!} = \prod_{l=1}^{K} (K-l+1)^{N_C^l} \tag{5}$$

where q_i denotes the number of nodes in the i-th connected component (if smaller than K, or K otherwise), and N_C^l denotes the number of connected component with l or more elements $N_C = N_C^1 \geq N_C^2 \geq ... \geq N_C^K$. Substituting (5) and (2) into (1) we get the second result:

Result 4.2
The information gain of positive over negative constraints satisfies

$$I \geq \sum_{l=2}^{K} N_C^l \log(K-l+1)$$

This bound is rather loose, as it is derived by assuming that each connected component has only one coloring solution. Typically, however, the situation is quite different: if a graph has any solution at all, it would typically (for random graphs) have an exponential number of solutions (Krivelevich, 2002). We can therefore state that,

If $N >> N_C$, the information content of positive constraints is exponentially larger than negative constraints.

5 Discussion

We investigated properties of PECs and NECs and their effects on performance in a classification task – in the context of human cognition and machine learning. Parallel theoretical analyses demonstrated that the use of NECs is computationally much more difficult than use of PECs, and that NECs convey less information than do PECs. In accordance with this theoretical result, our cognitive experiments found that humans can easily make use of randomly-chosen PECs, but random NECs do not provide any gain in performance compared to the no-constraints baseline condition. Computer experiments similarly found improved performance only with random PECs. While the EM algorithm does not necessarily simulate human categorization strategies, it does demonstrate that the difficulties in using NECs are inherent. The theoretical analysis implies that our results are general and not limited to the rule-based classification task (that assumes an object space whose dimensionality may be reduced in a consistent manner) or the EM algorithm (that assumes a Euclidean object space with proximity representing similarity).

If the limitation in using NECs derives from their properties when chosen at random, informative NECs should allow good performance. Surprisingly, we discovered that only about half of the participants succeeded in properly using highly informative NECs, selected to pinpoint a single relevant dimension. Our computer experiments found an improvement with highNECs, but not to the level achieved by highPECs. These results may derive from the good performing participants shifting their classification strategy, while the poor performers were unable to do so. The computer algorithm, also unable to change its strategy, similarly obtained only moderate improvement. The poor performance by many human participants is consistent with the hypothesis that since NECs are generally less informative than PECs, people lack experience in their use and many fail to use them even when they are informative. This hypothesis is supported by the finding that the provision of directions allowed all participants to achieve very good performance with highPECs.

If people are generally not experienced in the use of NECs for general classification scenarios, are NECs useful at all? One possibility is that NECs are important for the difficult task of identifying fine, yet important differences between highly similar categories – as in subordinate-level categories or perceptual learning requiring identification of subtle differences between stimuli. In these cases, informative NECs may increase the perceived dissimilarities [7] leading to refinement of the classifier conceptual knowledge.

References

[1] Ashby, F.G., Maddox, W.T.: Human category learning. Ann. Rev Psychology 56, 149–178 (2005)

[2] Bar-Hilel, A., Hertz, T., Shental, N., Weinshall, D.: Learning distance functions using equivalence relations. In: The 20th International Conference on Machine Learning (2003)

[3] Bilenko, M., Basu, S., Mooney, R.J.: Integrating constraints and metric learning in semi-supervised clustering. In: Banff Canada, AAAI press, Stanford, California, USA (2004)

[4] Bishop, C.M.: Neural Networks for Pattern Recognition. Oxford press, Oxford (1995)

[5] Cohen, A.L., Nosofsky, R.M.: An exemplar-retrieval model of speeded same-different judgments. Journal of Experimental Psychology: Human Perception and Performance 26, 1549–1569 (2000)

[6] Duda, R.O., Hart, P.E., Stork, D.G.: Pattern Classification. John Wiley and Sons Inc., Chichester (2001)

[7] Goldstone, R.L.: Influences of categorization on perceptual discrimination. Journal of Experimental Psychology: General 123(2), 178–200 (1994)

[8] Grier, J.B.: Nonparametric indexes for sensetivity and bias: Computing formulas. Psychological Bulletin 75, 424–429 (1971)

[9] Hammer, R., Hertz, T., Hochstein, S., Weinshall, D.: Category learning from equivalence constraints. Cognitive Processing (in press)

[10] Hertz, T., Bar-Hillel, A., Weinshall, D.: Boosting margin based distance functions for clustering. In: ICML (2004)

[11] Khanna, S., Linial, N., Safra, S.: On the hardness of approximating the chromatic number. Combinatorica 1(3), 393–415 (2000)

[12] Klein, D., Kamvar, S., Manning, C.: From instance-level constraints to space-level constraints: Making the most of prior knowledge in data clustering. In: Proceedings of the Nineteenth International Conference on Machine Learning (2002)

[13] Krivelevich, M.: Sparse graphs usually have exponentially many optimal colorings. Electronic Journal of Combinatorics 9 (2002)

[14] Shental, N., Bar-Hilel, A., Hertz, T., Weinshall, D.: Computing Gaussian mixture models with EM using equivalence constraints. In: Advances in Neural Information Processing Systems, vol. 16, MIT Press, Cambridge (2004)

[15] Stanislaw, H., Todorov, N.: Calculating signal detection theory measures. Behavior Research Methods, Instruments, & Computers 31(1), 137–149 (1999)

[16] Wagstaff, K., Cardie, C., Rogers, S., Schroedl, S.: Constrained K-means clustering with background knowledge. In: Proc. 18th International Conf. on Machine Learning, pp. 577–584. Morgan Kaufmann, San Francisco, CA (2001)

[17] Xing, E.P., Ng, A.Y., Jordan, M.I., Russell, S.: Distance metric learnign with application to clustering with side-information. In: Advances in Neural Information Processing Systems, vol. 15, MIT Press, Cambridge (2002)

A Graph-Based Clustering Method and Its Applications

Pasquale Foggia[1], Gennaro Percannella[2], Carlo Sansone[1], and Mario Vento[2]

[1] Dipartimento di Informatica e Sistemistica
Università di Napoli Federico II, Via Claudio, 21 I-80125 Napoli (Italy)
{foggiapa,carlosan}@unina.it
[2] Dipartimento di Ingegneria dell'Informazione ed Ingegneria Elettrica,
Università di Salerno, via P.te Don Melillo, I-84084 Fisciano (SA), Italy
{pergen,mvento}@unisa.it

Abstract. In this paper we present a graph-based clustering method particularly suited for dealing with data that do not come from a Gaussian or a spherical distribution. It can be used for detecting clusters of any size and shape, without the need of specifying neither the actual number of clusters nor other parameters.

The method has been tested on data coming from two different computer vision applications. A comparison with other three state-of-the-art algorithms was also provided, demonstrating the effectiveness of the proposed approach.

1 Introduction

In Pattern Recognition and Computer Vision there is a significant number of applications that use clustering algorithms [1]. The main drawback of most clustering algorithms is that their performance can be affected by the shape and the size of the clusters to be detected [2]. Some well-known clustering algorithms (e.g. *k-means* [2] or *self-organizing maps* [3]), for example, fail if data are distributed in the feature space along a non-smooth manifold [4]. Such algorithms, in fact, are based on the assumption that the data comes from a Gaussian or a spherical distribution. Moreover, in order to obtain an adequate clustering result, these algorithms sometimes require some *a priori* knowledge about the actual number of clusters, and/or require the setting of a threshold or a parameter, sometimes without a clear physical meaning.

On the other hand, in some applications there is the need of grouping, in one or more clusters, only a part of the whole dataset. This happens when samples of interest for the application at hand are present together with several *noisy* samples. We can refer to this case as to a *cluster detection* problem. It occurs, for example, when we want to find, in a mammografic image, one or more clusters of microcalcifications starting from the output of a microcalcification detection algorithm [5]. Such kind of algorithms typically yields some false detections (*false positives*) together with the true microcalcifications (*true positives*). The aim is then to cluster only true microcalcifications, discarding all the false positives that can be regarded, to some extent, as noise. Another case arises in the context of image segmentation, as described in [6]. Here, among all the edges coming from an edge detection algorithm, only the interesting ones have to be grouped together by a cluster detector, in order to use them for achieving a good segmentation result.

F. Mele et al. (Eds.): BVAI 2007, LNCS 4729, pp. 277–287, 2007.

In the above cited situations most clustering algorithms yield a not so useful result, as in any case they try to attribute each sample to a cluster. So, noisy samples, that are typically not similar to each other, are grouped together with true positives. Even if it would be theoretically possible to group together in some clusters only noisy samples, it is practically difficult because the number of clusters should be provided in advance. This cannot be effectively done, since the actual distribution of noisy samples cannot be easily modeled.

A particular family of clustering algorithms that can cope with these problems is the one based on graph theory. The algorithms of this family represent the problem data through an undirected graph. Each node is associated to a sample in the feature space, while to each edge is associated the distance between nodes connected under a suitably defined neighborhood relationship. A cluster is thus defined to be a connected sub-graph, obtained according to criteria peculiar of each specific algorithm. Algorithms based on this definition are capable of detecting clusters of various shapes and sizes, at least for the case in which they are well separated [4]. Moreover, isolated samples should form singleton clusters and then can be easily discarded as noise in case of cluster detection problems.

Usually graph-based clustering algorithms do not require the setting of the number of clusters, but need however some parameters to be provided by the user.

The algorithm proposed in this paper overcomes this limitation, proving to be an effective solution in some real applications where a completely unsupervised method is desirable. Our proposal is based on the algorithm described by Zahn in [7]. The original algorithm constructs the Minimum Spanning Tree (MST) of the graph representing the samples. After that, it identifies inconsistent edges and removes them from the MST. The remained connected components are then the clusters provided by the algorithm. An edge is inconsistent if the distance associated to it is greater than a predefined threshold. The Zahn algorithm does not suggest a criterion for deriving this threshold, leaving it as a manually provided parameter. In order to determine automatically the optimal value of this threshold, in this paper we propose a novel method based on the use of the *Fuzzy C-Means* algorithm [8].

The proposed algorithm has been compared with other three graph-based clustering algorithms, namely the Markov Clustering proposed by van Dongen [9], the Iterative Conductance Cutting proposed by Kannan *et al.* [10] and the Geometric MST Clustering introduced by Gaertler in [11]. The comparison has been made with reference to a cluster detection problem in two different applicative domains. In particular, the problems of detecting clusters of anchor shots in news videos [12] and of microcalcifications in mammographic images [5] have been considered. In both cases, the results obtained by all the algorithms have been reported and compared by using a suitably modified definition of the *recall* and *precision* figures, that are typically used for evaluating solutions of a detection problem.

The organization of the paper is as follows: in Section 2, the proposed clustering method is presented, while the other three graph-based clustering algorithms are presented in Section 3. In Section 4, the two considered Computer Vision applications are illustrated, together with the datasets used for comparing the chosen algorithms. Tests carried out in order to assess the performance of the proposed method are reported in Section 5, and, finally, some conclusions are drawn in Section 6.

2 The Proposed Graph-Based Clustering Method

The proposed clustering method (*Fuzzy c-means MST Clustering* algorithm - FMC) is based on graph theoretical cluster analysis. As stated in the introduction, this family of clustering algorithms is capable of detecting clusters of various shapes, at least for the case in which they are well separated.

The method starts by constructing the complete graph where each node is associated to a sample to be clustered. The weight of each edge accounts for the distance between the connected nodes. Then, the Minimum Spanning Tree (MST) is computed on the graph. By removing all the edges with weights greater than a threshold λ, we arrive at a *forest* containing a certain number of subtrees (clusters). In this way, the method automatically groups nodes into clusters. As demonstrated in [11], the clustering induced by the subtrees is independent of the particular MST. So the clustering results do not depend on the algorithm chosen for deriving the MST: in this paper, we used the Prim's algorithm [13].

It is worth noting that the optimal value of λ typically depends on the specific clustering problem. As a consequence, it is not possible to use a fixed value of λ for every case. Our proposal is then to determine the optimal value of λ by reformulating the problem as the one of partitioning the whole set of edges into two clusters, according to their weights. The cluster of the edges of the MST with small weights will contain edges to be preserved, while the edges belonging to the other cluster will be removed from the MST. In order to solve this problem we employ the *Fuzzy C-Means* (FCM) clustering algorithm [8].

FCM is a clustering technique based on the minimization of the following objective function:

$$J_m = \sum_{i=1}^{N} \sum_{j=1}^{C} u_{ij}^m \left(x_i - c_j\right)^2, \qquad 1 \le m < \infty$$

where m is any real number greater than 1, x_i is the i-th measured data (in our case the weight of the i-th edge of the MST), c_j is the center of the cluster, u_{ij} is the degree of membership of x_i to the cluster j, C is the number of clusters (in our case $C = 2$) and N is the number of objects to be clustered. Fuzzy partitioning is carried out through an iterative optimization of the objective function shown above, with the update of membership u_{ij} and the cluster centers c_j by:

$$u_{ij} = \frac{1}{\sum_{k=1}^{C} \left(\dfrac{x_i - c_j}{x_i - c_k}\right)^{\frac{2}{m-1}}} \qquad \text{and} \qquad c_j = \frac{\sum_{i=1}^{N} u_{ij}^m \cdot x_i}{\sum_{i=1}^{N} u_{ij}^m}$$

This iteration will stop when:

$$\max_{ij} \left\{ \left| u_{ij}^{(k+1)} - u_{ij}^{(k)} \right| \right\} < \varepsilon$$

where ε is a termination criterion between 0 and 1, whereas k are the iteration steps. This procedure converges to a local minimum or a saddle point of J_m. At the end of the procedure, each edge x_i has been assigned to the cluster r such that:

$$r = \arg \max_j u_{ij}$$

At this point, all the edges of the MST are separated into two clusters. Then, we remove from the MST all the edges belonging to the cluster s whose center exhibits the largest value, $i.e.$:

$$s = \arg \max_j c_j$$

In conclusion, the proposed clustering method can be summarized as follows:

1) construct a complete graph G such that:
   a) its nodes x_i correspond to the input samples;
   b) each of its edges $e = (x_i, x_j)$ is characterized by the weight $w(e) = d(x_i, x_j)$ that is the distance between the two nodes x_i and x_j in the feature space, according to a suitably chosen metric;
2) determine the MST of G;
3) remove from the MST the edges with large weights individuated by using the FCM algorithm.

The detected clusters are then the remaining subtrees of the MST.

Indeed, the FCM algorithm requires the termination criterion ε to be fixed. However, we have verified that good values for this parameter are substantially independent of the considered application. In this sense, the algorithm can be seen as completely unsupervised. In particular, the value of ε was fixed to 0.5 in all the tests reported in the paper.

3 Algorithms Selected for the Comparison

In this section we will provide a brief description of the three algorithms that will be used for our experimental comparison, together with the settings used for employing them in the two considered applications.

3.1 The Markov Clustering Algorithm

The Markov Clustering algorithm (MCL) was proposed by van Dongen in his PhD thesis [9] in 2000. The rationale of the method is based on the observation that if a group of nodes is strongly connected inside and has few connections to the outside (which is the property defining a cluster), a random walk starting from one of the nodes in the group is more likely to remain in the group after a few steps than to go outside. Conceptually, it is possible to define a clustering procedure as follows: each edge is assigned a probability, derived by the edge attribute. Then, a large number of random walks is simulated starting from each node i of the graph and measuring the frequency of the walk arriving at each node j after k steps. Finally, two nodes i, j are considered to be in the same cluster if the probability of the arrival at j starting from i is above a threshold; the transitive closure of this relation determines a partition of the whole graph into clusters.

While this *Monte-Carlo* approach is conceptually sound, it is unacceptably expensive from the computational point of view. So the MCL algorithm proposes a faster procedure to compute the probabilities of arrival. The algorithm has two parameters: an expansion exponent k (a natural number greater than 1) and an inflation exponent r (a positive real number, greater than 1). The algorithm alternates between two phases, expansion and inflation, until a fixed point is reached. In the expansion phase, the probability of the random walk is computed by raising the matrix of the edge probabilities to the k-th power. In the inflation phase, the matrix is renormalized after raising each element to r; the resulting matrix is used as input for the subsequent expansion. The goal of the inflation phase is to reduce towards 0 the smaller probabilities and to enhance towards 1 the larger ones. At the end, the clustering is determined by the resulting probabilities which are sensibly different from 0.

Notice that there is no formal proof of convergence of the algorithm, although in practice it has never occurred a case in which a fixed point was not achieved after a few tens of iterations.

3.2 The Iterative Conductance Cutting Algorithm

The Iterative Conductance Cutting algorithm (ICC) was proposed by Kannan et al. in 2000 [10]. This algorithm works in a hierarchical way: it starts with a single cluster comprising the whole graph and at each step it tries to split a cluster into two, as long as a performance measure computed on the two resulting parts is below a threshold α. The iteration stops when there are no more clusters that can be split remaining within the threshold.

The measure used to evaluate the opportunity of the split is *cluster conductance*, defined in the same paper. Basically, this measure compares the sum of the inter-cluster edges with the sum of all the edges incident to the nodes of the clusters. The lower the conductance, the better is the clustering; the maximum value of 1 is attained for degenerate cases such as one-node clusters or whole-graph clusters.

An interesting aspect of this algorithm is the determination of the split to perform among all the possible splits of a given cluster. An exhaustive search of the split minimizing the conductance would require an exponential time complexity with respect to the size of the cluster. The authors propose instead a polynomial approximation based on a spectral technique. In particular, the nodes of the cluster are sorted according to the corresponding component of the second largest eigenvector of the normalized adjacency matrix (whose values are a similarity measure between adjacent nodes). Only the cuts consistent with this ordering (i.e. in which all the nodes of a part are greater than all the nodes in the other) are considered, thus avoiding a combinatorial explosion. The claim of the authors is that this strategy usually gives a good approximation of the optimal split.

3.3 The Geometric MST Clustering Algorithm

The Geometric MST Clustering (GMC) algorithm is an extension of the Minimum Spanning Tree clustering algorithm by Zahn [7]. This method, introduced by Gaertler in his master thesis [11] and in the paper by Brandes et al. [14], solves the problem of finding a suitable threshold for cutting the edges of the minimum spanning tree by computing for each possible threshold a performance measure and choosing the optimal one (note that there are at most $n - 1$ distinct thresholds to be considered, where n is the number of nodes in the graph). For non-attributed graphs, the author propose the use of a *geometric graph embedding* to define a distance between nodes (hence the name of the algorithm); we have not used this part of the method since the edges of our graphs are already attributed with the distance. In the paper by Brandes et al. [14] several performance measures have been used in an experimental comparison.

3.4 Settings Used for the Algorithms

The MCL algorithm requires a transition probability matrix together with the two parameters k and r. We have derived the transition probabilities from the distances by assuming an exponential distribution. We have chosen $k = 3$ and $r = 2$ after some experiments on artificially generated clustering problems.

The ICC algorithm requires a similarity matrix, that we have defined by taking the inverse of the distance. Also, we have used the value 0.45 for the threshold α following the set-up presented in [14].

The GMC requires the choice of a performance measure; we have used *conductance* for this purpose. Since the computation of conductance requires a similarity matrix, we have defined one using the same technique adopted for ICC.

4 Computer Vision Applications

In order to assess the performance obtainable by the proposed method for cluster detection in real applications, two different applicative domains have been considered. In particular, the problems of detecting clusters of anchor shots in news videos [12] and of microcalcifications in mammographic images [5] have been considered. In the following we will illustrate how graph-based technique can be profitably used for cluster detection in such domains, as well as the datasets used for the tests.

4.1 Detecting Anchor Shot Clusters in News Videos

Segmenting news videos into *stories* is among the key issues for achieving efficient treatment of news-based digital libraries. The segmentation of a news video implies, at a first stage, the partition of the video into sequences of frames, called *shots*, obtained by detecting transitions that are typically associated to camera changes. Once the shots have been individuated by means of a shot change detection algorithm, they can be classified as *anchor shot* or *news-report shot* on the basis of their content. Successively, the entire news video can be divided into stories, by grouping each anchor shot with all the successive news-report shots, until another anchor shot will occur. Anchor shot detection is then a basic step for performing news video segmentation.

It is worth noting that anchor shots are typically characterized by similar visual contents, while this property should not hold for news-report shots [12]. So, it makes sense to try to group anchor shots in clusters, or, in other words, to detect anchor shot clusters among all the shots composing a news video. This approach also allows us to perform detection in an unsupervised way.

In order to obtain a graph-based representation of all the news video shots, a distinctive frame, called *key-frame*, is extracted from each shot. These key-frames can be seen as nodes of a graph in a suitable feature space. To do that, a distance between key-frames, based on the colour histograms, has to be defined. Such a distance is the weight associated to the edge that connects the two nodes representing the key-frames in the feature space. In particular, as proposed in [12], each key-frame has been divided into 16 regions of the same size; the histograms of corresponding regions in the two key-frames have been compared and the eight regions with the largest histogram differences have been discarded to reduce the effects of object motion and noise. The distance between these two key-frames is then defined as the sum of the histogram differences of the remaining regions.

By using this representation, shots are first assigned to candidate clusters by the considered graph-based clustering algorithm; then, clusters composed by less than two shots are eliminated, since they do not fit the hypothesis that anchor shots repeatedly occur during the whole news video [12].

As regard the dataset, we chose to make tests on news videos captured from a single broadcaster. A typical broadcaster, in fact, is interested in employing such a system to analyze all the editions of its news videos rather than the videos produced by other broadcasters. Furthermore, let us consider that, although some broadcasters nowadays already have the edit list for their own news videos, this is unlikely for the old materials. These ones still need to be segmented into news-stories for an effective indexing. Starting from these considerations, the database used in this paper is composed by 17 news videos extracted from the main Italian public TV-network, namely, RAI 1 (see Tab. 1). Special care has been taken to include in the database different editions of news videos from this TV-network.

4.2 Detecting Microcalcification Clusters in Mammografic Images

Microcalcifications are small accumulation of calcium in the breast tissue that appear as bright spots in a mammogram. Cluster of microcalcifications are used as diagnostic evidence for breast cancer. >From a clinical point of view, a microcalcification cluster is a group of at least three microcalcifications in a limited area (usually 1 cm^2) of the mammogram. From this definition, it derives that the Euclidean distance in the mammografic image is the most important feature for clustering microcalcifications. The microcalcifications are associated to the nodes of a completely connected graph, whose edges weights are the Euclidean distances between them. Nodes are first assigned to candidate clusters by the chosen algorithm; then, clusters composed by less than three microcalcifications are eliminated. It is clear that the detection of the candidate clusters constitutes the most critical phase of the whole process, especially in presence of falsely detected microcalcifications (*false positives*). In this application, in fact, the aim is to cluster only true microcalcifications, discarding all the false positives that can be regarded as noise.

In order to evaluate the performance of graph-based cluster detection methods in a real environment (i.e., when falsely detected microcalcifications occur), we chose and implemented the microcalcification detection algorithm proposed in [15]. Note that this method simply determines if a pixel of the image is likely to belong to a microcalcification, but does not reconstruct the whole microcalcification. So, we aggregate adjacent points by using a connected component algorithm to obtain the microcalcifications. Finally, each microcalcification is represented by means of its center of mass.

Tests on cluster detection were performed by using a standard database publicly available. It is made of 33 mammographic images, containing in the whole 77 clusters (see Tab. 1). Images were provided by courtesy of the National Expert and Training Centre for Breast Cancer Screening and the Department of Radiology at the University of Nijmegen, the Netherlands.

Table 1. Characteristics of the two considered Computer Vision applications

Application	# of samples	min # of graph nodes	max # of graph nodes	avg # of graph nodes	min # of true clusters	max # of true clusters	avg # of true clusters
μ-calcification Cluster Detection	33 images	12	283	65.8	1	14	2.33
News-Videos Segmentation	17 videos	46	263	92.5	1	2	1.71

5 Experimental Results

It is customary, in detection applications, to measure the effectiveness of detection using the figures of *precision* and *recall*, which are defined as follows:

$$precision = \frac{TP}{TP+FP} \qquad recall = \frac{TP}{TP+FN}$$

where *TP* is the number of *true positives*, that is objects correctly detected by the system; *FP* is the number of *false positives*, that is false objects detected by the system but not actually present; *FN* is the number of *false negatives*, that is actual objects that are not detected by the system. Sometimes it is preferable to have one single index for measuring the performance (e.g. for performance tuning of a parametric system); in this case some authors propose the *f-index*, defined as the harmonic mean of *precision* and *recall*:

$$f\text{-}index = \frac{2 \cdot precision \cdot recall}{precision + recall}$$

Harmonic mean is used instead of arithmetic mean because the former gives a small result even if only one of *precision* or *recall* has a small value.

The usual definition of *precision* and *recall* makes sense for applications in which detection is a crisp decision, that is, an object is either completely detected or completely missed. In our case, since we deal with clusters that are not atomic entities, intermediate situations may occur and must be considered when defining the performance indices. To this aim, we have extended the definition of *TP*, *FP* and *FN* to have a more "fuzzy" behaviour in our case. More formally, if we have a set *D* of detected clusters (where each cluster is in turn a set of nodes) and a set G of ground-truth clusters, we define:

$$TP = \sum_{g \in G} \sum_{d \in D} \frac{|g \cap d|}{|g \cup d|} \qquad FP = \sum_{d \in D} \frac{|d| - \max_{g \in G} |d \cap g|}{|d|} \qquad FN = \sum_{g \in G} \frac{|g| - \max_{d \in D} |d \cap g|}{|g|}$$

where $|\,.\,|$ denotes the cardinality of a set.

As it can be easily shown, these definitions reduce to the usual counts of true positives, false positives and false negatives when the detection provide an "all-or-nothing" result, but behave more smoothly in case of partial detections. Given the above defined values of TP, FP and FN, we have computed *precision*, *recall* and the *f-index* for the results of the four algorithms on the two datasets.

5.1 Results on News Videos and Mammographic Images

Table 2 summarizes the results on the first application, the detection of anchor shots in news videos. From the table, it can be seen that our method clearly outperforms ICC and MCL and has a slightly larger value than GMC with respect to *precision* and *f-index*, while GMC has a slightly larger *recall*. It can be noted that even the absolute *precision* of the best algorithms is not very high on this application; however, with the addition of application-specific heuristics (such as those proposed in [12]) that are out of the scope of this paper, we have been able to obtain a good anchor shot detection performance.

Table 2. Performance on news videos. Best results are reported in bold.

	ICC	MCL	GMC	FMC
precision	0.211	0.201	0.380	**0.418**
recall	0.812	0.857	**0.985**	0.946
f-index	0.303	0.313	0.508	**0.556**

An analysis of the statistical significance of the results presented in Table 2 has shown that the comparison of FMC with ICC and MCL is significant (using the Friedman test, the probability p that the difference is not significant is less than 0.1%), while the differences between GMC and FMC are too small to be considered significant given the small size of this data set (17 videos).

Table 3 presents the results on the detection of clusters of microcalcifications in mammographic images. FMC outperforms all the other algorithms with respect to both *precision* and *recall* (and consequently, with respect to the *f-index*). In particular,

Table 3. Performance on mammographic images. Best results are reported in bold.

	ICC	MCL	GMC	FMC
precision	0.465	0.592	0.561	**0.634**
recall	0.653	0.895	0.935	**0.997**
f-index	0.518	0.692	0.653	**0.744**

it has an extremely good *recall*, which is very important for diagnostic purposes, and at the same time a good *precision* (with respect to the other methods). It can be also noted that while the GMC method, like FMC, is based on a Minimum Spanning Tree approach, on this application it is surpassed by MCL with respect to *precision* and *f-index*.

Also for these data we have conducted a statistical significance analysis with the Friedman test. Within a significance threshold of 5%, all the differences presented in Table 3 are significant.

6 Conclusions

In this paper we presented a graph-based clustering algorithm (*FMC*) and its application to a cluster detection problem in two pattern recognition applications: anchor shot detection in news video and microcalcifications cluster detection in mammographic images. The proposed algorithm is different from other graph-based clustering algorithms in that it does not require the user to set any parameter or threshold.

A comparison with other three graph-based clustering algorithms (namely, *ICC*, *MCL* and *GMC*) has been also carried out on the considered applications, by using an extended definition of the traditional *precision* and *recall* measures, that takes into account the possibility of partially detected clusters.

While we can reasonably conclude that the ICC algorithm has proven to be inadequate for this kind of problem, both MCL and GMC have shown a good performance in at least a subset of the tests. Globally, however, our algorithm has demonstrated to be consistently better than the other two, except for a few cases in which its performance was however close to the one scoring the best result.

As a future work, we are going to extend the experimental comparison including both more data (especially for the news video application, where the statistical significance needs to be improved) and other graph-based algorithms.

References

[1] Jain, A.K., Murty, M.N., Flynn, P.J.: Data clustering: a review. ACM Computing Surveys 31(3), 264–323 (1999)

[2] Jain, A.K., Dubes, R.C.: Algorithms for clustering data. Prentice-Hall, Inc., Upper Saddle River, NJ, USA (1988)

[3] Kohonen, T.: Self-organizing maps. Springer, Heidelberg (1995)

[4] Juszczak, P.: Learning to recognise. A study on one-class classification and active learning, PhD thesis, Delft University of Technology (2006), ISBN: 978-90-9020684-4

[5] Cheng, H.D., Cai, X., Chen, X., Hu, L., Lou, X.: Computer-aided detection and classification of microcalcifications in mammograms: a survey. Pattern Recognition 36, 2967–2991 (2003)

[6] Wu, Z., Leahy, R.: An Optimal Graph Theoretic Approach to Data Clustering: Theory and Its Application to Image Segmentation. IEEE Trans. on PAMI 15(11), 1101–1113 (1993)

[7] Zahn, C.: Graph-theoretical methods for detecting and describing gestalt clusters. IEEE Transactions on Computers C-20, 68–86 (1971)

[8] Bezdek, J.C.: Pattern Recognition with Fuzzy Objective Function Algorithms. Plenum Press, New York (1981)

[9] van Dongen, S.M.: Graph Clustering by Flow Simulation. PhD thesis, University of Utrecht (2000)

[10] Kannan, R., Vampala, S., Vetta, A.: On Clustering: Good, Bad and Spectral. In: Foundations of Computer Science 2000, pp. 367–378 (2000)

[11] Gaertler, M.: Clustering with spectral methods. Master's thesis, Universitat Konstanz (2002)

[12] De Santo, M., Percannella, G., Sansone, C., Vento, M.: Combining experts for anchorperson shot detection in news videos. Pattern Analysis and Applications 7(4), 447–460 (2005)

[13] Horowitz, E., Sahni, S.: Fundamentals of Computer Algorithms. Computer Science Press (1978)

[14] Brandes, U., Gaertler, M., Wagner, D.: Experiments on Graph Clustering Algorithms. In: Di Battista, G., Zwick, U. (eds.) ESA 2003. LNCS, vol. 2832, pp. 568–579. Springer, Heidelberg (2003)

[15] Sajda, P., Spence, C., Pearson, J.: Learning contextual relationships in mammograms using a hierarchical pyramid neural network. IEEE Trans. on Medical Imaging 21(3), 239–250 (2002)

Neural Object Recognition by Hierarchical Learning and Extraction of Essential Shapes

Daniel Oberhoff and Marina Kolesnik

Fraunhofer Institut FIT, Schloss Birlinghoven, 53754 Sankt Augustin

Abstract. We present a hierarchical system for object recognition that models neural mechanisms of visual processing identified in the mammalian ventral stream. The system is composed of neural units organized in a hierarchy of layers with increasing complexity. A key feature of the system is that the neural units learn their preferred patterns from visual input alone. Through this "soft wiring" of neural units the system becomes tuned for target object classes through pure visual experience and with no prior labeling. Object labels are only introduced to train a classifier on the system's output. The system's tuning takes place in a feedforward path. We also present a neural mechanism for back projection of the learned image patterns down the hierarchical layers. This feedback mechanism could serve as a starting point for integration of what- and where-information processed by the ventral and dorsal stream. We test the neural system with natural images from publicly available datasets of natural scenes and handwritten digits.

1 Introduction

Even after many years of active research in computer vision, approaches to object recognition only seldomly yield the desired performance. This is despite the ease with which humans and many animals perform these tasks. In the hope to reach at least part of this performance, more attention is being paid to algorithms that, in more or less detail, model visual cortical organization as identified in humans and other mammals by means of psychophysics and neurophysiology.

There, several processing streams have been identified, of which ventral and dorsal are the most pronounced ones [1]. Each stream has a hierarchical multilayer structure in which the complexity of the neuron's selectivity increases gradually from bottom to top layers. The ventral stream mainly performs recognition and classification tasks [2] while the dorsal stream is specialized for the processing of motion and place as well as depth. The ventral stream on the other hand is largely ignorant to motion and place information as well as the exact arrangement of object features. The mechanism for this has been clearly identified in area V1 by Hubel and Wiesel [3] who found separate populations of simple and complex cells: Simple were found to act as detectors of oriented intensity variations with high specificity to the position, orientation, and phase of these stimuli, while complex cells exhibit the same selectivity but are tolerant to a limited amount of shift of these stimuli. Hubel and Wiesel were also the first to identify

F. Mele et al. (Eds.): BVAI 2007, LNCS 4729, pp. 288–297, 2007.

columnar organization of the visual cortex: Columns are assemblies of (simple and complex) cells that have receptive fields in mostly the same retinotopic area and cover the whole spectrum of different features.

This neural structure has been reflected in several schemes for learning and recognition of image patterns. Probably the first such network, called "Neocognitron", was suggested by Kunihiko Fukushima in 1980 [4]. Neocognitron consists of a series of S- and C-layers (mimicking simple and complex cell types, respectively) with shared weights for a set of local receptive fields and inhibitory and excitatory sub-populations of units with interactions resembling neural mechanisms. Neocognitron learns through a combination of winner-take-all and reinforcement learning, autonomously forms classes for presented characters, and correctly classifies some slightly distorted and noisy versions of these characters. In 1989 Yan LeCun et al. [5], introduced a similar but much more powerful successor to this network that generated local feature descriptors through backpropagation. A later version of this network, called "LeNet", has been shown to act as an efficient framework for nonlinear-dimensionality reduction of imagesets [6]. "LeNet" is similar in architecture to Neocognitron, but does not learn autonomously and requires labels to initiate the back-propagation. The latter is not biologically justified.

In 2003 Riesenhuber and Poggio [7] suggested a computational model for object recognition in the visual cortex with a similar layout called "hmax", initially focusing on the correspondence between model components and cortical areas. "hmax" employs Gaussian radial basis functions to model the selectivity of simple cells, and a nonlinear max-function, pooling input from a local population of simple cells, to model functionality of complex cells. Learning in hmax is constrained to the tuning of simple cells to random snapshots of local input activity while presenting objects of interest. It was, however, successfully applied to the modeling of V4 and IT neuron responses and also as an input stage to a classifier for object and face recognition yielding very good performance.

Another approach that focuses very much on the neural details of neural adaptation and learning and does not use weight sharing is found in "VisNet", presented by Deco and Rolls in 2002 [9]. The most interesting ingredient to their model is the fact that it can learn the shift invariance of the feature detectors autonomously through a temporal learning rule called the *trace rule*.

The system we present here, while structurally similar to hmax, incorporates an unsupervised learning strategy and feedback projections.

2   The Object Recognition System

The architecture of the system comprises a hierarchy of several processing layers representing the visual areas in the ventral stream (see Fig. 1). Each layer, analogously to most cortical visual areas, has a columnar organization, such that for every spatial location there are several units with distinct receptivity. The output of such a layer is arranged along 3 dimensions: horizontal/vertical displacement and feature index. The layers are arranged in pairs called (following established notation) S- and C- layers. The S-layers perform feature detection on their input while the C-layers reduce the resolution of the S-layer output by pooling over local spatial regions using a max-nonlinearity [7] while keeping the same columnar arrangement. This processing step performed by the C-layers makes their response position invariant to a limited degree. The area over which C-layer units pool is chosen to match the receptive field size of the preceding S-layer. The receptive fields of the S-layers only encompass a few spatial locations of their input (S1:5x5, S2-S3:3x3), but due to the hierarchical arrangement, the receptive fields of units in higher layers of the hierarchy (if projected all the way back to the first layer) become very large. This accounts for one of the important properties in the ventral stream: growing receptive field sizes and reduction of the information about the spatial origin of visual percepts.

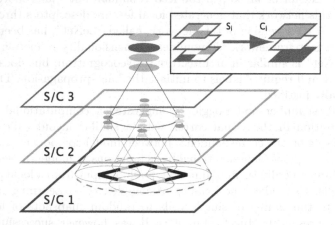

Fig. 1. Architecture of the shape extraction hierarchy. It is exemplarily shown how information reaches a single S3-unit, and how the large effective receptive field of this unit is constructed hierarchically.

The described hierarchy performs recognition of shapes in a multi-scale fashion: units on lower layers of the hierarchy are receptive for local shape features such as lines, curves, branches or corners, while units on higher levels are receptive to complex combinations of such low-level features. The first feature extracting layer, S0, employs a V1 simple cell model, based on Gabor filters and surround suppression, followed by a maximum pooling layer, C0, corresponding to the complex cells in V1. 8 sets of Gabor pairs were used, with spatial periods of 4 and 8 pixels and at 4 orientations. The following S-layers (S1-S3) perform autonomous learning as described in the next section.

2.1   Self-tuning Feature Extraction Layers

Layers S1-S3 of the system "tune themselves" to shape features elicited by visual input. Through an iterative learning process (Fig. 2) one column of selective units is generated and replicated across the whole spatial domain of the perceived image. The selectivity of the units in the column is modeled using Gaussian radial basis functions operating on the input within unit's receptive field:

$$a_i(x,y) = |I_r(x,y)| \times e^{\frac{(\hat{I}_r(x,y)-p_i)^2}{2\sigma_i}} \tag{1}$$

Here i is the index of the unit in the column, (x,y) is the retinotopic position of the column, p_i is the unit's preferred pattern, and $I_r(x,y)$ is the input within a radius r around (x,y). The tuning width, σ_i, defines the sharpness of the unit's selectivity. $\hat{I}$ denotes Euclidean normalization.

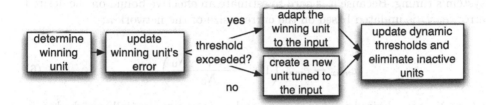

Fig. 2. Overview of one iteration of the learning process. These steps are performed for each input position for each presented image and for each layer.

To generate a representative set of unit's for each S-layer, images are presented to the system and the best responding unit is selected in the neighborhood $B_r(x,y)$ around each input location (x,y):

$$i'(x,y) = \underset{i}{\operatorname{argmax}} \left(\max_{(x',y')\in B_r(x,y)} a_i(x',y') \right). \tag{2}$$

The effect of this selection is that the receptive fields of selected units do not overlap. To initialize the system an arbitrary position with strong activity is selected in the input and a unit is generated that prefers exactly this pattern. The receptive field size r is kept constant for each layer.

Since only a single column is trained, all the image positions have to be visited in series, so, to avoid bias of any one region, the visiting order is randomized. Before the actual update is performed the difference of the experienced input and the winning unit's preferred pattern is measured and used to update an error variable for the unit:

$$e_i \leftarrow e^{-1/\tau} \left(e_i + \delta_{ii'} |I_r(x,y)| \cdot |\hat{I}_r(x,y) - p_i| \right) \tag{3}$$

where τ is a time constant determining the layer's speed of adaptation and $\delta_{ii'}$ is Kronecker's Delta. Using this update rule has the effect that e_i will take on high values when the unit wins repeatedly while experiencing input that is very different from its preferred pattern.

If the error exceeds a threshold e_{max} a new unit is generated, the error is distributed equally to the winning, and the new unit and both their tuning widths (σ) set to halve the winning unit's tuning width. Only when the error did not exceed e_{max}, the winning unit is updated according to:

$$p_{i'} \leftarrow p_{i'} + \alpha |I_r(x,y)| \left(I_r(x,y) - p_{i'}\right) \tag{4}$$

$$\sigma_{i'} \leftarrow \sigma_{i'} + \alpha |I_r(x,y)| \left(|I_r(x,y)| - p_i| - \sigma_{i'}\right) \tag{5}$$

were α is a constant learning rate. Note that the updates in (3-5) are weighed by the actual amount of input, $|I_r(x,y)|$, in the range of the unit's receptive field. Thus, only regions containing information will actually have an impact on the system's tuning. Because it is hard to estimate an effective bound on the desired error, e_{max} is updated based on the current size of the network n:

$$e_{max} \leftarrow e_{max} \left(1 + \frac{n + n_+ - N_0}{N_0}\right) \tag{6}$$

where N_0 is the desired number of units, and n_+ is an exponentially weighed moving average of the growth rate. Additionally to the tuning and growing process, units are removed from the system if they win the competition too infrequently. The threshold for removal is updated similarly to the one for growing:

$$f_0 \leftarrow f_0 \left(1 - \frac{n + n_+ - N_0}{N_0}\right) \tag{7}$$

The above steps have the effect that within a few time constants the column will reach the desired size and be appropriately tuned to the input patterns encountered during that time. Thus τ should be set a few times smaller than the training set size.

2.2 Feedback Projections

Anatomical studies have shown that virtually all connections between successive pairs of visual areas in the ventral stream are reciprocal[10]. The feedback projections are thought to serve top-down processing for object association and visual attention.

Our approach to feedback projections is based on the *Selective Tuning* model by John K. Tsotsos et. al. [11], but with a less strict selection scheme, and some adaptation to suit our architecture:

- Activation from the output of the S-layers and the perceptron is "cleaned up" in that (at every retinotopic position) only the unit with the maximum response projects back. The back-projection through the perceptron is furthermore rectified since negative activation is undesirable.
- Only the afferent that contributed to the output of the C-layers is propagated back. This introduces the spatial competition emphasized in [11].

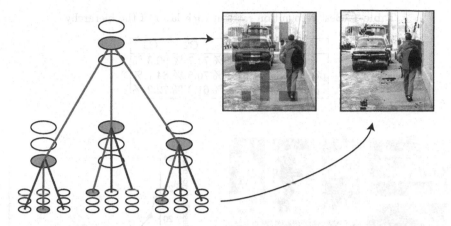

Fig. 3. Feedback begins at a selected output unit feeding back among it's afferents to that unit which yielded the strongest input in the forward sweep. The images show the output from a perceptron trained to recognize cars from C3-output (*left*), and the feedback result to the lowest layer, S0(*right*).

 – The actual selection is performed by multiplying the back-propagating signal with the forward traveling signal before each max-pooling layer.

Through these mechanisms we can recover the low level input responsible for a certain classification event (Fig. 3) .

3   Applications

The learning system has been applied to various datasets ranging from natural sceneries to images of handwritten digits. In all trials three pairs of S- and C-layers for learning and maximum pooling, respectively, were used. Learning layers were trained sequentially from bottom to top. For the learning of each layer the training set was presented twice: once to establish a codebook and another time to refine it.

3.1   Natural Images

Natural images of street scenes were selected from a publicly available database[1] together with image annotations. The annotations were refined to make sure all instances of pedestrians and cars were labeled. 600 crops were extracted with 10 pixels padding on each side. 200 crops per class featuring cars, pedestrians, and other randomly selected objects were split by half for the training and test set (Fig. 4,*left*). A linear classifier was employed for object classification. This classifier extracted the mean and covariance of the data for each class, and assigned unseen data to the class for which the corresponding normal distribution

---

[1] See http://labelme.csai.mit.edu/

Table 1. Best recognition rates at each layer of the hierarchy

layer	C0	C1	C2	C3
cars	63.3 %	68.7 %	74.7 %	90.3 %
people	46.4 %	57.6 %	76.5 %	84.7 %
other	48.9 %	50.4 %	61.3 %	72.2 %

 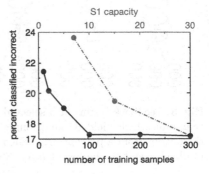

Fig. 4. *Left:* examples of crops obtained from the LabelMe database. *Right:* dependence of the total recognition error on N_0 (top axis, dashed line) and training set size (bottom axis, solid line).

yielded the highest posterior probability. Since the output of the last learning layer, C3, usually contained more than one spatial location (i.e. > 1x1 pixels), the location with maximum sum of activities over a column has been selected as input to the classifier. The adaptation time constant, τ, was fixed to 100.

To measure the increase in shape information as it travels up the hierarchy, we also trained and tested classifiers with the outputs from the lower C-layers, while adjusting the pooling in these layers to make the output resolution equal to that of C3. Table 1 lists the obtained recognition rates showing that the performance increases with each layer. A jump in performance occurs between layers C1 and C2 for pedestrians and between C2 and C3 for cars. This jump can be assigned to the fact, that the effective receptive field size is large enough to cover the whole instances of the respective class at their typical size. Best performances are **90%** for the car class and **84%** for the pedestrian class. Clearly, pedestrians are harder to classify because of their variable shapes. The obtained rates seem competitive for this kind of task, though we have not tried any established algorithms for comparison, but are planning to do so in the near future.

To test the influence of the layer capcity N_0 on the overall recognition performance, three different capacities of 7, 15, and 30 for the lowest layer were tried. The capacities were doubled for each higher layer (e.g. S1:30, S2:60, S3:120). For the largest capacity the size of the training set was varied between 10 and 300 (the whole set) while adjusting the number of presentations of the set to keep the total number of presented images constant. The whole training set was used for the

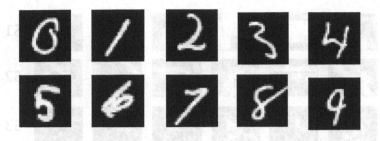

Fig. 5. Handwritten digits from the MNIST dataset

training of the classifier. The results (Fig 4, *right*) show that the system can generalize sufficiently well and shows no degradation in performance even for a training set of only 33 images per class. Reducing the N_0 causes strong degradation in performance, indicating a minimal capacity required for the task. Yet additional tests have shown that a further increase in N_0 tends to decrease performance. It thus remains to find a way for automatic tuning of the system's capacity.

3.2 Handwritten Digits

A sample of handwritten digits from the MNIST dataset[2] is shown in Fig.5. The dataset contains 60.000 training and 10.000 test examples, binarized, centered, and scaled to a common size. The speed of adaptation, τ, was set to 5000, and the capacities of the learning layers were (from lowest to highest in the hierarchy) 40, 80 and 160, respectively. No Gabor filtering stage was used in this trial because the images had low spatial resolution. Also, due to their near binary nature, these images could be directly processed by layer S1. The increasing complexity of the learned features is shown in Fig. 6. A two layer perceptron with 100 hidden units was employed for classification because the linear classifier failed to produce reasonable results (we also tried Support Vector Machines with Gaussian kernels and Gentle AdaBoost both yielding similar results). The necessity of a non-linear classifier indicates that the C3-layer outputs do not form single clusters for each of the ten digits. This is not so surprising since the digits appear in many and sometimes subtle variations.

Running our system on this dataset yields a recognition rate of **94.2%** on the test set with the perceptron. This is comparable with the results exhibited by state-of-the-art algorithms[2]. The system also exhibits some tolerance to rotation and scale changes(Fig. 7), even though only undistorted images were used for training. This tolerance is partly introduced by the C-layers discarding some information about the exact spatial origin of each feature. Rotation tolerance is also due to the facts that only a small number of units were part of the S1-column, so that a small rotation of the feature does not change the winning unit, and that some rotation variance was already present in the training set. The tolerance does not, however, hold for much larger rotations, which would have to be explicitly learned (see also [8]).

---

[2] See http://yann.lecun.com/exdb/mnist/

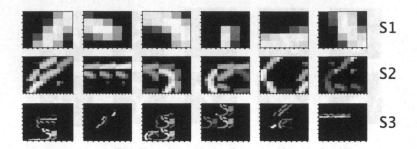

Fig. 6. Examples of receptive fields learned by units in (S1)-(S3) as back-projected to the retinal level. The projection is only approximate due to the position discarding nature of the C-layers. Nevertheless one can nicely observe how the complexity increases up to full digits.

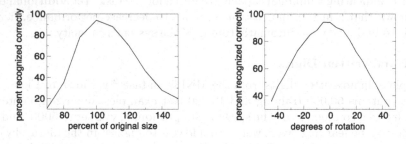

Fig. 7. Recognition rate as a function of change in size (*left:*) and rotation (*right*)

4 Conclusion

We have described the hierarchical learning system for shape based object recognition inspired by neurophysiological evidence on ventral stream processing in the mammalian brain. The system exhibits a robust capability to develop selectivity to frequently occurring input patterns with the only constraining parameters being it's capacity and the time constant of the adaptation. Especially no class information is required in the learning stage, in contrast to most current approaches to feature learning.

This learned selectivity to characteristic image patterns generates a unique set of features at the highest layer of the hierarchy. When these are passed to a final classifier, a respectable recognition performance, comparable to the state-of-the-art algorithms, is achieved for very different images ranging from natural scenes to artificial objects. This capability to adapt and perform consistently comes almost for free through natural tuning and with little change of a few parameters. We only know of one similar system that combines this kind of architecture with an unsupervised learning rule for object recognition [12]. There an energy minimization scheme has been used to generate a set of preferred patterns based on the reconstruction error and an additional term enforcing sparsity of the response of the feature selective layers, while we used a more biological competitive Hebbian learning rule. All other system either do not incorporate any unsupervised learning aside from random picking of input data as codebook entries or require a much more powerful classifier to perform similarly or both; or use supervised learning for the whole system [4,5,7,8,13].

We have also presented how the attention model of J. K. Tsotsos et al. [11] can be adapted to our system to recover the exact location of responsible stimuli for a recognition event in large scenes. Future work will investigate how these responsible stimuli could facilitate the learning and, ultimately, recognition.

References

1. Ungerleider, L.G., Mishkin, M.: Two cortical visual systems. In: Analysis of Visual Behavior, pp. 549–586. MIT Press, Cambridge (1992)
2. Hung, C.P., Kreiman, G., Poggio, T., DiCarlo, J.J.: Fast readout of object identity from macaque inferior temporal cortex. Science Reports (2005)
3. Hubel, D.H., Wiesel, T.N.: Receptive fields and functional architecture of monkey striate cortex. J. Physiol. 195 (1967)
4. Fukushima, K.: Neocognitron: A self-organizing neural network model for a mechanism of pattern recognition unaffected by shift in position. Biol. Cyb. V36(4), 193–202 (1980)
5. LeCun, Y., Jackel, L.D., Boser, B., Denker, J.S., Graf, H.P., Guyon, I., Henderson, D., Howard, R.E., Hubbard, W.: Handwritten digit recognition: Applications of neural net chips and automatic learning. IEEE Comm., 41–46 (invited paper, 1989)
6. Hadsell, R., Chopra, S., LeCun, Y.: Dimensionality reduction by learning an invariant mapping. In: Proc. CVPR, IEEE Press, Los Alamitos (2006)
7. Serre, T., Kouh, M., Cadieu, C., Knoblich, U., Kreiman, G., Poggio, T.: A theory of object recognition: Computations and circuits in the feedforward path of the ventral stream in primate visual cortex. CBCL Memo 259 (2005)
8. Deco, G., Rolls, E.T.: A neurodynamical cortical model of visual attention and invariant object recognition. Vis. Res. 44 (2004)
9. Rolls, E.T., Deco, G.: The Computational Neuroscience of Vision. Oxford University Press, Oxford (2002)
10. Felleman, D.J., Van Essen, D.C.: Distributed Hierarchical Processing in the Primate Cerebral Cortex. Cereb. Cortex 1, 1–a–47 (1991)
11. Tsotsos, J.K., Culhane, S.M., Wai, W.Y.K., Lai, Y., Davis, N., Nuflo, F.: Modeling visual attention via selective tuning. Artificial Intelligence 78, 507–545 (1994)
12. Mutch, J., Lowe, D.G.: Multiclass object recognition with sparse, localized features. In: Proc. CVPR, pp. 11–18 (2006)
13. Munder, S., Gavrila, D.M.: An experimental study on pedestrian classification. IEEE Trans. Pattern Analysis and Machine Intelligence 28, 1863–1868 (2006)

Increasing Efficiency in Disparity Calculation

Jarno Ralli, Francisco Pelayo, and Javier Diaz

University Of Granada, Escuela Técnica Superior de Ingenierías Informática y de
Telecomunicación, Departamento de Arquitectura y Tecnología de Computadores
Calle Periodista Daniel Saucedo Aranda s/n E-18071 Granada, Spain
jralli@atc.ugr.es, fpelayo@ugr.es, jdiaz@atc.ugr.es

Abstract. In this paper a trade-off between the computation effort and the
accuracy of the resulting disparity map, obtained using interpolation over
spatial domain, is presented. The accuracy of the obtained disparity map is
presented as the mean squared error calculated over the known disparity ground
truth of test images, while efficiency increase is presented in terms of algorithm
run-times. Even when reducing the search space for correspondences using
epipolar geometry, disparity calculation methods are considered computationally more expensive than interpolation. We show that substantial efficiency
increase can be gained using interpolation, in comparison to calculating the
dense disparity map directly. As will be shown interpolation also permits us to
approximate a disparity value for the occluded pixels. The main contribution of
our work is the disparity calculation efficiency increase using interpolation, that
fits the sparse disparity map as a 2D surface.

Keywords: Dense disparity map, interpolation, visual completion, computation
efficiency.

1 Introduction

Binocular vision for depth information retrieval can be considered as a special case of
motion parallax. Due to motion parallax the observed objects apparently shift as the
observing position changes [1]. The apparent shift of the object depends on the
distance between the object and the observer and the size of the motion parallax
(distance between the observing points). Thus if the size of the motion parallax is
known, the distance from the observer to the object can be deduced [1],[2],[3]. In the
binocular vision case the observer position distance (the distance between the left and
right eyes or cameras) is either fixed or known. While motion parallax refers to the
position change of the observer, disparity is the equivalent term in the image planes
[1],[2],[3]. One of the problems caused by motion parallax that biological binocular
vision systems have to deal with is that some parts of the image are not present in the
other image. This is known as occlusion. The problem is overcome in biological
visual systems by a process known as visual completion or interpolation [4],[5]. The
visual completion process results in an impression of a surface or contour in locations
where such information is not available in the image [4].

F. Mele et al. (Eds.): BVAI 2007, LNCS 4729, pp. 298–307, 2007.
© Springer-Verlag Berlin Heidelberg 2007

In machine vision the disparity is calculated by discovering the corresponding points or features in the left and right images which describe the same real-world object point [1],[2],[3]. One of the problems, as was mentioned earlier, is that for the occluded points the disparity cannot be calculated directly [2]. Even if interpolation is a widely used post-processing technique (for example improving the density and visual quality of image features such as stereo or motion) only a few studies exist indicating how to increase efficiency or accuracy (see [10]) via interpolation.

In this paper we present the results of using the interpolation property of biological binocular vision systems not only to approximate the disparity at the occluded points but also as a way of improving the disparity computation. In this sense the interpolation process can be seen as a tradeoff between the resulting disparity map accuracy and computation efficiency. Due to the fact that real world objects present in the images normally have continuous and smooth surfaces, except at the object edges, in geometrical sense it is justified to approximate these surfaces using interpolation. The interpolation methods that we have used to reconstruct the dense disparity map treat the sparse disparity map as a 2D surface.

2 System Overview

The system consists of two different parts: camera parameter calculation and the consecutive stages of disparity calculation. This is schematically shown in Fig. 1.

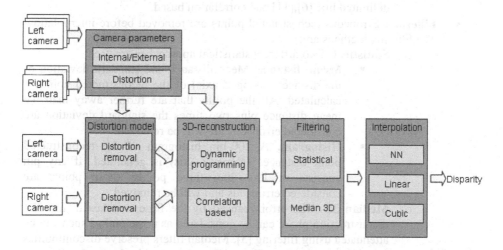

Fig. 1. System description. The consecutive stages take as input a pair of stereo images with the corresponding camera parameters and return a disparity map.

The image processing stages of the system are the following:

- **Camera parameters and lens distortion.** This stage consists of approximating the internal, external and camera-lens distortion parameters. Output from the distortion model stage is a pair of images without lens distortions.

- **3D-reconstruction.** In this stage the corresponding left and right image points are searched for using either dynamic programming (feature based) or correlation (area based) methods, after which triangulation is used for 3D-reconstruction. More detailed description can be found in [11].
  - o Correlation based method compares image patches in order to calculate where the intensity values are similar [2]. The similarity metrics used is normalized cross-correlation (NCC) [11]. An evenly spaced grid, called the search grid, for defining the points used for calculating the disparity is first defined. A point validation is used to discard possible false correspondences: first a corresponding point for the left point p_L is searched for in the right image, which shall be called p_{CR}. Then for the point p_{CR} the maximally correlating point in the left image is searched for, which shall be called p_{CL}. If p_L and p_{CL} describe the same point, then the point pair (p_L, p_{CR}) is accepted [2].
  - o Dynamic programming addresses the problem of finding corresponding points by converting it into an optimization problem and thus tries to find a more global solution [6],[11]. For the dynamic programming only intra scan-line search is employed, using two different kinds of metrics for optimization: edge delimited line [6],[11] and correlation based.
- **Filtering.** Erroneous reconstructed points are removed before interpolation. The filtering methods are:
  - o **Statistical.** Two different statistical approaches are used:
    - **Mean distance.** Mean distance and standard deviation of the distance (along Z-axis) of the reconstructed points is calculated. All the points that are further away than the mean distance plus two times the standard deviation are considered erroneous are will be removed.
    - **Histogram.** A 100-bin histogram of the reconstructed point distances (along Z-axis) is generated. If any pin consists of less than three points, those points are considered erroneous and will be removed.
  - o **Median 3D.** The errors caused by the false matches in the 3D-reconstruction phase can be considered as noise and as such can be attenuated using filtering [3]. Median filters preserve discontinuities better than averaging filters [3] and thus suits better for filtering disparity values, where the disparity on the object edges is discontinuous. The nearest points to a particular point of interest are deduced using Euclidean distance.
- **Interpolation.** Before interpolation sparse disparity map is constructed from the original image point position coordinates used for triangulation and the 3D-reconstucted Z-axis coordinate, which is inversely proportionate to disparity. The tested interpolation methods are:

- o   Nearest Neighbor (NN).
- o   Linear.
- o   Cubic.

3   Experiments and Results

Several tests were conducted with real and synthetic images in order to evaluate the effects of interpolation on the resulting dense disparity map accuracy and the corresponding increase in computation efficiency. The accuracy is calculated as a mean squared error (MSE) between the ground truth and the resulting disparity map. The programming and testing was done using Matlab running on a PC with Intel Core 2 Duo processor running at 2.4GHz and with 1 GB of RAM.

Fig. 2. Test images from left to right: Tsukuba (real) and Venus (synthetic). On the top row left-right stereo images are displayed. On the bottom row the ground truth disparity corresponding to each of the left-stereo-images is shown. The test images are available at Middlebury College, Stereo Vision Research Page [7].

3.1   Qualitative Analysis

In this experiment the disparity was calculated directly for all the image elements using both the correlation and dynamic programming methods (Fig. 3 and 4). The disparity values shown are in fact back-projected values from 3D-reconstructed points (Fig. 1) and thus due to inaccuracies in the back-projection the MSE is high. More important than the absolute value of MSE is the relative change of MSE between interpolated and non-interpolated case.

First the calculated disparity map, without interpolation, is displayed on the left. Then the same calculated disparity map is used as a basis for linear interpolation and the resulting disparity map is displayed on the right. The MSE is calculated using the pixels for which the disparity has been calculated (detected false matches are ignored). In the disparity-difference images a bright intensity denotes a big error between the ground truth and the obtained disparity.

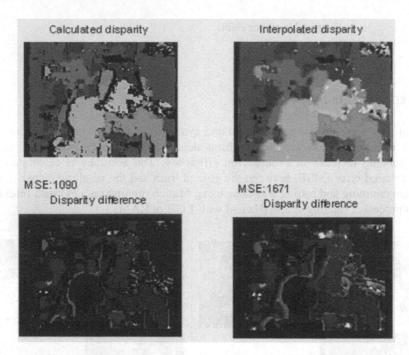

Calculated disparity   Interpolated disparity

MSE:1090   MSE:1671

Disparity difference   Disparity difference

Fig. 3. Correlation method. The experiment on the left side shows the resulting disparity map calculated directly for all the pixels, while the experiment on the right side demonstrates the resulting dense disparity map using linear interpolation. The images are from the experiments 11 and 12 in the table 1.

Fig. 3 demonstrates the effects of the interpolation on the resulting disparity map obtained using correlation. The MSE of the initial sparse disparity map (left) is relatively high which is due false positives that have not been filtered out. The MSE of the interpolated disparity map increases due to the spreading effect of the interpolation and thus the erroneous zones are spread, increasing the overall error. As can be observed from the other results in table 1, using a considerably sparser initial disparity map for interpolation can result in a more accurate disparity map. This means that the correctness of the initial disparity map greatly affects accuracy. Thus either a method producing less false-positive matches should be employed or more effective filtering should be applied prior to interpolation.

Fig. 4 demonstrates the effects of interpolating the disparity map from the results obtained using dynamic programming with correlation. Since dynamic programming is based on feature matching, features being edges in this case, disparity values can only be calculated for pixels where a feature is present. Disparity estimations for the edges can be observed in Fig 4, top row left image. The MSE of the interpolated disparity map is only slightly higher than that of the directly calculated. Even if the amount of pixels for which the disparity is known, is considerably lower in the dynamic programming than in the intensity correlation case (see Fig. 3 and 4), the resulting final disparity map is however notably better.

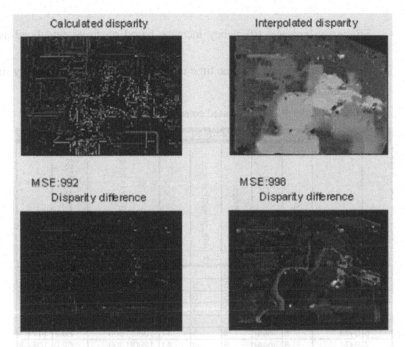

Fig. 4. Dynamic programming using correlation. The experiment on the left side shows the results of calculating the disparity for all the lines, while the experiment on the right side demonstrates the resulting dense disparity map using linear interpolation. The images are from experiments 13 and 14 in table 2.

3.2 Quantitative Analysis

Effects of the parameters on the resulting disparity map accuracy and algorithm run-times are similar for both of the test images and thus only results for the Tsukuba images are displayed in tables 1 and 2. Also the results using dynamic programming with correlation were always better than those of edge delimited line metrics, thus the results for the latter will not be presented. Because the interpolation times were negligible in comparison with the time taken for calculating the sparse disparity map, the computational complexity estimation is based on the time taken to calculate the initial dense disparity map in each case. In tables 1 and 2 the tests with best efficiency increase and lowest MSE have been highlighted.

Information related to the tables:

- Filter: Statistical, Median or S+M (statistical and then median).
- Median nn size: Neighborhood size for the median filter.
- Grid search length: The distance in pixels that each point in the search grid can be moved. Search points are moved, within search length limits, over pixels where an edge or change is present.
- Correlation window size: Size in pixels of the correlation window.
- N, P: correlation window size: $N \times P$ (table 2).
- Grid size: Size of the search grid (table 1).

- Efficiency increase: Efficiency increase based on time, calculated as $\dfrac{t_m}{t_n}$ where t_m and t_n refer to the time used for calculating the disparity map in the m:th and the n:th test.

Table 1. Results of intensity based correlation for the Tsukuba images

Method: Intensity correlation. Image: Tsukuba									
Test number	Filter	Median nn size	Interpolation method	Grid search length	Correlation window size	Grid size	Points found/Points total	Efficiency increase (t12/t1n)	MSE
1	None	5	linear	5	5	41	1271/1600	75,0	3540,7
2	Statistical	5	linear	5	5	41	1255/1600	76,1	1088,4
3	Median	5	linear	5	5	41	1271/1600	76,1	1755,3
4	S+M	5	linear	2	5	41	1261/1600	76,3	870,8
5	S+M	5	linear	0	5	41	1239/1600	76,2	820,2
6	S+M	5	linear	5	3	41	1080/1600	80,7	1171,5
7	S+M	5	linear	5	9	41	1290/1600	62,0	1054,8
8	S+M	5	linear	5	5	11	79/100	1213,4	925,4
9	S+M	5	linear	2	5	81	4901/6400	19,0	911,5
10	S+M	5	cubic	5	5	41	1255/1600	76,0	904,4
11	Statistical	5	none	2	5	0	85391/110592	1,0	1090,0
12	Statistical	5	linear	2	5	0	85391/110592	1,0	1670,7

Table 2. Results of dynamic programming with correlation, for the Tsukuba images

Method:DP intensity correlation. Image: Tsukuba										
Test number	N	P	Search lines	Occlucion threshold	Filter	Median nn size	Interpolation method	Points found/Points total	Efficiency increase (t14/tn)	MSE
1	5	5	41	0,1	S+M	5	linear	1826/2750	7,6	1060,0
2	5	5	41	0,3	S+M	5	linear	2126/2750	7,7	1018,3
3	5	5	41	0,5	S+M	5	linear	2182/2750	7,7	992,6
4	5	5	41	0,3	None	5	linear	2154/2750	7,7	8138,7
5	5	5	41	0,3	Statistical	5	linear	2126/2750	7,7	975,8
6	5	5	41	0,3	Median	5	linear	2154/2750	7,7	1005,3
7	5	5	11	0,3	S+M	5	linear	492/648	34,4	1130,6
8	5	5	81	0,3	S+M	5	linear	4430/5702	3,6	858,6
9	7	3	41	0,3	S+M	5	linear	2127/2750	7,7	1044,3
10	5	5	41	0,3	S+M	7	linear	2126/2750	7,7	1049,7
11	5	5	41	0,7	S+M	5	linear	2241/2750	7,7	1169,8
12	5	5	41	0,3	S+M	5	cubic	2126/2750	7,7	1084,4
13	5	5	0	0,3	Statistical	5	none	15606/19815	1,0	991,5
14	5	5	0	0,3	Statistical	5	linear	15606/19815	1,0	998,1

The Fig. 5 and 6 demonstrate the effects of using different amounts of points for disparity calculation on the efficiency and error between the resulting map and the ground truth. The fitted trend-lines are a second order polynomial and a "power" function of the form $y = cx^b$.

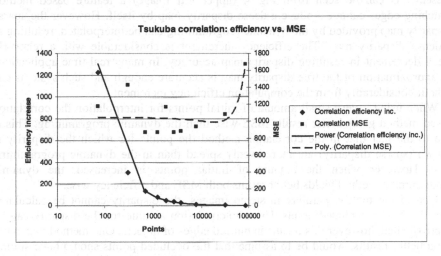

Fig. 5. Tsukuba images; efficiency vs. MSE using intensity correlation

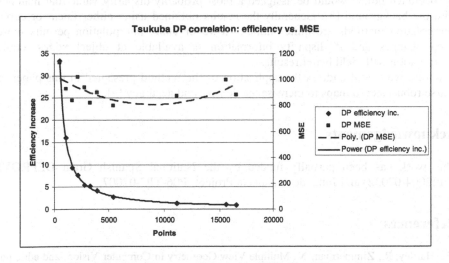

Fig. 6. Tsukuba images; efficiency vs. MSE using DP correlation

As can be seen from the Fig. 5 and 6, first the MSE decreases as more initial points are used for interpolation. However as the number of initial points is increased the MSE starts to rise. This is due to the inefficient filtering of false positives. As the number of initial points increases, the efficiency decreases rapidly.

4 Discussions

In this paper we have shown that interpolation can be employed for increasing the disparity map computation efficiency and for deducing a disparity value where not present. As can be seen from Fig. 4 (upper left image) a feature based method matching edges cannot produce a dense disparity map by itself. However the sparse disparity map provided by the dynamic programming can be interpolated, resulting in a dense disparity map. The efficiency increment is considerable with a relatively small decrement in resulting disparity map accuracy. In many real-time applications an approximation of the true disparity map is accurate enough and such systems can benefit considerably from the computation efficiency increment.

When using a very small amount of initial points for interpolation the correlation based method gives better results MSE wise than the dynamic programming. This is due to the fact that in the correlation method the points for which the disparity is known (sparse disparity) are more evenly spread than in the dynamic programming case. However when the amount of initial points is increased, the dynamic programming method yields better results both MSE and efficiency wise.

Due to the motion parallax in stereo images, the disparity cannot be calculated directly for the occluded points. Using interpolation a value for the disparity can be approximated, however this results in blurred edges of objects. One method that could yield better results, would be to assume that the occluded points should have similar disparity value that the nearest background points. Thus before the interpolation phase the occluded points would be assigned a most probably disparity value that matches with the background [8]. Generally the results obtained using either linear or cubic interpolation methods are quite similar. However cubic interpolation permits more steep changes and if disparity information is available at object edges, cubic interpolation will yield better results.

Future work will address the application of the method presented in this paper to sparse robust stereo maps to increase the density and accuracy [9].

Acknowledgements

This work has been partially funded by the National Spanish Grant DEPROVI (DPI2004-07032) and Junta de Andalucía Project: P06-TIC-02007.

References

1. Hartley, R., Zimmerman, A.: Multiple View Geometry in Computer Vision, 2nd edn., pp. 204–208. The Press syndicate of the University of Cambridge (2003)
2. Faugeras, O.: Three-Dimensional Computer Vision: A Geometric Viewpoint. MIT Press, Cambridge (1996)
3. Trucco, E., Verri, A.: Introductory Techniques for 3D Computer Vision. Prentice-Hall Inc., Englewood Cliffs (1998)
4. Anderson, B.L., Singh, M., Fleming, R.W.: The Interpolation of Object and Surface Structure. Cognitive Psychology 44, 148–190 (2002)

5. Wilcox, L., Duke, P.: Spatial and Temporal Properties of Stereoscopic Surface Interpolation. Perception 34, 1325–1338 (2005)
6. Ohta, Y., Kanade, T.: Stereo by Intra- and Inter-Scanline Search Using Dynamic Programming. IEEE Transactions on Pattern Analysis and Machine Intelligence 7(2), 139–154 (1985)
7. Middlebury College: Stereo Vision Research Page, URL: http://www.middlebury.edu/stereo
8. Park, J.-I., Um, G.M., Ahn, C.: Virtual Control of Optical Axis of the 3DTV Camera for Reducing Visual Fatigue in Stereoscopic 3DTV. ETRI Journal 26(6), 597–604 (2004)
9. Krüger, N., Felsberg, M.: An Explicit and Compact Coding of Geometric and Structural Information Applied to Stereo Matching. Pattern Recognition Letters 25(8), 849–863 (2004)
10. Boufama, B., Rastgar, H., Bouakaz, S.: Efficient Surface Interpolation with Occlusion Detection. In: JCIS-2006 Proceedings. Advances in Intelligent Systems Research (2006)
11. Brown, M.Z., Burschka, D., Hager, G.D.: Advances in Computational Stereo. IEEE Transactions on Pattern Analysis and Machine Intelligence 25(8), 993–1008 (2003)

Patterns of Binocular Disparity
for a Fixating Observer

Miles Hansard and Radu Horaud

INRIA Rhône-Alpes, 655 Avenue de l'Europe, Montbonnot 38330, France
miles.hansard@inrialpes.fr, radu.horaud@inrialpes.fr

Abstract. Binocular information about the structure of a scene is contained in the relative positions of corresponding points in the two views. If the eyes rotate, in order to fixate a different target, then the disparity at a given image location is likely to change. Quite different disparities can be produced at the same location, as the eyes move from one fixation-point to the next. The pointwise variability of the disparity map is problematic for biological visual systems, in which stereopsis is based on simple, short-range mechanisms. It is argued here that the problem can be addressed in two ways; firstly by an appropriate representation of disparity, and secondly by learning the typical pattern of image correspondences. It is shown that the average spatial structure of the disparity field can be estimated, by integrating over a series of binocular fixations. An algorithm based on this idea is tested on natural images. Finally, it is shown how the average pattern of disparities could help to put the images into binocular correspondence.

1   Introduction

Binocular disparity is the difference in position of a matched point, as it appears in the left and right images. This difference can be divided into two components; one that is due to the structure of the scene, and one that is imposed by cameras themselves. In particular, the pattern of binocular disparity is sensitive to the relative orientation of the sensors. This is important for active vision systems, in which binocular fixation is achieved by rotating the cameras, such that the left and right images are centred on the point of interest. It follows that the pattern of disparity will be different for each fixation, even in a static scene.

The effect of relative orientation on disparity is problematic for biological visual systems, in which stereopsis is based on the output of local filter-like mechanisms [7]. For example, binocular cells in primate V1 have relatively small receptive fields, and may be tuned to a single direction of disparity on the retina. Hence it would be desirable for the visual system to arrange these mechanisms according to the patterns of disparity that occur most often. This would have two clear advantages. Firstly, depth-sensitivity could be improved, by placing additional mechanisms in regions of highly variable disparity. Secondly, when the image data are ambiguous, it would be useful to have an implicit model of the most likely disparity at each point on the retina. There is experimental

F. Mele et al. (Eds.): BVAI 2007, LNCS 4729, pp. 308–317, 2007.

evidence to suggest that such an organization of disparity sensitivity exists in the primate visual cortex [1].

In section 2 it will be argued that the displacement of image-features between the left and right views is best represented with respect to the underlying epipolar geometry. However, as will be explained, the epipolar geometry depends on the relative orientation of the eyes. The question of whether the visual system uses this geometric information at the disparity-processing stage remains open. For this reason, we will consider both epipolar and non-epipolar representations in the present work.

If the visual system does estimate the epipolar geometry, then the pattern of disparities is largely determined by each fixation point; what remains to be estimated is the magnitude of each disparity. However, it is no less important to consider the average pattern of disparities in this case. The reason is simply that the same local mechanisms must be used during each fixation. Hence some arrangements of these mechanisms will be better than others, depending on which epipolar geometries are more likely to occur, as different points are fixated. This should make it clear that, although we use ideas from computer vision, the problems addressed here arise from *biological* constraints on visual processing. It should be emphasized that we are not directly investigating the distribution of scene depths [4] in this work. Rather, we are investigating the distribution of *disparity fields*, which is determined by the combination of eye-movements and scene structure.

Sections 2 and 3 describe the geometric and image-processing background that is subsequently required. Our main idea is presented in section 4, in which we show how a collection of disparity maps can be combined. This procedure is tested in section 5. A stereo image-pair is warped into a number of 'fixating' views, and the disparity field is recorded in each case. These maps are combined, to produce an average disparity map, with respect to the different fixation-points. We discuss, in section 6, how such a representation could be used by the visual system.

2 Disparity Models

The left and right eyes are modelled here by pinhole cameras, with centres of projection c_ℓ and c_r, respectively. It is convenient to represent image-points by their homogeneous coordinates $q_\ell = (x_\ell, y_\ell, 1)^\top$, and similarly for q_r. Suppose, without loss of generality, that the axes of the scene coordinate-system are aligned with the left eye. Then the image-points are related to the scene-point $\bar{q} = (x, y, z)^\top$ by the projections

$$z_\ell q_\ell = \bar{q} \quad \text{and} \quad z_r q_r = R(\bar{q} - c_r),\tag{1}$$

where R is the 3×3 rotation matrix that determines the relative orientation of the eyes. One possible representation of binocular disparity is simply the difference between q_ℓ and q_r. This is, in general, a vector with non-zero horizontal

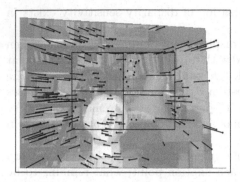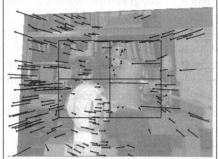

Fig. 1. A stereo image-pair that has been warped to simulate the fixation of a particular scene-point. The raw disparities of the matched points are indicated by the black vectors. The sharp-end of each vector marks the image feature; the blunt end marks the location of the same feature in the other view. No epipolar geometry has been imposed, and so the vectors do not follow a simple pattern. Images courtesy of the University of Tsukuba.

and vertical components [6]; we will call these the *raw* disparities. An example of a raw disparity field is shown in figure 1.

An alternative representation of disparity can be derived from the fact that the scene point $\bar{q}$ in equation (1) is equal to the back-projected image-point $z_\ell q_\ell$. It follows that the left and right image-points are related by the well-known equation

$$q_r \sim Rq_\ell + (1/z_\ell)e_r, \quad \text{where} \quad e_r = -Rc_r, \tag{2}$$

and '$\sim$' denotes equality up to a scalar multiple. The importance of this model is that if R is known, as well as q_ℓ and q_r, then only one degree of freedom, z_ℓ, remains for the unknown scene-point. The point e_r is the epipole, being the image of the left optical centre. Note that e_r varies with the relative orientation of the eyes, but not with the choice of scene-point $\bar{q}$. Another way to understand this is that the position of each point q_r is measured with respect to a corresponding reference-point Rq_ℓ in the same image. These reference points lie on the plane at infinity; however it can be shown that the same principles apply if the reference-points lie on any plane (not passing through either optical centre). This leads to the more general decomposition [2,8];

$$q_r \sim Hq_\ell + \delta e_r, \tag{3}$$

in which H is a homography containing R and the parameters of the plane, while δ is proportional to the scalar depth of $\bar{q}$ with respect to the plane. The vector δe_r will be called the *epipolar* disparity, including equation (2) as a special case. We emphasize that the epipolar disparity has one degree of freedom δ, whereas the raw disparity has two; d_x and d_y. The epipolar disparity has several other advantages; for example, the reference plane can be chosen in order to reduce the size of the disparities. In our experiments, we use a fronto-parallel plane

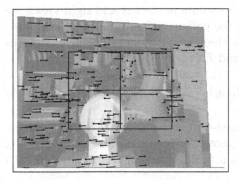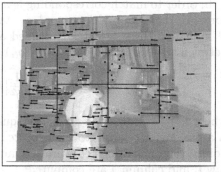

Fig. 2. The fixating stereo pair from figure 1 is shown again. The feature-correspondence is also identical, however, the epipolar geometry has been imposed. The blunt ends of the vectors now represent reference-positions on a virtual plane through the fixation-point. The disparities are organized along epipolar lines, and tend to be smaller than those in figure 1.

(with respect to the head), positioned at the fixation distance. An example of the resulting epipolar disparity field is shown in figure 2.

In order to recover the metric structure of the scene, it is necessary to know the relative orientation of the cameras, and to account for any geometric distortion imposed by the sensors. If these calibration parameters are unknown, then equation (3) can nonetheless be used to estimate non-metric properties of the scene. For example, it can be established whether a given scene-point is in front of or behind the reference plane encoded by H. The effect of the fixation plane can be seen in figure 2. The plane is at a depth between that of the face (in the lower-left quadrant) and the far wall. The disparities associated with these two parts of the scene are in opposite directions. It has been argued elsewhere that a qualitative representation of this kind could explain several aspects of biological stereopsis [9].

3   Image Matching

In order to generate disparity-fields, we must have a stereo image pair with corresponding points identified. We use a simple feature-matching process, as follows. First we apply a Gaussian filter G, of width λ, to smooth each image I. We then construct an outer-product matrix from the luminance-gradient at each point. These matrices are themselves smoothed at scale μ, and the response $Q(x, y)$ is computed;

$$Q(x,y) = \frac{\det(G_\mu \star S)}{\operatorname{tr}(G_\mu \star S)}, \quad \text{where} \quad S(x,y) = (\nabla G_\lambda \star I)(\nabla G_\lambda \star I)^\top,$$

and '$\star$' denotes 2-D convolution. This commonly-used operator produces maxima in $Q(x, y)$ at 'interest points' $q_{\ell i}$ and q_{rj} in the left and right images [3].

In order to match corresponding feature-points in the left and right views, we compare the colour of I_ℓ around $q_{\ell i}$, to the colour of I_r around q_{rj}. The 'cost' of matching these features is defined as the sum of squared colour-differences between the two image-patches $\mathcal{I}_\ell(q_{\ell i})$ and $\mathcal{I}_r(q_{rj})$;

$$F(q_\ell, q_r) = \frac{1}{\phi^2} |\mathcal{I}_\ell(q_\ell) - \mathcal{I}_r(q_r)|_{\mathcal{I}}^2, \tag{4}$$

where $|\cdot|_{\mathcal{I}}^2$ averages the pointwise squared-differences over the patches, and ϕ is a parameter relating to the expected photometric variation at corresponding points. The matching-costs are put into a table, F_{ij}, and the minima in each row i, and column j are computed:

$$m_{\ell i} = \arg\min_j F_{ij}, \quad \text{and} \quad m_{rj} = \arg\min_i F_{ij}.$$

We then enforce 'uniqueness' and 'compatibility' constraints on the matches, meaning that point $q_{\ell i}$ matches q_{rj} if

$$i = m_{rj}, \quad j = m_{\ell i}, \quad \text{and} \quad F_{ij} < T\phi^2,$$

where $T\phi^2$ is a threshold defining the maximum photometric incompatibility between matched points. The procedure described above produces very sparse, but relatively reliable matches. Note that the matching cost in equation (4) does not penalize implausibly large disparities. The average pointwise magnitude of the disparity field is investigated below, and in section 6 it is shown how the resulting probabilistic model could be incorporated into the matching algorithm.

Our experimental data was constructed by applying appropriate homographies to an original stereo image pair, in order to simulate fixating pairs of views. In principle, we could apply the matching process to each pair of warped images. In practice, we compute the correspondence only once, using the original images. The homographies are then used to map the coordinates of the matched points into the fixating images. This is done in order to avoid irrelevant effects of the warping on the correspondence process; for example, pixel-resampling may reduce the number of points that are matched in more strongly warped images. We also enforce the epipolar constraint on the matched points, by considering only horizontal displacements in the rectified images.

4   Disparity Processing

In this section we describe our model of the disparity data. We have measured, in each image, the disparity of $k = 1 \cdots M$ points, over $v = 1 \cdots N$ fixations. Hence we have image positions q_{kv} and their associated (raw or epipolar) disparity vectors d_{kv}. The procedures in this section apply to the left and right views independently, and so we suppress the ℓ, r indices, in order to simplify the notation.

We consider the data $\{q_{kv}, d_{kv}\}$ as a single vector field, and ask what structure, if any, it contains. Note that the points q_{kv} are not evenly distributed in the images, and that neighbouring points may be associated with quite different disparities. Hence we effectively wish to smooth and interpolate the observed vector-field. We are particularly interested in the local-orientation of the field, and so the smoothing-process must treat vectors that differ in orientation by 180° as being 'similar'. This can be achieved by representing the disparities as outer-products

$$D_{kv} = d_{kv} d_{kv}^{\mathsf{T}},$$ (5)

each of which is a 2×2 matrix of rank-one [5]. As described above, we would like to have a representation of the average disparity at an arbitrary location q, based on samples from points q_{kv}. We use a simple kernel-like estimator to obtain

$$D(q) \propto \sum_{k}^{M} \sum_{v}^{N} W(q_{kv}, q) D_{kv}.$$ (6)

This gives the disparity-matrix D at position q as a weighted average over all of the data. The average is subsequently normalized by the sum of the weights. The kernel could be any decreasing function of the separation between q_{kv} and q. We use an isotropic Gaussian, with width parameter w;

$$W(p, q) = \exp\left(\frac{-|p - q|^2}{2w^2}\right).$$ (7)

In general, the average matrices $D(q)$ will have rank-two. The local orientation and variability of the disparity-field at location q is obtained by eigen-decomposition of the corresponding matrix. The eigenvector associated with the larger eigenvalue, σ_1^2, is oriented along the characteristic direction of disparity. The smaller eigenvalue, σ_2^2, indicates the variability of the disparity around the characteristic direction.

5   Simulation Results

In this section we investigate the distribution of raw and epipolar disparity fields by a simulation, based on real images. We believe that this approach is worth-while, because it incorporates a number of effects that would be difficult to specify in a purely geometric simulation. For example, the joint distribution of feature-locations and scene-depths is naturally determined by the images them-selves. Furthermore, it is possible to demonstrate the robustness of the smoothing process to the false matches contained in the disparity field. Data was generated by synthetically fixating each scene-point that had been matched in the images, and recording the resulting disparity field. As described in section 3, there was a single underlying set of correspondences; only the relative orientation of the two views was varied.

The procedure is complicated by the fact that the warped images are incom-plete with respect to the original field of view (c.f. the edges of the images in figures 1 & 2). The results would be biased if this effect were ignored, because it is the same structure (the upper and lower epipolar lines on the side of the epipole) which is lost in each case. We avoid this artifact by analyzing only the central 25% of the original field of view, defined by the inner rectangle in figures 1 & 2. We reject any fixation that would leave this region incomplete. The drawback of the approach is that the more variable disparities tend to lie in the periphery, and so our results are conservative.

The procedure described in section 3 returned 404 interest-points in the left image, and 398 in the right. Of these features, $M = 207$ were matched between the left and right images. There were 25 scene-points that could be fixated such that the resulting disparity-maps were complete over the central 25% of both images, for the reason described above. A further nine fixations were valid for the left image only, and a further one fixation for the right image only. All data was used in the analysis, meaning that several thousand disparities ($M \times N$, $M = 207$; $N = 26, 34$) contributed to each of the average disparity maps.

The distributions of disparity magnitude and orientation are shown in figures 3 and 4. As expected, the epipolar disparities are on average shorter than the original vectors; the means are 0.104 and 0.065, respectively. This difference is attributable to the use of a appropriate reference plane, as described in the introduction. It was also found that the epipolar lines were much less variable in orientation than the original disparity vectors; the standard deviations of the angular data are 0.448 and 0.168, respectively.

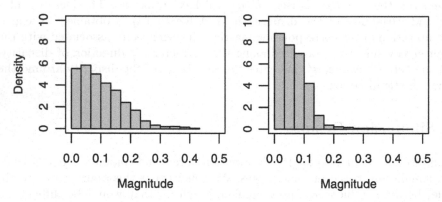

Fig. 3. Histograms of disparity magnitude for the raw (left) and epipolar (right) representations. The epipolar disparities are smaller, owing to the use of an appropriate reference plane.

Finally, we consider the spatial structure of the combined disparity maps. The estimator described in section 4 was used to resample the central region of the disparity maps on a regular grid, as shown in figure 5. The spatial width parameter w in equation (7) was set to one half of the grid spacing. It can be seen that raw disparity field is less regular than the epipolar field, as expected. The average vertical disparity increases with distance from the horizontal meridian, causing the local structure to become more variable.

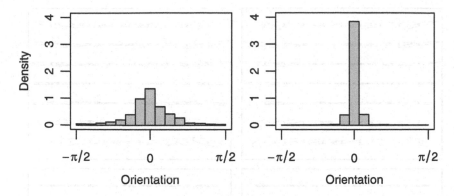

Fig. 4. Histograms of disparity orientation for the raw (left) and epipolar (right) representations. Angles are measured with respect to the horizontal axis of the image. Note that the local epipolar directions are much less variable than the raw disparities.

In contrast, the epipolar disparities are quite stable. The smoothing process recovers a structure that resembles a single, average epipolar geometry. In this simulation, the average epipolar lines are parallel, though this is not necessarily always the case. For example, a spatially concentrated distribution of fixation points could produce an asymmetric average map.

It is perhaps surprising that the raw and epipolar disparity maps appear quite similar in figure 5. This can be explained as follows. The difference between the raw and epipolar representations depends largely on the homography that expresses the relative orientation of the eyes. In the present simulation, this homography is not far from the identity, for two reasons. Firstly, we have applied a fixation constraint, which tends to limit the difference in orientation between the views, especially when the scene is relatively distant. Secondly, the field of view over which the homography applies is quite small in this simulation, as described above.

6   Discussion

We have reviewed the measurement of binocular disparity, and shown how it can be represented in relation to the underlying epipolar geometry. The novel contribution of this work is our analysis of the average disparity field, for a fixating observer. We have shown that this contains useful geometric structure, and that this can be extracted by a simple smoothing process.

The most interesting use of the average disparity field is as a *prior* model of the binocular correspondence field. It is straightforward to go from the scatter-matrices $D(q)$ defined in section 4 to a probabilistic model of the local disparity vector. This is done via the Mahalanobis distance, which we write as a cost function

$$E(q_0, q) = (q - q_0)^\top D(q_0)^{-1}(q - q_0), \tag{8}$$

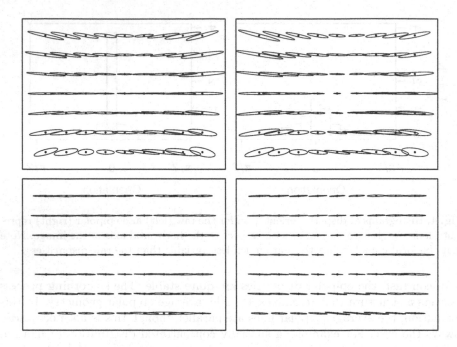

Fig. 5. Structure of the raw (top left & right) and epipolar (bottom left & right) disparity maps, combined over a series of fixations. The maps have been resampled, using the estimator in equation (6), over a region corresponding to the central rectangle that appears in figures 1 & 2. The axes of each ellipse, obtained from the eigen-decomposition of $D(q)$, represent the local variability of the disparity field.

where q is the measured feature position, and q_0 is the reference point, transferred from the other image, as described in section 1. Hence the candidate disparity is $q - q_0$, with length δ. Recall from section 4 that σ_1^2 and σ_2^2 are the eigenvalues of D. It follows that if the disparity is in the characteristic direction, then the cost will be δ/σ_1^2, whereas if it is in the perpendicular direction, the cost will be δ/σ_2^2. The cost is lower in the preferred direction, because $\sigma_1^2 > \sigma_2^2$, assuming that the average disparity has a definite orientation at q_0.

These considerations lead directly to a Gaussian model for the prior probability of the match between q_ℓ and q_r;

$$\mathrm{pr}\big(q_\ell, q_r\big) \propto \exp\Big(-\tfrac{1}{2}E_\ell\big(H^{-1}q_r, q_\ell\big) - \tfrac{1}{2}E_r\big(Hq_\ell, q_r\big)\Big).$$

The matrix H is the homography that includes the relative orientation of the cameras, as in equation (3). We use both the right-to left and left-to right costs, because the distance defined in equation (8) depends on the average disparity field, and the left and right versions may not be mutually consistent. Here we have constructed a geometric prior, which depends on the variable orientation of the eyes. This could be readily combined with the photometric prior

$\exp\left(-\frac{1}{2}F(q_\ell, q_r)\right)$, which is obtained from the matching-cost F, as defined in equation (4).

In our future work, we plan to incorporate the geometric prior into the image-matching process, as outlined above. We believe that this would improve the estimated binocular correspondences, especially in a biological model based on short-range disparity mechanisms, as described in the introduction. We also plan to evaluate our disparity-smoothing procedure across a wider range of images and fixation points. This will allow us to compare our average correspondence maps to the distribution of disparity-tuned cells in area V1 [1].

Acknowledgments

This work is part of the *Perception on Purpose* project, supported by EU grant 027268.

References

1. Cumming, B.G.: An Unexpected Specialization for Horizontal Disparity in Primate Primary Visual Cortex. Nature 418(8), 636–663 (2002)
2. Faugeras, O.: Stratification of 3-D Vision: Projective, Affine, and Metric Representations. Journal of the Optical Society of America A 12(3), 465–484 (1995)
3. Harris, C., Stephens, M.: A Combined Corner and Edge Detector. In: Proc. 4th Alvey Vision Conference, pp. 147–151 (1988)
4. Huang, J., Lee, A.B., Mumford, D.: Statistics of Range Images. In: Proc. Computer Vision and Pattern Recognition, pp. 324–331 (2000)
5. Knutsson, H.: Representing Local Structure Using Tensors. In: Proc. 6th Scandinavian Conference on Image Analysis, pp. 244–251 (1989)
6. Mayhew, J.E., Longuet-Higgins, H.C.: A Computational Model of Binocular Depth Perception. Nature 297, 376–378 (1982)
7. Ohzawa, I., Freeman, R.: Stereoscopic Depth Discrimination in the Visual Cortex: Neurons Ideally Suited as Disparity Detectors. Science 249, 1037–1041 (1990)
8. Shashua, A., Navab, N.: Relative Affine Structure: Canonical Model for 3-D from 2-D Geometry and Applications. IEEE Trans. Pattern Analysis and Machine Intelligence 18(9), 873–883 (1996)
9. Weinshall, D.: Qualitative Depth from Stereo, with Applications. Computer Vision, Graphics, and Image Processing 49(2), 222–241 (1990)

3D Reconstruction and Mapping from Stereo Pairs with Geometrical Rectification

Antonio Javier Gallego, Rafael Molina, Patricia Compañ, and Carlos Villagrá

Grupo de Informática Industrial e Inteligencia Artificial
Universidad de Alicante, Ap.99, E-03080, Alicante, Spain
{ajgallego,rmolina,company,villagra}@dccia.ua.es

Abstract. In this paper a new method for reconstructing 3D scenes from stereo images is presented, as well as an algorithm for environment mapping, as an application of the previous method. In the reconstruction process a geometrical rectification filter is used to remove the conical perspective of the images. It is essential to recover the geometry of the scene (with real data of depth and volume) and to achieve a realistic appearance in 3D reconstructions. It also uses sub-pixel precision to solve the lack of information for distant objects. Finally, the method is applied to a mapping algorithm in order to show its usefulness.

1 Introduction

Unknown environments reconstruction is a fundamental requirement in several fields of research. Stereoscopic vision opens new paths that in the future will allow to capture the three-dimensional structure of the environment, and take advantage of this to calculate the geometry, volume and depth of the objects in the scene. Range sensors can also acquire very detailed models [1], but these types of sensors are more expensive and they cannot provide information of both range and appearance, which is useful for reconstruction and texture mapping. For these reasons we will focus on stereo vision.

Several authors use stereo vision and disparity images to solve the 3D reconstruction or mapping problems. For instance, a first solution to three-dimensional reconstruction with stereo technology explores the possibility of composing several 3D views from the camera transforms [2]. There are other approaches which infer 3D grids from stereo vision, due to the fact that appearance information is not provided by range finders. Hence, they add an additional camera to their mobile robots [3,4]. Moreover, a module of 3D recognition could be added to identify some objects. This technique is not exclusive of robotics, but it could be used in other applications such as automatic machine guidance or also for detection and estimation of vehicle movement [5].

Stereo vision can improve the perception of scenes and world modelling, so there are some methods which work with disparity images due to their advantages. The problem is that these algorithms cannot be applied in a widespread manner with all types of structures; because the images (or the objects) obtained from a camera have no real size, since they are deformed by the conical

F. Mele et al. (Eds.): BVAI 2007, LNCS 4729, pp. 318–327, 2007.

perspective effect. In general, any image taken by a camera is deformed by this effect, so direct reconstruction generates scenes with unreal aspect. There are very few works which focus on creating a good reconstruction and on obtaining a real appearance of the scene. However, some interesting works can be found [6,7,8], but none of them makes any type of geometrical rectification. Specific objects are reconstructed instead of the whole scene, so the real structure of the environment is not recovered. Some naïve rectifications have already been used in other fields, to rectify roads and to obtain their real appearance [9].

This work is centred in the reconstruction of the structure of the scene showing its real aspect, using the information provided by the stereo images and the disparity maps (in fact depth maps, their duals, are used). Our proposal does not make assumptions about the scene nor the object structure, it does not segment objects trying to identify known shapes, only a stereo pair is needed and it is not correspondence dependent. Perspective rectification allows the method to eliminate the conical perspective of the scene and to remove the camera orientation. This way the algorithm recovers the structure of the scene and some crucial information such us object geometry, volume and depth. Moreover, the reconstruction method is also extended to manage a sequence of stereo images to map a whole environment.

2   Geometrical Rectification: Recovery of the Real Perspective

Perspective effect arises from the common appearance of the real world which surrounds us. This effect deforms the size and geometry of the space and the objects contained in it in order to create the depth effect. Figure 1(b) shows how the conical perspective effect changes the size with which the objects are represented according to their distance from the view point. Rectification is used for correcting this effect and recovering the real scene geometry. As an example, figure 1(a) shows an image of a corridor, in which, a pixel in the lower part of the image represents a small volume of the scene (it represents a part of the scene in the foreground); while a pixel in the centre of the same image represents a larger volume (because the part of the scene represented by the pixel is in the background). If the scene is directly reconstructed, the perspective is preserved. So, to correctly perform the 3D reconstruction the perspective must be rectified making a correction to the pixel's coordinates. This way the obtained result will show the same aspect as the real scene.

Rectification is performed on values of a depth map D calculated from a pair of stereo images. In principle the depth map can be obtained by any method, but in this approach the depth image is computed using multi-resolution and energy function [10]. Each value $D(x, y)$ of the depth map contains the depth associated to the pixel (x, y) of the reference image (left image) [11,12].

Figure 1(c) shows the scheme of the process. On the left hand side it illustrates the desired result of the left wall rectification, which is rotated $\alpha°$ to recover its real inclination. And on the right hand side, it shows the point Q (current

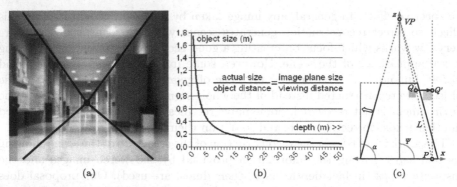

Fig. 1. (a) shows the effect of the conical perspective. (b) shows how the object size decreases as the depth is increased, due to the perspective's effect. (c) shows the rectification scheme on a non-rectified scene seen from above (x-z plane).

pixel being processed obtained from the input depth map) with coordinates $(x, y, D(x, y))$, which is rectified to obtain Q'. This pixel is a part of an object which is rectified to recover its real size. The first step to rectify Q is to obtain the line L, which links the points VP and Q. Next, the intersection of the line L with the x-y plane is calculated, obtaining in this way the point P. Starting from P, the line L is rotated to be perpendicular to the x-y plane. This way the coordinates (x, y) of Q' can be obtained. The calculation of the coordinate $z_{Q'}$ is shown in the section 2.1. In short, the equation 1 shows the calculation of the new rectified point $Q' = (x', y', z')$. Rectification is referred as π, where the new coordinates of Q are obtained as $Q' = \pi(Q)$.

$$\pi(Q) = \begin{cases} x_{Q'} = x_{VP} + z_{VP}\frac{x_{VP}-x_Q}{z_Q-z_{VP}} \\ y_{Q'} = y_{VP} + z_{VP}\frac{y_{VP}-y_Q}{z_Q-z_{VP}} \\ z_{Q'} = f\frac{T}{d\lambda}\rho \end{cases} \tag{1}$$

As can be seen in the equation 1, the vanishing point position has to be obtained. In general, the central point can be used as the vanishing point of the scene, obtaining a reconstruction that maintains the original angle of the camera. If the camera view is oblique, the real position of the vanishing point can be calculated. This way, the camera orientation is corrected and a frontal view is obtained after the reconstruction. When the perspective cannot be calculated (in non Manhattan Worlds), the central point is taken by defect.

For the depth of the real vanishing point VP the maximum depth value (D_{max}) of the whole depth map is used. The coordinates x and y of VP are calculated using the method proposed in [13]. It uses a Bayesian model which combines knowledge of the 3D geometry of world with statistical knowledge of edges in images. The method returns an angle (called as Ψ) which defines de orientation of the camera in direction $\cos\Psi i - \sin\Psi j$. Cartesian coordinates (x, y, z) of VP can be obtained from the following camera coordinates $\boldsymbol{u} = (u, v)$:

$$u = \frac{f \cdot (-x_{VP}\sin\Psi - y_{VP}\cos\Psi)}{x_{VP}\cos\Psi - y_{VP}\sin\Psi}, \quad v = \frac{f \cdot z_{VP}}{x_{VP}\cos\Psi - y_{VP}\sin\Psi} \tag{2}$$

2.1   Calculating the Error in the Rectification

Coordinate $z_{Q'}$ is obtained using a modified version of the equation $z = f\frac{T}{d}$ [14]. Where d is the disparity $(D(x,y))$ for this pixel, T is the length of the base line, f is the focal distance. The main problem is that disparity d is expressed in pixels, while the other parameters are expressed in metres. So, a conversion factor is used $\lambda = CCD$ *width in meters* / *Image width in pixels* to convert pixels into metres. To calculate the CCD width, its dimensions $(1/3")$ and its proportions $(\frac{x}{y} = \frac{4}{3})$ are needed (figure 2 (a)). Therefore, the value of x (total width in metres) can be isolated from the equation $x^2 + y^2 = (\frac{1}{3}")^2$. There is also an error that appears when the obtained distance is compared with the real one (figure 2(b)). This error is a small linear deviation due to the lens concavity and it is corrected adding a correction factor ρ to the equation (obtained empirically).

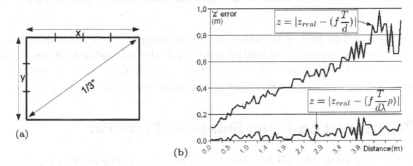

Fig. 2. (a) Camera lens proportions. (b) Comparison of the error made in the equations for the depth calculation.

Figure 3(b) shows the error in the objects size made when they are represented after de geometrical rectification. To obtain the error, a sequence of images of the same object (the sign in image 3(a)) were taken at different distances. A comparison between the representation size and the real size were done. The representation size can be easily calculated due to the fact that the coordinates of each point are known. In figure 3(b) the error made by the previous approach to the geometrical rectification is also shown [15].

3   Applications of the Geometrical Rectification

The proposed method can be useful in a wide range of applications, because some crucial information from the scene is retrieved, such as object geometry, volume and depth. For example, it could be applied in Augmented Reality (AR) systems to solve some problems related to this discipline, as well as to set out new applications and improvements.

Next, two possible applications are presented. The first one is the 3D reconstruction of scenes using sub-pixel precision and stereo images. The second one

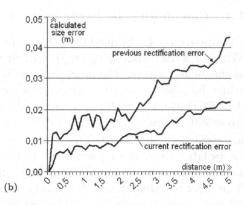

(a)

(b)

Fig. 3. (a) Sequence of images taken to calculate the error in the representation size. (b) Comparison of the error made in the representation as the depth increases.

is the map building from a sequence of stereo images. They both demonstrate the utility of the geometrical rectification and the advantages of its application to this kind of problems. For this reason simple methods are used. In the conclusions section more applications of these methods will be proposed.

4   Reconstruction Using Sub-pixel Precision

In the first step to do the 3D reconstruction of a scene, the depth map D is calculated from a pair of stereo images (LI and RI). The depth map D is obtained using the methods proposed in [10]. Based on D, the geometrical rectification process is applied in order to remove the effect of the conical perspective and recover the real structure of the scene (section 2). The result of this stage is a rectified matrix of voxels R, which is used in the reconstruction to represent the space occupation. R is initialized to zero and, then, it is filled as follows: $R(x', y', D(x, y)) = 1$ where (x', y') are the rectified coordinates of (x, y), $\forall x, y \in \mathbb{R}/\{0 \leq x \leq m - 1, 0 \leq y \leq n - 1\}$. The final step is obtaining the real units. Equation 1 shows how to obtain the equivalence in metres from a disparity value and the rectified coordinates.

The most important drawback is the fact that when the geometrical rectification corrects the pixels' coordinates, the voxels are separated in the 3D representation (see figure 4). This is due to the discreteness of depth maps. In fact, pixels corresponding to a distant object are split, leaving a hole whose dimensions increase as the distance to the object increases. To minimize these problems a sub-pixel precision technique is proposed to calculate the position of n fictitious pixels between two consecutive pixels. The precision used for the reconstruction is calculated using the equation $1 - (z/D_{max})$, which returns the minimum value when the pixel is in the foreground and the maximum one when it is in the background. All the steps of the sub-pixel reconstruction method can be summarized as follows:

1. $D := CalculateDepthMap(LI, RI)$
2. while ($x \le m - 1$)
   (a) while ($y \le n - 1$)
      i. $(x', y') := \pi(x, y)$
      ii. $R(x', y', D(\lfloor x \rfloor, \lfloor y \rfloor)) = 1$
      iii. $y = y + 1 - (D(\lfloor x \rfloor, \lfloor y \rfloor)/D_{max})$
   (b) $x = x + 1 - (D(\lfloor x \rfloor, \lfloor y \rfloor)/D_{max})$
3. $Display(R)$

4.1 Reconstruction Experimentation

In figure 4 two examples of reconstruction using sub-pixel precision are shown. The images on the left show the mesh used during the reconstruction, these images are obtained without and with sub-pixel precision respectively. On the right side, there is another example of reconstruction using voxels. The first image shows the reconstruction without using sub-pixel precision, in which the voxels are separated due to the geometrical rectification. In the second image

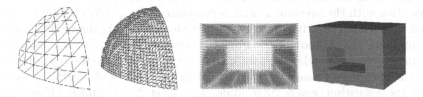

Fig. 4. Examples of reconstruction using sub-pixel precision

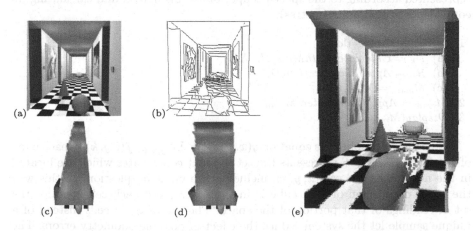

(a)   (b)

(c)   (d)   (e)

Fig. 5. Geometrical rectification comparison using a corridor depth map

the sub-pixel precision has been used. The result has a more realistic appearance because holes have been filled.

Figure 5 shows a 3D reconstruction comparison using a synthetic depth map (a) which simulates a corridor. This example clearly shows the effect of the geometrical rectification. Figure (b) shows the segmentation used to calculate the vanishing point, which is estimated to be -4°. The camera deviation is very small as it can be observed, so the real orientation could have been used avoiding so the VP calculation. In figures (c), (d) and (e) the rectification effect is compared: (c) shows a non-rectified reconstruction (seen from above), and (d) and (e) show a top and an oblique view of the correct result after the rectification. As it can be seen, the walls are perfectly rectified, becoming parallel as expected.

5   Mapping Algorithm

In order to do the 3D mapping of the scene, N stereo pairs (LI_0, RI_0), (LI_1, RI_1), ..., (LI_{N-1}, RI_{N-1}) of the environment are taken. Each of these images is captured at a fixed distance. Once a stereo pair (LI_k, RI_k) is obtained, its corresponding depth map D_k is calculated and added to the Σ list which stores all the depth maps. Next, the algorithm of geometrical rectification is used in order to compute the rectified matrix R_k of each depth map. For each matrix R_k its intersection with the previous matrix is calculated $(R_{k-1} \cap R_k)$, and its result is added to the main matrix M_{map} which represents the mapping of the scene. In this approach the position of the frames is obtained from robot odometry. The system only needs the relative position of the next frame to do the reconstruction from the sequence of images. In order to reduce the effect of possible odometry errors the algorithm uses a cubic filter. This filter F (explained below) is applied to the whole matrix M_{map}, which discretizes the three-dimensional matrix and transforms it into a grid of rectangular cubes. Lastly, the result (M_{map}) is represented according to the space occupation of this matrix and calculating its equivalence in real units (metres).

1. **for each** $D_k \in \Sigma$ **do**
    (a) $D_k := CalculateDepthMap(LI_k, RI_k)$
    (b) $R_k := ApplyRectification(D_k)$
    (c) $M_{map} := M_{map} \cap R_k$
2. $M_{map} := ApplyCubicFilter(M_{map})$
3. $Display(M_{map})$

Cubic filter F applies the equation $g(x, y, z) := \Sigma_{(i,j,k) \in S} f(i, j, k)$ to each cube of the matrix, where S represents the set of point coordinates which are located in the neighbourhood of $g(x, y, z)$, including the point in question. In this way the space occupation of each cube is in the centre, and each cell contains the set of readings of that portion of the space. The use of these cells instead of a unique sample let the system reduce the effect of possible odometry errors. The number of readings is referred to as "votes", and represents the probability of space occupation.

5.1 Mapping Experimentation

To do the mapping experimentation two sequences of 30 images obtained from two different corridors have been used (Figures 6 and 7). Figures 6(a) and 7(a) show the first three images of both sequences as well as their depth maps. The main objective is that the walls, floor and roof appear without slope in the reconstruction, and that there should not be any obstacle (noise) in the corridor. It is also important that the columns (represented by circles in the plan (Fig. 6(b))) and the coffee machine (represented by a rectangle in the plan (Fig. 7(b))) are detected correctly. In figures 6(c, d) and 7(c, d) the results are shown. In 6(c) and 7(c) there is no perspective rectification, consequently a wrong result is obtained: the in-between space of the corridors is not clear. In 6(d) and 7(d) the rectification has been applied. These results show a good definition of the corridors because the walls are limited and the in-between area can be seen. Moreover, the columns and the coffee machine can be distinguished on the right hand side of each one of the results. For these examples a cubic filter size of $3 \times 3 \times 3$ and a number of votes of 5 have been used.

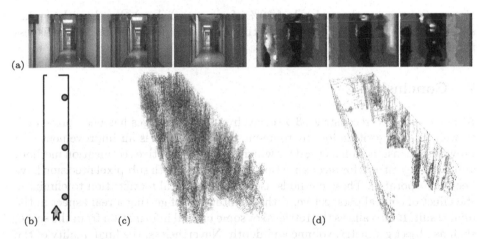

Fig. 6. (a) Sequence of images for the mapping. (b) Corridor sketch. (c, d) Mapping results of the corridor.

6 Performance Results

To conduct the experiments, a Pentium IV 3,20GHz with 2GB of RAM and a 512MB graphic card have been used. The reconstruction of the maps have been made using a $320 \times 240 \times 256$ voxels matrix and depth maps with a size of 320×240 pixels. Moreover, it is important to note that only non-null pixels (finite depth) in the depth map are processed. The computational cost linearly depends on the size of the input images and on the precision of the reconstruction. So the algorithm obtains a good performance: To process just one sequence of 30

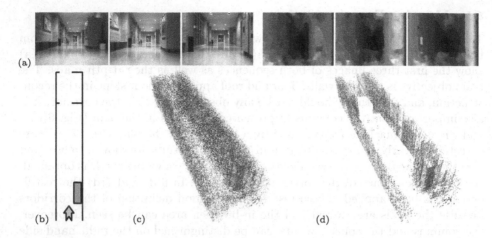

Fig. 7. (a) Sequence of images for the mapping. (b) Corridor sketch. (c, d) Mapping results of the corridor.

images (each image has a level of 70% of processed data) the algorithm takes approximately 9 seconds. The process time of an individual reconstruction is less than 0.3 seconds.

7   Conclusions

A new method to reconstruct 3D scenes from stereo images has been presented, as well as an algorithm for environment mapping. This is an improvement of a previous reconstruction method for which a new perspective rectification method, and news algorithms for reconstruction and mapping with sub-pixel precision have been incorporated. These methods use the geometrical rectification to eliminate the effect of conical perspective, with the intention of getting a real aspect in the final result. It also allows the retrieval of some crucial information from the scene, such as object geometry, volume and depth. Nevertheless, the final quality of the reconstructed image depends on the quality of the disparity map. In future experiments, better disparity images will improve the final result.

The results show how this process corrects the perspective effect and how it helps to improve the matching in the mapping algorithm. An advantage of this method is that it is not correspondence dependent. In addition, it could probably be used for real-time applications due to the low computational burden and to the good performance.

Current work is focused on applying the obtained results to an Augmented Reality system. So that it can take advantage from the geometry information in order to develop new applications (as new interfaces or games) and solve problems related to this discipline (visual tracking, hidden objects and alignment). This work will also be related with an autonomous robot system which uses the environment information to be able to identify specific areas.

Acknowledgments. This work has been done with the support of the Spanish Generalitat Valenciana, Project GV06/158.

References

1. Sanchiz, J.M., Fisher, R.B.: Viewpoint Estimation in Three-Dimensional Images Taken with Perspective Range Sensors. IEEE Transactions on Pattern Analysis and Machine Intelligence 22(11), 1324–1329 (2000)
2. Moravec, H.P.: Robot spatial perception by stereoscopic vision and 3D evidence grids. The Robotics Institute Carnegie Mellon University. Pittsburgh, PA (1996)
3. Stephen Se, D., Lowe, J.L.: Vision-based mobile robot localization and mapping using scale-invariant features. In: ICRA (2001)
4. Martin, C., Thrun, S.: Real-time acquisition of compact volumetric maps with mobile robots. In: ICRA (2002)
5. Martinsanz, G.P., de la Cruz García, J.M.: Visión por computador: imágenes digitales y aplicaciones. Ra-Ma, Madrid, D.L. (eds.) (2001)
6. Vogiatzis, G., Torr, P.H.S., Cipolla, R.: Multi-view stereo via Volumetric Graph-cuts. In: CVPR, pp. 391–398 (2005)
7. Zhang, L., Seitz, S.M.: Parameter estimation for MRF stereo. In: CVPR. IEEE Computer Society Conference on Computer Vision and Pattern Recognition, San Diego, CA, IEEE Computer Society Press, Los Alamitos (June 2005)
8. Sinha, S., Pollefeys, M.: Multi-view Reconstruction using Photo-consistency and Exact Silhouette Constraints: A Maximum-Flow Formulation. In: ICCV (2005)
9. Broggi, A.: Robust Real-Time Lane and Road Detection in Critical Shadow Conditions. In: Proceedings IEEE International Symposium on Computer Vision, Coral Gables, Florida, IEEE Computer Society Press, Los Alamitos (1995)
10. Compañ, P., Satorre, R., Rizo, R.: Disparity estimation in stereoscopic vision by simulated annealing. Artificial Intelligence research and development, pp. 160–167. IOS Press, Amsterdam (2003)
11. Trucco, E., Verri, A.: Introductory techniques for 3-D Computer Vision. Prentice-Hall, Englewood Cliffs (1998)
12. Cox, I., Ignoran, S., Rao, S.: A maximum lilelihood stereo algorithm. Computer Vision and Image Understanding 63 (1996)
13. Coughlan, J., Yuille, A.L.: Manhattan World: Orientation and Outlier Detection by Bayesian Inference. Neural Computation 15(5), 1063–1088 (2003)
14. Faugeras, O.: Three-dimensional computer vision: a geometric viewpoint. MIT Press, Cambridge, Massachusetts (1993)
15. Gallego Sánchez, A.J., Molina Carmona, R., Villagrá Arnedo, C.: Three-Dimensional Mapping from Stereo Images with Geometrical Rectification. In: Perales, F.J., Fisher, R.B. (eds.) AMDO 2006. LNCS, vol. 4069, pp. 213–222. Springer, Heidelberg (2006)

Noise Analysis for Depth Estimation

Aamir Saeed Malik and Tae-Sun Choi

Gwangju Institute of Science and Technology,
Oryong-Dong, Buk-Gu, Gwangju, 500712, Korea
{aamir,tschoi}@gist.ac.kr

Abstract. Depth estimation is an important parameter for three-dimensional shape recovery. There are many factors affecting the depth estimation including luminance, texture reflectance, noise etc. In this paper, we limit our discussion to noise. We present noise analysis by first pre-filtering the noisy images using well known Wiener filter and then using a robust focus measure for depth estimation. That depth map can further be used in techniques and algorithms leading to recovery of three dimensional structure of the object. The focus measure is based on an optical transfer function implemented in the Fourier domain and its results are compared with the earlier focus measures and presented in this paper. The additive Gaussian noise is considered for noise analysis.

Keywords: Noise, Pre-Filtering, Depth Map.

1 Introduction

There are many methods for the calculation of depth leading to 3D shape recovery. In this paper, we limit our discussion to one of such methods, i.e., Shape From Focus (SFF). The objective of shape from focus is to find out the depth of every point of the object from the camera lens. Hence, finally we get a depth map which contains the depth of all points of the object from the camera lens where they are best focused or in other words, where they show maximum sharpness.

The basic problem of imaging systems, such as the eye or a video-camera, is that depth information is lost while projecting a 3D scene onto 2D image plane. Therefore, one fundamental problem in computer vision is the reconstruction of a geometric object from one or several observations. Shape information that is obtained from the reconstruction of a geometric object is of critical importance in many higher level vision applications like mobile robot systems. For example, an unmanned spacecraft, in order to land safely on lunar surface, needs to estimate depth details of the terrain. Various image processing techniques retrieve the lost cue and shape information from the pictorial information. Shape from focus (SFF) is one of such image processing techniques that are used to recover such information.

Various techniques and algorithms have been proposed in the literature for the implementation of SFF. They include methods using focus image surface, Lagrange polynomial, neural networks, dynamic programming etc. But almost all the techniques start with the estimation of the depth map. Hence, the techniques for the estimation of this initial depth map become quite significant.

F. Mele et al. (Eds.): BVAI 2007, LNCS 4729, pp. 328–337, 2007.

Generally SFF scheme relies on a Focus Measure operator and an approximation technique. Focus Measure operator plays a very important role for three dimensional shape recovery because it is the first step in calculation of the depth map. So a focus measure operator needs to show robustness even in the presence of noise. Hence it should provide a very good estimate of the depth map.

2 Related Work

2.1 Focus Measure Methods

A Focus Measure operator is one that calculates the best focused point in the image. And focus measure is defined as a quantity to evaluate the sharpness of a pixel locally. Franz Stephan Helmli and Stefan Scherer [1] summarized the traditional focus measures while introducing three new focus measure operators.

Laplacian, the most commonly used operator, is suitable for accurate shape recovery because of being a point and symmetric operator, and is obtained by adding second derivatives in the x and y directions. Modified Laplacian (ML) [2,3] is computed by adding squared 2nd derivates. In order to handle possible variations, Shree K. Nayar and Yasuo Nakagawa suggested a variable spacing (step) between the pixels used to compute derivatives. In order to improve robustness for weak-texture images, Shree K. Nayar and Yasuo Nakagawa [2,3] presented focus measure at (x,y) as sum of ML values in a local window (about 5x5).

Tenenbaum Focus Measure is gradient magnitude maximization method that measures the sum of squared responses of horizontal and vertical Sobel masks. Variance Focus Measure is based on the variance of gray-level which is higher than that in a blur image. Mean Method Focus Measure [1] depends on the ratio of mean grey value to the center grey value in the neighborhood. The ratio of one shows a constant greylevel or absence of texture. Curvature Focus Measure [1] exploits that the curvature in a sharp image is expected to be higher than that in a blur image. Point Focus Measure [1] is approximated by a polynomial of degree four.

2.2 Approximation Methods

A more accurate depth range image can be obtained by using some optimization and approximation method. The results of the focus measures, defined in section 2.1, are refined using such a reconstruction scheme. First we discuss the traditional SFF method. In Traditional (TR) SFF, for each image in the sequence, focus measure at each pixel is computed by Sum Modified Laplacian in a 2D neighborhood around the pixel. The results of TR SFF are improved by Subbarao and Choi [4] who proposed a new concept termed Focused Image Surface (FIS) based on planar surface approximations. The FIS of an object is defined as the surface formed by the set of points at which the object points are focused by a camera lens. Joungil Yun and Tae-Sun Choi [5] summarized various approximation techniques.

FIS can be improved by a piecewise curved surface rather than piecewise planar approximation. This was proposed by Choi and J. Yun [6]. They estimated the piecewise curved surface by interpolation using second order Lagrange polynomial. Asif and Choi [7] used Neural Networks to learn shape of FIS by optimizing the focus measure over small 3-D windows. Bilal and Choi [8] proposed the use of Dynamic Programming (DP) to handle the complexity of FIS. DP is motivated by the Bellman's principal of optimality. A direct application of DP on a 3D data is impractical due computational complexity. Therefore, a heuristic model based on DP was proposed by Bilal and Choi.

3 Method

In this paper, we perform noise analysis using additive Gaussian noise. Only we consider focus measures for the depth estimation. Various focus measures are mentioned in section 2.1. Approximation techniques are out of the scope of this paper which are briefly discussed in section 2.2.

Since the focus measure calculates the sharpest pixels in the image hence their success depends on their ability to calculate the sharpness value of each pixel. In this noise analysis, we consider the Optical Focus Measure [9] that has been described to show robustness in the presence of noise. A depth map is made using this focus measure and its results are compared with the traditional focus measures. Further, all the processing has been done using optimum window size as described by [10].

The Optical Focus Measure is denoted as FM_O. It is based on bipolar incoherent image processing. Ting-Chung Poon and Partha P. Banerjee [11] has discussed bipolar incoherent image processing in detail. The sharpness of pixel values in the image is found by convolving the spectrum of the intensity image with the optical transfer function (OTF). The computed image [i_c (x, y)] is given as:

$$i_c (x, y) = Re \left[|I_0(x, y)|^2 * h_\Omega(x, y)\} \right] \qquad (1)$$

where '*' indicates convolution and:

$$|I_0(x, y)|^2 = \text{Spectrum of the Intensity Image}$$
$$h_\Omega(x, y) = \text{Transfer Function}$$

Transfer function is basically the OTF which is calculated in frequency domain using either Discrete Fourier Transform or Discrete Cosine Transform. For DFT, the transfer function $h_\Omega(x, y)$ is given as:

$$h_\Omega(x, y) = F^{-1} \{OTF_\Omega(k_x, k_y)\} \qquad (2)$$

where:

$$OTF_\Omega(k_x, k_y) = \text{Optical Transfer Function}$$
$$k_x, k_y = \text{Spatial frequencies}$$

So finally we can write the computed image as:

$$i_c (x, y) = Re \left[F^{-1} \{F \{ |I_0(x, y)|^2\} OTF_\Omega(k_x, k_y)\} \right] \qquad (3)$$

where F is for Fourier Transform and F^{-1} is for Inverse Fourier Transform. The OTF itself is calculated as:

$$OTF_\Omega (k_x, k_y) = \iint p_1(x', y') \, p_2(x' + f k_x/k_0, y' + f k_y/k_0) \, dx \,'dy' \qquad (4)$$

where f is the focal length of the lenses and k_0 is the wave number of light. The OTF is the cross correlation of the two pupils (p_1 and p_2) in the incoherent optical system [11]. Hence, the point spread function becomes bipolar.

In equation (4) above, p_1 is a difference of Gaussian aperture function and p_2 is a small pin hole aperture. p_1 is given as [11]:

$$p_1 = \exp[-a_1(x^2 + y^2)]-\exp[-a_2(x^2 + y^2)] \tag{5}$$

where a_1 and a_2 are constants. p_2 is given as [11]:

$$p_2 = \delta(x,y) \tag{6}$$

For implementation purposes, equation (4) can be rewritten as [11]:

$$OTF_\Omega\ (k_x, k_y) = \exp[-\sigma_1(k_x^2 +k_y^2)]-\exp[-\sigma_2(k_x^2 +k_y^2)] \tag{7}$$

where:

$$\sigma_1 = a_1\ (f/\ k_0)^2$$
$$\sigma_2 = a_2\ (f/\ k_0)^2$$

Equation 7 shows that OTF has two parameters as described above. These two parameters make OTF a band pass filter with gradual cut off frequency. The filtering operation depends upon σ_1 and σ_2. Sharp focus measure is obtained by adjusting these two parameters. The operator responds to the high frequency variations in the image intensity. The high frequency component of an image area is determined by processing in the Fourier domain and analyzing the frequency distribution. Fourier transform used to be computationally expensive but with high speed personal computers available today, this computational complexity has decreased exponentially and it is not a matter of concern anymore. The processing in the frequency domain is particularly useful for noise reduction as the noise frequencies are easily filtered out. Fig 1 shows the filter with σ_1= 0.01 and σ_2= 0.1. Fig 2 shows the Fourier spectrum of the "TEST" image which itself is shown in Fig 3.

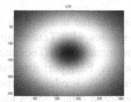

Fig. 1. Filter with σ_1= 0.01 and σ_2= 0.1   **Fig. 2.** Fourier Spectrum

The next step is to find the best focused pixel in the sequence of images. Equation 3 is used to find the focus measure at a point (i,j) in a small window around (i,j) and the value at (i,j) is replaced by the sum of computed values (by equation 3 & 7 above) of all pixels in that window. This operation is similar to that used for Sum of Modified Laplacian [2,3]. We have used optimum window size for our experiments because larger window size results in smoothing of the image and hence losing the actual sharp focused point [10]. Therefore, FM_O is calculated as:

$$FM_O\ (i, j) = \sum_{x=i-N}^{i+N} \sum_{y=j-N}^{j+N} i_c\ (x, y) \tag{8}$$

This focus measure is based on the conventional Difference of Gaussian Operator. A further improvement can be made by considering biologically motivated processing step, called surround suppression, which has been shown to provide better contour detection ability [12].

Most of the focus measures, discussed in section 2.1, are sensitive to noise. This has been discussed in detail by [9] for various types of noise. However, they did not perform any noise pre-filtering while performing experiments. In this paper, we perform the experiments by employing Wiener filter before the application of focus measure. We consider only additive Gaussian noise. We use Wiener filter because it filters an intensity image that has been degraded by constant power additive noise. Since we already know that this additive noise is Gaussian noise, therefore, we use this information for implementing this filter.

4 Results and Discussion

The comparison is made using various types of images including a "TEST" image, a sequence of 97 simulated cone images and a sequence of 97 real cone images. The size of the images is 360x360 pixels. The real cone is taken from the CCD camera system. The real cone object was made of hardboard with black and white stripes drawn on the surface so that a dense texture of ring patterns is viewed in the images. The comparison is made for three focus measure operators, namely, Sum of Modified Laplacian (SML), Tenenbaum (TEN) and Optical Focus Measure (FM_0).

Fig 3(a) shows the test image with uniform background of white color and "TEST" written in black over it. Fig 3(b) shows the same image with the Gaussian noise with zero mean and variance value of 0.5. In fig 4, the result for SML has deteriorated while that for Tenenbaum is still recognizable. However, the optical focus measure (FM_0) shows very good results.

Fig 5 shows the image with real cone, noise addition to the image with variance value equal to 0.01 and the corresponding processed images with Tenenbaum, SML and the FM_0. Hence, as clear from the figures, the performance of Tenenbaum and SML degrades when noise is added to the images. However, FM_0 performs satisfactorily well. In real time applications, various type of noise like Rayleigh, exponential, uniform, shot, speckle, Gaussian etc may occur. Therefore, a robust focus measure is required to deal with noisy situations.

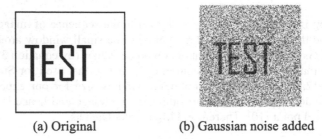

(a) Original   (b) Gaussian noise added

Fig. 3. Original Test Image & One with Gaussian Noise

(a) Tenenbaum   (b) SML   (c) FM$_O$

Fig. 4. Results with Gaussian noise addition

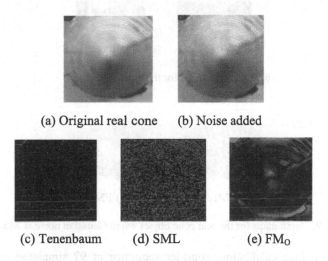

(a) Original real cone   (b) Noise added

(c) Tenenbaum   (d) SML   (e) FM$_O$

Fig. 5. Results for real cone image

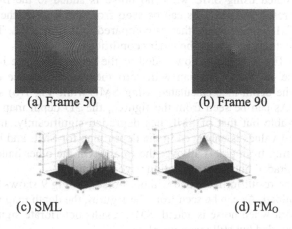

(a) Frame 50   (b) Frame 90

(c) SML   (d) FM$_O$

Fig. 6. Depth maps for the simulated cone object

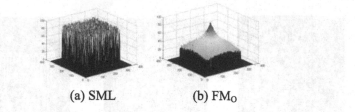

(a) SML   (b) FM$_O$

Fig. 7. Depth maps for the simulated cone object when Gaussian noise is added

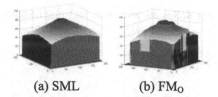

(a) SML   (b) FM$_O$

Fig. 8. Depth maps for the real cone object

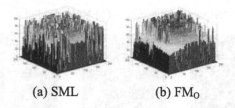

(a) SML   (b) FM$_O$

Fig. 9. Depth maps for the real cone object when Gaussian noise is added

As for depth map calculation, consider sequence of 97 simulated cone images. Fig 6(a) and 6(b) show two of the frames for the simulated cone. Fig 6(c) shows the depth map calculated using SML while no noise is added to the images. Fig 6(d) shows the same result for FM$_O$. As can be seen from the figures, the 3D depth map obtained using FM$_O$ is much smoother as compared to that of SML. The spikes seen in fig 6(c) are due to processing of boundary conditions.

Now consider Fig 7. Noise is now added to the sequence of the images of simulated cone. Noise added is Gaussian with zero mean and variance equal to 0.005. Fig 7(a) shows the depth map calculated using SML while Fig 7(b) shows the same result for FM$_O$. As can be seen from the figures, the 3D depth map obtained using FM$_O$ is recognizable but that of SML has degraded significantly. Infact, the noise added to the pixel values is enhanced in the depth map for SML and hence the result is spikes originating from pixels all over the image. On the other hand, the result for FM$_O$ has also degraded but that degradation is very minor.

Fig 8 shows the result for real cone without noise and Fig 9 shows the results with Gaussian noise added. As can be seen from the figures, the depth map without noise is almost similar. But when noise is added, SML results deteriorate significantly. Also, FM$_O$ result is degraded but still recognizable.

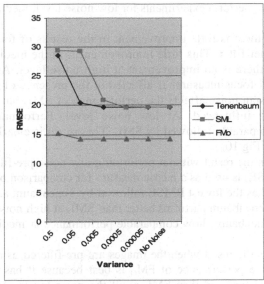

(a) Without noise Filtering

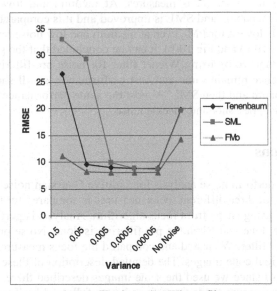

(b) Pre-filtering using Wiener filter

Fig. 10. Comparison of Focus Measures (Gaussian Noise)

Till now, no noise pre-filtering is done and the results are similar to those presented earlier [9]. However, generally some type of pre-filtering is performed for noisy images. Hence, we used Wiener filter since we already know that the noise type is additive Gaussian noise and Wiener filter performs well for this type of noise. We consider various noise levels for this experiment. We take five different noise levels with Gaussian noise of zero mean and variance of 0.5, 0.05, 0.005, 0.0005 and

0.00005. Hence, we perform experiments for low noise level, medium noise level and high noise level.

We found that there is little improvement in the results of focus measures after the usage of Wiener filter. This little improvement is at the medium and low noise levels. However, there is no improvement at high noise level. At high noise level, performance of all focus measures is affected in the presence of noise. At medium noise level, Gaussian noise affects the performance of SML but rests of the focus measures are not influenced. At low noise level, Performance of FM_O and Tenenbaum is comparable followed by SML. This result is clearly depicted for the simulated cone in Fig 10.

Fig 10(a) shows the result without performing any noise pre-filtering. Root Mean Square Error (RMSE) is used as a metric measure for comparison of the results. It can be seen that FM_O has the lowest RMSE followed by Tenenbaum and then SML at all the noise levels. Tenenbaum performs better than SML at high noise levels. However, both SML and Tenenbaum show comparable performance at medium and low noise levels.

Fig 10(b) shows the result when the images are pre-filtered using Wiener filter. It can be seen that the performance of FM_O is best because it has the lowest RMSE followed by Tenenbaum and then SML at all the noise levels. At high noise level, FM_O outperforms the other focus measures. At medium and low noise levels, the performance of Tenenabum and SML is improved and it is comparable to FM_O. However, still RMSE is lowest for FM_O even at medium and low noise levels.

Comparing Fig 10(a) and Fig 10(b), it can be concluded that the performance of all focus measures improve by using Wiener filter for noise pre-filtering. However, the order of performance remain same and best performance is still shown by FM_O followed by Tenenbaum and then SML. Almost the same performance was observed for other types of noise, i.e., shot and speckle noise.

5   Conclusions

In this paper, we perform noise analysis for additive Gaussian noise for depth estimation. Performance of three different focus measures is compared for their sensitivity to this type of noise using shape from focus algorithm. Analysis is performed both when no pre-filtering is done and when the pre-filtering is done. Noise pre-filtering is performed by Wiener filter. We tested and compared the focus measures using simulated cone images and real cone images. The detailed description of these image sequences can be found in [4] since we used the same images described there. The results show that optical focus measure tends to perform better followed by Tenenbaum and then Sum of Modified Laplacian focus measures.

Acknowledgement

This work was supported by the basic research project through a grant provided by the Gwangju Institute of Science and Technology in 2007.

References

1. Helmli, F.S., Scherer, S.: Adaptive Shape from Focus with an Error Estimation in Light Microscopy. In: 2nd Int'l Symposium on Image and Signal Processing and Analysis Croatia, pp. 188–193 (2001)
2. Nayar, S.K., Nakagawa, Y.: Shape from focus. IEEE Transactions on Pattern Analysis and Machine Intelligence 16(8), 824–831 (1994)
3. Nayar, S.K., Noguchi, M., Watanabe, M., Nakagawa, Y.: Real time focus range sensors. IEEE Transactions on Pattern Analysis and Machine Intelligence 18(12), 1186–1198 (1996)
4. Subbarao, M., Choi, T.-S.: Accurate recovery of three dimensional shape from image focus. IEEE Transactions on Pattern Analysis and Machine Intelligence 17(3), 266–274 (1995)
5. Yun, J., Choi, T.-S.: Accurate 3-D Shape Recovery using Curved Window Focus Measure. In: IEEE International Conference on Image Processing, vol. 3, pp. 910–914. IEEE Computer Society Press, Los Alamitos (1999)
6. Choi, T.-S., Asif, M., Yun, J.: Three-dimensional shape recovery from focused image surface. In: IEEE International Conference of Acoustics, Speech and Signal Processing, vol. 6, pp. 3269–3272. IEEE Computer Society Press, Los Alamitos (1999)
7. Asif, M., Choi, T.-S.: Shape from focus using multilayer feedforward neural network. IEEE Transactions on Image Processing 10(11), 1670–1675 (2001)
8. Ahmad, M.B., Choi, T.-S.: A Heuristic approach for finding best focused shape. IEEE Transactions on Circuits and Systems for Video Technology 15(4), 566–574 (2005)
9. Malik, A.S., Choi, T.-S.: A Novel Algorithm for Estimation of Depth Map using Image Focus for 3D Shape Recovery in the Presence of Noise. Pattern Recognition
10. Malik, A.S., Choi, T.-S.: Consideration of Illumination Effects and Optimization of Window Size for Accurate Calculation of Depth Map for 3D Shape Recovery. Pattern Recognition 40(1), 154–170 (2007)
11. Poon, T.-C., Banerjee, P.P.: Contemporary optical image processing, 1st edn. Elsevier Science Ltd., New York (2001)
12. Grigorescu, C., Petkov, N., Westenberg, M.A.: Contour and boundary detection improved by surround suppression of texture edges. Image and Vision Computing 22(8), 609–622 (2004)

Stimulus-Response Curves in Sensory Neurons: How to Find the Stimulus Measurable with the Highest Precision

Petr Lansky[1], Ondřej Pokora[1,2], and Jean-Pierre Rospars[3]

[1] Institute of Physiology, Academy of Sciences of Czech Republic, Videnska 1083, 142 20 Prague 4, Czech Republic
lansky@biomed.cas.cz
[2] Department of Mathematics and Statistics, Faculty of Science, Masaryk University, Janackovo namesti 2a, 602 00 Brno, Czech Republic
[3] UMR 1272 UMPC–INRA–AgroParisTech "Physiologie de l'Insecte Signalisation et Communication", INRA, 78026 Versailles Cedex, France

Abstract. To study sensory neurons, the neuron response is plotted versus stimulus level. The aim of the present contribution is to determine how well two different levels of the incoming stimulation can be distinguished on the basis of their evoked responses. Two generic models of response function are presented and studied under the influence of noise. We show in these noisy cases that the most suitable signal, from the point of view of its identification, is not unique. To obtain the best identification we propose to use measures based on Fisher information. For these measures, we show that the most identifiable signal may differ from that derived when the noise is neglected.

1 Introduction

Characterization of the input-output properties of sensory neurons and their models is commonly done by using the so called frequency (input-output) response functions, $R(s)$, in which the output is plotted against the strength of the signal, s. The output is usually the spiking frequency, or rate of firing, but it can be also the activity or level of any intermediate variable in the transduction cascade, e.g., effector enzyme concentration, ionic channel activity or receptor potential. The response curves are usually monotonously increasing functions (most often of sigmoid shape) assigning a unique response to an input signal (see Fig. 1 for illustration). In these curves, there are two special points – the threshold below which the neuron does not respond or only a spontaneous activity, r_{min}, is detected and the first level of the signal at which the response, r_{max}, is saturated. The range of signals between threshold and saturation is called dynamic range D (for detailed discussion and references see [25]). For formal treatment it is convenient to scale the range of responses, $[r_{min}, r_{max}]$, into interval $[0, 1]$.

The intuitive concept of "just noticeable difference" has been deeply studied in psychophysics ([9]). This concept is also implicitly involved in understanding

F. Mele et al. (Eds.): BVAI 2007, LNCS 4729, pp. 338–349, 2007.

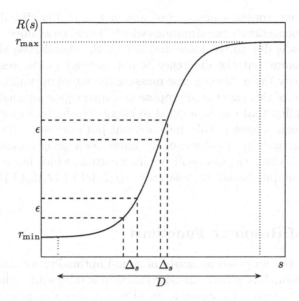

Fig. 1. A schematic example of transfer function. The dynamic range D, threshold response r_{min} and maximal discharge r_{max} are given. The concept of "just noticeable difference" ϵ is illustrated. The size of the corresponding "just noticeable difference" in the signal, Δ_s, depends on the slope of the transfer function and is smallest where the slope is highest.

of signal optimality in neurons. Having the transfer function $R(s)$ and minimum detectable increment ϵ of the response, we can calculate Δ_s which is the just noticeable difference in the signal. Following from the model given by the response curve, Δ_s depends on the slope of the response curve (Fig. 1). In the case of an abstract linear response curve $(R(s) = s/D)$ we have, $\Delta_s = D\epsilon$. If the response curve is nonlinear (for example sigmoidal as in Fig. 1) we can see that Δ_s varies along D and the smallest values of the just noticeable difference in the signal are achieved where the response curve is steepest (see Fig. 1). Therefore the stimulus intensity for which the signal is optimal, that is the best detectable, is where the slope of the transfer function is highest.

This measure of signal optimality is based on deterministic transformation of the signal into a response. In other words it applies to situations in which to each signal s corresponds a deterministically unique response $R(s)$. However, in practice, an identical signal does not always yield the same response. The variability can be intrinsic (on the way from signal to response) or extrinsic (in the stimulus or when reading the response). These two kinds of variability are not distinguished here and are collectively considered as noise acting upon the signal-to-response transfer. The presence of noise complicates the concept of signal optimality based on the "just noticeable difference". Not only a fixed response (e.g., firing rate) is assigned to every level of the stimulus (as in the classical frequency coding schema), but also a probability distribution of the responses. The noise causes two situations which should be avoided: (a) difference in the responses is due to the noise and not to the signal-false alarm, (b) the signals are different but the difference is not noticed in the response-missed signal. To quantify these effects a new measure for signal optimality is required.

The main aim of this paper is to propose and investigate alternative measures of signal optimality, that can be applied to noisy transfer in sensory neurons. It means, the measures have to take into account both factors – the slope of the transfer function and the amplitude of the noise. As a general measure of signal optimality in this case, we propose Fisher information, which has become a common tool in computational neuroscience ([1,2,3,6,10,11,12,13,15,16,19,20,23, 29,31,32,33]).

2   Model of Response Functions

For illustrating the proposed measures of signal optimality we study a descriptive statistical model. A generic transfer function is selected to which a suitable noise is added. Consider for example an olfactory receptor neuron, located in the nasal olfactory epithelium. When stimulated during, say, one second, odorant molecules interact with receptor proteins embedded at the membrane surface of receptor neurons. Binding of odorants to receptors triggers biochemical events that result in the opening of ionic channels, the generation of a locally spreading receptor potential, which in turn initiates a spike train. The relations between the concentration s of odorant molecules and the density of activated receptors, or the neuron depolarization, or its firing rates, are examples of transfer functions. We investigated several models of this system ([14,18,26,27,28]) and a generic stochastic variant is considered below. The most frequently studied neuron response is the firing rate, $R(s)$, as a function of stimulus intensity s, under the assumption of rate coding. The shape of $R(s)$ is usually sigmoidal, as shown in different sensory systems by [24,25,28] and others.

A typical sigmoid transfer function to which experimental data are fitted is the logistic function,

$$R(s) = \frac{r_{max}}{1 + \exp\left(-b(s - s_1)\right)} ,\tag{1}$$

where the parameter $r_{max} > 0$ gives the saturation firing rate, s_1 determines the location along the s axis, and $b > 0$ controls the steepness of the curve, or the width of the interval of predominant increase ([25]). Thus, the parameters b and s_1 determine the stimulus intensity at threshold and at saturation. The firing frequency is measured for different levels of s and parameters r_{max}, b and s_1 are estimated. For convenience of comparison with other measures, we set $r_{max} = b = 1$ in (1), and we locate the inflection point, s_1, at zero, so that $R(0) = R'(0) = 1/2$,

$$R(s) = \frac{1}{1 + \exp(-s)} .\tag{2}$$

Thus, the frequency saturates at level one and the slope of the transfer function at zero is fixed to one half.

The transfer function defined by (2) does not take into account random factors influencing the generation of a spike train. In order to obtain a more precise picture of reality, one would like to have a stochastic version of the model. Then, besides the mean firing rate, as it appears in (2), the distribution functions of the frequency as a function of the signal intensity would be required. For example, the random frequency in response to signal intensity, s, is of the form

$$R(s) = \frac{1}{1 + \exp(-s)} + \xi_s , \tag{3}$$

where ξ_s is the random component of the firing frequency, assuming that $E(\xi_s) = 0$. The simplest example which can be proposed is to assume that the noise has Gaussian distribution, thus

$$R(s) \sim N\left(\frac{1}{1 + \exp(-s)}, \ \mathrm{Var}(R(s))\right) , \tag{4}$$

with mean $E(R(s))$ given by (2) and variance $\mathrm{Var}(R(s)) = \mathrm{Var}(\xi_s)$ also depending on s. How the variance depends on s influences significantly the signal identification. For this reason we consider two different examples.

In the first example we assume

$$\mathrm{Var}(R(s)) = \sigma^2 \exp(-cs^2) , \tag{5}$$

where $c \geq 0$. For $s \to \pm\infty$, $\mathrm{Var}(R(s)) \to 0$, and for $s = 0$, $\mathrm{Var}(R(s)) = \sigma^2$. If $c > 0$, the variance tends to zero at the endpoints of the dynamic range and parameter c controls how fast the variance tends to zero for extremal values of s. If $c = 0$, the variance is a constant independent of signal intensity s.

In the second example we consider that the variance of the response function depends on s in the following way

$$\mathrm{Var}(R(s)) = 4\sigma^2 \frac{\exp(-s)}{(1 + \exp(-s))^2} . \tag{6}$$

Again, for $s \to \pm\infty$, $\mathrm{Var}(R(s)) \to 0$, and for $s = 0$, $\mathrm{Var}(R(s)) = \sigma^2$. The difference with respect to (5) is that the variance given by (6) decreases more slowly with s. For example, with $c = 1$, the ratio $\mathrm{Var}(R(1))/\mathrm{Var}(R(0))$ is 0.368 for (5) and 0.786 for (6).

Models (5) and (6) still permit observations outside the range of responses $[0, 1]$ and thus their modification may appear as useful, see Fig. 2. For example, one may require that the noise effect becomes asymmetric close to the endpoints of the dynamic range. It means that if $|s|$ is large, the distribution of the response is not symmetric around $E(R(s))$, but skewed away from the boundaries, i.e., from zero, resp., one. Such an example could be constructed by considering the Beta distribution for the response function, $R(s)$, with parameters depending on

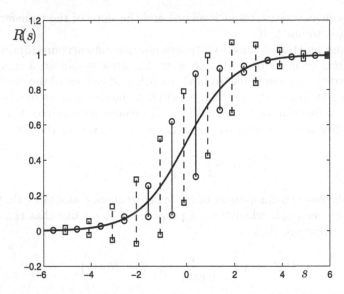

Fig. 2. Examples of transfer functions and their variability. Mean transfer function is plotted and variability is depicted by vertical bars giving standard deviations corresponding to the signal. Model is given by equations (4) and (5) for $\sigma^2 = 0.1$, $c = 1$ (solid bars and circles), and $\sigma^2 = 0.1$, $c = 0.25$ (dashed bars and squares). In the case $c = 0$ (not shown) the vertical bars are equal (with length $2\sigma = 0.632$) whatever s.

the signal. An advantage of the Beta distribution is that it completely prevents the response function to take values outside interval $[0, 1]$.

3   Optimality Criteria

Now, we introduce three criteria for optimum signal determination, J, J_1 and J_2, as follows.

Criterion J_1

Under the deterministic scenario there is a one-to-one correspondence between signal and response. In this case, as already mentioned, the region around the inflection point, where the function $R(s)$ is steepest and nearly linear, is the region of highest sensitivity to an increment of stimulation. In other words, the best identification of the signal is in the region where a small change in s implies a large change of the response $R(s)$. Therefore we are interested in the value of s for which the derivative, J_1, of the transfer function is maximal and we denote this value as s_1. This criterion can be extended to the stochastic models by maximizing the derivative of the mean of the transfer function, $E(R(s))$. Formally, we look for maxima of J_1,

$$J_1 = \frac{\partial E(R(s))}{\partial s} \ . \tag{7}$$

J_1 is the slope of the transfer function at stimulus intensity s. In the example of the spike frequency coding of olfactory receptor neuron this is the ratio of a firing rate (s^{-1}) to a concentration (molarity M), so J_1 is expressed in $s^{-1}M^{-1}$.

Criterion J

Under the stochastic scenario, for a signal s there is a family of responses, each of them appearing with predefined probability. The noise can be so large in the region of steep mean transfer function that signals outside this region can be identified with greater precision. We propose that Fisher information is used as a measure of how well a signal, s, can be estimated from the transfer function. Suppose that the random variable $R(s)$ has probability density function belonging to a parametric family $g(x; s)$. The Fisher information with respect to parameter s is

$$I = \int_{-\infty}^{\infty} \frac{1}{g} \left(\frac{\partial g}{\partial s} \right)^2 dx \ . \tag{8}$$

The use of Fisher information as a tool to locate the optimal signal for information transfer is theoretically motivated by Cramer-Rao inequality. It says that the variance of an unbiased estimate of the signal cannot be smaller than the inverse of the Fisher information, see [4],

$$\mathrm{Var}(\hat{s}) \geq \frac{1}{I} \ . \tag{9}$$

Formula (9) suggests that the larger the Fisher information, the better the estimate of s that can be achieved. This conclusion is very important from the point of view of how well one can hope to identify the signal. However, the best result will be obtained only if equality can be achieved in (9), $I = 1/\mathrm{Var}(\hat{s})$. In the example of the olfactory receptor neuron, $\mathrm{Var}(\hat{s})$ is expressed in M^2, so I is expressed in M^{-2}. For a better comparison with measure (8) we introduce the quantity $J = \sqrt{I}$, so for the best estimator holds

$$J = \frac{1}{\sqrt{\mathrm{Var}(\hat{s})}} \ , \tag{10}$$

which is expressed in M^{-1}. We denote the value of parameter s for which I (the Fisher information) and J reach their (common) maximum by s_0.

Criterion J_2

Criterion (8) requires a complete knowledge of the distribution $g(x; s)$, but an approximation of the Fisher information can also be used. It is a lower bound of J based on the first two moments of the random variable $R(s)$,

$$I_2 = \frac{1}{\mathrm{Var}(R(s))} \left(\frac{\partial E(R(s))}{\partial s} \right)^2 \ , \tag{11}$$

which can be obtained from the Cauchy-Schwarz inequality, see [4]. In fact for a large class of distributions, $I_2 = I$ (see [20]), and obviously I_2 is computationally much simpler as it requires only the first two moments but not the distribution of probability. We denote by s_2 the value of intensity s at which (11) reaches its maximum. Defining $J_2 = \sqrt{I_2}$ we note that

$$J_2 = \frac{J_1}{\sqrt{\mathrm{Var}(R(s))}} \tag{12}$$

and therefore, J_2 is also expressed in M^{-1}. Equation (12) shows that the effect of slope J_1 is modulated by the standard deviation of $R(s)$. If the standard deviation is large, J_2 will be small even if the slope is steep.

4   Results

For the simplest (J_1) of the three criteria defined above only the mean response function is needed. On the other hand, for the criterion based on the Fisher information (J) the distribution of responses is required. The criterion J_2 based on (12), which uses the first two moments of the response function, is a compromise. In the following we compare the criteria for the logistic model introduced above. The mean responses and their standard deviations for two models are plotted in Fig. 3.

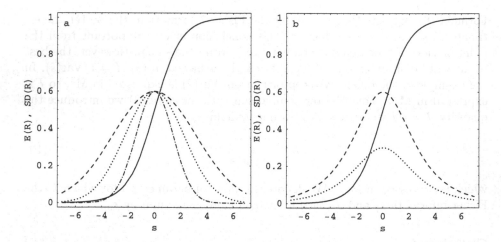

Fig. 3. (a) Mean response $\mathrm{E}(R(s))$ (solid line) and standard deviation of $R(s)$ for model given by (4) and (5) with $\sigma = 0.6$, $c = 0.1$ (dashed), $\sigma = 0.6$, $c = 0.2$ (dotted) and $\sigma = 0.6$, $c = 0.5$ (dot-and-dashed). In the case $c = 0$ (not shown) the standard deviation is a straight horizontal line at level 0.6. (b) Mean response $\mathrm{E}(R(s))$ (solid line) and standard deviation of $R(s)$ for model given by (4) and (6) with $\sigma = 0.6$ (dashed) and $\sigma = 0.3$ (dotted).

First Example

For the first model with variance (5), the optimality criterion $J(s)$ was evaluated numerically. The criteria J_1 and J_2 were calculated directly from (4) and (5),

$$J_1(s) = \frac{\exp(-s)}{(1 + \exp(-s))^2} \,, \tag{13}$$

$$J_2(s) = \frac{\exp(cs^2/2 - s)}{\sigma \, (1 + \exp(-s))^2} \,. \tag{14}$$

It can be shown that J_1 is unimodal and that its maximum is always located at $s_1 = 0$. Moreover, the two conditions, $J(0) = J_2(0) = \sigma^{-1}/4$ and $J(\pm\infty) = J_2(\pm\infty) = \infty$, hold. The behavior of J and $J_2(s)$ strongly depends on the parameter c.

Fig. 4a shows how the optimality criteria J_1 and J_2 depend on s. For $c \geq 0.5$, J_2 has only a local minimum in the center of the transfer function. The shape of $J_2(s)$ is mirror-like to the shape of $J_1(s)$. For these large values of c, the standard deviation is very low outside the central part of the transfer function and the optimum signal appears to be for the extreme values of the signal. If c is small ($c < 0.5$), the optimality curve $J_2(s)$ behaves identically for extremal values of s, but in addition, it has a local maximum at zero. Two other local minima appear approximately at $\pm 1/c$. Fig. 4b shows how the optimality criterion J depends on s. The shape of curve J is similar to the shape of criterion J_2. However, the value of the parameter c which evokes the change of shape of the curve J is not generally equal to 0.5 (as for J_2) and depends on σ.

Second Example

For the second model, with variance given by equation (6), the criterion J_1 is the same as in the previous case, see (13). Further, we can directly derive

$$J_2(s) = \frac{\exp(-s/2)}{2\sigma \, (1 + \exp(-s))} = \frac{\sqrt{J_1(s)}}{2\sigma} \tag{15}$$

and the Fisher information

$$I(s) = J^2(s) = \frac{\cosh(s) - 1 + \sigma^{-2}/4}{2 \, (\cosh(s) + 1)} \,. \tag{16}$$

Both criteria J_1 and J_2 reach their local maxima at $s_1 = s_2 = 0$, $J_1(0) = 1/4$, $J_2(0) = \sigma^{-1}/4$ and $J_1(\pm\infty) = J_2(\pm\infty) = 0$. For the criterion J, $J(0) = \sigma^{-1}/4$ and $J(\pm\infty) = \sqrt{2}/2$ hold.

Figs. 5a and 5b show how the criteria depends on the signal, s. The shape of the optimality curve J strongly changes in dependence on the parameter σ, while shapes of the curves J_1 and J_2 do not. The criterion function J is a constant $J(s) \equiv \sqrt{2}/2$ if $\sigma = \sqrt{2}/4$, it is unimodal with maximum at $s_0 = 0$ for $\sigma < \sqrt{2}/4$, and unimodal with minimum at zero for $\sigma > \sqrt{2}/4$. In case of optimality criterion J with $\sigma > \sqrt{2}/4$ the optimum signal appears to be for the extreme values.

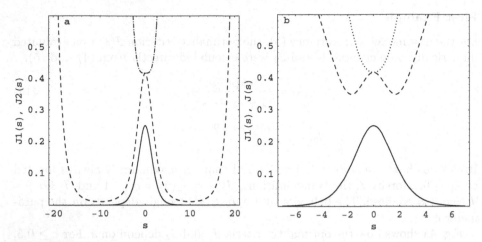

Fig. 4. Optimality criteria for the logistic model with a Gaussian distribution of noise given by (4) and (5). (a) Optimality criteria $J_1(s)$ (solid line) and $J_2(s)$ for $\sigma = 0.6$, $c = 0.5$ (dot-and-dashed) and for $\sigma = 0.6$, $c = 0.1$ (dashed). (b) Optimality criteria $J_1(s)$ (solid line) and $J(s)$ for $\sigma = 0.6$, $c = 0.2$ (dotted) and for $\sigma = 0.6$, $c = 0.1$ (dashed). In the case $c \approx 0$ (not shown), $J(s)$ is similar to the dashed curve, with same maximum at $s = 0$, with wings falling quickly to zero on both sides, and climbing to infinity outside the range of s values shown.

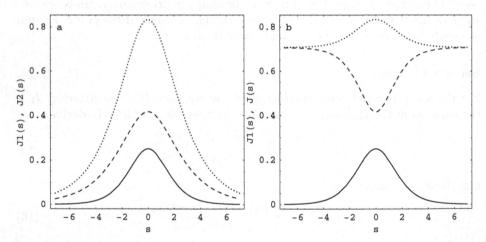

Fig. 5. Optimality criteria for logistic model with a Gaussian distribution of noise given by (4) and (6). (a) Optimality criteria $J_1(s)$ (solid line) and $J_2(s)$ for $\sigma = 0.6$ (dashed) and $\sigma = 0.3$ (dotted). (b) Optimality criteria $J_1(s)$ (solid line) and $J(s)$ for $\sigma = 0.6$ (dashed) and $\sigma = 0.3$ (dotted).

5   Conclusions

Response of many modalities in sensory neurons, especially spiking rate, are associated with sigmoid frequency transfer functions. Under the deterministic scenario, the optimum signal is defined as that one which induces the highest change in response for the smallest change in the input signal. Therefore, with a logistic response curve, the just noticeable difference in response corresponds to the smallest difference in stimulus at the inflection point, where the slope of the response curve is the steepest. This is not necessarily the case when the stochastic nature of the response is taken into account.

We investigated criteria to find an optimum signal which takes the stochastic fluctuation into account. The methods are based on Fisher information, which is the inverse of the minimum variance of an unbiased estimator. The level of Fisher information determines the quality of the signal identification – highest the Fisher information, the best the signal can be estimated.

Adding noise to the transfer function has significant consequences. In the two logistic models studied (Figs. 3a and 3b), the variances are similar, except that it decreases to zero faster in the former than in the latter case. However the optimal values of s are different. The shapes of the measures of identifiability in dependency on the signal are not only different, but also the values are reached with different speeds. This fact is important for identifying the dynamical range. If it is defined, for example, as the range of signals s greater than 10% and smaller than 90% of the maximum value, then each measure implies different dynamical range.

The identifiability of the signal is no longer proportional to the slope of the transfer function as in the deterministic case. The most unexpected results are obtained in the example where the variance, although not constant, does not vary much in the range of values of the stimulus intensity s corresponding to the dynamic range of the response studied. In this case the optimality criterion (which is best when it is large) has a wave shape (see Figs. 4a and 4b) with maxima for s at the middle and at the endpoints of the dynamic range.

It should be noted that the information value of the signal is not considered here. The mutual (Shannon) information between the stimulus and the response is not evaluated and thus the optimal signal may be useful from the point of view of its identifiability but not from the point of view of the transferred information.

Acknowledgments. AV0Z50110509, Center for Neurosciences LC554, Center for Statistics LC06024, Academy of Sciences of the Czech Republic (Information Society, 1ET400110401), ECO-NET 12644PF from French Ministère des Affaires étrangères and ANR-05-PNRA-1.E7 Aromalim from Agence Nationale de la Recherche.

References

1. Amari, S., Nakahara, H.: Difficulty of singularity in population coding. Neural Comput. 17, 839–858 (2005)
2. Bethge, M., Rotermund, D., Pawelzik, K.: Optimal short-term population coding: When Fisher information fails. Neural Comput. 14, 2317–2351 (2002)
3. Brunel, N., Nadal, J.-P.: Mutual information, Fisher information, and population coding. Neural Comput. 10, 1731–1757 (1998)

4. Cramer, H.: Mathematical Methods of Statistics. Princeton University Press, Princeton (1946)
5. Dayan, P., Abbott, L.F.: Theoretical neuroscience. MIT Press, Cambridge (2001)
6. Freund, J.A., Schimansky-Geier, L., Beisner, B., et al.: Behavioral stochastic resonance: How the noise from a Daphnia swarm enhances individual prey capture by juvenile paddlefish. J. Theor. Biol. 214, 71–83 (2002)
7. Getz, W.M., Lansky, P.: Ligand concentration coding and optimal Michaelis-Menten parameters in multivalent and heterogeneous receptor membranes. Chemical Senses 26, 95–104 (2001)
8. Gerstner, W., Kistler, W.: Spiking neuron models. Cambridge Univ. Press, Cambridge (2002)
9. Green, D.M., Swets, J.A.: Signal detection theory and psychophysics. Wiley, New York (1966)
10. Greenwood, P.E., Ward, L.M., Wefelmeyer, W.: Statistical analysis of stochastic resonance in a simple setting. Phys. Rev. E, Part B 60, 4687–4695 (1999)
11. Greenwood, P.E., Ward, L.M., Russel, D.F., Neiman, A., Moss, F.: Stochastic resonance enhances the electrosensory information available to paddlefish for prey capture. Phys. Rev. Lett. 84, 4773–4776 (2000)
12. Greenwood, P.E., Lansky, P.: Optimum signal in a simple neuronal model with signal-dependent noise. Biol. Cybern. 92, 199–205 (2005)
13. Greenwood, P.E., Lansky, P.: Information content in threshold data with non-Gaussian noise. Fluct. Noise Letters, L79–L89 (2007)
14. Krivan, V., Lansky, P., Rospars, J.-P.: Coding of periodic pulse stimulations in chemoreceptors. BioSystems 67, 121–128 (2002)
15. Jenison, R.L.: Decoding first-spike latency: A likelihood approach. Neurocomput. 38, 239–248 (2001)
16. Johnson, D.H., Ray, W.: Optimal stimulus coding by neural populations using rate codes. J. Comput. Neurosci. 16, 129–138 (2004)
17. Lam, H.S., Lampard, D.G.: Modeling of drug receptor interaction with birth and death processes. J. Math. Biol. 12, 153–172 (1981)
18. Lansky, P., Getz, W.M.: Sensitivity and coding range in olfactory sensory neuron. Role of heterogeneity of receptors. Bull. Math. Biol. 63, 885–908 (2001)
19. Lansky, P., Greenwood, P.E.: Optimal signal estimation in neuronal models. Neural Comput. 17, 2240–2257 (2005)
20. Lansky, P., Greenwood, P.E.: Optimal signal in sensory neurons under extended rate coding concept. BioSystems 89, 10–15 (2007)
21. Lansky, P., Rodriguez, R., Sacerdote, L.: Mean instantaneous firing frequency is always higher than the firing rate. Neural Comput. 16, 477–489 (2004)
22. Lansky, P., Rospars, J.-P.: Coding of odor intensity. BioSystems 31, 15–38 (1993)
23. Lansky, P., Sacerdote, L., Zucca, L.: Optimum signal in a diffusion leaky integrate-and-fire neuronal model. Math. Biosci. 207, 261–274 (2007)
24. McKeegan, D.E.F.: Spontaneous and odour evoked activity in single avian olfactory bulb neurones. Brain Res. 929, 48–58 (2002)
25. Nizami, L.: Estimating auditory neuronal dynamic range using a fitted function. Hearing Res. 167, 13–27 (2002)
26. Rospars, J.-P., Lansky, P., Duchamp-Viret, P., Duchamp, A.: Spiking frequency vs. odorant concentration in olfactory receptor neurons. BioSystems 58, 133–141 (2000)
27. Rospars, J.-P., Krivan, V., Lansky, P.: Perireceptor and receptor events in olfaction. Comparison of concentration and flux detectors: a modeling study. Chemical Senses 25, 293–311 (2000)

28. Rospars, J.-P., Lansky, P., Duchamp-Viret, P., Duchamp, A.: Relation between stimulus intensity and response in frog olfactory receptor neurons in vivo. European J. Neurosci. 18, 1135–1154 (2003)
29. Stemmler, M.: A single spike suffices: the simplest form of stochastic resonance in model neurons. Network 7, 687–716 (1996)
30. Wiener, M.C., Richmond, B.J.: Decoding spike trains instant by instant using order statistics and the mixture-of-Poisson model. J. Neurosci. 23, 2394–2406 (2003)
31. Wilke, S.D., Eurich, C.W.: Representational accuracy of stochastic neural populations. Neural Comput. 14, 155–189 (2002)
32. Wu, S., Amari, S., Nakahara, H.: Information processing in a neuron ensemble with the multiplicative correlation structure. Neural Networks 17, 205–214 (2004)
33. Zhang, K.C., Sejnowski, T.J.: Neuronal tuning: To sharpen or broaden? Neural Comput. 11, 75–84 (1999)

Molecular Mechanism of Glutamate-Triggered Brain Glucose Metabolism: A Parametric Model from FDG PET-Scans

Paola Lecca[1] and Michela Lecca[2]

[1] The Microsoft Research - University of Trento
Centre for Computational and Systems Biology
piazza Manci 17, 38100 Povo (Trento), Italy
lecca@cosbi.eu
[2] Fondazione Bruno Kessler - Centre for Scientific and Technological Research
via Sommarive 18, 38050 Povo (Trento), Italy
lecca@itc.it

Abstract. We present a computational model describing glutamate-stimulated glucose uptake and use into astrocytes. It consists of a set of ordinary differential equations, that specify the time-behavior of the main molecular species involved in the astrocytic glucose use (i. e. glutamate, glucose, Na^+, β-threohydroxyaspartate) and the dynamical rates of glutamate, glucose and Na^+ uptake. The kinetic rate constants of the model have been identified on a set of dynamic PET images. The relevance of such a model to the PET functional brain imaging consists in providing an *in silico* framework, in which to experiment the dynamics of glucose metabolism and its spatial mapping to elucidate their still elusive aspects.

1   Introduction

Positron Emission Tomography, also called PET imaging or PET scan is both a medical and research tool used to detect blood flow, oxygen consumption and energy metabolism. It consists in the acquisition of physiologic images based on the detection of radiation from the emission of positrons. To conduct the scan, a short-lived radioactive tracer isotope, that decays by emitting positrons, is chemically incorporated into a metabolically active molecule. Most commonly, this molecule is the fluorodeoxyglucose (FDG). Then the radioactive tracer attached to the metabolic molecule is injected into the blood circulation of the patient. After a waiting period time that the active metabolite needs to concentrate in the tissues, the patient is placed in the imaging scanner. The changing of regional blood flow in various anatomic structures as a measure of the injected positron emitter can been visualized and quantified with a PET scan. FDG-PET is widely used in clinical oncology, but is also an important research tool to map brain functions, since it is capable of detecting areas of molecular biology detail even prior to anatomic change. The kinetics of the FDG tracers are similar to the

F. Mele et al. (Eds.): BVAI 2007, LNCS 4729, pp. 350–359, 2007.
© Springer-Verlag Berlin Heidelberg 2007

glucose ones. It passes through the brain-blood barrier and is phosphorylated intracellularly in a process analogous to the glucose. The phosphorylized FDG compound does not enter in the Krebs cycle, thence it is effectively trapped.

Despite the striking advances in PET functional brain imaging [5,10], the molecular mechanisms that underlie the signals detected by this technique are still largely unknown. The basic physiological principle is represented by the tight coupling between neuronal activity and the associated increase in both blood flow and glucose metabolism. The development of the autoradiographic 2-deoxyglucose method by Sokoloff about 30 years ago, proved the coupling between synaptic activity and glucose use, the so-called neurometabolic coupling [11,12]. Wet experimental analyses *in vitro* have been carried out to investigate the neurotransmitter-regulated metabolic fluxes and to determine the cellular localization of enzymes and transporters involved in the glucose metabolism. At the same time *in vivo* approaches, as microdialysis and magnetic resonance approaches have recognized in the neurotransmitter glutamate and astrocytes, a specific type of glial cells, the key elements in the coupling between the synaptic activity and the glucose metabolism (for a detailed review about recent and less recent studies see [6]). Nevertheless, many aspects of the molecular interactions driving the glucose uptake and consumption are still elusive. In this article we present a mathematical model of the glutamate-triggered glucose uptake and metabolism by focusing on the emerging central role of the reaction occurring within astrocyrtes. At the best of our knowledge, this work is the first to provide a computational model related to the molecular basis of the use of the glucose in astrocytes. Our model consists of a set of seven differential equations, describing the time behavior of the glutamate and glucose use into the astrocyte. The synaptically released glutamate triggers glucose flux in astrocytes. The time course model of the glucose concentration inside that glial cell is related to the concurrency of the inhibitory action of the β-threohydroxyaspartate on the glutamate-stimulated glucose use and the activity of the Na^+/K^+-ATPase. The latter stimulates glucose uptake and glycolysis. The simulation parameters of the model, as the initial concentration of the reactants molecules and the kinetic rate constants, have been estimated by a slice-by-slice fit of the data of 31 PET-scans, each of which consisting of 15 horizontal slices, of a brain of a normal subject. The shapes of the brain activity curves, obtained by solving the equations, show a behavioral agreement with the typical measured blood activity curves of normal subjects [13]. Moreover, the results of our model simulations are in agreement with the simulations of the Sokoloff's model describing the kinetics of the compound FDG. This last fact, in particular, validates our model further on, since it is an additional confirmation that the model includes the most salient features of the molecular machinery of the astrocytic glucose metabolism. Finally, with respect to the model presented in this paper, the Sokoloff's model can be considered as a *black box* approach to the glucose metabolism kinetics, that Sokoloff indirectly obtained from the kinetics of the FDG tracer.

2 Glucose Use in Astrocytes

Astrocytes are sub-type of the glial cells in the brain. Following a group of recent studies, researchers have found an increasing amount of evidence that suggests that the astrocytes play a central role in brain function by affecting the activity of neurons, by taking an active part in the distribution of energy substrates from the circulation to neurons [14,15]. The ratio between neuronal and non-neuronal cells depends on species, brain areas or developmental ages. It is a well-established fact that neurons contribute at most 50% of cerebral cortical volume [2] and that the astrocytes outnumber the neurons ten to one.

Astrocytes are stellate cells (hence their name) with multiple fine processes, some of which are in close apposition to capillary walls. The entire surface of intraparenchymal capillaries is covered by these specialized processes, called astrocytic end-feet. This cytoarchitectural arrangement implies that astrocytes form the first cellular barrier encountered by the glucose entering the brain parenchyma. Therefore astrocytes are a likely site of prevalent glucose uptake. The uptake of glucose in astrocyte is triggered by glutamate. The glutamate is the main excitatory neurotransmitter of the cerebral cortex. Activation of afferent pathways by specific modalities (e. g. visual, auditory, somatosensory) results in a spatially and temporally defined local release of glutamate from the activated specific synapses. The action of glutamate on postsynaptic neurons terminates with the reuptake of glutamate in astrocytes [1,3,4]. Glutamate uptake

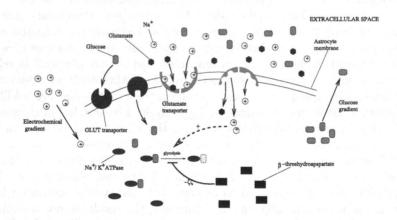

Fig. 1. A cartoon of the reactions governing the astrocytic glycolysis

into astrocytes is driven by the electro-chemical gradient of Na$^+$; it is an Na$^+$-dependent mechanism with a stoichiometry of three Na$^+$ ions cotransported with one glutamate molecule. A consequence of the glutamate uptake into astrocytes is the stimulation of glucose uptake and aerobic glycolysis in these cells, i. e. of glucose use [8]. Glutamate-stimulated increase in glucose uptake into astrocytes is abolished in the absence of Na$^+$ in the extracellular medium, consistently with the necessity for an electro-chemical gradient for the ion to drive glutamate uptake. A central role in the coupling between glutamate transporter activity and glucose uptake into the astrocytes is the activation of the Na^+/K^+-ATPase. The astrocytic Na^+/K^+-ATPase responds to increases in intracellular Na^+ concentration. Well established experimental observations [9] show that glutamate activates Na^+/K^+-ATPase. There is also an ample evidence from studies in a variety of cellular systems including brain, kidney, vascular smooth muscle and erythrocytes, that increases in the activity of the Na^+/K^+-ATPase stimulates glucose uptake and glycolysis [8]. Finally, the specific glutamate transporter inhibitor β-threohydroxyaspartate inhibits the glutamate-stimulate glucose use [6,8]. Figure 1 depicts the mechanism of glucose absorption and use inside the astrocyte.

3   The Kinetic Model

The rate equation of the concentration of glucose in the astrocyte ($GLUCOSE_{IN}$) is composed by three terms (Eq. (1)). The first term models the glutamate-stimulated glucose increase as a direct proportionality between the time derivative of glucose astrocytic concentration and the glutamate astrocytic concentration ($GLUTAM$). The second term is the product of the rate of glucose uptake and its astrocytic concentration. This term expresses the proportionality between the time change of astrocytic glucose and both the flux of incoming glucose (GL_{IN}) and the glucose astrocytic concentration. Finally, the third term in Eq. (1) represents the decrease of glucose in astrocyte due to the Na^+/K^+-ATPase - stimulated glycolysis. Since the astrocytic Na^+/K^+-ATPase is activated by glutamate in response to increases in intracellular Na^+ concentration, the rate equation for Na^+/K^+-ATPase (Eq. (3)) is given by a term proportional to the concentration of Na^+ in the astrocyte and by a negative term proportional to the amounts of β-threohydroxyaspartate and Na^+/K^+-ATPase. This term models the inhibition of glutamate-stimulated glucose use performed by β-threohydroxyaspartate. In Eq. (3) the inhibition of glycolysis is modeled by a decrement term in the rate equation of Na^+/K^+-ATPase. In fact a decrement of the amount of this enzyme causes a decrement of the glycolytic events.

The rate equation for the astrocytic glutamate concentration (Eq. (2)) is the product of the glutamate amount in the cell and the flux of incoming glutamate (GT_{IN}). The fluxes of glutamate and glucose entering the astrocyte (GL_{IN} and GT_{IN}, respectively) have been modeled as functions of time. Experimentally the rate at which glucose is transported into the cell is determined by the rate at which the concentration of glucose accumulates inside the cell in the absence of metabolism [7]. Thence, the temporal derivatives of the glucose and glutamate fluxes are given by Eq. (5) and Eq. (6) respectively. Eq. (5) contains a term accounting for the number of GLUT transporter in an open state ($GLUT_{OPEN}$), i. e. transporters that are facing the exterior of the cell and ready to receive a glucose molecule. Similarly, Eq. (6) contains a term proportional to the fraction of two types of glutamate transporters GLT_1 and $GLAST$ and a term proportional to the difference between the internal and external concentration of Na$^+$ (NA_{IN} and NA_{OUT}, respectively).

Glucose entering into the astrocyte (1)

$$\frac{dGLUCOSE_{IN}}{dt} = k_1 \; GLUTAM + k_2 \; GL_{IN} \cdot GLUCOSE_{IN} - k_3 \; NA\_K\_ATPase \cdot GLUCOSE_{IN}$$

Glutamate entering into the astrocyte (2)

$$\frac{dGLUTAM}{dt} = k_4 \; GT_{IN} \cdot GLUTAM$$

Na$^+$_K$^+$_ATPase (3)

$$\frac{dNA\_K\_ATPase}{dt} = k_5 \; NA_{IN} - k_6 \; GT\_INHIBIT \cdot NA\_K\_ATPase$$

β_threohydroxyaspartate (4)

$$\frac{dGT\_INHIBIT}{dt} = -k_7 \; NA_{IN} \cdot GT\_INHIBIT$$

Rate of glucose uptake into the astrocyte (5)

$$\frac{dGL_{IN}}{dt} = k_8 GLUT_{OPEN} \cdot GL_{IN}$$

Rate of glutamate uptake into astrocyte (6)

$$\frac{dGT_{IN}}{dt} = (k_9 \; GLT\_1 + k_{10} \; GLAST) GT\_IN + k_{11} \; (NA_{IN} - NA_{OUT})$$

Na$^+$ uptake into astrocyte (7)

$$\frac{dNA\_IN}{dt} = k_{12} \; GLUTAM$$

Eq. (4) is the rate equation for the β-threohydroxyaspartate ($GT\_INHIBIT$). The time derivative of this inhibitor is given by the product of its concentration and the concentration of Na$^+$. Namely, the inhibitory activity of the β-threohydroxyaspartate is consequent to the increase of the concentration of Na$^+$, that in turn is also responsible for the activation of the glycolytic activity of Na$^+$/K$^+$-ATPase. Finally, Eq. (7) describes the time behavior of the astrocytic concentration of Na$^+$. Its time derivative is proportional to the astrocytic concentration of glutamate. This equation expresses the direct relationship between glutamate and the co-transported Na$^+$. The coupling between synaptic glutamate release and its re-uptake into astrocyte is so tight that the determination of the Na$^+$ current generated in astrocytes by the co-transport of glutamate and Na$^+$ through the glutamate transporters provides an accurate estimate of glutamate release from the synapses [1].

3.1 PET Image Processing and Parameters Derivation

The dynamic FDG PET data used in this work have been provided by the Neurobiology Research Group, Righospitalet of Copenhagen. These data consist of 31 three-dimensional grey level images of the brain of a normal subject. The

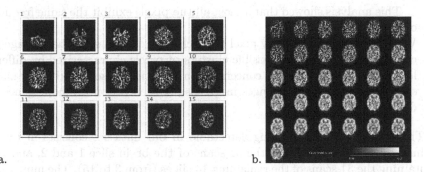

Fig. 2. a. A view of a set of brain slices. **b.** The red boundary encloses the regions R_j^k for $j = 1, \ldots 31$ and $k = 7$. The values on the grey level scale are measured in Bq/cc.

scans have been taken with a Scanditronix 4096 scanner on a time range of 3429 seconds. Figure 2(a) shows a set of brain slices of the database used in this work.

To identify the kinetic rates $k-$s of the model we used a standard fit procedure of the time-dependency of glucose concentration obtained from the PET images. For the fit we used a simple least squares cost function. Before obtaining the measured time-dependence of glucose concentration, the images have been processed in order to eliminate noise and border effects and identify exclusively the region corresponding to the brain. The identification of the brain region and the elimination of the noisy parts on the borders of the skull have been performed with the following procedure. Let I_j denote the 3D-scan taken at time t_j and $\{I_j^1, \ldots, I_j^{15}\}$ with $j = 1, \ldots, 31$, the set of 15 slices of the j-th scan. For each scan I_j and for each slice I_j^k ($k = 1, \ldots, 15$), we calculated the smallest polygon P_j^k, enclosing the pixels, whose grey-level is greater than zero (i. e. the pixels which do not belong to the background). The boundary of this polygon has been smoothed by a simple procedure of elimination of its parts having thickness larger than one pixel. Hence, for each slice I_j^k, the region R_j^k, we estimated as region effectively corresponding to the brain, is given by the topological internal part of P_j^k and the P_j^k boundary itself (see Figure 2(b)). Moreover, we defined $R_k \equiv \cup_{h=1}^{31} R_h^k$, $k = 1, \ldots, 15$, and we calculated the glucose concentration variation slice by slice using the following formula

$$\frac{dG_k}{dt}(t_i) = \frac{1}{\text{Area}(R_k)} \sum_{p \in R_k} \frac{|\sigma_p(t_i) - \sigma_p(t_{i+1})|}{t_{i+1} - t_i} \qquad (8)$$

where $\sigma_p(t_i)$ is the intensity of the pixel $p \in R_k$ at time t_i ($i = 1, \ldots, 31$).

Two kinds of analysis has been carried out pixel by pixel to reveal a possible partitioning of the brain slice in activation areas.

1. For each slice I_j^k of an image I_j we defined a *frequency map* $M : R_k \longrightarrow \mathbb{N}$ of pixel activation in the following way: $M[p] = 0$ if $p \notin R_k$, and $M[p] = m$ otherwise, where m is the number of intensity's changes occurred in pixel p.

This analysis showed that almost all the pixels exhibit the same frequency of intensity's change.

2. We also computed pixel by pixel for each slice of each scan the average glucose variation to detect possible clusters of pixels characterized by different levels of changes in glucose concentration variation. Also this kind of analysis showed that the time changes in glucose concentration are homogeneously distributed.

The only spatial partitioning detectable in our data set consists in two set of images: *set 1* consisting of the 31 scans of the brain slice 1 and 2, and *set 2* containing the 31 scans of the remaining 14 slices (from 3 to 15). The numeration of the slices refers to the one given in Figure 2a. This partitioning is pointed out by the different rates, with which the glucose concentration changes over time. Figures 3 a and b show the time behavior of glucose concentration for the slices of set 1 and set 2, respectively. In Table 1 the values of the initial concentrations of the reactants and the kinetic rates constants are shown. Figure 4a shows the model simulation of time-dependent glucose concentration for the slices of set 1. The set of equations of the model shows that the time behavior of the glucose concentration is mainly affected by the change of the values of k_1, k_2, k_3, k_6, and k_7. Increasing k_1 and k_2 (as well as increasing simultaneously k_6 and k_7 or k_7 only) means to decrease the speed of glucose metabolism (Figure 4b-c), whereas increasing k_3 speeds up the glucose use (Figure 4b).

Table 1. Parameter space of the model

Species	Initial concentration ($\times$ 0.0379016 Bq/cc)	Rate	Value (sec^{-1}) Set 1	Value (sec^{-1}) Set 2
$GLUCOSE_{IN}$	12.00	k_1	0.00003	0.00001
$GLUTAMATE_{IN}$	11.00	k_2	0.00003	0.00005
NA_K_ATPase	2.0	k_3	0.02000	0.04000
$GT\_INHIBIT$	0.01	k_4	0.00100	0.00030
GL_{IN}	0.10	k_5	0.00100	0.00020
GT_{IN}	0.10	k_6	0.00800	0.00080
NA_{IN}	0.70	k_7	0.00100	0.00003
Constants	Values	k_8	0.00100	0.00050
NA_{OUT}	0.1	k_9	0.01000	0.01000
$GLUT_{OPEN}$	0.1	k_{10}	0.01000	0.02000
GLT_1	0.1	k_{11}	0.01000	1.00000
$GLAST$	0.1	k_{12}	0.10000	0.00100

In our study, the exploration of the 12-dimensional parameter space of the model is exclusively driven by the experimental data of the dynamic PET scans. Curves of the time-glucose variation that are fitted by the equations of the model with different sets of rate coefficients may reveal different specific speeds of the metabolic kinetics in different brain regions. Since the simulations of the model are in agreement with the solutions of the set of ordinary differential equations

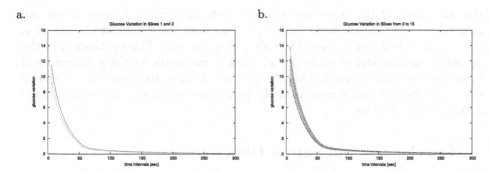

Fig. 3. a. Time behavior of glucose concentration in brain slice 1 and slice 2. **b.** Time behavior of glucose concentration for slices 3-15. In both figures the values on y-axis have to be multiplied by measured 0.0379016, that is a factor that converts the pixel intensity into the radioactivity concentration measured in Bq/cc.

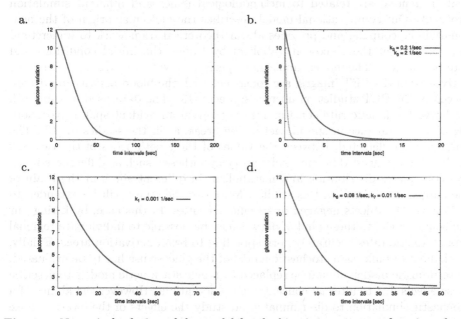

Fig. 4. a. Numerical solution of the model for the kinetic parameters of set 1 as show in Table 1. **b.** Two simulations with different values of k_2 (0.2 and 2 sec^{-1}). The other parameters maintain the values shown in Table 1. **c.** Simulations with $k_1 = 0.001$ sec^{-1} (the other parameters are fixed as in Table 1). **d.** Two simulations with increased values of k_6 and k_7 (0.08 and 0.01 sec^{-1}). (see in the text for more details).

of the Sokoloff's model and they also reproduce the typical behavior of the tracer density in arterial blood as in [13], the model can be used as a computational tool to estimate the astrocytic glucose metabolism by direct fitting to the measured data the rate constants. The curve of 18-FDG tracer differs from on subject to another in the value and the time of the maximum because of different blood circulation, presence of metabolic or neurological disorders, and variations in the way doses of the tracer are injected. Different tracer density curves can also be detected in the same subject, in this case the fitting of the model is able to provide a brain *map* of the glucose utilisation. The application of the model on healthy and ill subjects and, most importantly, on subjects employed in specific activities (visual, auditory, etc) will be able to reconstruct a kinetic rates distribution that decomposes the parameter space also into qualitatively different brain regions.

4   Conclusions and Future Directions

Functional neuroimaging techniques such as PET have provided valuable insights into the working brain. However, fundamental questions related to the cellular and molecular aspects of neurometabolic coupling are unresolved. Moreover, different PET studies provide discordant results about glycolytic metabolism, that in general are related to methodological issues and different simulation protocols. Our computational model describes the molecular origin of the neurometabolic coupling and provides also a theoretical framework to understand and experiment the glucose metabolism by tuning the initial conditions and rate parameters. The model simulations, performed with the kinetic parameters derived from the PET images, are consistent with the blood activity curves observed in the PET studies on normal subjects [13]. The data used in this work to derive the kinetic rate constants do not reveal an evident spatial partitioning of the brain slice in specific activation areas, as in the studies in [13]. The difference, we detected, between the values of the kinetic rates of the two sets of slices may suggest different explanatory hypotheses, such as differences in astrocytic spatial distribution and metabolism in different slices in the brain of the subject considered in this studies. Moreover the study will be extended to a data set of subjects engaged in specific activities. In this case, by fitting our molecular model to these kind of data it may be possible to individuate regional sets of kinetic rates accurately corresponding to brain activation areas. Finally, the benefit of building a stochastic model of the glucose use has to be evaluated. Deterministic models should be replaced by stochastic kinetic models to describe noise effects due to internal concentration fluctuations. However the ability of a stochastic simulation to discriminate and study the effects of the internal noise on the glucose variation time curve depends on the ratio between the levels of intrinsic and external noise of the measured radioactivity concentration. In fact, if the level of noise is too high it could mask the small stochastic fluctuations and therefore the information that we can extract from them. Such a situation recommends, as a future direction of work, the construction of a noise model and its validation on a sufficiently large database of PET scans before a plausible application and a correct interpretation of a stochastic approach. First such noise model, currently under development, will allow to obtain less noisy blood activity curves and consequently more accurate estimates of the rate parameters. Then it will allow to correctly interpret the outcomes of a sensitivity analysis of the kinetic model.

References

1. Bergles, D.E., Jahr, C.E.: Glials contribution to glutamate uptake at Schaffer collateral-commissural synapses in the hippocampus. J. Neurosci. 18, 7709–7716 (1998)
2. Bignami, A.: Glial cells in the central nervous system. Discussions in Neuroscience 8(1), 1–45 (1991)
3. Hertz, L., Peng, L., Dienel, G.A.: Energy metabolism in astrocytes: high rate of oxidative metabolism and spatiotemporal dependence on glycoslysis/glycogenolysis. J. of Cerebral Blood Flow & Metabolism 27, 219–249 (2007)
4. Kasiscke, K.A., Vishwasrao, H.D., Fisher, P.J., Zipfel, W.R., Webb, W.W.: Neuronal activity triggers neuronal oxidative metabolism followed by astrocytic glycolysis. Science 305(5680), 99–103 (2004)
5. Kimura, Y., Takabayashi, Y., Oda, K., Ishii, K., Ishiwata, K.: Functional image on glucose metabolism in brain using PET with short time scan. In: Procs of the 25th Annual International Conference of the IEEE EMBS, Cancun, Mexico, IEEE Computer Society Press, Los Alamitos (2003)
6. Magistretti, P.J., Pellerin, L.: Cellular mechanisms of brain energy metabolism and their relevance to functional brain imaging. Phil. Trans. R. Soc. Lond. B 354, 1155–1163 (1999)
7. Marland, E.S., Keizer, J.E.: Transporters and Pumps. In: Fall, C.P., Marland, E.S., Wagner, J.M., Tyson, J.J. (eds.) Computational Cell Biology, ch. 3, Springer, Heidelberg (2000)
8. Pellerin, L., Magistretti, P.J.: Glutamate uptake into astrocytes stimulates aerobic glycolysis: a mechanism coupling neuronal activity to glucose utilisation. Proc. Natl. Acad. Sci. 91, 10625–10628 (1994)
9. Pellerin, L., Magistretti, P.J.: Glutamate uptake stimulates Na^+/K^+-ATPase activity in astrocytes via an activation of the Na^+/K^+-ATPase. J. Neurochem. 69, 2132–2137 (1997)
10. Shulman, R.G.: Functional imaging studies: linking mind and basic neuroscience. Am. J. of Psychiatry (2001)
11. Sokoloff, L., Reivich, M., Kennedy, C., des Rosiers, M.H., Patlak, C.S., Pettigrew, K.D., Sakurada, O., Shinoara, M.: The [^{14}C]deoxyglucose method for the measurement of local cerebral glucose utilization: theory, procedure, and normal values in the conscious and anesthetized albino rat. J. of Neurochem. 26, 897–916 (1977)
12. Sokoloff, L.: Relationship between functional activity and energy metabolism in the nervous system: whether, where and why? In: Lassen, N.A., Ingvar, D.H., Raichle, M.E., Friberg, L. (eds.) Brain work and mental activity, pp. 52–64. Munskgaard, Copenhagen (1991)
13. Svarer, C., Iaw, I., Holm, S., Mørch, N., Paulson, O.: Estimation of the glucose metabolism from dynamic PET-scan using neural networks (1995), available at citeseer.ist.psu.edu/227145.html
14. Takano, T., Tian, G.F., Peng, W., Lou, N., Libionka, W., Han, X., Nedergaard, M.: Astrocytes mediated control of cerebral blood flow. Nat. Neurosci. 9, 260–267 (2006)
15. Volterra, A., Meldolesi, J.: Astrocytes, from brain glue to communication: the revolution continues. Nat. Rev. Neurosci 6, 626–640 (2005)

Steady-State Properties of Coding of Odor Intensity in Olfactory Sensory Neurons

Ondřej Pokora[1,2] and Petr Lansky[2]

[1] Department of Mathematics and Statistics, Faculty of Science, Masaryk University,
Janackovo namesti 2a, 602 00 Brno, Czech Republic
pokora@math.muni.cz
[2] Institute of Physiology, Academy of Sciences of Czech Republic, Videnska 1083,
142 20 Prague 4, Czech Republic
lansky@biomed.cas.cz

Abstract. Several models for coding of odor intensity in olfactory sensory neurons are investigated. Behavior of the systems is described by stochastic processes of binding (and activation). Characteristics how well the odorant concentration can be estimated from the knowledge of response, the concentration of bounded (activated) neuron receptors, are studied. This approach is based on the Fisher information and analogous measures. These measures are computed and applied to locate the coding range, levels of the odorant concentration which are most suitable for estimation. Results are compared with the classical (deterministic) approach to determine the coding range via steepness of the input-output transfer function.

1 Introduction and Methods

Models of coding of odor intensity in olfactory sensory neurons are studied. The response, concentration of bound (activated) receptors, depends on input signal, concentration of odorant in perireceptor space. The dependency of response on signal is realized through the input-output transfer function, $f(s)$. To obtain statistical characteristics of the models we use their discrete stochastic versions. We focus on the steady-state solutions and their properties.

How well the constant signal, s, which is assumed to be log-concentration of the odorant, can be determined from a knowledge of the response, $R_A(s)$, concentration of bound (or activated, $R_A^*(s)$) receptors and which signal levels are optimal, that means can be well determined from the knowledge of random sample of $R_A(s)$, is investigated. $R_A(s)$ is assumed to be a random variable with some (continuous) distribution dependent on scalar parameter s. In other words, we consider an experiment in which a fixed odorant concentration is applied k-times and steady-state responses of the system are observed. These are independent (it is random sample) realizations of random variable $R_A(s)$ from which we wish to determine s.

Note there are two properties limiting the optimal signal determination. First, the minimal resolution ability. The system cannot distinguish two response values that are near one another and the corresponding signal values are declared as equal. Moreover, there are two bounds of the response, the threshold and saturation, between them the neuron can reliably code the information. Corresponding range of signals (or its part) is called dynamic (coding) range (for details see [5]). Second, the fluctuation of realizations of the response. On the same signal level, observed responses are not equal.

In models we explore, the deterministic input-output transfer function, $f(s)$, is assumed to be equal to mean value, $E(R_A(s))$, of random variable describing the binding process stochastically. The classical, deterministic, approach to determine the optimal signal is based on the first derivative of the input-output transfer function, $f(s)$, with respect to s. As an optimality measure the quantity

$$J_1(s) = \frac{\partial E(R_A(s))}{\partial s} \tag{1}$$

is used. Higher the value of $J_1(s)$ the better determination of the odorant concentration, s, can be achieved.

An alternative approach, we use here, is based on statistical properties of the response. This method was used by [3] in analysis of statistical properties of generated interspike intervals. Let us suppose that the observed concentration of bound (activated) receptors in steady-state, $R_A(s)$ ($R_A^*(s)$), is a continuous random variable with a distribution belonging to the regular parametric family of probability density functions, $g(x; s)$, with the odorant log-concentration, s, as a parameter.

Determination of the signal, s, from known response, $R_A(s)$, corresponds to its estimation, $\hat{s}$, in chosen family of probability density functions. As a measure of signal optimality is used the Fisher information (see [4])

$$J(s) = \int \frac{1}{g(x; s)} \left(\frac{\partial g(x; s)}{\partial s} \right)^2 dx \tag{2}$$

with respect to signal, s. The Fisher information, $J(s)$, is the inverse asymptotic variance of the best unbiased estimator, $\hat{s}$, of s, $\mathrm{Var}(s) \geq J(\hat{s})^{-1}$. Hence, higher the Fisher information $J(s)$ the better estimation of s can be achieved. In some cases the analytical expression of the Fisher information may be difficult. Then we can use the lower bound, $J_2(s) \leq J(s)$, of the Fisher information, (see [3])

$$J_2(s) = \frac{1}{\mathrm{Var}(R_A(s))} \left(\frac{\partial E(R_A(s))}{\partial s} \right)^2 = \frac{J_1(s)^2}{\mathrm{Var}(R_A(s))} , \tag{3}$$

which only requires the knowledge of first two moments of the distribution g.

2   Models

We describe three models for odorant binding and receptor activation and corresponding steady-state moments. Let A, R, R_A and R_A^* denote the odorant, unbound (free), bound (occupied) and activated receptor, respectively. Let us suppose that the count (concentration), n, of receptor sites and the concentration, $[A] = \exp(s)$, of odorant A is constant during the binding (activation) process.

2.1 Basic Interaction

Unbound (free) receptors, R, compete for odorant molecules, A, through the interaction

$$A + R \underset{k_{-1}}{\overset{k_1}{\rightleftharpoons}} R_A , \tag{4}$$

where k_1 and k_{-1} are the association and dissociation rates. Every receptor can be either free or occupied. The model can be described as birth and death process with states $\{0, 1, \ldots, n\}$, initial probabilities $(1, 0, \ldots, 0)$, birth rates $\lambda_i = k_1(n - i)\exp(s)$ and death rates $\mu_i = k_{-1}i$, $i = 0, 1, \ldots, n$ (see [1,2] for details).

According to the probability distribution of stationary state of the process, the mean and variance in steady-state can be computed. Due to the fact, that values $R_A(s)$ are rather high, replacing a discrete variable by its continuous variant – by concentration – is justified. Then, if the maximal concentration of bound receptors is scaled to one ($n = 1$), the mean and variance are

$$E\left(R_A(s)\right) = \frac{1}{1 + K_1 \exp(-s)} , \tag{5}$$

$$\text{Var}\left(R_A(s)\right) = \frac{K_1 \exp(-s)}{n\left(1 + K_1 \exp(-s)\right)^2} , \tag{6}$$

where $K_1 = k_{-1}/k_1$ is the dissociation constant. The variance has its maximum located at $s = \log K_1$ and is symmetric around this point. Moreover, the variance tends to zero for extremal values of odorant concentration. The mean and standard deviation of R_A are plotted in Fig. 1a.

2.2 Basic Interaction with Simple Activation

In this more complex model it is assumed that binding of the odorant molecule is not sufficient to trigger the response, the bound receptor must be activated. Model described by [2] supposes that each occupied receptor can either become activated, R_A^*, with probability $p \in (0; 1)$, or stay inactive, R_A, with probability $1 - p$, independently of its past behavior and of the behavior of other receptors. Such an interaction corresponds to the following transition diagram,

$$
\begin{array}{ccc}
 & A + R & \\
k_{1n}\diagup\ k_{-1} & & k_{-1}\ \diagdown k_{1a} \\
R_A \underset{k_d}{\overset{k_a}{\rightleftharpoons}} & & R_A^*
\end{array}
\tag{7}
$$

where $k_{1a} = pk_1$ and $k_{1n} = (1 - p)k_1$ are association rates for the activated and inactivated state, $k_a = pc$ and $k_d = (1 - p)c$ are rates of activation and deactivation and $c > 0$ is a constant controlling the rate of activation-deactivation

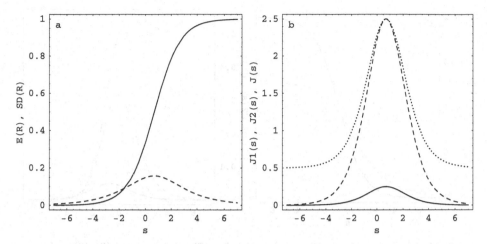

Fig. 1. Model of basic interaction (4) with moments (5), (6) and parameters $K_1 = 2$, $n = 10$. (a) Mean $E(R_A(s))$ (solid line) and standard deviation of $R_A(s)$ (dashed). The standard deviation of R_A tends to zero for extremal odorant concentrations. (b) Optimality criteria $J_1(s)$ (solid line), $J_2(s)$ (dashed) and $J(s)$ (dotted). All their maxima are located at $s_1 = 0.693$.

process. We are interested in the concentration of activated receptors, R_A^*. Its steady-state moments are (see [2])

$$E\left(R_A^*(s)\right) = \frac{p}{1 + K_1 \exp(-s)} \ , \tag{8}$$

$$\mathrm{Var}\left(R_A^*(s)\right) = \frac{p(1-p)}{n(1 + K_1 \exp(-s))} + \frac{p^2 K_1 \exp(-s)}{n\left(1 + K_1 \exp(-s)\right)^2} \ . \tag{9}$$

Limit moments are $E\left(R_A^*(\infty)\right) = p$ and $\mathrm{Var}\left(R_A^*(\infty)\right) = p(1-p)/n$. The variance is purely ascending from zero to $p(1-p)/n$ for $p \in (0, 0.5]$. For $p \in (0.5, 1]$, it increases from zero to maximal value $n^{-1}/4$ achieved at $s = \log K_1 - \log(2p - 1)$ and then decreases to $p(1-p)/n$. Both the mean and standard deviation of R_A^* are depicted in Figs. 2a and 3a.

2.3   Double Step Interaction

In the double-step interaction, which is an extension of model (7), the interaction between free, R, bound, R_A, and activated receptors, R_A^*, is formed by the transitions via schema

$$L + R \underset{k_{-1}}{\overset{k_1}{\rightleftharpoons}} R_A \underset{k_{-2}}{\overset{k_2}{\rightleftharpoons}} R_A^* \ , \tag{10}$$

where two further parameters, rate constants k_2 and k_{-2}, characterise the activation (deactivation) process (see [6] for details). In contrast with the model (7),

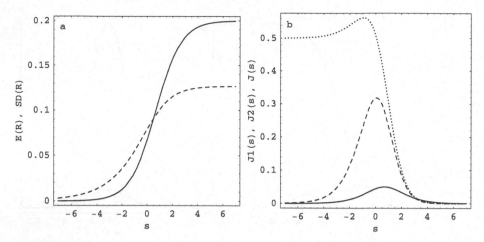

Fig. 2. Model of interaction with simple activation (7) with moments (8), (9) and parameters $K_1 = 2$, $n = 10$, $p = 0.2$. (a) Mean $E(R_A^*(s))$ (solid line) and standard deviation of $R_A^*(s)$ (dashed). The variability of R_A^* remains positive for high odorant concentrations. (b) Optimality criteria $J_1(s)$ (solid line), $J_2(s)$ (dashed) and $J(s)$ (dotted). J_1 achieves its maximum at $s_1 = 0.693$, J_2 at $s_2 = 0.072$ and J at $s_0 = -0.931$.

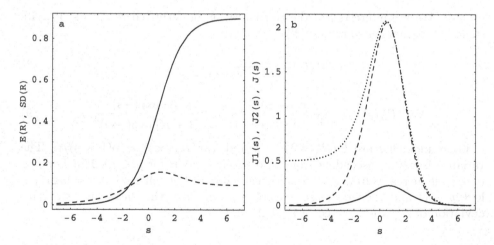

Fig. 3. Model of interaction with simple activation (7) with moments (8), (9) and parameters $K_1 = 2$, $n = 10$, $p = 0.9$. (a) Mean $E(R_A^*(s))$ (solid line) and standard deviation of $R_A^*(s)$ (dashed). The standard deviation has a maximum located at $s = 0.916$ and remains positive for high odorant concentrations. (b) Optimality criteria $J_1(s)$ (solid line), $J_2(s)$ (dashed) and $J(s)$ (dotted). J_1 achieves its maximum at $s_1 = 0.693$, J_2 at $s_2 = 0.535$ and J at $s_0 = 0.467$.

in this model it is unable to pass between the unbound and activated state without crossing the bound inactivated state. Discrete version of the model (with n receptors) can be represented as an Markovian process with states

$\{(i,j);\ 0 \leq i+j \leq n\}$ and its moments can be computed using stationary probability distribution. Scaling the maximal concentration to one, the steady-state mean value of the concentration of activated receptors, R_A^*, is

$$E\left(R_A^*(s)\right) = \frac{1}{1 + K_2\left(1 + K_1 \exp(-s)\right)}\ , \qquad (11)$$

where $K_2 = k_{-2}/k_2$ is the dissociation constant of the activation-deactivation process. It is difficult to express the variance analytically, nevertheless it can be computed numerically and fitted by a smooth function. A function of the form

$$\frac{a + b \exp(-s)}{1 + c \exp(-s) + d \exp(-2s)} \qquad (12)$$

with estimated parameters $a > 0, b, c, d$ seems to be a good approximation of the variance $\mathrm{Var}(R_A^*(s))$. Then, the relations $\mathrm{Var}(R_A^*(-\infty)) = 0$ and $\mathrm{Var}(R_A^*(\infty)) = a$ hold. The mean and standard deviation of R_A^* are depicted in Fig. 4a.

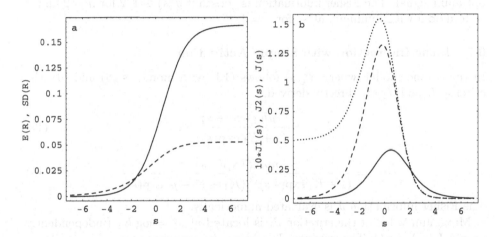

Fig. 4. Model of the double-step interaction (10) with mean (11) and dissociation constants $K_1 = 2$, $K_2 = 5$. The variance is approximated by fitted function $\mathrm{Var}(R_A^*(s)) = (0.00278 + 0.00084 \exp(-s)) / (1 + 1.628 \exp(-s) + 0.483 \exp(-2s))$. (a) Mean $E(R_A^*(s))$ (solid line) and standard deviation of $R_A^*(s)$ (dashed). The variability of R_A^* remains positive for high odorant concentrations. (b) Optimality criteria $10\,J_1(s)$ (solid line), $J_2(s)$ (dashed) and $J(s)$ (dotted). J_1 achieves its maximum at $s_1 = 0.511$, J_2 at $s_2 = -0.158$ and J at $s_0 = -0.379$.

3   Results

We assume that R_A and R_A^* have Gaussian distribution,

$$R_A^{(*)}(s) \sim \mathrm{N}\big(E(R_A^{(*)}(s)), \mathrm{Var}(R_A^{(*)}(s))\big)\ , \qquad (13)$$

with the mean and variance in accordance with the specific binding model.

3.1 Basic Interaction

In the first model, where $R_A(s)$ follows (13) with moments (5) and (6), all the optimality criteria are directly derived,

$$J_1(s) = \frac{K_1 \exp(-s)}{(1 + K_1 \exp(-s))^2} \; , \tag{14}$$

$$J_2(s) = \frac{nK_1 \exp(-s)}{(1 + K_1 \exp(-s))^2} = nJ_1(s) \; , \tag{15}$$

$$J(s) = \frac{1}{2} + \frac{(n-2)K_1 \exp(-s)}{(1 + K_1 \exp(-s))^2} . \tag{16}$$

All the criteria are unimodal and always achieve their maxima for $s_1 = \log K_1$, $J_1(s_1) = 1/4$, $J_2(s_1) = J(s_1) = n/4$ (J holds this for $n > 2$ only). Moreover, they are symmetric around the point s_1 and the conditions $J_1(\pm\infty) = J_2(\pm\infty) = 0$ and $J(\pm\infty) = 1/2$ hold. As depicted in Fig. 1b, all the criteria give the same optimum signal. The Fisher information is constant $J(s) \equiv 1/2$ for $n = 2$ and it is unimodal with minimum at s_1 for $n = 1$.

3.2 Basic Interaction with Simple Activation

In the second model, where $R_A^*(s)$ follows (13) with moments (8) and (9), the criteria J_1 and J_2 are directly derived,

$$J_1(s) = \frac{pK_1 \exp(-s)}{(1 + K_1 \exp(s))^2} \; , \tag{17}$$

$$J_2(s) = \frac{npK_1^2 \exp(-s)}{(1 + K_1 \exp(-s))^2 (K_1 + (1 - p) \exp(s))} . \tag{18}$$

The Fisher information J is evaluated numerically.

Maximum value of the criterion J_1 is located at $s_1 = \log K_1$ (independently on p), $J_1(s_1) = p/4$. The criterion J_2 achieves its maximum for

$$s_2 = \log K_1 - \log \frac{4(1 - p)}{\sqrt{9 - 8p} - 1} . \tag{19}$$

For $p \in (0, 1)$, the relation $s_1 - \log 2 < s_2 < s_1$ holds. For lower probabilities p the location of maximum of J_2 is shifted to lower levels of the signal. As plotted in Figs. 2b and 3b, the criterion J holds this feature, too. Limit values of the criteria are $J_1(\pm\infty) = J_2(\pm\infty) = J(\infty) = 0$, $J(-\infty) = 1/2$.

3.3 Double Step Interaction

Considering the model (10), where $R_A^*(s)$ follows (13) with mean (11), the criterion J_1 is equal to

$$J_1(s) = \frac{K_1 K_2 \exp(-s)}{(1 + K_2 (1 + K_1 \exp(-s)))^2} \tag{20}$$

and its maximum $J_1(s_1) = (1 + K_2)^{-1}/4$ is located at $s_1 = \log K_1 + \log K_2 - \log(1 + K_2)$. Comparing this point of maxima with the model of basic interaction with the same dissociation constant K_1, where $s_1 = \log K_1$ holds, point of maximum in the double-step interaction is shifted to lower levels of the signal.

Conditions $J_1(\pm\infty) = J_2(\pm\infty) = J(\infty) = 0$ and $J(-\infty) = 1/2$ hold. Fitted variance $\mathrm{Var}(R_A^*)$ and the criteria J_2 and J are computed numerically. All the optimum criteria are plotted in Fig. 4b. Maximum values of J_2 and J appear to be shifted to the lower levels of signal than s_1.

4   Conclusions

In the model of basic interaction all three criteria give the same result. In two other models the measures based on Fisher information and its lower bound are more sensitive to lower concentrations. The variance of concentration of activated receptors remains positive for high odorant concentrations, that means the receptors oscillate between activated and inactivated state. It should be noted, that using other then Gaussian probability distribution, the results obtained using the Fisher information may differ.

Acknowledgments. This work was supported by European Biophysics' Societies Association, Center for Theoretical and Applied Statistics LC06024, Center for Neuroscience LC554, Research project AV0Z50110509 and by the Academy of Sciences of the Czech Republic Grant (Information Society, 1ET400110401).

References

1. Lam, H.S., Lampard, D.G.: Modelling of Drug Receptor Interaction with Birth and Death Processes. Journal of Mathematical Biology 12, 153–172 (1981)
2. Lansky, P., Rospars, J.-P.: Coding of odor intensity. BioSystems 31, 15–38 (1993)
3. Lansky, P., Greenwood, P.E.: Optimal Signal Estimation in Neuronal Models. Neural Computation 17, 2240–2257 (2005)
4. Lehmann, E.L.: Theory of Point Estimation. Wiley, New York (1983)
5. Nizami, L.: Estimating auditory neuronal dynamic range using a fitted function. Hearing Research 167, 13–27 (2002)
6. Rospars, J.-P., Krivan, V., Lansky, P.: Perireceptor and Receptor Events in Olfaction. Comparison of Concentration and Flux Detectors: a Modeling Study. Chem. Senses 25, 293–311 (2000)
7. Stemmler, M.: A single spike suffices: The simplest form of stochastic resonance in model neurons. Network: Computation in Neural Systems 7, 687–716 (1996)

Input Identification in the Ornstein-Uhlenbeck Neuronal Model with Signal Dependent Noise

Laura Sacerdote[1], Cristina Zucca[1], and Petr Lánský[2]

[1] Dept. of Mathematics, University of Torino
Via Carlo Alberto 10, 10123 Torino, Italy
[2] Institute of Physiology, Academy of Sciences of Czech Republic
Videnská 1083, 142 20 Prague 4, Czech Republic

Abstract. The Ornstein-Uhlenbeck neuronal model is investigated under the assumption that the amplitude of the noise depends functionally on the signal. This assumption is deduced from the procedure in which the model is built and it corresponds to commonly accepted understanding that with increasing magnitude of a measured quantity, the measurement errors (noise) are also increasing. This approach based on the signal dependent noise permits a new view on searching an optimum signal with respect to its possible identification. Two measures are employed for this purpose. The first one is the traditional one and is based exclusively on the firing rate. This criterion gives as an optimum signal any sufficiently strong signal. The second measure, which takes into the account not only the firing rate but also its variability and which is based on Fisher information determines uniquely the optimum signal in the considered model. This is in contrast to the Ornstein-Uhlenbeck model with constant amplitude of the noise.

1 Introduction

Noise is unavoidable in any living system and the experimental results, supported by theoretical investigations, show the prominent role of noise in the transfer of information in neural systems (Cecchi et al. 2000; and others). In most of the studies aimed on effects of noise in neural models, it has been assumed that the amplitude of the noise is independent of the incoming signal. This follows from the fact that the models were originally deterministic and simply modified by adding some type of noise. To overcome this lack of realism we investigated one of the most common neuronal models under the condition that the amplitude of the noise depends on the signal (Lánský and Sacerdote 2001; Sacerdote and Lánský 2002). There we do not employed artificial relationship between signal and noise, but we established it by pointing to an analogous version of the model with discrete state-space.

The so called frequency (input-output) transfer functions, in which the frequency of firing is plotted against the strength of the input signal, is commonly used to characterize the input-output properties of neurons and neuronal models, for a constant signal or under stedy state conditions.

F. Mele et al. (Eds.): BVAI 2007, LNCS 4729, pp. 368–377, 2007.
© Springer-Verlag Berlin Heidelberg 2007

By constructing the transfer functions, it is implicitly presumed, that the information in the investigated neuron is coded by the frequency of the action potentials (Adrian 1928). From this point of view, the steep part of the transfer function represents the optimum signal because a small change in the signal implies the largest change in the response. An alternative criterium to the optimum signal determination is based on the application of Fisher information measure. In this approach, the signal plays the role of an unknown parameter which should be estimated from observation of a random variable, in our case the interspike interval. The Fisher information in evaluating neural models has become a common tool recently (e.g., Stemmler 1996; Greenwood et al. 1999, 2000; Johnson and Ray 2004; Amari and Nakahara 2005 and many others).

In this paper we compare results based on these two measures applied on the stochastic leaky integrate-and-fire (LIF) model under the condition that the amplitude of noise is signal dependent. We show that the introduced dependency of noise magnitude from the signal is substantial for searching an optimum signal in the neuronal models. Indeed when the noise is independent of the signal there is no globally a unique level of optimal signal and finally the investigations end up with a search for an optimum noise under certain intensity of the signal. On the contrary here we obtain, under the knowledge of the properties of the model, a unique optimum signal.

2   The Model and Its Properties

The LIF model is common concept in computational neuroscience and the number of direct and indirect references to it would be very large (Tuckwell 1988; Gerstner and Kistler 2002; Burkitt 2006 and others). Here we consider the Stein model (1965), where the membrane depolarization is described as a one-dimensional stochastic process, $X = \{X(t), t \geq 0\}$, for which holds

$$dX(t) = -\frac{X(t)}{\tau} + adP^+(t) + idP^-(t) ; X(0) = 0. \tag{1}$$

Here $\tau = RC > 0$ is the membrane time constant ($\tau = RC$, where R is the membrane resistance and C is its capacitance); time zero is the moment of the last generated action potential; $i < 0 < a$ are constants; $P^+(t)$, $P^-(t)$ are two independent homogeneous Poisson processes with intensities λ and ω, respectively, reflecting the time dynamics of all excitatory and inhibitory inputs acting upon the neuron. The values a and i represent the mean amplitudes of excitatory and inhibitory postsynaptic potentials. The initial depolarization is assumed to be equal to the equilibrium level shifted to zero. The first and second infinitesimal moments of X defined by (1) are

$$M_1(x) = \lim_{\Delta \to 0} \frac{E\left[\Delta X(t) \mid X(t) = x\right]}{\Delta} = -\frac{x}{\tau} + \lambda a + \omega i, \tag{2}$$

$$M_2(x) = \lim_{\Delta \to 0} \frac{E\left[(\Delta X(t))^2 \mid X(t) = x\right]}{\Delta} = \lambda a^2 + \omega i^2, \tag{3}$$

where $\Delta X(t) = X(t + \Delta) - X(t)$.

In diffusion neuronal models, the membrane depolarization is described by a scalar diffusion process X given by the Itô-type stochastic differential equation specified by two real-valued functions (called a drift and an infinitesimal variance)(e.g. Tuckwell 1988). The drift coefficient reflects the local average rate of displacement and local variability is represented by the infinitesimal variance. These two coefficients coincide with the infinitesimal moments. Therefore, identifying infinitesimal moments (2) and (3) of model (1) with the infinitesimal moments of the diffusion model, a suitable diffusion approximation of the Stein's model is the O-U process

$$dX(t) = \left(-\frac{X(t)}{\tau} + \mu\right) dt + \sigma dW(t); \ X(0) = 0, \tag{4}$$

where μ, $\sigma > 0$ and $\tau > 0$ are constants; τ plays the same role as in equation (1) and W is the standard Wiener process. The parameters μ and σ^2 in (4) reflect the input signal and its variability resulting from the stochastic dendritic currents generated by action of other neurons (or by external stimulation in sensory neurons). As seen from (2) and (3), the parameter μ is a linear function of the rates λ and ω of the incoming excitatory and inhibitory postsynaptic potentials and σ depends on these intensities in a square root manner.

In models (1) and (4), the interspike intervals are identified with the first-passage time, T_μ, of the stochastic process X across a constant threshold, S,

$$T_\mu = \inf\{t \geq 0, X(t) > S \mid X(0) = 0 < S\}, \tag{5}$$

where index μ is used to stress that we investigated the FPT in dependency on the input μ. The time origin is the moment of the last firing. At these moments, the membrane potential is repeatedly reset to its initial value and the ISIs form a renewal process. The means of X given by (1) and (4) coincide, $E(X(t)) = \mu\tau\left(1 - \exp\left(-t/\tau\right)\right)$. If $E(X(\infty)) = \mu\tau \leq S$, then the regimen is called subthreshold and in absence of noise the neuron never fires. When $\mu\tau > S$, the stimulation is called suprathreshold and the neuron fires even in absence of the noise.

For suprathreshold stimulation in model (4) and for $\sigma \to 0$, the transfer function is

$$f(\mu) = \begin{cases} \left(\tau \ln\left(\frac{\mu\tau}{\mu\tau - S}\right)\right)^{-1} & \mu\tau > S \\ 0 & \mu\tau \leq S \end{cases}. \tag{6}$$

The asymptote of function (6) is

$$f_a(\mu) = (2\tau\mu - S)/2\tau S. \tag{7}$$

A complete solution of the first-passage-time problem in model (4) is not a simple task and therefore numerical (Ricciardi and Sato 1990) and simulation (Giraudo and Sacerdote 1999; Giraudo et al. 2001) techniques were proposed. In order to compute the mean $E(T_\mu)$ we directly applied so called Siegert formula

$$E(T_\mu) = \sqrt{\frac{\pi\tau}{\sigma^2}} \int_{-\mu\tau}^{S-\mu\tau} \left(1 + Erf\left(\frac{z^2}{\sigma^2\tau}\right)\right) \exp\left(\frac{z^2}{\sigma^2\tau}\right) dz \tag{8}$$

where $Erf(.)$ is the error function. For large μ we used the approximation

$$E(T_\mu) \approx \tau \ln\left(\frac{\mu}{\mu - S}\right) - \frac{\tau\sigma^2}{4}\left(\frac{1}{(\mu - S)^2} - \frac{1}{\mu^2}\right) \tag{9}$$

and

$$Var(T_\mu) \approx \frac{\tau^2\sigma^2}{2}\left(\frac{1}{(\mu - S)^2} - \frac{1}{\mu^2}\right), \tag{10}$$

found in Ditlevsen and Lánský (2005).

3 The Method

The spiking of a neuron from which the signal should be deduced is considered as a renewal process. Then the interspike intervals which lengths depend on signal μ, are independent realization of a random variable, T_μ. The transfer function is usually expressed as

$$f(\mu) = \frac{1}{E(T_\mu)}, \tag{11}$$

In this way the highest precision in determining the signal corresponds to the highest derivative of function (11). Hence we define a function

$$I_\mu^{(1)} = \frac{\partial}{\partial\mu}\left(\frac{1}{E(T_\mu)}\right) \tag{12}$$

and our criterion recognizes, as signal detected with the highest precision, the maximum of this function.

In order to measure information about μ in a more complete way than by (12), one has to consider the entire probability distribution, and not only the mean, $E(T_\mu)$, as a function of the signal. For this purpose we employ Fisher information. Under the condition that the random variable T_μ has probability density function belonging to a parametric family $g(t; \mu)$, the Fisher information with respect to the parameter μ is defined by

$$J_\mu = \int_0^\infty \frac{1}{g}\left(\frac{\partial g}{\partial\mu}\right)^2 dt. \tag{13}$$

The Fisher information is the inverse of the asymptotic variance of the normalized error from an asymptotically efficient estimator (Rao 2002). Thus, higher the Fisher information - more accurate estimate of μ can be achieved.

The Fisher information is used here under the renewal process assumption. In this case the Fisher information in n observations is just n-times the information per single observation, given by equation (13). For this reason it is clear that the information about μ is proportional to the number of spikes. The mean time required to obtain n measurements is $nE(T_\mu)$. Thus a measure of information per time unit is obtained by dividing J_μ by $E(T_\mu)$ (Lánský and Greenwood 2005). The normalized Fisher information with respect to the parameter μ is defined as

$$I_\mu = J_\mu / E(T_\mu). \tag{14}$$

To simplify the calculation a lower bound for the Fisher information can be introduced,

$$J_\mu^{(2)} = \frac{1}{Var(T_\mu)} \left(\frac{\partial E(T_\mu)}{\partial \mu} \right)^2, \tag{15}$$

where $Var(T_\mu)$ is the variance of the random variable T_μ. Analogously to the function given by equation (15), we define

$$I_\mu^{(2)} = J_\mu^{(2)} / E(T_\mu) \tag{16}$$

and search for its maximum to find an optimum signal. In general, three measures $I_\mu^{(1)}$, $I_\mu^{(2)}$ and I_μ differ by the order of moments required for their evaluation.

4   Results and Discussion

Before any attempt to determine the signal, intrinsic parameters of model (4), which do not depend on the input, should be specified. In accordance with generally accepted ranges, we fixed the firing threshold $S = 10\,\mathrm{mV}$ and the value of the time constant we set $\tau = 10\,\mathrm{ms}$. With this choice $\mu < 1$ represents a subthreshold signal and in the opposite case the signal is suprathreshold.

The procedure of diffusion approximation leading from equation (1) to (4) requires that the rates λ and ω are large and parameters a and i are small. Assuming the same relative effect of excitatory and inhibitory postsynaptic potentials, $a = -i$, from equations (2) and (3) we obtain

$$\mu = a(\lambda - \omega) \tag{17}$$

and

$$\sigma^2 = a^2(\lambda + \omega). \tag{18}$$

These formulas permit us to reinterpret the results obtained for the O-U model in terms of excitation and inhibition (λ and ω are the excitatory and inhibitory input rates).

In Lánský and Sacerdote (2001) we presented some hints about the values of the input parameters μ and σ, $\mu = 0.5\mathrm{mV/msec}$, $\sigma \cong 0.4\mathrm{mVmsec}^{-1/2}$. Another source of information about the input parameters in the O-U model should come immediately from the experimental data, but these estimates are quite rare. In Inoue et al. (1995) the estimated values of the parameter μ ranges from -6.77 to $3\mathrm{mV/msec}$ and σ goes from values close to zero up to $15\mathrm{mVmsec}^{-\frac{1}{2}}$. In other paper oriented on investigation of the parameters in the O-U model (Lánský et al. 2006), we concluded that parameter μ varies around 0.3 mV/msec. In that paper the estimation of σ was highly influenced by the fact that the data were filtered before the estimation. For a general discussion about the parameters of model (1) see Tuckwell and Richter (1978).

In general, changing (increasing) the net input μ can be achieved in two basic ways in model (4). Either the increase of excitation and inhibition is proportional or it is not. The proportional increase leads to a linear relationship between μ and σ^2. We use in this study

$$\sigma^2(\mu) = k\mu + \sigma_0^2, \tag{19}$$

where $k > 0$ is a constant of proportionality and σ_0^2 is the minimum level of noise. With this functional connection between signal and noise, we investigate the decoding ability of the neuron, i.e. identification of the signal, in any range, be it sub or suprathreshold. In nonproportional change we can observe a paradoxical result in which an increase of the net input μ decreases the firing frequency (Lánský and Sacerdote 2001). To achieve it, the increase of μ has to be accompanied by appropriate decrease of σ. This situation seems to be unprobable and is not investigated here.

Simple dependency (19) reminds Weber's law, often applied in psychophysics (Laming 1973). It implies, in particular, that when there is practically no signal there is no noise. So the model investigated here is

$$dX(t) = \left(-\frac{X(t)}{\tau} + \mu\right) dt + \left(k\mu + \sigma_0^2\right) dW(t), \tag{20}$$

and the question is how well μ can be deduced from the realization of the FPT.

The approximations for the mean and the variance of T_μ can be obtained simply substituting (19) in (9) and (10), while to obtain $\partial E(T_\mu)/\partial\mu$, required for the Fisher information evaluation (see below), the Siegert formula was applied, which gives

$$\frac{\partial E(T_\mu)}{\partial\mu} = \sqrt{\pi}\tau \left\{ \left(\sqrt{\tau}\xi - \frac{\mu k\sqrt{\tau}\xi^3}{2}\right) \left(1 - Erf\left(\mu\sqrt{\tau}\xi\right)\right) \exp\left(\mu^2\tau\xi^2\right) \right. \tag{21}$$
$$\left. - \left(\sqrt{\tau}\xi + \frac{(S-\mu\tau)k\xi^3}{2\sqrt{\tau}}\right) \left(1 + Erf\left(\frac{(S-\mu\tau)\xi}{\sqrt{\tau}}\right)\right) \exp\left(\frac{(S-\mu\tau)^2\xi^2}{\tau}\right) \right\},$$

where $\xi = 1/\sqrt{k\mu + \sigma_0}$.

We aim to find how well the signal, which is directly μ in equation (20) can be determined on the basis of observation of random variable T_μ defined by (5). For this purpose we investigate measures, $I^{(1)}$ and $I^{(2)}$, which were introduced above. As mentioned, despite we were not able to prove it analytically, all the numerical calculations suggested that $J_\mu^{(2)} = J_\mu$ for the first-passage-time distribution of the O-U process. Therefore, we restrict ourselves on calculation of the lower bound $J_\mu^{(2)}$ because it is numerically less demanding than calculation of the Fisher information.

In the inlet of Fig. 1 are presented the frequency transfer functions for our model in which the amplitude of noise increases with the signal in accordance with equation (19). We fixed the parameter k in such a way, that at $\mu = -4$, the

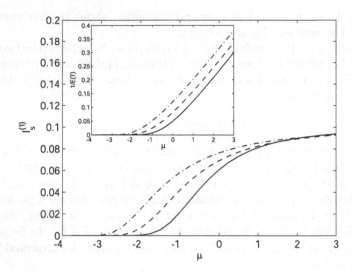

Fig. 1. Dependency of $I_\mu^{(1)}$ on the signal μ for the model with the noise amplitude changing with the signal. In the inlet the corresponding frequency transfer functions are given. Full line: $\sigma^2 = 5\mu+21$, dashed line: $\sigma^2 = 10\mu+41$, dash-dot line: $\sigma^2 = 17.32\mu+70$.

noise amplitude is equal to one. We can see that the transfer functions are similar to those obtained for LIF model with constant amplitude of noise (e.g. Lansky et al. 2007, Fig. 2b). It can be shown by using formula (8) that with increasing μ the transfer function becomes linear with asymptote given by equation (7).

Thus this measure reaches no unique optimum (see Fig. 1). With increasing signal the measure achieves a constant value. Taking the derivative of the asymptote with respect of μ, we obtain the asymptotic inverse value of $I_\mu^{(1)}$. It means that by using this criterion, there is no unique optimum level for the signal μ. Even before crossing the threshold stimulation $\mu = 1$ mV/msec, the transfer function becomes almost linear. It means that any sufficiently strong signal can be determined equally well if only the firing frequency is taken into account.

The evaluation of the lower bound of Fisher information $J_\mu^{(2)}$ and of its normalized version $I^{(2)}$ is illustrated in Fig. 2 and 3. We can see in Fig. 2 that the Fisher information steeply decreases with increasing μ. The decrease is even faster than for the model with constant infinitesimal variance, as was shown in Lánský et al. (2007, Fig. 1). There is no direct implication from this result, but if we combine Fig. 1 and Fig. 2, we obtain Fisher information in natural time (see Fig. 3) and we can see that the measure reaches its maximum. This is a surprising result because as the firing frequencies were compared (Lánský and Sacerdote 2001), signal-dependent noise did not bring too much change into the behavior of the neuron. We can see in Fig. 3 several features:

1. There is always a unique maximum of this measure. Hence there exists an optimal level of the signal and a range of signals, i.e. a coding range, around this optimum can be determined similarly well.

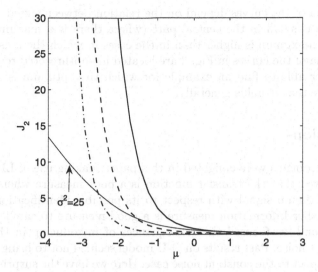

Fig. 2. Dependency of the Fisher information on the signal μ for the model in which the noise amplitude changes with the signal. Full line: $\sigma^2 = 5\mu + 21$, dashed line: $\sigma^2 = 10\mu + 41$, dash-dot line: $\sigma^2 = 17.32\mu + 70$. Comparison with the Fisher information where the noise amplitude is constant $\sigma^2 = 25$.

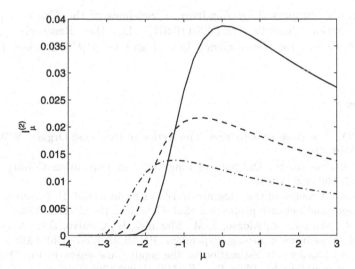

Fig. 3. Dependency of $I_\mu^{(2)}$ on the signal μ for the model in which the noise amplitude changes with the signal. Full line: $\sigma^2 = 5\mu + 21$, dashed line: $\sigma^2 = 10\mu + 41$, dash-dot line: $\sigma^2 = 17.32\mu + 70$.

2. Since the curves in Fig. 3 are asymmetrical the coding range is narrow in the left part (low intensity) but quite broad on the right part (strong signal).

3. The maxima of the curves depend on the relation between signal and noise. If the noise is small in the central part (where there is a maximum of the curve), the maximum is higher than in the cases in which the noise is large.
4. The maxima of the curves in Fig. 3 are located in subthreshold regimen. We were neither able to find an example for which the optimum is above one nor to prove that it holds generally.

5   Conclusions

Two different problems were enlighted in this paper making use of LIF models. Firstly we showed that the transfer function is a poor measure when one wish to detect an optimum signal with respect to its possible identification. On the contrary the Fisher Information measure is a good measure to catch the signal optimality. Second we focused the consequences of introducing in the models signal dependent noise. Past results on O-U model seemed not to bring too much change with respect to the constant noise case. Here we have the surprising result that there exists always an optimal level of the signal and that there is a range of signals around this optimum that can be determined similarly well. All our results are refered to the O-U process because its simplicity but we expect similar features also with more complex diffusion models.

Acknowledgments. Supported by Academy of Sciences of the Czech Republic Grant (Information Society, 1ET400110401), by the Research project AV0Z5011922, Center for Neuroscience LC554 and by MIUR Project PRIN-Cofin 2005.

References

1. Adrian, E.D.: The Basis of Sensation: The Action of the Sense Organs. WW Norton, New York (1928)
2. Amari, S., Nakahara, H.: Difficulty of Singularity in Population Coding. Neur. Comput. 17, 839–858 (2005)
3. Burkitt, A.N.: A review of the integrate-and-fire neuron model. II. Inhomogeneous synaptic input and network properties. Biol. Cybernet. 95, 97–112 (2006)
4. Cecchi, G.A., Sigman, M., Alonso, J.-M., Martinez, L., Chialvo, D.R., Magnasco, M.O.: Noise in neurons is message dependent. PNAS 97, 5557–5561 (2000)
5. Ditlevsen, S., Lánský, P.: Estimation of the input parameters in the Ornstein-Uhlenbeck neuronal model. Phys. Rev. E 71(3), 11907 (2005)
6. Gerstner, W., Kistler, W.M.: Spiking neuron models. Single neurons, populations, plasticity. Cambridge University Press, Cambridge (2002)
7. Giraudo, M.T., Sacerdote, L.: An improved technique for the simulation of first passage times for diffusion processes. Commun. Statist.- Simula. 28, 1135–1163 (1999)
8. Giraudo, M.T., Sacerdote, L., Zucca, C.: A Monte Carlo method for the simulation of first passage times of diffusion processes. Methodol. Comput. Appl. Probab. 3, 215–231 (2001)

9. Greenwood, P.E., Ward, L., Russell, D., Neiman, A., Moss, F.: Stochastic resonance enhances the electrosensory information available to paddlefish for prey capture. Phys. Rev. Lett. 84, 4773–4776 (2000)
10. Greenwood, P.E., Ward, L., Wefelmeyer, W.: Statistical analysis of stochastic resonance in a simple setting. Phys. Rev. E 60, 4687–4695 (1999)
11. Inoue, J., Sato, S., Ricciardi, L.M.: On the parameter estimation for diffusion models of single neurons' activities. Biol. Cybern. 73, 209–221 (1995)
12. Johnson, D.H., Ray, W.: Optimal Stimulus Coding by Neural Populations Using Rate Codes. J. Comput. Neurosci. 16, 129–138 (2004)
13. Laming, D.R.J.: Mathematical psychology. Academic Press, New York (1973)
14. Lánský, P., Sacerdote, L.: The Ornstein-Uhlenbeck neuronal model with signal-dependent noise. Phys. Lett. A 285, 132–140 (2001)
15. Lánský, P., Sacerdote, L., Zucca, C.: Optimum signal in a diffusion leaky integrate-and-fire neuronal model. Mathematical Biosciences 207(2), 261–274 (2007)
16. Lánský, P., Greenwood, P.E.: Optimal signal estimation in neuronal models. Neur. Comput. 17, 2240–2257 (2005)
17. Lánský, P., Sanda, P., He, J.: The parameters of the stochastic leaky integrate-and-fire neuronal model. J. Comput. Neurosci. 21, 211–223 (2006)
18. Rao, R.C.: Linear Statistical Inference and its Applications. John Wiley, New York (2002)
19. Ricciardi, L.M., Sacerdote, L.: The Ornstein-Uhlenbeck process as a model of neuronal activity. Biol. Cybern. 35, 1–9 (1979)
20. Ricciardi, L.M., Sato, S.: Diffusion processes and first-passage-time problems. In: Ricciardi, L.M. (ed.) Lectures in Applied Mathematics and Informatics, Manchester Univ. Press, Manchester (1990)
21. Sacerdote, L., Lánský, P.: Interspike interval statistics in the Ornstein-Uhlenbeck neuronal model with signal-dependent noise. BioSys. 67, 213–219 (2002)
22. Stein, R.B.: A theoretical analysis of neuronal variability. Biophys. J. 5, 173–195 (1965)
23. Stemmler, M.: A single spike suffices: The simplest form of stochastic resonance in model neurons. Network: Comput. Neur. Syst. 7, 687–716 (1996)
24. Tuckwell, H.C.: Introduction to Theoretical Neurobiology. Cambridge Univ. Press, Cambridge (1988)
25. Tuckwell, H.C., Richter, W.: Neuronal interspike time distribution and the estimation of neurophysiological and neuroanatomical parameters. J. Theor. Biol. 71, 167–183 (1978)

Numerical Results on the Hodgkin-Huxley Neural Network: Spikes Annihilation

Dragos Calitoiu[1], John B. Oommen[2], and Doron Nussbaum[3]

[1] Carleton University, Ottawa, K1S 5B6, Canada
dcalitoi@scs.carleton.ca
[2] *Chancellor's Professor*; *Fellow: IEEE* and *Fellow: IAPR*, Carleton University,
Ottawa, K1S 5B6, Canada
oommen@scs.carleton.ca
[3] Carleton University, Ottawa, K1S 5B6, Canada
nussbaum@scs.carleton.ca

Abstract. One of various families of Neural Networks (NN) that have
been used in the study and development of the field of Artificial Intelligence (AI) is the Hodgkin-Huxley (HH) Network. In addition to the
computational properties of the HH neuron, it also can be used to reasonably model biological phenomena, and in particular, in modeling neurons
which are "synchronized/desynchronized". The HH Neuron is a nonlinear system with two equilibrium states: A fixed point and a limit cycle.
Both of them co-exist and are stable. By using a perturbation method,
the behavior of this neuron can be switched between these two equilibria,
namely *spiking* and *resting* respectively. The process of changing from
spiking to resting is referred to as *Spike Annihilation*. In this paper, we[1]
numerically prove the existence of a brief excitation (input) which, when
delivered to the HH neuron during its repetitively firing state, annihilates
its spikes. We also derive the characteristics of this brief excitation.

1 Introduction

Hopfield and Grossberg suggested that the process of coding information using
neural networks (NN) can be developed around the regime involving fixed point
attractors. There are also alternative philosophies, motivated by clinical neurologists, that indicated that brain dynamics is characterized by cyclic and weakly
chaotic regimes. Some theories proposed in Artificial Intelligence (AI) have attempted to exploit cyclic attractors for information encoding. One of these theories consists of indexing the "attractor information items" by means of external
stimuli rather than by using initial conditions as proposed by Hopfield. This
algorithm implies the existence of alternative responses to external stimuli and
a switching process from one of these potential attractors to another in response

---

[1] The second author also holds an *Adjunct Professorship* with the Department of
Information and Communication Technology, Agder University College, Grooseveien
36, N-4876 Grimstad, Norway. The work of this author was partially supported by
the Natural Sciences and Engineering Research Council of Canada.

F. Mele et al. (Eds.): BVAI 2007, LNCS 4729, pp. 378–387, 2007.

to any input stimulus. The process of retrieving the information stored in the cycles depends on the model chosen for the investigation: A more realistic model for the neuron will have a richer range of non-linear behaviors (represented by stable or unstable limit cycles). Our paper investigates the process of retrieving the information stored in the cycles, namely that of controlling the neuron (to be more specific, a Hodgkin-Huxley (HH) neuron).

We present now a few considerations about the dynamical properties of the HH neuron. This neural model can be in one of two states: A resting state (corresponding to a stable fixed point) and a state that fires in response to certain forms of stimulation (corresponding to a stable limit cycle). One problem to be considered here is the switching of the neuron from one equilibrium mode to the other, which is a phenomenon which can occur without modifying the number and the stability of the equilibria.

From a classical system theory point of view, the equilibrium point of a non-linear dynamical system may disappear or may lose its stability if a control parameter is changed, depending on the type of bifurcation displayed by the system. In our research, the HH neuron is considered to be a dynamical nonlinear system whose equilibrium states are not to be radically changed with regard to its stability. We investigate the case when both equilibria, namely the fixed point and the limit cycle, co-exist and remain stable. In this particular situation, the system is bi-stable, and with a carefully chosen synaptic input, it is possible to switch the behavior from being resting to one which demonstrates spiking, or from being spiking to a resting (spike annihilation) mode.

This above stimulus, chosen to be a brief pulse of current, is not a control parameter. Its behavior affects neither the existence of the equilibrium points, nor their stability. The control parameter is the strength of the constantly applied current and, during our investigation, it is set to be constant. We argue that injecting a constant current into the axon is not equivalent to injecting a brief pulse of current. In the former, the system can go through a bifurcation of the equilibrium by changing the existence of the equilibria or by affecting their stability. In the latter, however, the system can jump to an alternate location in the state space, which is achieved by the system resetting the initial condition. The neuron is driven to a state of "shock", and consequently, the membrane potential instantly switches to a new value. The fixed point, corresponding to the resting state, co-exists with the limit cycle, which corresponds to the spiking state, and the system continues to be bistable.

1.1 Contribution of the Paper

As we stated before, our paper investigates only one stage of the process of retrieving the information stored in the cycles, namely that of controlling the HH neuron. In contrast to the previous pieces of work, which validated experimentally or anticipated theoretically that annihilation is possible, we achieve the followings: (i) We numerically prove that the problem of spike annihilation has a well defined solution. (ii) We formally derive the characteristics of the proposed solution.

2   The Bistable HH Neuron

In this section we investigate the stability-related characteristics of the HH neuron. In the previous section, we stated that the HH neuron can be perceived as a dynamical nonlinear system with two stable equilibria. We intend to explore, *numerically*, the system defined by Equations (1) and (2) proposed by Rinzel and Wilson [2], which, indeed, approximate the Hodgkin-Huxley neuron:

$$\frac{dV}{dt} = \frac{1}{\tau}[-(a_1 + b_1V + c_1V^2)(V - d_1) - e_1R(V + f_1) + +B + \sigma], \quad (1)$$

$$\frac{dR}{dt} = \frac{1}{\tau_R}(-R + a_2V + b_2), \quad (2)$$

where $a_1, a_2, b_1, b_2, c_1, d_1, e_1, f_1, \tau$, and τ_R are constants[2], B is the background activity[3], and σ is an excitation stimulus. Consequently, we propose to discover, *numerically*, the number and the positions of the limit cycles. The numerical approach to yield the number and the relative positions of the limit cycles of the system described by Equations (1) and (2), is the only reasonable strategy (instead of an analytical one) to tackle the problem.

To render our consideration meaningful, in the following, we shall derive:

1. The fixed points of the HH neuron by solving the system of equation described by the isoclines,
2. The Jacobian corresponding to the system described by Equations (1) and (2), at the fixed points,
3. The eigenvalues of the Jacobian, by solving the characteristic equation associated with the Jacobian, and
4. The requirements on the eigenvalues as specified by the *Hopf Bifurcation Theorem* for identifying the limit cycle.

2.1   Computing the Equilibrium States

Consider a system described by Equations (1) and (2). We compute the the equilibrium states by solving the system of equations described by their isoclines. Using the settings of Rinzel and Wilson [2], assigned to mimic real-life brain phenomena, Equations $\frac{dV}{dt}$ and $\frac{dR}{dt}$ become:

$$\frac{1}{\tau}[-(17.81 + 47.71V + 32.63V^2)(V - 0.55) - 26R(V + 0.92) + +B] = 0 \quad (3)$$

---

[2] In their experiments, Rinzel and Wilson [2] set the constants as: $a_1 = 17.81$, $b_1 = 47.71$, $c_1 = 32.63$, $d_1 = 0.55$, $e_1 = 0.55$, $f_1 = 0.92$, $a_2 = 1.35$, $b_2 = 1.03$, $\tau = 0.8$ ms and $\tau_R = 1.9$ ms. The stimulus σ was expressed in $\mu A/100$, and V was measured in deci-volts.

[3] The background activity generates limit cycles in the system. Without this value, the system will converge through the stable spiral point.

and

$$\frac{1}{\tau_R}(-R + 1.35V + 1.03) = 0. \tag{4}$$

The equilibrium states can thus be computed as solutions of Equations (3) and (4) leading to the resulting cubic polynomial equation:

$$-32.6304V^3 - 64.8632V^2 - 50.6416V + Bk - 14.8424 = 0. \tag{5}$$

The roots of the Equation (5) can be computed for specific values of B.

2.2 Computing the Jacobian

Using the same settings of Rinzel and Wilson [2], the Jacobian matrix of the "real-life" HH neural system becomes:

$$J(V,R) = \begin{pmatrix} \frac{\partial V(V,R)}{\partial V} & \frac{\partial V(V,R)}{\partial R} \\ \frac{\partial R(V,R)}{\partial V} & \frac{\partial R(V,R)}{\partial R} \end{pmatrix},$$

where $\frac{\partial V(V,R)}{\partial V} = -122.36V^2 - 74.40V + 10.55 - 32.5R$; $\frac{\partial V(V,R)}{\partial R} = -32.5V - 29.9$; $\frac{\partial R(V,R)}{\partial V} = 0.71053$ and $\frac{\partial R(V,R)}{\partial R} = -0.52632$.

The Equation (4) can be used to eliminate R from the partial derivatives and thus, the Jacobian becomes:

$$J(V) = \begin{pmatrix} -122.36V^2 - 118.28V - 22.937 & -32.5V - 29.9 \\ 0.71053 & -0.52632 \end{pmatrix}.$$

2.3 Finding the Bifurcation Point

We shall now consider the problem of finding the neuron's bifurcation point by using the dynamical matrix of the system. This value of the bifurcation point is used to "set" the neuron so as to render it to be bi-stable. As before, using the same settings of Rinzel and Wilson [2], the condition to have imaginary roots applied to the Jacobian, generates the equation: $-122.36V^2 - 118.28V - 22.937 - 0.52632 = 0$, whose roots are -0.6879 and -0.2788.

From Equation (5), we can compute the value of B that corresponds to the root $V = -0.6879$. This value[4], of $B = 0.0777$, generates a bifurcation in the system. The second root, -0.2788, does not have any biological significance, being distant from the resting potential of the neuron.

The values of the roots (and the corresponding stability consequences) are tabulated in Table 1 as a function of b. Examining Table 1, we can conclude (using the notation of the *Hopf Bifurcation Theorem*) that $\alpha = 0.0777$. Thus, if $B < 0.0777$ (namely, $\beta < \alpha$) the system has an stable spiral point. If $B > 0.0777$, the stable spiral point became unstable and the system has a stable limit cycle.

---

[4] The more exact value is 0.07773267 and it is obtained for V=-0.687930 and R=0.101295. The Largest Lyapunov exponent for this Hopf bifurcation is 1.000287e-002.

Table 1. Eigenvalues of the Jacobian computed from the real root of the equilibrium equation obtained with particular values of the background stimulus B. Last column describe the stability of the equilibrium, namely S (stable) and U (unstable).

B	$V_{equilib}$	λ_1	λ_2	
0	-0.6979	-0.2565+2.2485i	-0.2565-2.2485i	S
0.025	-0.6947	-0.1731+2.2534i	-0.1731-2.2534i	S
0.05	-0.6915	-0.0909+2.2554i	-0.0909-2.2554i	S
0.06	-0.6902	-0.0579+2.2555i	-0.0579-2.2555i	S
0.065	-0.6896	-0.0909+2.2554i	-0.0909-2.2554i	S
0.07	-0.6889	-0.0909+2.2554i	-0.0909-2.2554i	S
0.075	-0.6883	-0.0100+2.2548i	-0.0100-2.2548i	S
0.08	-0.6876	+0.0075+2.2543i	+0.0075-2.2543i	U
0.085	-0.6870	0.0225+2.2537i	0.0225-2.2537i	U
0.1	-0.6850	0.0721+2.2514i	0.0721-2.2514i	U
0.125	-0.6818	0.1504+2.2456i	0.1504-2.2456i	U
0.15	-0.6785	0.2299+2.2372i	0.2299-2.2372i	U
0.2	-0.6720	0.3825+2.2138i	0.3825-2.2138i	U
0.25	-0.6655	0.5300+2.1820i	0.5300-2.1820i	U

The value $B = 0.0777$ is a subcritical or hard Hopf bifurcation point. The system has an unstable limit cycle for $B < 0.0777$, and this is a point that is not observable in the real world due to its instability. It is only possible to *detect* the *consequences* of its presence.

2.4   The Stable and Unstable Limit Cycles

If we consider B to be a control parameter, we can analytically compute the equilibrium point, which, for certain values of σ, leads to a *spiral stable point*, and which, for other values of σ, leads to an *unstable spiral point*. The behavior around a specific value, namely the change of the stability of the equilibrium point, induces the concept of a *subcritical (hard) Hopf bifurcation*.

Let us focus on the issue of the limit cycles themselves. By plotting the evolutions of the numerical solutions of the system (Equations (1) and (2)), we discover that for the settings of Rinzel and Wilson [2], there is a stable limit cycle to the right of the bifurcation point. To identify a hypothetical unstable limit cycle, we can modify the system's equations to make time run "backwards". The modification, which consists of rendering the sign of the two constants, τ and τ_R, to be negative, changes the unstable limit cycle to become asymptotically stable. In this way, by using a numerical method, we can identify the position of a second limit cycle, which happens to be unstable. The stable spiral point is surrounded by this unstable limit cycle which, in turn, acts as a *separatrix* defining a basin of attraction for the stable point.

In Figure 1 we present the stable and unstable limit cycles, together with the isoclines ($\frac{dV}{dt} = 0$ and $\frac{dR}{dt} = 0$). The trajectory starts at the point indicated by '1' and follows the arrowed curves. Observe that in the case of Figure 1 Left, the trajectory of the HH neuron trajectory follows the stable limit cycle,

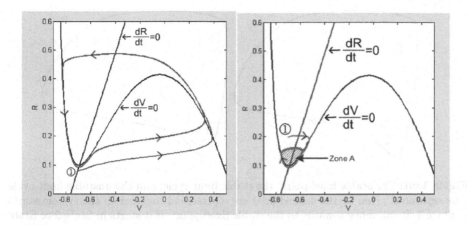

Fig. 1. Left: The phase space representing the *stable* limit cycle and the resulting isoclines ($\frac{dV}{dt} = 0$ and $\frac{dR}{dt} = 0$) obtained by using Rinzel and Wilson settings for the HH neuron. The starting point, (represented with '1') is $V_0 = -0.7$, and $R = 0.08$. In addition, $B = 0.08$. **Right:** The phase space representing the *unstable* limit cycle and the isoclines for Rinzel and Wilson settings for the HH neuron. In this graph, the starting point (represented with '1') is $V_0 = -0.7$, and $R_0 = 0.2$ and must be outside the zone called $Zone_A$, defined by the cycle. In addition, $B = 0.08$.

and in Figure 1 Right, the trajectory follows the unstable limit cycle. When B is increased from the resting value, the steady state remains asymptotically stable and the spikes are generated only after the bifurcation point is reached, by increasing the value of B. In other words, the HH neuron indicates spiking at $B = 0.0777$, and the spiking process continues for all values of $B > 0.0777$.

3   The Problem of Annihilation

The problem of the annihilation of spikes for the HH neuron involves moving the state of the system, by using a pulse stimulus, from outside a particular zone (denoted as $Zone_A$) to being inside $Zone_A$, where $Zone_A$ is a basin of attraction of the stable spiral point which is described by an unstable limit cycle. For example, if the system is characterized by the settings specified by Rinzel and Wilson [2], $Zone_A$ is contained in the region given by $V \in [-0.6, -0.8]$ and $R \in [0.1, 0.15]$, as depicted in Figure 1, Right. Figure 2 contains all the steady states of the system, including the stable spiral point, and the stable and unstable limit cycles.

The success of the annihilation process depends on four crucial issues: (i) What should be the initial point (V, R) for the system to exhibit annihilation? (ii) When should the pulse stimulus, σ, be applied to the system to annihilate it? (iii) What should the amplitude of the pulse stimulus be for the annihilation

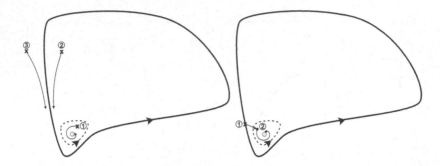

Fig. 2. Left: The stable fixed point, the stable limit cycle, and the unstable limit cycle (the *separatrix* given by the dashed line) are represented together. If the system starts in State 1, it will move towards to the stable fixed point. If it starts in State 2 or State 3, it will converge to the stable limit cycle. **Right:** If the system starts in a carefully chosen configuration at State 1 on the stable limit cycle, the system can be driven to State 2 by applying a carefully chosen stimulus. From this state, it will then go to the stable fixed point.

to be achieved? (iv) What should the duration of the pulse stimulus be for the annihilation to be achieved[5]?

The solution of the annihilation problem consists of determining a stimulus which adequately responds to all the above questions. In Figure 2 Left, we present the annihilation process. If the system starts in a carefully chosen configuration at State 1 on the stable limit cycle, the system can be driven to State 2 by applying a carefully chosen stimulus. From this state, it will then go to the stable fixed point.

We propose to solve the problem of annihilation using a numerically computation of the characteristics of the stimuli that achieve annihilation, for the settings of Rinzel and Wilson [2]. The strategy consists of proposing an algorithm for computing the moment of insertion, the magnitude, and the duration of the stimulus used to annihilate the system.

3.1 The HH Neuron Annihilation Theorem

Since we are interested in annihilating the spikes, we shall demonstrate that this can be done by invoking a discretized time model. To achieve this, first of all, we rewrite the dynamical system of equations for a bistable model of the HH neuron in a discrete-time manner as:

$$V[n+1] = V[n] + \tfrac{1}{\tau}[-(a_1 + b_1 V[n] + c_1 V^2[n])(V[n] - d_1)$$

$$- e_1 R[n](V[n] + f_1) + Bk + \sigma], \tag{6}$$

$$R[n+1] = R[n] + \frac{1}{\tau_R}(-R[n] + a_2 V[n] + b_2). \tag{7}$$

---

[5] In this paper, we consider the duration of the stimulus to be equal to unity.

The general **Theorem of Annihilation** is formally written below.

Theorem 2 (HH Neuron Annihilation)

Consider a system described by its discretized dynamical equations:
$$\begin{pmatrix} V[n+1] \\ R[n+1] \end{pmatrix} = \begin{pmatrix} V[n] \\ R[n] \end{pmatrix} + \begin{pmatrix} f_1(V[n], R[n]) \\ f_2(V[n], R[n]) \end{pmatrix} + \underline{S}[n], \text{ with } n = 0, 1, ..$$

(8)

where f_1 and f_2 specify the unexcited dynamics, and $\underline{S}[n]$ is the excitation applied to the system.

If the system has a stable limit cycle, a stable spiral point and an unstable limit cycle which separates the fixed point and the stable limit cycle, then, there exists an excitation function $\underline{S}[n]$, which equals 0 everywhere except at a specific point $(V[0], R[0])$ on the stable limit cycle, at which point $\underline{S}[0]$ has the value $[A, 0]^T$ for a duration of one iteration, and which when applied to the system, forces it from the stable limit cycle to the stable spiral point.

The proof can be found in [1].

In order to discover the properties of the stimulus which achieves the spikes annihilation, we have also opted to simulate this numerically. To do this, we have to work towards controling the model, namely, to move the system to a bi-stable state, in the neighborhood of the bifurcation point. All these steps will be discussed in the next Section.

4   Experiments

In this Section, the results described in Section 3 are experimentally evaluated to verify their validity, and to explore the state space characteristics for each parameter of the annihilation stimulus. If a background stimulus B is applied to create a train of spikes, we demonstrate that it is possible to annihilate the limit cycle with an additional *brief* stimulus, and to move the system from a stable limit circle to an unstable spiral point.

The solution to this problem has to respond to the following questions: (i) What is the amplitude of the stimulus? (ii) What is the suitable phase when the stimulus should be applied? (iii) How long should the stimulus be?

In order to analyze the effect of the stimulus, we have to choose initial values for V and R. We have studied this for various numerical settings, but present only one scenario here, in the interest of brevity. We consider an example of train spikes that we propose to annihilate with a stimulus. This train of spikes started from $V = -0.7043$ and $R = 0$, and was generated with $B = 0.08$.

For generating a spike train, we chose the background stimuli B to be between 0.68 and 0.7. We here chose $V = -0.7043$ and $R = 0$ as initial values for the subsequent simulations.

Table 2. The amplitude and the moment of insertion of the stimulus σ in order to annihilate the spikes

ms	$B(0.68)$		$B(0.69)$		$B(0.7)$	
	σ_{min}	σ_{max}	σ_{min}	σ_{max}	σ_{min}	σ_{max}
3.0	0.4	1.54				
3.1	0.14	1.57				
3.2	0.06	1.47	0.47	1.15		
3.3	0.028	1.34	0.19	1.23	0.50	0.97
3.4	0.014	1.21	0.09	1.17	0.21	1.08
3.5	0.008	1.09	0.05	1.06	0.11	1.02
3.6	0.005	0.97	0.03	0.95	0.062	0.93
3.7	0.003	0.85	0.018	0.84	0.03	0.83
3.8	0.002	0.74	0.016	0.73	0.027	0.72
3.9	0.002	0.63	0.01	0.63	0.02	0.62
4.0	0.002	0.53	0.008	0.53	0.016	0.52
4.1	0.002	0.45	0.007	0.44	0.015	0.43
4.2	0.002	0.35	0.007	0.34	0.015	0.33
4.3	0.002	0.25	0.008	0.25	0.017	0.25
4.4	0.002	0.16	0.011	0.15	0.024	0.14

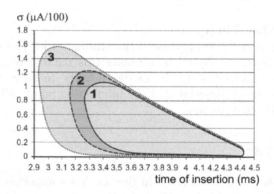

σ (μA/100)

time of insertion (ms)

Fig. 3. The three areas for the three different values for the background, B, namely 0.70 (*Area 1*), 0.69 (*Area 2*) and 0.68 (*Area 3*)

For an additional stimulus σ, namely, a pulse of 0.1 ms duration, we identified its position of insertion and its amplitude. In Table 2, we present the range of values for σ (the minimum and the maximum values) for which we can annihilate the spikes. Each range is computed for different times of insertion of the stimulus (from 3.0 ms to 4.4 ms) and for different values of the quantity B. The neuron exhibited spikes only for a range of B, which spanned values from 0.68 to 0.70 μA/100. The results from Table 2 are depicted in Figure 3.

From this simulation we can conclude that: (i) The neuron spikes only for a specific range of values of B; (ii) If the neuron generates spikes, these can be annihilated with particular stimuli found in the area plotted in Figure 3.

Consider now the problem of finding the vulnerable phase of the neuron. For a value of $\sigma = 0.7$, we see from Figure 3 that the length of the vulnerable phase is between 3 ms to 4.4 ms, namely a width of 1.4 ms. Since the period is 6 ms, the neuron has an interval of 23.33% of its period where one can insert a proper stimulus to achieve this annihilation.

The reader can observe that for the experimental results reported, we conducted experiments with three different background stimuli in order to to generate a bi-stable neuron, namely with $B = 0.68$, $B = 0.69$ and $B = 0.70$. For all these values, we present in Figure 3 three areas, namely those depicted by *Area 1*, *Area 2*, and *Area 3*. Fortunately, there seems to be an inclusion relationship between these three areas, namely *Area 1* is included in *Area 2* and *Area 3*. Consider now the scenario when a population of neurons from the brain receives a constant stimulus with the magnitude having a minimum value of 0.68 for an interval of time. If the task is to annihilate this population, choosing a stimulus with a magnitude corresponding to the minimum background is successful because such a stimulus is common for all background stimuli greater than this minimum one. For example, the area corresponding to a $B = 1$ includes the area corresponding to the minimum $B = 0.68$ - simplifying the choice of the stimulus.

5   Conclusions

This paper briefly described the HH neuron and formally derived various properties of its stability. It also described numerically that the problem of spike annihilation has a well defined solution, and presented an algorithm for computing the properties of the stimulus. We add that the method of perturbation with brief stimuli differs from the classical approach of modifying the control parameter and changing the Jacobian of the system. In our approach, we keep the system bi-stable all the time, and our task is to switch between these two states without modifying their stability. To conclude, we analyzed the properties of this pulse, namely, the range of time when it can be inserted and its magnitude.

References

1. Calitoiu, D.: Chaotic Systems for Pattern Recognition and Brain Modelling. Ph.D. Thesis, Carleton University (2006)
2. Wilson, H.: Spikes decisions and actions: Dynamical foundations of neuroscience. Oxford University Press (1999)

Excitatory Synaptic Interaction on the Dendritic Tree

Vito Di Maio

Istituto di Cibernetica "E. Caianiello" del CNR
Via Campi Flegrei, 34, 80078 Pozzuoli (NA), italy
vdm@biocib.cib.na.cnr.it, v.dimaio@cib.na.cnr.it
http://www-biocib.cib.na.cnr.it/DiMaio/dimaio.html

Abstract. A neuron in the Central Nervous System receives thousands of synaptic inputs arriving both from close and long distance neurons. Synaptic activity modulates the electrical potential of the neuronal membrane producing an output which is regulated by a threshold mechanism. The crossing of the threshold produces a sequence of spikes which, very likely, is the neural representation of the stimulus. Dendrites usually receive the larger amount of synaptic inputs and their role in synaptic integration and code formation in the single neuron cannot be neglected. In the present paper, the mutual interaction of a couple of excitatory synapses connected to the same, terminal, dendritic trunk will be analyzed and some aspects of the computational ability of the "dendritic machinery" will be discussed.

1 Introduction

The problem of how the brain processes and stores information is one of the most important challenges of the modern neurobiology. The information processing implies that the stimuli (physical or chemical) arriving to the brain are converted (coded) in a language understandable to the neurons which are the building blocks of the brain. It is very likely that the code is embedded into the sequence of spikes generated by a neuron when it receives information by means of active synaptic contacts. How the code is embedded into the spikes sequence is, however, still unclear. According to the "coincidence detector" theory, the stimulus produces a coincidence of synaptic activation on the receiving neuron which emits a precise sequence of spikes that is the neural representation of the code [1,2, among others]. Some evidences seem to support this hypothesis. For example, some neurons, located in the auditory system of birds, behave like "coincidence detectors" because they fire a precise sequence of spikes only when they receive the input from both ears with a delay of $10 - 100\mu s$ between the two ears [3]. On the other side, the "rate code" hypothesis is based on the idea that code is embedded in the spike frequency (ϕ) defined as the number of spikes (N) emitted in the time unit (s) computed on an adequate time window (i.e., $\phi = \frac{N}{s}$). This hypothesis is supported by several evidences demonstrating that the times between the spikes in the sequence (Inter Spikes Intervals, *ISIs*) can be fitted by

F. Mele et al. (Eds.): BVAI 2007, LNCS 4729, pp. 388–397, 2007.
© Springer-Verlag Berlin Heidelberg 2007

a Poissonian distribution and, hence, it is not a precise time sequence but a random sequence. The "rate code" hypothesis, then, assumes that not the precise sequence but a frequency of spike is the neuronal representation of the stimulus. Many models based on this idea have been proposed [7,12,14,27, among many others]. More recently, however, the idea that several different coding systems, ranging from the "coincidence detector" to the "rate code", could be simultaneously active in the brain, is becoming very common among the neuroscientists. What is the nature of the code and what are the relationships between the code and the stimulus properties are interesting research topics for experimental and theoretical investigators. In the theoretical field, computational experiments are carried with different approaches and using different models, the simplest of which is the so called Leaky Integrate-and-Fire (LIF) model. Usually, in this model, synapses are simulated as periodic inputs (those located on the soma or in its proximity) or a stochastic noise (dendritic synapses) and the neuron is simply considered a linear integrator of these signals. The integration process generates variations of the membrane potential which can reach a threshold level producing a spike sequence [4,5,13,15,16]. Other models, with different degrees of complication, are often used. For example, some very detailed models consider a large number of variables as the geometry of the neuron, the precise synaptic spatial distribution, the intrinsic synaptic variability, and many others [28].

Code generation and information processing implie a sort of computational ability by the system. Starting from McCullogh and Pitts [19] the largest part of computational ability is traditionally assigned to a network of neurons, considered as virtually able to perform any kind of computation, more than to the single neuron to whom only a low computational ability is attributed. Neuron has always been considered only as simple linear integrator with a threshold mechanism necessary to have a point of non linearity to perform a minimal computation [18,31]. A relevant observation in this contest is that, to perform a good level of computation, a system needs essentially non linear mechanisms [31] and the threshold system do not represent the unique non linear mechanism in the dynamics of the neuron. For example, since the pioneering work of Rall [21,22], it has been shown that synaptic inputs arriving to dendritic tree can sum non linearly. The activity of any synapse, in fact, can influence the activity of the others, located in the proximity, by changing the driving force which generate the Post Synaptic Current (PSC). This force is the difference between the membrane potential (V_m) and the equilibrium potential of ions (E_{ions}) involved in the PSC generation (see equation 3). Due to the high input impedance of the membrane in small dendrites and spines (in the $G\Omega$ order [23,24,25,26]), the PSC generated by the activation of a synapse produces a significant Post Synaptic Potential (PSP) and this variation of V_m modify the driving force for any close synapse producing the non linear summation of the single PSPs. For two (or more) excitatory synapses, located very close each other, this effect consist in a reduction of the driving force and consequently a reduction of the efficacy (amplitude) of the Excitatory Post Synaptic Potential (EPSP) of any other active synapses. Synapses sum linearly only if they are located very far from each other because the PSP decreases with distance according to the cable equation [23,24]. If we consider the activation of excitatory and inhibitory synapses in an appropriate time window, then this mutual interaction become much more evident. Inhibitory synapses, in fact, can have a shunting or also a *"veto"* effect on excitatory synapses depending on their relative position and on the activation time. This effect is maximized when the inhibitory synapse is located on the path of the current flow of the active excitatory synapses [17]. Other mechanisms able to modify the "normal" synaptic behavior in the dendritic tree can be found in several different types of neurons. For example, backpropagation of spikes from the axon to the soma and dendrites can, in some cases, produce dramatic changes of membrane potential in the dendritic region because of the activation of voltage dependent channels. The activation of these channels can sustain for a longer time the membrane potential depolarization with a consequent long lasting modification of the driving force for all the synapses in the region. A similar effect is produced by Ca^{++} spikes which can be generated in the dendrites of some neurons. This effect, when present, can produce variation of membrane potential so strong to be able to trigger normal spikes at the hillock (which is the region of the axon where usually spikes arises). These are only few examples of possible sources of non linearity in dendritic tree of the neurons. Both passive and active dendritic properties seem, then, to play a key role in the computation ability of the single neuron [8,9,11,17,18,26].

In the present paper will be shown some regulatory effects that two active excitatory synapses can have each other. Ideally, it will be shown that a dendritic branch can be considered as a special kind of *"electrical synapse"* which can modulate the activity of another branch to whom it is grafted on. These mechanisms, in a hierarchy of dendritic branches and synapses, can determine the output behavior of the neuron.

2   Model

The simplest way to represente a dendritic branch is to consider it as a cylinder. In Fig. 1 there is a schematic representation of a dendritic branch (B) with diameter d_B connected to a major branch (A) with diameter d_A (i.e., $d_A > d_B$). Although A and B can have both excitatory (connected mainly on the spines) and inhibitory (10% of the total and connected mainly on the shaft [20]) synapses, in the present paper only excitatory synapses are considered and are labeled as S_A and S_B depending on the branch (A or B) to which they are connected. The branch B of Fig. 1 can be considered as a special case of *"electrical synapse"* of the branch A. In fact, although the current can flow in both directions ($B \Rightarrow A$ or $A \Rightarrow B$) and mainly depends on the difference of potential between the two branches ($V_A - V_B$), there is a preferential flux of current from B to A due to the minor axial resistance in A with respect to B (the axial resistance is inversely proportional to the diameter). In order to simplify, let us assume that at time $t = 0$ the two branches are isopotential and that $\frac{dV}{dt} = 0$ (i.e., no current flows in any direction). Let us also assume

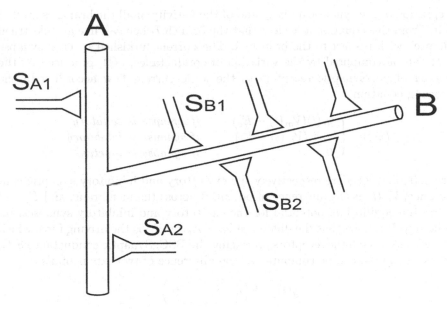

Fig. 1. Schematic representation of a dendritic brach B grafted on a larger dendritic branch A. Synapses are labeled according to the branch A or B (S_A or S_B) respectively.

that at any time $t > 0$ one or more excitatory synapses on branch B become active producing an Excitatory Post Synaptic Current (EPSC). Being the EPSC a depolarizing current, the resulting EPSP will increase the membrane potential. This transient variation of potential will produce a current flowing from B to A. The total current generated on branch B with n synapses will be given by

$$I_B(t) = \sum_{j=1}^{n} I_{S_{B_j}}(t) \tag{1}$$

where $I_{S_{B_j}}(t)$ is the current produced at time t by the j_{nd} synapses on branch B. Equation (1) assumes some simplifications which are: a) it consider B as a terminal branch with no further ramification; b) it considers the length of B negligible with respect to the space constant λ and c) it considers the active synapses so closed each other that the effect of one synapse can be "experienced" simultaneously by neighboring synapses without filtering of the signal.

For the branch A, which is not a terminal branch, and for a short segment around the point where B is grafted on A, we can consider

$$I_A(t) = I_B(t) + \sum_{i=1}^{n} I_{S_{A_i}}(t) \tag{2}$$

where $I_{S_{A_i}}(t)$ is the current contribution given by i_{nd} synapse connected to the branch A. In general, the activity produced by a branch is given by the integration of the synaptic activity and of the activity of all the branches grafted on it. From this equation it is clear that the branch B behaves like an "electrical synapse" with respect to the branch A. The current furnished by each synapse $I_S(t)$ can be computed by the variation of conductance, $g(t)$, produced by the opening of postsynaptic receptors to the ionic current flow according to the following equation

$$I_S(t) = \begin{cases} g_e(t)(V_m(t) - E_e) & \text{if synapse is ecitatory} \\ g_i(t)(V_m(t) - E_i) & \text{if synapse is inhibitory} \\ 0 & \text{if synapse is inactive} \end{cases} \quad (3)$$

here $g_e(t)$ and $g_i(t)$ are respectively the excitatory and inhibitory synaptic conductance, $V_m(t)$ is the difference of potential across the membrane, and E_e and E_i are the equilibrium potential for the excitatory and inhibitory synapses, respectively. It follows that the difference $V_m - E_e$ (or E_i) is the driving force which moves ions through the receptors producing the PSC. Synaptic conductance $g(t)$, for each synapse, can be computed as the difference of two exponentials

$$g(t) = k \left(e^{-\frac{t}{\tau_2}} - e^{-\frac{t}{\tau_1}} \right) \quad (4)$$

where τ_1 and τ_2 are the rise and decay time constants respectively and k is a constant related to the maximal value of the conductance ($\bar{g}$). Since the goal of the present paper is to show the mutual interaction of excitatory synapses placed on a small terminal branch, the activity of only two excitatory synapses, positioned on the branch B of Fig. 1, has been simulated. The initial value of the membrane potential was assumed equal to the resting potential (V_r) of the neurons ($\sim -70mV$) and then computation of $V(t)$ was made by the Ohm's law

$$V(t) = V_r + R_{in} I_B(t) \quad (5)$$

where R_{in} is the input resistance of the dendritic branch and $I_B(t)$ is computed according to equation (1). It has to be noted that this is an oversimplified system. For long segments, for example, one has to consider the mutual distance between synapses because the signal decays with distance as predicted by the cable equation

$$\lambda^2 \frac{\partial^2 V}{\partial X^2} = V + \tau \frac{\partial V}{\partial t} \quad (6)$$

where X is the distance from the origin, $\lambda = \sqrt{\frac{R_m}{R_i} \frac{d}{4}}$ is the space constant depending on the membrane resistance (R_m), the axial resistance (R_i) and the diameter (d) of the dendrite and $\tau = R_m C_m$ is the time constant, being C_m the membrane capacitance expressed in Farad.

3   Simulation and Results

Simulations were carried by a C^{++} program under Linux. As a first approximation, the interaction of only two excitatory synapses, very close each other,

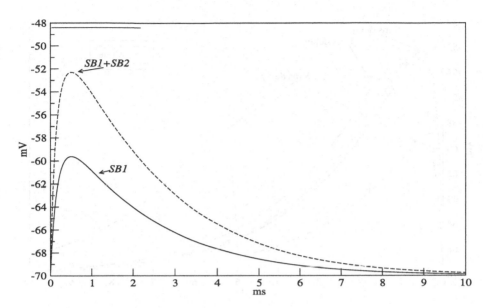

Fig. 2. cEPSP obtained by the simultaneous activation of two excitatory synapses on branch B. The horizontal line indicates the peak value that should be reached if the two synapses would sum linearly.

on a short dendritic branch (as for example S_{B_1} and S_{B_2} in Fig. 1) has been considered. The input resistance R_{in} was kept constant at $5Gohm$ and the resting potential was $V_r = -70mV$. For the computation of $g(t)$ of both synapses, the same values of τ_1 and τ_2 have been used (0.2 and 2.0ms, respectively). The equilibrium potential for excitatory synapses E_e was set to $-10mV$ and k was kept such to have $I(t)$ with a peak amplitude and time course comparable with electrophysiological evidences [6,10] and with the results of computational experiments [29,30] on glutamatergic synapses. The total simulation time was $10ms$ and the simulation time step (dt) was $0.001ms$ for all the experiments. In a first set of computational experiments, two excitatory synapses (S_{B_1} and S_{B_2} of Fig. 1) were simultaneously activated. The results are shown in Fig. 2 where the horizontal line indicates the level that the peak should reach if the two synapses would be independent and linearly summing (i.e., if $I_{B_1}(t) + I_{B_2}(t) \simeq 2I_{B_1}(t)$). In a second set of experiments, one of the two synapses (S_{B_1}) has been activated at time $t_1 = 0$ while S_{B_2} with a delay time $t_1 \geq 0$ ($\Delta T = t_2 - t_1$). In Fig. 3 the results of computational experiments with activation delay (ΔT) ranging from 0 to $5ms$ are shown. For three values of ΔT (0, 1 and $5ms$, respectively) the potential has been labeled and plotted by dashed lines to show some important differences in the produced outputs. An important value to consider in this case is the time to peak (t_{p_1}) of the EPSP produced by S_{B_1}. If we consider the time interval $\Delta'T = t_{p_1} - t_1$, it is evident that for $\Delta T < \Delta'T$, the effect of the two synapses seems to be synergic although the composite peak decreases linearly as a function ΔT. For $\Delta T > \Delta'T$ the progressive separation of the two traces

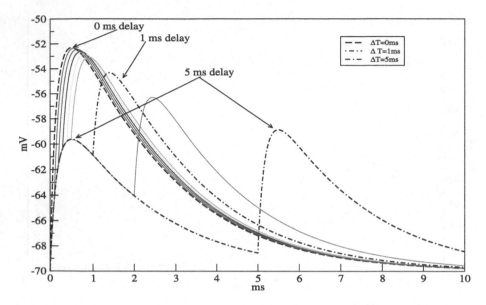

Fig. 3. Activation of S_{B_1} and S_{B_2} of Fig.1 with different delay time (ΔT) of activation. Three major traces (dashed lines) are labeled corresponding to $\Delta T = 0, 1$ and $5ms$. Non dashed lines correspond to intermediate values of ΔT $(0.1, 0.2, 0.3, 0.4, 0.5$ and $2.0ms)$.

produces different patterns which seem more addressed to mantain an higher level of potential in B than to give a "strong" electrical signal to A.

4 Discussion

The results presented here, although simulating only the most elementary configuration possible for synaptic arrangements on a dendritic branch, give some useful indications on the role that dendrites play in the fine regulation of the activity of the neuron. Just considering two synapses for the short time of $10ms$, it is evident that a large range of possible signals can be generated and used to control the activity not only of synapses co-localized on the same dendritic shaft but also of those positioned on a different branch. Each active synapse can influence the activity of the others by modulating the membrane potential and, consequently, the driving force acting on the dynamics of all the active synapses. The most evident effect of this is shown in Fig. 2 where the mutual effect of two simultaneously activated synapses is shown. The results presented in Fig. 3 show that different kinds of output are produced depending on the delay times of activation of the synapses (ΔT). The non linear summation of the EPSPs produces a composite EPSC (cEPSC) that for $\Delta T \leq \Delta'T$ is smaller than the linear sum of two single EPSPs but able to produce a strong change of membrane potential with a flow of a transient current from the minor branch to the major one ($B \Rightarrow A$, in our example). The amplitude of the cEPSP decreases by increasing the activation delay time for $\Delta T \leq \Delta' T$. For $\Delta T > \Delta' T$, the peaks of the two EPSPs separate and the cEPSP shows patterns with different characteristics. These are some possible configurations produced by the activation of two excitatory synapses. The activation of many excitatory synapses on a dendritic branch can produce a large variety of different patterns. If we consider also the inhibitory synapses, then the number of different electrical patterns that can be generated is very large. In fact, while on one side the Inhibitory Post Synaptic Current (IPSC), being an iperpolarizing current, can reduce or abolish the EPSP (which is produced by a depolarizing current), on the other side the iperpolarization or ripolarization of the membrane potential increases the driving force acting on the excitatory synapses. For the case of only excitatory synapses, it has to be stressed that a paradoxical effect could be the inversion of their role. In fact, if many excitatory synapses, close each other, become active in a short time window (synchronization) the depolarization can drive the voltage (V_m) to become greather then equilibrium potential (E_e) and this effect can invert the direction of the EPSC (see equation 3). E_e is then another threshold used by the neuron to create a point of non linerarity which is an important factor for neural computation. A strong synaptic activity on a branch can have an important effect on the branches closely related to it. These effects, added to the large variability observed in synaptic quantal transmission and to the extremely complex machinery of synaptic activation, neurotransmitter diffusion, re-uptake, spillover, and presynaptic regulation of vesicle release [6,10,29,30], configure a greatly complex system. Is it reasonable to assume that all these complex and fine mechanisms of regulation of synaptic activity on dendrites produce only a simple noise influencing the neuronal activity? Can the electrical patterns, generated by the different combinations of activation of excitatory and inhibitory synapses on dendrites, be considered as a sort of language (code) by the means of which synapses and dendritic branches comunicate each other to produce the neuronal output? These questions should be considered in the formulation of theories on neural code.

In summary, the precise timing of synaptic activation, the number and organization of dendritic branches, the relative synaptic positions, the mechanisms of the quantal neurotransmitter release, the presence of voltage dependent channels, etc., are important factors working in synergy to shape the signal arriving at the hillock and to determine the spikes generation. The branches of the dendritic tree, from the largest to the smallest, work in a sort of hierarchy of systems, modulating each others. A consequence of this hierarchical system is that by increasing the number and complexity of branches and the type of synapses connetcted to them, increases the complexity of the regulatory mechanism of the neuronal output. If this is not a condition necessary to increase the computational ability of the neuron it seems likely that it is a mechanism able to increase the precision of the neuronal computational and code generation.

Aknowledgements

I am grateful to Mr Salvatore Piantedosi of Institute of Cybernetics for his valuable help in figure's drawing.

References

1. Abeles, M.: Role of the cortical neuron: integrator or coincidence detector? Isr. J. Med. Sci. 18, 83–92 (1982)
2. Abeles, M.: Corticonics: neural circuits of the cerebral cortex. Cambridge University Press, Cambridge, New York (1991)
3. Agmon-Snir, H., Carr, C.E., Rinzel, J.: The roles of dendrites in auditory coincidence detection. Nature 393, 268–272 (1998)
4. Cecchi, G.A., Alonso, J.-M., Martinez, L., Chialvo, D.R., Magnasco, M.O.: Noise in neurons is message dependent. Proc. Acad. Sci. USA 97, 5557–5561 (2000)
5. Di Maio, V., Lánský, P., Rodriguez, R.: Different types of noise in leaky integrate-and-fire model of neuronal dynamics with discrete periodical input. Gen. Physiol. Biophys. 23, 21–38 (2004)
6. Forti, L., Bossi, M., Bergamaschi, A., Villa, A., Malgaroli, A.: Loose patch recordings of single quanta at individual hippocampal synapse. Nature 388, 874–878 (1997)
7. Gerstein, G.L., Mandelbrot, B.: Random walk models for the spike activity of single neuron. Biophys. J. 71, 41–68 (1964)
8. Golding, N.L., Spruston, N.: Dendritic sodium spikes are variable triggers of axon action potential in hippocampal CA1 pyramidal neurons. Neuron 21, 1189–1200 (1998)
9. Golding, N.L., Staff, N.P., Spruston, N.: Dendritic spikes as mechanism for cooperative long term potentiation. Nature 418, 326–331 (2002)
10. Jonas, P., Major, G., Sakman, B.: Quantal components of unitary EPSCs at the mossy fibre synapse on CA3 pyramidal cells of rat hippocampus. J. Physiol. 472, 615–663 (1993)
11. Kock, C., Segev, I.: The role of sinlge neurons in information processing. Nat. Neurosci. 3, 1171–1177 (2000)
12. Lánský, P.: On approximation of Stein's neuronal model. J. Theor. Biol. 107, 631–647 (1984)
13. Lánský, P.: Source of periodical force in noisy integrate-and-fire model of neuronal dynamics. Phys. Rev. E. 55, 2040–2043 (1997)
14. Lánský, P., Lánská, V.: Diffusion approximation of the neural model with synaptic reversal potentials. Biol. Cybern. 56, 19–26 (1987)
15. Lánský, P., Rospar, J.-P.: Ornstein-Uhlenbeck model neuron revisited. Biol. Cybern. 72, 397–406
16. Lánský, P., Sacerdote, L.: The Ornstein-Uhlenbeck neuronal model with the signal dependent noise. Phys. Let. A 285, 132–140 (2001)
17. Liu, G.: Local structural balance and functional interaction of excitatory and inhibitory synapses in hippocampal dendrites. Nat. Neurosci. 7, 373–379 (2004)
18. London, M., Häusser, M.: Dendritic computation. Ann. Rev. Neurosci. 28, 503–532
19. McCullogh, W.S., Pitts, W.H.: A logical calculus of the ideas immanent in nervous activity. Bull. Math. Biophys. 5, 115–133 (1943)

20. Megías, M., Emri, Z.S., Freund, T.F., Gulyás, A.I.: Total number and distribution of inhibitory and excitatory synapses of hippocampal CA1 pyramidal cells. Neurosc. 102, 527–540 (2001)
21. Rall, W.: Branching dendritic tree and motorneuron membrane resistivity. Exp. Neurol. 1, 491–527 (1959)
22. Rall, W.: Theoretical significance of dendritic trees for neuronal input-output relationship. In: Reis, R.F. (ed.) Neural theory and Modeling, Stanford University Press, Palo Alto (1964)
23. Rall, W., Rinzel, J.: Branch input resistance and steady attenuation for input to one branch of a dendritic neuron model. Biophys. J. 13, 648–688 (1973)
24. Rinzel, J., Rall, W.: Transient response in a dendritic neuron model for current injected at one branch. Biophys. J. 14, 759–790 (1974)
25. Segev, I., London, M.: Untangling dendrites with quantitative models. Science 290, 744–750 (2000)
26. Segev, I., Rinzel, J., Shepherd, G.M.: The theoretical foundation of dendritic function. The MIT Press, Cambridge, London (1995)
27. Tuckwell, H.C.: Determination of the inter-spike times of neurons receiving randomly arriving post synaptic potentials. Biol. Cybern. 18, 225–237 (1975)
28. Ventriglia, F., Di Maio, V.: Neural code and irregular spike trains. In: De Gregorio, M., Di Maio, V., Frucci, M., Musio, C. (eds.) BVAI 2005. LNCS, vol. 3704, pp. 89–98. Springer, Heidelberg (2005)
29. Ventriglia, F., Di Maio, V.: Stochastic fluctuation of the synaptic function. Biosystems 67, 287–294 (2002)
30. Ventriglia, F., Di Maio, V.: Stochastic fluctuation of the quantal EPSC amplitude in computer simulated excitatory synapses of hippocampus. Biosys. 71, 195–204 (2003)
31. Zador, A.M.: The basic units of computation. Nat. Neurosci. 3, 1167 (2000)

Ghost Stochastic Resonance for a Neuron with a Pair of Periodic Inputs

Maria Teresa Giraudo, Laura Sacerdote, and Alessandro Sicco

Dept. of Mathematics University of Torino,
Via C.Alberto 10, 10123 Torino, Italy
{mariateresa.giraudo,laura.sacerdote,alessandro.sicco}@unito.it

Abstract. A small network like that proposed in [8] and [9] is studied when a pair of periodic signals are carried by the two different input neurons to verify the arising of ghost stochastic resonance phenomena in the third processing neuron. Suitable modifications of the stochastic leaky integrate-and-fire model are employed to describe the membrane potential of the input neurons while the processing neuron is modeled by means of a jump-diffusion process. A stochastic resonance behavior is detected for the processing neuron in correspondence with the "ghost" frequencies both in the harmonic and in the anharmonic case. The range of parameter values under which this behavior occurs is specified and an interpretation of the coincidence detection mechanism involved is provided.

Keywords: Leaky integrate-and-fire model, fundamental frequency, jump-diffusion process, coincidence detection.

1 Introduction

The processing of multiple input signals by sensory neurons is an important task accomplished by the nervous systems in the case for example of auditory perception of complex sounds. On the other hand, two-frequency signals are commonly employed for diagnostic purposes like the analysis of evoked potentials in human visual cortex (cf. for example [2] and references quoted therein).

For this reason the response of a neuron to several sinusoidal inputs has been considered in different settings by means of suitable models (cf. [3], [4], [2], [5]). In all the models proposed the phenomenon of "ghost" stochastic resonance arises. Indeed an excitable neuron driven by (at least) two sinusoidal inputs, harmonic of the same fundamental frequency, responds also to the missing fundamental one. Moreover the response is optimized for a suitable amount of noise. If the signals are rendered anharmonic by adding the same shift to all the input frequencies the neuron responds with a shift in the missing frequency perceived.

The results in [3], [4] and [5] concern the response to multiple periodic inputs of single neuron models. In [2] a small network based on noisy Morris-Lecar model neurons is proposed. In the harmonic case, two periodic inputs of frequencies multiple of a fundamental one determine the spiking activity of two model

F. Mele et al. (Eds.): BVAI 2007, LNCS 4729, pp. 398–407, 2007.
© Springer-Verlag Berlin Heidelberg 2007

neurons that stimulate a third one. The resulting activity of this last processing neuron exhibits a ghost stochastic resonance behavior.

Following the small neuron network model proposed in [8] and [9], we consider in this work a model where a pair of periodic input signals is carried by two different neurons acting on a third processing one. While the membrane potential of the input neurons is described by means of a modification of the stochastic leaky integrate-and-fire model (cf. [6]), the time course of the membrane potential for the third receiving neuron follows a jump-diffusion process. The rationale to study this further model is related to the advantages remarked in the use of these stochastic processes to study the single neuron activity. Indeed they facilitate the understanding of the leading features of spiking activity and the analysis of underlying phenomena such as the coincidence detection of signals coming from the input neurons.

A synthetic description of the model proposed and of the methods employed is provided in Section 2. In Section 3 we illustrate by means of examples the detection of the missing frequencies by the processing neuron and the arising of ghost stochastic resonance phenomena in both the harmonic and the anharmonic case. We conclude in Section 4 with a brief discussion of the results.

2   The Model

We use here the small network of three neurons arranged in two different layers proposed in [8] and [9]. The first layer is composed of two input neurons, both with an excitatory function, whose spiking behavior acts on a third processing neuron on the second layer. The coupling between the two layers is unidirectional from the input neurons to the processing one.

The evolutions of the membrane potential of the input neurons are described by means of modifications of the Ornstein-Uhlenbeck diffusion process (cf. [6]). In particular, periodic signals with frequencies respectively $f^{(1)}$ and $f^{(2)}$ are added to the drift coefficients. In analogy with the leaky integrate-and-fire model (cf. [6]) for each of the two resulting processes $X_t^{(i)}$, $i = 1, 2$, a spike is generated at the times $\Lambda_n^{(i)}$, $n = 1, 2, \ldots$ when the process $X_t^{(i)}$ first reaches the given constant threshold $S > 0$, the same for the two neurons. After each spike the membrane potential is instantaneously reset to its resting value, set for simplicity to $X_0^{(i)} = 0$, $i = 1, 2$. The time course of the input modulations is not reset after each spike. Hence the time intervals between successive spikes (interspike intervals, ISIs) $\left\{ \Gamma_1^{(i)}, \Gamma_2^{(i)}, \ldots, \Gamma_n^{(i)}, \ldots \right\}$, $i = 1, 2$, with $\Gamma_1^{(i)} \equiv \Lambda_1^{(i)}$ and $\Gamma_n^{(i)} = \Lambda_n^{(i)} - \Lambda_{n-1}^{(i)}$, $n = 2, \ldots$, give rise to time series.

The membrane potential of the two input neurons is then solution for $t \in \left[0, \Gamma_j^{(i)} \right]$, $j = 1, 2, \ldots, i = 1, 2$ to the following stochastic differential equations (SDEs):

$$dX_t^{(i)} = \left(-\frac{1}{\theta} X_t^{(i)} + \mu + A \cos \left(2\pi f^{(i)} \left(t + \Lambda_{j-1}^{(i)} \right) \right) \right) dt + \sigma dW_t, \quad X_0^{(i)} = 0; \ i = 1, 2.$$

$$(1)$$

Here μ and σ^2 are constants representing respectively the net input and the noise amplitude, θ is the membrane time constant, A is the modulation amplitude (the same constant for both neurons) and W_t is a standard Wiener process.

We analyze the case where the input neurons are in the sub-threshold regime. As can be shown by employing the methods in [1] this corresponds to fulfilling in each interval $\left[0, \Gamma_j^{(i)}\right]$, $j = 1, 2, ..., i = 1, 2$, provided that $2\pi f^{(i)} \geq \frac{\sqrt{A^2 - \mu^2}}{\theta \mu}$ and independently from the values assumed by $\Lambda_{j-1}^{(1)}$, the constraint

$$\max_{t \in \left[0, \Gamma_j^{(i)}\right]} \{\mathbb{E}(X_t^{(i)})\} = \theta \left(\mu + \frac{A}{\sqrt{1 + (2\pi f^{(i)})^2 \theta^2}}\right) < S, \ i = 1, 2. \quad (2)$$

In this instance the neurons do not fire in the absence of noise and for small intensity of the noise the corresponding ISI distributions are much broader then in the analoguous super-threshold regime. As an example, the plot of $\mathbb{E}(X_t^{(1)})$ is shown in Fig. 1 for the same parameter choice as in Case (a) of Section 3 below and a value assumed by $\Lambda_{j-1}^{(1)}$ corresponding to $10 \, ms$.

The normalized ISI count plots for model (1) show several peaks centered at integer multiples of the periods corresponding to the driving frequencies $f^{(i)}$ (cf. [10] and references quoted therein) with a dispersion related both to the noise amplitude σ^2 and to the modulation amplitude A.

To model the behavior of the processing neuron we assume that in the absence of activity from both input neurons the membrane potential evolves according to an Ornstein-Uhlenbeck process (cf. [6]) with parameters μ^{OU}, σ_{OU}^2 and θ^{OU}. Whenever a spike is elicited by either of the input neurons the membrane potential Y_t of the processing neuron undergoes a jump increasing its value by a constant amount H. Hence the model Y_t reaches the threshold S either by pure diffusion or by effect of an upward jump at time $\hat{t}$ when $Y_{\hat{t}-} \in [S - H, S)$.

The study is performed via computer simulation of the firing times both for the input neurons and for the processing one.

For the spiking times of the input neurons we employ an algorithm similar to the one described in [5].

To obtain the spiking times for the processing neuron we use a jump-adapted simulation procedure analoguous to the one described in [8]. For every case $N = 50000$ simulation runs for the processing neuron are executed and normalized count plots of the simulated ISIs are drawn to represent the ISI distribution.

To estimate the coherence of the output with the frequencies of interest we analyze whether peaks arise at the corresponding periods in the normalized count plots. Stochastic resonance is recognized by studying whether the ISI distribution heights at the period corresponding to the missing frequency go through a maximum when the noise intensity σ_{OU}^2 is varied while keeping all the other parameters of the model fixed.

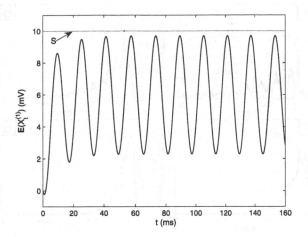

Fig. 1. Plot of $\mathbb{E}(X_t^{(1)})$ for $\mu = 0.6\ mVms^{-1}$, $\theta = 10\ ms$, $S = 10\ mV$, $\sigma^2 = 0.6\ mV^2ms^{-1}$, $f^{(0)} = 0.03125\ ms^{-1}$, $A = 1.5\ mVms^{-1}$ and $\Lambda_{j-1}^{(1)}$ assuming a value of $10\ ms$.

3   Results

To understand the response of the model processing neuron to the double stimulus in various conditions we distinguish among two different settings for the periodic stimuli.

(a) Harmonic case: $f^{(1)} = 2f^{(0)}$, $f^{(2)} = 3f^{(0)}$ where $f^{(0)}$ denotes the fundamental frequency.

(b) Anharmonic case: $f^{(1)} = 2f^{(0)} + \delta$, $f^{(2)} = 3f^{(0)} + \delta$ where $f^{(0)}$ is as above and δ denotes the common shift in frequency.

To investigate on the ISI distribution for the processing model neuron we consider here some examples in the two harmonic and anharmonic instances.

We choose the parameters for the input neurons and for the processing one so that the mean firing frequencies, computed as the inverse of the mean ISIs, lie in most instances between 5 and 30 spikes per second, which is generally accepted as reasonable. In particular we select $\mu = \mu^{OU} = 0.6\ mVms^{-1}$, $\theta = \theta^{OU} = 10\ ms$, $S = 10\ mV$, $\sigma^2 = 0.6\ mV^2ms^{-1}$ and $f^{(0)} = 0.03125\ ms^{-1}$ as in [5] and we vary the values of A, H, δ and σ_{OU}^2 as required by the different criteria of analysis chosen.

Case (a). A preliminary analysis was performed to find the value of A that produces a good phase-locking of the spiking times with the modulation frequencies for both input neurons. The optimal value results to be $A = 1.5\ mVms^{-1}$. Throughout this study the jump amplitude H ranges between 2.5 mV and 3.5 mV since for values lower then 2.5 mV the effects of jumps vanishes while for $H > 3.5\ mV$ almost each upward excitatory jump causes the crossing of the threshold.

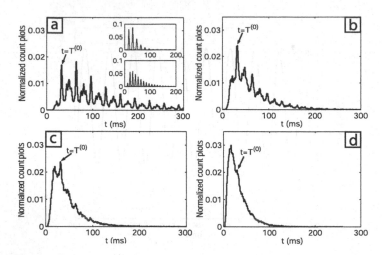

Fig. 2. Normalized count plots of the simulated ISIs in the harmonic case for $\mu = \mu^{OU} = 0.6\ mVms^{-1}$, $\theta = \theta^{OU} = 10\ ms$, $S = 10\ mV$, $\sigma^2 = 0.6\ mV^2ms^{-1}$, $f^{(0)} = 0.03125\ ms^{-1}$, $A = 1.5\ mVms^{-1}$, $H = 2.5\ mV$ and (panel a to d) $\sigma_{OU}^2 = 0.1, 0.5, 1, 2\ mV^2ms^{-1}$

In Fig. 2, panels $a - d$, we show the normalized count plots of the simulated ISIs corresponding respectively to the different values of $\sigma_{OU}^2 = 0.1, 0.5, 1$ and $2\ mV^2ms^{-1}$. Here the jump amplitude is set to $H = 2.5\ mV$. The upper and lower insets in panel a show the normalized count plots for the simulated ISIs of the input neurons with frequencies respectively $f^{(1)}$ and $f^{(2)}$ that determine the spiking activity of the processing neuron illustrated in the four panels of Fig. 2. Note that the distributions in the inset panels show a dispersion with respect to the peak values although the small dimension of the Figures gives the false intuition of a sharp periodic behavior.

Here and in all the cases considered the ISI normalized count plots exhibit peaks at integer multiples of the period $T^{(0)} = \frac{1}{f^{(0)}}$ corresponding to the fundamental frequency. Depending upon the value assumed by σ_{OU}^2 peaks may appear also at multiples of the two harmonic frequencies $f^{(1)}$ and $f^{(2)}$.

In Fig. 3 the height of the peaks in the simulated ISI normalized count plots at $T^{(0)}$ is represented as a function of the noise intensity σ_{OU}^2 for the three values of $H = 2.5, 3.0$ and $3.5\ mV$.

A maximum in the peak height at $T^{(0)}$ as a function of σ_{OU}^2 appears for all the values of H considered, revealing that a stochastic resonance phenomenon arises in correspondence with the "ghost" fundamental frequency which is missing in the input. The level of noise that maximizes the processing neuron response to the fundamental frequency $f^{(0)}$ decreases for increasing values of $H = 2.5, 3.0$ and $3.5\ mV$.

The analysis on the height of the peaks that arise in the ISI normalized count plots shows a stochastic resonance-like behavior also in correspondence with the

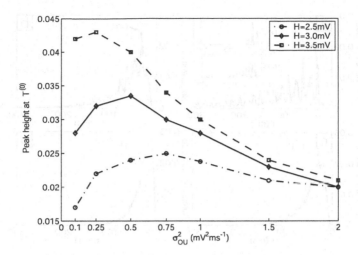

Fig. 3. Height of the peaks at $T^{(0)} = \frac{1}{f^{(0)}}$ in the simulated ISI normalized count plots for the harmonic case as a function of σ^2_{OU} for (bottom to top) $H = 2.5, 3.0, 3.5\ mV$. Other parameters as in Fig. 2.

frequency $\frac{f^{(1)}}{3}$. However in this case the peak heights at $t = \frac{3}{f^{(1)}}$ are always much lower than the peaks at $T^{(0)}$.

An analoguous study conducted in the super-threshold regime (data not shown) evidentiates that for the same value of H the peak height at $T^{(0)}$ are much higher than in the case considered here. Furthermore the ghost stochastic resonance behavior arises only for smaller values of H with respect to the sub-threshold regime when the input neurons are in the super-threshold regime.

Case (b). We study here the case where the two frequencies $f^{(1)}$ and $f^{(2)}$ are shifted with respect to $2f^{(0)}$ and $3f^{(0)}$, respectively, by a common value δ. Our aim is now to ascertain whether the processing neuron simply detects the frequency difference $f^{(1)} - f^{(2)}$ or whether the response depends on the frequency shift δ. In analogy with Case **(a)** we choose a value of $A = 1.5\ mVms^{-1}$ and we vary the jump amplitude H in the range between 2.5 and 3.5 mV. We set the shift value to $\delta \cong \frac{1}{10} f^{(0)}\ ms^{-1}$. A motivation for this choice is presented in the Appendix.

In Fig. 4, panels $a - d$, the normalized count plots of the simulated ISIs corresponding respectively to $\sigma^2_{OU} = 0.1, 0.5, 1$ and $2\ mV^2 ms^{-1}$ are represented when $H = 2.5\ mV$. As in Fig. 2, the upper and lower insets in the first panel show the normalized count plots for the simulated ISIs of the input neurons with frequencies $f^{(1)} = 2f^{(0)} + \delta$ (upper inset) and $f^{(2)} = 3f^{(0)} + \delta$ (lower inset).

The ISI normalized count plots exhibit peaks in correspondence to integer multiples of a missing frequency $f^{(r)} \neq f^{(0)}$. An approximated value for $f^{(r)}$ can be obtained by means of a theoretical analysis of the possible coincidence detection of the spikes from the two input neurons by the processing one. A sketch of the analysis is given in the Appendix. For intermediate values of the

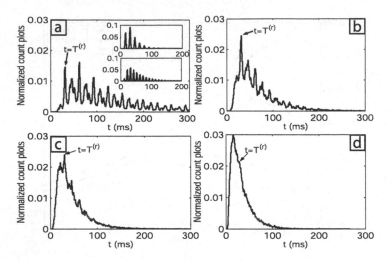

Fig. 4. Normalized count plots of the simulated ISIs in the anharmonic case. Same parameters as in Fig. 2, $\delta = \frac{1}{10} f^{(0)}$ and (panel a to d) $\sigma_{OU}^2 = 0.1, 0.5, 1, 2 \, mV^2 ms^{-1}$.

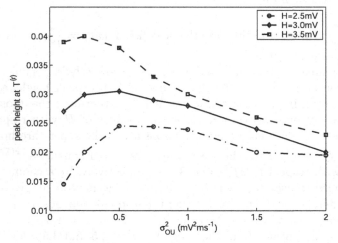

Fig. 5. Height of the peaks in the simulated ISI normalized count plots at $T^{(r)} = \frac{1}{f^{(r)}}$ in the anharmonic case as a function of σ_{OU}^2 for (bottom to top) $H = 2.5, 3.0, 3.5 \, mV$. Other parameters as in Fig. 4.

noise intensity σ_{OU}^2 for the processing neuron the peak heights at $T^{(r)} = \frac{1}{f^{(r)}}$ are higher than the corresponding values at $T^{(0)}$ in the harmonic regime thus hinting to a stronger effect of the input composition in this range.

In Fig. 5 we show the height of the peaks in the simulated ISI normalized count plots at $T^{(r)} = \frac{1}{f^{(r)}}$ as a function of the noise intensity σ_{OU}^2 for the three values of $H = 2.5, 3.0$ and $3.5 \, mV$.

A maximum appears for all the values of H considered, shifting towards lower levels of the processing neuron noise intensity σ_{OU}^2 for the highest value of H.

4   Conclusions

We have investigated the response of a processing neuron whose membrane potential is modeled by means of a jump-diffusion process where the jumps are determined by the spiking activity of two model neurons subject to sub-threshold periodic stimuli.

The processing neuron detects the missing fundamental frequency in the harmonic case and a different missing frequency in the anharmonic setting. Moreover a ghost stochastic resonance behavior has been observed in both cases in correspondence with such frequencies for a suitable range of noise levels and jump amplitude values. The processing neuron seems thus able to detect the coincident arrival of spikes from each input neuron. This coincidence produces an effect which is analoguous to the composition of periodic inputs in a single neuron model (cf. [5] and references therein).

The features illustrated by means of examples are common to more general instances since they are maintained also in cases with different fundamental frequencies $f^{(0)}$ or different noise intensities σ^2 for the two input neurons as well as when the input neurons are in the super-threshold regime. However in this last instance a more straightforward interpretation of the resulting spiking behavior can be provided.

Acknowledgments. Work partially funded by PRIN 2005.

References

1. Arnold, L.: Stochastic Differential Equations: Theory and Applications. Wiley, New York (1974)
2. Balenzuela, P., Garcia-Ojalvo, J.: Neural mechanism for binaural pitch perception via ghost stochastic resonance. Chaos 15(023903), 1–8 (2005)
3. Chialvo, D.R., Calvo, O., Gonzales, D.L., Piro, O., Savino, G.V.: Subharmonic stochastic synchronization and resonance in neuronal systems. Phys. Rev. E 65(5) (2002), Art. No. 050902(R)
4. Chialvo, D.R.: How we hear what is not there: A neural mechanism for the missing fundamental illusion. Chaos 13(4), 1226–1230 (2003)
5. Giraudo, M.T., Sacerdote, L.: Ghost stochastic resonance for a single neuron model. Sc. Math. Jap. 64(2), 299–312 (2006)
6. Ricciardi, L.M., Di Crescenzo, A., Giorno, V., Nobile, A.G.: An outline of theoretical and algorithmic approaches to first passage time problems with application to biological modeling. Math. Japonica 50(2), 247–322 (1999)
7. Ricciardi, L.M.: On the trasformation of diffusion processes into the Wiener process. J. Math. Anal. Appl. 54, 185–199 (1976)
8. Sirovich, R.: Mathematical models for the study of synchronization phenomena in neuronal networks. PhD Thesis, University of Torino and University of Grenoble (2006)

9. Sacerdote, L., Sirovich, R., Villa, A.E.P.: Multimodal inter-spike interval distribution in a jump diffusion neuronal model, pp. 1–22 (preprint)
10. Shimokawa, T., Pakdaman, K., Sato, S.: Time-scale matching in the response of a stochastic leaky integrate-and-fire neuron model to periodic stimulus with additive noise. Phys. Rev. E 59(3), 3427–3443 (1999)

Appendix

Let us consider the processes $X_t^{(i)}$, $i = 1, 2$ solutions to the SDEs (1). Furthermore let us define $T^{(i)} = \frac{1}{f^{(i)}}$, $i = 1, 2$ where the frequencies $f^{(i)}$, $i = 1, 2$ are defined as in Case (b) of Section 3.

By means of a suitable space transformation we can throw the problem of determining the time at which $X_t^{(i)}$, $i = 1, 2$ first cross the constant threshold $S > 0$ into the problem of finding the time at which the Ornstein-Uhlenbeck process X_t^{OU} first crosses suitable modulated boundaries $S^{(i)}(t)$, $i = 1, 2$.

Indeed employing the method introduced in [7] one can look for space-time transformations $x^{(i),OU} = \psi(x^{(i)}, t)$, $t^{OU} = \phi(t)$ that map the processes $X_t^{(i)}$, $i = 1, 2$ with corresponding threshold S into Ornstein-Uhlenbeck processes with corresponding thresholds $S^{(i)}(t)$, $i = 1, 2$. In this particular case it is easy to check that the transformations do not affect the time variables while for the space variables one gets

$$\psi(x^{(i)}, t) = x^{(i)} + \nu^{(i)}(t), \ i = 1, 2 \tag{3}$$

where $\nu^{(i)}(t)$, $i = 1, 2$ are solutions to the following first order differential equations:

$$\frac{d\nu^{(1)}(t)}{dt} - \frac{1}{\theta}\nu^{(1)}(t) + A\cos\left(\left(4\pi f^{(0)} + \delta\right)t\right) = 0; \tag{4}$$

$$\frac{d\nu^{(2)}(t)}{dt} - \frac{1}{\theta}\nu^{(2)}(t) + A\cos\left(\left(6\pi f^{(0)} + \delta\right)t\right) = 0. \tag{5}$$

Denoting as $\alpha = \frac{1}{\theta}$, the transformed thresholds are then obtained as:

$$S^{(1)}(t) = S + \frac{A\alpha\cos\left(\left(4\pi f^{(0)} + \delta\right)t\right) - \left(2Af^{(0)} + A\delta\right)\sin\left(\left(4\pi f^{(0)} + \delta\right)t\right)}{\alpha^2 + 4(f^{(0)})^2 + 4f^{(0)}\delta} \tag{6}$$

and

$$S^{(2)}(t) = S + \frac{A\alpha\cos\left(\left(6\pi f^{(0)} + \delta\right)t\right) - \left(3Af^{(0)} + A\delta\right)\sin\left(\left(6\pi f^{(0)} + \delta\right)t\right)}{\alpha^2 + 9(f^{(0)})^2 + 6f^{(0)}\delta}. \tag{7}$$

A coincidence in the times at which both processes $X_t^{(i)}$, $i = 1, 2$ reach the threshold S will be more likely to occur if $S^{(1)}(t)$ and $S^{(2)}(t)$ are in phase. By inspection of the plots of (6) and (7) or by using numerical procedures one can determine $\min\left\{(h,k),h=1,2,...;k=1,2,...:\left|hT^{(1)}-kT^{(2)}\right|\leq\lambda\right\}$ for a suitable small value of λ. Note that λ must be much smaller then both $T^{(1)}$ and $T^{(2)}$. Choosing in particular $\lambda=\frac{T^{(1)}}{16}$, under the condition $\delta\leq\frac{1}{5}f^{(0)}$ one gets $(h,k)=(2,3)$. The time at which the probability that both processes $X_t^{(1)}$ and $X_t^{(2)}$ reach their thresholds is maximized can then be approximated as

$$T^{(r)}\cong\frac{\left(2T^{(1)}+3T^{(2)}\right)}{2}. \tag{8}$$

For a choice of the parameter values as in Section 3 one gets $T^{(r)}\cong30.7\,ms$ that coincides with the results obtained from the simulations.

In Fig. 6 the shapes of $S^{(1)}(t)$ and $S^{(2)}(t)$ corresponding to the examples in Section 3 are shown together with the value of $T^{(r)}$.

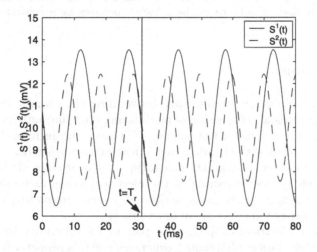

Fig. 6. Plots of $S^{(1)}(t)$ and $S^{(2)}(t)$ corresponding to the examples in Section 3.

Coincidence Detector Properties of Small Networks of Interneurons

Angelo Di Garbo, Michele Barbi, and Santi Chillemi

Istituto di Biofisica CNR, Sezione di Pisa,
Via G. Moruzzi 1, 56124 Pisa, Italy
{angelo.digarbo,michele.barbi,santi.chillemi}@pi.ibf.cnr.it
http://www.pi.ibf.cnr.it

Abstract. We study the transmission of excitatory synaptic inputs by a
network of interneurons, coupled by electrical and inhibitory synapses, in
the cases in which the network consists of three and four coupled units.
It is shown that in both cases the network behaves as a coincidence
detector.

1 Introduction

The main task of inhibitory interneurons, innervating the somatic and periso-
matic region of pyramidal cells, is that of modulating the firing activities of these
neurons [1]. Paired recordings of fast spiking (FS) interneurons have shown that
they are interconnected with electrical and inhibitory synapses [2,3]. The relevance of the electrical synapses for the generation of synchronous discharges was
shown experimentally: the impairing of the electrical synapses between cortical interneurons disrupts synchronous oscillations in the gamma frequency band
that seem to be associated to cognitive functions [4].

The presence of electrical coupling in a pair of FS inhibitory interneurons
promotes synchronization at all spiking frequencies and this property is enhanced
when the strength of the electrical coupling increases [5]. Additional experiments
suggest that FS cells play a relevant role in the detection of synchronous activity
[6] and are involved in the feed-forward inhibition of pyramidal cells as a direct
consequence of their fast and reliable response to excitatory inputs [7].

Recently we have shown that a pair of FS cells, coupled by electrical and
inhibitory synapses, is capable to detect and transmit synchronous excitatory
inputs [9]; here we extend this study to the case of three or four coupled cells.
A motivation to study a small population of interneurons, coupled by electrical coupling , comes from recent experimental findings [8,10,11,12]. In fact the
inhibitory interneurons of the thalamic reticular nucleus are interconnected by
electrical synapses and form clusters that are quite small compared with those in
the neocortex; moreover it was shown that the electrical coupling coordinates the
rhythmic activity of these neural netwoks [10]. An additional contribution to the
synchronization properties of thalamic reticular neurons probably comes from
the excitatory inputs that they receive from neocortex and thalamic relay nuclei

F. Mele et al. (Eds.): BVAI 2007, LNCS 4729, pp. 408–417, 2007.

[10]. Another example is that of the Inferior Olive region: the corresponding experimental results indicate that the presence of gap junctions between neurons plays a key role in promoting synchronization[11,12]. In this paper we study how the output of a network of coupled cells is affected by the time delay between its excitatory input pulses. In particular, by using a computational approach, we investigate the capability of a network of three and four coupled interneurons of transmitting their input signal mimicking an excitatory synaptic pulse. Our choice of the size of the network is a compromise between computational requirements and biological relevance. A simple neurobiological justification of this choice comes from the experimental results reported in [10]: it was shown that the soma size of the interneurons in the thalamic reticular nucleus ranged from 141 to 503 μm^2. From these data we estimate the average soma area as $S_A = \frac{141+503}{2} \mu m^2 = 322 \mu m^2$. Moreover it was shown that the distance $d_{i,j}$ between the soma of all electrical coupled cells of the thalamic reticular nucleus satisfies $d_{i,j} \leq 2R = 40 \mu m$ [10]. Thus, an estimation of the number of interneurons contained within a circle of diameter $2R$ is given by $n_{Int} = \frac{\pi R^2}{S_A} \cong 3.9$. This estimation of the size of the network of electrically coupled interneurons in the thalamic reticular nucleus shows that our choice is compatible with the biological data.

2   Methods

2.1   Model Description

To model an isolated FS cell receiving an excitatory synaptic pulse, we use the following single compartment biophysical model studied in [9]:

$$C\frac{dV}{dt} = I_E - g_{Na}m^3h(V - V_{Na}) - g_K n(V - V_K) - g_L(V - V_L) + g_{Exc}P(t - t^*) \quad (1)$$

$$\frac{dx}{dt} = \frac{x_\infty - x}{\tau_x}, \quad x_\infty = \frac{\alpha_x}{\alpha_x + \beta_x}, \quad \tau_x = \frac{1}{\alpha_x + \beta_x}, \quad (x = m, h, n) \quad (2)$$

where $C = 1$ $\mu F/cm^2$, I_E is the external stimulation current. The maximal specific conductances and the reversal potentials are respectively: $g_{Na} = 85$ mS/cm^2, $g_K = 60$ mS/cm^2, $g_L = 0.15$ mS/cm^2 and $V_{Na} = 65$ mV, $V_K = $ -95 mV, $V_L = $ - 72 mV. The kinetic of the Na^+ current is described by the following activation and deactivation rate variables: $\alpha_m(V) = 3.exp[(V+25)/20]$, $\beta_m(V) = 3.exp[-(V + 25)/27]$, $\alpha_h(V) = 0.026exp[-(V + 58)/15]$, $\beta_h(V) = 0.026exp[(V + 58)/12]$. The kinetics of the potassium current K^+ is defined by: $\alpha_n(V) = [-0.019(V$-4.2$)]/exp[-(V$-4.2$)/6.4]$-1, $\beta_n(V) = 0.016exp(-V/vAHP)$, where vAHP $= 13$ mV. The term $g_{Exc}P(t - t^*)$ represents the excitatory pulses starting at time t^* and it is defined by: $g_{Exc}P(t - t^*) = g_{Exc}H(t - t^*)\{N[e^{-(t-t^*)/\tau_D} - e^{-(t-t^*)/\tau_R}]\}$ where, $H(*)$ is the Heaviside function, N is a normalization constant ($| P | \leq 1$), $\tau_D = 2ms$ and $\tau_R = 0.4ms$ are, respectively, realistic values of the decay and rise time constants of the excitatory pulse and g_{Exc} is its amplitude. For a network of coupled cells, the j-*th* interneuron receives the excitatory pulse at time t_j with: $t_j \leq t_{j+1}$. Moreover, the time delays between two consecutive pulses will be adopted to be equal: i.e. $t_{j+1} = t_j + \Delta t$. In keeping with the experiments, the simulations are carried out to reproduce the membrane potential fluctuations occurring in *in vitro* conditions [13]. Thus, the $j - th$ cell model is injected with a noisy current: $\sigma \xi_j(t)$, $\xi_j(t)$ being an uncorrelated Gaussian random variable of zero mean and unit standard deviation ($< \xi_i(t), \xi_j(t) >= \delta_{ij}, i \neq j = 1, 2, 3$). The values of the stimulation current I_E and of σ are chosen in such a way that no firing occurs in absence of the excitatory pulse. We investigate the network of coupled interneurons in realistic conditions: i.e. when, in the absence of coupling, the firing probability of each cell receiving the excitatory pulse is lower than 1. With this in mind the parameters values I_E, σ and g_{EXC} are so chosen that the firing probability of each cell is $\cong 0.75$ (see [6]). Lastly, to get accurate firing statistics the stimulation protocol is repeated ($N_{Trials} = 400$) by using independent realizations of the applied noisy current.

2.2   Synaptic Coupling

The electrical coupling between a pair of interneuron is modeled as follows:

$$I_{El,1} = -g_{El}(V_1 - V_2),\tag{3}$$

where g_{El} is the maximal conductance of the gap junction (in mS/cm^2 unit). In the case of a network of N coupled interneurons the electrical coupling current of the $i - th$ cell is defined as follows:

$$I_{El,i} = -\frac{1}{N-1}\sum_{k} g_{El}(i,k)(V_i - V_k)\tag{4}$$

where $g_{In}(i, k) = g_{In}(k, i)$ is the electrical coupling conductance between interneuron i and k.

The inhibitory postsynaptic current (IPSC) is given by:

$$I_{In}(t) = -g_{In}s_{Pre}(t)(V_{Post}(t) - V_{Rev}),\tag{5}$$

where g_{In} is the specific maximal conductance of the inhibitory synapse (in mS/cm^2 unit), $s_{Pre}(t)$ is determined by the equation $\dot{s}_{Pre} = \alpha_0 T(V_{Pre})(1 - s_{Pre}) - \tau_{Decay}^{-1}s_{Pre}$, V_{Pre} (V_{Post}) is the membrane potential of the presynaptic (postsynaptic) neuron, τ_{Decay} is the decay time constants of the IPSC, $\alpha_0 = 6ms^{-1}$ and $T(V_{Pre}) = (1 + e^{-V_{Pre}})^{-1}$. For FS interneurons the IPSC is characterized by a reversal potential $V_{Rev}= -80$ mV and a mean decay time constant $\tau_{Decay} = 2.6$ ms [13]. For a network of N coupled cells the total inhibitory current of the $i - th$ unit is defined as:

$$I_{In,i}(t) = -\frac{1}{N-1}\sum_{k} g_{In}(i,k)s_k(t)(V_i(t) - V_{Rev})\tag{6}$$

where the first sum is over the $N - 1$ interneurons and $g_{In}(i, k) = g_{In}(k, i)$ is the inhibitory conductance value between cell i and k.

For all simulations the adopted value of the parameters $g_{In}(i, k)$ and $g_{El}(i, k)$ were all within the physiological range [2,3,13]. Then, for the $i - th$ cell model, the total coupling current $I_{El,i} + I_{In,i}$ was added to the right-hand side of equation 1.

3   Results

3.1   Three Coupled Interneurons

Let us consider a set of three interneurons, coupled by electrical synapses alone. We study how the excitatory synaptic pulses are transmitted by this network. To get a more clear understanding, it is useful and meaningful from the neurobiological point of view, to think these inputs to be the postsynaptic currents generated by the presynaptic activities of excitatory neural networks. Thus, the input to the network is the set of all excitatory pulses, while the output is represented by the firing activity generated by this input. To characterize quantitatively the information transmission property of each cell we proceed as follows.

Let $p_j = \frac{n_j}{N_{Trials}}$ be the firing probability of the $j - th$ cell receiving the excitatory pulses, where n_j represents the total number of spikes generated during the N_{Trials} trials. The quantity p_j is used here as a measure of the information transmission of the excitatory synaptic pulses. Then, the quantity $p_A = \frac{\sum_j p_j}{N}$ represents the information transmission measure of a network of N coupled cells. The results, in the case in which the electrical conductances among interneurons are all equal, are reported in figure 1.

When the time delay between the pulses is $\Delta t = 0.5ms$, the spikes histograms show that all cells respond to the excitatory pulses synchronously. Thus, in this case the excitatory pulses are transmitted by the network of coupled cells efficiently ($p_A \cong 0.81$): i.e. each interneuron fires with high probability and this leads to a very powerful control of the timing of pyramidal cells arising from the network output. When the time delay between the pulses increases to $\Delta t = 4ms$ there is a strong (slight) reduction of the firing activity of cell 1 (cell 2), while that of cell 3 increases slightly. Thus, for $\Delta t = 4ms$ the information transmission of the excitatory pulses is smaller ($p_A \cong 0.57$) of that occurring in the case $\Delta t = 0.5ms$. The neurobiological meaning of this last result is that the control of the firing activity of the excitatory cells, arising from the output of the network of inhibitory interneurons, reduces. To get a better understanding of the transmission properties of the network, in the left panel of figure 2 are reported the firing probabilities of the three coupled interneurons against the time delay between the excitatory pulses. The adopted values of the delay times were: $\Delta t = \{0.5, 1, 2, 4, 8, 10, 12, 15, 18, 20, 25, 30\}\,(ms)$.

Inspection of these data implies that the higher capability of transmission of the excitatory inputs occurs when the time delay between them is in the range $0 - 2ms$: i.e. the network behaves as a coincidence detector and, therefore the maximal

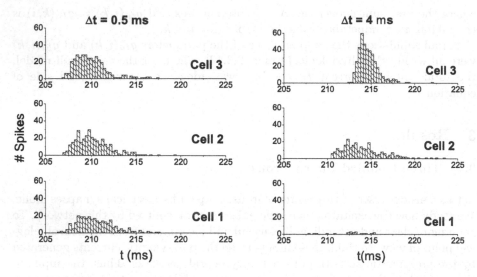

Fig. 1. Signal transmission properties of a network of three coupled interneurons for two values of the time delay between the excitatory pulses and in absence of inhibitory coupling. Cell 1 receive the excitatory pulse at the time $t_1 = 200ms$, cell 2 at $t_2 = t_1 + \Delta t$ and cell 3 at $t_3 = t_2 + \Delta t$. For the left panel it is: $p_A \cong 0.81$, while for the right one it is $p_A \cong 0.57$. For all panels the parameter values are: $t_1 = 200ms$, $g_{Exc} = 5.5\mu A/cm^2$, $\sigma = 0.3\mu A/cm^2$, $I_E = 0.5\mu A/cm^2$, $N_{Trials} = 400$, $g_{El}(1,2) = g_{El}(1,3) = g_{El}(2,3) = 0.02mS/cm^2$; the bin size is $0.3ms$.

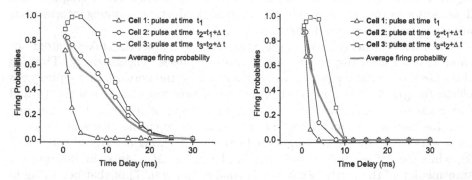

Fig. 2. Firing probabilities of three coupled interneurons against the time delay between the excitatory pulses and in absence of inhibitory coupling. Left panel: $g_{El}(1,2) = g_{El}(1,3) = g_{El}(2,3) = 0.02mS/cm^2$; right panel: $g_{El}(1,2) = g_{El}(1,3) = g_{El}(2,3) = 0.06mS/cm^2$. For all panels the parameter values are: $t_1 = 200ms$, $g_{Exc} = 5.5\mu A/cm^2$, $\sigma = 0.3\mu A/cm^2$, $I_E = 0.5\mu A/cm^2$, $N_{Trials} = 400$. The gray line represents the average firing probability of the network (p_A).

network response (measured by the p_A value) occurs when the excitatory inputs are near synchronous. By increasing the electrical coupling conductance value (see right panel of figure 2) promotes the information transmission for Δt values

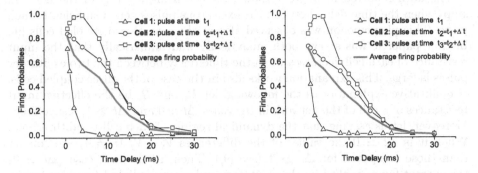

Fig. 3. Firing probabilities of three coupled interneurons against the time delay between the excitatory pulses. The parameter values are: $t_1 = 200ms$, $g_{Exc} = 5.5\mu A/cm^2$, $\sigma = 0.3\mu A/cm^2$, $I_E = 0.5\mu A/cm^2$, $N_{Trials} = 400$. For the left panels it is $g_{El}(1,2) = 0.02379mS/cm^2$, $g_{El}(1,3) = 0.02047mS/cm^2$, $g_{El}(2,3) = 0.01522mS/cm^2$ and $g_{In}(1,2) = g_{In}(1,3) = g_{In}(2,3) = 0mS/cm^2$, while for the right panel it is $g_{El}(1,2) = g_{El}(1,3) = g_{El}(2,3) = 0.02mS/cm^2$ and $g_{In}(1,2) = g_{In}(1,3) = g_{In}(2,3) = 0.1mS/cm^2$. For both panels the gray line represents the average firing probability of the network (p_A).

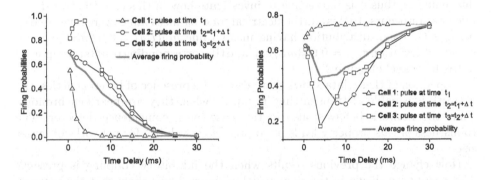

Fig. 4. Firing probabilities of three coupled interneurons against the time delay between the excitatory pulses. The parameter values are: $t_1 = 200ms$, $g_{Exc} = 5.5\mu A/cm^2$, $\sigma = 0.3\mu A/cm^2$, $I_E = 0.5\mu A/cm^2$, $N_{Trials} = 400$. For the left panels it is $g_{El}(1,2) = g_{El}(1,3) = g_{El}(2,3) = 0.02mS/cm^2$, $g_{In}(1,2) = g_{In}(1,3) = g_{In}(2,3) = 0.1mS/cm^2$ and $\tau = 6ms$, while for the right panel it is $g_{El}(1,2) = g_{El}(1,3) = g_{El}(2,3) = 0mS/cm^2$, $g_{In}(1,2) = g_{In}(1,3) = g_{In}(2,3) = 0.1mS/cm^2$ and and $\tau = 2.6ms$. For both panels the gray line represents the average firing probability of the network (p_A).

in the range $0 - 3ms$. For $\Delta t > 3ms$ the information transmission for the case $g_{El}(i,j) = 0.02mS/cm^2$ is larger than that for $g_{El}(i,j) = 0.06mS/cm^2$.

The present results are a generalization of that found in the case of two coupled cells, experimentally [6] and theoretically [9]. Moreover the results obtained in the case of two coupled cells can be used to explain why it is $p_1 < p_2 < p_3$ for $\Delta t \neq 0$ (see figures 1 and 2).

The data reported in figure 2 show that the firing activity of the network stops when the time delay between the excitatory pulses gets a sufficiently high value. This phenomenon was observed also in the case of two coupled cells [9]. In that paper it was shown both analytically and numerically that the input resistance of each cell decreases when the time delay between the two excitatory pulses is large. This explanation works also in the case of the three coupled cells. A qualitative explanation is the following: let R_i and $\bar{R}_i$ be the effective input resistances of a cell of the network in the cases $\Delta t \simeq 0$ and $\Delta t \gg 1$, respectively. Moreover, let us assume that the dynamical regime of each cell is subthreshold. When it is $\Delta t \simeq 0$ the values of the differences $V_i - V_j$ ($i \neq j$) are smaller than those computed for $\Delta t \gg 1$ (see [9]). Then, in the first case ($\Delta t \simeq 0$) the current fluxes evoked by the excitatory pulse are mediated (mainly) by the capacitive and leakage conductances, while in the second case ($\Delta t \gg 1$) there are additional current fluxes through the electrical synapses. Therefore, it follows that it is $R_i > \bar{R}_i$. Thus, the amplitude of the depolarization evoked by the pulse will be greater in the case $\Delta t \simeq 0$ than for $\Delta t \gg 1$.

The results presented up to now were obtained in the case $g_{El}(1,2) = g_{El}(1,3) = g_{El}(2,3) = 0.02 mS/cm^2$, how change they when the electrical conductances values are not equal? The presence of heterogeneity in the electrical coupling conductances is a more realistic representation of a real network of coupled interneurons; thus it is interesting to investigate how in this case the transfer of information occurs. To this aim the electrical conductances values were generated by using a Gaussian distribution having mean value $g_{El}(i,j) = 0.02 mS/cm^2$ and standard deviation $\sigma_{g_{El}} = 0.003 mS/cm^2$ and the corresponding results are reported in the left panel of figure 3.

Inspection of these data shows that, also in the presence of heterogeneties, the network is capable of transmitting its inputs when they are near synchronous. Thus the network behaves, also in this case, as a coincidence detector. The robustness of this property leads us to predict its validity for networks of larger size.

How change the previous results when the inhibitory coupling is present? The results are shown in the right panel of figure 3 and show that the network behaves as a coincidence detector also in this case. The results do not change qualitatively when heterogeneity is introduced (data not shown).

Next we investigate how the results reported in the right panel of figure 3 change when the decay time constant of the inhibitory postsynaptic current increases. The results, for the case $\tau_{Decay} = 6ms$, are reported in the left panel of figure 4 and show that are similar to those reported in the right panel of figure 3. An interesting question is to see whether the coincidence detector property of the network is preserved when the interneurons are coupled by inhibitory synapses alone. The results are reported in right panel of figure 4 and show that the signal transmission properties of the network (measured by the p_A value) are different from those obtained in the presence of electrical coupling. In particular, these data show that, for small time delay values ($\Delta t < 2ms$), it is $p_A \cong 0.63$ while for figure 2 and 3 the corresponding p_A values are greater than 0.63. For time delay values $\Delta t \gg 1$ the p_A value approaches, as expected, 0.75 that was obtained in absence of coupling among the cells (see 2.1). In conclusion the network does not behave as a typical coincidence detector in this case.

3.2 Four Coupled Interneurons

Let us now consider the case of a network of four inhibitory interneurons coupled by electrical and inhibitory synapses. As in the previous section we investigate the signal transmission properties of the network when each cell receives an excitatory input pulse. The results for the case in which the cells are coupled by electrical synapses alone are reported in the left panel of figure 5, while those obtained in the presence of both types of coupling are in the right panel. These data indicate, as the previous ones, that the network behaves as a coincidence detector. The results do not change when heterogeneity is introduced in the coupling (data not shown). Results similar to those reported in figures 3 and 4 were also obtained in the presence of inhibitory coupling (data not shown). Therefore, the findings obtained for the networks of three and four coupled cells, suggest that the presence of the electrical coupling confers to the network the capability to detect synchronous inputs.

The experimental studies on coupled interneurons showed that the presence of electrical synapses between the cells promotes their firing synchrony [2,3,5,6]. In particular it was shown that the presence of electrical coupling in a pair of coupled interneurons confers to the network the capability to detect synchronous inputs [6,8]. Our results agree with these experimental findings. For instance, the All Amacrine cells in the mammalian retina are coupled by electrical synapses and receive excitatory inputs from Rod Bipolar cells [8]. A recent experimental

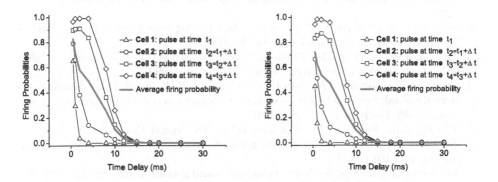

Fig. 5. Firing probabilities of four coupled interneurons against the time delay between the excitatory pulses. The parameter values are: $t_1 = 200ms$, $g_{Exc} = 5.5\mu A/cm^2$, $\sigma = 0.3\mu A/cm^2$, $I_E = 0.5\mu A/cm^2$, $N_{Trials} = 400$. For the left panels it is $g_{El}(i,j) = 0.02mS/cm^2 (i \neq j = 1,2,3,4)$ and $g_{In}(i,j) = 0mS/cm^2 (i \neq j = 1,2,3,4)$, while for the right panel it is $g_{El}(i,j) = 0.02mS/cm^2 (i \neq j = 1,2,3,4)$ and $g_{In}(i,j) = 0.1mS/cm^2 (i \neq j = 1,2,3,4)$. For both panels the gray line represents the average firing probability of the network (p_A).

paper analysed the information transmission properties of a pair of coupled All Amacrine cells: i.e. the firing probability of each cell when receiving excitatory inputs [8]. It was found that when the two excitatory pulses were applied asynchronously the firing probability of the cells was low, while it was significantly higher when the two pulses were synchronous [8]. Thus, the results reported here (see figures 2,3,4 and 5) agree qualitatively with those experimental findings.

4   Conclusions

The excitatory synaptic communication among neurons is the basis for the transmission and coding of the sensory information [7]. This neural activity is modulated by the discharge of inhibitory interneurons [1]. Moreover it is now established that interneurons are coupled also by gap junctions and play a key role for the processing of the neural information [2,3,14]. In this paper we considered networks of three or four interneurons coupled by electrical and inhibitory synapses and we studied how excitatory synaptic inputs are transmitted by the networks. It was found, both in the case of three and of four coupled cells, that the network behaves as a coincidence detector when the electrical synapses are set on: the transmission of the information is high when the excitatory pulses are near synchronous, while it is low when the inputs are asynchronous. These simulations results suggest that this property holds in general for networks of larger size.

References

1. Fisahn, A., McBain, C.J.: Interneurons unbound. Nat. Rev. Neurosci. 2, 11–23 (2001)
2. Galarreta, M., Hestrin, S.: A network of fast-spiking cells in the cortex connected by electrical synapses. Nature 402, 72–75 (1999)
3. Gibson, J.R., Beierlein, M., Connors, B.W.: Two networks of electrically coupled inhibitory neurons in neocortex. Nature 402, 75–79 (1999)
4. Deans, M.R., Gibson, J.R., Sellitto, C., Connors, B.W., Paul, D.L.: Synchronous activity of inhibitory networks in neocortex requires electrical synapses containing connexin36. Neuron 31, 477–485 (2001)
5. Gibson, J.R., Beierlein, M., Connors, B.W.: Functional Properties of Electrical Synapses between Inhibitory Interneurons of Neocortical Layer 4. J. Neurophysiol. 93, 467–480 (2005)
6. Galarreta, M., Hestrin, S.: Spike transmission and synchrony detection in networks of GABAergic interneurons. Science 292, 2295–2299 (2001)
7. Povysheva, N.V., Gonzalez-Burgos, G., Zaitsev, A.V., Kroner, S., Barrionuevo, G., Lewis, D.A., Krimer, L.S.: Properties of excitatory synaptic responses in fast-spiking interneurons and pyramidal cells from monkey and rat prefrontal cortex. Cerebral Cortex 16, 541–552 (2006)
8. Veruki, L.M., Hartveit, E.: AII (Rod) amacrine cells form a network of electrically coupled interneurons in the mammalian retina. Neuron 33, 935–946 (2002)
9. Di Garbo, A., Barbi, M., Chillemi, S.: Signal processing properties of fast spiking interneurons. BioSystems 86, 27–37 (2002)

10. Long, M.A., Landisman, C.E., Connors, B.W.: Small clusters of electrically coupled neurons generate synchronous rhythms in the thalamic reticular nucleus. J. Neurosci. 24, 341–349 (2004)
11. Leznik, E., Llinas, R.: Role of gap junctions in the synchronized neuronal oscillations in the inferior olive. J. Neurophysiol. 94, 2447–2456 (2005)
12. Placantonakis, D.G., Bukovsky, A.A., Aicher, S.A., Kiem, H., Welsh, J.P.: Continuous electrical oscillations emerge from a coupled network: a study of the inferior olive using lentiviral knockdown of connexin36. J. Neurosci. 26, 5008–5016 (2006)
13. Galarreta, M., Hestrin, S.: Electrical and chemical Synapses among parvalbumin fast-spiking GABAergic interneurons in adult mouse neocortex. PNAS USA 99, 12438–12443 (2002)
14. Galarreta, M., Hestrin, S.: Electrical synapses between GABA-releasing interneurons. Nat. Neurosci. 2, 425–433 (2001)

Computing the Maximum Using Presynaptic Inhibition with Glutamate Receptors

Dražen Domijan and Mia Šetić

Department of Psychology, Faculty of Philosophy, University of Rijeka
Ivana Klobučarića 1, 51000 Rijeka, Croatia
ddomijan@ffri.hr, mia-setic@ffri.hr

Abstract. Neurophysiological investigations suggest that presynaptic ionotropic receptors are important mechanism for controlling synaptic transmission. In this paper, presynaptic kainate receptors are incorporated in a feedforward inhibitory neural network in order to investigate their role in the cortical information processing. Computer simulations showed that the proposed mechanism is able to compute the function maximum by disinhibiting the cell with the maximal amplitude. The maximum is computed with high precision even in the case where inhibitory synaptic weights are weak and (or) asymmetric. Moreover, the network is able to track time-varying input and to select multiple winners. These capabilities do not depend on the dimensionality of the network. Also, the model is able to implement the winner-take-all behaviour.

Keywords: glutamate receptors; winner-takes-all; maximum operator; synaptic modulation; presynaptic inhibition.

1 Introduction

The maximum (MAX) function returns the magnitude of the largest of its arguments. It is a basic non-linear operator from which more complex algorithms and models can be built [15]. Theoretical considerations about object recognition in the visual cortex suggest that computing the maximum can be an important step in achieving invariant neural responses with respect to variations in input [11]. Neurophysiological investigations showed that the cells in the inferotemporal cortex and V4 may indeed compute maximum of their inputs [5,12]. Yu *et al.* [15] analysed biophysical mechanisms which can support the maximum computation. They investigate various combinations of feedforward, feedback, subtractive, shunting, firing rate and spiking neural models. The general conclusion was that feedforward networks are not able to suppress the non-maximal input for a wide variety of inputs and parameter choices. On the other hand, the shunting feedback model is very robust with respect to parameter change. However, the feedback model has a drawback because it shows independence from initial conditions and it is consequently insensitive to the changes in the input after the convergence to the stable state.

Networks for computing the maximum are closely related to more familiar winner-take-all (WTA) networks [8,16]. WTA networks select the cell which receives the largest input without information about the magnitude of its activation. They are

F. Mele et al. (Eds.): BVAI 2007, LNCS 4729, pp. 418–427, 2007.
© Springer-Verlag Berlin Heidelberg 2007

important component of many neural models such as competitive learning algorithms, models of visual selective attention, perceptual processing and motor control [6,8,13,14]. Previous proposals for biologically realistic models of WTA behaviour relied on a feedback (or recurrent) lateral inhibition. Such models had limited success because they are dynamical systems which require symmetry and strong connection weights in order to remain stable and to select appropriate input [3,6]. If symmetry is violated, the dynamical instabilities may arise and the network may select the wrong input or it may not reach the equilibrium value at all [6,8]. Such difficulties clearly show that the feedback lateral inhibition is not sufficient to ensure robust MAX and WTA computation.

The aim of the present paper is to provide a computational analysis of a new model for computing MAX and WTA based on presynaptic inhibition from excitatory neurotransmitter glutamate. Yuille and Grzywacz [16] introduce the feedback presynaptic inhibition where competition is achieved using axo-axonic synapses between the feedback inhibitory cells and excitatory axons from the input layer. Here, it is shown that the introduction of glutamate receptors on the axonal terminals of the feedforward inhibitory pathway allows computation of the maximum which is more robust compared to the model of Yuille and Grzywacz [16]. In particular, the proposed mechanism is able to select the largest input even if the network connections are weak and (or) asymmetric. Moreover, the network is able to track time-varying input without need to reset itself. Sensitivity to input fluctuations is an important property for real biological systems because they are immersed in dynamic environments [8].

2 Methods

We consider a neural network with shunting feedforward inhibition. The model is illustrated in Figure 1. Feedforward inhibitory axons from the input layer project to the excitatory cells in the output layer. Output from the excitatory cell forms an axo-axonic synapses with axons of inhibitory cells (Fig 1a). We assume that inhibitory axon terminals are endowed with kainate receptors which are able to reduce inhibitory transmission from the axonal terminal when they are stimulated by glutamate [7]. Another possibility is that glutamate spill-over occurs at certain glutamergic synapses [2]. In that case, glutamate may freely diffuse into space around the cell and bind to the kainate receptors at axonal terminals of inhibitory interneurons (Fig 1b). Mathematically, the model is described as

$$\tau_x \frac{dx_i}{dt} = -Ax_i + I_i - (B + x_i)\sum_j w_{ji} f\big[g(y_j) - z_{ij}h(x_i) - Tr\big] \qquad (1)$$

and

$$\tau_y \frac{dy_i}{dt} = -y_i + I_i \qquad (2)$$

where x_i is the firing rate of the excitatory (pyramidal) cell at the spatial position i which sends excitatory output to the inhibitory axons projecting from the cells in the input layer whose firing rate is denoted with y_i.

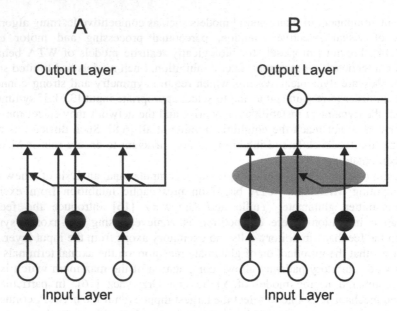

Fig. 1. A model for computing the MAX function based on presynaptic inhibition of feed forward inhibitory pathways. Open circles are excitatory cells and filled circles are inhibitory cells. A) Implementation of the model using axo-axonal synapses from excitatory cells to inhibitory axons with presynaptic kainate receptors. B) Implementation of the model using glutamate spill-over which binds the presynaptic kainate receptors. The grey area indicates space where glutamate is spilled around the target cell.

Time constants, τ_x, and, τ_y, control the speed of evolution of the activity of excitatory and inhibitory cells, respectively. Parameter, A, controls the speed of passive decay ($-x_i$) for the excitatory cells which drives activity toward zero if there is no input; I_i is the input from the sensory receptors or earlier network layer; B defines the inhibitory saturation point, that is, the lower bound for activity level that could be obtained; w_{ji} is a synaptic weight of feedforward inhibitory connection from cell j in the input layer to cell i in the output layer; z_{ij} is a synaptic weight of presynaptic inhibition from the excitatory cell to inhibitory axons; the sum is taken from j=1,..., N where N is the dimension of the network; f(x), g(x) and h(x) are output functions given by·[x]=x if x>0 and ·[x]=0 if x ≤ 0 where stands for f, g, or h. Tr is a threshold for feedforward inhibitory transmission. Output functions describe simple rectification, which is necessary in a biologically plausible model, because they prevent excitatory connection from becoming inhibitory and vice versa.

Term $-h(x_i)$ describes presynaptic inhibition by glutamate receptors. It acts on inhibitory signals from the input layer, y_i, before they can perturb the target excitatory cell. Therefore, the feedforward inhibitory signal, y_i, may trigger neurotransmitter release only if it is stronger than the retrograde signal from postsynaptic cell, x_i. As a consequence, the excitatory cell with a certain activity level can inhibit all inhibitory signals form the cells with lower activity level, but it cannot inhibit signals from cells with stronger activity. The cell with the highest activity level does not receive any inhibition and therefore converges to the value proportional to the input strength. All other cells receive a certain amount of inhibition which gradually increases and drives cell activity below the threshold. Presynaptic inhibition induces an ordering of activity values that corresponds to the magnitude of inputs. This allows the network to select the largest input even if the inhibitory connection strengths between cells are weak and (or) non-symmetric.

The same mechanism can be applied for implementing WTA behavior when eqn (1) is replaced with

$$\tau_x \frac{dx_i}{dt} = -Ax_i + (C - x_i)I_i - (B + x_i)\sum_j w_{ji} f[g(y_j) - z_{ij}h(x_i) - Tr] \quad (3)$$

where all network parameters have the same meaning as for eqn (1) and constant C describes upper saturation point for x_i. Therefore, x_i is no longer proportional to the input magnitude but it will saturate to a value close to the C. Also, it is possible to replace feedforward inhibition with feedback inhibition when we change eqn (2) into

$$\tau_y \frac{dy_i}{dt} = -y_i + x_i. \quad (4)$$

In this case, inhibition will be even stronger compared to the feedforward case, but all desirable properties described here will be retained.

3 Results

Network equations (1) and (2) are numerically solved using the 4.5 Runge-Kutta method. Parameters were set to the following values: $\tau_x=1$; $\tau_y=2$; A=1; B=1; $z_{ij}=1$ for all i and j; Tr=0; N=30. With respect to the inhibitory synaptic weights, wji, we consider two cases: full connectivity with $w_{ji}=.5$ for all j and i, and nearest neighbour connectivity with $w_{ji}=.5$ for $j = \{i\text{-}1, i, i\text{+}1\}$ and $w_{ji}=0$ for all other j. Fig 2 illustrates the model behaviour when tested on two different input patterns. Fig 2a shows the evolution of network responses when input has Gaussian distribution which is often the case in biological networks. Three objects centred at i = {8, 15, 22} were used with standard deviation, $\sigma = 2$ and with different amplitudes. As can be seen, network with full connectivity finds the global maximum in the input. On the other hand, the network with the nearest neighbour connectivity computes the local maximum. It shows three distinct winners corresponding to the centres of the three objects. Despite the fact that amplitudes of the objects are widely different they are nevertheless represented separately indicating that the nearest neighbour connectivity is sufficient to obtain sharp contrast enhancement.

Fig 2a shows another interesting point regarding the time needed to achieve convergence. In the model, the speed of selection is not dependent on the number of different elements in the input as it is in the case with WTA network based on oscillatory activity. However, reducing the distinctiveness (i.e., the difference between maximal and non-maximal input) of input elements increases the time necessary for convergence. In the network with full connectivity this is seen in response to the Gaussian input. The cells corresponding to the objects with smaller amplitudes are inhibited before the cells in the neighbourhood of the cell with the maximal input. In general, the speed of selection is very fast due to the fact that the cell with the maximal input does not receive any inhibitory input. Therefore it exponentially converges to its equilibrium state without interference form the other cells.

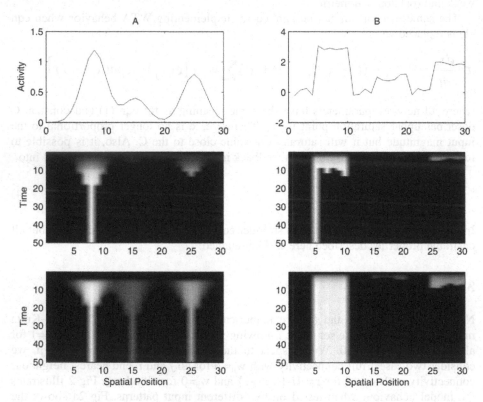

Fig. 2. Computer simulations illustrating the model behaviour on two different input patterns. A) Input with Gaussian shape tested on the network with full connectivity (middle row) and on the network with nearest neighbour connectivity (bottom row). B) Input with uniform random noise. Network is tested with Tr set to 0 (middle row) and with Tr set to .5 (bottom row).

Fig 2b shows the network ability to handle noisy input and to select a group of locations with similar activity level. Here, the input is an intensity staircase with three distinct levels, $I_i = \{1, 2, 3\}$ but it is obscured by the uniform noise in the range [-.25, .25]. Simulations in Fig 2b are performed using full connectivity but the value of the threshold for feedforward inhibition, Tr, is varied. In the Fig 2b, Tr=0, which forces the network to select one node with maximal activity. In this case, it is not justified to select a single location because noise prevents the network from detecting the full pattern (all locations with intensity value around I_i=3). When Tr is set to .5, all locations which receive input around I_i=3 will be selected. Similar arguments led to the construction of k-WTA networks which are able to select k winning cells [4]. However, in the k-WTA networks, the number of active cells is chosen in advance. Proposed network shows greater flexibility because the number of active cells will depend on the characteristics of the input and not on the network parameters. If there are many cells with similar values they all will be selected together. If a single location with maximal input is distinctive it will be selected alone.

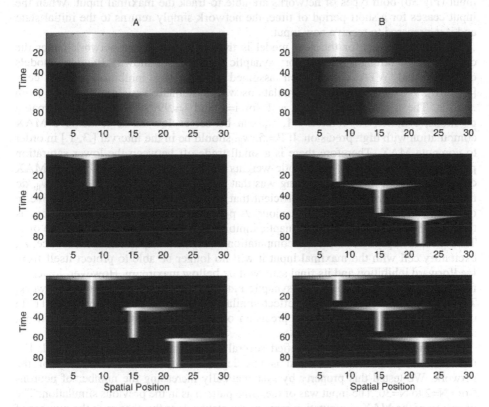

Fig. 3. Computer simulation illustrating the model ability to track time-varying input. A) Continuously changing input. B) Input with short delays between input presentations. Middle row shows output of the network with full connectivity. Bottom row shows output of the network with nearest neighbour connectivity.

Fig 3 illustrates the network sensitivity to the alternations in the input pattern. Again, we consider separately the network with full connectivity (middle row) and the network with the nearest neighbour connectivity (bottom row). Input (top row) consists of a symmetric intensity staircase with value 1 at the position i=8. Intensity is reduced in constant steps of .1 to the left and to the right from the position i=8. At t=30 input shifts to the right for 8 locations. At t=60 it makes another shift to the right for another 8 locations. Parameter setting was the same as in previous simulations except for the time constant for excitatory cells which is set to τ_x=.1. When the input continuously changes (Fig 3a) the network with full connectivity is not able to track these changes. The reason is that the inhibitory cells are continuously active and they prevent new excitatory cells to become active and to build enough activity to use presynaptic inhibition. This does not happen to a network with the nearest neighbour connectivity provided that new input pattern is sufficiently different from the old pattern. In that case, previously active inhibitory cells will be further away from the new maximal input and therefore they will not interfere with computing MAX at the new location. However, when there are delays between presentations of different input (Fig 3b) both types of networks are able to track the maximal input. When the input ceases for a short period of time, the network simply returns to the initial state and it is prepared to receive new input.

An important test for the new model is the behaviour of the network under the changes of the strength of inhibitory synaptic weights (not shown). Previous models of MAX and WTA computation assumed very strong inhibition among cells [4,15,16]. We made parametric simulations with systematic variation of the w_{ji} from .1 to 1. The input pattern was $I_i = 1$ for i=1 and $I_i=.999999$ for all other spatial positions, i=2, ..., N. With B =1, w_{ji} can be set as low as .2 to achieve MAX computation with high precision. If B=.5, w_{ji}, should be in the interval [.3, 1.] in order to compute MAX. Therefore there is a small trade-off between the lower saturation point, B, and the strength of synaptic weights necessary to achieve the precise MAX computation. An interesting finding was that the inhibitory synaptic weights, w_{ji}, do not need to be symmetric. It is sufficient that, w_{ji}, is in the range specified above in order to achieve the desirable behaviour. A potential critique of these simulations is that, z_{ij}, synaptic weights for presynaptic inhibition are kept constant at the value of 1. This choice simply allows precise computation of the MAX operator. If we reduce, z_{ij}, excitatory cell with the maximal input it will no longer be able to protect itself from feedforward inhibition and its final state will be bellow maximum. However, lowering the strength of connections for presynaptic inhibition will not destabilise the network. These connections will have the effect similar to the effect of the threshold, Tr. In other words, they will reduce the precision of MAX computation but they will not abolish it completely.

Computer simulations also verified several other features of the new model. For instance, the proposed mechanism is not dependent on the dimensionality of the network. We tested this property by systematically increasing the number of neurons from N=2 to N=30. The input was of the same pattern as in the previous simulation. The precision of the MAX computation remains constant across the change in the number of active cells. Fukai and Tanaka [4] suggest that competitive networks should be able to ignore the noise present at the start of the simulation. In other words, when initial values for the simulations are set to some small random values the network should nevertheless find the cell with the maximal input. The present model is consistent with this requirement providing further evidence for noise tolerance. It is interesting to note that the proposed model achieves the desired behaviour using the linear output function (above the threshold) and the same behaviour is obtained even if f() is slower-than-linear. This is in contrast with many previous models which usually require faster-than-linear output function in order to achieve MAX or WTA computation.

4 Discussion

Yuille and Grzywacz [16] proposed that a presynaptic inhibition of excitatory input pathways is a biophysical mechanism for MAX and WTA computation. However, their model has several deficiencies. Firstly, it depends on the parameter λ which controls the amount of competition. If λ is chosen small, model does not exhibit WTA behaviour. The best performance is achieved when λ is set to a biophysically unrealistic value. Also the model uses a non-linear exponential output function. Secondly, the model depends on the dimensionality of the network. That is, performance of the model is degraded when more cells are introduced in the network. Thirdly, the network does not reset its activity when input is removed. This is undesirable because the network is not able to respond to the changes in the input pattern. It may be argued that such behaviour is useful when the winning node must be stored in short-term memory but it is problematic for modelling many other aspects of the cortical processing related to motion perception, and attention. We proposed a new model with presynaptic inhibition of feedforward inhibitory pathways. The new model addressed all issues which arise for Yuille and Grzywacz's model as it is verified by computer simulations. Moreover, it is more robust with respect to the changes in parameter settings.

Presynaptic inhibition of inhibitory pathways effectively computes the activity difference between the input to the target cell and the input from the rest of the network. In the context of modelling visual selective attention Tsotsos et al. [13] proposed a WTA mechanism based on computing activity difference between nodes. However, they do not specify neural mechanisms which are able to compute difference and they do not use real-time formalism. Therefore, their model did not deal with the issues of the connectivity, symmetry, and output functions. Modulation of inhibitory synaptic transmission by kainate receptors may be understood as a real-time biophysically realistic extension of their proposal.

Fukai and Tanaka [4] and Wang [14] argued that in many situations WTA behaviour is not sufficient and the output with multiple winners is more desirable. For instance, Wang [14] introduced a selection network based on relaxation oscillators which can select the representation of the whole object and not just a single point. The present approach is compatible with the requirements for multiple winners. When there are more inputs with the same maximal amplitude, all excitatory cells receiving such input will be selected due to the fact that their presynaptic inhibition will cancel all feedforward inhibition. Another possibility for insuring multiple winners in a noisy environment is to set the threshold for inhibitory transmission, Tr, to some small positive value. In the case, Tr > 0, all cells whose activity is in the interval between x_{max} and x_{max} - Tr, will be selected because they will not receive inhibition. In other words, all cells which are similar in magnitude to the winning cell will be selected. It is also possible that the threshold could be modulated in a task dependent manner or modulated depending on the statistics of the input. Such schemes will further increase the flexibility of the network.

Presynaptic inhibition is sensitive on the time of arrival of excitatory and inhibitory signals. If excitatory signals arrive before inhibitory, depolarization will initiate presynaptic inhibition which will prevent the following feedforward inhibition. On the other hand, if feedforward inhibitory signals arrive before the excitatory ones, they may prevent the cell from depolarizing enough to reach the threshold and to initiate disinhibition by presynaptic inhibition on glutamate receptors. Therefore, the proposed mechanism can be used for computing WTA and MAX in a temporal domain. This is true under the assumption that input signals convey information about the input magnitude by delays of initiation of single spikes across axon. In this coding scheme, the cell which receives the largest input will fire first; second largest cell will fire second and so on. When the first spike arrives at the corresponding target cell it depolarizes the cell and induces presynaptic inhibition on inhibitory axons projecting to it. Presynaptic inhibition will protect the cell from inhibitory spikes arriving latter. When the second spike arrives on the corresponding target cell it will not induce presynaptic inhibition on this cell because the cell is already inhibited from the previously activated cell. The same is true for all other spikes that will arrive later in time on all other cells.

Disadvantage of the proposed mechanism is that it requires a large number of axo-axonic connections between nodes in the output layer and feedforward inhibitory pathway. This type of connectivity is not supported by physiological data. We presented this version of the model in order to facilitate comparison with the model of Yuille and Grzywacz [16]. Biophysically plausible version of the model which does not require extensive connectivity uses glutamate spill-over instead (Fig 1b). Potential problem with glutamate spill-over is that a large amount of glutamate needs to be concentrated in the extra-cellular space which may have harmful effect on the neural tissue. Therefore, usefulness of the glutamate spill-over is restricted to small networks. However, there is possibility that other neurotransmitters such as GABA may use spill-over in order to influence inhibitory axonal terminals. Another possibility is that postsynaptic cell excretes neurotransmitter which binds to presynaptic receptor and reduces the amount of inhibition from presynaptic terminal [1,9]. This is known as depolarization-induced suppression of inhibition (DSI). It has been studied in the cerebellum and the hippocampus but it could be a general neural mechanism which allows the postsynaptic cell to control the amount of neurotransmitter release. Investigations showed that GABA and endocannabinoids are involved in this type of retrograde signalling [1,9]. Therefore, functional description of the mechanism presented here could have different biophysical realisations in real neural networks.

In conclusion, computer simulations showed that presynaptic inhibition of feedforward inhibitory pathways allows the network to compute the MAX function with greater flexibility compared to the model where presynaptic inhibition is applied on excitatory pathways [16]. In particular, the new model can achieve MAX computation even when the inhibitory snypatic weights are weak and (or) asymmetric. The model behaviour is not dependent on the dimensionality of the network and it can handle multiple winners, input noise and time-varying input. With slight modification, the model is able to show WTA behaviour. Therefore, presynaptic inhibition of inhibitory transmission may significantly increase the computational power and robustness of competitive network [10]. Biophysical implementation of the proposed model could involve kainate receptors located on axonal terminals of inhibitory cells [2,7]. These receptors are found to inhibit GABA release and effectively disinhibit the postsynaptic cell. Due to the fact that kainate receptors are ionotropic receptors, a time-scale of their activation is appropriate for fast sensory processing.

Acknowledgments. This work is supported by the Bial Foundation research grant No. 80/06.

References

1. Alger, B.E., Pitler, T.A.: Retrograde signaling at GABAA-receptor synapses in the mammalian CNS. Trends Neurosci. 18, 333–340 (1995)
2. Binns, K.E., Turner, J.P., Salt, T.E.: Kainate receptor (GluR5)-mediated disinhibition of responses in rat ventrobasal thalamus allows a novel sensory processing mechanism. J. Physiol. 551, 525–537 (2003)
3. Ermentrout, B.: Complex dynamics in winner-take-all neural nets with slow inhibition. Neural Netw. 5, 415–431 (1992)
4. Fukai, T., Tanaka, S.: A simple neural network exhibiting selective activation of neuronal ensembles: from winner-take-all to winners-share-all. Neural Comput. 9, 77–97 (1997)
5. Gawne, T.J., Martin, J.M.: Responses of primate visual cortical V4 neurons to simultaneously presented stimuli. J. Neurophysiol. 88, 1128–1135 (2002)
6. Grossberg, S.: Nonlinear neural networks: Principles, mechanisms, and architectures. Neural Netw. 1, 17–61 (1988)
7. Huettner, J.E.: Kainate receptors and synaptic transmission. Prog. Neurobiol. 70, 387–407 (2001)
8. Kaski, S., Kohonen, T.: Winner-take-all networks for physiological models of competitive learning. Neural Netw. 7, 973–984 (1994)
9. Kreitzer, A.C., Regehr, W.G.: Retrograde signalling by endocannabinoids. Curr. Opin. Neurobiol. 12, 324–330 (2002)
10. MacDermott, A.B., Role, L.W., Siegelbaum, S.A.: Presynaptic ionotropic receptors and the control of transmitter release. Annu. Rev. Neurosci. 22, 443–485 (1999)
11. Riesenhuber, M., Poggio, T.A.: Hierarchical models of object recognition in cortex. Nat. Neurosci. 2, 1019–1025 (1999)
12. Sato, T.: Interactions of visual stimuli in the receptive fields of inferior temporal neurons in awake macaques. Exp. Brain Res. 77, 23–30 (1989)
13. Tsotsos, J., Culhane, S., Wai, W., Lai, Y., Davis, N., Nuflo, F.: Modeling visual attention via selective tuning. Artif. Intel. 78, 507–545 (1995)
14. Wang, D.L.: Object selection based on oscillatory correlations. Neural Netw. 12, 579–592 (1999)
15. Yu, A.J., Giese, M.A., Poggio, T.A.: Biophysically plausible implementations of the maximum operation. Neural Comput. 14, 2857–2881 (2002)
16. Yuille, A.L., Grzywacz, N.M.: A winner-take-all mechanism based on presynaptic inhibittion feedback. Neural Comput. 1, 334–347 (1989)

Bounds of the Ability to Destroy Precise Coincidences by Spike Dithering

Antonio Pazienti[1], Markus Diesmann[1], and Sonja Grün[1,2]

[1] Computational Neuroscience Group
RIKEN Brain Science Institute
Wako, Japan
[2] Bernstein Center for Computational Neuroscience
Berlin, Germany
antonio.pazienti@neurobiologie.fu-berlin.de

Abstract. Correlation analysis of neuronal spiking activity relies on the availability of distributions for assessing significance. At present, these distributions can only be created by surrogate data. A widely used surrogate, termed dithering, adds a small random offset to all spikes. Due to the biological noise, simultaneous spike emission is registered within a finite coincidence window. Established methods of counting are: (i) partitioning the temporal axis into disjunct bins and (ii) integrating the counts of precise coincidences over multiple relative temporal shifts of the two spike trains. Here, we rigorously analyze for both methods the effectiveness of dithering in destroying precise coincidences. Closed form expressions and bounds are derived for the case where the dither range equals the coincidence window. In this situation disjunct binning detects half of the original coincidences, the multiple shift method recovers three quarters. Thus, only a dither range much larger than the detection window qualifies as a generator of suitable surrogates.

Keywords: multi-channel recording, spike train, Monte-Carlo, surrogate data, correlation.

1 Introduction

The only way to identify information processing in biological neuronal networks is to simultaneously record from many neurons at a time. Nowadays multi-channel recordings are a standard technique in electrophysiological laboratories. Correlation analysis of such data has demonstrated that neurons exhibit correlated spiking activity on a fine temporal scale (ms precision) and in relation to the experimental protocol [1,2]. This has been interpreted as indicative for an involvement of correlated spiking activity in brain processing.

However, the presence of correlated spiking activity is not obvious from visual inspection. At first sight, the data appear to originate from a stochastic process with large variability in the number and the timing of spikes in responses to an identical stimulus. Furthermore, the rate of spike emission typically exhibits a

F. Mele et al. (Eds.): BVAI 2007, LNCS 4729, pp. 428–437, 2007.

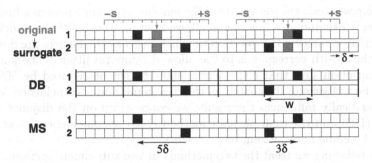

Fig. 1. Spike dithering and two methods of coincidence detection. Filled bins indicate spike occurrence, the width of the bins indicates the time resolution δ (typically 1 ms). Top: Generation of surrogate data. Original simultaneous spike data (grey bins) of neuron 1 and 2. Coincidences are assumed to be precise (within the same bin). In surrogate spike trains (black bins) all original spikes are independently dithered with uniform probability in the range $\pm s$ (in units of δ). Middle: In the disjunct binning (DB) method coincidences are detected in exclusive windows of width w to allow a temporal jitter of the spikes. Only spikes within the same window (between thick vertical lines) are counted as a coincidence. Bottom: In the multiple shift (MS) method spike coincidences are detected if the distance between spikes is smaller than or equal to an a-priori parameter (see Sec. 3).

complex temporal profile. Clearly, spike coincidences with millisecond precision can also occur as chance events. Thus, the empirical number of joint-spike events needs to be compared to the distribution of coincidence counts resulting from independent spike trains. This distribution can only be derived using strong assumptions about the statistics of the spike trains [3] typically not fulfilled by electrophysiological data. Therefore, Monte-Carlo methods are widely used to construct the distribution of coincidence counts from surrogate data [4] that maintain certain statistical properties of the original data but do not include correlations [5].

Various methods are in use for the generation of surrogate data [6,4,7,8,9]. All of them fulfill the condition to destroy the correlation, but also have the draw-back to simultaneously destroy one or the other statistical feature of the data [8,10], e.g. the Poissonian nature or the exact spike counts. Date and colleagues proposed the method of spike dithering to generate surrogates which currently best meets the criterion to destroy the correlation between spike trains and simultaneously to maintain as many statistical properties of the data as possible [11]. The approach is to randomly re-place each spike within a small time window around its original position, thereby almost perfectly preserving the other statistical features of the single neuron data. Meanwhile, the method is in routinely use in the correlation analysis of neuronal spike trains [12,13]. Strategies have been developed to reduce the perturbation of the inter-spike interval statistics for moderate dithers [10,14].

However, it is not well understood how much dither is required to destroy the spike correlation, in particular if joint-spike events are allowed to have a temporal jitter. Here we study the decay rate of the number of coincidences as a function of the dither width and as a function of allowed temporal jitter of the coincidences. In particular we answer the question to which degree coincidences are destroyed, if the dither width corresponds to the allowed temporal jitter of the joint-spike events. Intuition says that coincidences should then be reduced by 50%. This needs to be analyzed in the context of the chosen method of coincidence detection since it critically influences the result: we concentrate on the disjunct binning method (DB) and the multiple shift method (MS) of coincidence detection [15] (cf. Fig. 1 middle and bottom, respectively).

In the following we treat the two methods in two subsequent sections, in each of which we briefly introduce the respective method, and derive analytically the probability of detecting coincidences given originally precise coincidences as a function of dither and of the allowed coincidence width. The results section compares the two methods for the particular case of the applied dither being equal to the allowed coincidence width. We show that the probability of detection decays with increasing dither, however much faster for DB as compared to the MS method. We also compare to the case where only one spike train is dithered.

2 Disjunct Binning

The original spike data are discretized into bins of width δ, such that the total duration T of the recording is divided into N bins ($T = \delta \cdot N$). Each bin is assumed to contain at most one spike. As a result the activity of each neuron is represented by a binary sequence (Fig. 1) of zeros (no spikes) and ones (spikes). We define coincident events (or simply coincidences) as the joint firing of the two neurons within a coincidence window of w bins, thereby allowing coincidences to have a certain temporal jitter. In order to detect the total number of coincident events, the DB method sections T into disjunct, adjacent time segments (coincidence windows) $W_k, k = 1, ..., \lceil N/w \rceil$ each containing w bins of width δ. With bins numbered from 1 to N, the first coincidence window W_1 is composed of bins $\{1, 2, ..., w\}$, the second W_2 of $\{w + 1, w + 2, ..., 2w\}$, and so on.

We assume the original coincidences (i.e., before dithering) to be perfectly synchronous joint-events, i.e., both neurons have a spike in the very same bin. Due to an applied dither in the range of $[-s, s]$ bins a spike may trespass the border of a coincidence window and fall into another coincidence window. The *dither factor* $D = \lceil \frac{s}{w} \rceil$, i.e., the next integer larger than (or equal to) $\frac{s}{w}$, defines in how many coincidence windows the spike may fall and thus how many borders it might cross.

Next we are interested in the probability to detect a coincidence after dithering. The result depends on whether dithering is applied to both neurons (*2-neuron dithering*) or only one neuron (*1-neuron dithering*). The approaches are treated separately in the next two sections.

2.1   2-Neuron Dithering

In 2-neuron dithering each spike of both spike trains is randomly displaced in the range of $[-s, s]$ bins with uniform probability.

In order to calculate the probability that a coincidence after dithering is still detected as a coincidence, we need to consider all coincidence windows W_k into which the dithered spikes may be scattered. The number of windows is given by the dither factor D. If we assume the original coincidence to be in window W_0, spikes may be dithered into coincidence windows W_k with $k = 0, \pm 1, \pm 2, ..., \pm D$. Therefore, the probability is the sum of the probabilities that the spikes fall into the same window W_k.

The probability to detect a coincidence within a particular coincidence window W_k depends on the number of bins that may be reached from the original coincidence position given a particular dither s. The probability to fall in a single bin δ within the dither interval $[-s, +s]$ is $1/(2s + 1)$. Depending on the initial position $\alpha = 1, 2, ..., w$ of a spike in the coincidence window, a different number of bins is reachable in the surrounding coincidence windows. In the coincidence windows where all w bins can be reached ($k \in [-D + 2, ..., D - 2]$), the probability of a spike to fall into the window is $\Delta w_k^{\alpha} \cdot \frac{1}{2s+1}$, with $\Delta w_k^{\alpha} = w$. In the remote windows $\{W_{-D}, W_{-D+1}, W_{D-1}, W_D\}$, the probability corresponds to the number of reachable bins, i.e., $\Delta w_{k'}^{\alpha} \cdot \frac{1}{(2s+1)}$ with $k' = -D, -D + 1, D - 1, D$, respectively.

Because the two coincident spikes are dithered independently, the joint probability of both spikes being in window W_k is the product of the probabilities $(\Delta w_k^{\alpha} \cdot \frac{1}{2s+1})$ for the individual spikes. Then the total probability to detect the coincidence after dithering is given by the sum of the joint probabilities across all reachable coincidence windows:

$$P_{\alpha}^{[2-n]}(w, s) = \sum_{k=-D}^{k=D} \left(\frac{\Delta w_k^{\alpha}}{2s + 1} \right)^2. \tag{1}$$

The closure relation is given by the condition that the total dither involves $2s+1$ bins:

$$\sum_{k=-D}^{k=D} \Delta w_k^{\alpha} = 2s + 1 \quad \Rightarrow \quad \sum_{k=-D}^{k=D} \frac{\Delta w_k^{\alpha}}{2s + 1} = 1. \tag{2}$$

Fig. 2A,B show the coincidence detection probability $P_{\alpha}^{[2-n]}(w, s)$ as a function of the initial position α of the spikes in the coincidence window, for different values of the dither s. Surprisingly, the probability of detection $P_{\alpha}^{[2-n]}(w, s)$ depends on the distance of the initial coincidence from the borders of the coincidence window. For $s = w$ (Fig. 2A) the probability $P_{\alpha}^{[2-n]}(w, s)$ reaches its minimum if the initial coincidence is in the center of the window, and is maximal when the initial coincidence is just at the window border. This counterintuitive result holds true for all values of w. However, it can be understood by considering that if spikes were originally in the proximity of the border of the coincidence

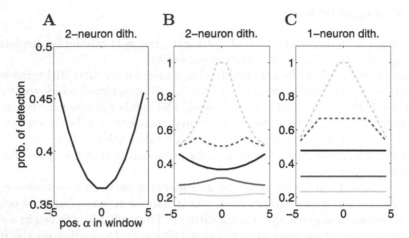

Fig. 2. Probability of detecting coincidences after dithering for DB as a function of the position α of the original coincidences measured from the center of the coincidence window W_0. A,B: For 2-neuron dithering. C: For 1-neuron dithering. Black curves: case $w = s$ (enlarged ordinate in A), solid grey curves: $w < s$, dashed grey curves: $w > s$. Parameter values: $w = 10$, $s = 15$ (solid, dark grey), $s = 21$ (solid, light grey), $s = 7$ (dashed, dark grey), and $s = 4$ (dashed, light grey).

window the number of destination windows is generally smaller than for originally centered spikes. As a consequence, spikes fall in larger stretches of successive bins, and thus the probability for the fission of coincidences by the borders of the coincidence windows is reduced. The total probability $P_\alpha^{[2-n]}(w, s)$, which is constrained by Eq. 2, is maximized if few increments Δw_k^α are large and is minimal if all increments have intermediate values. In other words, the number of ways of arranging the two spikes in a destination window increases quadratically with the number of involved bins (cf. Eq. 1), hence the α-dependance observed in Fig. 2A.

As shown in Fig. 2B, the overall probability $P_\alpha^{[2-n]}(w, s)$ progressively increases with decreasing s from $s > w$ to $s < w$, shown here for a fixed w. For decreasing s the spikes have a decreasing chance to trespass the window border and to escape from their original window. In extreme, for $s \ll w$ the spikes may not reach any other windows and thus stay coincident. In contrast, for $s > w$ the coincidence has an increasing probability to be destroyed because of the large number of potential destination windows. The probability $P_\alpha^{[2-n]}(w, s)$ shows different shapes depending on the exact relationship between s and w.

2.2   1-Neuron Dithering

In case only the spikes of one spike train are dithered (e.g. only the spikes of neuron 2, [6]) the probability of detecting the coincidences after dithering only depends on the new positions of the spikes of train 2. This method leads to a total probability

$$P_\alpha^{[1-n]}(w, s) = \begin{cases} w/(2s+1) & \text{if } s \geq w-1 \\ \Delta w_k^\alpha/(2s+1) & \text{if } s < w-1, \end{cases} \tag{3}$$

where we assumed the initial coincidence window to be W_k and Δw_k^α to be the associated number of bins reachable by a spike from neuron 2. Again, this number depends on the initial position α of the spike.

For $s \geq w-1$ both sides of the dither window $[-s, s]$ are larger than the coincident window W_k and thus the probability for the two original spikes to stay coincident after dithering depends on the probability for the dithered spike to stay in that window. Its probability is given by the number of bins in the window w relative to the total number of possible bins, i.e., $2s+1$, the spike may be dithered into (upper relation in Eq. 3). This obviously does not depend on the initial position α of the coincidence.

If both sides of the dither window are smaller than the coincident window ($s < w-1$), only a fraction of the bins may receive a spike after dithering and depends on the original position α of the spike (Fig. 2C). For $s < w-1$ the probability of detecting the coincidence after dithering increases progressively as s decreases, with a maximum at the central bins of the window. The maximal detection probability $w/(2s+1)$ is attained if the whole dither window $[-s, s]$ is included in the coincidence window W_k.

3   Multiple Shift

This method provides a different way of counting coincident spikes of two neurons, avoiding the arbitrarily located "hard" borders. The multiple shift method defines a maximum allowed shift b. Assuming again the spike trains to have resolution δ, the procedure begins with counting all precise coincidences. Then spike train 2 is shifted with respect to spike train 1 by δ and again all precise coincidences are counted. The procedure continues for all positive shifts $2\delta, 3\delta, .., b\delta$ and for the negative shifts $-\delta, -2\delta, ..., -b\delta$. Consequently, spikes with a distance of up to $\pm b$ bins are counted as coincident. The parameter b is analogous to the coincident width w, however with the substantial difference that there are no fixed borders and the initial position of the coincidence α is meaningless.

Consider both spikes constituting a coincidence to be dithered in the range $\pm s$ and the origin of the temporal axis to be located at the position of the initial coincidence. After dithering the probability to find spike 2 at distance k from spike 1 is given by the probability to find 1 at i times the probability to find 2 at $k+i$ summed over all possible positions i:

$$J(k, s) = \frac{1}{2s+1} \sum_{i=-s}^{s} p(k+i). \tag{4}$$

However, $p(k+i)$ is subject to further constraints. If e.g. spike 1 is at $-s$, spike 2 can only be coincident or to the right of spike 1, requiring $p(k-s)$ to vanish for negative k. Therefore, the effective limits of the sum also depend on k, collapsing Eq. 4 to

$$J(k,s) = \begin{cases} 1/(2s+1) & \text{for } k = 0 \\ \frac{2s+1-|k|}{(2s+1)^2} & \text{for } |k| \leq 2s \\ 0 & \text{for } |k| > 2s . \end{cases} \tag{5}$$

The probability of dithering two initially coincident spikes to a distance $|k|$ reaches its maximum at zero offset and decreases linearly with $|k|$ before it drops to zero at $\pm 2s$.

In the MS method all spikes dithered up to a distance $k = \pm b$ are classified as coincident. To obtain the probability to detect an initially coincident event after dithering $P^{[MS]}(b, s)$ we have to sum the probabilities $J(k, s)$ of all possible dithering results for k in the range $-b, ..., b$

$$P^{[MS]}(b,s) = \begin{cases} 1/(2s+1) & \text{for } b = 0 \\ \frac{1}{2s+1} + \sum_{k=-b}^{b} \frac{2s+1-|k|}{(2s+1)^2} & \text{for } b \leq 2s \\ 1 & \text{for } b > 2s \end{cases}$$

$$= \begin{cases} \frac{2b+1}{2s+1} - \frac{b(b+1)}{(2s+1)^2} & \text{for } b \leq 2s \\ 1 & \text{for } b > 2s . \end{cases} \tag{6}$$

4   Results

In this section we will derive the expected probability of detecting a coincidence after dithering given a large number of coincidences occurring in the spike trains at random times.

In the disjunct binning framework the assumption of many coincidences occurring at random times implies that the original coincident events will cover, in expectation, all possible initial positions $\alpha \in [1, ..., w]$. Therefore we have to average the results of Secs. 2.1 and 2.2 (Eqs. 1, 3) over α. For 2-neuron dithering this yields

$$\langle P_{\alpha}^{[2-n]}(w,s) \rangle_{\alpha} = \frac{1}{w} \sum_{\alpha=1}^{w} \sum_{k=-D}^{k=D} \left(\frac{\Delta w_k^{\alpha}}{2s+1} \right)^2 . \tag{7}$$

Using similar arguments we derive the expected probability for the case of DB after 1-neuron dithering utilizing Eq. 3:

$$\langle P_{\alpha}^{[1-n]}(w,s) \rangle_{\alpha} = \begin{cases} w/(2s+1) & \text{if } s \geq w - 1 \\ \Delta w_k^{\alpha}/(2s+1) & \text{if } s < w - 1 , \end{cases} \tag{8}$$

whereas in the case of the MS method there is no α-dependence of the probability. For convenience however we also rewrite Eq. 6:

$$\langle P^{[MS]}(b,s) \rangle = \begin{cases} \frac{2b+1}{2s+1} - \frac{b(b+1)}{(2s+1)^2} & \text{for } b \leq 2s \\ 1 & \text{for } b > 2s . \end{cases} \tag{9}$$

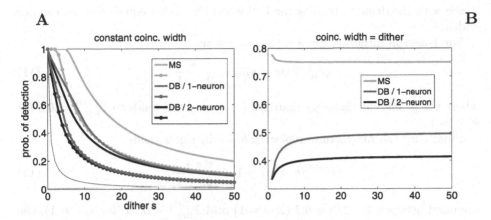

Fig. 3. Expected probability of detecting coincidences with DB and MS as a function of dither range. $\langle P^{[\mathrm{MS}]}(b,s)\rangle$ (light grey), $\langle P_\alpha^{[1-\mathrm{n}]}(w,s)\rangle_\alpha$ (dark grey), $\langle P_\alpha^{[2-\mathrm{n}]}(w,s)\rangle_\alpha$ (black). A: Three values of constant coincidence width. Thin curve: $b=0, w=1$ (MS and 1-/2-neuron, respectively), thick curves with knobs: $w=b=5$, thick curves: $w=b=10$. B: Bounds for coincidence width corresponding to dither width, $w=s$ and $b=s$ respectively.

Fig. 3A shows $\langle P_\alpha^{[2-\mathrm{n}]}(w,s)\rangle_\alpha$, $\langle P_\alpha^{[1-\mathrm{n}]}(w,s)\rangle_\alpha$ and $\langle P^{[\mathrm{MS}]}(b,s)\rangle$ as functions of the dither s and for three different values of allowed coincidence width. The expected probability declines with increasing dither in all cases. Detecting only precise coincidences ($w=1$ or $b=0$, respectively) the dither has a strong effect and destroys coincidences already at small values of s.

With increasing coincidence width the different cases deviate from each other, the 2-neuron dithering being the more effective way of destroying coincidences. For $w=b=10$ the 2-neuron dithering destroys about 80% of the original coincidences for dither values of about $s=20$. In this situation, the 1-neuron dithering leads to similar but slightly higher probabilities of detection, whereas for a similar loss of detected coincidences with the MS method a dither of about $s=50$ is required.

Let us now investigate the special case in which the dither equals the coincidence width, i.e., $s=w$, in order to obtain closed form expressions and limits. For the 2-neuron dithering setting $w=s$ and dither factor $D=1$ reduces Eq. 7 to

$$\langle P_\alpha^{[2-\mathrm{n}]}(w=s)\rangle_\alpha = \frac{1}{w}\sum_{\alpha=1}^{w}\sum_{k=-1}^{k=1}\left(\frac{\Delta w_k^\alpha}{2s+1}\right)^2$$

$$= \frac{1}{3} + \frac{s(s-1)}{3(2s+1)^2}. \tag{10}$$

For non-zero values of dithering Eq. 10 assumes values between $1/3$ (for $s, w=1$) and $\frac{1}{3}+\frac{1}{12}$ (for $s, w \gg 1$), that is $\frac{1}{3} \leq \langle P_\alpha^{[2-\mathrm{n}]}(w=s)\rangle_\alpha < 0.41\bar{6} = P_{\mathrm{lim}}^{[2-\mathrm{n}]}$. Therefore $P_{\mathrm{lim}}^{[2-\mathrm{n}]}$ is the maximum probability of detecting a 2-neuron dithered coincidence with the disjunct binning method when the dither equals the coincidence width.

For 1-neuron dithering Eq. 8 with $w = s$ is just

$$\langle P_\alpha^{[1-n]}(w = s)\rangle_\alpha = \frac{s}{2s+1} , \qquad (11)$$

where the probability is larger than $1/3$ $(s, w = 1)$ and tends to $P_{\text{lim}}^{[1-n]} = 0.5$ for $s, w \gg 1$.

Finally for the MS method replacing $b = s$ in Eq. 9 yields

$$\langle P^{[\text{MS}]}(b = s)\rangle = 1 - \frac{s(s+1)}{(2s+1)^2} , \qquad (12)$$

bounded between $1 - 2/9 = 0.\bar{7}$ $(b, w = 1)$ and $P_{\text{lim}}^{[\text{MS}]} = 0.75$ (for $b, s \gg 1$), the difference being only about 4%. The above results are visualized in Fig. 3B.

5   Discussion

In this contribution we have rigorously analyzed the effectiveness of 2-neuron dithering for the disjunct binning and the multiple shift detection methods and for comparison also 1-neuron dithering for DB. The analysis is restricted to precise coincidences. Further studies are required to investigate the biologically more relevant case of jittered (i.e., imprecise) coincidences [15], the presence of background activity, and processes with a biologically realistic inter-spike interval statistics [10]. Nevertheless, the present study provides detailed new insight in the dithering process. After uniform 2-neuron dithering of coincident spikes, the distribution of spike distances $|k|$ is not uniform, favoring the survival of coincidences. Furthermore, in DB the probability of detection after dithering depends on the initial location of the coincidence in a complex manner.

We provide analytic expressions for the expected probability of detection in the different scenarios. In DB and MS the expressions reduce to simple closed forms for $w = s$ and $b = s$, respectively. Under these constraints we obtain in the limit $s \to \infty$ the bounds $P_{\text{lim}}^{[2-n]} = 0.41\bar{6}$, $P_{\text{lim}}^{[1-n]} = 0.5$, and $P_{\text{lim}}^{[\text{MS}]} = 0.75$. These asymptotic values are monotonically approached. Thus, for 1-neuron dithering analyzed by DB the intuition that a dither width equal to the coincidence window destroys 50% of the coincidences is confirmed. For 2-neuron dithering the rate of destruction is slightly larger. Counter to intuition, for MS the effect is much less pronounced. At $b = s$ still 3/4 of the coincidences survive. For example, with $b = 10$ and $s = 50$ the probability of detection still is at $P^{[MS]}(b, s) \simeq 0.2$. Thus, for detection methods like MS which essentially evaluate the central peak of the cross-correlation, a dither width much larger than the detection window is required to destroy a relevant fraction of the coincidences.

Acknowledgements. We enjoyed inspiring discussions with George Gerstein during his stay in our laboratory at RIKEN BSI. Partially funded by BMBF

Grant 01GQ0413 to the BCCN Berlin, the Stifterverband für die deutsche Wissenschaft, DIP F1.2, and EU Grant 15879 (FACETS).

References

1. Riehle, A., Grün, S., Diesmann, M., Aertsen, A.: Spike synchronization and rate modulation differentially involved in motor cortical function. Science 278(5345), 1950–1953 (1997)
2. Nowak, L.G., Munk, M.H., Nelson, J.I., James, A., Bullier, J.: Structural basis of cortical synchronization. I. Three types of interhemispheric coupling. J. Neurophysiol. 74(6), 2379–2400 (1995)
3. Grün, S., Diesmann, M., Aertsen, A.: 'Unitary events' in multiple single-neuron spiking activity: I. Detection and significance. Neural Comput. 14(1), 43–80 (2002)
4. Pipa, G., Grün, S.: Non-parametric significance estimation of joint-spike events by shuffling and resampling. Neurocomputing 52–54, 31–37 (2003)
5. Ikegaya, Y., Aaron, G., Cossart, R., Aronov, D., Lampl, I., Ferster, D., Yuste, R.: Synfire chains and cortical songs: temporal modules of cortical activity. Science 5670(304), 559–564 (2004)
6. Hatsopoulos, N., Geman, S., Amarasingham, A., Bienenstock, E.: At what time scale does the nervous system operate? Neurocomputing 52–54, 25–29 (2003)
7. Pipa, G., Diesmann, M., Grün, S.: Significance of joint-spike events based on trial-shuffling by efficient combinatorial methods. Complexity 8(4), 79–86 (2003)
8. Grün, S., Riehle, A., Diesmann, M.: Effect of cross-trial nonstationarity on joint-spike events. Biol. Cybern. 88(5), 335–351 (2003)
9. Pipa, G., Riehle, A., Grün, S.: Validation of task-related excess of spike coincidences based on neuroxidence. Neurocomputing 70(10–12), 2064–2068 (2007)
10. Davies, R.M., Gerstein, G.L., Baker, S.N.: Measurement of time-dependent changes in the irregularity of neuronal spiking. J. Neurophysiol. 96, 906–918 (2006)
11. Date, A., Bienenstock, E., Geman, S.: On the temporal resolution of neural activity. Technical report, Divison of Applied Mathematics, Brown University (1998)
12. Abeles, M., Gat, I.: Detecting precise firing sequences in experimental data. J. Neurosci. Methods 107(1–2), 141–154 (2001)
13. Maldonado, P., Babul, C., Singer, W., Rodriguez, E., Berger, D., Grün, S.: Dissociation between discharge rates and synchrony in primary visual cortex of monkeys viewing natural images (submitted)
14. Gerstein, G.L.: Searching for significance in spatio-temporal firing patterns. Acta Neurobiol. Exp (Wars.) 2(64), 203–207 (2004)
15. Grün, S., Diesmann, M., Grammont, F., Riehle, A., Aertsen, A.: Detecting unitary events without discretization of time. J. Neurosci. Methods 94(1), 67–79 (1999)

Non-invasive Brain-Actuated Interaction

José del R. Millán[1,2], Pierre W. Ferrez[1,2], Ferran Galán[1,2], Eileen Lew[1,2],
and Ricardo Chavarriaga[1,2]

[1] IDIAP Research Institute, Rue du Simplon 4, 1920 Martigny, Switzerland
[2] Ecole Polytechnique Fédérale de Lausanne (EPFL), Switzerland
{jose.millan,pierre.ferrez,ferran.galan,eileen.lew,
ricardo.chavarriaga}@idiap.ch

Abstract. The promise of Brain-Computer Interfaces (BCI) technology is to augment human capabilities by enabling interaction with computers through a conscious and spontaneous modulation of the brainwaves after a short training period. Indeed, by analyzing brain electrical activity online, several groups have designed brain-actuated devices that provide alternative channels for communication, entertainment and control. Thus, a person can write messages using a virtual keyboard on a computer screen and also browse the internet. Alternatively, subjects can operate simple computer games, or brain games, and interact with educational software. Work with humans has shown that it is possible for them to move a cursor and even to drive a wheelchair. This paper briefly reviews the field of BCI, with a focus on non-invasive systems based on electroencephalogram (EEG) signals. It also describes three brain-actuated devices we have developed: a virtual keyboard, a brain game, and a wheelchair. Finally, it shortly discusses current research directions we are pursuing in order to improve the performance and robustness of our BCI system, especially for real-time control of brain-actuated robots.

Keywords: Brain-computer interfaces, electroencephalogram, asynchronous protocols, brain-actuated devices, statistical classifiers, feature selection.

1 Introduction

The idea of controlling machines not by manual operation, but by mere "thinking" (i.e., the brain activity of human subjects) has fascinated humankind since ever, and researchers working at the crossroads of computer science, neurosciences, and biomedical engineering have started to develop the first prototypes of *brain-computer interfaces (BCI)* over the last decade or so [1], [2], [3], [4], [5]. A BCI monitors the user's brain activity and translates their intentions into actions—such as moving a wheelchair [6], [7] or selecting a letter from a virtual keyboard [8], [9]—*without* using activity of any muscle or peripheral nerve. The central tenet of a BCI is the capability to distinguish different patterns of brain activity, each being associated to a particular intention or mental task.

Such a kind of BCI is a natural way to augment human capabilities by providing a new interaction link with the outside world and is particularly relevant as an aid for paralyzed humans, although it also opens up new possibilities in natural and direct interaction for able-bodied people. Figure 1 shows the general architecture of a BCI.

F. Mele et al. (Eds.): BVAI 2007, LNCS 4729, pp. 438–447, 2007.
© Springer-Verlag Berlin Heidelberg 2007

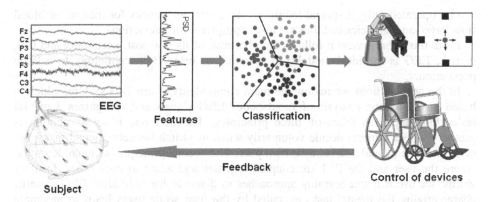

Fig. 1. General architecture of a brain-computer interface (BCI) for controlling devices such as a cursor, a robotic arm, or a motorized wheelchair. In this case the BCI measures electroencephalogram (EEG) signals recorded non-invasively from electrodes placed on the subject's scalp.

Brain electrical activity is recorded with a portable device. These raw signals are first processed and transformed in order to extract some relevant features that are then passed on to some mathematical models (e.g., statistical classifiers or neural networks). This model computes, after some training process, the appropriate mental commands to control the device. Finally, visual feedback, and maybe other kinds such as tactile stimulation, informs the subject about the performance of the brain-actuated device so that they can learn appropriate mental control strategies and make rapid changes to achieve the task.

A BCI may monitor brain activity via a variety of methods, which can be coarsely classified as invasive and non-invasive. In invasive BCI systems the activity of single neurons (their spiking rate) is recorded from microelectrodes implanted in the brain. Less invasive approaches are based on the analysis of electrocorticogram (ECoG) signals from electrodes implanted under the skull. For humans, however, it is preferable to use non-invasive approaches to avoid the risks generated by permanent surgically implanted devices in the brain, and the associated ethical concerns. Most non-invasive BCI systems use electroencephalogram (EEG) signals; i.e., the electrical brain activity recorded from electrodes placed on the scalp. The main source of the EEG is the synchronous activity of thousands of cortical neurons. Measuring the EEG is a simple noninvasive way to monitor electrical brain activity, but it does not provide detailed information on the activity of single neurons (or small brain areas). Moreover, it is characterized by small signal amplitudes (a few μVolts) and noisy measurements (especially if recording outside shield rooms).

Besides electrical activity, neural activity also produces other types of signals, such as magnetic and metabolic, that could be used in a BCI. Magnetic fields can be recorded with magnetoencephalography (MEG), while brain metabolic activity— reflected in changes in blood flow—can be observed with positron emission tomography (PET), functional magnetic resonance imaging (fMRI), and optical imaging. Unfortunately, such alternative techniques require sophisticated devices that can be operated only in special facilities. Moreover, techniques for measuring blood flow have long latencies and thus are less appropriate for interaction.

From this short review it follows that, because of its low cost, portability and lack of risk, EEG is the ideal modality if we want to bring BCI technology to a large population.

In the next sections we review the main components of our BCI system, which is based on the online analysis of spontaneous EEG signals and recognizes 3 mental tasks. Our approach relies on three principles. The first one is an asynchronous protocol where subjects decide voluntarily when to switch between mental tasks and perform those mental tasks at their own pace. The second principle is mutual learning, where the user and the BCI are coupled together and adapt to each other. In other words, we use machine learning approaches to discover the individual EEG patterns characterizing the mental tasks executed by the user while users learn to modulate their brainwaves so as to improve the recognition of the EEG patterns. Finally, the third principle is the combination of the user's intelligence with the design of intelligent devices that facilitate interaction and reduce the user's cognitive workload. This is particularly useful for mental control of robots. We also describe the three brain-actuated applications we have developed. Finally, we discuss current research directions we are pursuing in order to improve the performance and robustness of our BCI system, especially for real-time control of brain-actuated robots.

2 Spontaneous EEG and Asynchronous Operation

Non-invasive EEG-based BCIs can be classified as "evoked" or "spontaneous". An evoked BCI exploits a strong characteristic of the EEG, the so-called evoked potential, which reflects the immediate automatic responses of the brain to some external stimuli. Evoked potentials are, in principle, easy to pick up with scalp electrodes. The necessity of external stimulation does, however, restrict the applicability of evoked potentials to a limited range of tasks. In our view, a more natural and suitable alternative for interaction is to analyze components associated with spontaneous "intentional" mental activity. This is particularly the case when controlling robotics devices. Spontaneous BCIs are based on the analysis of EEG phenomena associated with various aspects of brain function related to mental tasks carried out by the subject at his/her own will. Such a kind of BCI can exploit two kinds of spontaneous, or endogenous, brain signals, namely slow potential shifts [10] or variations of rhythmic activity [6], [8], [11], [12], [13], [14]. We will focus on the latter that are the most common.

EEG-based BCIs are limited by a low channel capacity[1]. Most of the current systems have a channel capacity below 0.5 bits/s [3]. One of the main reasons for such a low bandwidth is that they are based on synchronous protocols where EEG is time-locked to externally paced cues repeated every 4-10 s and the response of the BCI is the overall decision over this period [10], [12], [13]. Such synchronous protocols facilitate EEG analysis since the starting time of mental states are precisely

---

[1] Channel capacity is the maximum possible information transfer rate, or bit rate, through a channel.

known and differences with respect to background EEG activity can be amplified. Unfortunately, they are slow and BCI systems that use them normally recognize only 2 mental states.

On the contrary, we utilize more flexible asynchronous protocols where the subject makes self-paced decisions on when to stop doing a mental task and start immediately the next one [6], [8], [15]. In such asynchronous protocols the subject can voluntarily change the mental task being executed at any moment without waiting for external cues. The time of response of an asynchronous BCI can be below 1 second. For instance, in our approach the system responds every 1/2 second. The rapid responses of our asynchronous BCI, together with its performance (see Section 3), give a theoretical channel capacity between 1 and 1.5 bits/s.

3 The Machine Learning Way to BCI

A critical issue for the development of a BCI is training—i.e., how users learn to operate the BCI. Some groups have demonstrated that some subjects can learn to control their brain activity through appropriate, but lengthy, training in order to generate fixed EEG patterns that the BCI transforms into external actions [10], [13]. In this case the subject is trained over several months to modify the amplitude of their EEG signals. We follow a mutual learning process to facilitate and accelerate the user's training period. Indeed, our approach allows subjects to achieve good performances in just a few hours of training in the presence of feedback [8].

Most BCI systems deal with the recognition of just 2 mental tasks [11], [12], [14], [15]. Our approach achieves error rates below 5% for 3 mental tasks, but correct recognition is 70%. In the remaining cases (around 20-25%), the classifier doesn't respond, since it considers the EEG samples as uncertain. The incorporation of rejection criteria (see below) to avoid making risky decisions is an important concern in BCI. From a practical point of view, a low classification error is a critical performance criterion for a BCI; otherwise users can become frustrated and stop utilizing it.

We use machine learning techniques at two levels, namely feature selection and training the classifier embedded into the BCI. The approach aims at discovering subject-specific spatio-frequency patterns embedded in the continuous EEG signal— i.e., EEG rhythms over local cortical areas that differentiate the mental tasks. At the first level, we select those features that are more relevant for discriminating among the mental tasks. The selected features are those that satisfy two criteria: maximization of the separability of the mental tasks and stability over time. Indeed, EEG signals are non-stationary and, so, change over time. Feature selection is based on canonical variates analysis [16]. This procedure yields a sample, or input vector, x composed of the power of some frequency components from some electrodes.

We use a statistical Gaussian classifier (see [6] for more details). The output of this statistical classifier is an estimation of the posterior class probability distribution for a sample; i.e., the probability that a given single trial belongs to each mental task (or class). Each class is represented by a number of Gaussian prototypes, typically less than four. That is, we assume that the class-conditional probability function of class C_k is a superposition of N_k Gaussian prototypes. We also assume that all classes have equal prior probability. All classes have the same number of prototypes N_p, and for each class each prototype has equal weight $1/N_k$. Then, dropping constant terms, the activity a_k^i of the ith prototype of class C_k for a given sample $\mathbf{x}$ is the value of the Gaussian with centre μ_k^i and covariance matrix Σ_k^i. From this we calculate the posterior probability y_k of the class C_k. The posterior probability y_k of the class C_k is now the sum of the activities of all the prototypes of class k divided by the sum of the activities of all the prototypes of all the classes.

The classifier output for input vector $\mathbf{x}$ is now the class with the highest probability, provided that the probability is above a given threshold, otherwise the result is "unknown".

Usually each prototype of each class would have an individual covariance matrix Σ_k^i, but to reduce the number of parameters the model has a single diagonal covariance matrix common to all the prototypes of the same class. During offline training of the classifier, the prototype centers are initialized by any clustering algorithm or generative approach. This initial estimate is then improved by stochastic gradient descent to minimize the mean square error $E = \frac{1}{2}\sum_k (y_k - t_k)^2$, where $\mathbf{t}$ is the target vector in the form 1-of-C; that is, if the second of three classes was the desired output, the target vector is (0,1,0). The covariance matrices are computed individually and are then averaged over the prototypes of each class to give Σ_k.

4 Hardware and Signal Acquisition

We acquire EEG potentials with a portable BioSemi system using a cap with either 32 or 64 integrated electrodes arranged in the modified 10/20 International System. The EEG recordings are monopolar and taken at 512Hz.

EEG signals are characterized by a poor signal-to-noise ratio and spatial resolution. Their quality is greatly improved by means of spatial filtering techniques. We use the common average reference (CAR) procedure, where at each time step the average potential over all the channels is subtracted from each channel. This re-referencing procedure removes the background activity, leaving activity from local sources beneath the electrodes. Alternatively, raw EEG potentials can be transformed by means of a Surface Laplacian (SL) derivation. The SL estimate yields new potentials that represent better the cortical activity originated in radial sources immediately below the electrodes. The superiority of SL- and/or CAR-transformed signals over raw potentials for the operation of a BCI has been demonstrated in different studies [11], [17].

5 Brain-Actuated Devices

BCI systems are being used to operate a number of brain-actuated applications that augment people's communication capabilities, provide new forms of entertainment, and also enable the operation of physical devices. In this section we briefly describe some of the brain-actuated devices we have developed over the years. All these systems have been largely demonstrated publicly.

Our asynchronous BCI can be used to select letters from a virtual keyboard on a computer screen and to write a message [8], [9]. Initially, the whole keyboard (26 English letters plus the space to separate words, for a total of 27 symbols organized in a matrix of 3 rows by 9 columns) is divided in three blocks, each associated to one of the mental tasks. The association between blocks and mental tasks is indicated by the same colors as during the training phase. Each block contains an equal number of symbols, namely 9 at this first level (3 rows by 3 columns). Then, once the statistical classifier recognizes the block on which the subject is concentrating, this block is split in 3 smaller blocks, each having 3 symbols this time (1 row). As one of this second-level blocks is selected, it is again split in 3 parts. At this third and final level, each block contains 1 single symbol. Finally, to select the desired symbol, the user concentrates in its associated mental task as indicated by the color of the symbol. This symbol goes to the message and the whole process starts over again. Thus, the process of writing a single letter requires three decision steps.

The second brain-actuated device is a simple computer game [9], or "brain game", but other educational software could have been selected instead. It is the classical Pacman. For the control of Pacman, two mental tasks are enough to make it turn left of right. Pacman changes direction of movement whenever one of the mental tasks is recognized twice in a row. In the absence of further mental commands, Pacman moves forward until it reaches a wall, where it stops and waits for instructions.

Finally, it is also possible to control mentally robots and prosthesis. Until recently, EEG-based BCIs have been considered too slow for controlling rapid and complex sequences of movements. But we have shown for the first time [6], [8] that asynchronous analysis of EEG signals is sufficient for humans to continuously control a mobile robot—emulating a motorized wheelchair—along non-trivial trajectories requiring fast and frequent switches between mental tasks (see Fig. 2). Two human subjects learned to mentally drive the robot between rooms in a house-like environment visiting 3 or 4 rooms in the desired order. Furthermore, mental control was only marginally worse than manual control on the same task. A key element of this brain-actuated robot is shared control between two intelligent agents—the human user and the robot—so that the user only gives high-level mental commands that the robot performs autonomously. In particular, the user's mental states are associated with high-level commands (e.g., "turn right at the next occasion") and that the robot executes these commands autonomously using the readings of its on-board sensors. Another critical feature is that a subject can issue high-level commands at any moment. This is possible because the operation of the BCI is asynchronous and, unlike synchronous approaches, does not require waiting for external cues. The robot relies on a behaviour-based controller to implement the high-level commands to guarantee obstacle avoidance and smooth turns. In this kind of controller, on-board sensors are read constantly and determine the next action to take.

More recently, we have extended this work to the mental control of both a simulated and a real wheelchair (see Fig. 3). This has been done in the framework of the European project MAIA (http://www.maia-project.org) and in cooperation with

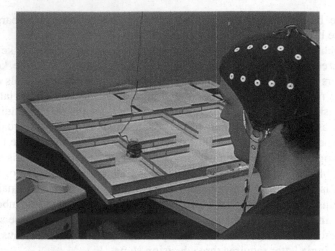

Fig. 2. One of the users while driving mentally the robot through the different rooms of the environment, making it turn right, turn left, or move forward. The robot has 3 lights on top to provide feedback to the user and 8 infrared sensors around its diameter to detect obstacles.

Fig. 3. Subject driving the wheelchair in a natural environment from non-invasive EEG. Note the laser scanner in front of the wheelchair, in between the subject's legs.

the KU Leuven. In this case, we have incorporated shared control principles into the BCI [18], [19]. In shared control, the intelligent controller relieves the human from low level tasks without sacrificing the cognitive superiority and adaptability of human beings that are capable of acting in unforeseen situations. In other words, in shared control there are two intelligent agents—the human user and the robot—so that the user only conveys intents that the robot performs autonomously. Although our first brain-actuated robot had already some form of cooperative control, shared autonomy is a more principled and flexible framework. Shared autonomy is also an essential component of any high-performance brain-actuated space device of the future.

6 Current Directions of Research

For brain-actuated robots, contrarily to augmented communication through BCI, fast decision-making is critical. In this sense, real-time control of brain-actuated devices, especially robots and neuroprostheses, is the most challenging application for BCI. While brain-actuated robots have been demonstrated in the laboratory, this technology is not yet ready to be taken out and used in real-world situations. A critical issue is how to improve the robustness of BCIs with the goal of making it a more practical and reliable technology. A first avenue of research is online adaptation of the interface to the user to keep the BCI constantly tuned to its owner [20], [21]. The point here is that, as subjects gain experience, they develop new capabilities and change their brain activity patterns. In addition, brain signals change naturally over time. In particular, this is the case from a session (with which data the classifier is trained) to the next (where the classifier is applied). Thus, online learning can be used to adapt the classifier throughout its use and keep it tuned to drifts in the signals it is receiving in each session. Preliminary work shows the feasibility and benefits of this approach.

The second line is the analysis of neural correlates of high-level cognitive and affective states such as errors, alarms, attention, frustration, confusion, etc. Information about these states is embedded in the EEG together with the mental commands intentionally generated by the user. The ability to detect and adapt to these states would enable the BCI to interact with the user in a much more meaningful way. One of these high-level states is the awareness of erroneous responses, whose neural correlate arises in the millisecond range. Thus, user's commands are executed only if no error is detected in this short time. Recent results have shown satisfactory single-trial recognition of errors that leads to significant improvement of the BCI performance [22], [23]. In addition, this new type of error potential—which is generated in response to errors made by the BCI rather than by the user—can provide with performance feedback that, in combination with online adaptation, allows improving the BCI while it is being used [24].

Acknowledgments. This work is supported by the Swiss National Science Foundation through the National Centre of Competence in Research on "Interactive Multimodal Information Management (IM2)" and also by the European IST Programme FET Project FP6-003758. This paper only reflects the authors' views and funding agencies are not liable for any use that may be made of the information contained herein.

References

1. Nicolelis, M.A.L.: Actions from Thoughts. Nature 409, 403–407 (2001)
2. Millán, J.d.R.: Brain-Computer Interfaces. In: Arbib, M.A. (ed.) Handbook of Brain Theory and Neural Networks, pp. 178–181. MIT Press, Cambridge, Massachusetts (2002)
3. Wolpaw, J.R., Birbaumer, N., McFarland, D.J., Pfurtscheller, G., Vaughan, T.M.: Brain-Computer Interfaces for Communication and Control. Clin. Neurophysiol. 113, 767–791 (2002)
4. Wickelgren, I.: Tapping the Mind. Science 299, 496–499 (2003)
5. Dornhege, G., Millán, J.d.R., Hinterberger, T., McFarland, D., Müller, K.-R. (eds.): Towards Brain-Computer Interfacing. MIT Press, Cambridge, Massachusetts (2007)
6. Millán, J.d.R., Renkens, F., Mouriño, J., Gerstner, W.: Non-Invasive Brain-Actuated Control of a Mobile Robot by Human EEG. IEEE Trans. Biomed. Eng. 51, 1026–1033 (2004)
7. Galán, F., Nuttin, M., Lew, E., Ferrez, P.W., Vanacker, G., Philips, J., Van Brussel, H., Millán, J.d.R.: An Asynchronous and Non-Invasive Brain-Actuated Wheelchair. In: 13th International Symposium on Robotics Research, Hirsoshima, Japan (2007)
8. Millán, J.d.R., Renkens, F., Mouriño, J., Gerstner, W.: Brain-Actuated Interaction. Artif. Intell. 159, 241–259 (2004)
9. Millán, J.d.R.: Adaptive Brain Interfaces. Comm. ACM 46, 74–80 (2003)
10. Birbaumer, N., Ghanayim, N., Hinterberger, T., Iversen, I., Kotchoubey, B., Kübler, A., Perelmouter, J., Taub, E., Flor, H.: A Spelling Device for the Paralysed. Nature 398, 297–298 (1999)
11. Babiloni, F., Cincotti, F., Lazzarini, L., Millán, J.d.R., Mouriño, J., Varsta, M., Heikkonen, J., Bianchi, L., Marciani, M.G.: Linear Classification of Low-Resolution EEG Patterns Produced by Imagined Hand Movements. IEEE Trans. Rehab. Eng. 8, 186–188 (2000)
12. Pfurtscheller, G., Neuper, C.: Motor Imagery and Direct Brain-Computer Communication. Proc. IEEE 89, 1123–1134 (2001)
13. Wolpaw, J.R., McFarland, D.J.: Control of a Two-Dimensional Movement Signal by a Noninvasive Brain-Computer Interface in Humans. PNAS 101, 17849–17854 (2004)
14. Blankertz, B., Dornhege, G., Krauledat, M., Müller, K.R., Kunzmann, V., Losch, F., Curio, G.: The Berlin Brain-Computer Interface: EEG-based Communication without Subject Training. IEEE Trans. Neural Sys. Rehab. Eng. 14, 147–152 (2006)
15. Birch, G.E., Bozorgzadeh, Z., Mason, S.G.: Initial On-Line Evaluation of the LF-ASD Brain-Computer Interface with Able-Bodied and Spinal-Cord Subjects using Imagined Voluntary Motor Potentials. IEEE Trans. Neural Sys. Rehab. Eng. 10, 219–224 (2002)
16. Galán, F., Ferrez, P.W., Oliva, F., Guàrdia, J., Millán, J.d.R.: Feature Extraction for Multi-class BCI using Canonical Variates Analysis. In: IEEE International Symposium on Intelligent Signal Processing, Alcalá de Henares, Spain (2007)
17. Mouriño, J.: EEG-based Analysis for the Design of Adaptive Brain Interfaces. Ph.D. thesis, Centre de Recerca en Enginyeria Biomèdica, Universitat Politècnica de Catalunya, Barcelona, Spain (2003)
18. Philips, J., Millán, J.d.R., Vanacker, G., Lew, E., Galán, F., Ferrez, P.W., Van Brussel, H., Nuttin, M.: Adaptive Shared Control of a Brain-Actuated Simulated Wheelchair. In: 10th International Conference on Rehabilitation Robotics, Noordwijk, The Netherlands (2007)
19. Vanacker, G., Millán, J.d.R., Lew, E., Ferrez, P.W., Galán, F., Philips, J., Van Brussel, H., Nuttin, M.: Context-based Filtering for Assisted Brain-Actuated Wheelchair Driving. Computational Intelligence and Neuroscience (2007)

20. Buttfield, A., Ferrez, P.W., Millán, J.d.R.: Towards a Robust BCI: Error Recognition and Online Learning. IEEE Trans. Neural Sys. Rehab. Eng. 14, 164–168 (2006)
21. Millán, J.d.R., Buttfield, A., Vidaurre, C., Krauledat, M., Schögl, A., Shenoy, P., Blankertz, B., Rao, R.P.N., Cabeza, R., Pfurtscheller, G., Müller, K.-R.: Adaptation in Brain-Computer Interfaces. In: Dornhege, G., Millán, J.d.R., Hinterberger, T., McFarland, D., Müller, K.-R. (eds.) Towards Brain-Computer Interfacing, MIT Press, Cambridge, Massachusetts (2007)
22. Ferrez, P.W., Millán, J.d.R.: You Are Wrong!—Automatic Detection of Interaction Errors from Brain Waves. In: Proc. 19th International Joint Conference on Artificial Intelligence (2005)
23. Ferrez, P.W., Millán, J.d.R.: Error-Related EEG Potentials in Brain-Computer Interfaces. In: Dornhege, G., Millán, J.d.R., Hinterberger, T., McFarland, D., Müller, K.-R. (eds.) Towards Brain-Computer Interfacing, MIT Press, Cambridge, Massachusetts (2007)
24. Perrin, X., Chavarriaga, R., Siegwart, R., Millán, J.d.R.: Bayesian Controller for a Novel Semi-Autonomous Navigation Concept. In: European Conference on Mobile Robotics, Freiburg, Germany (2007)

Decomposition Approach to Solve Dial-a-Ride Problems Using Ant Computing and Constraint Programming

Broderick Crawford[1,2], Carlos Castro[2], Eric Monfroy[2,3], and Claudio Cubillos[1,*]

[1] Pontificia Universidad Católica de Valparaíso, Chile
FirstName.Name@ucv.cl
[2] Universidad Técnica Federico Santa María, Valparaíso, Chile
FirstName.Name@inf.utfsm.cl
[3] LINA, Université de Nantes, France
FirstName.Name@univ-nantes.fr

Abstract. In this paper we solve the Dial-A-Ride Problem (DARP). The main objective of the DARP is to minimize operation costs for renting pieces of work from the transportation service providers. The resolution approach considered in this work, starting from a network formulation of the DARP, decomposes the problem in two phases: Clustering and Chaining. We model both phases like a Set Partitioning Problem (SPP) and solve them with an interesting sinergy between two different optimization methods: Ant Computing and Constraint Programming.

Keywords: Dial-A-Ride Problem, Ant Colony Optimization, Constraint Programming.

1 Introduction

Transportation on demand problems is concerned with the transportation of passengers or goods between specific origins and destinations at the request of users. The research on Optimization has deserved an increasing interest in this context, providing models and techniques to solve them. For example, many real life problems can be formulated as Set Partitioning Problems (SPP). Although the best known application of the SPP is Airline Crew Scheduling [2], several other applications exist, including Vehicle Routing Problems (VRP) [20,3] and Query Processing [18]. The main disadvantage of SPP-based models is the need to explicitly generate a large set of possibilities to obtain good solutions. Additionally, in many cases a prohibitive time is needed to find the exact solution.

* The authors had been partially supported by the following projects: the first author by PUCV 209.745/2007 project, the second by the Chilean National Science Fund through the project FONDECYT 1070268, the third author by FONDECYT 1060373 project and the fourth author by PUCV 209.746/2007 project.

F. Mele et al. (Eds.): BVAI 2007, LNCS 4729, pp. 448–457, 2007.
© Springer-Verlag Berlin Heidelberg 2007

In relation with VRP was proposed in 1964 [3] and recent contributions are including the use of metaheuristic to solve it [9]. Furthermore, Set Partitioning Problems occur as subproblems in various combinatorial optimization problems. In Airline Scheduling, a subtask called Crew Scheduling, takes as input data a set of crew pairings, where the selection of crew pairings which cause minimal costs and ensure that each flight is covered exactly once, can be modelled as a set partitioning problem [2]. In [6] solving a particular case of VRP, the Dial-a-ride Problem (DARP), also uses a SPP decomposition approach. Because, the SPP formulation have demonstrated to be useful modeling VRP problems (or their phases), it is our interest to solve it with novel techniques, in [9] there is a review of the scientific literature on the DARP. In this work, we solve some test instances of SPP with Ant Colony Optimization (ACO) algorithms and some hybridizations of ACO with Constraint Programming (CP) techniques. A direct implementation of the basic ACO framework is unable of obtaining feasible solutions for many SPP standard tested instances [25]. The best performing metaheuristic for SPP is a genetic algorithm due to Chu and Beasley [7]. There already exists some first approaches applying ACO to Subset Problems (Set Partitionong, Set Covering and Set Packing) [22,19,17]. Taking into account these results, it seems that the incomplete approach of Ant Computing could be considered as a good alternative to solve these problems when complete techniques are not able to get the optimal solution in a reasonable time. Although the idea of obtaining sinergy from hybridization of ACO with CP is not novel [27,16,26], we are working in the addition of a Constraint Programming mechanism in the construction phase of ACO thus only feasible partial solutions are generated. The CP mechanism allows the incorporation of information about the instantiation of variables after the current decision.

This paper is organised as follows: Section 2 is dedicated to the presentation of the problem and its mathematical model. The section 3 describes the solution approach: SPP decomposition of DARP. In Section 4, we describe the applicability of the ACO algorithms for solving SPP. In Section 5, we present the basic concepts to adding Constraint Programming techniques to ACO algorithms. In Section 6, we present our results solving benchmarks available in the OR-Library of Beasley [4]. Finally, in Section 7 we conclude the paper and give some perspectives for future research.

2   Problem Description

DARP belongs to a huge family of vehicle routing problems. In its canonical form: VRP, requires the design of a set of minimum cost routes originating and terminating at a central depot for a fleet of vehicles that has to service a set of customers with known demands. Examples of VRP application domains are the mail distribution, garbage collection and school bus problem among others. Furthermore, the vehicle routing problem is a generalization of the traveling salesman problem (TSP), the well-known combinatorial problem known to be NP-hard. For instance, the single uncapacitated vehicle version of the VRP problem with the objective of minimizing total travel time reduces to a Traveling Salesman Problem. The Pickup and Delivery Problem (PDP) arise when a vehicle is required to pickup an entity (e.g. a passenger or a good) at one location and then deliver it to another location. In this case, some pairing and precedence constraints must be preserved. Precedence constraints deal with the restriction that each pickup location has to be visited prior to visiting the corresponding delivery location. Pairing constraints restrict the set of admissible routes such that one vehicle has to do both the pickup and the delivery of the passengers of one transportation request. PDP is sometimes called vehicle routing problem with pickup and delivery (VRPPD), as it is a generalization of the vehicle routing problem. Practical problems that can be modeled as PDP are dial-a-ride problems and courier company pickup and delivery problems (CCPDP). In this sense, DARP can be seen as an application area of the pickup and delivery problem devoted to passengers. DARP distinguishes itself from the basic PDP by its focus on controlling user inconvenience, in the form of constraints or objective function terms (e.g. waiting time, ride time, desired departure/arrival time deviations). Most practical problems impose time restrictions related to when the vehicle has to be at the pickup or delivery stop, these restrictions can be applied to all of the above mentioned problems.

2.1   Mathematical Formulation

The early work on mathematical formulation of the problem was done in the late 1970s, the formulation has since changed and improved [28,8,9].

Let n denote the number of users (or requests) to be served. The DARP may be defined on a complete directed graph $G = (N, A)$ where $N = P \cup D \cup \{0, 2n+1\}$, $P = \{1, ..., n\}$ and $D = \{n+1, ..., 2n\}$. Subsets P and D contain pick-up and drop-off nodes, respectively, while nodes 0 and $2n + 1$ represent the origin and destination depots. With each user i are thus associated an origin node i and a destination node $n + i$. Let K be the set of vehicles and let $m = |K|$. Each vehicle $k \in K$ has a capacity Q_k and the total duration of its route cannot exceed T_k. With each node $i \in N$ are associated a load q_i and a non-negative service duration d_i such that $q_0 = q_{2n+1} = 0$, $q_i = -q_{n+i}(i = 1, ..., n)$ and $d_0 = d_{2n+1} = 0$. A time window $[e_i, l_i]$ is also associated with node $i \in N$ where e_i and l_i represent the earliest and latest time, respectively, at which service may begin at node i. With each arc $(i, j) \in A$ are associated a routing cost c_{ij} and a travel time t_{ij}. Finally, denote by L the maximum ride time of a user. For each arc $(i, j) \in A$ and each vehicle $k \in K$, let $x_{ij}^k = 1$ if vehicle k travels from node i to node j. For each node $i \in N$ and each vehicle $k \in K$, let B_i^k be the time at which vehicle k begins service at node i, and Q_i^k be the load of vehicle k after visiting node i. Finally, for each user i, let L_i^k be the ride time of user i on vehicle k. The formulation is as follows:

$$Minimise \qquad \sum_{k \in K} \sum_{i \in N} \sum_{j \in N} C_{ij}^k X_{ij}^k \qquad (1)$$

Subject to

$$\sum_{k \in K} \sum_{j \in N} X_{ij}^k = 1 \qquad\qquad \forall i \in P \qquad\qquad (2)$$

$$\sum_{j \in N} X_{ij}^k - \sum_{j \in N} X_{n+i,j}^k = 0 \qquad\qquad \forall i \in P, k \in K \qquad\qquad (3)$$

$$\sum_{j \in N} X_{0j}^k = 1 \qquad\qquad \forall k \in K \qquad\qquad (4)$$

$$\sum_{j \in N} X_{ji}^k - \sum_{j \in N} X_{ij}^k = 0 \qquad\qquad \forall i \in P \cup D, k \in K \qquad\qquad (5)$$

$$\sum_{i \in N} X_{i,2n+1}^k = 1 \qquad\qquad \forall k \in K \qquad\qquad (6)$$

$$B_j^k \geq (B_i^k + d_i + t_{ij})x_{ij}^k \qquad\qquad \forall i \in N, j \in N, k \in K \qquad\qquad (7)$$

$$Q_j^k \geq (Q_i^k + q_j)x_{ij}^k \qquad\qquad \forall i \in N, j \in N, k \in K \qquad\qquad (8)$$

$$L_i^k = B_{n+i}^k - (B_i^k + d_i) \qquad\qquad \forall i \in P, k \in K \qquad\qquad (9)$$

$$B_{2n+1}^k - B_0^k \leq T_k \qquad\qquad \forall k \in K \qquad\qquad (10)$$

$$e_i \leq B_i^k \leq l_i \qquad\qquad \forall i \in N, k \in K \qquad\qquad (11)$$

$$t_{i,n+i} \leq L_i^k \leq L \qquad\qquad \forall i \in P, k \in K \qquad\qquad (12)$$

$$max\{0, q_i\} \leq Q_i^k \leq min\{Q_k, Q_k + q_i\} \qquad\qquad \forall i \in N, k \in K \qquad\qquad (13)$$

$$X_{ij}^k \in \{0,1\} \qquad\qquad \forall i \in N, j \in N, k \in K \qquad\qquad (14)$$

The objective function (1) minimizes the total routing cost. Constraints (2) and (3) ensure that each request is served exactly once and that the origin and destination nodes are visited by the same vehicle. Constraints (4)-(6) guarantee that the route of each vehicle k starts at the origin depot and ends at the destination depot. Consistence of the time and load variables is ensured by constraints (7) and (8). Equalities (9) define the ride time of each user which is bounded by constraints (12). It is worth mentioning that the latter also act as precedence constraints because the non-negativity of the L_i^k variables ensures that node i will be visited before node $n+i$ for every user i. Finally, inequalities (10) bound the duration of each route while (11) and (13) impose time windows and capacity constraints, respectively. This formulation is non-linear because of constraints (7) and (8).

3   Solution Approach

The solution approach considered in this work can be categorized like a Decomposition Strategy. Decomposition methods range from relatively simple *cluster-first, route-second* idea known as the two phase method. Starting from a network formulation of the DARP, a decomposition approach decomposes the problem into a Clustering and a Chaining phase, solving both phases like SPP. In [6] it is suggested the following two step decomposition approach to the DARP:

- Clustering Step: Construct a set of feasible clusters.
- Chaining Step: Chain clusters to a set of tours that constitute a feasible schedule.

The decomposition is based on the concept of a cluster. A cluster is a segment of a vehicle tour satisfying the local constraints: Pairing precedence, time windows, no stop, and capacity. Clusters are useful for vehicle scheduling because they can serve as the building blocks of vehicle tours. Then, we can chain clusters to feasible tours just as we constructed clusters from the individual requests. As the clusters already satisfy the local constraints, the chaining can concentrate on the remaining global constraints. Clustering and Chaining SPP are of identical structure. The objective of the clustering step is to construct a set of clusters that can be chained to an optimal solution of the DARP. Then DARP results in the following optimization problem over clusters: *Given the customer requests, find a set of clusters such that each request is contained in exactly one cluster and the sum of the cluster objectives is minimal.*

The formulation of the clustering step aims at inputs for the chaining phase and can be formulated as a Set Partitioning Problem. SPP is the NP-complete problem of partitioning a given set into mutually independent subsets while minimizing a cost function defined as the sum of the costs associated to each of the eligible subsets. In the SPP matrix formulation we are given a $m \times n$ matrix $A = (a_{ij})$ in which all the matrix elements are either zero or one. Additionally, each column is given a non-negative cost c_j. We say that a column j can cover a row i if $a_{ij} = 1$. Let J denotes the set of the columns and x_j a binary variable which is one if column j is chosen and zero otherwise. The SPP can be defined formally as follows:

$$Minimize \quad f(x) = \sum_{j=1}^{n} c_j \times x_j \tag{15}$$

$$Subject \ to \quad \sum_{j=1}^{n} a_{ij} \times x_j = 1; \quad \forall i = 1, \ldots, m \tag{16}$$

These constraints enforce that each row is covered by exactly one column. In this formulation, each row represents a customer request that must be contained in exactly one cluster. The columns represent clusters. c_j is the vector of cluster objectives. Having decided for a set of clusters we can treat the chaining step in exactly the same way as we just did with the clustering step.

Approximating the objective value of the DARP as a sum of objectives of individual tours, the DARP for fixed clusters simplifies to the following optimization problem over tours: *Given a clustering, find a set of vehicle tours such that each cluster is contained in exactly one tour and the sum of the tour objectives is minimal.* Natural objectives associated to tours are operation costs for vehicles and/or customer satisfaction criteria like accumulated waiting time. It can also be modelled as a set partitioning problem.

4   Solving Set Partitioning Problem with Ant Computing

ACO can be applied in a very straightforward way to SPP. The columns are chosen as the solution components and have associated a cost and a pheromone trail [14,13]. Each column can be visited by an ant only once and then a final solution has to cover all rows. A walk of an ant over the graph representation corresponds to the iterative addition of columns to the partial solution obtained so far. Each ant starts with an empty solution and adds columns until a cover is completed. A pheromone trail τ_j and a heuristic information η_j are associated to each eligible column j. A column to be added is chosen with a probability that depends of pheromone trail and the heuristic information. The most common form of the ACO decision policy (*Transition Rule Probability*) when ants work with components is:

$$p_j^k(t) = \frac{\tau_j * \eta_j^\beta}{\sum\limits_{l \notin S^k} \tau_l [\eta_l]^\beta} \quad \text{if } j \notin S^k \tag{17}$$

where S^k is the partial solution of the ant k. The β parameter controls how important is η in the probabilistic decision [14].

Pheromone trail τ_j. In this work the pheromone trail is put on the problems component (each eligible column j) instead of the problems connections. And setting a good pheromone quantity is not a trivial task either. The quantity of pheromone trail laid on columns is based on the idea: *the more pheromone trail on a particular item, the more profitable that item is* [22]. Then, the pheromone deposited in each component will be in relation to its frequency in the ants solutions. In this work we divided this frequency by the number of ants obtaining better results.

Heuristic information η_j. In this paper we use a dynamic heuristic information that depends on the partial solution of an ant. It can be defined as $\eta_j = \frac{e_j}{c_j}$, where e_j is the so called cover value, that is, the number of additional rows covered when adding column j to the current partial solution, and c_j is the cost of column j. In other words, the heuristic information measures the unit cost of covering one additional row. An ant ends the solution construction when all rows are covered.

In this work, we use two instances of ACO: Ant System (AS) and Ant Colony System (ACS) algorithms, the original and the most famous algorithms in the

ACO family [14]. ACS improves the search of AS using: a different transition rule in the constructive phase, exploiting the heuristic information in a more rude form, using a list of candidates to future labelling and using a different treatment of pheromone. A direct implementation of the basic ACO framework is incapable of obtaining feasible solution for many SPP instances [10]. Each ant starts with an empty solution and adds columns until a cover is completed. But to determine if a column actually belongs or not to the partial solution ($j \notin S^k$) is not good enough. The traditional ACO decision policy, Equation 17, does not work for SPP because the ants, in this traditional selection process of the next columns, ignore the information of the problem constraints when a variable is instantiated. And in the worst case, in the iterative steps is possible to assign values to some variable that will make impossible to obtain complete solutions. To improve it, we use a procedure similar to the Constraint Propagation technique from Constraint Programming [5,1].

```
1   Procedure ACO+CP_for_SPP
2   Begin
3     InitParameters();
4     While (remain iterations) do
5       For k := 1 to nants do
6         While (solution is not completed) and TabuList <> J do
7           Choose next Column j with Transition Rule Probability
8           For each Row i covered by j do              /* constraints with j    */
9             feasible(i):= Posting(j);                 /* Constraint Propagation */
10          EndFor
11          If feasible(i) for all i then AddColumnToSolution(j)
12                              else Backtracking(j); /* set j uninstantiated   */
13          AddColumnToTabuList(j);
14        EndWhile
15      EndFor
16      UpdateOptimum();
17      UpdatePheromone();
18    EndWhile
19    Return best_solution_founded
20  End.
```

Fig. 1. ACO+CP algorithm for SPP

5   Integrating Constraint Programming to Ants

Recently, some efforts have been done in order to integrate Constraint Programming techniques to ACO algorithms [26,15]. An hybridization of ACO and CP can be approached from two directions: we can either take ACO or CP as the base algorithm and try to embed the respective other method into it. A form to integrate CP into ACO is to let it reduce the possible candidates among the not yet instantiated variables participating in the same constraints that the actual variable. A different approach would be to embed ACO within CP. The point at which ACO can interact with CP is during the labelling phase, using ACO to learn a value ordering that is more likely to produce good solutions. In this work, ACO use CP in the variable selection (when adding columns to partial solution). The CP algorithm used in this paper is Forward Checking with Backtracking [11]. It performs Arc Consistency between pairs of a not yet instantiated variable and an instantiated variable, i.e., when a value is assigned to the current variable, any value in the domain of a future variable which conflicts with this assignment is removed from the domain. The Forward Checking procedure, taking into account the constraints network topology (i.e. wich sets of variables are linked by a constraint and wich are not), guarantees that at each step of the search, all constraints between already assigned variables and not yet assigned variables are arc consistent. Then, adding Forward Checking to ACO for SPP means that columns are chosen if they do not produce any conflict with the next column to be chose. Figure 1 describes the hybrid ACO+CP algorithm to solve SPP [10].

6 Experiments and Results

The first five columns of Table 1 present the problem code (from Orlib [4]), the number of rows (constraints), the number of columns (decision variables), the best known cost value for each instance (IP optimal), and the density (percentage of ones in the constraint matrix) respectively. The next three columns present the results obtained by better performing metaheuristics with respect to SPP: Genetic Algorithm of Chu and Beasley [7], Genetic Algorithm of Levine [24] and the most recent algorithm by Kotecha et al. [21]. And the last four columns present the cost obtained when applying Ant Algorithms, AS and ACS, and combining them with Forward Checking. An entry of "X" in the table means no feasible solution was found. The algorithms have been run with the following parameters settings: influence of pheromone (alpha)=1.0, influence of heuristic information (beta)=0.5 and evaporation rate (rho)=0.4 as suggested in [22,23,14]. The number of ants has been set to 120 and the maximum number of iterations to 160, so that the number of generated candidate solutions is limited to 19.200. For ACS the list size was 500 and Qo=0.5. Algorithms were implemented using ANSI C, GCC 3.3.6, under Microsoft Windows XP Professional version 2002.

The effectiveness of Constraint Programming is showed to solve SPP, because the SPP is so strongly constrained the stochastic behaviour of ACO can be improved with lookahead techniques in the construction phase, so that almost

Table 1. Results of SPP benchmarks

Problem	Rows	Columns	Optimum	Density	Beasley	Levine	Kotecha	AS	ACS	AS+FC	ACS+FC
sppnw06	50	6774	7810	18.17	7810	-	-	9200	9788	8160	8038
sppnw08	24	434	35894	22.39	35894	37078	36068	X	X	35894	36682
sppnw09	40	3103	67760	16.20	67760	-	-	70462	X	70222	69332
sppnw10	24	853	68271	21.18	68271	X	68271	X	X	X	X
sppnw12	27	626	14118	20.00	14118	15110	14474	15406	16060	14466	14252
sppnw15	31	467	67743	19.55	67743	-	-	67755	67746	67743	67743
sppnw19	40	2879	10898	21.88	10898	11060	11944	11678	12350	11060	11858
sppnw23	19	711	12534	24.80	12534	12534	12534	14304	14604	13932	12880
sppnw26	23	771	6796	23.77	6796	6796	6804	6976	6956	6880	6880
sppnw32	19	294	14877	24.29	14877	14877	14877	14877	14886	14877	14877
sppnw34	20	899	10488	28.06	10488	10488	10488	13341	11289	10713	10797
sppnw39	25	677	10080	26.55	10080	10080	10080	11670	10758	11322	10545
sppnw41	17	197	11307	22.10	11307	11307	11307	11307	11307	11307	11307

only feasible partial solutions are induced. In the original ACO implementation the SPP solving derives in a lot of unfeasible labelling of variables, and the ants can not complete solutions.

7   Conclusions

In order to be able to solve any combinatorial optimization problem it seems that a good idea is to use both incomplete and complete techniques together. When problems are easy enough to allow searching for the optimal solution, complete techniques can be used. When problems become harder, incomplete techniques represent a good alternative in order to solve approximately the problem. Particularly, promising possibilities of combining ACO metaheuristic with Constraint Programming were pointed out in this work. Indeed, a complete search can guide a constructive metaheuristic: constraint propagation can be applied in order to restrict the neighborhood or prune the search space. Complete techniques are also used in order to explore the neighborhood of the current configuration helping to select the next moves. Following these ideas, we solved some benchmarks of SPP in the context of DARP decomposition. We are working in the development of a computational application that can integrate the resolution for both Clustering and Chaining in order to provide a whole solver for DARP.

References

1. Apt, K.R.: Principles of Constraint Programming. Cambridge University Press, Cambridge (2003)
2. Balas, E., Padberg, M.: Set partitioning: A survey. SIAM Review 18, 710–760 (1976)
3. Balinski, M.L., Quandt, R.E.: On an integer program for a delivery problem. Operations Research 12(2), 300–304 (1964)
4. Beasley, J.E.: Or-library:distributing test problem by electronic mail. Journal of Operational Research Society 41(11), 1069–1072 (1990)
5. Bessiere, C.: Constraint propagation. Technical Report 06020, LIRMM (March 2006), also in Rossi, F., van Beek, P., Walsh, T. (eds.) ch. 3 of the Handbook of Constraint Programming, Elsevier (2006)
6. Borndorfer, R., Grotschel, M., Klostermeier, F., Kuttner, C.: Telebus berlin: Vehicle scheduling in a dial-a-ride system. Technical Report SC 97-23, Konrad-Zuse-Zentrum fur Informationstechnik (1997)
7. Chu, P.C., Beasley, J.E.: Constraint handling in genetic algorithms: the set partitioning problem. Journal of Heuristics 4, 323–357 (1998)
8. Cordeau, J.-F.: A branch-and-cut algorithm for the dial-a-ride problem. Oper. Res. 54(3), 573–586 (2006)
9. Cordeau, J.-F., Laporte, G.: The dial-a-ride problem (darp): Variants, modeling issues and algorithms. Journal 4OR: A Quarterly Journal of Operations Research 1(2), 89–101 (2003)
10. Crawford, B., Castro, C., Monfroy, E.: A hybrid ant algorithm for the airline crew pairing problem. In: Gelbukh, A., Reyes-Garcia, C.A. (eds.) MICAI 2006. LNCS (LNAI), vol. 4293, pp. 381–391. Springer, Heidelberg (2006)

11. Dechter, R., Frost, D.: Backjump-based backtracking for constraint satisfaction problems. Artificial Intelligence 136, 147–188 (2002)
12. Dorigo, M., Birattari, M., Blum, C., Gambardella, L.M., Mondada, F., Stützle, T. (eds.): ANTS 2004. LNCS, vol. 3172. Springer, Heidelberg (2004)
13. Dorigo, M., Gambardella, L.M.: Ant colony system: A cooperative learning approach to the traveling salesman problem. IEEE Transactions on Evolutionary Computation 1(1), 53–66 (1997)
14. Dorigo, M., Stutzle, T.: Ant Colony Optimization. MIT Press, USA (2004)
15. Focacci, F., Laburthe, F., Lodi, A.: Local search and constraint programming. In: Handbook of metaheuristics, Kluwer, Dordrecht (2002)
16. Gagne, C., Gravel, M., Price, W.: A look-ahead addition to the ant colony optimization metaheuristic and its application to an industrial scheduling problem. In: Sousa, J.P., et al. (eds.) MIC'01. Proceedings of the fourth Metaheuristics International Conference, pp. 79–84 (July 2001)
17. Gandibleux, X., Delorme, X., T'Kindt, V.: An ant colony optimisation algorithm for the set packing problem. In: Dorigo, et al. [12], pp. 49–60
18. Gopal, R.D., Ramesh, R.: The query clustering problem: A set partitioning approach. IEEE Trans. Knowl. Data Eng. 7(6), 885–899 (1995)
19. Hadji, R., Rahoual, M., Talbi, E., Bachelet, V.: Ant colonies for the set covering problem. In: Bosma, W. (ed.) Algorithmic Number Theory. LNCS, vol. 1838, pp. 63–66. Springer, Heidelberg (2000)
20. Kelly, J.P., Xu, J.: A set-partitioning-based heuristic for the vehicle routing problem. INFORMS J. on Computing 11(2), 161–172 (1999)
21. Kotecha, K., Sanghani, G., Gambhava, N.: Genetic algorithm for airline crew scheduling problem using cost-based uniform crossover. In: Manandhar, S., Austin, J., Desai, U., Oyanagi, Y., Talukder, A.K. (eds.) AACC 2004. LNCS, vol. 3285, pp. 84–91. Springer, Heidelberg (2004)
22. Leguizamón, G., Michalewicz, Z.: A new version of ant system for subset problems. In: CEC'99. Congress on Evolutionary Computation, Piscataway, NJ, USA, pp. 1459–1464. IEEE Press, Los Alamitos (1999)
23. Lessing, L., Dumitrescu, I., Stützle, T.: A comparison between aco algorithms for the set covering problem. In: Dorigo, et al. [12], pp. 1–12
24. Levine, D.: A parallel genetic algorithm for the set partitioning problem. Technical Report ANL-94/23 Argonne National Laboratory (May 1994), available at http://citeseer.ist.psu.edu/levine94parallel.html
25. Maniezzo, V., Milandri, M.: An ant-based framework for very strongly constrained problems. In: Dorigo, M., Di Caro, G.A., Sampels, M. (eds.) Ant Algorithms. LNCS, vol. 2463, pp. 222–227. Springer, Heidelberg (2002)
26. Meyer, B., Ernst, A.: Integrating aco and constraint propagation. In: Dorigo, et al. [12], pp. 166–177
27. Michel, R., Middendorf, M.: An island model based ant system with lookahead for the shortest supersequence problem. In: Eiben, A.E., Bäck, T., Schoenauer, M., Schwefel, H.-P. (eds.) Parallel Problem Solving from Nature - PPSN V. LNCS, vol. 1498, pp. 692–701. Springer, Heidelberg (1998)
28. Savelsbergh, M.W.P.: The general pickup and delivery problem. Transportation Science 29(1), 17–29 (1995)

Logic as Energy: A SAT-Based Approach

Priscila M. V. Lima[1], M. Mariela M. Morveli-Espinoza[2,3], and
Felipe M. G. França[1,3]

[1] LAM – Computer Architecture and Microelectronics Laboratory
Universidade Federal do Rio de Janeiro, Brazil
priscilamvl@lam.ufrj.br
http://www.lam.ufrj.br/
[2] Departament d'Informàtica
Universitat Autònoma de Barcelona, Spain
fourme@gmail.com
http://upiia.uab.es/
[3] COPPE – Systems Engineering and Computer Science Program
Universidade Federal do Rio de Janeiro, Brazil
{mme,felipe}@cos.ufrj.br
http://www.cos.ufrj.br/~felipe

Abstract. This paper presents the implementation of ARQ-PROP II, a limited-depth propositional reasoner, via the compilation of its specification into an exact formulation using the SATyrus platform. SATyrus' compiler takes as input the definition of a problem as a set of pseudo-Boolean constraints and produces, as output, the Energy function of a higher-order artificial neural network. This way, SATisfiability of a formula can be associated to global optima. In the case of ARQ-PROP II, global optima is associated to Resolution-based refutation, in such a way that allows for simplified abduction and prediction to be unified with deduction. Besides experimental results on deduction with ARQ-PROP II, this work also corrects the mapping of SATisfiability into Energy minima originally proposed by Gadi Pinkas.

Keywords: ARQ-PROP II, higher-order neural networks, propositional reasoner, satisfiability, SATyrus.

1 Introduction

Plenty of research has been carried out on how neural networks learn and create implicit knowledge from perceptual experience. On a smaller scale, come the efforts on rule extraction from such knowledge. In the next scale degree, fewer works on how neural networks perform logical reasoning are noticed. However, with very few exceptions [1], not much has been done towards integrating these three approaches. This paper presents the implementation of ARQ-PROP II [8], a neural-based propositional reasoner possessing a writable area so that knowledge coming from outside, e.g., perceptual areas, could be integrated in the reasoning process.

F. Mele et al. (Eds.): BVAI 2007, LNCS 4729, pp. 458–467, 2007.

In order to handle ARQ-PROP II's complex architecture, its implementation was realized through the use of the SATyrus' platform [11]. In previous works, it was shown how optimization problems, such as TSP (*Traveling Salesperson Problem*) and graph colouring, could be specified as sets of pseudo-Boolean constraints and easily combined through the concatenation of their respective specifications, plus the addition of other pseudo-Boolean constraints specifying the combination's intentionality [10]. ARQ-PROP II's architecture, declared as pseudo-Boolean constraints, is taken as input to the SATyrus' compiler which produces, as output, an Energy function that can be directly mapped into a higher-order artificial neural network.

SATyrus' compilation process, described in the next section, is based on the mapping of SATisfiability of a formula into global optima of an Energy function, which was originally proposed by Gadi Pinkas [9]. However, such mapping was proven to produce spurious global minima in more complex problems, such as in the case of ARQ-PROP II, and this is corrected in Section 2.2. ARQ-PROP II, presented in Section 3, works by associating global optima to Resolution-based refutation, so that different logical reasoning styles such as abduction, deduction and prediction can be performed in a uniform way. Experimental results from ARQ-PROP II performing deduction are described and discussed in Section 4, followed by our conclusions, presented in the last section.

2   SATyrus: A SATisfiability-Based Architecture for Constraint Processing

SATyrus platform is basically composed by two modules: a *compiler* and a *solver* [10] [11]. A problem specification is fed to the compiler as a set of pseudo-Boolean constraints, representing both the problem's search space and the cost function, and a *penalty scale* modulating the whole set of constraints. The object code produced by the compiler consists of an Energy function, which can also be seen as a single exact formulation to the problem in question. Global minima of this Energy function, corresponding to the desired set of solutions, are obtained through the use of a solver. The current SATyrus' solver is based on symmetric higher-order neural networks.

2.1   SATyrus' Language and Compiler

Input to SATyrus' compiler consists of a problem specification written in the SATyrus' declarative language. The general structure of a problem specification is divided in four main parts: (i) neural structures, (ii) integrity constraints, (iii) optimality constraints and (iv) a penalty scale associated to the different groups of constraints defined within (ii) and (iii).

Constructs are provided to express the specification of different data structures of binary elements. These structures are, basically, multi-dimensional arrays. The elements of these arrays play the role of propositional variables in the constructs that specify constraints and will be identified as binary neurons in the neural solver. The replication of such constraints is facilitated by other constructs. The objective function sentences are defined in a similar way and may be read from a file. Also provided are constructs for the association of an identifier to a group of both integrity and optimality constraints, in order to enable the attribution of a same penalty level to them.

2.2   Energy Function Generation

The compiler translates the file containing the problem specification into an intermediate representation composed by one header and a record for each term of the Energy function. Each record has the following information: penalty level, weight, connection arity and list of neighboring neurons. The header provides a table with penalty identifiers and respective values. Only the penalty identifiers and their levels are informed by the user, their values and neurons attributes result from the compilation process.

The association of SATISFIABILITY (SAT) to global minima of a function requires the consideration of the basic mapping of truth values of propositional formulae to the domain $\{0, 1\}$:

$$H(true) = 1$$
$$H(false) = 0$$
$$H(\neg p) = 1 - H(p)$$
$$H(p \wedge q) = H(p) \times H(q)$$
$$H(p \vee q) = H(p) + H(q) - H(p \wedge q)$$

If a logical formula is converted to an equivalent in *Conjunctive Normal Form* (CNF), the result being a conjunction φ of disjunctions φ_i, it is possible to associate energy to $H(\neg\varphi)$. Nevertheless, energy calculated in this way would only have two possible values: *one*, meaning solution not found (if the network has not reached global minimum), and *zero* when a model has been found. Intuitively, it would be better to have more "clues", or degrees of "non-satisfiabililty", on whether the network is close to a solution or not. This measure also prevents the Energy equation from having an exponential number of terms which could result from the conversion of the outermost disjunction in the negated formula.

Let $\varphi = \wedge_i \varphi_i$ where $\varphi_i = \vee_j l_{ij}$, and l_{ij} is a literal (either p_{ij} or $\neg p_{ij}$). Therefore $\neg\varphi = \vee_i \neg\varphi_i$ where $\neg\varphi_i = \wedge_j \neg l_{ij}$. Instead of making $E = H(\neg\varphi)$, consider $E = H^*(\neg\varphi) = \sum_i H(\neg\varphi_i)$. So, $E = \sum_i H(\wedge_j \neg l_{ij}) = \sum_i \prod_j H(\neg l_{ij})$, where $H(p)$ will be referred to as p. Informally, E counts the number of clauses that are *not satisfied* by the interpretation represented by the network's state.

A simple example demonstrates how SAT can be mapped to EM. Let φ be the formula, expressed as a conjunction of clauses:

$$\varphi = (p \vee \neg q) \wedge (p \vee \neg r) \wedge (r)$$

SAT (φ) can be translated to the minimum of the following energy function:

$$
\begin{aligned}
E &= H(\neg(p \vee \neg q)) + H(\neg(p \vee \neg r)) + H(\neg r) \\
&= H(\neg p \wedge q) + H(\neg p \wedge r) + H(\neg r) \\
&= (1 - p) * q + (1 - p) * r + (1 - r) \\
&= q - pq - pr + 1
\end{aligned}
$$

where $H(p) = p$.

Another source of potentially exponential space cost occurs when a clause c_i is required by the modeling to have a number of literals equal to the size n of the problem. The simplification displayed by function $H^*(\neg\varphi)$ could not be applied in this case. In some situations, however, only one of the disjuncts should be allowed to be true at a time, constituting an exclusive-OR. The definition of a set of so-called *Winner-Takes-All* (WTA) constraints helps to prevent violation of the exclusiveness. This prevention can only be achieved by the attribution to the WTA-constraints of a penalty level higher than c_i. Penalty values should be calculated in such a way that no violation of a constraint of level i could be traded for the satisfaction of constraints of lower levels. This can be done automatically, provided that the user informs an upper bound for the optimality constraints, if there are any. It is also worth mentioning that Pinkas' mapping did not consider tackling optimization problems, only logical reasoning ones.

Up to this point, the mapping proposed by Gadi Pinkas has been described. Nevertheless, an important mapping rule has been left unspecified by him, leading to potential spurious global minima. This work proposes the addition of a rule that states that clause c_i should be broken into n singleton clauses s_{ij}, $1 \leq j \leq n$. The set $\{s_{ij}\}$ should be associated to a new penalty level, immediately lower than that of the original c_i, but still higher than the other lower penalty levels.

2.3 SATyrus' Neural Solver

Once the Energy function is defined, one could apply a number of different solvers in order to find its global minima. In the present work, it is assumed a generalization of Hopfield neural networks [5], where a stochastic behaviour [6] is introduced into its binary neurons, i.e., output $ON = 1$ or $OFF = 0$. It is worth noticing that the symmetric neural network associated to the mapping introduced in the previous subsection may have higher-order connections. This means that the resulting Energy function may have terms with more than two propositional variables, what would imply on having synaptic weights involving more than two neurons each, e.g., neurons i, j and k such that $w_{ijk} = w_{jik} = w_{kij}$. This does not constitute a hindrance as has been demonstrated that, with higher-order connections, Boltzmann Machines still converge to energy minima [4]. Parallel and distributed simulation of networks [2] with higher-order connections can be done by substituting each higher-order connection by a completely-connected subgraph. Alternatively, [9] converts the higher-order network to a

binarily connected one that preserves the order of energy values of the different
network states.

3   ARQ-PROP II: A Goal-Driven Propositional Reasoner

It is possible to use the mechanism described in Section 2 to design a neural engine that is capable of performing propositional Resolution-based reasoning with
both complete and incomplete knowledge. The modeling has to define the sets
of propositional variables to be associated to binary neurons and a set of constraints that provides the reasoner with the ability to perform sound Resolution
steps. Additionally, in order to reason with incomplete knowledge and to have
the flexibility that the knowledge base does not be pre-encoded as constraints,
the engine has to be able to create new sentences (clauses).

3.1   ARQ-PROP II Architecture

The data structures of ARQ-PROP II are displayed in Figure 1. The meaning
of the states of the elements of the ARQ-PROP II in Figure 1 will be explained
in Section 4. The interpretation of ARQ-PROP II structures is the following:

- IN ($n \times 1$): indicates if the line is part of the selected proof or not; $i =$ line
  number in the proof area;
- PROOF ($n \times n \times \{+, -\}$): proof area; $i =$ line number; $j =$ nameprop; $k =$
  literal sign;
- CB-RES-INV ($n \times 3$): reason for belonging to the selected proof for a line in
  the proof area; it can either be an instance of a clause of the Clause Base
  (CB), the result of a resolution step (RES), or an invention in the case of
  reasoning with incomplete knowledge (INV); $i =$ line number; $j =$ reason;
- EMPTY ($n \times 1$): indicates whether the line is the empty clause or not; $i =$ line
  number;
- CBMAP ($n \times n$): maps proof lines to the internal names of clauses of the Clause
  Base that they derive from; $i =$ line number; $j =$ clause;
- PARENT ($n \times n \times \{1, 2\}$): indicates the parents (parent1 or parent2) of a line,
  resulting from a resolution step, in the proof; $i =$ parent line number; $j =$
  line number; $k =$ parent1 or parent2;
- CANCELED ($n \times n$): indicates which proposition has been canceled in the proof
  lines that result from resolution steps; $i =$ line number; $j =$ nameprop;
- CLCOMP ($n \times n \times \{+, -\}$): indicates clause composition for each clause (internal
  name) of the selected Clause Base; $i =$ clause number; $j =$ nameprop, $k =$
  literal sign;
- ORIG ($n \times 1$): indicates that the clause belongs to the original knowledge
  base; $i =$ clause number.

It is worth pointing out that structures PROOF, CLCOMP and PARENT are tri-
dimensional with $n \times n \times 2$ elements, each. In the first two structures, the third dimension indicates the sign of the propositional literal, while in structure PARENT,

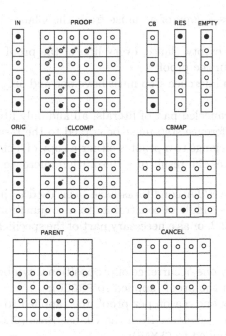

Fig. 1. General structures of ARQ-PROP II having a proof depth limit of 6. Final states of neurons after deduction of $\square$ from $\{p \vee \neg q, p \vee \neg r, q\} \cup \{\neg p\}$. The IN-PROOF lines compose a refutation for $\neg p$, thus proving p: line 1: $\square$ (empty clause), line 3: q, line 4: $\neg q$, line 5: $\neg q \vee p$, line 6: $\neg p$ (query).

the third dimension is used to enforce the participation of two different clause instances on a Resolution step. Clauses composition must be indicated explicitly by fixing the values of the nodes of structure CLCOMP. The structure INV is used to indicate that a proof could be generated provided that sentence(s) were incorporated to the knowledge base.

3.2 Set of Constraints of ARQ-PROP II

In general, the set of integrity and optimality constraints of ARQ-PROP II must account for the specification of a Resolution step (Resolution step constraints, Parent line constraints and Resolvent composition constraints) and specify the conditions for a line in the PROOF area to actually belong to the result of the computation (In-proof constraints). In order to accomplish that, it is necessary to add constraints for the enforcement of clause syntax (Clause instance constraints, Clause syntax constraints, Empty clause constraints, Clause-invention constraints). The whole set of constraints, the detailing of which has been revised in [14], can be informally stated as:

1. Every line of PROOF resulting from an inference step, i.e., one that is not a copy of a clause from CLCOMP, must have exactly two different parents, which are also lines of PROOF;

2. Every line that is a copy of a clause from the Clause Base, `CLCOMP` has no parents;
3. Except from the empty clause, every line of the proof must be a parent of exactly one line in the proof;
4. Every Resolution inference step must have one and only one pair of canceled literals;
5. Apart from the canceled pair of literals, all and only literals of both parents involved in an inference step must be copied to the resulting proof line;
6. Every line that belongs to a proof is either a copy of a clause from the Clause Base or constitutes the result of a Resolution inference step;

Additionally, some WTA conditions have been used to justify the conversion of disjunctions in the middle of constraints to a conjunction of the disjuncts, as explained in Section 2.2, or as a necessary part of the specification of ARQ-PROP II:

7. WTA-1-sign: only one occurrence of propositional symbol (i.e., of its internal name) per line in the proof (applied to `PROOF`);
8. WTA-2-line: only one reason per proof line (applied to `CB-RES-INV`);
9. WTA-3-line: only one clause from the Clause Base (`CLCOMP`) copied per line of `PROOF` area (applied to `CBMAP`);
10. WTA-4-(column, parent1/2): a line can have only one parent1 and only one parent2 (applied to `PARENT`);
11. WTA-5-line: a line in the proof may take part in a resolution step (i.e., be one of the parents of another line) only once (applied to `PARENT`);
12. WTA-6-parent1/2: two different proof lines must be involved in a resolution step (applied to `PARENT`);
13. WTA-7-line: only one pair of literals (i.e., propositional symbol) canceled per line number resulting from a resolution step (applied to `CANCELED`);
14. WTA-8-sign: only one occurrence of propositional symbol (i.e., of its internal name) per clause (applied to `CLCOMP`).

The specification of a pure-deduction reasoner would be complete if constraints 1 to 14 were satisfied. For a simple version of reasoning with incomplete knowledge to take place, the invention of a clause must be penalized, as it is usually more desirable to have a complete deduction of the empty clause. The penalty has to be such that energy of a sentence that belongs to a proof will be smaller if it is possible to choose it from the knowledge base or to generate it from a Resolution step. This is achieved by attributing the lowest penalty level to these constraints, making them optimality constraints.

4   Compiling and Running ARQ-PROP II with SATyrus

This section presents two experiments exercising ARQ-PROP II on performing deduction over two small clause bases, both having $\neg p$ as query:

$$\Delta_1 = \{p \vee \neg q, p \vee \neg r, q\}$$
$$\Delta_2 = \{p \vee \neg q \vee \neg r, q, r\}$$

As previously shown in Figure 1, the compilation of ARQ-PROP II, assuming a depth limit of 6 in the proof area, resulted in a network having 318 neurons (note that fields PROOF and CLCOMP have two layers – "+" and "−", as well as field PARENT – parent1 and parent2). The clause base $\Delta_1 \cup \{\neg p\}$ was written in the clause base (CLCOMP) area. The graphical conventions adopted for the neurons' output are: **black** means the neuron is clamped *ON*; within lines having black neurons, **white** nodes are clamped *OFF*; **grey** neurons are *ON* as a result; within lines having grey neurons, **white** nodes are *OFF* as a result; positions having no output doesn't matter for the current result. Notice that, as illustrated in Figure 1, there are *ON* neurons in the proof area (PROOF) representing no input clauses. Such neurons, specially the ones in line 2, should not be considered since their corresponding neurons in field IN were set to *OFF*. Those neurons producing *ON* values do not have any influence on the final calculus of the Energy function.

Both experiments were conducted using the same initial temperature $T_i = 10000$, final temperature $T_f = 1$, and a geometrical cooling factor of 0.99. Figure 2 illustrates the behaviour of Energy function in the experiment with ARQ-PROP II performing deduction of $\square$ from $\Delta_1 \cup \{\neg p\}$. In the second experiment, the compilation of ARQ-PROP II assumed a depth limit of 8 in the proof area, resulting in a network having 552 neurons. The clause base $\Delta_2 \cup \{\neg p\}$ was written in the clause base (CLCOMP) area and Figure 3 illustrates the behaviour of Energy in this case.

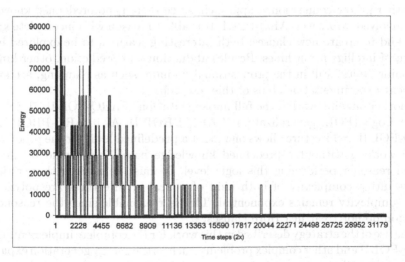

Fig. 2. Trajectory of the Energy for deduction of $\square$ from $\Delta_1 \cup \{\neg p\}$; final Energy: 169

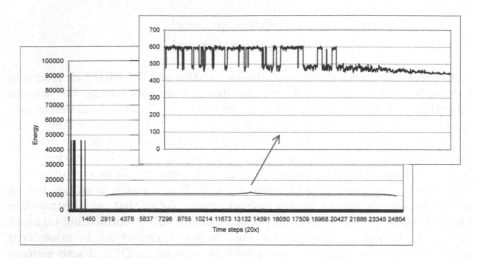

Fig. 3. Trajectory of the Energy for deduction of $\square$ from $\Delta_2 \cup \{\neg p\}$; final Energy: 433

5 Conclusion

Apart from the recent resurgence of interest in SATISFIABILITY as a means of overcoming the inherent difficulty of many NP-hard problems [3], interest on Pinkas' original mapping, such as in *Markov Logic Networks* (MLNs) [13], are relatively recent. The main contribution of MLNs lies on the amalgamation of learning by examples with inferencing. On the other hand, the conception of ARQ-PROP II as a generic propositional reasoner is unique when compared to any other purely connectionist approach, since there is no predefined knowledge base involved. Moreover, ARQ-PROP II is able to reason with incomplete knowledge and to create new clauses; both interesting features to be explored in the design of intelligent machines. Besides abduction and prediction, other kinds of reasoning styles, still in the propositional domain, such as planning, are among the next experimentation steps of this research.

Another ongoing work is the full implementation of ARQ-FOL II [7], the First Order Logic (FOL) generalization of ARQ-PROP II. As in ARQ-PROP II, the ARQ-FOL II architecture allows one to set a predefined limit for the proof depth, while working without a predefined knowledge base. Such would be the first neural reasoner performing this logic level. It must be noticed that, although the resulting complexity of both kind of neural architectures are polynomial, time complexity remains exponential. This is reasonable since the reasoners in question do not treat just Horn clauses.

The use of the strategy described in this work for the complete implementation of ARQ-FOL II and other complex problems, such as the energy generation expansion [15] and the molecular geometry reconstruction [12], can only be carried out via an automated process. This is due to the number of terms of the Energy function generated by the SATyrus compiler, as would be the case of other logical/opmization methods. Adjustment of the search mechanisms of the SATyrus neural solver and exploration of other meta-heuristics constitute ongoing work as well.

Acknowledgments. This work was supported by CNPq, CEDERJ (EELA project) and FEST (SCAE project).

References

1. Aleksander, I., Evans, R.G., Sales, N.: Towards intentional neural systems: experiments with MAGNUS. In: Proc. of the Fourth Int. Conf. on Artificial Neural Networks, pp. 122–126 (1995)
2. Barbosa, V.C, Lima, P.M.V.: On the distributed parallel simulation of Hopfield's neural networks. Software-Practice and Experience 20(10), 967–983 (1990)
3. Dixon, H.E., Ginsberg, M.L., Parkes, A.J.: Generalizing Boolean Satisfiability I: Background and Survey of Existing Work. J. of Art. Intelligence Research 21, 193–243 (2004)
4. Geman, S., Geman, D.: Stochastic relaxation, Gibbs distribution, and the Bayesian restoration of images. IEEE Trans. on Pattern Analysis and Machine Intelligence PAMI-6, 721–741 (1984)
5. Hopfield, J.J.: Neural networks and physical systems with emergent collective computational abilities. Proc. of the Nat. Acad. of Sciences USA 79, 2554–2558 (1982)
6. Kirkpatrick, S., Gellat Jr., C.D., Vecchi, M.P.: Optimization via Simulated Annealing. Science 220, 671–680 (1983)
7. Lima, P.M.V.: Resolution-Based Inference on Artificial Neural Networks. Ph.D. Thesis, Department of Computing. Imperial College London, UK (2000)
8. Lima, P.M.V.: A Goal-Driven Neural Propositional Interpreter. International Journal of Neural Systems 11, 311–322 (2001)
9. Pinkas, G.: Logical Inference in Symmetric Neural Networks. D.Sc. Thesis, Sever Institute of Technology, Washington University, Saint Louis, USA (1992)
10. Lima, P.M.V., Pereira, G.C., Morveli-Espinoza, M.M.M., França, F.M.G.: Mapping and Combining Combinatorial Problems into Energy Landscapes via Pseudo-Boolean Constraints. In: De Gregorio, M., Di Maio, V., Frucci, M., Musio, C. (eds.) BVAI 2005. LNCS, vol. 3704, pp. 308–317. Springer, Heidelberg (2005)
11. Lima, P.M.V., Pereira, G.C., Morveli-Espinoza, M.M.M., França, F.M.G.: SATyrus: A SAT-based Neuro-Symbolic Architecture for Constraint Processing. In: Proc. of the Fifth Int. Conf. on Hybrid Intelligent Systems, pp. 137–142 (2005)
12. Lima, P.M.V., Pereira, G.C., Morveli-Espinoza, M.M.M., França, F.M.G., Lavor, C.C.: Mapping Molecular Geometry Problems into Pseudo-Boolean Constraints. In: Proc. of the Int. Work. on Genomic Databases – IWGD '05 (2005), http://www.biowebdb.org/iwgd05/proceedings/index.html
13. Richardson, M., Domingos, P.: Markov Logic Networks. Machine Learning 62, 107–136 (2006)
14. Morveli-Espinoza, M.M.M.: Compiling Problems Resolution to Energy Minimization. M.Sc. dissert. COPPE/PESC, Universidade Federal do Rio de Janeiro (2006)
15. Silva, E.F., Lima, P.M.V., Diacovo, R., França, F.M.G.: Aggregating energy scenarios using the SATyrus neuro-symbolic tool. In: Abstracts of the 19th Int. Symp. on Mathematical Programming, pp. 146–146 (2006)

Towards a Formal Approach to Generative Design: An Assistant System for the Creation of Artefact Models

Antonio Calabrese[1], Carlo Coppola[3], Salvatore Masecchia[2], Francesco Mele[1], Antonio Origlia[2], Antonio Sorgente[1], and Oliviero Talamo[1]

[1] Institute of Cybernetics, CNR, Naples, Italy
[2] University of Naples "Federico II", Naples, Italy
[3] SUN of Naples, Naples, Italy

Abstract. In this paper we propose a formal approach to the generative design of artefacts. The founding idea, bridging the gap between the domain of architectural artefacts and the field of ontologies, is to represent the notion of species as it exists in the context of generative design by the concept of class existing in the field of formal ontologies. In this paper we propose an artefact design methodology and a system based on it that assists a designer in the building process of artefact 3D models. The implemented system is structured in three conceptual levels: the Design Strategy, the Computational Model, and the 3D graphical rendering system. The Computational model has been defined and developed using the Frame Logic formalism. The proposed methodology is independent of specific modelling environments. In this paper we also present methodological directions to couple artefact representations with 3D rendering systems.

Keywords: Intelligent System, Human Computer Interaction, Generative Design.

1 Introduction

Generative design is an architectural design operating method. While this methodology covers a wide set of design strategies, in this paper we focus on artefacts design, specifically on the design of every-day use artefacts [1]. We do not consider technical artefacts even if we are aware that also in the design of the simplest artefact at least a small set of functionalities (technical qualities) has to be considered.

Generative design is an approach to the architectural design that allows to control the generative process of the production of artefacts [2]. A key concept of generative design of artefacts is the notion of species. This notion has in this context a meaning similar to the biological one, where each animal species includes a high number of different creatures, all different but individually recognizable and identifiable.

Through the notion of species, generative design can be seen as a generation procedure of shapes and relations producing objects (artefacts) all belonging to a single set of individuals (species) sharing the same object idea.

Therefore, generative design is not the design of a single specific artefact but the design of a species of artefacts. In the creative generative process the conjectured

F. Mele et al. (Eds.): BVAI 2007, LNCS 4729, pp. 468–479, 2007.

species is intensively tested by simulating the generation of a high number of individuals of the species. This *population* is used to modify the generative code of the process to obtain, finally, the code considered by the designer the most suitable to produce the compositive result identified as the recurring characteristics in each individual artefact.

In this paper we try to make explicit and formal the generative design approach using a formal ontological representation [3]. The founding idea, bridging the gap between the domain of architectural artefact and the field of ontologies, is to represent the notion of species as it exists in the context of generative design by the concept of class existing in the field of formal ontologies. We formalized in Frame Logic [4] most of the generative approach concepts. This formalization has been critical to build a computational model defining the proposed generative design aid system. We present an artefact design methodology and a system based on it that assists a designer in the building process of artefact 3D models. In the definition and development of the implemented system, three conceptual levels have been considered (fig. 1): the Design Strategy, the Computational Model, and the 3D primitives used to render the artefact's model.

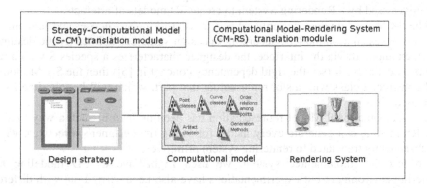

Fig. 1. The system's three levels

The Design Strategy adopts a methodology belonging to the set of generative approaches to the creation of artefacts and allows to design the artefact through a set of qualitative and quantitative spatial relations among the component parts of the artefact [7]. The designer is aware of such a strategy and the implemented system provides an interface acting as a guide to define the design strategy. In our opinion, the explicit use of relations in the generation cycle increases *competence* in the generative process because structural and functional choices are directly connected to the theory used in the design process. The Computational Model is composed by an artefacts representation and a set of inferential services offered by the aid system. It is not critical for the designer to be aware of the representation. In our system we adopt a frame-based representation: for each artefact's species, defined by the designer in the design strategy, the system builds an ontological class. To represent the computational model we used the FLORA-2 language [5].

The third level is composed by rendering primitives interpreted by Rendering System. These are basic functions provided by the modeling environment used to build and render artefact's 3D model. Such functions are activated following the Design Strategy ontological representation introduced in the Computational Model.

Through the system interface the designer controls the models generation process by means of explicit definitions for species (artefact classes). Every species is represented as a whole composed by a set of parts and a set of relations among parts. These relations are mainly of spatial type, both qualitative and quantitative.

Using ontological representations in the generative design of artefacts, the generation process is described by producing class instances. Each instance represents an artefact and artefacts belonging to the same species are represented as instances of the same class. So, species can be defined by varying the composing parts set and by modifying the relations among parts set.

In the proposed architecture there are two translation modules (fig. 1). The first one, the Strategy-Computational_Model (S-CM) translation module, translates the designer's *directives* expressed via the interface to the computational model (S-CM module in the figure). The second one, the Computational_Model-Rendering_System (CM-RS) translation module, translates the Computational Model in a set of modeling primitives used by a Rendering System to create 3D models of artefacts.

The S-CM module does not only act as a translator: it also chooses and implements specific representation models, according to design strategies defined by the designer. As an example, if, via the interface, the designer characterizes a species S with a part that is essential for it (see the rigid dependency concept in [6]) then the S-CM module will construct a class with a slot representing that part, which will be inherited by all subclasses of S.

The Computational Model representation has been defined in such a way that the CM-RS module can generate every model following the designer's directives, which is subsequently translated to rendering system primitives.

To test the implemented system, we used LightWave as 3D modeling and rendering environment but experimentations have also been carried out with different environments (Rhyno, Wmrl, X3D and Java 3D).

2 Design Strategy

The Design Strategy is expressed in the implemented system interface. Even if the proposed design strategy adopts a methodology belonging to the set of generative approaches to the creation of artefacts we introduced a specific characterization. The strategy cycle is expressed via the iterative cycle shown in figure 2 and is structured in various phases.

In *Phase A* an artefact is defined through species definition (a class in the computational model) or as parts aggregation. By aggregation we mean a whole represented by a set of composing parts and relations among parts (wholes are explicitly expressed and each definition contains part names [7]).

A specialization is obtained by introducing new whole descriptors or by adding new relations (constraints) among parts. A specializing process consists in a definitions *chain* for species-subspecies couples in which essential parts are distinguished from non-essential parts (each new species is defined only if at least one part or at least one relation/constraint is marked as essential).

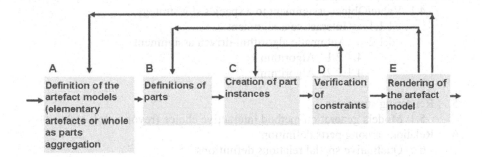

Fig. 2. Design Strategy Cycle

In the proposed methodology an abstraction is the action of deleting a description (essential or not). In practice, an abstraction is a temporary reference to an existing species and, followed by a specialization, it defines a revision operation.

In *Phase B* parts are defined as elementary artefacts or as aggregations. In *Phase C* parts and relations instantiations are performed. This way single artefacts or artefact families are obtained. In *Phase D* a consistency check for introduced instantiations relatively to owning classes is performed.

Next, the generated artefact is rendered and the designer evaluates if the obtained geometry conforms to his intentions. If discrepancies or second thoughts occur, the designer will have to revise parts or relations definitions. We wish to highlight that, in the cycle, the S-CM translation module hides the Computational Model to the designer while the CM-RS module hides functions activations executed by the Rendering System and used to build models.

In the following list we summarize all design project operations available in the proposed methodology.

1. Species definition strategies
    1.1 Specialization strategy
        1.1.1   Specialization by adding descriptors
        1.1.2   Specialization by constraining descriptors
            1.1.2.1   Specialization by constraining parts dimensions (numeric constraints on lengths)
            1.1.2.2   Specialization by relating a whole's parts (parts relations or parts spatial constraints)
    1.2 Abstraction strategy
        1.2.1   Abstraction by deleting non-essential descriptors
        1.2.2   Abstraction by deleting non-essential constraints
    1.3 Existing species definition revising strategy
        1.3.1   An abstraction followed by a specialization
2. Whole/Part definition strategies
    2.1 Parts aggregation strategy

2.2 New species definition strategy
3.   Parts aggregation
      3.1 Parts definition + Parts relations (constraints)
4.   Instantiation strategies
      4.1 Value/Object assignment to a species slot strategy
            4.1.1   Interactive assignment
            4.1.2   Automatic algorithm-driven assignment
                  4.1.2.1   Algorithm 1
                  4.1.2.2   Algorithm
                        , . . . ,
5.   Rendering strategies
      5.1 Models generation method interactive choice (revolve, loft etc)
6.   Relations among parts definition
      6.1 Qualitative spatial relations definitions
      6.2 Quantitative spatial relations definitions
      6.3 Frontiers definitions
7.   Constraints check
      7.1 Interactive checking
      7.2 Algorithm-driven checking

(For interactive checking of constraints we mean operations similar to those of PAL plugin [8]). In the implemented design strategy management interface a subset of these project options has been made available. This interface, shown in section 6, provides a number of interactors to activate project functionalities.

3 Computational Model

In the Computational Model each artefact class is represented by means of an ontological class. Our computational model has two primary generation procedures for an artefact:

1.   Elementary objects generation
2.   Parts aggregation

3.1 Representing Elementary Artefacts

Elementary artefacts are represented as primitive shape classes (box, sphere, etc.) or as shape generating methods classes (revolve, loft, sweep, etc.). Generation methods available in the ontology are: revolve, sweep and loft.

Revolve is a function used to describe shapes as spin solids given a profile curve and a spin axis. Sweep is an operation of profile curve extrusion guided by a second curve named rail. Sweep can be considered a revolve generalization if a circular rail is instantiated as extrusion guide. Loft is a function to generate a 3D model given a curves set and an order among them.

In our system, we describe curves as result of points interpolation. It is critical to the loft function that input curves are described with the same number of points. The 3D model is obtained by connecting control points of curves following the defined order. Points connections are also performed following the order of the curves control points (the first point of the first curve is connected to the first point of the second curve, the second point of the first curve is connected with the second point of the second curve and so on).

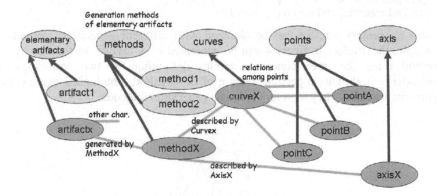

Fig. 3. Computational Model basic classes

In our approach some basic classes exist to describe artefact models through generation methods (fig. 3). These classes are: elementary artefacts, methods, curves, points and axis. Each elementary artefact class is defined by a generation method and a set of other characteristics like colour, texture, etc. In figure the symbol "arrow" connecting the two oval forms, say c1 and c2, represents a taxonomic relation meaning "c1 is subclass of c2" (in the Frame Logic formalism represented as c1::c2), while the symbol "simple line" represents an association relation between two classes.

Methods are defined as classes having specific method-depending arguments as slots. The revolve generation method, for example, has an axis and a curve spinning around that axis as properties (slots of a frame-based ontological class) while a loft generation method has a curves set and an order relations set as properties.

```
loft::methods.      %loft method is a subclass of methods
revolve::methods. %revolve method is a subclass methods
%every method has a name of type string
methods[name *=> string].
%curve used by revolve belongs to the class curves
%spin axis of the curve belongs to the class axisClass
revolve[curve *=> curves,
        axis *=> axisClass].
loft[curveSet *=>> curves, relOrdCurve *=>> relOrd].
%artefactx is a subclass of elementaryArtefacts
artefactx::elementaryArtefacts.
freeForms::curves. %freeForms is a subclass of curves
%verticalAxis is a subclass of axisClass
verticalAxis::axisClass.
artefactx[genByRevolve *=> revolve,
        otherC *=>> characteristics].
%artefactx'sinstances are generated by revolve
a:artefactx[genByRevolve -> r1, otherC ->> {c1,c2,c3}].
```

```
r1:revolve[curve -> abc, axis -> axis1].
%the curve is abc, axis is axis1
abc:freeForms[points ->> {p1,p2,p3}].
p1:points[x -> 2, y -> 2, z -> 0].
p2:points[x -> 4, y -> 4, z -> 0].
p3:points[x -> 2, y -> 6, z -> 0].
axis1:verticalAxis[x -> 1].
```

An elementary artefact can be obtained with different generation methods. For example, the artefact in figure 4 can be generated by a revolve method or by a loft method using the three concentric circles delimiting the two cone logs. This coincidence highlights a peculiar feature of our method: ontological classes do not represent artefacts. They represent artefacts generation methods.

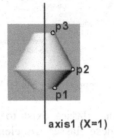

Fig. 4. Revolve (or Loft) artefact generation

3.2 A Whole as Parts Aggregation

The methodology we are presenting in this paper provides generation of wholes by the composition of parts.

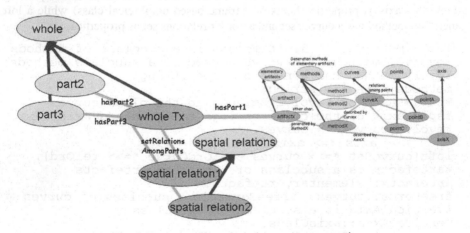

Fig. 5. Representation of whole as parts aggregation

In our computational model wholes are defined by a set of parts and a set of spatial relations among parts. In the following figure we show, as an example, a class Tx composed by three parts: artefactx, part2, part3. artefactx is an elementary artefact while part2 and part3 can be the result of elementary artefacts aggregations or simply elementary artefacts.

4   From Design Strategy to Computational Model

The S-CM system module works as a filter and translator between Design Strategy and Computational Model.

4.1   Parts and Wholes

An S-CM module basic rule states that, given N parts describing a whole T through aggregation, a class T with N attributes representing parts is built in the Computational Model.

S-CM has some *good constructing* rules to follow for artefacts composed of parts. One of the main translation rules is stated as: if in the design management interface the designer marks one or more parts as essential (see [6] for artefact's essentiality), S-CM builds a concrete class with one or more non-inherited attributes. S-CM builds artefact's specializations (subclasses) following definitions of parts essentiality, introduced by the designer via the interface.

S-CM, aided by some interface functions, rejects non-consistent design operations. For example, it is not allowed to specialize an artefact class A by creating a subclass if the designer did not define at least one new descriptor or at least one new relation among parts or at least one new constraint.

4.2   Points into Spatial Regions as Constraints

S-CM translates as constraints some of the specifics defined by the designer via the interface. For each spatial limitation for a point named Px (for example a point constrained to remain in a given region R) S-CM builds a class for Px by defining a constraint set on its coordinates. This way each instance in the Px class has its coordinates localized into the region.

If the designer defines curve points spatially constrained and related among themselves (for example, a point constrained to have an Y-value lower than the Y-value of another point) S-CM builds two constraint sets: a region-type constraint group, as previously explained (by points constraining) and a constraint group on the curve's class.

4.3   Frontiers as Parts Spatial Relations

In our design approach special relations among parts named frontiers can be descrybed. A frontier is a points sharing relation between two parts of a whole.

We considered three frontier kinds: frontiers sharing a) points, b) curves and c) surfaces. Given a designer declaration of frontier relation, the S-CM module builds the appropriate representations in the computational model. In figure 6 a b-type frontier is shown.

The Figure 7 shows as an example two parts sharing the same curveX curve class while a constraintX constraint is defined to force the two curves instances to be the same.

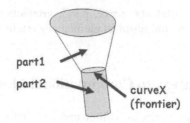

Fig. 6. B-type frontier between part1 and part2

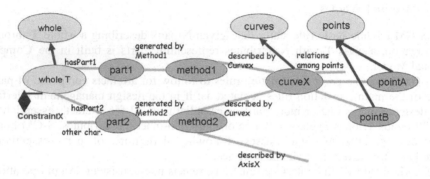

Fig. 7. B-type frontier representation

5 From Computational Model to Rendering System

The Computational Model is designed to provide an environment to represent 3D modeling common concepts. This representation has been studied to effectively represent design concepts so that it could transmit everything defined through the design interface to the chosen modeling environment to build and render defined artefact models.

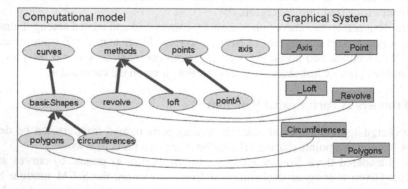

Fig. 8. Correspondences between Computational Model and modeling environment

Generation methods represented into the computational model are in correspondence with the tools provided by modeling environment (fig. 8). The CM-RS system module is responsible of data transferring from the Computational Model to the modeling environment. We have chosen LightWave Modeler [9] to implement the specific solution presented in this paper, however the computational model is completely independent of the associated modeling environment.

6 Design Interface, Graphical Models and Artefact Representation

Our system's interface is designed to explicitly show the generation cycle of an artefact.

To perform a generation of artefacts belonging to a defined class, the designer goes through the Design phase to define species and subspecies using the design strategies we formalized, then, during the instantiation phase, constraints are used to generate a subset of instances of an artefact class and, finally, a connection with a modeling environment is established to model and render generated artefacts. In figure 9 a layout of design strategy interface is shown. In figure 10 three basic artefact shapes and their aggregation result obtained by coupling LiteWave Modeler with the Computational Model are shown.

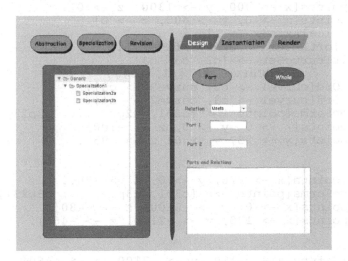

Fig. 9. A layout of design strategy interface

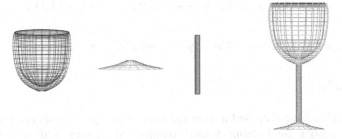

Fig. 10. Parts (cup, base and stem) and whole models of a glass representation

The following FLORA-2 formalism is the correspondent glass representation stored in our system's computational model.

```
cylinderArtefacts::elementaryArtefacts.
revolveArtefacts::elementaryArtefacts.
loftArtefacts::elementaryArtefacts.
cylinderArtefact[height *=> float, weight *=> float,
                 dept *=> dept].
revolveArtefact[genByRevolve *=> revolve].
loftArtefact[genByLoft *=> loft].

stemx:cylinderArtefact[height -> 2200,
                       weight -> 200, dept -> 200].
cupx:revolveArtefact[genByRevolve -> r1].
r1:revolve[curve -> c1, axis -> a1].
c1:freeForms[points ->> {c1p1, c1p2, c1p3, c1p4,
             c1p5}].
c1p1:points[x -> 0, y -> 200, z -> 0].
c1p2:points[x -> 700, y -> 700, z -> 0].
c1p3:points[x -> 1000, y -> 2500, z -> 0].
c1p4:points[x -> 900, y -> 1300, z -> 0].
c1p5:points[x -> 0, y -> 400, z -> 0].
a1:verticalAxis[x -> 1].
basex:loftArtefact[genByLoft -> l1].
l1:loft[curveSet ->>{c2, c3, c4} ,
        relOrdCurve ->> {r1, r2}].
r1:relOrd[curve1 -> c2, curve2 -> c3].
r2:relOrd[curve1 -> c3, curve2 -> c4].
c2:freeForms[points ->> {c2p1, c2p2, ..., c2p23}].
c2p1:points[x -> 0, y -> 0, z -> -100].
c2p2:points[x -> 25, y -> 0, z -> -95].
...
...
c2p23:points[x -> -26, y -> 0, z -> -96].
c3:freeForms[points ->> {c3p1, c3p2, ..., c3p23}].
c3p1:points[x -> 0, y -> -2100, z -> -480].
c3p2:points[x -> 120, y -> -2100, z -> -460].
...
...
c3p23:points[x -> -120, y -> -2100, z -> -460].
c4:freeForms[points ->> {c4p1, c4p2, ..., c4p23}].
c4p1:points[x -> 0, y -> -2200, z -> -980].
c4p2:points[x -> 250, y -> -2200, z -> -940].
...
...
c4p23:points[x -> -250, y -> -2200, z -> -940].
```

7 Remarks

In this paper we have proposed a representation of the species concept existing in the generative design field using formal ontological classes and a new artefacts generation methodology *directly* connected to 3D models building.

About representation, an approach similar to the one we presented here has been described in [12], but in that work the design strategy problem is treated only as a parts aggregation process without considering the generation process of the artefact 3D model. In other works theories based on artefact functionalities are proposed [10, 11]. Functionalities have not been considered in this paper. However, we think the representation we proposed can be used by an abstract level theory concerning artefacts functional and behavioural properties, leaving to a low level theory, like ours, the artefacts 3D generation methods management.

References

1. Pintori, E.: Design delle interfacce. Forme di ibridazione semiotica, Ocula-7, Giugno (2006)
2. Soddu, C.: http://www.generativedesign.com/progettazionegenerativa2003/index.html
3. Guarino, N.: Formal Ontology in Information Systems. In: Proceedings of FOIS'98, Trento, Italy, IOS Press, Amsterdam (1998)
4. Kifer, M., Lausen, G., Wu, J.: Logical Foundations of Object-Oriented and Frame-Based Languages. Journal of ACM (1995)
5. FLORA-2: An Object-Oriented Knowledge Base Language - http://flora.sourceforge.net/
6. Guarino, N., Welty, C.: Evaluating Ontological Decisions with Ontoclean. Communications of the ACM 45, 61 (2002)
7. Calabrese, A., Licenziato, L., Mele, F., Minei, G., Sorgente, A., Talamo, O.: Spatial reasoning for 3D visualization and reconstruction of architectonic artefacts. In: Workshop AI*IA Milano (19-Ott-2005)
8. Protégé Axiom Language - http://protege.stanford.edu/plugins/paltabs/pal-quickguide/
9. LightWave - www.newtek.com/lightwave
10. Gero, J., Kannengiesser, U.: The situated function–behaviour–structure framework–Artificial Intelligence. In: Design '02, pp. 89–104. Kluwer Academic Publisher, Dordrecht, printed in the Netherlands (2002)
11. Borgo, S., Carrara, M., Vermaas, P.E., Garbacz, P.: Behavior of a Technical Device: An Ontological Perspective in Egineering. In: FOIS 2006. International Conference on Formal Ontology in Information Systems, Baltimore, Maryland, USA (November 9-11, 2006)
12. Colombo, G., Cugini, U., Pugliese D., Pulli M.: Metodi di rappresentazione della conoscenza nella progettazione generativa, www.ingegraf.es/pdf/titulos/Comunicaciones%20aceptadas/p20.pdf

Using Software Agent Negotiation
for Service Selection

Claudia Di Napoli

Istituto di Cibernetica "E. Caianiello" - C.N.R.
Via Campi Flegrei, 34
80078 Pozzuoli (Napoli) - Italy
C.Dinapoli@cib.na.cnr.it

Abstract. The management of computational resources is becoming a crucial aspect in new generation distributed computing systems like the Grid because of the decentralized, heterogeneous and autonomous nature of these resources. As such they cannot be managed by adopting a centralized approach, but more sophisticated computing methodologies are necessary. In this paper we propose to use software agent negotiation to select services necessary to compose Grid applications. In particular, we propose an automated negotiation mechanism to select the service providers that meet the requirements of service consumers on the provision of multiple interconnected services. The negotiation mechanism allows for the evaluation of dependent issues that are negotiated upon when multiple interconnected services are required, and it relies on an iterative process so to improve the possibility of reaching an agreement by letting both service consumers and providers to exchange more proposals and counter–proposals in order to accommodate to the dynamic and changing nature of Grid environments.

1 Introduction

Computational grids [1] represent the new research challenge in the field of distributed computing. They aim at providing a unified computational infrastructure composed of networked heterogeneous resources that provide dependable, consistent, pervasive, and inexpensive access to high–end computational capabilities in the same way as electric power grids provide power to devices in a relatively efficient, low–cost, and reliable fashion. Resources use standard, open, general–purpose protocols and interfaces (i.e. not application–specific), and more importantly are not subject to centralized control, i.e. they exist within different control domains and they do not rely on a central management system. Resources need to be combined in order to deliver non–trivial services so that the utility of the resulting system is significantly greater than the sum of its parts. Users will be able to access and share these computing resources on demand over the Internet, relying on an infrastructure that is expected to be resilient, self managing and always available.

In order to make computational grids a viable approach, middleware mechanisms are necessary to enable the sharing, selection, and aggregation of services

F. Mele et al. (Eds.): BVAI 2007, LNCS 4729, pp. 480–489, 2007.
© Springer-Verlag Berlin Heidelberg 2007

distributed across different administrative domains, depending on their availability, capability, performance, cost and users' quality-of-service requirements.

The focus of the present work is to provide a middleware mechanism to allow for the selection of grid services, among the ones available, necessary for the execution of complex distributed applications in terms of dependencies occurring their components. In traditional computing systems the selection of resources is guaranteed by resource management systems designed to operate under the assumption that they have complete control of a resource and thus they implement mechanisms and policies necessary for the effective use of that resource in isolation. In environments like the grid this assumption cannot be made. This is why it is necessary to adopt more sophisticated computational methodologies for managing services that are heterogeneous, located across scparately administrated domains, and that inevitably adopt different policies for their use without relying on a centralized control. Furthermore, once computational grids become commercially available, it is likely that the provision of computational services will be regulated by market-based mechanisms. This implies that it becomes necessary to adopt methodologies that can take into account both users and providers requirements when accessing resources and not only the optimization of the resource usage [2,3]. We propose that the middleware mechanism to select the services necessary for composing complex distributed applications is based on *software agent negotiation* both to guarantee the autonomy of services, their coordination, and the satisfaction of both users and providers requirements in respectively requiring and providing them.

The paper is organised as follows. Section 2 motivates the use of software agent methodologies to regulate grid service provision. Section 3 describes the problem addressed and the proposed solution. Section 4 describes some preliminary results. Finally some conclusion and future work are reported.

2   Agent-Orientation for the Grid

In the present work any grid computational resource is considered a *grid service* i.e. a computational capability defined through a set of well-defined interfaces, and a set of standard protocols used to invoke them from those interfaces [4]. A service may be information or a virtual representation of some physical good or processing capability, and it has to be identified, published, allocated, and scheduled [5]. In this view, a service is provided by the *body* responsible for offering it, that we refer to as *service provider*, for consumption by others that we refer to as *service consumers*.

The strength of grid computing is the possibility of aggregating services provided by different service providers in order to build more complex applications (*workflows*) that provide high-level functionality to end users and whose components are not subject to a centralized control management system. This is why the automated composition of loosely coupled grid services is emerging as a critical requirement for grid systems. The first step for the automated composition of grid services is their selection since it is very likely that in grid-based systems there will be a large number of services that can provide the same functionality but with variable availability, quality of service and cost.

In this work we represent a *grid workflow* as a *Directed Acyclic Graph* (*DAG*) whose nodes are the required services, and arcs are dependencies among them. An arc $s_i \mapsto s_j$ means that the service s_i should complete its execution before service s_j can start its execution. There are *sequential* and *parallel* worflows whose components services can be executed respectively in sequential or parallel way.

In Figure 1 an example of sequential workflow is reported where for each required service, i.e. a node of the graph, several services, reported in square boxes, are potentially available.

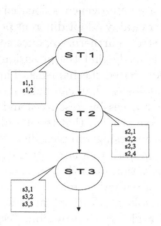

Fig. 1. A sequential workflow

In order to allow for the automated selection of grid services they need to be equipped with middleware technology able to represent providers and consumers and to model their behaviour.

Software agents are a natural way to represent service providers and consumers and their defining characteristics are essential to realize the full potential of the grid [6]. Software agents are autonomous problem solving entities, situated in an environment, able to reach their own objectives, and are equipped with flexible decision making capabilities [7]. The above characteristics make software agents a useful computational paradigm to model respectively providers that offer services (which they have total control on) at given conditions, and consumers that require services at other sometimes conflicting conditions. Providers and consumers interoperate according to specified protocols and interfaces and establish their own conditions to provide or consume services, and they can adopt different decision making mechanisms to accommodate to the dynamic and changing nature of the open environment in which they operate.

Furthermore software agents are able to cooperate by providing their capabilities in an aggregated and coordinated manner so that more sophisticated capabilities can be provided to service consumers when required. This aspect of agency maps the Virtual Organisation concept underlying the grid, i.e. the possibility of sharing computers, software, data, and other resources according to well established sharing rules [8]. So, aspects of agency become even more useful when composition of services are required, i.e. when service consumers cannot interact just with a single service provider for what they need. In fact, in such a case service providers need to coordinate the provision of their services and also to accommodate to the needs of consumers that refer to the provision of the whole composition and not of the individual components.

Software agents allow us to represent:

- the distributed nature of the provided services through the location of service provider agents in different control domains,
- the different behaviours service providers may have in providing their services through the possibility of adopting different and autonomous decision making mechanisms for the different service providers,
- the available services through *agent capabilities*, i.e. tasks that providers are able to accomplish,
- the provision of services through *agent actions*,
- the request of services through *agent interactions*,
- the quality–of–services as *agent preferences*.

We refer to agents representing service providers as *Service Agents* (SAs), and agents acting on behalf of service consumers as *Service Market Agents* (SMAs). The agents are modelled as self–interested software agents since they are autonomous and independent business entities that do not usually have common objectives, but they are more likely to have conflicting interests. The Service Market Agent can play the role of a Service Agent and viceversa.

A composition of services $cs = \{s_1 \mapsto s_2 \mapsto \ldots \mapsto s_n\}$ is a workflow of n services, each one provided by a service provider, so it corresponds to an aggregation of Service Agents that provide the components of the composition of services according to established conditions they agreed upon. This aggregation can be seen as a *Virtual Organisation* formed to provide a single reference provider for the entire composition.

3   Selecting Services Through Agent Negotiation

The scenario we refer to in our work consists of users requiring compositions of services with the constraint that they have to be delivered within a certain deadline specified as their preference:

$UsReq = \langle Workflow, Deadline \rangle$

When a composition of services is required, it is necessary to coordinate its provision so that both dependencies among the service components, and the required deadline can be successfully met.

In this scenario, the time at which services need to be provided should be established and agreed upon before service execution because the unavailability of one service at the right time results in the failure of the entire composition.

This is why the possibility of establishing *Service Level Agreements* (SLAs) [9] between service consumers and service providers is emerging as a key feature in the provision of services. An SLA is a contract between a user and provider stating the conditions under which the service is provided. These conditions have to be negotiated upon between service consumers and service providers in order to obtained a better exploitation of grid infrastructures [10,3]. The focus of the present work is the negotiation process preceding the establishment of an SLA.

In order to deal with the dynamic and distributed nature of services and with the possibility of establishing the conditions at which these services are provided *software agent negotiation* is a quite mature technology to suggest solutions [11].

Nevertheless, most of the efforts in this area concentrate on negotiation between a service consumer and a service provider, i.e. on a form of bilateral negotiation [12,13]. In our scenario settling the time for the provision of one service cannot be done without considering settling the times for the provision of the other services in the composition because of the dependencies that occur among the required services. Only when all Service Agents agree on these issues, the composition of services can be successfully delivered to the end user according to its preferences.

For this reason we propose a negotiation protocol that allows for the concurrent evaluation of bids coming from the Service Agents, assuming that more Service Agents are able to provide the same service required in the composition but at different conditions. The outcome of the negotiation, if successful, is the selection of the Service Agents, one for each service required in the composition, able to provide services at time conditions that meet both the user requirements and the dependencies specified in the composition.

In order to deal both with the dependencies that occur among the service attributes that are negotiated upon (i.e. the time to deliver), and with the varying conditions under which the negotiation takes place, we propose a flexible negotiation protocol that we call a *Multi-Phase-Multi-Iteration Negotiation*.

It consists of three phases:

1. *Exploratory Phase*, that allows the Service Market Agents to find out the number of Service Agents available to enter negotiation, and their initial preferences over the issues to be negotiated upon,
2. *Intermediate Phase*, that allows to iterate the process of alternating announcements and bids for a variable number of times, so to accommodate time constraint requirements on negotiation duration,
3. *Final Phase*, that allows to end the negotiation either with a success leading to a signed contractual agreement, or with a failure.

The Exploratory phase and each iteration of the Intermediate phase are based on a variation of the Contract Net Protocol (CNP) [14]. The Service Market Agent sends a set of n announcements $A = \{a_{s_1}, \ldots, a_{s_n}\}$ to the Service Agents, where n is the number of required services in the workflow.

The main difference between CNP and our proposed negotiation protocol is that a contract is not awarded after the potential contractors send back their bids to offer the service they are able to provide. The reason why we introduced this

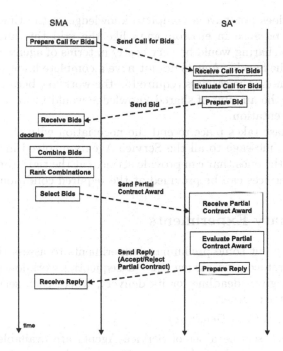

Fig. 2. The basic protocol

variation is due to the necessity of evaluating the combination of bids (because of the dependencies that can occur among the service attributes that are negotiated upon), and so each bid cannot be evaluated independently from the others.

The Service Market Agent initiates the negotiation as soon as it receives a user's request (Figure 2) by sending as many announcements a_{s_i} as the number of services in the composition, requiring the $time_{start}$ and $time_{end}$ for each of them. The corresponding Service Agents that decide to take part in the negotiation process (SA^* in Figure 2) reply with bids to announcements specifying when they can provide the service. So, an announcement is split in as many proposals as the number of services required in the composition. The compositions of bids form a *feasible* composition of services when both the required deadline and the time constraints coming from the required execution order of its components are met.

The flexibility of the protocol consists in varying the number of times the exchange of announcements and bids can occur in the Intermediate Phase depending on conditions that can be only determined at run–time, i.e. the number of participants, their strategies, the time within which the negotiation should end, and so on.

Furthermore, at each iteration it is possible for the Service Market Agent to collect more information examining the proposals sent back by the Service Agents, so that it can adjust its announcements trying to propose time intervals that are more likely to be accepted by the Service Agents. In fact, the Service

Market Agent does not have a complete knowledge of the time availability of Service Agents because in environments like the grid this knowledge is very dynamic and its sharing would be very costly in terms of agents interactions. At the same time the Service Agents do not have a complete knowledge of the time dependencies among the services required in the workflow because again in very large workflows the amount of shared knowledge would be very costly in terms of agent implementation.

The Final phase takes place to end the negotiation with the Service Market Agent sending a message to all the Service Agents involved in the negotiation either to award the ones that can provide services at the right time, or to declare a failure if no services can be provided at the required conditions.

4 Preliminary Experiments

In order to carry out some preliminary experiments to assess the feasibility of the proposed protocol, we assume that a sequential workflow of 3 services is required with a given deadline for its delivery, where each service need to be executed one after another:

$$UsReq = \langle Workflow, Deadline \rangle$$

and that for each service a set of Service Agents are available to provide it. We considered sequential worflows since they are the ones that present more dependencies coming from the sequential order of execution of its components than the parallel ones. We varied the number of iterations from 0 to 2 in the Intermediate Phase and the number of Service Agents available for each required service from 2 to 10. That means that the number of possible combinations of services provided by the available service providers varies accordingly from 8 to 1000.

We represent the workload of Service Agents as a random distribution of *free* and *busy* time slots in the time interval $[0, Deadline]$, where free time slots are the ones which the Service Agent can provide the service within, and as such they can be proposed in bids. The length of time slots varies for each required service and represents the maximum expected execution time of each service.

Service Agents adopt a simple strategy when replying to an announcement by proposing in a bid the free time slot closest in time to the time slot proposed by the Service Market Agent in the announcement. Even though this represents a strong requirement on the Service Agent behaviour, we believe that it is reasonable to assume that Service Agents try to meet user requirements because all of them have to come to an agreement with the Service Market Agent otherwise no one will be able to provide their own services. In other words there is a form of cooperation driven by a self-interested behaviour.

Also the Service Market Agent adopts a very simple decision making mechanism in building announcements by trying to propose, at every iteration, time slots for each service in the composition that are closer to the ones proposed in the first received bids, but still compliant with the time constraints required by the workflow and by the user preference.

The simulation results in Figure 3 report on the Y–axis the percentage of feasible combinations and on the X–axis the total number of possible combinations coming from the available service providers for each service required in the composition. The results show that the number of feasible combinations increases when more iterations of the protocol are allowed. This is an expected behaviour, since with more iterations in the negotiation the possibility of obtaining feasible combinations increases because Service Agents are allowed to propose different time intervals that could meet the time constraints.

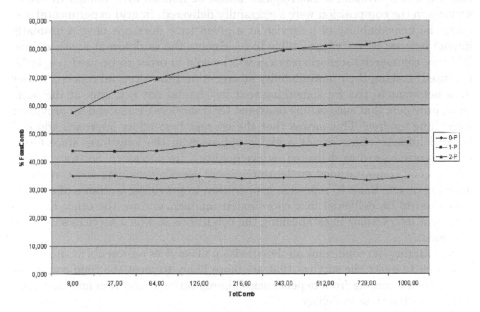

Fig. 3. Preliminary tests

We interpret the number of obtained feasible combinations as a percentage of successful negotiations.

These preliminary results give an idea of the feasibility of the proposed protocol, even though we are aware that in order to be significant in terms of performance decision making mechanisms have to be specified for the Service Market Agent in determining at each iteration of the protocol which intervals to propose next according to the time constraints on each service in the composition and the received bids.

5   Conclusions

Agent negotiation is crucial when grid resources cannot be considered constantly "ready to use", as in the case of today research grid infrastructures. When these infrastructures are commercially available, it will be necessary to provide sets of services on demand in response to dynamic requirements and circumstances.

In today computational grids enactment engines rely on simple scheduling techniques that do not consider neither the cost nor the quality for providing services since they are based on a First Come First Served (FCFS) policy. Only recently, the possibility to include user preferences when managing grid resources has been investigated including user preferences that concern the price and the usage time of resources, as it is reported in several works in the area [15,16,3,17]. In fact, a First Come First Served approach in providing the single services is not advisable because if a component service scheduled for the execution is not available when it is invoked, a user request cannot be fulfilled even though the other services in the composition were successfully delivered. In grid experimental settings the unavailability of a service at a given time does not have a dramatic impact because it is always possible to re–execute the workflow at another time. But in a commercial scenario services will be sold in order to be used (i.e. to be executed) making their unavailability at execution time a crucial concern: a user does not want to pay for something that he/she did not get, and, at the same time, providers that successfully delivered their services cannot end up providing something for free! This means that the current best–effort approach adopted by grid infrastructures is not a viable approach in the long term since forms of guarantee regarding delivered service qualities are necessary. Software agents offer a good computational model to represent service providers and consumers allowing on one hand to represent cooperation in providing worflows of services that need to be delivered in a coordinated manner, and on the other hand to represent interactions in establishing the conditions at which services should be provided.

Negotiating the conditions on the provision of services represents an appealing approach to select the services that are more likely to meet the time constraint requirements coming from dependencies among service execution and user preferences on the time to deliver.

The negotiation protocol proposed in this work allows for the management of interdependent issues trying to disclose as little knowledge as possible, but still allowing for different types of negotiation according to run–time decisions.

We plan to further investigate the performance of the protocol by assigning utility functions to the Service Market Agent and more sophisticated strategies to forming announcements based on constraint–based satisfaction techniques. At the same time different distributions of the Service Agents workloads will be adopted to simulate their different behaviours.

We aim at collecting results that can help in determining the parameters that drive run–time decisions on the protocol to adopt.

References

1. Foster, I., Kesselmann, K.: The Grid: Blueprint for a New Computing Infrastructure. Morgan Kaufmann, San Francisco (1998)
2. Buyya, R., Abramson, D., Giddy, J.: An economy driven resource management architecture for global computational power grids. In: PDPTA 2000. Proceedings

of The 2000 International Conference on Parallel and Distributed Processing Techniques and Applications, Las Vegas, USA (2000)

3. Schwiegelshohn, U., Wieder, P., Yahyapour, R.: Resource management for future generation grids. CoreGRID Series 3, 99–112 (2006)
4. Foster, I., Kesselman, C., Nick, J., Tuecke, S.: The physiology of the grid: An open grid service architecture for distributed system integration. Technical report Open Grid Service Infrastructure WG (2002)
5. De Roure, D., Jennings, N.R., Shadbolt, N.: The Semantic Grid: A future e–Science infrastructure, pp. 437–470. Wiley, Chichester (2003)
6. Foster, I., Jennings, N.R., Kesselman, C.: Brain meets brawn: Why grid and agents need each other. In: Proc. 3rd AAMAS, pp. 8–15 (2004)
7. Jennings, N.: An agent–based approach for building complex software systems. Communication of the ACM 44(4), 35–41 (2001)
8. Foster, I., Kesselman, C., Tuecke, S.: The anatomy of the grid: Enabling scalable virtual organizations. The International Journal of High Performance Computing Applications 15(3), 200–222 (2001)
9. Czajkowski, K., Foster, I., Kesselman, C., Sander, V., Tuecke, S.: Snap: A protocol for negotiating service level agreements and coordinating resource management in distributed systems. In: Feitelson, D.G., Rudolph, L., Schwiegelshohn, U. (eds.) JSSPP 2002. LNCS, vol. 2537, pp. 153–183. Springer, Heidelberg (2002)
10. WG, G.: Grid resource allocation agreement protocol (graap) working group, http://www.fz-juelich.de/zam/RD/coop/ggf/graap/graap-wg.html
11. Lomuscio, A., Wooldridge, M., Jennings, N.R.: A classification scheme for negotiation in electronic commerce. Int. Journal of Group Decision and Negotiation 12(1), 31–56 (2003)
12. Li, J., Yahyapour, R.: Negotiation strategies for grid scheduling. In: Chung, Y.-C., Moreira, J.E. (eds.) GPC 2006. LNCS, vol. 3947, pp. 42–52. Springer, Heidelberg (2006)
13. Li, Z., Parashar, M.: An agent–based infrastructure for autonomic composition of grid applications. An International Journal 1(4), 183–195 (2005)
14. Smith, R.G.: The contract net protocol: High–level communication and control in a distributed problem solver. IEEE Trans. on Computers 29(12), 1104–1113 (1980)
15. Nassif, L.N., Nogueira, J.M., de Andrade, F.V.: Distributed resource selection in grid using decision theory. In: CCGrid '07. Seventh IEEE International Symposium on Cluster Computing and the Grid, pp. 327–334. IEEE, Los Alamitos (2007)
16. Ouelhadj, D., Garibaldi, J., MacLaren, J., Sakellariou, R., Krishnakumar, K.: A multi–agent infrastructure and a service level agreement negotiation protocol for robust scheduling in grid computing. In: Sloot, P.M.A., Hoekstra, A.G., Priol, T., Reinefeld, A., Bubak, M. (eds.) EGC 2005. LNCS, vol. 3470, pp. 651–660. Springer, Heidelberg (2005)
17. Buyya, R., Vazhkudai, S.: Compute power market: Towards a market–oriented grid. In: CCGrid 2001. Proceedings of First IEEE/ACM International Symposium on Cluster Computing and the Grid, Brisbane, Australia (2001)

A Genetic Algorithm for the Quadratic Multiple Knapsack Problem

Tugba Saraç and Aydin Sipahioglu

Eskişehir Osmangazi University, Department of Industrial Engineering, 26030, Bademlik Eskişehir, Turkey
{tsarac,asipahi}@ogu.edu.tr

Abstract. The Quadratic Multiple Knapsack Problem (QMKP) is a generaliz-ation of the quadratic knapsack problem, which is one of the well-known combinatorial optimization problems, from a single knapsack to k knapsacks with (possibly) different capacities. The objective is to assign each item to at most one of the knapsacks such that none of the capacity constraints are violated and the total profit of the items put into the knapsacks is maximized. In this paper, a genetic algorithm is proposed to solve QMKP. Specialized crossover operator is developed to maintain the feasibility of the chromosomes and two distinct mutation operators with different improvement techniques from the non-evolutionary heuristic are presented. The performance of the developed GA is evaluated and the obtained results are compared to the previous study in the literature.

Keywords: Quadratic Multiple Knapsack Problem, Genetic Algorithm, Com-binatorial Optimization.

1 Introduction

The knapsack problem (KP) is a well-known combinatorial optimization problem. The classical KP seeks to select, from a finite set of items, the subset, which maximizes a linear function of the items chosen, subject to a single inequality constraint. In many real life applications it is important that the profit of a packing also should reflect how well the given items fit together. One formulation of such interdependence is the quadratic knapsack problem. The Quadratic Knapsack Problems (QKP) ask to maximize a quadratic objective function subject to a single capacity constraint. Some application areas of the QKP are; the determination of the optimal sites for communication satellite earth stations with a budget constraint, and similarly the determination of the location of railway stations and freight handling terminals and airports.

QKP has been introduced and the first branch-and-bound algorithm using the bounds based on upper planes has been presented by Gallo, Hammer and Simeone [1]. In 1986, a branch and bound algorithm for QKP proposed, the computation of an upper bound was based on Lagrangean relaxation by Chaillou, Hansen and Mahieu [2]. Two upper bounds based on Lagrangean decomposition have been presented for

F. Mele et al. (Eds.): BVAI 2007, LNCS 4729, pp. 490–498, 2007.
© Springer-Verlag Berlin Heidelberg 2007

QKP by Michelon and Veuilleux [3]. In the same year, Billionnet and Calmels [4] presented a branch-and-cut approach for QKP. An exact algorithm for QKP has developed by Caprara, Pisinger and Toth [5]. In 2000, Helmberg, Rendl and Weismantel [6] proposed a number of upper bounds for QKP based on semi definite programming. In 2003, an exact method based on computation of an upper bound by Lagrangean decomposition has been presented by Billionnet and Soutif [7]. This method allows finding the optimum of instances with up to 150 variables whatever their densities are, and with up to 300 variables for medium and low densities. In 2005, a greedy Genetic Algorithm (GA), applies operators that implement the strategies of the two QKP greedy heuristics proposed by Julstrom [8]. By using the greedy GA, near optimal solutions with very small error were obtained for the test instances with 100 and 200 variables in a reasonable short time.

The quadratic multiple knapsack problem (QMKP) extends the QKP with k knapsack, each with its own capacity c_k. The QMKP is defined as follows:

$$\max \quad z = \sum_{j=1}^{n} p_j x_{jk} + \sum_{i=1}^{n-1} \sum_{j=i+1}^{n} \sum_{k=1}^{m} p_{ij} x_{ik} x_{jk}$$

subject to

$$\sum_{j=1}^{n} w_j x_{jk} \leq c_k, \quad k = 1,\ldots\ldots,m$$

$$\sum_{k=1}^{m} x_{jk} \leq 1, \quad j = 1,\ldots\ldots,n$$

$$x_{jk} \in \{0,1\}, \quad j = 1,\ldots\ldots,n, \ k = 1,\ldots\ldots,m$$

Where, n items to pack in k knapsacks of capacity c_k. Each item j has a weight w_j and profit p_j which is the profit achieved if item j is selected for any knapsack. p_{ij} is the profit achieved if both items i and j are selected to a same knapsack and the objective is to assign each item to at most one of the knapsacks such that none of the capacity constraints are violated and the total profit of the items put into knapsacks is maximized. Because of this, the QMKP is harder than the other knapsack problems.

Best of our knowledge, there is only one paper presented by Hiley and Julstrom [9] about QMKP in the literature. QMKP has been introduced and the first solution approaches have been produced by them. They developed three heuristic approaches; a greedy heuristic, a stochastic hill-climber and a Genetic Algorithm (GA). Greedy heuristic fills the knapsacks one at a time, always choosing the unassigned item with the highest ratio of values with other items to its own weight that fits in the knapsack. The hill-climber's neighbor operator removes objects from each knapsack, and then refills the knapsack greedily as in the greedy heuristic. The hill-climber's neighbor operator also serves as the GA's mutation. By using these approaches, results were obtained for the test instances composed of two different densities (0.25, 0.75), two different numbers of items (100, 200) and three different numbers of knapsacks (3, 5, 10). It is remarkable that the GA only outperforms the hill-climber on the smaller instances with density d=0.25, with n=100 items and k=3 or 5 knapsacks. Consequently, we aimed to develop a GA which is more successful on the larger instances.

Many optimization problems are combinatorial in nature as QMKP and quite hard to solve by conventional optimization techniques. Recently, GAs have received considerable attention regarding their potential as an optimization technique for combinatorial optimization problems. Consequently, many researchers [8-11] have described evolutionary algorithms for different types of knapsack problems. Kellerer, Pferschy, and Pisinger [12] have provided a thorough introduction to knapsack problems and their variants.

In this paper, a genetic algorithm is proposed to solve QMKP. Specialized crossover operator is developed to maintain the feasibility of the chromosomes and two distinct mutation operators with different improvement techniques from the non-evolutionary heuristic are presented. Unlike Hiley and Julstrom [9], we have no assumption that all the knapsack capacities are the same. And it is demonstrated that obtained solutions are better than the solutions of Hiley and Julstrom [9]. Besides, success of the developed GA increases when the number of knapsacks increases.

The organization of this paper is as follows. In section two, developed genetic algorithm is explained. Computational results are reported in section three and conclusions are offered in the fourth section.

2   A New Genetic Algorithm for QMKP

GAs are powerful and broadly applicable in stochastic search and optimization techniques based on principles from evolution theory [13]. GAs, which are different from normal optimization and search procedures: (a) Work with a coding of the parameter set, not the parameters themselves. (b) Search from population of points, not a single point. (c) Use payoff (objective function) information, not derivatives or other auxiliary knowledge. (d) Use probabilistic transition rules, not deterministic rules [14].

KPs that are combinatorial optimization problems belong to the NP-hard type problems [15]. QMKP is NP-hard by restriction to KP; set all the quadratic values p_{ij} to zero and the number of knapsack to one. An efficient search heuristic will be useful for tackling such a problem. For that reason, in this study, a GA is proposed to solve QMKP. The developed GA is discussed in detail below.

2.1   Representation

It is used an n bit integer string to represent of candidate solutions to the QMKP where the integer number $\{1,2,...,k\}$ means the number of knapsack, inclusion of the item in, and zero the exclusion of one of the n items from all of the knapsacks. For example, a solution for the 7-item problem can be represented as the following bit string: [0201002]. It means that items 2 and 7 are selected to be filled in the knapsack two and item 4 is selected to be filled in the knapsack one. This representation may yield an infeasible solution.

2.2   Handling Constraints

The central question in applying genetic algorithms to the constrained optimization is how to handle constraints because the genetic operators used to manipulate the chromosomes often yields infeasible offspring. The existing techniques can be roughly classified as rejecting strategy, repairing strategy, modifying genetic operators strategy and penalizing strategy. In this study a modified genetic operators strategy is chosen to generate feasible solutions.

Initial population. Since without having feasible initial solutions using modified genetic operators would be useless, only strings whose selections of items have total weight no more than the knapsacks' capacities are generated. To generate a chromosome, the knapsacks are ordered according to their capacities and starting from the knapsack with smallest capacity, each knapsack fills with randomly selected items which have smaller weight than the remaining knapsack capacity.

2.3 Genetic Operators

The feasibility of the chromosomes that are generated by the initialization procedure must be satisfied while they are being processed by the genetic operators. Genetic operators are introduced to prevent us from having this infeasibility as explained below.

Reproduction. The reproduction operator allows individual strings to be copied for possible inclusion in the next generation. The chance that a string will be copied is based on the string's fitness value, calculated from a fitness function. 2-tournament selection method is used as reproduction operators.

Crossover. Crossover enables the algorithm to extract the best genes from different individuals and recombine them into potentially superior children. A specialized uniform based crossover operator is developed to maintain the feasibility of chromosomes. Randomly selected two parents chromosomes are used to generate two offspring. Randomly selected gene of the first chromosome is interchanged to the corresponding gene that is placed in the same order of the second chromosome, if the capacities of the knapsacks are available for both of the chromosomes. If any capacity of knapsack exceed by adding a new gene, came from the other parent chromosome, the value of this gene change as zero. The capacity of the offspring is completed by considering the remaining items which is not included by any knapsack according to their profit which is provided by including in the offspring.

Mutation. Reproduction and crossover alone can obviously generate a staggering amount of differing strings. However, depending on the initial population chosen, there may not be enough variety of strings to ensure the GA searches the entire problem space, or the GA may find itself converging on strings that are not quite close to the optimum it seeks due to a bad initial population. Some of these problems may be prevented by introducing a mutation operator into the GA. Developed GA contains two independent mutation operators each with its own mutation rate. Martello and Toth [16] proposed a polynomial time approximate algorithm for multiple knapsack problems with linear objective function. We modified the improvement techniques of this approximate algorithm for QMKP. Both of the mutation operators are used these techniques explained below. Mutation 1, improves on the solution though local exchanges. First, it considers all pairs of items assigned to different knapsacks and, if possible and if the total profit increases, interchanges them. The procedure of the mutation 1 is given below:

Mutation_1 Procedure.

```
begin
for i := 1 to ps do if m1 > random number from [0,1]
then
   begin
   for j := 1 to ng do if gene_ij > 0 then
      for k := j + 1 to ng do if 0 < gene_ij ≠ gene_ik then
         begin
         h := arg max {w_j, w_k}; l := arg min {w_j, w_k};
         d := w_h - w_k ;
         if d ≤ rcapacity_l and
         Σ_{l≠m} P_{lm} + Σ_{h≠r} P_{hr} ≥ Σ_{h≠m} P_{hm} + Σ_{l≠r} P_{lr} : m ∈ knapsack
         gene_ih , r ∈ knapsack gene_il then
            begin
            g := gene_il ; gene_il := gene_ih ; gene_ih := g ;
            rcapacity_h := rcapacity_h + d ;
            rcapacity_l := rcapacity_l - d ;
            end
      end;
   end
end.
```

ps: population size, $m1$: mutation_1 rate, nk: number of knapsacks, $capacity_k$: capacity of the knapsack k, $rcapacity_{ik}$: remaining capacity of the knapsack k of chromosome i, $gene_{ir}$: value of the gene r of chromosome i.

Mutation 2, removes s included items randomly. s is the parameter of the mutation 2. Then the capacity of the chromosome is completed as in crossover. The procedure of the mutation 2 is given below:

```
Mutation_2 Procedure.
begin
for i := 1 to ps do if m2 > random number from [0,1]
then
   for t:= 1 to s do gene_it := 0   (randomly selected
   t:gene_it>0)
      for k := 1 to nk do
         begin
         find r := arg min{ w_j: gen_ij = 0 };
         while w_r ≤ ( capacity_k - tw_k ) do
            begin
            for j := 1 to ng do
               begin
               find q := max { P_j + Σ_{l≠j} P_jl : gene_ij = gene_il = k,

               tw_k + w_j ≤ capacity_k };
```

```
                gene_iq := k ; tw_k := tw_k + w_q ;
                end
            if r = q  then find r:= arg min{w_j: gene_ij =0};
            end
        end
    end.
```

$m1$: mutation_1 rate, tw_k: total weight of the items of the knapsack k.

When creating a new generation, there is always a risk of losing the most fit individuals. Using elitism, the most fit individuals are copied to the next generation. The other ones undergo the crossover and mutation. Since the elitism selection improves the efficiency of a GA considerably, as it prevents losing the best results, it is used in developed GA.

We use two type termination conditions with together. One of them checks whether the algorithm has run a fixed number (nf) of generations. And the other one stops the algorithm if the solution is same during an identical number (ni) of generation even if ni is smaller then the nf.

The test instance described in the next section, the GA's population contained 30 chromosomes. The probability that crossover generated offspring chromosomes was determined as 0.80, and mutation 1 and mutation 2 rates were chosen as 0.40 and 0.10 respectively. Parameter of the mutation 2 was 4. Finally, the values of the termination parameters were ni=200 and nf=300.

3 Computational Results

In this section, it is reported the solution results obtained by using developed GA for forty two QMKP instances given in the literature. Additionally, the results are compared with the results of the GA presented by Hiley and Julstrom [9]. All computational experiments were conducted on HP6000 workstation with Excel/Visual Basic Application.

An instance of the QMKP consists of its number n of available items and k knapsacks. A significant feature of a QMKP instance is the density of its linear values p_i and quadratic values p_{ij} which are non-zero. We solved instances composed of two different densities (0.25, 0.75), two different numbers of items (100, 200) and three different numbers of knapsacks (3, 5, 10). All QKP instances are available on the web site[1] and the number of knapsacks and the capacities of the knapsacks, which are exactly the same values with the values used by Hiley and Julstrom [9], used to modify these QKP instances to QMKP instances, are given in Table 1.

Computational results for forty two QMKP instances are also illustrated in Table 1. The left part of the table summarizes the instances' features. For each instance, the table lists its number of knapsacks (k), density (d), and number of items (n), instance number given in the web site (no) and capacities of the knapsacks (c). The second and third parts contain GA$_{HJ}$ results were given by Hilley and Julstrom (2006) and developed GA$_{SS}$ results respectively. Mean values of the results of 5 trials and

---

[1] http://cermsem.univ-paris1.fr/soutif/QKP/

Table 1. Performance of the GA$_{SS}$ on the forty two QMKP instance

K	d	n	no	cap.	GA$_{HJ}$ best	GA$_{HJ}$ values mean	GA$_{SS}$ best	GA$_{SS}$ values mean	% (GA$_{SS}$ best - GA$_{HJ}$ best) / GA$_{HJ}$ best
10	0.25	100	1	206	13521	12499	**15778**	15505,2	16,69%
10	0.25	100	2	221	12859	12019	**14835**	14601,2	15,37%
10	0.25	100	3	199	11790	11245	**14348**	14136,2	21,70%
10	0.25	100	4	241	13316	12593	**15495**	15178,8	16,36%
10	0.25	100	5	217	11909	11389	**14770**	11665,8	24,02%
10	0.25	200	1	414	42016	39791	**48119**	47652,8	14,53%
10	0.25	200	2	373	45483	42739	**51666**	50410,2	13,59%
10	0.25	200	4	424	41623	39446	**48792**	47906,8	17,22%
10	0.25	200	5	407	46811	42399	**49504**	48698	5,75%
10	0.75	100	1	200	26603	25681	**28767**	27723,2	8,13%
10	0.75	100	2	214	28663	27815	**29824**	29344,4	4,05%
10	0.75	100	3	205	26176	25038	**27960**	27281,6	6,82%
10	0.75	100	4	200	29701	28592	**30712**	29134,6	3,40%
10	0.75	200	1	393	102002	98962	**106008**	100939,6	3,93%
5	0.25	100	1	413	21914	21315	**22039**	21734,6	0,57%
5	0.25	100	2	442	21216	20472	**21249**	20723,8	0,16%
5	0.25	100	3	398	20243	19763	**20862**	20444,4	3,06%
5	0.25	100	4	482	**21698**	20923	21601	21417	-0,45%
5	0.25	100	5	434	20808	20248	**20928**	16779	0,58%
5	0.25	200	1	828	70731	68705	**73619**	72600,2	4,08%
5	0.25	200	2	747	**76297**	72924	74883	74403,2	-1,85%
5	0.25	200	4	848	70264	67416	**71936**	71338,8	2,38%
5	0.25	200	5	815	72745	69978	**73825**	72006	1,48%
5	0.75	100	1	401	**48663**	47678	47449	45902	-2,49%
5	0.75	100	2	428	**48990**	48175	47766	47031,8	-2,50%
5	0.75	100	3	411	47512	46623	**48008**	46586,8	1,04%
5	0.75	100	4	400	**49845**	49194	46921	46063	-5,87%
5	0.75	200	1	786	**179525**	177438	173905	170447,2	-3,13%
3	0.25	100	1	688	28665	27904	**28807**	28514,4	0,50%
3	0.25	100	2	738	28059	27044	**28456**	28225,2	1,41%
3	0.25	100	3	663	**26780**	25991	26754	26573,8	-0,10%
3	0.25	100	4	804	28199	27265	**28383**	28035,4	0,65%
3	0.25	100	5	723	27550	26683	**27582**	22043	0,12%
3	0.25	200	1	1381	97469	95497	**99853**	99216	2,45%
3	0.25	200	2	1246	**106162**	100521	104277	101179	-1,78%
3	0.25	200	4	1413	95649	93968	**97700**	97525	2,14%
3	0.25	200	5	1358	**99458**	96077	98326	97979,6	-1,14%
3	0.75	100	1	669	**69769**	68941	64335	63757,2	-7,79%
3	0.75	100	2	714	**69146**	68639	68164	66584,8	-1,42%
3	0.75	100	3	686	**68763**	67557	67643	66257	-1,63%
3	0.75	100	4	666	**69907**	69101	68626	65018,4	-1,83%
3	0.75	200	1	1311	**268919**	265523	261106	254300,8	-2,91%

obtained best solutions are reported. Better solutions of the algorithm's best are signed as bold and underlined. Last column of the Table 1 shows that the performance of developed GA. The positive value means obtained best objective value by using the GA_{SS} much better than the GA_{HJ}'s best value, in percent.

As shown in Table 1, the GA presented in this study is more successful than the GA presented by Hiley and Julstrom [9] especially while the number of knapsack (k) increases. For example, the GA_{SS} results are totally superior for $k=10$ regardless number of items and densities of the instances. Furthermore, obtained best solution by using the GA_{SS} is better than the best of the GA_{HJ} at least 3.4%, and at most 24.02%. These are good consequences. On the other hand, the GA_{SS} results superior only 8 of 14 instances for $k=5$, and superior only 6 of 14 instances for $k=3$. Besides, the difference of the best solutions is not quite big. For example the range of best solution differences is 0.16%-5.87% for $k=5$ and 0.10%-7.79% for $k=3$. These comparisons show that the success of developed GA depends on the number of knapsack, strongly. Moreover, the density of matrix affects the success of developed GA. It is apparent that, the developed algorithm's success increase when the density decrease for small number of knapsack such as 3 and 5.

4 Conclusions

In this study, a new genetic algorithm is presented to solve the QMKP. The contribution the new GA is proposing specialized crossover operator and two new distinct mutation operators. Proposed crossover operator maintains feasibility of chromosomes. Mutation operators use the improvement techniques from modified non-evolutionary heuristic which is proposed for multi knapsack problems with linear objective function.

Unlike Hiley and Julstrom [9], there is no assumption that all the knapsack capacities are the same. And it is demonstrated that the GA_{SS} is more successful than the GA_{HJ} on the instances with large number of knapsacks. Very successful results are obtained for number of knapsacks is equal to 10 regardless the numbers of items and densities. For example, the difference between the best solutions of the algorithms is bigger then 20% for some instances. Additionally, it is demonstrated that the developed GA is more successful with low densities for small number of knapsacks such as 3 and 5. Since the efficiency of the GA_{SS} depends on its parameters, it is recommended that an analysis to decide on the best values of the parameters of GA may be made, which is one of the ideas for further research on this subject.

References

1. Gallo, G., Hammer, P.L., Simeone, B.: Quadratic Knapsack Problems. Mathematical Programming Study 12, 132–149 (1980)
2. Chaillou, P., Hansen, P., Mahieu, Y.: Best network flow bound for the quadratic knapsack problem. In: Combinatorial Optimization. Lecture Notes in Mathematics, vol. 1403, pp. 225–235 (1986)
3. Michelon, P., Veuilleux, L.: Lagrangean methods for the 0-1 quadratic knapsack problem. European Journal of Operational Research 92, 326–341 (1996)
4. Billionnet, A., Calmels, F.: Linear programming for the 0-1 quadratic knapsack problem. European Journal of Operational Research 92, 310–325 (1996)

5. Caprara, A., Pisinger, D., Toth, P.: Exact solution of the quadratic knapsack problem. INFORMS Journal on Computing 11, 125–137 (1999)
6. Helmberg, C., Rendl, F., Weismantel, R.: A semidefinite programming approach to the quadratic knapsack problem. Journal of Combinatorial Optimization 4, 197–215 (2000)
7. Billionnet, A., Soutif, E.: An exact method based on Lagrangean decomposition for the 0-1 quadratic knapsack problem. European Journal of operational research 157(3), 565–575 (2003)
8. Julstrom, B.A.: Greedy, genetic, and greedy genetic algorithms for the quadratic knapsack problem. Proceedings of the Genetic and Evolutionary Computation Conference 1, 607–614 (2005)
9. Hiley, A., Julstrom, B.A.: The Quadratic multiple knapsack problem and three heuristic approaches to it. In: Proceedings of the Genetic and Evolutionary Computation Conference, pp. 547–552 (2006)
10. Cotta, C., Troya, J.: A hybrid genetic algorithm for the 0-1 multiple knapsack problem. Artificial Neural Networks and Genetic Algorithms 3, 250–254 (1998)
11. Anagun, A.S., Saraç, T.: Optimization of performance of genetic algorithm for 0-1 knapsack problems using Taguchi method. In: Gavrilova, M., Gervasi, O., Kumar, V., Tan, C.J.K., Taniar, D., Laganà, A., Mun, Y., Choo, H. (eds.) ICCSA 2006. LNCS, vol. 3982, pp. 678–687. Springer, Heidelberg (2006)
12. Kellerer, H., Pferschy, U., Pisinger, D.: Knapsack Problems. Springer, Heidelberg (2004)
13. Gen, M., Cheng, R.: Genetic Algorithms and Engineering Design. John Wiley & Sons, New York (1997)
14. Goldberg, D.E.: Genetic Algorithms in Search, Optimization, and Machine Learning. Addison-Wesley, Reading (1989)
15. Martello, S., Toth, P.: Knapsack Problems Algorithms and Computer Implementations. John Wiley & Sons, England (1990)
16. Martello, S., Toth, P.: Heuristic algorithms for the multiple knapsack problem. Computing 27, 93–112 (1981)

The Application of Neural Networks in Classification of Epilepsy Using EEG Signals

Cenk Sahin[1], Seyfettin Noyan Ogulata[1], Kezban Aslan[2], and Hacer Bozdemir[2]

[1] Department of Industrial Engineering, Faculty of Engineering and Architecture, Cukurova University, 01330, Adana, Turkey
[2] Department of Neurology, Faculty of Medicine, Cukurova University, 01330, Adana, Turkey

Abstract. Epilepsy is a disorder of cortical excitability and still an important medical problem. The correct diagnosis of a patient's epilepsy syndrome clarifies the choice of drug treatment and also allows an accurate assessment of prognosis in many cases. The aim of this study is to evaluate epileptic patients and classify epilepsy groups by using Multi-Layer Perceptron Neural Networks (MLPNNs). 418 patients with epilepsy diagnoses according to International League against Epilepsy (ILAE, 1981) were included in this study. The correct classification of this data was performed by two expert neurologists before they were executed by MLPNNs. The MLPNNs were trained by the parameters obtained from the EEG signals and clinic properties of the patients. We classified the epilepsy into two groups such as partial and primary generalized epilepsy and we achieved an 89.2% correct prediction rate by using MLPNN model. The parameters of the loss of consciousness in the course of seizure, the duration and ritmicity of abnormal activities found in EEG constituted the most significant variables in the classification of epilepsy by using MLPNN. These results indicate that the classification performance of MLPNN model for epilepsy groups is satisfactory and we think that this model may be used in clinical studies as a decision support tool to confirm the classification of epilepsy groups after they are developed.

Keywords: Epilepsy, EEG, Multilayer Perceptron Neural Network (MLPNN), Levenberg-Marquardt.

1 Introduction

Epilepsy is a disorder of cortical excitability and interictal electroencephalography (EEG) remains the most convenient and the least expensive way to demonstrate physiological manifestations of this disorder [1-3].

Epilepsy is classified as either generalized or partial with several subcategories in each class. In the management of patients with established epilepsy, the concept of epilepsy syndrome based on age at onset, seizure type or types, EEG findings and etiology has been an important advancement [4]. The correct diagnosis of a patient's epilepsy syndrome clarifies the choice of drug treatment and also allows an accurate assessment of prognosis in many cases [3-5].

F. Mele et al. (Eds.): BVAI 2007, LNCS 4729, pp. 499–508, 2007.
© Springer-Verlag Berlin Heidelberg 2007

About 50 % of the patients with epilepsy show interictal epileptiform discharge on EEG. Epileptiform activity is specific, but not sensitive for diagnosis of epilepsy [1,3,6].

The trend is to develop new methods for computer assisted decision-making in medicine and to evaluate critically these methods in clinical practice. Artificial neural networks (ANNs) have been used extensively in many different problems in medicine [7-11]. ANNs have also been used for the detection of seizure activity [12-14]. The results of these studies on detection of seizure events in EEGs of epileptic patients showed that ANNs are capable of capturing qualitative information from an EEG with over 90% accuracy. In addition to these studies, Walczak and Nowack [15] were the first to use ANNs for the diagnosis of epilepsy. However, they did not obtain high categorization accuracy. Some authors also applied neural network and statistical recognition methods to EEG analysis [16-18]. Their results confirmed that the proposed model has potential in classifying the EEG signals.

Although ANNs have been used for the detection of seizure activity related to video EEGs analysis before, none of the previous works classify the epilepsy groups. In this study, we both categorized the EEG findings and combined the clinic properties of the patients along with these EEG findings. We have tested to what extent we could determine the epilepsy classification of the patients with the method of ANN.

2   Material and Methods

2.1   Collection and Processing of Data

579 patients with epilepsy diagnoses according to International League against Epilepsy (ILAE, 1981) are included in this study. The patients at the clinic of epilepsy outpatients of Cukurova University Medical School, Neurology Department between the years of 2002-2005 were examined and included in the study. The epilepsy diagnosis was based on the medical history, clinical findings, electrophysiological reports, radiological and biochemical analysis.

This study considers the categorization of sex, age of seizure onset groups, seizure types, the loss of consciousness in the course of seizure time and the properties of the first interictal EEG analysis of epileptic patients. In the classification belonging to age of seizure onset : the patients between 0-20 year olds were classified as group 1, between 21-60 year olds were classified as group 2, and 61 and over year olds were classified as group 3. The EEG records were detected by 12 channel Nihon-Kohdem EEG machine. Each EEG record was done for 20 minutes, but the EEG of the activated sleep was recorded for 2 hours. The patients who had pseudo seizures and EEG from out of our electrophysiology laboratory were excluded from the study. Eventually, we reevaluated 418 patients with their first EEGs and clinical properties. All the EEGs examined in this study were recorded after postictal period of seizure. EEG signals contain a wide range of frequency components; this range is classified approximately in a number of frequency bands as follows: δ (0.5–4 Hz), θ (4–8 Hz), α (8–13 Hz), β (13–30 Hz). The δ, θ waves were accepted as abnormal activities, whereas α, β waves were accepted as normal. On the other hand, sharp, sharp and wave, spike, spike and wave activities were accepted as abnormal signals as well. While the frequency component of delta and theta activities as stated above is a limited application, the frequency of the other abnormal activities is not limited [19]. The activity properties of EEG findings were classified in the direction of group 1: sharp and/or spikes; group 2: delta and/or theta, group 3: normal. In the course of EEG, the physiological conditions of the patients were determined as either awake or sleep and the properties of ritmicity of the abnormal activities were categorized as yes or no. The localization of abnormal activities was categorized; either they are focal (frontal, temporal, parietal, occipital or in more fields than one) or generalized or normal. On the other hand, abnormal activities were categorized from the point of hemispheric lateralization as right, left, diffuse and normal. We determined the frequency of abnormal waves (how many times a second these activities have been repeated), and duration of the abnormal signals (how long abnormal signals take during the EEG recording) on the EEG. On the other hand we checked the parameter of whether the loss of consciousness in the course of seizure time was being identified (yes/ no/ sometimes reported but not in all seizure). The data were evaluated with independent samples one-way analysis of variance using SPSS 10.0 statistical program, p value of less than 0.05 was considered statistically significant.

2.2 Multilayer Perceptron Neural Networks (MLPNNs)

The architecture of MLPNN may contain two or more layers. Each layer consists of units which receive their input from a layer directly below and send their output to units in a layer directly above the unit. The connections between the neurons are arranged by using a "learn" algorithm. There are many training algorithms used to train an MLPNN and a frequently used one is called backpropagation (BP) training algorithm [20]. Although the BP algorithm has been a significant milestone in neural network research area of interest, it has been known as an algorithm with a very poor convergence rate. Many attempts have been made to speed up the BP algorithm. A significant improvement on realization performance can be observed by using various second order approaches namely Newton's method, conjugate gradient's, or the Levenberg-Marquardt (LM) optimization technique [21-23]. LM can be thought of as a combination of the steepest descent and the Gauss-Newton method. In the last years, the LM method, directly taken from the Optimization field, has been increasing its popularity within the neural networks community. The difference between optimization and neural network applications of the method comes from the fact that in the latter there is usually a great deal of parameters to be estimated [24,25].

3 Results

3.1 Statistical Analysis and Results

418 patients who had been diagnosed with epilepsy were included in this study. The data set was summarized in Table 1.

Table 1. Demographic and Disease Properties of the Patients

Sex	n	%
Female	229	54.8
Male	189	45.2
Total	418	
Age groups		
0-20	237	56.7
21-60	141	33.7
61- ↑	40	9.6
Epilepsy groups		
Partial epilepsy	339	81.9
Primary generalized epilepsy	79	18.9

Table 2. The Activity Properties of EEG Findings According to Epilepsy Groups

	Epilepsy groups						
EEG findings	PE	%	PGE	%	Total	%	p
Sharp and /or spike	121	35.7	43	54.4	164	39.2	
Delta and / or theta	128	40.7	24	30.4	162	38.8	
Normal	80	23.6	12	25.2	92	22	
Total	339	100	9	100	418	100	0.009

*PE: Partial epilepsy, PGE: Primary generalized epilepsy

The analysis of the first interictal EEGs revealed sharp and/or spike activity in 164 (39.2%), delta and/or theta activity in 162 (38.8%) of all patients. It was normal in 92 (22%) of all patients. The EEG findings of the patients whose seizures were classified as a partial epilepsy revealed sharp and/or spike activity in 121 (35.7%) and delta and/or theta activity in 128 (40.7%) of the patients whereas the EEG findings of the patients who were diagnosed as primary generalized epilepsy revealed sharp and/or spike activity in 43 (54.4%) and delta and/or theta activity in 24 (30.4%) of the patients. The sharp and/or spike activity was seen more often in the primary generalized epilepsy, and the delta and/or theta activity was seen more often in the partial epilepsy (p value is 0.009, Table 2).

Table 3. Major Localization of Activities According to Epilepsy Groups

	Localization of abnormal activities							
Epilepsy Groups	Generalized discharge		Local discharge		Normal		Total	p
	n	%	n	%	n	%	n	
PE	61	17.9	198	58.5	80	23.6	339	
PGE	32	40.5	35	44.3	12	15.2	79	
Total	93	22.3	233	55.7	92	22	418	0.001

*PE: Partial epilepsy, PGE: Primary generalized epilepsy

The EEG findings belonging to the partial epilepsy group revealed localized discharge in 198 (58.5%) (frontal=27; temporal=81; parietal=5, occipital=11, more than one area: 74), normal in 80 (23.6%) and generalized discharge in 61 (17.9%) of the patients. On the other hand, EEG findings of the patients whose seizures were classified as primary generalized epilepsy revealed generalized discharge in 32 (40.5%), localized epileptic or slow activity in 35 (44.3%) (frontal=3; temporal=17; parietal=2, occipital=5, more than one area=8) and normal in 12 (15.2%) of the patients. This result also showed that the localization of EEG activity is in correlation with epileptic groups (p value is 0.001, Table 3).

According to the localization of abnormal activities, EEG findings of the patients whose EEGs showed generalized discharge (n=93) revealed sharp and/or spike in 59 (63.4%), delta and/or theta activity in 34 (36.6%) of the patients. This result showed that most of generalized discharge was constituted mostly by sharp and/or spike activity, and local discharge was constituted mostly by delta and / or theta activity (p<0.000).

3.2 Neural Networks Analysis and Results

3.2.1 Training and Testing of MLPNNs for the Classification of Epilepsy Groups

The learning of the network was executed by applying the input and output vectors. In this classification, the output of the network was the epilepsy groups (partial and primary generalized epilepsy which are coded as 0 and 1, respectively). In the present study, the activation functions in the hidden layer and the output layer were selected as sigmoid and softmax functions, respectively.

In using the MLPNNs, The MLPNNs were trained with the training set, cross validated with the cross validation set and checked with the test set. The cross validating stopping rule was used for terminating training in this research. When the error in the cross validation increased, the training was stopped because the point of the best generalization was reached [18,26]. The MLPNN models for classifying epilepsy groups were developed using the 167 training examples, while the remaining 251 examples were used for testing of the model. A practical way to find a point of better generalization is to use a small percentage (around %20) of the training set for the cross validation. For obtaining a better generalization 34, training examples were randomly selected to be used as a cross validation set. It is very important to determine the architecture of MLPNNs having the best generalization. Therefore, we have formed different MLPNNs composed of different number of nodes in the hidden layer in order to find optimal topologies of MLPNNs. The most popular approach to finding the optimal number of nodes in hidden layer is by trial and error. In the present study, each formed MLPNN having different number of node in the hidden layer from 1 to 100 was trained for classifying the epilepsy groups. In order to evaluate the performance of the neural networks, classifications were done by the expert neurologists and the classification results calculated at the output of neural network were compared. Classification success of the neural networks on unseen test data was shown in figure 1.

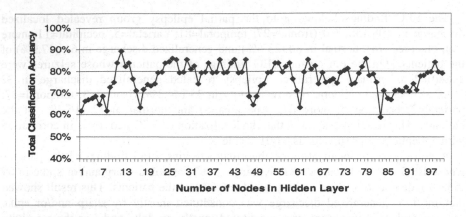

Fig. 1. Total Classification Accuracy of Tested MLPNNs

According to these results, the MLPNN having 12 nodes in the hidden layer had the best total classification accuracy of 89.2%. The classification success of the best MLPNN was evaluated in detail by examining the table called the confusing matrix. The 2nd and 3rd columns of Table 4 represented confusing matrix. According to confusing matrix, 9 out of 47 primary generalized epilepsy samples were classified incorrectly by the MLPNN as partial epilepsy and 18 out of 204 partial epilepsy samples were classified as primary generalized epilepsy. The test performance of the MLPNN was determined by computation of the statistical parameters such as sensitivities of partial epilepsy and primary generalized epilepsy, and total classification accuracy.

Table 4. Confusing Matrix and Statistical Parameters for Epilepsy Groups

	Result (PE)	Result (PGE)	Sensitivity (%)
Result (PE)	186	9	91.1
Result (PGE)	18	38	80.8
Total	204	47	89.2

*PE: Partial epilepsy, PGE: Primary generalized epilepsy

The values of the statistical parameters were given in the 3rd column of Table 4. The MLPNN classified partial and primary generalized epilepsy with the accuracy of 91.1% and 80.8%, respectively. In addition, it succeeded in classifying the epilepsy groups with the total classification accuracy of 89.2%.

Additionally, ten new MLPNNs were constructed for determining significant variables. Significant variable will cause the classification accuracy of MLPNN to decrease when it is omitted from the input vector. As the results shown in Table 5, all variables were significant because the classification accuracy of MLPNN decreased when one of them was omitted from the input vector. Therefore, no variables were excluded. The loss of consciousness in the course of seizure time variable caused the largest decrease in the classification accuracy when it was left out.

Table 5. Ten Variables Classification Accuracy

Missing Value	Total Classification Accuracy
The loss of consciousness in the course of seizure time	76,1
Duration of the abnormal signals	79,3
Ritmicity of the abnormal activities	80,9
Localization	80,9
The activity properties of EEG findings	82,5
Frequency of abnormal waves	82,5
Age of seizure onset groups	82,5
Hemispheric lateralization	83,3
Sex	83,3
The physiological conditions of the patients in the course of EEG	84,9

4 Discussion

EEG findings enhance the multi-axial diagnosis of epilepsy in terms of whether the seizure disorder is partial or generalized. As other laboratory tests, it should be used in conjunction with clinical data. However, partial and generalized seizure disorders show some overlap both clinical and EEG manifestation. The conceptual classification of seizures as partial or primary generalized epilepsy is important and clinically useful because the knowledge of an individual patient's epilepsy group allows the assessment of prognosis and the choice of the most effective antiepileptic drug. On the other hand, EEG has relatively low sensitivity in epilepsy ranging from 25% to 56%. Specificity is better, but it varies between 78-98% [3]. As most authors suggest, only interictal epileptiform discharge (IED) are associated with seizure disorder [3,5,6].

The category of partial seizures was found as one of the most controversial aspects of the ILAE classification [5]. In this study, we found that seizures were classified as partial epilepsy in 339 (81.9%) of all patients whereas primary generalized epilepsy in 79 (18.9%) of all patients. This distribution is not uniform as our epilepsy clinic treats mostly adult patients.

The performed EEGs revealed sharp and/or spike activity in 164 (39.2%), delta and/or theta activity in 162 (38.8%) patients. It was normal in 92 (22%) of all patients. The timing of EEG recording is important because the EEG record within 24 hours of seizure revealed interictal epileptiform discharge in 51% as compared to 34% who had EEG later. Only 50% of patients with epilepsy show IED in the first EEG test [3]. These results showed that our finding was the same as the ratio which was recorded after 24 hours of seizures. According to Pedley et al. [1], only IED and perhaps periodic lateralized epileptiform discharge (PLED) are associated with epilepsy at rates sufficiently high to be clinically useful. The percentage of normal EEG findings determined in our study is less than Hopkins et al. [27] and King et al. [4] studies. On the other hand, Walczak and Nowack [15] suggest that it is possible to achieve a classification accuracy of 62% and 68% with further refinement in epileptic seizures using lateralized burst of theta activity with an initial backpropagation ANN.

Focal slow–wave activity and generalized slowing of background rhythms are common findings in patients with partial seizures and symptomatic epilepsy [1,28]. In this study, the EEG findings of partial epilepsy group revealed normal in 80 (23.6%), sharp and/or spike activity in 121 (35.7%) and delta and/or theta activity in 128 (40.7%) of the patients (Table 2). This result suggests that the slow activity should be a considerable finding in partial epilepsy. The EEG findings belonging to the partial epilepsy group revealed localized discharge in 198 (58.5%) (frontal=27; temporal=81; parietal=5, occipital=11, more than one area: 74), generalized discharge in 61 (17.9%) of the patients (Table 3). The bilateral generalized spike and wave discharge is not absolute diagnostic feature of primary subcortical epilepsy [6]. In our study, EEG finding of the partial epileptic patients showed especially localized discharge and sharp and/or spike activity as well.

The IEDs in primary generalized epilepsy are always widespread, bilaterally synchronous and more or less symmetrical EEG finding can be recorded [6]. The sharp and/or spike activity was found more common in primary generalized epilepsy (54.4%) than partial epilepsy (35.7%)(Table 2). This result show that there is a statistically significant relation between the epileptic group and the abnormal EEG activities (p=0.009, Table 2). On the other hand, EEG findings of the patients whose seizures were classified as primary generalized epilepsy revealed generalized discharge in only 32 (40.5%) (p=0.001, Table 3). The interictal EEG is normal in 15-40% of the cases with idiopathic generalized epilepsy. The interictal focal abnormalities are also described in up to 40-56% of these cases [3]. This result shows that our result is similar to other studies [3-5]. These findings are important for primary generalized epilepsy since insufficient history or EEG asymmetries including focal slowing, amplitude asymmetries or secondary bilateral synchrony are major risk factors for misdiagnosis or delay of diagnosis in this group [29,30]. That is why there should be a different methodology for finding accurate diagnosis in these patients.

Most of the studies done earlier focused on the epileptic seizure detection and the classification of EEG signals through ANN using some of EEG properties. In this study, the neural network is trained by the parameters obtained from not only the EEG signals, but also the demographic properties of patients and the parameter of the loss of consciousness in the course of seizure. This is the first study to classify the epilepsy groups using the neural network according to these parameters. To achieve this aim, the demographic properties, the loss of consciousness in the course of seizure and the first EEGs of 418 patients were evaluated and applied to neural network as independent variables. Subsequently, the MLPNNs trained with Levenberg-Marquardt algorithm were used to classify epilepsy groups.

The MLPNN having the best classification accuracy classified correctly 91.1% of patients having partial epilepsy, and also 80.8% of patients having primary generalized epilepsy. Overall, we had an 89.2% correct prediction rate for the 251 test data set. The classification performances of ten new MLPNNs were used to identify the significant variables for the classification of the epilepsy groups. Walczak and Nowack [15] investigated when two variables which were temporal lobe location and prevalence were excluded; the performance of neural network was improved. In our study, all variables we studied were significant and no variable was removed. On the other hand, the parameters of the loss of consciousness in the course of seizure, the duration and ritmicity of abnormal activities found in EEG constituted the most significant variables in the classification of epilepsy groups by using MLPNN (Table 5).

When the confusion matrix and statistical table are examined, the MLPNNs have obtained acceptable classification success. The classification performance of MLPNN models for epilepsy groups have been found satisfactory and we think that this model can be used in clinical studies as a decision support tool to confirm the classification of epilepsy groups after they are developed.

References

1. Pedley, T.A., Mendiratta, A., Walczak, T.S.: Seizures and epilepsy. In: Ebersole, J.S., Pedley, T.A. (eds.) Current Practice of Clinical Electroencephalography, pp. 506–587. Lippincott Williams & Wilkins Comp., USA (2002)
2. Smith, S.J.M.: EEG in neurological conditions other than epilepsy: When does it help, what does it add? J. Neurol. Neurosurg. Psychiatry 76, 8–12 (2005)
3. Smith, S.J.M.: EEG in diagnosis, classification, and management of patients with epilepsy. J. Neurol. Neurosurg. Psychiatry 76, 2–7 (2005)
4. King, M.A., Newton, M.R., Jackson, G.D., et al.: Epileptology of the first -seizure presentation: a clinical, electroencephalographic and magnetic resonance imaging study of 300 consecutive patients. Lancet 352, 1007–1011 (1998)
5. Trescher, H.W., Lesser, R.P.: The Epilepsies. In: Bradley, G.W., Daroff, B.R. (eds.) Neurology in Clinical Practice, pp. 1745–1779. Buterworth-Heineman, USA (2000)
6. Kiloh, L.G., McComas, A.J., Osselton, J.W.: Clinical Electroencephalography, pp. 168–200. Butterworht & Co ltd., Great Britain (1972)
7. Selvi, S.T., Arumugam, S., Ganesan, L.: BIONET: An artificial neural network model for diagnosis of diseases. Pattern Recognition Letters 21, 721–740 (2001)
8. Tomida, S., Hanai, T., Koma, N., Suzuki, Y., Kobayashi, T., Honda, H.: Artificial neural network predictive model for allergic disease using neural network nucleotide polymorphisms data. Journal of Bioscience and Bioengineering 93(5), 470–478 (2002)
9. Zhang, G.P., Berardi, V.L.: An investigation of neural networks in thyroid function diagnosis. Health Care Management Science 1, 29–37 (1998)
10. Itchhaaporia, D., Snow, P.B., Almassy, R.J., Oetgen, W.J.: Artificial neural networks: current status in cardiovascular medicine. JACC 28(2), 515–521 (1996)
11. Abe, H., Ashizawa, K., Li, F., Matsuyama, N., Fukushima, A., Shiraishi, J., Macmahon, H., Dio, K.: Artificial neural networks for differential diagnosis of interstitial lung disease: results of a simulation test with actual clinical cases. Acad Radiol 11, 29–37 (2004)
12. Webber, W.R.S., Lesser, R.P., Richardson, R.T., Wilson, K.: An approach to seizure detection using an artificial neural network. Electroencephalography and Clinical Neurophysiology 98, 250–272 (1996)
13. Pradhan, N., Sadasivan, P.K., Arunodaya, G.R.: Detection of seizure activity in EEG by artificial neural network: A preliminary study. Computers and Biomedical Research 29, 303–313 (1996)
14. Gabor, A.J.: Seizure detection using a self-organizing neural network: validation and comparison with other detection strategies. Electroencephalography and Clinical Neurophysiology 107, 27–32 (1998)
15. Walczak, S., Nowack, W.J.: An artificial neural network to diagnosing epilepsy using lateralized burst of theta EEGs. Journal of Medical Systems 25(1), 9–20 (2001)
16. Subasi, A., Ercelebi, E.: Classification of EEG signals using neural network and logistic regression. Computer Methods and Programs in Biomedicine 78, 87–99 (2005)

17. Alkan, A., Koklukaya, E., Subasi, A.: Automatic seizure detection in EEG using logistic regression and artificial neural network. Journal of Neuroscience Methods 148, 167–176 (2005)
18. Guler, I., Ubeyli, E.D.: Adaptive neuro-fuzzy inference system for classification of EEG signals using wavelet coefficients. Journal of Neuroscience Methods 48(2), 113–121 (2005)
19. Kellaway, P.: Orderly approach to visual analysis: Elements of the normal EEG and their characteristics in children and adults. In: Ebersole, J.S., Pedley, T.A. (eds.) Current practice of clinical electroencephalography, pp. 100–159. Lippincott Williams & Wilkins, Philadelphia (2002)
20. Haykin, S.: Neural Networks: A Comprehensive Foundation. Macmillan, New York (1994)
21. Bernand, E.: Optimization training neural nets. IEEE Trans. Neural Networks 3(2), 989–993 (1992)
22. Hagan, M.T., Menhaj, M.B.: Training feedforward networks with the Marquardt algorithm. IEEE Trans. Neural Networks 5(6), 989–993 (1994)
23. Wilamowki, B.M., Iqlikci, S., Kaynak, O., Onder, E.M.: An algorithm for fast converges in training neural networks. In: IEEE Proceedings of International Joint Conference on Neural Networks, pp. 1778–1782 (2005)
24. Lera, G., Pinzolas, M.: A quasi-local Levenberg-Marquardt algorithm for neural network training. IEEE World Congress on Computational Intelligence 3, 2242–2246 (1998)
25. Manolis, I.A.L., Antonis, A.A.: Is Levenberg-Marquardt the most efficient optimization algorithm for implementing bundle adjustment? IEEE Proceedings of International Conference on Computer Vision 2, 1526–1531 (2005)
26. Gaafar, L.K., Choueiki, M.H.A.: Neural network model for solving the lot sizing problem. The International Journal of Management Science 28, 175–184 (1999)
27. Hopkins, A., Garman, A., Clarke, C.: The first seizure in adult life. Value of clinical features, electroencephalography, and computerized tomographic scannig in prediction of seizure recurrence. Lancet 1, 721–726 (1988)
28. Drake, M.E., Padamadan, H., Newll, A.S.: Interictal quantitative EEG in epilepsy. Seizure 7, 39–42 (1998)
29. So, M.G., Thiele, A.E., Sanger, T., et al.: Electroencephalogram and clinical facilities in juvenile myoclonic epilepsy. J. Child Neurol. 13, 541–545 (1998)
30. Grünewald, R.A., Chroni, E., Panayiotopoulos, P.P.: Delayed diagnosis of juvenile myoclonic epilepsy. J. Neurol. Neurosurg. Psychiatry 55, 487–490 (1992)

Moving Creative Words

Oliviero Stock, Carlo Strapparava, and Alessandro Valitutti

Istituto per la Ricerca Scientifica e Tecnologica, FBK-irst, I-38050, Povo,
Trento, Italy
{stock,strappa,alvalitu}@itc.it

Abstract. Among forms of creative language, verbal humor has received
some attention in the computational *milieu*. Some aspects of irony and
wordplay could be experimented in automated systems. For instance we
developed a system that makes fun of existing acronyms, based mainly
on lexical reasoning. The dimension of emotion in words is also starting
to be understood among computational linguists. The challenge of electronic advertisements offers in particular a great opportunity for getting
now deeper into creative language expression and emotion. An advertising message induces in the recipient a positive or negative attitude
toward the object to advertise. A prototype we have developed for advertising professionals has two steps: (i) the creative variation of familiar
expressions, taking into account the affective content of the produced
text, (ii) the automatic animation (semantically consistent with the affective text content) of the resulting expression, using kinetic typography
techniques. Validation prospects are also challenging and will be briefly
discussed.

1   Introduction

In recent times the landscape of natural language processing has been enriched
with elements of emotion-related processing. A text often reflects the opinions
and the affect of the writer, characters in a story may use specific lexical terms to
denote a certain emotional state, a dialogue is strongly affected by the evolution
of the affective states of the participants.

One puzzling topic at the border of affective communication is humor. Humor has been studied since ancient times and in the Twentieth Century various
theories have been proposed in fields such as philosophy, linguistics, and psychology. Yet, a deep understanding of the mechanisms is beyond the state of the
art. We believe the computational approach can contribute something here, as
it has happened with other areas of artificial intelligence. We also believe that
verbal humor touches on aspects of aesthetics and also from that point of view
a realization of some of the linguistic creative processes may help us understand
communication in a broad sense.

If we look at things from a different, applied perspective we can well say
that humor is a need in our relation with our fellow humans. As computers will
be able to yield autonomous contributions to communication, they will not be
accepted as full partners without displaying some humor capabilities of their own.

F. Mele et al. (Eds.): BVAI 2007, LNCS 4729, pp. 509–522, 2007.

In concrete terms computational humor has the potential to change computers into extraordinarily creative and motivational tools.

Computer-human interaction needs to evolve beyond usability and productivity. There is a wide perception in the field that the future is in themes such as entertainment, fun, emotions, aesthetic pleasure, motivation, attention, engagement and so on. Humor is an essential element in communication: it is strictly related to the themes mentioned above. While it is generally considered merely a way to induce amusement, humor provides an important way to influence the mental state of people to improve their activity. Even though humor is a very complex capability to reproduce, it is realistic to model some types of humor production and to aim at implementing this capability in computational systems. Let us now review a few elements that make humor so important from a cognitive point of view.

Humor and emotions. Humor is a powerful generator of emotions. As such, it has an impact on people's psychological state, directs their attention [1], influences the processes of memorization [2] and of decision-making [3], and creates desires. Actually, emotions are an extraordinary instrument for motivation and persuasion because those who are capable of transmitting and evoking them have the power to influence other people's opinions and behaviour. Humor, therefore, allows for conscious and constructive use of the affective states generated by it. Affective induction through verbal language is particularly interesting; and humor is one of the most effective ways of achieving it. Purposeful use of humorous techniques enables us to induce positive emotions and mood and to exploit their cognitive and behavioural effects. For example, the persuasive effect of humor and emotions is well known and widely employed in advertising. Advertisements have to be both short and meaningful, to be able to convey information and emotions at the same time.

Humor and beliefs. Humor acts not only upon emotions, but also on human beliefs. A joke plays on the beliefs and expectations of the hearer. By infringing on them, it causes surprise and then hilarity. Jesting with beliefs and opinions, humor induces irony and accustoms people not to take themselves too seriously. Sometimes simple wit can sweep away a negative outlook that places limits on people desires and abilities. Wit can help people overcome self-concern and pessimism that often prevents them from pursuing more ambitious goals and objectives.

Humor and creativity. Humor encourages creativity as well. The change of perspective caused by humorous situations induces new ways of interpreting the same event. By stripping away clichés and commonplaces, and stressing their inconsistency, people become more open to new ideas and points of view. Creativity redraws the space of possibilities and delivers unexpected solutions to problems. Actually, creative stimuli constitute one of the most effective impulses for human activity. Machines equipped with humorous capabilities will be able to play an active role in inducing users' emotions and beliefs, and in providing motivational support.

2   Background

While humor is relatively well studied in scientific fields such as linguistics [4] and psychology [5,6], to date there is only a limited number of research contributions made toward the construction of computational humor prototypes. A good review of the field can be found in [7]. Almost all the approaches try to deal with incongruity theory at various levels of refinement [8,9,4]. Incongruity theory focuses on the element of surprise. It states that humor is created out of a conflict between what is expected and what actually occurs in the joke. Underlying incongruity is one of the obvious features of a large part of humor phenomena: ambiguity or double meaning.

One of the first attempts that deals with humor generation is the work described in [10], where a formal model of semantic and syntactic regularities was devised, underlying some types of puns (punning riddles). A punning riddle is a question-answer riddle that uses phonological ambiguity. The three main strategies used to create phonological ambiguity are syllable substitution, word substitution and metathesis. *Syllable substitution* is the strategy to confuse a syllable in a word with a similar or identical sounding word. An example of syllable substitution is shown in the following joke: "What do shortsighted ghosts wear? Spooktacles" [11]. *Word substitution* is the strategy to confuse an entire word with another similar- or identical-sounding word. An example of a joke with word substitution is : "How do you make gold soup? Put fourteen carrots in it" [11]. *Metathesis* is a strategy very different to syllable or word substitution. It uses reversal of sounds and words to suggest a similarity in meaning between two semantically distinct phrases. An example is "What is the difference between a torn flag and a postage stamp? One's a tattered banner and the other's a battered tanner." [10].

Punning riddles based on these three strategies are all suitable for computer generation. Ritchie and Binsted focussed on the word substitution based punning riddles, as lists of homophones (i.e. phonetically identical words) are already available.

The assumptions about the contents and the structure of the lexicon are as follows. The lexicon consists of a finite set of *lexemes* and of *lexical relations*. A lexeme is an abstract entity corresponding to the meaning of a word. If a word has two meanings, it has two corresponding lexemes. Every lexeme has a set of properties about the representation and the type of word. A lexical relation can be an explicit relation between two lexemes, like synonym or homophone, or a general inter-lexeme relation, applicable to more than one pair of lexemes.

In order to describe a punning riddle, two sorts of symbolic description have to be used: *schema* and *template*. A schema stipulates a set of relations which must hold between the lexemes used to build a joke. A template indicates the information necessary to turn a schema and lexemes into a piece of text. It contains fixed segments of text that are to be used and syntactic details of how lexemes have to be expressed.

In [10], this model was then exploited to implement a system called JAPE, able to automatically generate amusing puns.

In a recent work [12] automatic production of a funny and appropriate punchline at the end of short jokes is proposed. The authors present a model that describes the relationship between the connector (part of the set-up) and the disjunctor (the punchline). In particular they have implemented this model in a system which, given a joke set-up, can select the best disjunctor from a list of alternatives.

Another humor-generation project was HAHAcronym [13], whose goal was to develop a system able to automatically generate humorous versions of existing acronyms, or to produce a new funny acronym constrained to be a valid vocabulary word, starting with concepts provided by the user. The humorous effect was achieved mainly on the basis of incongruity. We will provide examples of output of this system in Section 3.

Humor recognition has received less attention. In [14] the application of text categorization techniques to humor recognition has been investigated. In particular the authors show that classification techniques are a viable approach for distinguishing between humorous and non-humorous text, through experiments performed on very large data sets. They restrict their investigation to the type of humor found in *one-liners*. A one-liner is a short sentence with comic effects and a peculiar linguistic structure: simple syntax, deliberate use of rhetoric devices (e.g. alliteration, rhyme), and frequent use of creative language constructions meant to attract the readers' attention. In fact, while longer jokes can have a relatively complex narrative structure, a one-liner must produce the humorous effect "in one shot", with very few words.

The humor-recognition problem is formulated as a traditional classification task, feeding positive (humorous) and negative (non humorous) examples to some automatic classifiers. The humorous data set consisted of a corpus of 16,000 one-liners collected from the Web using an automatic bootstrapping process. The non-humorous data were selected such that it is structurally and stylistically similar to the one-liners. In particular, four different corpora were selected, each composed by 16,000 sentences: (1) Reuters news titles [15]; (2) proverbs; (3) sentences picked from the British National Corpus (BNC)[16]; and (4) commonsense statements from the Open Mind Common Sense (OMCS) corpus [17]. The features taken into account were both content-based features, usually considered in traditional text categorization tasks, and humor-specific stylistic features, such as alliteration, presence of antonymy and adult slang. The classification results were really encouraging. Regardless of the non-humorous data set playing the role of negative examples, the performance of the automatically learned humor-recognizer was always significantly better than apriori known baselines. Surprisingly, comparative experimental results showed that in fact it is more difficult to distinguish humor from regular text (e.g. BNC sentences) than from the other data sets.

Another related work is the study reported in [18], focussing on a very restricted type of wordplays, namely the "Knock-Knock" jokes. The goal of the study was to evaluate to what extent wordplay can be automatically identified in "Knock-Knock" jokes, and if such jokes can be reliably identified from other non-humorous texts. The algorithm is based on automatically extracted structural patterns and on heuristics heavily based on the peculiar structure of this particular type of jokes. While the wordplay recognition gave satisfactory results, the identification of jokes containing such wordplays turned out to be significantly more difficult.

Worth mentioning is also a formalization, based on a cognitive approach (the belief-desire-intention model), distinguishing between real and fictional humor [19].

Finally [20] proposes a first attempt to recognize the humorous *intent* of short dialogs. According to the authors, computational recognition of humorous intent can be divided into two parts: recognition of a humorous text, and recognition of the intent to be humorous. The approach is based on detecting ambiguity both in the setup and in the punchline.

3   HAHAcronym

HAHAcronym was the first European project devoted to computational humor[1]. The main goal of HAHAcronym was the realization of an acronym ironic re-analyzer and generator as a proof of concept in a focalized but non restricted context. In the first case the system makes fun of existing acronyms, in the second case, starting from concepts provided by the user, it produces new acronyms, constrained to be words of the given language. And, of course, they have to be funny.

The realization of this system was proposed to the European Commission as a project that we would be able to develop in a short period of time (less than a year), that would be meaningful, well demonstrable, that could be evaluated along some pre-decided criteria, and that was conducive to a subsequent development in a direction of potential applicative interest. So for us it was essential that:

1. the work could have many components of a larger system, simplified for the current setting;
2. we could reuse and adapt existing relevant linguistic resources (e.g. WordNet Domains, assonance tools, parser, etc.);
3. some simple strategies for humor effects could be experimented.

One of the purposes of the project was to show that using "standard" resources (with some extensions and modifications) and suitable linguistic theories of humor (i.e. developing specific algorithms that implement or elaborate theories), it is possible to implement a working prototype.

3.1   Examples

Here below some examples of acronym re-analysis by HAHAcronym are reported. As far as semantic field opposition is concerned we have slightly tuned the system

[1] EU project IST-2000-30039 (partners: ITC-irst and University of Twente), part of the Future Emerging Technologies section of the Fifth European Framework Program.

towards the domains FOOD, RELIGION and SEX. We report the original acronym, the re-analysis and some comments about the strategies followed by the system.

ACM - Association for Computing Machinery
→ Association for Confusing Machinery
FBI - Federal Bureau of Investigation
→ Fantastic Bureau of Intimidation

The system keeps all the main heads and works on the adjectives and the PP head, preserving the rhyme and/or using the a-semantic dictionary.

CRT - Cathodic Ray Tube
→ Catholic Ray Tube
ESA - European Space Agency
→ Epicurean Space Agency
PDA - Personal Digital Assistant
→ Penitential Demoniacal Assistant
→ Prenuptial Devotional Assistant
MIT - Massachusetts Institute of Technology
→ Mythical Institute of Theology

Some re-analyses are RELIGION oriented. Note the rhymes.

As far as generation from scratch is concerned, a main concept and some attributes (in terms of Wordnet synsets) are given as input to the system. Here below we report some examples of acronym generation.
Main concept: *processor* (in the sense of CPU);
Attribute: *fast*

OPEN - On-line Processor for Effervescent Net
PIQUE - Processor for Immobile Quick Uncertain Experimentation
TORPID - Traitorously Outstandingly Rusty Processor for Inadvertent Data_ processing
UTMOST - Unsettled Transcendental Mainframe for Off-line Secured Tcp/ip

We note that the system tries to keep all the expansions of the acronym coherent in the same semantic field of the main concept (COMPUTER_SCIENCE). At the same time, whenever possible, it exploits incongruity in the lexical choices.

4   Creative Messages and Optimal Innovation

Variating familiar expressions (proverbs, movie titles, famous citations, etc.) in an evocative way has been an effective technique in advertising for a long time [21]. A lot of efforts by professionals in the field goes into producing ever novel catchy expressions with some element of humor. Indeed it is common of "creatives" to be recruited in pairs formed by a copywriter and an art director. They work in a creative partnership to conceive, develop and produce effective advertisement. While the copywriter is mostly responsible for the textual content of the creative product, the art director focalizes efforts on the graphical presentation of the message. Advertising messages tend to be quite short but, at the same time, rich of emotional meaning and persuasive power.

We combined some computational functionalities for the semiautomatic production of creative advertising messages. In particular, we implemented a strategy for the creative variation of familiar expressions. This strategy is articulated in two steps. The first consists of the selection and creative variation of familiar or common sense expressions. The second step consists of the presentation of the headline through automated text animation, and it is based on the use of kinetic typography.

An advertising message induces in the recipient a positive (or negative) attitude toward the subject to advertise, for example through the evocation of a appropriate emotion. Another mandatory characteristic of an advertisement is its memorizability. These two aspects of an ads increase the probability to induce some wanted behaviours, for example the purchase of some product, the choice of a specific brand, or the click on some specific web link. In the last case, it is crucial to make the recipient curious about the subject referred by the URL. The best way to realize in an ads both attitude induction and memorizability is the generation of surprise, generally based on creative constraints.

In order to develop a strategy for surprise induction, we considered an interesting property of pleasurable creative communication that was named by Rachel Giora as the *optimal innovation hypothesis* ([22]). According to this assumption, when the novelty is in a complementary relation to salience (familiarity), it is "optimal" in the sense that it has an aesthetics value and "induce the most pleasing effect".

Therefore the simultaneous presence of novelty and familiarity makes the message potentially surprising, because this combination allows the recipient's mind to oscillate between what is known and what is different from usual. For this reasons, an advertising message must be original but, at the same time, connected to what is familiar [21]. Familiarity causes expectations, while novelty violates them, and finally surprise arises.

With "varied familiar expression" we indicate an expression (sentence or phrase) that is obtained as a linguistic change (e.g. substitution of a word, morphological or phonetic variation, etc.) of an expression recognized as familiar by recipients (e.g. selected by some collection of proverbs, famous movie titles, etc.). In this work we limited the variation to the word substitution.

Moreover, a successful message should have a semantic connection with some concept of the target topic. At the same time, it has to be semantically related with some emotion of a prefixed valence (e.g. positive emotion as joy or negative emotion as fear).

5   Resources

5.1   Affective Semantic Similarity

All words can potentially convey affective meaning. Each of them, even those more apparently neutral, can evoke pleasant or painful experiences. While some words have emotional meaning with respect to the individual story, for many others the affective power is part of the collective imagination (e.g. words "mum", "ghost", "war" etc.).

We are interested in this second group, because their affective meaning is part of common sense knowledge and can be detected in the linguistic usage. For this reason, we studied the use of words in textual productions, and in particular their co-occurrences with the words in which the affective meaning is explicit. As claimed by Ortony et al. [23], we have to distinguish between words directly referring to emotional states (e.g. "fear", "cheerful") and those having only an indirect reference that depends on the context (e.g. words that indicate possible emotional causes as "killer" or emotional responses as "cry"). We call the former *direct affective words* and the latter *indirect affective words* [24].

In order to manage affective lexical meaning, we (i) organized the direct affective words and synsets inside WORDNET-AFFECT, an affective lexical resource based on an extension of WORDNET, and (ii) implemented a selection function (named *affective weight*) based on a semantic similarity mechanism automatically acquired in an unsupervised way from a large corpus of texts (100 millions of words), in order to individuate the indirect affective lexicon.

Applied to a concept (e.g. a WORDNET synset) and an emotional category, this function returns a value representing the semantic affinity with that emotion. In this way it is possible to assign a value to the concept with respect to each emotional category, and eventually select the emotion with the highest value. Applied to a set of concepts that are semantically similar, this function selects subsets characterized by some given affective constraints (e.g. referring to a particular emotional category or valence).

As we will see, we are able to focus selectively on positive, negative, ambiguous or neutral types of emotions. For example, given "difficulty" as input term, the system suggests as related emotions: IDENTIFICATION, NEGATIVE-CONCERN, AMBIGUOUS-EXPECTATION, APATHY. Moreover, given an input word (e.g. "university") and the indication of an emotional valence (e.g. positive), the system suggests a set of related words through some positive emotional category (e.g. "professor" "scholarship" "achievement") found through the emotions ENTHUSIASM, SYMPATHY, DEVOTION, ENCOURAGEMENT.

This fine-grained affective lexicon selection can open up new possibilities in many applications that exploit verbal communication of emotions. For example, [25] exploited the semantic connection between a generic word and an emotion for the generation of affective evaluative predicates and sentences.

5.2 Database of Familiar Expressions

The base for the strategy of "familiar expression variation" is the availability of a set of expressions that are recognized as familiar by English speakers.

We considered three types of familiar expressions: proverbs, movie titles, clichés. We collected 1836 familiar expressions from the Web, organized in three types: common use proverbs (628), famous movie titles (290), and clichés (918). Proverbs were retrieved in some of many web sites in which they are grouped (e.g. http://www.francesfarmersrevenge.com/stuff/proverbs.htm

or www.manythings.org /proverbs). We considered only proverbs of common use. In a similar way we collected clichés, that are sentences whose overuse often makes them humorous (e.g. home sweet home, I am playing my own game). Finally, movie titles were selected from the Internet Movie Database (www.imdb.com). In particular, we considered the list of the best movies in allo sorts of categories based on votes from users.

The list of familiar expressions is composed mostly of sentences (in particular, proverbs and clichés), but part of them are phrases (in particular, movie title list includes a significant number of noun phrases)

5.3 Assonance Tool

To cope with this aspect we got and reorganized the CMU pronouncing dictionary (http://www.speech.cs.cmu.edu/cgi-bin/cmudict) with a suitable indexing. The CMU Pronouncing Dictionary is a machine-readable pronunciation dictionary for North American English that contains over 125,000 words and their transcriptions.

Its format is particularly useful for speech recognition and synthesis, as it has mappings from words to their pronunciations in the given phoneme set. The current phoneme set contains 39 phonemes; vowels may carry lexical stress.

5.4 Kinetic Typography Scripting Language

Kinetic typography is the technology of text animation, i.e. text that uses movement or other changes over time. The advantage of kinetic typography consists in a further communicative dimension, combining verbal and visual communication, and providing opportunities to enrich the expressiveness of static texts. According to [26], kinetic typography can be used for three different communicative goals: capturing and directing attention of recipients, creating characters, and expressing emotions. A possible way of animating a text is mimicking the typical movement of humans when they express the content of the text (e.g. "Hi" with a jumping motion mimics exaggerated body motion of humans when they are really glad).

We have realized a development environment for the creation and visualization of text animations based on Kinetic Typography Engine (KTE), a Java package developed at the Design School of Carnegie Mellon University [26].Our model for the animation representation is a bit simpler than the KTE model. The central assumption consists of the representation of the animation as a composition of elementary animations (e.g. linear, sinusoidal or exponential variation). In particular, we consider only one operator for the identification of elementary animations (K-BASE) and three composition operators: kinetic addition (K-ADD), kinetic concatenation (K-JOIN), and kinetic loop (K-LOOP).

6 Algorithm

In this section, we describe the algorithm developed to perform the creative variation of an existing familiar expression.

1. **Insertion of an input concept.** The first step of the procedure consists of the insertion of an input concept. This is represented by one or more words, a set of synonyms, or a WordNet synset. In the latter case, it is individuated through a word, the part of speech (noun, adjective, verb, or adverb), and the sense number, and it corresponds to a set of synonyms. Using the pseudo-document representation technique described above, the input concept is represented as a vector in the LSA vectorial space. For example, say that a cruise vacation agency seeks to produce a catchy message on the topics "vacation" and "beach".

2. **Generation of the target-list.** A list (named *target-list*) including terms that are semantically connected (in the LSA space) with the input concept(s) is generated. This target list represents a semantic domain that includes the input concept(s).For example, given the vector representing "vacation", "beach", the LSA returns a list "sea", "hotel", "bay", "excursion", etc.

3. **Association of assonant words.** For each word of the target-list one or more possible *assonant words* are associated. Then a list of word pairs (named *variation-pairs*) is created. The list of variation-pairs is filtered according to some constraints. The first one is syntactic (elements of each pair must have the same part of speech). The second one is semantic (i.e. the second element of each pair must not be included in the target-list), and its function is to realize a semantic opposition between the elements of a variation pair. Finally, to each variation pair an *emotion-label* (representing the emotional category most similar to the substituting word) is provided with the corresponding affective weight. Some possible assonant pairs for the example above are: *(bay, day), (bay, hay), (hotel, farewell)*, etc.

4. **Creative variation of familiar expressions.** In this step, the algorithm gets in input a set of familiar expressions (in particular, proverbs and movie titles) and, for each of them, generates all possible variations. The list of variated expressions is ordered according to the global affective weight.

Following the example, a resulting ad is *Tomorrow is Another Bay* as a variation of the familiar expression *Tomorrow is Another Day*. Note that for moment the final choice among the best resulting expressions proposed by the system is left to human selection.

At this point, the variated expression is animated with kinetic typography. In particular, words are animated according to the underlying emotion to emphasize the affective connotation.

7   Examples

In this section we show some examples of creative variations.

Starting from an input concept (e.g. *disease*) we can obtain, using the semantic similarity, a list of related terms (Table 1).

Table 1. Input word: "disease"

Name	POS	Similarity to the input
symptom	noun	0.971
therapy	noun	0.969
metabolism	noun	0.933
analgesic	noun	0.899
suture	noun	0.851
thoracic	adjective	0.782
extraction	noun	0.623

Table 2. Affective weight

Name	fear	joy	anger	sadness
disease	0.357	0.201	0.135	0.679
symptom	0.423	0.293	0.164	0.685
therapy	0.374	0.315	0.170	0.691
metabolism	0.372	0.258	0.082	0.552
analgesic	0.280	0.241	0.173	0.526
suture	0.237	0.299	0.227	0.490
thoracic	0.157	0.135	0.134	0.448
extraction	0.126	0.245	0.177	0.366

Using the affective weight function, it is possible to check for their affective characterization (in Table 2 only four emotions are displayed), selecting those affectively coherent with the input term. Subsequently, the system searches for assonant words (Table 3) and checks for affective opposition with the original words (Table 4).

Table 3. Phonetic associations

Name	Assonant Words
suture	*future*
thoracic	Jurassic
extraction	abstraction, attraction, contraction, diffraction, distraction, inaction, reaction, retraction, subtraction, transaction

At this point, the system retrieves familiar expressions that include the word to be substituted.

Table 5 shows the final word substitution in several examples. The system can then automatically animate the resulting expression emphasizing the novel affective connotation through kynetic typography techniques as shown in [27].

Table 4. Affective difference

Name	fear	joy	anger	sadness
suture	0.237	0.299	0.227	**0.490**
future	0.467	**0.571**	0.417	0.462

Table 5. More Examples

Input Words	Varied Expression	Word Substitution
vacation, beach	Tomorrow is another bay	day → bay
disease	Back to the Suture	future → suture
	Thoracic Park	jurassic → thoracic
	Fatal Extraction	attraction → extraction
crash	Saturday Fright Fever	night → fright
fashion	Jurassic Dark	park → dark

8   Humor and Neuroimaging

Deep evaluation of achieved results is not an easy task. Normally it is performed with user's direct feedback. Recent advances in cognitive neuroscience are worth examining as a potential new approach. In particular, there are a number of experiments of functional neuroimaging aimed at individuating neural correlates of humour comprehension and appreciation. These results were compared to studies on patients with brain lesions, leading in some cases to different outcomes, but in general the cognitive model was validated (for a complete review, see [28],). Generally the framework within which neuroimaging studies are interpreted is the Incongruity-Resolution Theory of Humour [29]. It is based on a two-stage model of humour comprehension. The first stage is the detection of an incongruity in some joke or pun. Incongruity is perceived when some expectation is disconfirmed and surprise arises. The second stage is the reinterpretation of the situation expressed in the text in a way that is congruous and funny.

Illustrative of the neuroimaging approach to humour are experiments by Mobbs et al. [30] and Bartolo et al. [31], based on event-related functional MRI (efMRI) study of humour comprehension. Both studies aimed at measuring hemodynamic increases in regions associated with cartoons considered to be funny. The results are coherent with previous analog experiments, and allow us to identity different clusters of brain areas with a significant BOLD signal, corresponding to the cognitive-affective components of humour comprehension: humour detection (including incongruity detection and incongruity resolution), motor response and affective response.

The most important feature of humour appreciation is reward, the amusement that follows the humorous stimulus. At the moment there are not results that conclusively demonstrate the subcortical correlates of reward, but there are a number of fMRI studies on different rewarding tasks (for review, see Schultz [32]).

Functional neuroimaging of humour appreciation could be useful for the evaluation of computational humour systems. The possibility of integrating information coming from subjects reports and direct neural functional activity is certainly appealing.

9 Conclusion

In this paper, we have presented some recent developments in automatic verbal humor production. We have described a prototype that produces creative variation of familiar expressions, exploiting state-of-the-art natural language processing techniques, and animates them according to the affective content. The creative textual variations rely on semantic and affective similarity, while animation makes use of a kinetic typography dynamic scripting language. The multimodal dynamic result is supposed to have a stronger effect. Evaluation is still preliminary and it may be worth looking into novel methodologies for appreciating the effects.

Acknowledgments

This work was developed in the context of HUMAINE Network of Excellence and partially sponsored by MUR FIRB-project number RBIN045PXH.

References

1. Kitayama, S., Niedenthal, P.: The Heart's Eye: Emotional influences in Perception and Attention. Academic Press, London (1994)
2. Kahneman, D.: Attention and Effort. Prentice-Hall, Englewood Cliffs (1973)
3. Isen, A.: Positive affect and decision making. In: Lewis, M., Haviland, J. (eds.) Handbook of Emotion, Guilford, New York (1993)
4. Attardo, S.: Linguistic Theories of Humor. Mouton de Gruyter, Berlin (1994)
5. Freud, S.: Der Witz und Seine Beziehung zum Unbewussten. Deutike, Leipzig and Vienna (1905)
6. Ruch, W.: Computers with a personality? lessons to be learned from studies of the psychology of humor. In: [33] (2002)
7. Ritchie, G.: Current directions in computational humour. Artificial Intelligence Review 16(2), 119–135 (2001)
8. Koestler, A.: The act of creation. Hutchinson, London (1964)
9. Raskin, V.: Semantic Mechanisms of Humor, Dordrecht, Boston, Lancaster (1985)
10. Binsted, K., Ritchie, G.: Computational rules for punning riddles. Humor 10(1) (1997)
11. Webb, K. (ed.): The Crack-a-Joke Book. Puffin, London (1978)
12. Stark, J., Binsted, K., Bergen, B.: Disjunctor selection for one-line jokes. In: Maybury, M., Stock, O., Wahlster, W. (eds.) INTETAIN 2005. LNCS (LNAI), vol. 3814, Springer, Heidelberg (2005)
13. Stock, O., Strapparava, C.: Getting serious about the development of computational humour. In: IJCAI-03. Proceedings of the 18th International Joint Conference on Artificial Intelligence, Acapulco, Mexico (August 2003)

14. Mihalcea, R., Strapparava, C.: Laughter abounds in the mouths of computers: Investigations in automatic humor recognition. In: Maybury, M., Stock, O., Wahlster, W. (eds.) INTETAIN 2005. LNCS (LNAI), vol. 3814, Springer, Heidelberg (2005)
15. Lewis, D., Yang, Y., Rose, T., Li, F.: RCV1: A new benchmark collection for text categorization research. The Journal of Machine Learning Research 5, 361–397 (2004)
16. BNC-Consortium: British national corpus (2000), http://www.hcu.ox.ac.uk/bnc/
17. Singh, P.: The public acquisition of commonsense knowledge. In: Proceedings of AAAI Spring Symposium: Acquiring (and Using) Linguistic (and World) Knowledge for Information Access, Palo Alto, CA (2002)
18. Taylor, J., Mazlack, L.: Computationally recognizing wordplay in jokes. In: Proceedings of CogSci 2004, Chicago (August 2004)
19. Mele, F.: Real and fictional ridicule. In: [33] (2002)
20. Taylor, J., Mazlack, L.: Toward computational recognition of humorous intent. In: COGSCI 05. Proc. of the 27th Annual Conference of the Cognitive Science Society, Stresa, Italy (July 2005)
21. Pricken, M.: Creative Advertising. Thames & Hudson (2002)
22. Giora, R.: On Our Mind: Salience, Context and Figurative Language. Oxford University Press, New York (2003)
23. Ortony, A., Clore, G.L., Foss, M.A.: The psychological foundations of the affective lexicon. Journal of Personality and Social Psychology 53, 751–766 (1987)
24. Strapparava, C., Valitutti, A., Stock, O.: The affective weight of lexicon. In: LREC 2006. Proceedings of the Fifth International Conference on Language Resources and Evaluation, Genoa, Italy (May 2006)
25. Valitutti, A., Strapparava, C., Stock, O.: Lexical resources and semantic similarity for affective evaluative expressions generation. In: Tao, J., Tan, T., Picard, R.W. (eds.) ACII 2005. LNCS, vol. 3784, Springer, Heidelberg (2005)
26. Lee, J., Forlizzi, J., Hudson, S.: The kinetic typography engine: An extensible system for animating expressive text. In: Proc. of ACM UIST 2002 Conference, ACM Press, New York (2002)
27. Strapparava, C., Valitutti, A., Stock, O.: Dances with words. In: IJCAI-07. Proceedings of the 20th International Joint Conference on Artificial Intelligence, Hyderabad, India (January 2007)
28. Wild, B., Rodden, F.A., Grodd, W., Ruch, W.: Neural correlates of laughter and humour. Brain (126), 2121–2138 (2003)
29. Suls, J.M.: A two-stage model for the appreciation of jokes and cartoons. In: Goldstein, P.E., McGhee, J.H. (eds.) The psychology of humour. Theoretical perspectives and empirical issue, pp. 81–100. Academic Press, New York (1972)
30. Mobbs, D., Greicius, M.D., Abdel-Azim, E., Menon, V., Reiss, A.L.: Humor modulates the mesolimbic reward centers. Neuron 40, 1041–1048 (2003)
31. Bartolo, A., Benuzzi, F., Nocetti, L., Baraldi, P., Nichelli, P.: Humor comprehension and appreciation: An fmri study. Journal of Cognitive Neuroscience 18(11), 1789–1798 (2006)
32. Schultz, W.: Getting formal with dopamine and reward. Neuron (36), 241–263 (2002)
33. Stock, O., Strapparava, C., Nijholt, A. (eds.): TWLT20. Proceedings of the The April Fools Day Workshop on Computational Humour, Trento (2002)

Applying Neural Networks to Knowledge Representation and Determination of Its Meaning

Mladen Stanojević and Sanja Vraneš

The Mihailo Pupin Institute, Volgina 15,
11060 Belgrade, Serbia and Montenegro
{Mladen,Sanja}@lab200.imp.bg.ac.yu

Abstract. Knowledge representation is one of the first challenges AI community was confronted with. To be applicable, knowledge representation techniques must be able not only to represent the knowledge, but also to provide
means to determine its meaning. The proposed knowledge representation techniques solve the problem of meaning determination by naming, i.e. by describing the meaning of represented knowledge. These descriptions are provided by
database, knowledge base, ontology designers, which give names to tables,
fields, classes, properties, relationships, etc. An alternative approach to the
problem of determining the meaning would be a neural network approach applied to knowledge representation in a natural language that does not use
names, but semantic categories. In this paper we propose a Hierarchical Semantic Form (HSF), a modification of localist approach of connectionist model,
which, together with Space of Universal Links (SOUL) algorithm, is capable of
representing knowledge in a natural language and interpreting its meaning by
using the semantic categories.

Keywords: Knowledge Representation, Natural Language, Neural Networks,
Localist Approach.

1 Introduction

One of the main obstacles to further development of information sciences lies in the
inability to automatically process and search a vast quantity of information available
in a natural language on the Web and in various kinds of documents in digital form.

Web community has recognized the importance of the problem and launched Semantic Web [1] in an attempt to allow computer programs (esp. intelligent agents) to
search the Web (using semantic categories instead of keywords) and find the needed
information for a user. However, computers are not able to extract semantic categories from Web pages in their current form (HTML), hence new knowledge representation techniques have been proposed to represent the meaning of Web pages.

Currently there are billions of Web pages and their manual annotation (translation) using any of the proposed Semantic Web formalism is not feasible. Some attempts to provide automatic annotations of Web pages have achieved success in limited domains, but
the automatic annotation of domain unlimited contents has proved to be a very hard prob-

F. Mele et al. (Eds.): BVAI 2007, LNCS 4729, pp. 523–532, 2007.

lem. Furthermore, even if automatic annotation was provided, computers would still not be able to understand the meaning of the represented knowledge.

If the automatic annotation is so hard, maybe the solution of this problem could be found elsewhere. Actually the problem of translation is generated by the application of knowledge representation techniques which use names to describe the meaning of represented knowledge. The problem would be solved if we could use a knowledge representation technique that would enable the structured representation in a natural language where all semantic relationships and concepts would be automatically identified and extracted from the plain text. The semantic relationships in plain text are implicit, while in the supposed knowledge representation they would be made explicit. The plain text form and the represented forms would be completely equivalent, except that the represented form would be structured with all semantic relationships extracted. The plain text could then be automatically converted to a structured form and vice versa with no loss of information.

Basically there are two possible ways to determine the meaning of semantically related knowledge: declarative and procedural. Declarative techniques, representing the main stream, are successfully applied in many applications to represent semantically related knowledge and include a wide variety of classical (e.g. relational [2] and object-oriented [3]) databases, AI techniques [4], [5] (e.g. logic formalism, semantic nets, conceptual dependencies, frames, scripts, rules, etc.), Semantic Web ontology and schema languages [6] (e.g. XOL [7], SHOE [8], OML [9], RDFS [10], DAML+OIL [11], OWL [12]) and distributed approach of the connectionist model. These techniques assume that the meaning of knowledge can be described independently and separately from the knowledge itself. They try to represent the meaning explicitly by naming or tagging the representational vehicles. In applications using declarative techniques, a database (knowledge base, ontology) designer provides the understanding of represented data, while a programmer, with the understanding of represented data and the understanding of user's requests, enables a productive use of these data.

On the other side are radical connectionists [13], which claim that a natural language (naming) is not used as a representational, but rather as a communicational medium. In procedural techniques the meaning is determined by matching the parts of represented knowledge with semantic categories and complex patterns. The localist approach of connectionist model [14] could be used to implement the ideas of radical connectionism. In the applications based on procedural techniques, the understanding of represented data and user's requests is not borrowed from database (knowledge base, ontology) designers and programmers, but represents an intrinsic capability of the application provided by the corresponding algorithm, which is used to interpret the meaning of represented knowledge.

Hierarchical Semantic Form (HSF) represents a modification of localist approach, where each node uniquely describes the meaning depending on the context it appears in. HSF overcomes the limitation of localist approach expressed by the inability to represent the structure [15] and the context of the node.

The Space Of Universal Links (SOUL) algorithm is used to create and maintain HSF, but also to interpret the meaning of the knowledge represented by HSF. The applicability of HSF with SOUL was tested on an example of Semantic Web service prototype [16] that provides information about flights from flight timetables defined in a natural language within an ordinary HTML file using natural language queries.

2 Knowledge Representation

The basics of how Hierarchical Semantic Form (HSF) and Space Of Universal Links (SOUL) algorithm are used in knowledge representation are given in [17]. However, the approach represented in [17] was a hybrid solution, where connectionist approach was used for knowledge representation, while classicist approach was applied to define and name semantic categories. In this paper we will present the pure connectionist solution where semantic categories are not named.

HSF is using two types of nodes, *groups* and *links*. Groups are used to uniquely represent letters, syllables, words, groups of words, sentences, etc., while links are used to represent groups in different contexts (e.g. the same word can appear in different contexts, and for each context one link representing that word is used). The SOUL algorithm is used to create and organize HSF. When a plain text is fed to it, SOUL automatically identifies repeated sequences (syllables, words, groups of words, etc.) and determines semantic structures and relationships between them.

Formally, the knowledge in HSF can be represented by the space S defined by the triple of groups G, links L and sequences Q (composed of links from L):

$$S = \{G, L, Q\}, \ g_i \in G, i = 1, r \ , \ l_j \in L, j = 1, s \ , \ q_k \in Q, k = 1, t \tag{1}$$

Initially G contains only groups corresponding to letters, L contains only links corresponding to these atomic groups and Q is an empty set of sequences.

HSF with SOUL follows the two basic principles in knowledge representation, the principle of locality and the principle of unique representation.

Principle of locality defines the transition T from the link l_t, which is the last link in the subsequence q_i, to the link l_u, when group g_c belonging to the same hierarchical level appears at the end of subsequence q_i:

$$l_u = T(l_t, g_c), \ q_p = q_i l_u, \ l_u \rightarrow g_c, \ q_i, q_p \in Q, \ g_c \in G, \ l_t, l_u \in L \tag{2}$$

The link l_u represents the group g_c in the subsequence q_p, which extends the subsequence q_i. If g_c is a new group, or link l_u does not exist, then the new link l_u must be created. The principle of locality enables learning of new sequences.

This principle is related to the representation of sequences at different levels of hierarchy (words, phrases, sentences, paragraphs, etc.). It basically says that paragraphs are composed of sentences and not of letters or words.

Principle of unique representation states that each subsequence (q_x) that repeats in two different sequences (contexts, q_i, q_j) must be uniquely represented by the corresponding group (g_u):

$$g_s \rightarrow q_i, q_i = q_a q_x q_b, \ g_s \in G, \ q_a, q_b, q_i, q_s, q_x \in Q$$
$$g_t \rightarrow q_j, q_j = q_c q_x q_d, \ g_t \in G, \ q_c, q_d, q_j, q_t, q_x \in Q \tag{3}$$
$$g_u \rightarrow q_x, \ l_p, l_q \rightarrow g_u, \ l_p, l_q \in L, \ g_u \in G, \ q_x \in Q$$

$$g_s \rightarrow q_i, q_i = q_a l_p q_b$$
$$g_t \rightarrow q_j, q_j = q_c l_q q_d$$

Hereby subsequences q_a or q_b, q_c or q_d may be empty, i.e. they may contain no links. When a subsequence q_x repeats in two sequences (q_i, q_j), a new group g_u will be created corresponding to this subsequence, as well as two new links (l_p, l_q) representing this subsequence in two different contexts (q_i, q_j). This is an example of selforganization of the space S, which allows an automatic identification of semantic concepts, structures and relations.

If we would like to apply HSF with SOUL to represent the following sentence:

John is a boy.
Mary is a girl.
John loves Mary.

we would have first to feed single words to SOUL: "John", "Mary", "is", "boy", "girl", "loves" (Fig. 1).

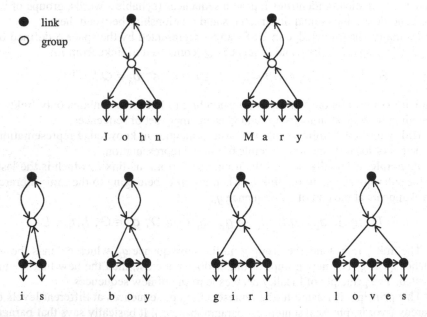

Fig. 1. Representation of single words in HSF

We can then feed the whole sentences to the SOUL algorithm and it will modify HSF correspondingly, identify and represent all semantic relationships between words (Fig. 2). It notices that the phrase "is a" occurring in the first statement is repeated in the second one, so it will create a new group representing this phrase. Each word and phrase "is a" is uniquely represented in HSF and for each statement they appear in, the corresponding link is created.

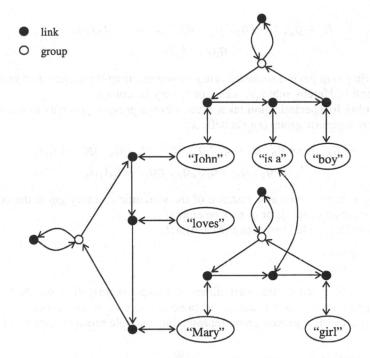

● link
○ group

Fig. 2. Representation of statements in HSF

The main difference between HSF and declarative techniques is that no names are used (groups in Fig. 2 are not named) and no designing is needed to get the representation in HSF. SOUL algorithm automatically creates the structure in HSF from plain text. However, a computer is still not able to understand the meaning of knowledge represented by HSF.

3 Determining the Meaning

To enable computers to understand the HSF representation, we will use semantic categories. To be able to represent semantic categories the space S must be accordingly extended:

$$S = \{G, L, Q, GG, GL, GQ\}, \ g_i \in G, i = 1, r \ , \ l_j \in L, j = 1, s \ , \ q_k \in Q, k = 1, t$$
$$gg_l \in GG, l = 1, u \ , \ gl_m \in GL, m = 1, v \ , \ gq_n \in GQ, n = 1, w \tag{4}$$

where *GG* represents a set of generic groups corresponding to semantic categories, *GL* a set of generic links representing generic groups in generic sequences belonging to the set *GQ*.

SOUL is able to learn semantic categories from the context. Two types of learning by example are supported, learning by generalization and learning by specialization.

Learning by generalization can be applied when different groups (g_a, g_b) represented by the corresponding links (l_i, l_j) occur in the same context (q_m, q_n):

$$l_i \rightarrow g_a,\ l_j \rightarrow g_b,\ q_u = q_m l_i q_n,\ q_v = q_m l_j q_n$$
$$gg_f \rightarrow l_i, l_j \tag{5}$$

Generic group gg_f is a semantic category representing the meaning of groups g_a, g_b in the context. Hereby subsequence q_m or q_n may be empty.

Learning by specialization takes place when a group (g_c) occurs in the same context where a generic group (gg_f) is defined:

$$l_i \rightarrow g_a,\ l_j \rightarrow g_b,\ q_u = q_m l_i q_n,\ q_v = q_m l_j q_n,\ gg_f \rightarrow l_i, l_j$$
$$l_k \rightarrow g_c,\ q_w = q_m l_k q_n,\ gg_f \rightarrow l_i, l_j, l_k \tag{6}$$

Group g_c represents a new instance of the semantic category gg_f in the context q_m, q_n, where subsequence q_m or q_n may be empty.

Suppose that we fed two sentences to SOUL:

John is a boy.
Bill is a boy.

SOUL will discover that two different groups representing words "John" and "Bill" appear at the same place in the same context, so it will generalize these two groups by creating a generic group representing a simple semantic category (Fig. 3).

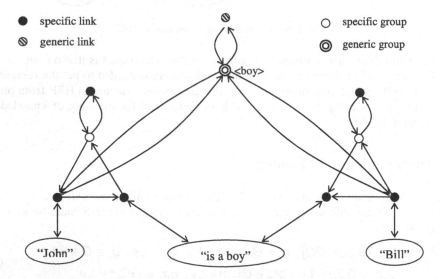

Fig. 3. Simple semantic category

This generic group is not named, but for the sake of clarity we will denote it as <boy>. Each time the words "John" or "Bill" are matched, the <boy> semantic category will also be matched, and this is how the meaning of these words will be interpreted. To each generic group correspond one or more generic links, which represent this generic group in complex semantic categories. On the other hand specific groups and links are used to represent semantic structures and relationships found in natural language statements.

To enable SOUL to understand a question:

Who does John love?

we would have to define the following semantic categories in a similar way as for the <boy> semantic category: <interrogative-pronoun> ("who"), <present-tense-do> ("does"), <emotional-relationship> ("love").

When we have defined these semantic categories, we can feed the question "Who does John love?" to SOUL and it will create the corresponding HSF representation (Fig. 4).

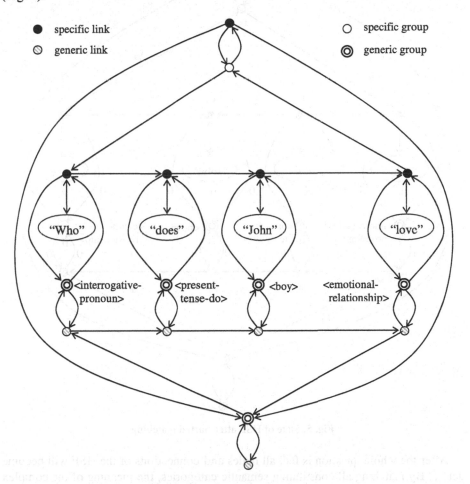

Fig. 4. Complex semantic category

In the process of understanding HSF acts as a recurrent neural network. Although nodes and connections can be in more states, for the purpose of this example we will assume that they can be only in one of the three states: active (1), semi-active (½) and inactive (0).

After the word "Who" is matched and the signals are propagated through the HSF, nodes and connections will be in the state as represented in Fig. 5. The generic group representing the complex semantic category will be in the semi-active state indicating that this group may potentially become active if the expected input is fed to HSF. The same holds for the specific group that represents the whole question.

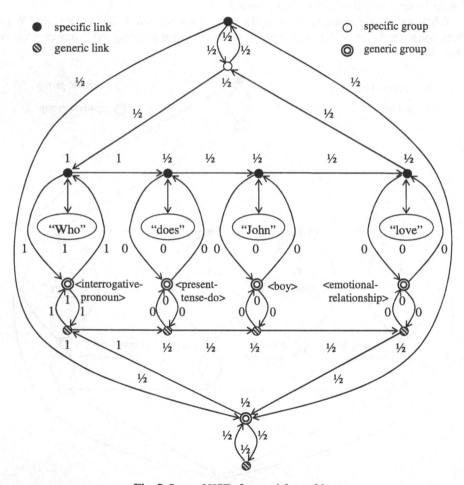

Fig. 5. State of HSF after partial matching

After the whole question is fed, all nodes and connections of the HSF will become active. By matching all constituting semantic categories, the meaning of the complex semantic category representing the question is understood.

The understanding of complex semantic categories is dependent only on the constituting semantic categories and not on their order. This provides a great flexibility of understanding, because not only syntactically correct inputs can be recognized, but also the ones such as "John does love who?". Moreover the queries containing some unknown words can also be recognized (e.g. "Could you please tell me who John does love?".

The understanding of questions can be used to find the corresponding answers by propagating the signals through the rest of HSF, but due to the limited space this will be described in greater details in some other paper.

4 Conclusions

According to the way they determine the meaning of the represented knowledge, knowledge representation techniques can be generally divided into declarative and procedural techniques. At present the declarative knowledge representation techniques constitute the main stream. Relational and object-oriented databases, AI knowledge representation techniques (e.g. frames, O-A-V triplets, semantic nets), Semantic Web techniques (ontology and schema languages) are all representatives of declarative approach. The main characteristic of declarative techniques is that they use descriptions to determine the meaning of represented knowledge. These descriptions are provided by giving names to tables, fields, classes, instances, properties, relations, etc.

However these techniques are limited in three ways: 1) unlike human brain which has domain unlimited knowledge representation capabilities, the knowledge representation capabilities of these techniques are defined and limited by their design; 2) vast quantities of data represented in a natural language must be translated into one of these formalisms; 3) computers are able to read the knowledge represented by declarative techniques, but are not able to understand it. As a consequence, highly specialized experts are required to describe the domain of description (database, knowledge base, ontology designers) and to create the applications that will use the represented knowledge (programmers).

An alternative approach to the problem of determining the meaning of represented knowledge is offered by procedural techniques. Procedural techniques do not describe the meaning of represented knowledge, but only provide means for the representation of its structure and semantic relations between them. The meaning of represented knowledge is determined through the process of matching semantic structures with simple and complex semantic categories.

In this paper we have proposed a kind of recurrent neural network, a modification of localist approach to connectionist model, Hierarchic Semantic Form (HSF), which is a hierarchical, structured equivalent of plain text form, where all semantic structures and semantic relations are explicitly represented. HSF and SOUL (Space of Universal Links) algorithm can be used to automatically translate the knowledge represented in a natural language (plain text) into a structured form, whereby all semantic structures and relations are automatically identified and represented.

The meaning of knowledge is determined by matching the simple and complex semantic categories with semantic structures represented in HSF. The matching is performed by propagating the signals through HSF as plain text is fed to it.

We have used a very simple example to illustrate how declarative techniques are used to describe the meaning of the knowledge and how HSF and SOUL are used to represent the same knowledge and to determine its meaning.

References

1. Berners-Lee, T., Hendler, J., Lassila, O.: The Semantic Web. Scientific American 284(5), 34–43 (2001)
2. Date, C.J.: Database in Depth: Relational Theory for Practitioners. O'Reilly Media, Inc., Sebastopol, CA (2005)
3. Russell, C., et al.: The Object Data Standard: ODMG 3.0. Morgan Kaufmann, San Francisco, CA (2000)
4. Sowa, J.: Knowledge Representation: Logical, Philosophical, and Computational Foundations. Brooks/Cole Publishing Co., Pacific Grove, CA (2000)
5. Vraneš, S., Stanojević, M.: Prolog/Rex - A Way to Extend Prolog for Better Knowledge Representation. IEEE Transactions on Knowledge and Data Engineering 6(1), 22–37 (1994)
6. Fensel, D., Hendler, J.A., Lieberman, H., Wahlster, W. (eds.): Spinning the Semantic Web: Bringing the World Wide Web to Its Full Potential. MIT Press, Cambridge, MA (2003)
7. Karp, R., et al.: XOL: An XML-Based Ontology Exchange Language (version 0.4) (February 26, 2007), www.ai.sri.com/pkarp/xol/
8. Heflin, J., et al.: SHOE: A Knowledge Representation Language for Internet Applications. Technical Report. CS-TR-4078 (UMIACS TR-99-71), Dept. of Computer Science, University of Maryland (1999)
9. Kent, R.: Ontology Markup LanguageVersion 0.3 (February 26, 2007), www.ontologos.org/OML/OML%200.3.htm
10. Brickley, D., Guha, R.V.: RDF Vocabulary Description Language 1.0: RDF Schema. W3C Recommendation (February 26, 2007), www.w3.org/TR/rdf-schema/
11. McGuinness, D., Fikes, R., Handler, J., Stein, L.: DAML+OIL: An Ontology Language for the Semantic Web. IEEE Intelligent Systems 17(5), 72–80 (2002)
12. McGuinness, D., van Harmelen, F. (eds.): OWL Web Ontology Language – Overview. W3C Recommendation (February 26, 2007), www.w3.org/TR/owl-features/
13. O'Brien, G., Opie, J.: Radical connectionism: thinking with (not in) language. Language & Communication 22, 313–329 (2002)
14. Hinton, G.E.: Mapping Part-Whole Hierarchies into Connectionist Networks. Artificial Intelligence 46(1-2), 47–75 (1990)
15. Fodor, J., Pylyshyn, Z.: Connectionism and Cognitive Architecture: A Critical Analysis. Cognition 28, 3–71 (1988)
16. Stanojević, M., Vraneš, S.: Semantic Web Services with Soul. In: De Gregorio, M., Di Maio, V., Frucci, M., Musio, C. (eds.) BVAI 2005. LNCS, vol. 3704, pp. 338–346. Springer, Heidelberg (2005)
17. Stanojević, M., Vraneš, S.: Knowledge representation with SOUL. Expert Systems with Applications 33(1), 122–134 (2007)

New Frameworks to Boost Feature Selection Algorithms in Emotion Detection for Improved Human-Computer Interaction

Halis Altun and Gökhan Polat

Nigde University, Electrical and Electronics Department, Kampus, 51100, Nigde, Turkey
halisaltun@nigde.edu.tr, gpolat51@yahoo.com

Abstract. One of the primary aims in human-computer interaction research is to develop an ability to recognize affective state of the user. Such ability is indispensable to have a more human-like nature in human-computer interaction. However, the researches in this direction are not mature and intensive efforts have only been witnessed recently. This work envisages the possibility of enhancing feature selection phase of emotion detection task to obtain robust parameters which will be determined from verbal information to achieve an improved affective human-computer interaction. As highly informative feature selection is believed to be a more critical factor than classifier itself, recent studies have increasingly focussed on determining features that contribute more to the classification problem. Two new frameworks for multi-class emotion detection problem are proposed in this paper, so as to boost the feature selection algorithms in a way that the selected features will be more informative in terms of class-separability. Evaluation of the selected final features is accomplished by multi-class classifiers. Results show that the proposed frameworks are successful in terms of attaining lower average cross-validation error.

Keywords: Human-Computer Interaction, Emotion Detection, Affective Computing, Pattern Recognition.

1 Introduction

Human Computer Interaction is defined as "a discipline concerned with the design, evaluation and implementation of interactive computing systems for human use and with the study of major phenomena surrounding them" [1]. It is an interdisciplinary field which arose from the intertwined roots in computer science, software engineering, image processing, human factors, cognitive science, psychology etc [2]. One of the primary aims in human-computer interaction research is to develop an ability to recognize affective state of a user. The new generation computers will recognize the affective state of users, such as nervousness, fear, happiness, concentration, eager etc., using verbal and nonverbal information [3,4]. This ability is the first step to have a more humanlike interaction between the users and computers. Such ability is indispensable to have a more human-like nature in human-computer

F. Mele et al. (Eds.): BVAI 2007, LNCS 4729, pp. 533–541, 2007.

interaction [5,6]. However, the researches in this direction are not mature and intensive efforts have only been witnessed recently. For human beings, recognition of affective state of a person is a trivial task, which can be accomplished by computer through integration of methods from tremendously diverse research fields such as image processing, speech processing, artificial intelligence, cognitive science and psychology.

As emotion recognition from speech signal can be considered as a pattern classification problem, an automatic emotion detection system might be composed of at least three main components: feature extraction, feature selection and classification. Although, a large amount of research has been conducted into feature selection to determine what aspects of the speech signal are more informative in emotion detection, it is still an open problem to identify reliable discriminating features for this task [7]. In this respect, feature selection in pattern recognition and classification becomes an important area of research as it is highly critical to select the best subset of high-dimensional data to reduce the classification error [8]. In many pattern recognition applications enormous amounts of multivariate data is currently available. However, classification algorithms are unable to attain high classification accuracy if there is a large number of weakly relevant and redundant features, which is attributed to "the curse of dimensionality". Many algorithms suffer from a computational load incurred by the high dimensional data. On the other hand, once a good small set of features are obtained, even simple algorithms such as 1-kNN is able to attain high accuracy [9]. Thus, feature selection is widely used to reduce the number of features and to remove irrelevant and redundant data [10].

The selection of a subset of features is based on an evaluation criterion and the quality of a feature subset is measured by this criterion. In this respect, feature selection algorithms broadly fall into three categories: the wrapper model, the filter model and the hybrid model. In the wrapper model, the performance of a specific algorithm is used to evaluate the subset of features. As the accuracy rate of the algorithm is determined for the selected subsets in each step, the wrapper model tends to be more computationally expensive. In the filter model, the classification performance is indirectly estimated using intrinsic characteristics of data such as distance measures. Despite the intensified research on finding the best representative features that give a higher accuracy, the subset of the selected best features are completely dependent on the ability of the algorithms used to rank the features. So it is not surprising if one end up with a completely different set of features as the best subset when a different feature selection algorithm is used. Therefore, there is an obvious need to define a framework within which it is more likely to obtain a reliable subset of features. This paper proposes two frameworks within which determining a subset of features with high informative power in terms of class-separability is made possible. The underlying property of the frameworks is to decompose a multi-class classification problem into binary classification as either one-vs-rest or one-vs-one problem. Although some variable selection methods, such as Sequential Forward Selection (SFS) method, treat the multi-class case directly rather than decomposing it into several two-class problems, it will be shown that decomposing the problem into binary-classification and reconstruction of a final feature subset from a set of candidate feature subsets results in an improved performance in terms of classifier accuracy.

Feature selection algorithms to evaluate the proposed frameworks are chosen to be one wrapper type, one filter type and two recently proposed embedded feature selection algorithms. The SFS algorithm with Leave-One-Out Cross Validation (LOOCV) error of a k-Nearest Neigbour (kNN) classifier is chosen as a wrapper type feature selection algorithm. The embedded type algorithms are two state of the art feature selection algorithms based on an Support Vector Machine (SVM) classifier, namely the algorithm based on Least Squared SVM Bound (LSBOUND) [11] and on W2R2 concept [12]. Finally, a filter approach based on Mutual Information (MUTINF) is used [13].

2 Emotion Detection Problem from Speech Signals

Recognition of emotion in human speech is an active research area, which has attracted the interest of the research community [14-19]. Despite of large amount of research carried out in literature to determine what aspects of the speech signal are more informative in emotion detection, identifying reliable discriminating features for this task remains still an open problem [7]. Fernandez and Picard in [20] highlighted results from an extensive investigation developing new features, and comparing them with classical features using machine learning techniques to recognize 5 emotional states. Sequential Floating Forward Selection (SFFS) with the leave-one-out (LOO) generalization error of a K-nearest neighbor (kNN) classifier was used in the feature selection phase to rank 87 features. Feature selection for emotion detection in noisy speech has been discussed by Schuller et al in [21]. They employed Information Gain Ratio based feature selection to select the best features, out of a set of 4000.

The feature set used in this study is extracted from the Berlin Emotional Speech Database-EmoDB [22]. 338 samples corresponding to four emotional classes have been used. Fifty-eight features have been extracted from the speech samples as explained in [23]. 17 of them are related to prosodic features based on statistical properties of the fundamental frequency F0. Five features are obtained from the sub-band energies of the utterances, using 6th order elliptic filters with center frequencies of 400, 800, 1200, 1600 and 3200 Hz, respectively. 20 Mel-Frequency Cepstrum Coeffients (MFCC) and 16th order Linear Predictive Coding (LPC) parameters have been included into feature vectors.

3 Proposed Frameworks for Feature Selection

The underlying properties of the proposed frameworks are to decompose multi-class classification problem into binary classification problem and then perform feature selection for each sub-problem. Then two feature construction strategies; namely intersection and unification, are defined to construct the final feature set. The proposed frameworks are depicted in Figure 1. In the first framework, labeled as FRM1, the multi-class emotion detection problem is cast into a "one-vs-rest" binary classification problem to discriminate one class of emotion from the rest. In this framework, class-specific features are expected to be selected by feature selection algorithm. As there are M classes of emotional states, M subsets of features are selected by each of the feature selection algorithms. In the second framework, the classification problem is organized as a "one-vs-one" binary classification task and it is labeled as FRM2. In this approach the feature selection algorithms are expected to select highly class-specific features which are informative in discriminating one class of emotion form another class of emotion. The number of subsets produced in FRM2 is M(M-1)/2 in this case.

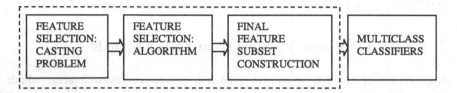

Fig. 1. Proposed framework for feature selection. Casting Problem refers to organising the emotion detection problem into either "one-vs-rest" or "one-vs-one" binary classification scheme. Then a number of subsets of features are selected by the feature selection algorithms.

Each feature selection algorithm will produce four subsets of features, S_i , each corresponding to one of four decomposed binary classification problems in FRM1, or six subsets of features in FRM2. In the feature construction stage, these subsets, S_i, are processed to finally obtain the "best feature subset". In this stage, two strategies in construction of a final feature set have been employed. Firstly, the intersection operator given in (1) is performed on the subsets to form the "best final subset" from the features that occurs more than one in the subsets, S_i. This final subset of features is labeled as SET1

$$SET1 = \bigcup_{\substack{i,j=1 \\ i \neq j}}^{N} S_i \cap S_j \tag{1}$$

where N=M is equal to the total number of subsets, S_i in FRM1.

In the second strategy, the subsets of features, S_i, are simply combined together. This task corresponds to performing a unification operation on the subsets S_i as given in (2)

$$SET2 = \bigcup_{i=1}^{N} S_i \tag{2}$$

where N=M equals the total number of subsets, S_i in FRM1.

In FRM2, as the emotion detection is organised as "one-vs-one" binary classification problem, there will be six binary classification problems. Each of the feature selection algorithms will then produce six subsets of features. Then the same steps are followed as in the construction of a final feature subset in FRM1: two final subsets are formed from the subsets of features, S_i, by performing the intersection and union operation as given in (1) and (2) where N=M(M-1)/2. These final best feature subsets are labeled as SET1 and SET2, respectively, following the convention employed in the FRM1. For the two final subsets produced by a feature selection algorithm, two multi-class classifiers are employed in the frameworks. 16 final features subsets (8 SET1s and 8 SET2s) are employed to train the multi-class classifiers in each framework, resulting in 32 classifications to carry out a comprehensive comparison.

Figure 2 shows the average percentage of features being selected from the feature groups by feature selection algorithms used in FRM1 and FRM2. Also the accuracy in terms of 5-fold Cross Validation (CV) error for multi-class classifiers are given in Table 1. In the table, average CV errors for each multi-classifier are shown in the first row using 58 features where no feature selection has been performed yet. Also the average CV error for multi-classifiers is given to indicate the performance of the SFS feature selection algorithm in the classical way. From the features selected by SFS in classical way, classification is performed using the only first 6, 15, 18 and 28 features in the rank. The results show that the SFS algorithm does not perform well. In most of the cases, the accuracy of the classifiers is worse, producing higher CV error compared to the no-feature selection case. On the other hand, when the features selected in the proposed frameworks are employed, the classifiers produces outperforming results, reducing CV error by 17.4% for the one-vs-one SVM, SVM(one-vs-one), classifier and 17.3% for the one-versus-rest SVM, SVM(one-vs-rest), classifier. The improvements indicate that SFS in the proposed framework selects more informative features.

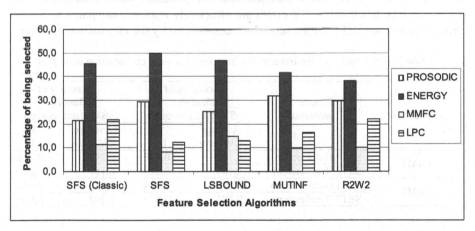

Fig. 2. Normalized percentage of features selected from the feature groups by the feature selection algorithms

As it is seen from Figure 2, SFS in the proposed framework is able to select more features from the prosodic and subband-energy related groups, while SFS in the classical way emphasis LPC parameters. This result is in line with the results reported in literature that prosodic and energy related features are more informative [8,24].

Table 1. Accuracy of SVM classifiers for SFS feature selection algorithm with and without the proposed frameworks

FRAMEWORK		Feature Selection Algorithm	# of features	Accuracy of Classifier: SVM(one-vs-one)		Accuracy of Classifier: SVM(one-vs-rest)	
				CV Error	Std Dev	CV Error	Std Dev
NO FRAMEWORK		*NOTAPPLIED*	**58**	**0,201**	**0,010**	**0,219**	**0,008**
		SFS(classic)	6	0,263	0,022	0,269	0,034
		SFS(classic)	15	0,231	0,025	0,237	0,026
		SFS(classic)	18	0,219	0,020	0,207	0,030
		SFS(classic)	28	0,190	0,029	0,196	0,031
SET1	FRM2	SFS(proposed)	6	0,281	0,031	0,311	0,025
	FRM1	SFS(proposed)	15	0,172	0,026	0,181	0,018
SET2	FRM2	SFS(proposed)	18	0,186	0,017	0,201	0,023
	FRM1	SFS(proposed)	28	0,166	0,022	0,187	0,027

The effectiveness of the proposed framework is illustrated in Table 2, Table 3 and Table 4 in terms of construction strategies, multi-class classifers and feature selection algorithms employed. Table 2 is organised to emphasise the effect of the feature construction strategies, namely Unification and Intersection. It shows average CV error of the classifiers for the final feature sets labelled as SET1 which are produced by the intersection operator, and for SET2 features produced by the unification operator. As it is seen, the unification operator produces more informative final feature subsets. In all cases, CV errors are effectively reduced, compared to the CV errors achieved for SET1 feature sets which constructed by the intersection operator.

Table 2. Performance of the frameworks in terms of feature construction strategies

Framework	Feature Construction	Accuracy of Classifier: SVM(one-vs-one)		Accuracy of Classifier: SVM(one-vs-rest)	
		Average CV Error	Std Dev	Average CV Error	Std Dev
FRM1	SET1 (Intersection)	0,182	0,022	0,202	0,022
	SET2 (Unification)	0,167	0,023	0,189	0,031
FRM2	SET1 (Intersection)	0,199	0,024	0,222	0,028
	SET2 (Unification)	0,174	0,023	0,192	0,026

A comparison between the multi-class classifiers is highlighted in Table 3. The results shows that irrespective of frameworks, the one-vs-one multi-class classifiers outperform the one-vs-rest classifier. It is seen that in the first framework, FRM1, all of the classifiers are more successful in terms of reducing average CV error. Among them SVM(one-vs-one) is able to produce an average CV error as low as $0,1745\pm0,0224$. The success of SVM(one-vs-one) is also apparent in the second framework producing an error level of $0,1866\pm0,0231$.

Table 3. Average accuracy of classifiers in the feature selection frameworks

Framework	Classifier	Average CV Error	Standard Deviation of CV Error
FRM1	SVM(one-vs-one)	0,1745	0,0224
	SVM(one-vs-rest)	0,1951	0,0264
FRM2	SVM(one-vs-one)	0,1866	0,0231
	SVM(one-vs-rest)	0,2071	0,0271

The effectiveness of the proposed frameworks are also evaluated with a comparison between feature selection algorithms with respect to the two feature selection frameworks. In both cases, the newly proposed LSBOUND based feature selection algorithm clearly outperforms the rest of the algorithms generating significantly lower average CV errors. The best accuracy, out of 32 experiments, is obtained by SVM(one-vs-one) with an CV error of 0.145 ± 0.02, when the LSBOUND based feature selection algorithm is employed.

Table 4. Average accuracy of all classifiers associated with particular feature selector in the feature selection frameworks

Framework	Feature Selection	Average CV Error	Standard Deviation of CV	Average # of features
FRM1	LSBOUND	0,175	0,020	23
	MUTINF	0,215	0,029	20,5
	R2W2	0,173	0,025	23,5
FRM2	LSBOUND	0,171	0,019	22
	MUTINF	0,183	0,033	23
	R2W2	0,190	0,024	22,5

4 Conclusion

In this paper, evaluation of the proposed feature selection frameworks and the construction approaches are carried out using four feature selection algorithms and two multi-class classifiers to improve emotion detection for human-computer interaction. It is shown that the algorithms tend to select more informative features in the proposed frameworks, which gives higher accuracy rates for the classifiers. Results show that the first framework where more informative features have been selected in terms of distinguishing one emotional state from the rest is more suitable in achieving higher accuracy. It has also been shown that among all of the four different feature selection algorithms, the recently proposed LSBOUND based feature selection is superior in terms of reducing average CV error. The best accuracy among 32 experiments is obtained by SVM(one-vs-one) with an CV error as low as 0.145 ± 0.02, when the LSBOUND feature selection algorithm is employed. Furthermore, the results have shown that SVM(one-vs-one) multi-classification scheme outperforms the other type of multi-task classifiers investigated and is consistently able to give higher accuracy in emotion detection. The results obtained suggest that the proposed frameworks are very effective in the emotion classification problem which is indispensable to achieve a more natural human-computer interaction.

Acknowledgement

This work has been sponsored by TUBITAK Project under the contract of 104E179. Corresponding author also would like to thank Prof. Dr. J Shawe-Taylor for his hospitality and guidance during the academic visit in the summer of 2006 granted by TUBİTAK at University of Southampton and at University College of London.

References

1. Hewett, C.: Curricula for Human Computer Interaction. ACM SIGCHI 1514 Broadway 10036, 15 (2002)
2. Vonada, N.A.: Introduction of Human Computer Interaction in Modern Education. In: Proc. of ISECON 2004. 21st Annual Information Systems Education Conference (2004), accessed via http://isedj.org/isecon/2004/3442/ISECON.2004.Vonada.pdf
3. Pantic, M., Rothkrantz, L.J.M.: Expert system for automatic analysis of facial expressions. Image and Vision Computing 8, 881–905 (2000)
4. Pantic, M., Rothkrantz, L.J.M.: Toward an affect-sensitive multimodal human-computer interaction. Proceedings of the IEEE 91(9), 1370–1390 (2003)
5. Altun, H.: Human computer interaction and its impact on e-learning in engineering education. In: The Proceeding of 1 Int. Conference on Innovations in Learning for the Future: e- learning, Istanbul, pp. 433–440 (2004)
6. Fasel, I., Stewart-Bartlett, M., Littelwort-Ford, G., Movellan, J.R.: Real time fully automatic coding of facial expressions from video. In: Proceedings of the 9th Symposium on Neural Computation, California Institute of Technology (May 2002)
7. Juslin, P.N., Scherer, K.R.: Vocal expression of affect. In: Harrigan, J., Rosenthal, R., Scherer, K. (eds.) The New Handbook of Methods in Nonverbal Behavior Research, Oxford University Press, Oxford, UK (2005)
8. Cowie, R., Douglas-Cowie, E., Tsapatsoulis, N., Votsis, G., Kollias, S., Fellenz, W., Taylor, J.G.: Emotion Recognition in Human-Computer Interaction. IEEE Signal Processing Magazine 18(1), 32–80 (2001)
9. Gilad-Bachrach, R., Navot, A., Tishby, N.: Margin Based Feature Selection: Theory and Algorithms. In: ICML. Proceeding of the 21'st International Confereence on Machine Learning, pp. 337–344 (2004)
10. Liu, H., Yu, L.: Toward Integrating Feature Selection Algorithms for Classification and Clustering. IEEE, Trans. on Knowledge and Data Engineering 17(4), 491–502 (2005)
11. Zhou, X., Mao, K.Z.: LS Bound based gene selection for DNA microarray data. Bioinformatics 21(8), 1559–1564 (2005)
12. Weston, J., Mukherjee, S., Chapelle, O., Pontil, M., Poggio, T., Vapnik, V.: Feature Selection for SVMs. In: Advances in Neural Information Processing Systems 13. Neural Information Processing Systems (NIPS), pp. 668–674 (2000)
13. Zaffalon, M., Hutter, M.: Robust feature selection by mutual information distributions. In: Darwiche, A., Friedman, N. (eds.) UAI-2002. Proceedings of the 18th Conference on Uncertainty in Artificial Intelligence, pp. 577–584. Morgan Kaufmann, San Francisco (2002)

14. Reynolds, C., Ishikawa, M., Tsujino, H.: Realizing Affect in Speech Classification in Real-Time. Aurally Informed Performance: Integrating Machine Listening and Auditory Presentation in Robotic Systems. In: conjunction with AAAI Fall Symposia, Washington, DC, USA (October 13-15, 2006)
15. Pantic, M., Sebe, N., Cohn, J.F., Huang, T.: Affective Multimodal Human-Computer Interaction. In: Proc. of ACM Int. Conf. on Multimedia, pp. 669–676. ACM Press, New York (2005)
16. Wang, Y., Guan, L.: An investigation of speech based human emotion recognition. In: IEEE 6th Workshop on Multimedia Signal Processing, pp. 15–18 (2004)
17. Ververidis, D., Kotropoulos, D.: Emotional speech classification using Gaussian mixture models and the sequential floating forward selection algorithm. In: ICME 2005. IEEE International Conference on Multimedia and Expo, pp. 1500–1503 (2005)
18. Ververidis, D., Kotropoulos, Y.: Automatic speech classification to five emotional states based on gender information. In: Proc. 12th European Signal Processing Conf., pp. 341–344 (2004)
19. Fragopanagos, N., Taylor, J.G.: Emotion recognition in human–computer interaction. Neural Networks 18, 389–405 (2005)
20. Fernandez, R., Picard, R.W.: Classical and Novel Discriminant Features for Affect Recognition from Speech. In: Interspeech 2005. Eurospeech 9th European Conference on Speech Communication and Technology (2005)
21. Schuller, B., Arsic, D., Wallhoff, F., Rigoll, G.: Emotion Recognition in the Noise Applying Large Acoustic Feature Sets. Speech Prosody, Dresden (2006)
22. Burkhardt, F., Paeschke, A., Rolfes, M.: Walter Sendlmeier und Benjamin Weiss, A Database of German Emotional Speech. In: Proceedings Interspeech (2005)
23. Dogan, G.: Emotion Detection Using Neural Networks. MSc Thesis, Nigde University (2006)
24. Xiao, Z., Dellandrea, E., Dou, W., Chen, L.: Features extraction and selection for emotional speech classification. In: Proceedings of IEEE Conference on Advanced Video and Signal Based Surveillance, pp. 411–416 (2005)

The Significance of Empty Speech Pauses: Cognitive and Algorithmic Issues

Anna Esposito[1], Vojtěch Stejskal[2], Zdeněk Smékal[2], and Nikolaos Bourbakis[3]

[1] Seconda Università di Napoli, Dipartimento di Psicologia, and IIASS, Italy
anna.esposito@unina2.it, iiass.annaesp@tin.it
[2] Brno University of Technology, Dept. of Telecommunications, Czech Republic
[3] ATRC / College of Engineering, Wright State University, Dayton Ohio, USA

Abstract. This study investigates pausing strategies, focusing attention on empty speech pauses. A cross-modal analysis (video and audio) of spontaneous narratives produced by male and female children (9 years old ±3 months) and adults showed that a remarkable amount of empty speech pauses (91% in male and 84% in female children, and 95% in adults of both sexes) was related to the amount of added information conveyed in the speech flow. Both adults and children consistently exploited pausing strategies to signal discourse boundaries such as clauses (marked by empty speech pauses for 73% and 70% of cases in male and female children, respectively, and 56% in adults) and paragraphs (97% and 96% in male and female children, respectively, and 94% in adults). The high consistency, among subjects, in the distribution of speech pauses suggests that, at least in the Italian context, the speaker in narration makes use of an intrinsic timing behavior, probably a general pattern of rules, to control speech flow for discourse organization. The implications of these findings for the development of improved speech recognition and speech synthesis systems are discussed and procedures for the automatic detection of speech pauses are proposed.

1 Introduction

A characteristic of spontaneous speech, as well as of other types of speech, is the presence of silent intervals (empty pauses) and vocalizations (filled pauses) that do not have a lexical meaning. Several studies have been conducted to investigate the system of rules that underlie the speaker's pausing strategies and their psychological bases. Research in this field has shown that pauses may play several communicative functions, such as building up tension or raising expectations in the listener about the rest of the story, assisting the listener in her/his task of understanding the speaker, signalling anxiety, emphasis, syntactic complexity, degree of spontaneity, and gender, and transmitting educational and socio-economic information [1, 5, 12, 25, 26, 32].

Studies on speech pause distribution in language production have produced evidence of a relationship between pausing and discourse structure. Empty and filled pauses are more likely to coincide with boundaries, realized as a silent interval of varying length, at clause and paragraph level [6, 22, 27, 42]. This is particularly true

F. Mele et al. (Eds.): BVAI 2007, LNCS 4729, pp. 542–554, 2007.

of narrative structures, where it has been shown that pausing marks the boundaries of narrative units [8-10, 15-17, 34-36, 42].

Several cognitive psychologists have suggested that pausing strategies reflect the complexity of neural information processing. Pauses will surface in the speech flow as the end product of a "planning" process that cannot be carried out during speech articulation, and the amount and length of pausing reflect the cognitive effort related to lexical choices and semantic difficulties in generating new information [7, 8, 15-17, 25].

We can conclude from the above considerations that pauses in speech are typically a multi-determined phenomenon [3, 7, 20], attributable to physical, socio-psychological, communicative, linguistic and cognitive causes. Physical pauses are normally attributed to breathing or articulatory processes (i.e. pauses due to a momentary stoppage of the breath stream caused by vocal-tract constrictions or the closure of the glottis). Socio-psychological pauses are caused by stress or anxiety [3]. Communicative pauses are meant to permit the listener to comprehend the message or to interrupt and ask questions or make comments. Linguistic pauses are used as a means for discourse segmentation. Finally, cognitive pauses are related to mental processes connected with the flow of speech, such as replacing the current mental structure with a new one in order to continue the production [8-10] or difficulties in conceptualization [25].

An accurate detection of empty speech pauses appears to be crucial for most of today's speech processing methods. For example, in *speech recognition*, the correct detection of word, clause, and paragraph boundaries has a significant impact on the final recognizer efficiency [29] and we will see, from the data reported below, that a significant percentage of such linguistic structures is marked by empty speech pauses. Furthermore, the detection of non-speech regions is of utmost importance in *speech enhancement* [38], and in *speech coding* [24] applications since automatic procedures, especially those devised for the reduction of noise and of the average bit rate by means of a variable transmission mode, exploit acoustic information extracted from silent intervals. A practical use of these features is reported in the definitions provided by the European Telecommunication Standards Institute (ETSI) and the International Telecommunication Union (ITU) standards [19, 30].

The interest in developing improved methods for empty pause detection also arises from the need to develop better interactive dialog systems and intelligent avatars that are able to engage in a natural interaction with the user. In this context, as already said, speech pauses play several functions that guide the flow of the interaction. Furthermore, the frequency and the length of empty pauses provide useful biometrical information on the emotional state of the speaker, since it has been shown that in stressed situations (for example, when the speaker is telling a lie) the silent intervals in speech flow tend to be more numerous and relatively longer than in non-stressed situations [13]. In this respect, a machine communicator can exploit empty pause detection to detect the register the speaker is using or to produce more natural sounding synthesized speech.

The discrimination between speech and non-speech segments is not as trivial as it might appear at first sight: most of the detection algorithms fail due to the combination of background noise and speaker's coarticulation effects. Former algorithms were frequently based on energy thresholding [23], pitch detection [11], zero-crossing rate [30], periodicity measure [47], cepstral features [46], spectrum analysis [33], and Linear Prediction Coding (LPC) [39] or combinations of these parameters. The efforts to enhance detection performance have led to the implementation of statistical models with decision rules derived from the Likelihood Ratio Test (LRT) applied to a set of hypotheses [19]. Recently, the Gaussian statistical model improved with the incorporation of an effective hang-over scheme based on the Hidden Markov Model (HMM) was applied in order to achieve more reliable results [43-44]. A different approach exploits a set of fuzzy rules implemented into the detection algorithm [4]. It has also been shown that algorithm robustness can be improved by using the signal-to-noise ratio (SNR) parameter and long-term information about the speech/non-speech signal measured separately on each filtered spectral band to formulate the appropriate decision rule for the problem under examination [40].

Each of the above proposed solutions has proved to give a satisfactory performance when tested on standard databases, such as TIMIT [21], NTIMIT [31], or Aurora framework [28], where noise has constant attributes that do not change from one record to another or during recording. However, the performance of the above algorithms decreases when environmental noise changes due to variations in the recording environment. The main problem for a correct empty pause detection is caused by local energy fluctuations, not only due to transient consonants but also to the presence of environmental noise. Fixed threshold methods are scarcely effective [23] because of high-level energy variations across the speech signal.

To overcome this problem, we propose an adaptive energy thresholding algorithm, where empty pause detection takes the form of measuring, in time, variations in the speech signal energy in different frequency regions. The rationale is that high-energy regions can be assigned to speech segments, whereas low-energy regions can be attributed to an empty pause. Threshold values are continuously adjusted on the basis of long-term speech and noise energy information as well as additional parameters that will be described below.

2 Materials and Methods for the Psycholinguistic Analysis

The video recordings on which our analysis is based are of narrations by 4 male and 4 female children (9 years old ±3 months) and 4 adults (2 males and two females, average age 28 years ±3 years). The speakers told the story of a 7-minute animated colour cartoon they had just watched. The cartoon, centered on a cat and a bird, was familiar to Italians (adults and children). The listeners in the case of children were the teacher and the other children also participating in the experiment, whereas in the adults' case the listener was the experimenter, who was also a close friend of their. Children's recordings were made after the experimenter had spent two months with the children in order to become familiar with them and after several preparatory recordings had been made in various contexts for the children to get used to the camera. In the case of adults, the recordings were made by the experimenter, in a friendly environment (at the experimenter's house after a relaxing dinner) and justifying the story-telling elicitation as a memory-recall experiment. This kept out stranger-experimenter inhibitions from the elicitation setting; i.e., factors that could result in stress and anxiety. Limiting these factors allowed us to rule out the *socio-psychological* type of pauses [3].

The cartoon had an episodic structure, each episode characterized by a "cat that tries to catch a bird and is foiled" narrative arc. Because of the cartoon's episodic structure, typically children and adults would forget entire episodes. In this case the experimenter was allowed to give suggestions in order to help them remember the story. However, given the length and the difficulty of the analytical procedure, in the present paper only two episodes were analyzed both for children and adults. The video was analyzed using commercial video analysis software (VirtualDub™) that allows viewing video-shots and forward/backward movements through the shots. The speech waves, extracted from the video, were sampled at 16 kHz and digitized at 16 bits. The audio was analyzed using Speechstation2™ from Sensimetrics. For the audio measurements the waveform, energy, spectrogram, and spectrum were considered together, in order to identify the beginnings and endings of utterances, filled and empty speech pauses, and phoneme lengthening. The details of the criteria applied to identify the boundaries in the speech waveform are described in Esposito and Stevens [18]. In this study, empty pauses are simply defined as a silence (or verbal inactivity) in the flow of speech equal to or longer than 120 milliseconds, whereas filled pauses, phoneme lengthening, and interruption are considered disfluencies (see Esposito [15-17] for details).

Both the video and audio data were analyzed perceptually, the former frame-by-frame and the latter clause-by-clause, where a *clause* is assumed to be "*a sequence of words grouped together on semantic or functional basis*", whereas a *paragraph* is considered "*a sequence of several clauses connected together by the same subject or scene*" [17]. Moreover, *added information* is considered "*any verbal material that produces a modification in the listener's conscious knowledge*", and therefore the *given* verbal material was intended not to produce such a modification [8].

3   Psycholinguistic Results

Table 1 reports the occurrences of the two pausing means considered (empty speech pauses and disfluencies) and their percentage (in brackets) computed as the ratio of empty speech pauses and disfluencies, respectively, to their total number of occurrences. Table 1 also reports the empty pause rate computed as the ratio of the numbers of speech pauses to the length of the subject's narrations measured in seconds. From Table 1 it can be observed that, overall, empty pauses are considerably frequent (43%, 42%, in male and female children, respectively, and 44% in adults) accounting for approximately two quarters of the total. Moreover, the empty pause rate in the children is higher in the females than in the males, the latter in turn being higher than in adults, suggesting that the three groups adopt different pausing strategies, depending on their language skills and their ability to structure the discourse.

Table 1. Occurrence of empty pauses, disfluencies, and empty pause rates in child and adult narratives. In brackets the percentage is reported as computed on the total number of empty pauses and disfluencies.

Male Children	Empty Pauses	Disfluency	Total	Empty Pause rate
S1 (77.94s)	28 (37)	47 (63)	75	36
S2 (84.47s)	32 (44)	40 (56)	72	38
S3 (114.5s)	39 (54)	33 (46)	72	34
S4 (121.0s)	39 (38)	63 (62)	102	32
Total (397.92s)	**138 (43)**	**183 (57)**	**321**	**35**
Female Children				
S1 (124.43s)	45 (47)	60 (63)	95	36
S2 (133.75s)	54 (46)	64 (54)	118	40
S3 (95.70s)	29 (31)	64 (69)	93	30
S4 (137.50s)	64 (42)	89 (58)	153	47
Total (353.88s)	**192 (42)**	**277 (60)**	**459**	**54**
Adults				
S1 (121.57s)	35 (51)	34 (49)	69	29
S2 (174.44s)	43 (40)	64 (60)	107	25
S3 (117.30s)	30 (46)	36 (55)	66	26
S4 (121.56s)	33 (43)	43 (57)	76	27
Total (543.87s)	**141 (44)**	**177 (56)**	**318**	**26**

Table 2 gives the occurrences of clauses and paragraphs as well as the number of clauses and paragraphs marked by an empty pause in children and adults. In brackets is reported the percentage of clauses and paragraphs, respectively, marked by an empty pause and computed as the ratio of the number of clauses (or paragraphs) marked by an empty pause to the total number of clauses (or paragraphs). Note that empty pauses marking a clause boundary can also mark a paragraph boundary. The results in Table 2 show a more reliable pattern at clause and paragraph level where both male and female children mark with a pause more than 70% of clause and 96% of the paragraph boundaries, whereas adults mark with a pause 56% of clause and 94% of paragraph boundaries. In contrast to the major difference between adults and children in the percentage of empty pauses marking clause boundaries, no difference was recorded between the two groups at the paragraph level. Both in adults' and children's speech, empty pauses were used to identify changes in scene, time and event structures, with the functional role of delimitating paragraphs. The difference between adults and children at clause level may depend on the fact that adults, in planning their utterances, may use gesture pauses (see Esposito & Marinaro [14]) for punctuating the spoken discourse in the absence of empty speech pauses, whereas children, being less skilled in assembling bodily and verbal information, tend to exploit both synchronously.

Table 3 reports the number of empty pauses that follow the *given*, and *added* speech material.

Table 2. Occurrences of empty pauses, disfluencies, and empty pause rates in child and adult narratives. In brackets the percentage is reported as computed on the total number of empty pauses and disfluencies (# = *quantity of*).

Male Children	#Clauses	# Clauses marked by Empty Pauses	# Paragraphs	# Paragraphs marked by Empty Pauses
S1	21	16 (76)	13	13 (100)
S2	21	19 (91)	11	11 (100)
S3	36	24 (68)	15	14 (93)
S4	38	26 (68)	16	15 (94)
Total	**116**	**85 (73)**	**55**	**53 (96)**
Female Children				
S1	42	29 (69)	17	16 (94)
S2	47	34 (72)	15	15 (100)
S3	34	20 (59)	14	13 (93)
S4	47	36 (77)	26	26 (100)
Total	**170**	**119 (70)**	**72**	**70 (97)**
Adults				
S1	58	28 (48)	17	16 (94)
S2	57	31 (54)	18	17 (94)
S3	42	26 (62)	17	16 (94)
S4	37	24 (65)	16	15 (94)
Total	**194**	**109 (56)**	**68**	**64 (94)**

Table 3. Absolute number of empty pauses associated with *given* and *added* information. The percentage (in brackets) is computed over the number of empty pauses for children and adults.

Male Children	Given	Added
S1	1 (4)	23 (82)
S2	0 (0)	30 (94)
S3	1 (3)	35 (90)
S4	0 (0)	38 (97)
Total	**2 (1)**	**126 (91)**
Female Children		
S1	3 (6)	37 (82)
S2	3 (5)	43 (80)
S3	0 (0)	26 (90)
S4	4 (6)	55 (86)
Total	**10(5)**	**161(84)**
Adults		
S1	2 (6)	33 (94)
S2	1 (2)	40 (93)
S3	0 (0)	30 (100)
S4	0 (0)	31 (94)
Total	**3(2)**	**134(95)**

Both children and adults pause to recover from memory the new information they wish to convey. Most of the empty pauses are made to convey *added* rather than *given* information. Most of the empty pauses made when no *added* or *given* information is produced, are a succession of filled and empty pauses signaling the enhanced cognitive recovery effort. The relationship between these pauses and the cognitive effort is evident examining the amount of empty pauses associated with changes of scene, time and event structure (see Table 2). The above data suggest a predictive scheme for the alternating pattern of cognitive rhythm in the production of spontaneous narratives. In this alternating pattern, empty speech pauses account for the highest percentage of paragraphs, and clauses. This is generally true of all subjects, hence suggesting that children and adults use a similar pause strategy to highlight different discourse units.

4 Adaptive Threshold Algorithm

Given the psycholinguistic significance of empty speech pauses we proposed an algorithm for their detection. To this aim the input speech signal was divided into frames using a 20 ms Hamming window with 10 ms overlap, and the sample log-energy values were computed for each window using the Fast Fourier Transform (FFT). Next, the computed spectrum was divided into four *Mel Frequency Scale* [37] sub-bands to match the human psycho-acoustical ability to resolve sounds with respect to frequency. The signal parameters of interest were described in the [0-4 kHz] frequency range containing an adequate amount of vocal activity, vocal tract articulatory features, and non-speech segment information (see details in [2- 45]).

A decision on whether the processed frame is a speech or non-speech segment was made by applying to the output of each filter a thresholding algorithm based on the following principles:

1) The thresholds, T_s and T_p, are computed, and if the energy value of the boundary regions exceeds the value T_s, a speech frame is detected; on the contrary, a non-speech frame is detected when the energy value falls below the T_p value. T_s and T_p are recomputed only when a non-speech frame is detected.

2) The computation starts by computing the threshold T as a mean of all first-frame energy values in the first band and the first silent segment is detected when all the band energy features fall below T. Initially T_s is set equal to T. This initial set-up may result in a minor misclassification when the first detected silent frame shows a slight offset with respect to its manually detected position.

Several algorithms for threshold calculation and adaptation were designed and experimentally tested due to the difficulty of identifying a procedure capable of preventing threshold value fluctuations that might arise from either a random noise or long-term silent segments. Among them we devised the Min/Max and the Spectral Flatness methods that were able to adapt to signal fluctuations.

Min/max method
The *min/max* algorithm is based on the ratio of predicted minimal noise energy in a detected non-speech region to the maximal noise energy computed on recently detected non-speech regions. Since the entire detection system runs in real-time, the processing of minimum noise value must be predicted on-line in concurrence with the

detection of silent pauses. The min/max ratio allows an adaptation of the generalized threshold level in response to changes in the noise level. The computation of the generalized threshold is described by Eq. (1):

$$T_k(n) = \overline{N} + \overline{N} \cdot \left(1 - \frac{N_{max}}{N_{min}^p}\right)$$ (1)

where T_k is the threshold value computed for k^{th} band and n^{th} frame, $\overline{N}$ is the mean of the noise energy computed on recently detected pauses, N_{max} and N^p_{min} are, respectively, the maximum noise energy value from recently detected pauses and the minimum noise energy value in the current detected silent pause p. T_s and T_p are set to $T_k(n) = T_{ks}(n) = 1.2 \cdot T_{kp}(n)$ and are protected against overflow and underflow through appropriate energy levels computed respectively on the previous 10s and 2s of input signal.

Spectral Flatness Method
This method introduces into the adaptive algorithm a correction factor described by Eq.(2):

$$T_k(n) = \lambda \overline{N} + \frac{\gamma}{4}(1 - F_c(n))$$ (2)

where F_c is the threshold correction obtained from the spectral flatness function described in Eq.(3):

$$F_c(n) = \int \log(S(f, n))df - \log\left(\int S(f, n)df\right)$$ (3)

where λ is the constant SNR correction estimated only once during the first detected non-speech segment. The SNR is computed as the ratio of the average speech energy to the noise energy in the first detected silent pause and reflects energy variations in the speaker's voice and in the environment; f is a spectral log-energy; n is the time window; γ is a constant taking on two different values, $\gamma_{Ts} = 1$ when processing speech frames and $\gamma_{Tp} = 1.6$ otherwise. Fig. 1 illustrates how the silent pause detection algorithm exploits the spectral flatness information to compute the different thresholds involved in the identification of speech and non-speech segments.

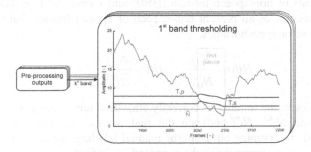

Fig. 1. Spectral flatness thresholding

Post-processing
The output of the detection algorithm is a vector of $J=4$ binary thresholded outputs that is then processed by a mapping algorithm indicating if the frame under examination is a speech or a silent segment. The mapping algorithm is exemplified in Figure 2. A frame is assumed to belong to a silent segment when almost all the components of the binary vector outputted by the filter bank will take a value of 1. Backward analysis is performed after each new detected silent pause to avoid including in the energy and slope vector computation the acoustic features of speech segments (such as weak fricatives and/or reduced vowels) whose energy may fall below the threshold defined for silent intervals.

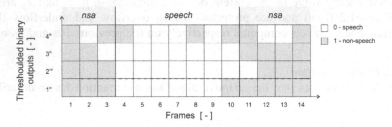

Fig. 2. Mapping algorithm

Comparative Tests
The system efficiency was tested on the narration recordings of eleven Italian and 1 American English female speakers (9 Italian males and 2 females). All the narrations referred to an episodic cartoon that the speakers had seen and were reporting to a friend (see section 3). For this purpose, speakers were videotaped at different environmental noise levels with a digital video-camera, and the audio to test our proposed algorithms was extracted directly from the video. The average narration length was 5 minutes ± 2.5 (standard deviation). The audio was sampled at 32 kHz and quantized at 16 bits. Noise sources included color noise, babble, echo and environmental noise. The minimum average SNR was 3dB. For reference, the signal was manually labeled for speech and silent pauses using Speechstation2™A cleaned version of the audio was obtained using the Adobe Audition™noise cancellation techniques and the proposed algorithm was also tested on this cleaned version. Detection performance was assessed in terms of non-speech hit-rate (HR0) and speech hit-rate (HR1) defined in Eq. (4) as a fraction of all present non-speech or speech frames that were correctly detected as pause or speech frames.

$$HR0 = \frac{N_{0,0}}{N_0^{\text{ref}}}, \quad HR1 = \frac{N_{1,1}}{N_1^{\text{ref}}} \tag{4}$$

$N_{0,0}$ and $N_{1,1}$ refer to the number of correctly classified non-speech and speech frames, respectively, and N_0^{ref}, N_1^{ref} indicate the real number of non-speech and speech frames, respectively, coming out from the manual labeling. Results are summarized in Table 4, where the performance of the proposed algorithms on both noisy and cleaned speech is reported. The Likelihood Ratio Test (LRT) algorithm [43] (with first order

Hidden Markov Model hang-over) was tested for comparison, since it has been proved to outperform most of the well known proposed VAD detection algorithms (see [41, 44]). The average accuracy of speech pause detection with 100 ms tolerance for the spectral flatness algorithm was 55% and 57% for noisy and clean speech, respectively, whereas for the min/max method it was 36% in noisy and 39% in clean speech. We can notice relatively high values of the non-speech frame hit-rate (HR0) for the spectral flatness algorithm, due to the fact that the SNR computation allows adapting the threshold to varying environmental and speaker characteristics, and therefore the pause boundaries are more appropriately detected, especially the pause onsets, which represent one of the main difficulties in accurate pause detection and significantly increase the HR0 value. Also, it should be noticed that both the proposed algorithms outperform LRT on male data (LRT's performance on female data were not reported because of the huge amount of training data required for LRT's statistics and the small number of records in our female database). It is worth noting that the pause detection performance does not vary significantly in noisy or clean conditions due to the difficulty of the task, and supports the robustness of our algorithms as regards the presence of noise.

Table 4. Average speech/non-speech hit-rates

Input files	Detectors	Min/max		Spectral flatness		LRT
		Male	Female	Male	Female	Male
Original	HR1 (%)	95.95	96.59	98.91	98.34	73.38
noisy speech	HR0 (%)	62.19	54.78	74.21	67.85	53.50
Cleaned	HR1 (%)	96.60	96.42	97.91	98.47	87.72
speech	HR0 (%)	62.37	60.27	77.49	68.90	56.34

5 Conclusions

This study is devoted to the investigation of the system of rules that underlie child and adult pausing strategies and their psychological bases, and to the proposal of an automatic algorithm for their detection The reported data show that empty pauses are largely used by the speaker to signal new information to the listeners' conscious knowledge and only a few among them mark the *given* information. This suggests that children pause, like adults [25, 34-36, 42], to recover from their memory the new information they are trying to convey. Moreover, pauses are not only generated by psychological motivations but they are also used as a linguistic means for discourse segmentation. Pauses are used by children and adults to mark the clause and paragraph boundaries. This result favors the hypothesis of a universal model for discourse structure otherwise we would expect children, being less skilled in the use of the lexis, to make more pauses at word level than at clause and paragraph levels. This hypothesis is further supported by previous data [15-17] showing that 56% of child pauses occur right after the first word in a clause, i.e. right after a filler conjunction that signals a major transition in the speech flow and serves to plan the message content for the continuation of the discourse. The consistency among the subjects in the use of pausing means seems to suggest a very coarse and general timing model that speakers use to regulate speech flow and discourse organization. More data are needed to make sense on how this model works, to allow its mathematical formulation for the implementation of more natural speech synthesis and interactive dialog systems, intelligent avatars.

We are currently able to propose a software system for silent speech pause detection in noisy and cleaned conditions, which exploits two adaptive log-energy based thresholding methods. Both methods show similar performance and their efficacy is comparable with standard VADs [19, 30, 40-41, 44]. No significant performance differences are noticed in the cleaned and noisy speech conditions suggesting that the reliability of the proposed methods does not depend on the signal quality even though, according to the results obtained, silent pause detection remains a difficult task that should be further investigated. The advantage of the proposed methods is in their robustness as regards high-energy noise randomly localized in sub-bands and the low energy wideband noise, even though they cannot handle high-energy noise spread widely over the band. Furthermore, no a priori knowledge of SNR and threshold values is required. In our future works the methods will be embedded in a multimodal pause detection system using both speech and gestures to improve the naturalness of human-machine interaction.

Acknowledgements

Acknowledgements go to Miss Tina Marcella Nappi for her editorial help. The authors want to express their deep sense of gratitude to Professor Roberto Ligrone for his useful comments and suggestions. The paper has been partially supported by COST Action 2102: *"Cross Modal Analysis of Verbal and Nonverbal Communication"* (CAVeNC), /www.cost.esf.org/index.php?id=110&action_number=2102 and partially by the National Research Project *"Information Society"* No. 1ET301710509.

References

1. Abrams, K., Bever, T.G.: Syntactic Structure Modifies Attention during Speech Perception and Recognition. Quarterly Journal of Experimental Psychology 21, 280–290 (1969)
2. Aversano, G., Esposito, A., Esposito, A.M., Marinaro, M.: A New Text-Independent Method for Phoneme Segmentation. In: Ewing, R.L., et al. (eds.) Proceedings of the IEEE Int. Workshop on Circuits and Systems, vol. 2, pp. 516–519 (2001)
3. Beaugrande, R.: Text Production. Text Publishing Corporation, Norwood, NJ (1984)
4. Beritelli, F., Casale, S., Cavallaro, A.: Adaptive Voice Activity Detection for Wireless Communications Based on Hybrid Fuzzy Learning. Proceedings of IEEE Global Telecommunications Conference 3, 1729–1734 (1998)
5. Bernstein, A.: Linguistic Codes, Hesitation Phenomena, and Intelligence. Language and Speech 5, 31–46 (1962)
6. Brotherton, P.: Speaking and not Speaking: Process for Translating Ideas into Speech. In: Siegman, A., Feldestein, S. (eds.) Of Time and Speech, Hillsdale, NJ, pp. 179–209 (1979)
7. Butterworth, B.L.: Evidence for Pauses in Speech. In: Butterworth, B.L. (ed.) Language Production, 1, Speech and Talk, pp. 155–176. London Academic Press, London (1980)

8. Chafe, W.L.: Cognitive Constraint on Information Flow. In: Tomlin, R. (ed.) Coherence and Grounding in Discourse, pp. 20–51. John Benjamins, Amsterdam (1987)
9. Chafe, W.L.: The Deployment of Consciousness in the Production of a Narrative. In: Chafe, W.L. (ed.) The Pear Stories, Norwood, NJ, Ablex, pp. 9–50 (1980)
10. Chafe, W.L.: Language and Consciousness. Language 50, 111–133 (1974)
11. Chengalvarayan, R.: Robust Energy Normalization Using Speech/Nonspeech Discriminator for German Connected Digit Recognition. In: Proceedings of EUROSPEECH, Budapest, Hungary, pp. 61–64 (1999)
12. O'Connell, D.C., Kowal, S.: Pausology. Computers in Language Research 2(19), 221–301 (1983)
13. Ekman, P.: Telling lies. W.W. Norton & Company, Inc., NY (2001)
14. Esposito, A., Marinaro, M.: What Pauses Can Tell Us about Speech and Gesture Partnership. In: Esposito, A., et al. (eds.) Fundamentals of Verbal and Nonverbal Communication and the Biometric Issue, vol. 18, pp. 45–57. IOS press, The Netherlands (2007)
15. Esposito, A.: Children's Organization of Discourse Structure through Pausing Means. In: Faundez-Zanuy, M., Janer, L., Esposito, A., Satue-Villar, A., Roure, J., Espinosa-Duro, V. (eds.) NOLISP 2005. LNCS (LNAI), vol. 3817, pp. 108–115. Springer, Heidelberg (2006)
16. Esposito, A.: Pausing Strategies in Children. In: Proceedings of the Int. Conference in Nonlinear Speech Processing, Cargraphics, Barcelona, Spain, April 19-22, 2005, pp. 42–48 (2005)
17. Esposito, A., Marinaro, M., Palombo, G.: Children Speech Pauses as Markers of Different Discourse Structures and Utterance Information Content. In: Proceedings of the Int. Conference: From Sound to Sense.., June 10-13, 2004, pp. C139–C144. MIT, Cambridge, USA (2004)
18. Esposito, A., Stevens, K.N.: Notes on Italian Vowels: An Acoustical Study (Part I). Research Laboratory of Electronic, Speech Communication Working Papers 10, 1–42 (1995)
19. ETSI: Voice Activity Detector (VAD) for Adaptive Multi-Rate (AMR) Speech Traffic Channels. In: ETSI EN 301 708 Recommendation (1999)
20. Garman, M.: Psycholinguistics. Cambridge University Press, Cambridge (1990)
21. Garofolo, J., et al.: DARPA TIMIT Acoustic-Phonetic Continuous Speech Corpus. National Institute of Standards and Technology, NTIS Order No. PB91-505065, CD-ROM (1990)
22. Gee, J.P., Grosjean, F.: Empirical Evidence for Narrative Structure. Cognitive Science 8, 59–85 (1984)
23. Gerven, S., Xie, F.: A Comparative Study of Speech Detection Methods. In: Proceedings of 5th EUROSPEECH, Rhodos, vol. 3, pp. 1095–1098 (1997)
24. Goldberg, R., Riek, L.: A Practical Handbook of Speech Coders. CRC Press, Boca Raton (2000)
25. Goldmar Eisler, F.: Psycholinguistic: Experiments in Spontaneous Speech. Academic press, London, New York (1968)
26. Green, D.W.: The Immediate Processing of Sentence. Quarterly Journal of Experimental Psychology 29, 135–146 (1977)
27. Grosz, B., Hirschberg, J.: Some Intentional Characteristics of Discourse Structure. In: Proceedings of Int. Conference on Spoken Language Processing, Banff, pp. 429–432 (1992)
28. Hirsch, H.G., Pearce, D.: The AURORA Experimental Framework for the Performance Evaluation of Speech Recognition Systems Under Noise Conditions. In: Proceedings of ISCA ITRW ASR (2000)
29. Huang, X., Acero, A., Hon, H.: Spoken Language Processing: a Guide to Theory, Algorithm, and System Development, pp. 375–463. Prentice-Hall, New Jersey (2001)

30. ITU: A Silence Compression Scheme for G.729 Optimized for Terminals Conforming to Recommendation V.70. In ITU-T Recommendation G.729, Annex B (1996)
31. Jankowski, et al.: NTIMIT: A Phonetically Balanced, Continuous Speech, Telephone Bandwidth Speech Database. In: Proc. of ICASSP (1990)
32. Kowal, S., O'Connell, D.C., Sabin, E.J.: Development of Temporal Patterning and Vocal Hesitations in Spontaneous Narratives. Journal of Psycholinguistic Research 4, 195–207 (1975)
33. Marzinzik, M., Kollmeier, B.: Speech Pause Detection for Noise Spectrum Estimation by Tracking Power Envelope Dynamics. IEEE Trans. Speech Audio Process. 10(6), 341–351 (2002)
34. O'Shaughnessy, D.: Timing Patterns in Fluent and Disfluent Spontaneous Speech. In: Proceedings of ICASSP Conference, Detroit, pp. 600–603 (1995)
35. Oliveira, M.: Prosodic Features in Spontaneous Narratives. Ph.D. Thesis, Simon Fraser University (2000)
36. Oliveira, M.: Pausing Strategies as Means of Information Processing Narratives. In: Proceedings of the Int. Conference on Speech Prosody, Ain-en-Provence, pp. 539–542 (2002)
37. Quatieri, T.: Discrete Time Speech Signal Processing. Prentice Hall, New Jersey (2002)
38. Rabiner, L., Juang, B.: Fundamentals of Speech Recognition. Prentice-Hall, Englewood Cliffs (1993)
39. Rabiner, L.R., Sambur, M.R.: Voiced-Unvoiced-Silence Detection Using Itakura LPC Distance Measure. In: Proceedings of IEEE Int. Conference in Acoustics, Speech, and Signal Processing, pp. 323–326. IEEE Computer Society Press, Los Alamitos (1977)
40. Ramírez, J., Segura, J., Benítez, C., Torre, A., Rubio, A.: Efficient Voice Activity Detection Algorithms Using Long-term Speech Information. Speech Communication 42(3-4), 271–287 (2004)
41. Ramírez, J., Segura, J.C., Benítez, C., Garcia, L., Rubio, A.: Statistical Voice Activity Detection Using a Multiple Observation Likeliood Ratio Tese. IEEE Signal Processing Letters 12(10), 689–692 (2005)
42. Rosenfield, B.: Pauses in Oral and Written Narratives. Boston University Press (1987)
43. Sohn, J., Kim, N.S., Sung, W.: A Statistical Model-Based Voice Activity Detection. IEEE Signal Processing Letters 6(1), 1–3 (1999)
44. Stadermann, J., Stahl, V., Rose, G.: Voice Activity Detection in Noisy Environments. In: Proceedings of EUROSPEECH, Aalborg, Denmark, pp. 1851–1854 (2001)
45. Stejskal, V., Smékal, Z., Esposito, A.: Fundamentals of Verbal and Nonverbal Communication and the Biometrical Issue. In: Esposito, A., et al. (eds.) Fundamentals of Verbal and Nonverbal Communication and the Biometrical Issue, IOS press, The Netherlands, IOS Press, Amsterdam (in press)
46. Stouten, F., Martens, J.: A Feature-Based Filled Pause Detection System for Dutch. In: Proceedings of IEEE Automatic Speech Recognition and Understanding, St. Thomas, USA, pp. 309–314. IEEE Computer Society Press, Los Alamitos (2003)
47. Tucker, R.: Voice Activity Detection Using a Periodicity Measure. Proceedings of Instrumental Electrical Engineering 139, 377–380 (1992)

Human Robot Interactions:
Towards the Implementation of Adaptive
Strategies for Robust Communication

Stanislao Lauria

Brunel University,
School of Information Systems, Computing and Mathematics
Uxbridge, UB8 3PH, UK
stasha.lauria@brunel.ac.uk
http://www.brunel.ac.uk

Abstract. Verbal communication is the most efficient way to communicate between humans, and yet it is not widely used in Human Computer Interactions (HCI). In this work-in-progress paper, some aspects related to the lack of success for speech-based HCI systems are firstly discussed and then, two adaptive strategies, developed by the author and currently under test, are introduced.

Keywords: Adaptive dialogue systems, HCI, robotics, Intelligent Systems.

1 Introduction

Currently human computer interactions (HCI) are mainly performed using keybord, mouse and screen. But this is not the most natural way humans interact and therefore it is sometimes inefficace and frustrating. In theory, Natural Language (NL) (sometime also referred as verbal communication or spontaneous speech) could be very efficient as an interaction paradigm with machines. It is the most spontaneous and efficient way humans communicate and there are several reasons to use speech also in computer interactions. For example, in mobile-related applications (such as driving or walking) or tedious application (searching information) a verbal-based paradigm would be more efficient and more spontaneous.

In general, NL-based communication is fast and therefore quite succesful in handling errors and uncertainties, since *interactions* with the other interlocutor are facilitated. Therefore, speech is quite efficient between humans since it allows the use of different recovery strategies and, at the same time, it can handle some degree of imprecision. However, these arguments can also be used to explain the difficulties in implementing the same strategy for human-machine interactions.

Recently there has been a remarkable progress in speech-based human machine interactions. Yet, only few working systems have been released and they have not outperformed standard interfaces. Therefore, they are considered less intuitive and users tend to dislike them after the first attempt (see for example the voice dialling option for mobile phones which is almost never used).

F. Mele et al. (Eds.): BVAI 2007, LNCS 4729, pp. 555–565, 2007.

Broadly speaking, a speech-based interface requires the following components: an Automatic Speech Recogniser (ASR), a Dialogue Manager (DM), a Natural Language Understanding (NLU) and a text to speech generator (TTS). Speech based systems are error prone, but the management of error corrections, the lack of suitable feedback and the lack of flexibility in artificial systems are probably the causes of the initial frustration among the users. While each user has a different way to interact, speech based interface offers little adaptability to the user profile. For instance, most ASRs do not try to adapt to an individual user during a dialogue session since it is very difficult to train ASRs on the fly. Therefore, their performance can vary significantly for different users and even for the same user across different dialogues. Managing the dialogue between humans and machines is another area where lack of adaptivity is a contributing factor of user frustration. The strategies are often very rigid and do not handle problematic situations very well. They do not try to improve their performance by dynamically adapting the system behaviour to the user profile during the dialogue.

For these critical situations described above, no error free solutions have yet been found. To tackle this lack of flexibility both at ASR and at DM level, we present here a strategy based on some adaptive capabilities manifested by the paradigm used. The strategy proposed here is based on *repairs*. That is, unsolved situations occurring during the interaction, being solved through cyles of clarifications. Then, using the *perceptive* abilities of the system, it will be possible to adapt to the user behaviour during the interactions.

2   The Basic Architecture

In the remaining we will mainly focus on a domain consisting of users giving route instructions to robots . [3,15,8,4,11] have developed systems able to translate verbal user instructions (or utterances) into machine procedures. In [15,8] the verbal interaction allows the robot both to update its current knowledge about its position and to plan the shortest path for a location given by the user. In [4] a display interface allows also graphical input/outputs, while in [11] the system suffers from a lack of parsing and grounding.

The paradigm used in this paper is the Instruction Based Learning (IBL) described in [3]. With the IBL project, a system has been developed to use spontaneous speech to instruct a robot to learn new routes. The system is able to build new sequences of actions (or procedures) starting from an initial set of pre-defined basic primitives. As shown in figure 1, an IBL system requires the following components: an *Automatic Speech Recogniser* (ASR) to convert speech utterances into some semantic representation using a corpus based grammar, a *Dialogue Manager* (DM) to produce an abstract discourse representation struc-ture (DRS) of the dialogue between the user and the robot using the results from the ASR, a *Robot Manager* (RM) to either map the DRS with an existing procedure/primitive or to build a new procedure if the route is unknown and finally a robot to verify and/or execute the primitive or procedure, and finally a

Text To Speech generator (TTS) to communicate back to the user. A key point
for the successful translation (or *grounding*) of a user's instruction into robot
actions is that the system should be able to produce appropriate feedback to
increase its level of perception.

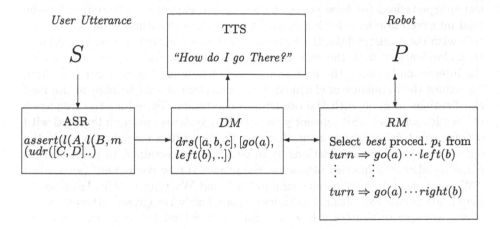

Fig. 1. IBL Block Diagram

IBL *feedback* enables the system to deal with grounding of utterances through
a dialogue. The user is informed about the system's evaluation of utterance understanding with feedback produced by the IBL components. Positive feedback
indicates a successful evaluation and therefore the ability to execute that instruction, whereas a negative feedback indicates a need for some clarification.

In the next section we will discuss the new adaptive strategies introduced
into the IBL architecture. The startegies introduced are based on the use of the
feedback produced by the system to change the state of the system.

3   Adaptive Speech Recognition

For human-robot communication to reach a satisfactory level of success rate, it
is necessary to possess some error correction capabilities . Feedback can increase
robustness and although it is already used during the grounding process (for
example, to evaluate whether a sequence of actions can be successfully executed),
it is possible to increase its influence further.

It has emerged that the rate of success in converting user instructions into
robot executable programs is dependent on the ASR accuracy . Hidden Markov
Models (HMMs) are currently used for ASRs. For example such models are implemented in Nuance [9], which is used with IBL systems (version 8.0). In [3]
the advantages of using Nuance have been discussed. However, some problems
cannot be solved with the rule-based approach so far used for Nuance in IBL
systems. For instance while testing IBL systems, it has been noticed that the

same command (i.e. the same sequence of words) can be repeated several times by the same user, but due to changes in pitch or intensity of the voice, a different interpretation could be produced every time and most of these interpretations could be very implausible. The reason being that each intermediate state (i.e. each component) of the grounding process could have produced competing partial interpretations (or *hypotheses*). Uncertainty is expected to be reduced in the final interpretation by selecting mutually supportive hypotheses that are consistent with the acoustic data. If uncertainty is still unresolved (i.e. no grounding), then clarifications with the user are needed. However, clarifications are making the interaction between the user and the robot tedious if they occur too often. To reduce the frequency of clarifications, the system should be able to use past clarifications to cope with the occurring uncertainty. To reduce the frequency of clarifications the ASR currently used in IBL systems can be integrated with a novel robot-driven component. The novelty being in a new way to apply the outcome of previous clarifications to an occurring uncertainty. In particular, to correctly identify a queried utterance, the proposed new component (also called TW component in this paper) employs a Time Warping (TW) algorithm to match utterances exploiting a database of previously recognised utterances.

An example to illustrate how uncertainty is solved by using the proposed hybrid approach is the following: if the standard HMM-based ASR produces **pass left pass the bridge** as an interpretation for the utterance **turn left after the bridge**, no mutually supportive hypothesis can be selected. Therefore, a negative feedback is generated (for example, the Robot Manager (RM) component cannot translate the command into a suitable robot procedure and therefore produces some negative feedback). In this case, a clarification dialogue starts (for example, the user will be requested to repeat the command again) and once the user utterance is grounded (i.e. the repeated utterance can be translated into the corresponding robot procedure), the system will produce positive feedback (for example, the user is informed that the command has been understood). At this point, if in a following session the user is going to repeat that command again, it is possible that the same sequence of events (i.e. wrong interpretation, request to repeat, etc) appears again. However, the system is not using the past events to avoid it. That because the utterances produced during the clarification dialogue cannot be used with standard ASR components to increase their accuracy.

However, the TW component is capable to re-use the past interactions to avoid this repetition of similar sequence of events by indexing the processed utterances based on the perceptive capabilities of the robot. In this way, if in a following session the user is going to repeat that command again, then the queried utterance can be successfully matched with a similar utterance already indexed to avoid further clarifications. As a result, the hybrid approach proposed (standard ASR and the TW-based component) unveils the ability to recover from a wider range of audio signals improving the recognition robustness.

The TW component, discussed in more details in [2], processes the time domain waveform of the signal S of the user's utterance U. By introducing the TW component in the IBL architecture as shown in figure 2, it is possible to complement the standard ASR. That is, if the *standard* ASR component rejects a new utterance U_1 (i.e. a speech signal S_1 containing the same sequence of instructions as U but with $S_1 \neq S$ due, for example, to change in pitch), then the TW-based component proposed here will associate the same grounding G as U to U_1 by successfully matching S_1 with S.

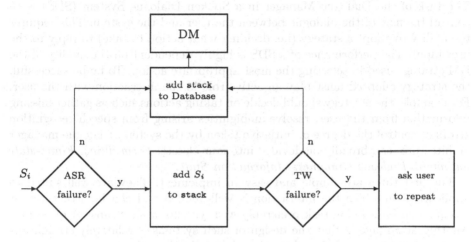

Fig. 2. Hybrid ASR model

Time warping is a pattern matching method which measures similarities between speech input by computing the best matches with a pre-defined database of speech data [12]. The recognition process consists of matching the incoming speech with stored templates. The template with the lowest distance measure from the input pattern is the recognised one. Rather than using a straightforward technique of comparing the value of the input signal at time t to the template signal at time t, an algorithm is used to search the space of mappings from the time sequence of the input signal to that of the template signal, so that the total distance is minimised. A side effect of this approach is that the algorithm can be applied to time series of different length therefore, appropriate for spontaneous speech domains where signals have different length.

Time warping algorithms have been used in the past for ASR until statistical-based methods (i.e. HMMs) gradually have taken over, although very recently there has been a growing interest back to time warping based methods. For example, in [10] the advantages of a hybrid approach based on both time warping and conventional statistical approaches have been demonstrated for a two stage approach to classify an artificial set of data (instead of speech ones). Computational complexity is one problem associated with time warping approaches. In [2] it has been proposed a strategy to reduce the computational complexity by reducing the dimension of the signal and some initial tests have shown that the hybrid approach proposed has been effective. In particular, preliminary tests have demonstrated that the TW component can complement the standard speech recognition component, improving the overall performance of the system (see [2] for further details).

4   The Adaptive Information State

The task of the Dialogue Manager in a Spoken Dialogue System (SDS) is to control the flow of the dialogue between the user and the system. This requires the ability to adopt a stategy (i.e. deciding what action to take) to reply to the user input. The performance of a SDS is highly dependent on the quality of the DM strategy used in selecting the most appropriate action. To be be successful, the strategy adopted must play an active role in the interaction with the user. For example, the strategy should decide on taking actions such as gather missing information from the user, resolve ambiguities arising from speech recognition errors or control the degree of initiative taken by the system. Dialogue manager architectures can broadly be devided into four classes: *Form filling, Finite-state automata, Dialogue Grammars, Information State.*

The first three are simple and easy to implement. They are well suited to applications in which the interaction is well-defined and can be structured as a sequential form-filling task preferably with yes/no or short answer questions. Another advantage is that the design of such systems is relatively straightforward and intuitive and their behaviour is predictable. However, they can lead to unnatural dialogue, where the information is elicited from user in the form of a sequence of questions. The dialogue strategy is very inflexible: the user must follow the structure of the dialogue and answer the system questions. Any additional provided information is ignored by the system. Attempting to extend the system to enable repair mechanisms (reaction to misunderstanding, clarification, etc) could lead to combinatorial explosion of states and transitions. The Information State (IS) approach is more versatile than the other three models and attempt to overcome their limitations. These approaches are not mutually exclusive and often they are used together. Since the architecture used in this paper is based on the IS model, we will not describe in details the other three models. The information state model describes dialogue as a coordinated effort to maintain an agreed record of the state of the conversation. It is based on the *Information State Update* (ISU) paradigm for dialogue managment [1]. The dialogue's *information state* represents the acquired information during previous dialogue actions. In this way, it is possible to both differentiate between dialogue states and prompt future actions [16].

The IS dialogue management used here is called DIPPER and it is available at http://www.ltg.ed.ac.uk/dipper. DIPPER is not a dialogue system itself, but it supports building spoken dialogue systems, by offering interfaces to speech recognisers, speech synthesisers, parsers and other kinds of agents. More specifically, the IS approach provides a programming paradigm for dialogue managers which centres around a well-structured information state model - a model that works with classes of declarative rules which effect information state transitions. The information state approach is characterised by the following components: *a specification of the contents of the information state of the dialogue, the datatypes used to structure the information state, a set of update rules covering the dynamic changes of the information state, a control strategy for information state updates.* With the DIPPER's record structure and datatypes, it is possible to define information states. An information state is normally defined as a recursive structure of the form **Name:Type**, where **Name** is an identifier, and **Type** a datatype. Datatypes include records, stacks and queues. An example of information state is in figure 3a. This example defines an information state as

```
is:record([history:queue(atomic),
      robot:stack(message),
      mode:stack(atomic),
      grammar:atomic,
      contact:atomic,
      input:queue(move),
      nxtmv:record([
                  utterance:queue(atomic),
                  act:queue(atomic)
                  ]),
      lastmoves:record([
                  string:stack(word),
                  act:stack(atomic),
                  udr:stack(udr),
                  conf:stack(atomic),
                  int:list(interpretation)
                  ]),
      drs:stack(drs),
      temp:drs
      ])
```

```
urule(rejection,
      [
      val(is^contact,yes),
      non_empty(is^nxtmv^utterance),
      non_empty(is^nxtmv^act),
      first(is^input,reject)
      ],
      [
      dequeue(is^nxtmv^utterance),
      dequeue(is^nxtmv^act),
      set(is^counter,0),
      dequeue(is^input),
      enqueue(is^history,user:'?'),
      enqueue(is^nxtmv^act,req_repeat),
      enqueue(is^nxtmv^utterance,'Repeat!')
      ]).
```

a) Information State   b) Update Rule

Fig. 3.

a record named **is**, consisting of the fields **history**, **robot**, **mode**, **grammar**, ..., **udr**, **conf**, **int**. For instance, the field **utterance** is defined as a queue of atomic typed structures, and the field **nxtmv** is defined as a record containing the fields **utterance** and **act**. The term a^b refers to the value of field **b** in record **a**. For instance, the path **is^history** in the above example refers to a queue of terms of type **atomic**. Note that paths can be arbitrarily long and may be used in conjunction with functions defined in the update language.

With terms, it is possible to refer to a specific value within the information state (for example, as explained below, either for testing a condition, or for applying an effect). There are two kinds of terms: *standard* terms and *anchored* terms. The standard terms define the data structures for the types (atomic types, queue, stack, records, etc), whereas the anchored terms allow us to refer to substructures of the information state (such as **first** and **last** to refer to the first respectively last item of a queue).

Update rules (see the example in Figure 3b) specify in a declarative way how information state changes. Hence, applying an update rule to an information state results in a new state. An update rule is a triple <*name, conditions, effects*>. The *conditions* and *effects* are defined by an update language, and both are recursively defined over terms. *conditions* is a set of tests on the current information state, while *effects* is an ordered set of operations on the information state. *name* is a rule identifier.

Conditions do not change the content of the information state, and are only used to inspect values in the record defining the information state (such as checking whether a queue is empty). *Effects*, on the other hand are responsible for changing the information state. There are two kinds of effects: operations (defined over terms), and solvables. The former include assignments of values to information state attributes and operations on datatypes such as stacks and queues. The latter are a useful way of incorporating procedural attachment to fulfil requests. The effects are ordered, because the information state is updated after each single effect, and hence the order in which the effects are applied to the information state matters. Conditions in update rules, however, are not ordered. As a result, external actions are able to update the information state, giving the properties of an asynchronous architecture while maintaining a central unit for data processing. If the conditions of a given updaterule have been satisfied then its effects are implemented.

For instance, the urule in figure 3b, `rejection`, deals with a situation where a user utterance has not been rejected by the speech recognition component. So, first step is to check the conditions. That means inspecting if: there is an ongoing dialogue, a (rejected) utterance has been produced, the dialogue is in a given state (`non_empty(is^nxtmv^act)`) and the response from the speech recogniser has been negative (`first(is^input,reject)`). If these conditions are true, the effects will then be implemented. With the update rule shown in figure ??, the dialogue strategy chosen for a rejected utterance is to ask the user to repeat the sentence. To achieve this, information concerning the last turn is removed (through the effects produced by `dequeue`) while new elements are placed in the queues with `enqueue`. As a consequence, the dialogue is now in a state where the system is ready to inform the user that last utterance should be repeated. After the user has been informed (through a speech synthesizer), a different update rule will change the state of the dialogue so that, the system is then ready to listen and try to recognize the new utterance (through the speech recogniser).

Different strategies can be used to decide which rule to select at a given point. the following are some types of update stratgies: *Take the first rule that applies, apply each (applicable) rule in sequence, apply rules according to class, Select a rule using probabilistic information, Let user decide.*

[5,6,13,14,18] are examples of a growing interest on introducing learning for dialogue managment strategies. These techniques model dialogue as a Markov Decision Process assigning rewards to various dialogue states and then finding the dialogue policy which leads to the maximum expected reward starting from any dialogue state. [7] have investigated how users could control the adaption of the system's dialogue strategies. The focus is on optimizing performance during a single dialogue. Unfortunately, a user-controlled adaptation system is not ideal for many applications, as it requires an initial (although minimal) training session for users. However, probably due to their complexity, none of these efforts has been integrated with a structured, formal account of the dynamics of dialogue context, such as that developed under IS-based models. [4] has investigated the use of reinforcment learning for IS models. They investigate two different methods for predicting the next user action based on the history of the information state. The system proposed requires some initial training and it would not be able to change its rules while interacting with the user. Another problem is the large size of the state space obtained.

In introducing adaptive policies able to adapt the dialogue managment behaviour while interacting with the user, we aim at tackling the problem of changing the strategy *on the fly*. That is, at any given time, the dialogue manager being able to change its strategy of *what to say next* based on past events. To implement this adaptive paradigm, we introduce a specific field in the information state record to map a state S to a single number. The value v assigned to S indicates the desirability of that state with v being modified by the effect's section of the update rules. As a consequence of the interactions, v can be modified by the selected rule applied to the state. In other words, v could be used to evaluate the desirability of the present state by the condition's section of the rule.

```
urule(request_repeat,
  [
  first(is^nxtmv^act,request_repeat),
  empty(is^input),
  val(is^contact,yes)
  ],
  [
  solve(s2s(first(is^nxtmve^uttrn)),[rep(n)]),
  prolog(rmXML(first(is^nxtmv^uttrn),Utt)),
  enqueue(is^history,robot:Utt),
  prolog(utterTime(Utt,N)),
  solve(rec(val(is^grammar),T,[M|_]),[rep(y)]),
  enqueue(is^input,M)
  ]).
```

a) Standard Rejection Rule

```
urule(request_repeat,
  [
  first(is^nxtmv^act,request_repeat),
  empty(is^input),
  prolog(val(is^desirability) < THRESHOLD),
  val(is^contact,yes)
  ],
  [
  solve(s2s(first(is^nxtmve^uttrn)),[rep(n)]),
  prolog(rmXML(first(is^nxtmv^uttrn),Utt)),
  enqueue(is^history,robot:Utt),
  prolog(utterTime(Utt,N)),
  increase(is^desirability),
  solve(rec(val(is^grammar),T,[M|_]),[rep(y)]),
  enqueue(is^input,M)
  ]).
```

b) Adaptive Rejection Rule

Fig. 4. Update rules triggering a request to repeat an utterance

The following example illustrate a possible case explaining the importance of introducing this concept of desirability. When the speech recogniser keeps failing to recognise an utterance, the standard dialogue manager would react with keeping asking the user to repeat the unrecognised utterance. This repetitive behaviour is caused by the fact that, the information state would return to the same state since the same sequence of rules has been applied (that is, the rejection and the request_repeat rules showed in figures 3b and 4a respectively). However, with the introduction of a desirability measure intoduced above, it is possible to break this loop whenever it is considered necessary. Indeed, as shown in figure 4b, in the condition's section of the new rule request_repeat_desir we have added a condition on the desirability of the produced state. In the effect's section we are also controlling the desirability (in this example by incrementing the value of is^desirability). In this way, it is possible to decide when to stop asking the user to repeat the sentence (by setting THRESHOLD to the desired value). So when is^desirability ≥ THRESHOLD, then the rule in figure 4b is not longer appplicable to the state S_i and a new rule will be selected for S_i. In this way, a different strategy will be adopted for the next interactions with the user. Since rules can trigger states where it is possible to change the information state rules, the dialogue manager can dynamically control the setting of the thresholds in any IS rule fields and therefore adapt its beavhiour while the system is interacting with the user. At the moment, several tests are being developed to define the best strategy to design the optimal dialogue manager. In particular, a Wizard of Oz approach is currently being implemented to collect human performance data. The general idea is that users communicate with a human *wizard* under the illusion that they are interacting with an artifact. The aim is to investigate how humans use adaptive strategies during dialogue sessions. The collected corpus is used to shape the design of the adaptive strategies. Information state *meta*-rules are being defined to modify existing IS rules to adapt the dialogue strategy in the way described above. Moreover, the possibility of creating on real-time new rules (instead of modifying old ones) by the system itself is currently under investigation. To evaluate the system the PARADISE [17] approach will be adopted. With this method, it is possible to separates how an agent uses dialogue strategies (e.g. confirm, summarise) from what an agent achieves in terms of task requirements. Therefore, it is expected to obtain an accurate evaluation of the dialogue management startegies implemented. At the moment, corpora of data with users interacting with the system and with a Wizard of Oz are being collected.

5   Conclusions

In this work-in-progress paper some aspects regarding the use of spontaneous speech for human machine interactions have been discussed. In particular, attention has focused on introducing an adaptive paradigm for a more robust interaction between the user and the system. The paradigm proposed uses the feedback produced by the system to both drive the recognition component and to control the dialogue strategies of the system. Some initial results have been discussed and current test briefly introduced.

References

1. Larsson, S., Traum, S.: Information state and dialogue management in the TRINDI dialogue move engine toolkit. Natural Language Engineering 6 (2000)
2. Lauria, S.: Talking to machines: introducing robot perception to resolve speech recognition uncertainties. Circuits, Systems and Signal Processing (accepted for publication, 2007)
3. Lauria, S., Bugmann, G., Kyriacou, T., Klein, E.: Training personal robots using natural language instruction. IEEE Intelligent Systems, 38–45 (2001)
4. Lemon, A., Bracy, A., Gruenstein, Peters, S.: The witas multi-modal dialogue system 1. In: Proceedings EuroSpeech-2001, pp. 1559–1562 (2001)

5. Levin, E., Pieraccini, R., Eckert, W.: A stochastic model of human-machine interaction for learning dialog strategies. IEEE Transactions on Speech and Audio Processing. 8(1), 11–23 (2000)
6. Litman, D., Kearns, M., Singh, S., Walker, M.: Automatic optimization of dialogue management. In: Proceedings of the 18th conference on Computational linguistics, Morristown, NJ, USA, pp. 502–508. Association for Computational Linguistics (2000)
7. Litman, D., Pan, S.: Empirically evaluating an adaptable spoken dialogue system. In: UM '99. Proceedings of the seventh international conference on User modeling, Secaucus, NJ, USA, pp. 55–64. Springer, Heidelberg (1999)
8. Matsui, T., Asoh, H., et al.: Integrated natural spoken dialogue system of jijo-2 mobile robot for office services. In: Proc. of the AAAI-99, pp. 621–627 (1999)
9. (2004), www.nuance.com
10. Oates, T., Firoiu, L., Cohen, P.: Clustering time series with hidden markov models and dynamic time warping. In: Proceedings of the IJCAI-99 Workshop on Neural, Symbolic and Reinforcement Learning Methods for Sequence Learning, pp. 17–21 (1999)
11. Pulasinghe, K., Watanabe, K., Izumi, K., Kiguchi, K.: Modular fuzzy-neuro controller driven by spoken language commands. IEEE Transactions on Systems, Man and Cyber. Part B 34(1), 293–302 (2004)
12. Rabiner, J.: Fundamentals of speech recognition. Prentice-Hall, Upper Saddle River, NJ, USA (1993)
13. Schatzmann, J., Weilhammer, K., Stuttle, M., Young, S.: A survey of statistical user simulation techniques for reinforcement-learning of dialogue management strategies. Knowl. Eng. Rev. 21(2), 97–126 (2006)
14. Scheffler, K., Young, S.: Automatic learning of dialogue strategy using dialogue simulation and reinforcement learning. In: Proceedings of HLT, San Diego, USA (2002)
15. Theobalt, C., Bos, J., Chapman, T., Espinosa-Romero, A., Fraser, M., Hayes, G., Klein, E., Oka, T., Reeve, R.: Talking to godot: Dialogue with a mobile robot. In: Proceedings of IEEE/RSJ (IROS 2002) International Conference on Intelligent Robots and System, pp. 1338–1343 (2002)
16. Traum, D., Bos, J., Cooper, J., Larsson, S., Lewin, I., Matheson, C., Poesio, M.: A model of dialogue moves and information state revision. Technial Report.Deliverable D2.1. TRINDI project, Goteborg University (1999)
17. Walker, M., Litman, D., Kamm, C., Abella, A.: Paradise: a framework for evaluating spoken dialogue agents. In: Proceedings of the 8th conference on European chapter of the Association for Computational Linguistics, pp. 271–280 (1997)
18. Young, S.: Probabilistic methods in spoken dialogue systems. Philosophical Transactions of the Royal Society (Series A) 358(1769), 1389–1402 (2000)

A Neurosymbolic Hybrid Approach for Landmark Recognition and Robot Localization

Paolo Coraggio[1] and Massimo De Gregorio[2]

[1] Robot Nursery Laboratory, DSF, Università di Napoli "Federico II", Naples, Italy
pcoraggio@na.infn.it
[2] Istituto di Cibernetica "Eduardo Caianiello", CNR, Pozzuoli (NA), Italy
m.degregorio@cib.na.cnr.it

Abstract. Robot self localization is a crucial issue in autonomous robotic research. In the last years, several approaches have been proposed to solve this problem. In this paper, we describe a landmark based neurosymbolic hybrid approach to tackle the global localization problem. We use the same approach to cope with the whole problem: from landmark recognition to position estimation. The map given to the robot is interpreted by a neurosymbolic system (formed by a weightless neural network and a BDI agent) for extracting landmark information. A "virtual neural sensor" is used, during robot navigation, for detecting the landmarks in the real environment. These information (map and detected landmarks) are finally processed by a unified neurosymbolic hybrid system (NSP) for determining the robot location on the given map.

1 Introduction

The robot self localization problem is the ability, for a robot, to autonomously localize itself in its environment. This problem can be, at a first glance, divided in two main subproblems: the position tracking and the global positioning. The first one deals with the odometric errors correction during the robot navigation, while the latter is the skill, for the robot, to recognize its pose starting from an unknown position on a given map [1]. The global position problem is considered the most difficult: although it needs more computational power, it gives less accurate results in terms of robot pose estimation [2].

During the last years several solutions have been proposed. The Markov Localization (ML) approach [3] uses a first order Markov Chain–based process to carry out the robot pose estimation. Monte Carlo Localization (MCL)[4][5] can be considered the "natural" development of ML. In this case the robot pose is expressed in terms of a multimodal probability distribution so preserving more than one plausible hypothesis on robot location.

Other approaches are based on the detection and recognition of particular environmental features [6][7][8]. These so called landmark–based methods make use of some (natural or artificial) a priori known characteristics of the environment. In a landmark based approach, the robot position is generally evaluated

F. Mele et al. (Eds.): BVAI 2007, LNCS 4729, pp. 566–575, 2007.

in four different steps. A sensor system acquires environmental data; an image processing unit recognizes the landmarks; a procedure establishes the correspondence between the detected landmarks and their location on a previously given map; a routine computes the robot position and its error on the map.

In this paper an autonomous mobile robot global localization system is presented. The robot, equipped with a stylized map (see Section 3) navigates in an office–like environment. The system is able to recognize the corners between walls as distinctive landmarks. These landmarks are detected and, above all, classified by a weightless neural network (WiSARD [9]). In order to improve the vision system performances, the neural network does not processes the whole camera frames but only the portions of the most promising image (see Section 4). During its navigation, all the information gathered by the robot is processed by a neurosymbolic–based control module that infers the robot locations (see Section 5). It is worth noticing that all the steps accomplishing the robot self localization are exploited by means of neurosymbolic hybrid systems. We thus obtain a unified framework to tackle the robot global localization problem.

2   System Architecture

The robot acts in an office–like environment without steps or stairs. The presence of furniture with well defined shapes is allowed (e.g. wardrobes, cabinets, etc). In this case, a 2D map representation is suitable and sufficient to represent the environmental information the robot needs. Moreover it turns plausible to use the corners formed by walls intersection as "natural" landmarks of the environment[1]. Once a metric map is provided to the system, it is processed by an Agent WiSARD–like system [10] that extracts the main (from the localization system point of view) information. Agent WiSARD is able to detect and classify the corners on the given map and to build up a stylized map of the environment (a closed polygonal composed by the detected corners).

The navigation strategy starts with the robot wandering the room looking for the first corner to be detected. When the sonars reveal a wall (or what the system can interpret as a wall), the robot begins a clockwise coastal navigation trying to keep itself aligned with the wall.

The robot vision system has to detect the landmarks in the environment. To this aim a "virtual neural sensor" (a WiSARD–like system) processes the frames grabbed by the camera looking for corners.

When the virtual neural sensor detects a corner, it passes these information to the NSP [11] control module that determines whether the robot can be localized on the map. If these information are not sufficient to localize the robot on the map (i.e. the end computation is not reached by the NSP), the robot keeps on following the walls looking for other corners. As soon as the available information are enough to determine the robot location, the robot motors stop and the final

---

[1] For "natural" landmark we mean that an office "naturally" possesses these features and, in order to localize the robot, we do not need to artificially introduce other landmarks in the environment.

location is outputted. It is worth noticing that, as described in 5.4, the output can be formed by more than one location. In particular, in case of symmetric maps it is not possible to establish the final location in a unique manner (for instance, in Fig. 6 each corner has its symmetric correspondent).

The whole localization system (Fig. 1) can be divided in three main blocks: a map input module; a virtual neural sensor (a WiSARD–like system) capable of detecting the office landmarks; an NSP control module whose aim is to infer the robot location and to decide whether the robot must continue its navigation.

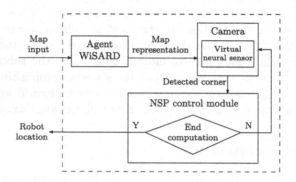

Fig. 1. Localization system architecture

3   The Agent WiSARD for Maps Interpretation

The robot is endowed with a metric map that has to be appropriately processed in order to establish a suitable relationship between the real environment and the map itself. We have adopted a modified version of the Agent WiSARD proposed in [10], for extracting the information the robot need to localize itself.

The neural network of Agent WiSARD has been trained with different instances of corners; its role is twofold: in one direction it is able to recognize the corners on the map and, reversely, it is able to produce a pictorial representation of what has been classified. In this way, the system is able to build up a stylized map from the metric one given as input. We notice that the same stylized map is used by the system to show the place where the robot localize itself.

Agent WiSARD labels all the corners that have been recognized and considered belonging to a plausible closed polygonal. We thus obtain a final system that, processing the initial image (left side of Fig. 2), recognizes a closed polygonal (right side of Fig. 2) and produces the following information:

- the list $C = [c_1, \ldots, c_l]$ of corners detected on the 2D map;
- the list $C^O = [c_1, \ldots, c_m]$ of outward corners;
- the list $C^I = [c_1, \ldots, c_n]$ of inward corners ($l = m + n$);
- the number H of possible ambiguities ($H = 1$ for non symmetric maps).

From these information, a devoted NSP is automatically generated and ready to be used in the control module.

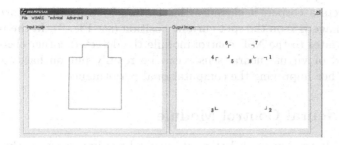

Fig. 2. Agent WiSARD map reconstruction

4 The Virtual Neural Sensor

In most robotic application the vision system plays a fundamental role in sensory data acquisition and usually it is the slowest and most computationally heavy module of the whole system. It comes as a consequence that having a fast processing vision system could be a crucial point for a generic robotic system. In order to reduce the elaboration time, it is sometime convenient not to process the whole image. In this case, the vision system is designed and implemented taking into account the particular environment in which the robot acts and its main goal (self localization).

The robot camera tilt inclination has been fixed to -15 degrees; this means that the landmarks to be detected are going to be only in the lowest part of the image (see Fig. 3). Moreover, the virtual neural sensor takes advantage of a squared spot (a sort of "attention window") that scans just that part of the image trying to detect and classify the landmarks.

The squared spot content is processed by the virtual neural sensor only if it contains a certain amount of black pixels. So doing, we obtain a vision system capable of quickly detect the landmarks. More precisely, it is a modified version of the one used in a previously designed hybrid neurosymbolic system [12].

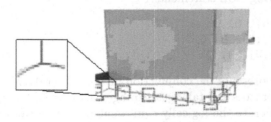

Fig. 3. Landmarks detection

The adopted WiSARD processes black and white images so that a frame preprocessing phase is necessary to first transform the RGB 24-bit image into a b/w binary image. The spot actively looks for landmarks and each time the virtual sensor detects a corner, it classifies this feature by putting the corresponding "mental" image [13] on the spot current position (see Fig. 3). In the meanwhile, it communicates to the NSP control module the detected corner class.

This kind of virtual neural sensor can be readily put on hardware (i.e. on RAMs) further improving the computational performances.

5   The Neural Control Module

In order to determine the robot position, we have implemented the self localization strategy on an NSP by means of the language NSL [14]. This language allows one to write logical programs [15] and to execute them in parallel on a devoted hardware (i.e. FPGA [16]).

Each time the virtual sensor detects a landmark, the NSP runs in order to determine, whether possible, the robot location on the map. In such a case, the NSP communicates that the position has been determined. The whole process stops and the system shows the robot position on the virtual map (in case of symmetric map, it outputs all the plausible positions).

Before going into details of the NSP architecture, we would like to remind the reader about some NSL definitions. As reported in [14], some operators have been defined to automatically generate the logically equivalent NSP. In this paper, we refer only to the following operators: $IMPLY$, $ATLEAST$ and $ATMOST$.

Let P be a set of literals, statements as:[2]

- "q is true if $P_\wedge$ is true";
- "q is true if at least h literals belonging to P are true";
- "q is true if at most h literals belonging to P are true";

are denoted respectively by the following NSL operators:

- $IMPLY(P_\wedge, q)$
- $ATLEAST(P_{\wedge\vee}, h, q)$
- $ATMOST(P_{\wedge\vee}, h, q)$

and by the following NSL statements:

- IMPLY(P[1..N], Q)
- ATLEAST(P[1..N], H, Q)
- ATMOST(P[1..N], H, Q)

where P[1..N] represents the conjunction of the n literals in P.

With these operators and taking advantages of other NSL constructs[3], we can automatically generate the logically equivalent neural networks. As reported in Section 3, NSP receive C, C^O, C^I, H and l as input from Agent WiSARD. From these information, the corresponding NSP is generated and made ready to receive, step by step, the corners detected by the virtual neural sensor.

---

[2] We denote the conjunction and the disjunction of P elements as $P_\wedge$ and with $P_\vee$ respectively ($P_{\wedge\vee}$ will denote either $P_\wedge$ or $P_\vee$).

[3] Further NSL constructs are: FOR, IF THEN ELSE, WHILE DO and REPEAT UNTIL.

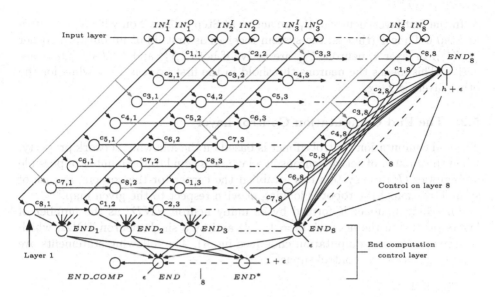

Fig. 4. Input layer, control on layer 8, end computation control layer, and the other l layers

5.1   The Input Layer

The input layer is formed by $2l$ neurons representing the possible inputs the system can receive during robot navigation. Since the system cannot decide in advance what kind of corner is going to be detected at step j, both corners (I, O) are represented for each step (IN_j^I, IN_j^O). In order to trace the overall reasoning carried out by the NSP, the input neurons fire on themselves an excitatory impulse (see Fig. 4). The following code generates the network input layer:

```
FOR J=1 TO L
    IMPLY(INOJ, INOJ)
    IMPLY(INIJ, INIJ).
```

Other l layers have to be generated in order to deal with the corners detected during the exploration. The layer 1 (Step 0) is generated by the following code:

```
FOR J=1 TO M   IMPLY(INO1, CO[J]1)
FOR J=1 TO N   IMPLY(INI1, CI[J]1)
```

and represents the set of all possible first detected corners; while, the other $l-1$ layers are generated by:[4]

```
FOR K=2 TO L
    FOR J=2 TO M   IMPLY((INOK, PREV(CO[J])K-1), CO[J]K)
    FOR J=2 TO N   IMPLY((INIK, PREV(CI[J])K-1), CI[J]K).
```

---

[4] $PREV$ operator is defined as: $PREV(c_i) = c_{i-1}$ for $i = 2 \ldots l$ and $PREV(c_1) = c_l$.

In the first layer, neurons $c^O_{j,1}$ are active at Step 0 Time 2 only if IN^O_1 is active at Step 0 Time 1 (that is, the system receives as first input an outward corner (IN^O_1)). In layer k, neurons $c^O_{j,k}$ are active if both IN^O_k and $PREV(c^O_j)_{k-1}$ are active. This means the neurons threshold in the first layer is $1 - \epsilon$ while for the other layers is $2 - \epsilon$.

5.2   The End Computation Control Layer

The end computation control subnet is based on the following network property: when the number of active neurons in a layer k is equal to the number of possible ambiguities (H) the system can establish the corner (or the corners, in case of symmetric maps) the robot is looking at with respect to the given map.

The control subnet is formed by as many neuron END_j as the number of layers present in the network $(j = 1 \ldots l)$ and by a single neuron END, which is active when the computation ends (see fig. 4). The following statements are used to generate the control subnet:

```
FOR K=1 to L
    ATMOST(C[1..L]K, H, ENDK)
ATMOST(END1..K, 1, END)
IMPLY(END, END_COMP).
```

The neuron END is active when no more than 1 neuron END_k is active, while neuron END_k is active when no more than H neurons of layer k are actives (IMPLY(END, END_COMP) sentence is just used to synchronize the outputs). Part of the control subnet is sketched in fig. 4.

5.3   The Output Layer

In order to show the results of the network computation, an output subnet is generated by the following code:

```
FOR K=1 TO L
    FOR J=1 TO L  IMPLY((ENDK,C[J]K), COUT[J]K)
FOR J=1 TO L  ATLEAST(COUT[J]1..K, 1, COUT[J]).
```

The neuron $cout_{j,k}$ is active if the neurons END_k (that is, the computation is ended in layer k) and $c_{j,k}$ (that is, the neuron associated to corner label c_j is active in layer k) are both actives. Furthermore, the neuron $cout_j$ is active if at least one of the corresponding $cout_{j,k}$ is active. To sum up, the output layer is formed by the neuron END_COMP and by the set of neurons $cout_{1,\ldots,l}$. Part of the output subnet is reported in fig. 5; in particular, it is reported only the part establishing whether the robot has stopped in front of corner c_7.

5.4   On a Simmetric Map

Suppose robot R placed in an environment like the one represented in Fig. 6. From its starting position, the robot begins to navigate in a wandering way (dash

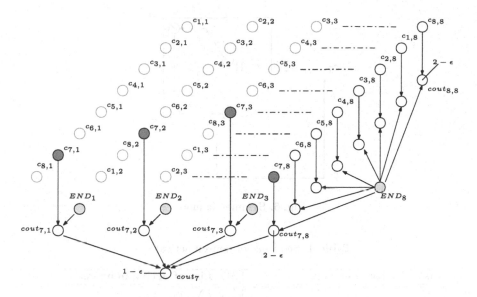

Fig. 5. c_7 output subnet

dotted line) just looking for a wall (or furniture if any). When the sonars reveal a wall, the robot turns on the right, gets aligned to the wall, and keeps following the wall (dashed line). During its navigation, c_1 is the first corner the virtual neural sensor detects (Step 0). Since c_1 is an outward corner, the virtual neural sensor activates neuron IN_1^O as first input for the NSP. (We remind the reader that the virtual sensor classifies the corner the robot is looking at but cannot establish its position.)

In table 1, the list of active neurons are reported with respect to the detected corner (Step) and to the time of activation (Time). One can notice that in Step 0 at Time 3 a neuron End^* is active (i.e. End_1^*). This means that the system cannot establish the robot position and the robot has to keep on navigating.

In Step 1 another outward corner is detected and neuron IN_2^O is activated (the neurons actives at Time 3 of Step 0 are still actives).

At Step 2 the robot reaches the corner c_3, and at Time 3, for the first time, a neuron END_j (in particular, END_3 and END_7) is activated instead of an END_j^* neuron. This means that in layer 3, the number of active neurons is equal to H ($H = 2$ and the active neurons in layer 3 are $c_{3,3}$ and $c_{7,3}$).

Neuron END is activated at Time 4 while the network outputs ($cout_3$ and $cout_7$) will be ready at Time 5. In order to have the neurons of the output layer actives at the same time, the neuron END_COMP has been added. In this way, at Step 2 and Time 5 the network ends its computation and determines where the robot is located ("$cout_3$, $cout_7$" stands for "the robot could be in c_3 or c_7").

Due to the localist representation nature of this network, we can even trace back all the corners the robot encountered during its navigation. In fact, one can notice that the active neurons $c_{3,3}$ and $c_{7,3}$ belong to the "rows" of neurons

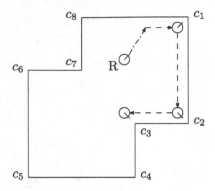

Fig. 6. Symmetric map

Table 1. Sequence of neuron activations

S	T	List of active neurons	S	T	List of active neurons
0	1	IN_1^O	2	2	IN_3^I, $c_{3,3}$, $c_{7,3}$
	2	IN_1^O, $c_{1,1}$, $c_{2,1}$, $c_{4,1}$, $c_{5,1}$, $c_{8,1}$		3	IN_1^O, $c_{1,1}$, $c_{2,1}$, $c_{4,1}$, $c_{5,1}$, $c_{8,1}$, END_1^*
	3	IN_1^O, $c_{1,1}$, $c_{2,1}$, $c_{4,1}$, $c_{5,1}$, $c_{8,1}$, END_1^*			IN_2^O, $c_{1,2}$, $c_{2,2}$, $c_{5,2}$, $c_{6,2}$, END_2^*
1	1	IN_1^O, $c_{1,1}$, $c_{2,1}$, $c_{4,1}$, $c_{5,1}$, $c_{8,1}$, END_1^*			IN_3^I, $c_{3,3}$, $c_{7,3}$, END_3, END_7
		IN_2^O		4	IN_1^O, $c_{1,1}$, $c_{2,1}$, $c_{4,1}$, $c_{5,1}$, $c_{8,1}$, END_1^*
	2	IN_1^O, $c_{1,1}$, $c_{2,1}$, $c_{4,1}$, $c_{5,1}$, $c_{8,1}$, END_1^*			IN_2^O, $c_{1,2}$, $c_{2,2}$, $c_{5,2}$, $c_{6,2}$, END_2^*
		IN_2^O, $c_{1,2}$, $c_{2,2}$, $c_{5,2}$, $c_{6,2}$			IN_3^I, $c_{3,3}$, $c_{7,3}$, END_3, END_7
	3	IN_1^O, $c_{1,1}$, $c_{2,1}$, $c_{4,1}$, $c_{5,1}$, $c_{8,1}$, END_1^*			$cout_{3,3}$, $cout_{7,3}$, END
		IN_2^O, $c_{1,2}$, $c_{2,2}$, $c_{5,2}$, $c_{6,2}$, END_2^*		5	IN_1^O, $c_{1,1}$, $c_{2,1}$, $c_{4,1}$, $c_{5,1}$, $c_{8,1}$, END_1^*
2	1	IN_1^O, $c_{1,1}$, $c_{2,1}$, $c_{4,1}$, $c_{5,1}$, $c_{8,1}$, END_1^*			IN_2^O, $c_{1,2}$, $c_{2,2}$, $c_{5,2}$, $c_{6,2}$, END_2^*
		IN_2^O, $c_{1,2}$, $c_{2,2}$, $c_{5,2}$, $c_{6,2}$, END_2^*			IN_3^I, $c_{3,3}$, $c_{7,3}$, END_3, END_7
		IN_3^I			$cout_{3,3}$, $cout_{7,3}$, END
	2	IN_1^O, $c_{1,1}$, $c_{2,1}$, $c_{4,1}$, $c_{5,1}$, $c_{8,1}$, END_1^*			END_COMP, $cout_3$, $cout_7$
		IN_2^O, $c_{1,2}$, $c_{2,2}$, $c_{5,2}$, $c_{6,2}$, END_2^*			

formed respectively by $(c_{1,1}, c_{2,2}, c_{3,3})$ and $(c_{5,1}, c_{6,2}, c_{7,3})$. These "rows" represent the two possible paths followed by the robot during its navigation.

6   Conclusions

In this paper we have presented a neurosymbolic hybrid based approach for solving the robot global localization problem. With this approach we have reduced the computational time both for the robot visual system and for robot decision system. The use of a virtual neural sensor for analyzing part of the input image, gave the first contribution in speeding up the visual processes. Furthermore, the NSP module, devoted to the location estimation, has the advantage of being a parallel processor of rule–based system. Eventually, these two module can be both implemented on hardware. Thanks to the modularity of the neurosymbolic hybrid approach here proposed, we can easily modify the whole system to improve its performances: the virtual neural sensor can be trained with other features in order to detect more landmarks; while the NSP control can be enriched with other rules to obtain a more flexible robot decision system.

References

1. Borenstein, J., Everett, H.R., Feng, L.: Navigating Mobile Robots: Systems and Techniques. A.K. Peters, Ltd., Natick, MA, USA (1996)
2. Thrun, S., Burgard, W., Fox, D.: Probabilistic Robotics (Intelligent Robotics and Autonomous Agents). The MIT Press, Cambridge (2005)
3. Simmons, R., Koenig, S.: Probabilistic robot navigation in partially observable environments. In: Proc. of the IJCAI, pp. 1080–1087 (1995)
4. Fox, D., Thrun, S., Burgard, W., Dellaert, F.: Particle filters for mobile robot localization (2001)
5. Jensfelt, P., Wijk, O., Austin, D., Andersson, M.: Experiments on augmenting condensation for mobile robot localization. In: IEEE ICRA, pp. 2518–2524. IEEE Computer Society Press, Los Alamitos (2000)
6. Motomura, A., Matsuoka, T., Hasegawa, T.: Self-localization method using two landmarks and dead reckoning for autonomous mobile soccer robots. In: Polani, D., Browning, B., Bonarini, A., Yoshida, K. (eds.) RoboCup 2003. LNCS (LNAI), vol. 3020, pp. 526–533. Springer, Heidelberg (2004)
7. Sim, R., Dudek, G.: Learning and evaluating visual features for pose estimation. ICCV (2), 1217–1222 (1999)
8. Se, S., Lowe, D., Little, J.: Local and global localization for mobile robots using visual landmarks. In: Proc. of the IEEE/RSJ IROS, Hawaii, pp. 414–420 (2001)
9. Aleksander, I., Thomas, W., Bowden, P.: WISARD, a radical new step forward in image recognition. Sensor Rev. 4, 120–124 (1984)
10. Burattini, E., Coraggio, P., De Gregorio, M.: Agent WiSARD: A hybrid system for reconstructing and understanding two-dimensional geometrical figures. In: Abraham, A., Köppen, M., Franke, K. (eds.) HIS. Frontiers in Artificial Intelligence and Applications, vol. 105, pp. 887–896. IOS Press, Amsterdam (2003)
11. Burattini, E., De Gregorio, M., Ferreira, V.M.G., França, F.M.G.: NSP: A neurosymbolic processor. In: Mira, J.M., Álvarez, J.R. (eds.) IWANN 2003. LNCS, vol. 2687, pp. 9–16. Springer, Heidelberg (2003)
12. Burattini, E., Coraggio, P., De Gregorio, M., Staffa, M.: Agent WiSARD in a 3D world. In: Mira, J.M., Álvarez, J.R. (eds.) IWINAC 2005. LNCS, vol. 3562, pp. 272–280. Springer, Heidelberg (2005)
13. Burattini, E., De Gregorio, M., Tamburrini, G.: Generation and classification of recall images by neurosymbolic computation. In: ECCM98. Second European Conference on Cognitive Modelling, pp. 127–134 (1998)
14. Burattini, E., de Francesco, A., De Gregorio, M.: NSL: A neuro-symbolic language for a neuro-symbolic processor (NSP). Int. J. Neural Syst. 13, 93–101 (2003)
15. Burattini, E., Datteri, E., Tamburrini, G.: Neuro-symbolic programs for robots. In: Proc. of the IJCAI05. Workshop on Neural-Symbolic Learning and Reasoning, Edimburgh, Scotland, pp. 7–14 (2005)
16. Burattini, E., De Gregorio, M., Tamburrini, G.: Neurosymbolic processing: Nonmonotonic operators and their FPGA implementation. In: Fourth Brazilian Symposium on Neural Networks, Rio de Janeiro, Brasil, pp. 93–101 (2000)

A Robotic Architecture with Innate Releasing Mechanism

Ernesto Burattini and Silvia Rossi

Dipartimento di Scienze Fisiche
Università degli Studi di Napoli "Federico II" – Napoli, Italy
ernb@na.infn.it, silrossi@unina.it

Abstract. In this paper we analyze the influence of the frequency of sensor data readings on the behaviours of a Robotic System (RS). This is done in the framework of behaviour based architectures drawing inspiration from biological and ethological evidences. In the first part of this paper we recall some notions on biological clocks, showing how to represent those clocks in terms of Schema Theory. Then, we propose an architecture in which the frequency of access to the sensory system is modified in accordance with environmental changes. We evaluate the results obtained in experiments with simple behaviour based systems in unknown environments with obstacles. In the last part of the paper, we briefly discuss the possibility of extending the proposed model to more complex robotic systems and to teams of robots.

1 Introduction

The presence of oscillatory mechanisms in living organisms is well known since the 18th century. In 1751, Carolus Linnaeus, Swedish botanist/naturalist, designed a flower garden clock, a botanical clock, using certain diurnal species of flowering plants. But it is only starting from the seminal work of Aschoff [1], in the 1960s that biologists have identified a series of biological rhythms, connected to each other, and triggered both by exogenous and endogenous factors. Nowadays, biologists still try to understand the origin of such mechanisms [2] and they have been turning their focus to genetic aspects [3].

The robotic community has always paid attention to living systems, as sources of inspiration for the design of their artefacts. On the one hand, with reactive architectures [4], and with behaviour based architectures in particular [5], roboticists tried to remove the complex problem of symbolic knowledge representation, which is computationally expensive, inspiring themselves directly to biological systems. On the other hand, other representations of the perception-action cycle, such as Schema Theory (ST) [6], tried to offer formal instruments for studying behaviour based systems. The ST, in particular, introducing the schema concept, already used in psychology [7], ethology, and early cognitive science [8], proposes a model in which the perception and action aspects are separated, adding the presence of a releaser, well known in the ethological studies [9], that controls behaviour activations.

F. Mele et al. (Eds.): BVAI 2007, LNCS 4729, pp. 576–585, 2007.

Referring to this model, we tried to connect the concept of releaser to the concept of biological clocks with the aim of taking into account the variability of the same behaviour according to the circumstances in which it is activated. For instance, a behaviour controlling the activity of a pedestrian crossing a urban street will regulate the access to the sensor data and consequently the speed of movements as a function of the presence or absence of upcoming vehicles. Moreover, in any robotic system there is the necessity of having a synchronization process between the readings of sensor data and the actions produced by different behaviours. Releasers, organized according to a common phase, enable one to manage this synchronization. Finally, whenever there is a robot equipped with complex sensors and behaviours, which requires many computational resources, such resources must be managed in an efficient way.

2 Biological Clocks

Biological rhythms are cyclic patterns of physiological changes or changes in activity in living organisms, most often synchronized with daily, monthly, or annual cyclical changes in the environment [10]. Jürgen Aschoff [1] postulated an innate biological trigger in living systems, and introduced the notion of "Zeitgeber" referring to any external cue that may entail the internal rhythm. His experimental and theoretical work in the 1950s and 1960s laid the basis for viewing circadian rhythms as the product of endogenous oscillators which derive their functional significance from the maintenance of a constant phase relationship with the light-dark cycle. Many biological rhythms are endogenous, e.g. core body temperature, sleep-wake cycle, and locomotor activity patterns, and will be maintained even when the environmental cues are removed. However, such external cues serve to refine and adjust rhythms, which, in the absence of such cues, will gradually drift out of phase with the environment. So, Biological Clocks can be reset and adjusted backwards and forwards by what is called a Zeitgeber - an environmental or other periodic influence. By entraining or being reset by a Zeitgeber the clock ensures that the rhythms it generates are most suitable for its surroundings.

The exact nature of the internal mechanism, or "biological clock", which controls such rhythms is not clearly understood. Living alone the general questions related to the identification of external cues, the origin of such internal rhythms, and their interaction, we observe that many biological systems act upon the stimulation provided by an internal clock whose period depends on some external and internal variables. Moreover, such clocks take into account the passage of time and consequently they act as an alarm by triggering some event to occur [11]. For example, a clocks may periodically control the activity of an organism to induce the feeding stimulus. In this way, the concept of biological clocks can be interpreted as a control system - i.e., they behave activating or inhibiting behaviours (like for example feeding or sleeping) - and can be related to a process of Innate Releasing Mechanisms in robotic architectures.

Finally, we want to point out that there are some particular rhythms, for example some electrical waves in the brain [12] or the rhythm controlling the beating of the heart, whose activity may change, accordingly to some circumstances, not just with an adjustment of its phase, but also changing its period. In the case of heartbeats, for example, we have that during physical activity the period decreases (i.e., the frequency of beating increases). Changing the period of the rhythms, which control the releasing activities of behaviours in a robotic architecture, may have as results that, depending on circumstances, the robot may show an adaptive emergent behaviour. The embedding of such controlled rhythms within a Robotic System (RS) allows for the realization of flexible behaviour which can realize timed activation of the behaviour itself. Furthermore, it may modify its activity according to its internal state and sensorial information.

3   Emergent Behaviour

Let us now turn to consider how some functional roles of biological clocks can be fruitfully deployed in robotics. As reported by Benjamin, Lonsdale and Arbib [13] the current behaviour-based robot generation is, generally, arranged in order to pursue a prefixed goal. In such systems, poor cognitive assumptions about the environment are made while the focus is just on sensory information, closely following the subsumption architecture model [4], where reactive actions and the absence of explicit models are fundamental. This is enough for modeling simple behaviours also in unstructured environments. However, if it is necessary to achieve more complex behaviours then, at every time instant, we need tools to select the best action in order to pursue a fixed goal.

The behaviour of a mobile robot, when it operates in some environment, is the result of three fundamental factors [14]:

1. The program that works on the robot in order to accomplish a given task;
2. The physical structure of the robot (sensors, motors, batteries, ...);
3. The environment in which it works (how much the objects are detectable, what is the lay of the land, what is the dumping factor of the land,...).

In fact the behaviour may change if the hardware is modified, or is malfunctioning, or if the control program works badly or the task changes, or simply if there are some changes in the environment.

Actually it is almost impossible to exactly forecast the behaviour of a robot since there is no available model that takes into account all relevant variables [14]. These difficulties are found even if we consider the biological world where it is difficult to forecast the behaviour, for instance, of an animal to the sight of a predator (e.g., in what direction it will escape, how quick, and so on). *A fortiori* the evaluation of the behaviour is more difficult to perform than the forecasting and analysis of the behaviour itself.

We assumed, in accordance with ADAPT [15], the hypotheses of a cognitive architecture with a perception system depending on the environments in which the robot is immersed and on some releasing mechanisms of activation that, according to the environment and to the goals, speeds up or slows down gradually the reading frequency of the sensors. In other words, we want to consider another element, already present in biological living systems: biological clocks. We surmise, therefore, that the explicit introduction of a control system of this sort can lead to adaptive performance of a RS. If the intelligence in robotic behaviour-based architectures appears only in the interaction with the environment, what it would seem to be of great importance is that the behaviours themselves, in some way, have to be affected by such interactions. Other sub-symbolic approaches, for instance neural nets [16,17], allow the data coming from the outside, once converted in output signals, to become a feedback for the system itself. In our model feedback is included in the fluctuation of the period of releaser activation, according to the environment and to the behaviour of the robot itself.

Moreover, it is well-known that synchronization between sensors readings and performed actions is fundamental for accomplishing a task. As an example, in a hybrid system in which perceptual information can modify the planning of actions, sensors readings must occur with a frequency that does not excessively slow down the RS, since more readings one makes more accesses to the deliberative system are performed. At the same time, however, one must keep in mind that the RS takes risks if one allows sensor readings with long time intervals. In fact, in between two consecutive sensors readings, the environment may have changed and, therefore, the RS may no longer behave appropriately. We argue that the period, between two consecutive readings of the values supplied by the sensory system, can be modified according to the trend of the displayed values. In particular, there is the need of managing the monitoring of the environment by sensors, in such way that the answer of the robot could be related to the rate of environmental changing. Finally, when a single robot is equipped with complex behaviours and sensors requiring a lot of computational resources (for instance a robot provided with a video-camera for image recognition processes) there is the need of managing resources for sensing and processing behaviours in an efficient way according to the circumstances.

Let us suppose that a RS, designed for navigation in open environments, works in a flat environment with few obstacles. Then we may suppose that it is sufficient to perform sensor readings separated by long intervals, since it is unlikely that troublesome situations will arise along the path. However, if the environment is not flat, or there are many obstacles, the time interval between two consecutive readings may be shortened. A RS could be immersed in an environment in which plains and hills, obstacles and empty spaces are alternated, and therefore it is convenient to assume a different reading interval according to the circumstances.

Our working hypothesis is that the RS has a general clock with period (p_b) that operates with a baseline period playing as a benchmark for other clocks whose period is a multiple or submultiple of the basic period. Such general clock must not to be confused with the machine clock, whose period is supposed to be constant and which fixes the time ascissa for the RS behaviour. We may think that one of the releasers managing the various macro-behaviours is activated by an individual clock, according to the main Zeitgeber and to the sensors involved in the behaviour. We suppose to have a simple RS wandering in an unknown environment with obstacles. At the beginning, the robotic system evaluates the range finder's values which are available at every p_b interval of time. Once it finds an obstacle, the period of reading decreases, thus allowing one to apply the strategies of avoidance on more frequently updated data. After moving around the obstacle and in the absence of a new obstacle, the readings of the range finder are less frequent and the process of wandering can be fully resumed. Therefore, in an environment with many obstacles we will have a cautious wandering, since we make many readings, while in the case of few obstacles, the wandering will be faster. We will have similar patterns of behaviour if, instead of a `wander`, we have a `move_to_goal`, or a `follow_wall`, etc.

3.1   A Zeitgeber for Robotic Artefacts

In order to describe our attempt to introduce a Zeitgeber $\mathcal{ZG}$ in a robotic architecture we use a Schema Theory representation for the behaviours of the robot [6]. There is a schema for each behaviour constituted by a coordinated control program, in which there is a releasing function, a perceptual schema and a motor schema, obtained through the application of a transfer function on sensory inputs and on a releasing state (see Fig. 1). More specifically, our releasing function takes in input sensor data and actuator commands (e.g. as feedback) and returns a releasing state for the behaviour.

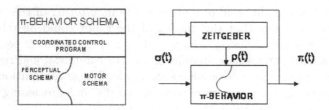

Fig. 1. Schemas for a Zeitgeber-Controlled Behaviour or π-Behaviour

Let us assume that:

- the RS has a baseline period (p_b);
- $\sigma(t)$ is a function that represents data coming from sensors at each time interval p_σ, which is set according to the machine clock;
- $\rho(t)$ is a function that, with periodicity p_β, is equal to 1 (0 otherwise), and notifies the robot when the perceptual schema has to process and send inputs to the motor schema.

We will have that: $p_\sigma \leq p_\beta(t) \leq p_b$.

Suppose that a SR has a behaviour with a sensor input $\sigma(t)$, a function $\rho(t)$ as releaser, and a function $\pi(t)$ as motor percept. $1[x]$ is the Heaviside function (it is equal to 1 for $x > 0$, 0 otherwise). The function $\rho(t)$ is equal to: $\rho(t) =$

$1[cos(p_\beta * t) - \epsilon]$ (for each arbitrarily small $\epsilon > 0$), which implies that the releaser is on ($\rho(t) = 1$) when the value of the periodic function $cos(p_\beta * t)$ is equal to 1. The function $\sigma'(t)$ is equal to: $\sigma'(t) = 1[\sigma(t) - \gamma]$ (γ = sensor's error) which implies that we have to analyze incoming sensor values only if they are greater than the error threshold γ.

We define as motor percept the function:

$$\pi(t) = \varphi(\sigma(t) * \sigma'(t) * \rho(t) + (1 - \rho(t)) * \sigma(t - 1) * \sigma'(t - 1))$$

where the function $\pi(t)$ represents the percept sent to the motors, and evaluated using the function $\varphi(t)$. Such function with a releaser $\rho(t)$, takes the input signal, evaluates the input using the function φ and then returns the output value, keeping it constant until the next clock (see Fig. 1). $\sigma(t)$ is a function that depends upon the surrounding environment of the RS (see Fig. 2). In the case of range finders, used as sensor inputs for the AVOID behaviour, if we have an increasing function[1], we have to reduce the period $p_\beta(t)$ and we have to increase it in case of decreasing signal. Accordingly, we assume that $p_\beta(t)$ depends on the output value of $\pi(t)$ as follows. Let $d_p(t) = 1[\pi(t) - \pi(t - 1)]$ be a function whose value is equal to 1 only if we have an increasing $\pi(t)$, we have:

$$p_\beta(t) = \begin{cases} \rho(t) * p_\beta(t-1) * (d_p(t)/k + (1 - d_p(t)) * k') + (1 - \rho(t)) * p_\beta(t-1) & \text{if } < p_b \\ p_\sigma & \text{if } < p_\sigma \\ p_b & \text{otherwise} \end{cases}$$

where k e k' are two multiplication factors for the period p_β .

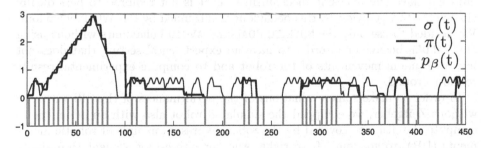

Fig. 2. Example of a motor percept $\pi(t)$ with an input signal $\sigma(t)$ and a period $p_\beta(t)$

In Fig. 2 we show a plot of $\pi(t)$. We observe that starting from a baseline period p_b, the period $p_\beta(t)$, whenever the releasing system is active, decreases if we have an increasing input $\sigma(t)$. In this way we have more frequent readings of sensor data, and therefore a more frequent modification of the motor percept until the upper bound, set by the period p_σ, is reached. As soon the input signal decreases then the period slowly decreases to the baseline value p_b.

---

[1] In order to have a more intuitive representation of the input function in our system the range finder data increases while approaching an obstacle.

3.2 A Simple Case Study

Our long term goal is the evaluation of a robotic architecture that is based on the concept of adaptive biological clocks. In particular we want to understand how this kind of approach can be useful for robots within a dynamic environment. What we attempt to do, as a main step toward our goal, is to evaluate how the introduction of variable clocks, coded in our architecture as adaptive releasers, can influence the behaviour of an individual robot that is equipped with sensors, even when particular computational abilities are not required. A positive result, albeit on a simple experiment, is a significant demonstration encouraging one to pursue this approach on more complex systems. What we expect, as result of our experiment, is that in simple environments the global behaviour of the robot, equipped with adaptive releasers, is comparable with the global behaviour of a robot without releasers showing better performances in terms of less elaboration of sensor data.

In order to test our working hypotheses we simulated a PIONEER 3DX robot, using Pyro [18], equipped with 8 sonars, whose task is the cross-walking of an environment with obstacles. Fig. 3 shows our subsumption architecture of a simple RS that has the task of traveling through an environment from a vertex to the opposite one, while avoiding obstacles. The sensory system is made by sonars, that provide the $\sigma(t)$ percept. The output percept $\pi(t)$ is obtained taking into account a Zeitgeber $\mathcal{Z}_{AV}(\sigma(t), p_b)$, that is, a function of the sensory input. The simulated environments have an attractor in the top–right angle, and the RS has the task of reaching that position. In this case, the MOVE_TO_GOAL behaviour does not have any releasing mechanism - i.e. it is not required to periodically change the task. Obviously, this behaviour is subsumed by the AVOID behaviour. We decided to use only the MOVE_TO_GOAL and AVOID behaviours without using any WANDER behaviour in order to have an experimental setting that does not involve random movements of the robot and to compare experimental results round to round.

In order to make some evaluations of the performances of this RS with and without Zeitgeber, we equipped the simulated robot also with an odometer to compute the distance covered by the robot, expressed as unit of robotic movements (UR), to go from left to right. Another interesting element to evaluate the performances is the number of accesses to the sensors, and consequently the number of percepts sent to the motors. It is obvious that the greater is the number of accesses to the sensors, the greater are the resources required by the robot for computing the output, and the greater will be the number of commands sent to the motors. Thus a longer time will be required to complete the task, while, with a high probability, many sensory readings, which inherently suffer of errors, may induce longer paths. We believe that it is interesting to report also the number of activations of AVOID behaviour, because this is an indicator of how the robot keeps close to the obstacles with the two methods.

In Tab. 1 the average values of 30 experiments on 3 different environments are reported, comparing the results obtained with ($p_b = p_\sigma = 1$) and with two general clocks having different values of p_b ($p_b = 4$ and $p_b = 8$). First of all let

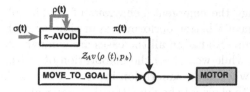

Fig. 3. A subsumption architecture for our experimentation

us highlight that in the case of $p_b = p_\sigma \neq 1$ – i.e. the period of the releasing function does not change and it is greater than the machine clock – we have that the robot may get stuck due to oscillatory mechanisms (the AVOID behaviour sets a direction, the next step the MOVE_TO_GOAL sets the opposite direction, and so on). Second, while approaching an obstacle, the robot must give the control of the global behaviour just to the AVOID behaviour, in order to safely move around the obstacle and so it is not possible to have a fixed releasing period for such single behaviour. In Table 1, for each of the three scenarios and for each of the three settings, we reported the average value for the number of times the releaser was activated ($\sharp\rho_{avr}$), the average number of time steps (t_{avr}), the time steps required to complete the task without having any obstacles on the path (t_{min}), the average value of the distance covered by the robot (d_{avr}), the minimum distance from the starting point to the target without obstacles (d_{min}), and the average number of times the AVOID behaviour was activated ($\sharp avoid_{avr}$).

As a result of our experimentation we notice that in presence of a Zeitgeber the global performance improves, in the sense that even though distances covered by the RS are comparable (we surmise that this happens because of the small distances that divide starting and arrival points) the number of accesses to sensor data, in general, is halved or it is reduced according to the selected p_b. Moreover, the results show that the introduction of an adaptive releasing system does not

Table 1. Results of the experiments

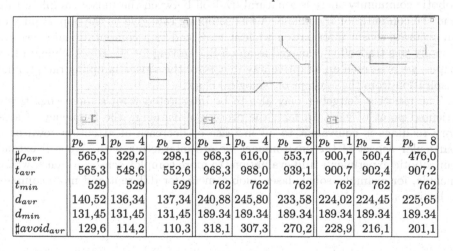

	$p_b = 1$	$p_b = 4$	$p_b = 8$	$p_b = 1$	$p_b = 4$	$p_b = 8$	$p_b = 1$	$p_b = 4$	$p_b = 8$
$\sharp\rho_{avr}$	565,3	329,2	298,1	968,3	616,0	553,7	900,7	560,4	476,0
t_{avr}	565,3	548,6	552,6	968,3	988,0	939,1	900,7	902,4	907,2
t_{min}	529	529	529	762	762	762	762	762	762
d_{avr}	140,52	136,34	137,34	240,88	245,80	233,58	224,02	224,45	225,65
d_{min}	131,45	131,45	131,45	189.34	189.34	189.34	189.34	189.34	189.34
$\sharp avoid_{avr}$	129,6	114,2	110,3	318,1	307,3	270,2	228,9	216,1	201,1

substantially change the emergent behaviour of simple robots. In conclusion, while we do not have a better performance in time or path it is important to notice that the results we had in all the cases are comparable. The fundamental point here is that, while we halved the elaboration of the sensor data (this can be a bigger result when such elaboration involves a heavy computational load), our system is able to show a behaviour that is comparable to a pure behaviour-based subsumption architecture. So, from one hand we have two architectures that show similar emergent behaviour, in terms of safety also, on the other hand we are able to save computational resources. Finally, we expect that in the case of a real prototype a small number of sensor readings will induce a smaller overall error coming from the sensors and so a bigger improvement of the global performances of the robot may be achieved.

4   Conclusions and Future Work

One of the main motivations for our research activity is, from the point of view of the individual robot, to have the capability of adapting to the frequency of change of a dynamic environment - e.g. to be able to change the velocity of reaction to the external stimuli in a coherent way to the changes occurring in the external environment. The search for an adaptive behaviour for a dynamic environment comes also from the necessity of having coordination and synchronization processes between groups of robots. Moreover, even a simple block environment becomes a dynamic one, when we are in the presence of other robots. The achievement of adaptive processes for coordination and synchronization between groups of robots is one of the main issues in multi-robot research. Moreover, in this kind of approach one can deal with problems of synchronization of behaviours in a natural way, and one can include the fundamental concept of feedback within the robotic architecture. In conclusion, the use of a variable Innate Releasing Mechanism (IRM) for the access to the sensor system gives rise to better performances of the RS in terms of access to the sensor data. In the robotic community there is a natural tradeoff between the sensor sampling rate and the computational demand. A fast sampling rate give us the opportunity of an accurate sensor information while it may lead to a computational overload. Usually this tradeoff is managed as an off-line setting for the robot while, in this paper, we presented an adaptive way to control the sensor sampling rate, taking inspiration from the concept of biological clock.

The use of a Zeitgeber may also to be interpreted from a more cognitively oriented point of view. In fact, the process of changing the frequency of sensory readings is equivalent to an increase or decrease of attention towards a particular aspect of the environment we are interacting with. We will extend our robotic experiments and evaluations to more complex sensor systems, which include, for example, sonar, laser, blob camera, for different and more complex behaviours.

References

1. Aschoff, J.: Circadian Clocks. North Holland Press, Amsterdam (1965)
2. Ishida, N., Kaneko, M., Allada, R.: Biological clocks. In: First Japanese American Foundation of Science Symposium, Irvine, CA (August 1998)
3. Hastings, M.: The brain, circadian rhythms, and clock genes. BMJ 317, 1704–1707 (1998)
4. Brooks, R.S.: A robust layered control system for a mobile robot. In: Readings in uncertain reasoning, pp. 204–213. Morgan Kaufmann Publishers Inc., San Francisco, CA, USA (1990)
5. Arkin, R.C.: Behaviour Based Robotics. MIT Press, Cambridge, Massachusetts (1991)
6. Arbib, M.A.: Schema theory. In: The handbook of brain theory and neural networks, pp. 830–834. MIT Press, Cambridge, MA, USA (1998)
7. Piaget, J.: Biology and knowledge. University of Chicago Press, Chicago (1971)
8. Craik, K.: The Nature of Explanation. Cambridge University Press, Cambridge (1943)
9. Tinbergen, N.: The study of instinct. Oxford University press, Oxford (1951)
10. Koukkari, W.L., Sothern, R.B.: Introducing Biological Rhythms. Springer, Heidelberg (2006)
11. Mirolli, M., Parisi, D.: Artificial organisms that sleep. In: Banzhaf, W., Ziegler, J., Christaller, T., Dittrich, P., Kim, J.T. (eds.) ECAL 2003. LNCS (LNAI), vol. 2801, pp. 377–386. Springer, Heidelberg (2003)
12. Biological Rhythm. In: Columbia Electronic Encyclopedia (2007)
13. Benjamin, D.P., Lonsdale, D., Lyons, D.: Integrating perception, language and problem solving in a cognitive agent for a mobile robot. In: Proceedings of the Third International Joint Conference on Autonomous Agents and Multiagent Systems, pp. 1310–1311. IEEE Computer Society, Washington, DC, USA (2004)
14. Nehmzow, U.: Scientific Methods in Mobile Robotics - Quantitative Analysis of Agent Behaviour. Springer, Heidelberg (2006)
15. Benjamin, D.P., Lyons, D., Lonsdale, D.: Adapt: A cognitive architecture for robotics. In: International Conference on Cognitive Modeling, Pittsburgh, PA (July 2004)
16. Carpenter, G.A., Grossberg, S.: A neural theory of circadian rhythms: Ashoff's rule in diurnal and nocturnal mammals. Am. J. Physiol. Regul. Integr. Comp. Physiol. 247, 1067–1082 (1984)
17. Burattini, E., Datteri, E., Tamburrini, G.: Neuro-symbolic programs for robots. In: The proceedings of NeSy'05 Neural-Symbolic Learning and Reasoning, Workshop at IJCAI-05, Edinburgh, Scotland (August 2005)
18. Blank, D.S., Kumar, D., Meeden, L., Yanco, H.: The pyro toolkit for ai and robotics. AI Magazine 27(1) (2006)

An Application of Vision Systems to the Path Planning of Industrial Robots

Vincenzo Niola, Cesare Rossi, and Sergio Savino

Department of Mechanical Engineering for Energetics
University of Naples "Federico II"
Napoli, Via Claudio, 21 – 80125 – Italy
cesare.rossi@unina.it

Abstract. In this paper the early results on the possibility to use a video system for the robot's trajectories planning is presented. By means of this application it is possible to plan the trajectories by a PC monitor, just clicking with the mouse on the monitor. In order to obtain a three dimensional vision a couple of cameras has been used. A software was developed that by means of each couple of frames make possible to select a desired point in the work space, obtaining three cartesian coordinates. These last are given to the control system and recorded by this last. Finally the control system will move the robot in a work cycle that is described by means of the points selected and recorded as described above. Tests have been carried on with a robot prototype that was designed and built at our Laboratory and showed a very good behaviour of the system.

1 Introduction

Industrial robots are a part of a production system and are used for a large number of application. Industrial application are referred to technological fields (assembly or dismounting, cut or stock removal; electrochemical processes; abrasive trials; cold or warm moulding; design with CAD techniques; metrology), or about several processes (control of the row material; workmanship of the component; assemblage; packing or storages; controls of quality; maintenance).

The main advantages of this technique are:

1) elimination of the human errors, particularly in the case of repetitive or monotonous operations;
2) possibility to vary the production acting on the power of the automatic system (the automatic machines can operate to high rhythms day and night every day of the year);
3) greater informative control through the acquisition of historical data; these data can be used for successive elaborations, for the analysis of the failures and to have statistics in real time;
4) quality control founded on objective parameters in order to avoid dispute, and loss of image.

F. Mele et al. (Eds.): BVAI 2007, LNCS 4729, pp. 586–594, 2007.

In any case a work cycle of a robot will be made by a number of points and sub-trajectories that can be planned in several ways.

The "Artificial Vision" permits industrial automation and system vision able to act in the production activities without humane presence and can be usefully connected with robotic systems; in fact the vision for a robot system can significantly increase the robot capability to interact with the environment and also can evaluate, analyze and manage the robot's movements.

In this paper the early results on the possibility to use a video system for the robot's trajectories planning is presented. By means of this application it is possible to plan the trajectories by a PC monitor, just clicking with the mouse on the monitor.

2 The Path Planning

A path planning algorithm, using as inputs: path definition and constraints due to the path and due to the robot's structure, will compute the trajectories in the joint space as arrays of positions and, also, velocities and accelerations of the joint themselves.

At the Robot Mechanics Laboratory of the Department of Mechanical Enginecring for Energetics, has been developed a complete procedure that permits to give to a robot arm all the parameters to describe an assigned path; this by means of a vision system. The procedure gives to the operator the possibility to fix start and end points of a working cycle, the intermediate points and the obstacles, by means of a couple of images on the monitor of a PC.

This procedure starts from a software, developed at the same Laboratory, that permits to recognize a point of three dimensional work space, starting from its two dimensional frame (image plane). This needs, obviously, at least a couple of images, taken from two different points of view (stereoscopic vision).

2.1 The Vision System

A vision system essentially consists in a frame grabber, a (television) camera and an host computer. Each point of the observed scene has a corresponding point on the image; the linkage between the "scene points" and the "image points" is a merely geometric transform, as schematically shown in figure 1.

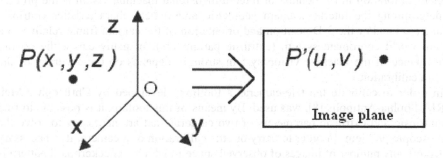

Fig. 1. Geometric transform

A (tele)camera model is necessary; this means to find the geometrical relations that describe the transform mentioned above, tacking onto account all the involved parameters. These last are intrinsic parameters (optics and camera sensors) and extrinsic parameters that essentially depend on the position of the camera reference frame respect to an external frame.

The simplest (tele)camera mathematical model is the pin-hole that is schematically reported in figure 2.

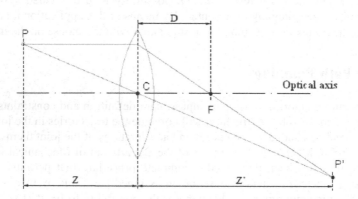

Fig. 2. Pin hole model

If the coordinates of a point P(X,Y,Z) in the scene and the focal length are known, it is possible to asses the coordinates of a point P'(u, v) that is the "image" of P on the image plane. Obviously the opposite is not possible: from a point on the image plane it isn't possible to obtain its corresponding coordinates in the space. This last aspect becomes possible only if, at least, a couple of images of the same scene are available; in this case, in fact, it is possible to obtain a stereoscopic vision, that allows to reconstruct a three-dimensional object by a number n (n ≥2) of different images. In our case a couple of tele-cameras was used.

2.2 The Camera Calibration

Camera calibration in the context of three-dimensional machine vision is the process of determining the internal camera geometric and optical characteristics (intrinsic parameters) and/or the 3-D position and orientation of the camera frame relative to a certain world coordinate system (extrinsic parameters). In many cases, the overall performance of the machine vision system strongly depends on the accuracy of the camera calibration.

In order to calibrate the tele-cameras a toolbox, developed by Christopher Mei, INRIA Sophia-Antipolis [8], was used. By means of this toolbox it is possible to find the intrinsic and extrinsic parameters of two cameras that are necessary to solve the stereoscopic problem. In order to carry out the calibration of a camera, it is necessary to acquire any number of images of observed space in which a checkerboard pattern is placed with different positions and orientations [9, 10].

In each acquired image, after clicking on the four extreme corners of a checkerboard pattern rectangular area, a corner extraction engine includes an automatic mechanism for counting the number of squares in the grid. These points are used like calibration points. The dimensions dX, dY of each of squares on the checker board are always kept to their original values in millimeters, and represent the parameters that put in relation the pixel dimensions with observed space dimensions (mm).

After corner extraction, calibration is done in two steps: first initialization, and then nonlinear optimization.

The initialization step computes a closed-form solution for the calibration parameters based not including any lens distortion.

The non-linear optimization step minimizes the total reprojection error (in the least squares sense) over all the calibration parameters (9 DOF for intrinsic: focal (2), principal point (2), distortion coefficients (5), and 6*n DOF extrinsic, with n = images number).

The calibration procedure allows to find the 3-D position of the grids with respect to the camera, like shown in fig. 3.

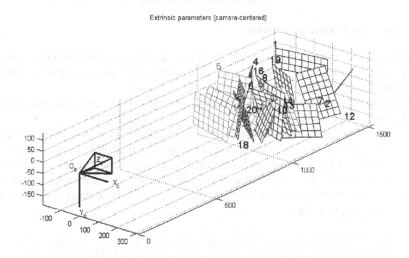

Fig. 3. Position of the grids for the calibration procedure

With two camera calibration, it is possible to carry out a stereo optimization, by means of a toolbox option, that allows to do a stereo calibration for stereoscopic problem.

The global stereo optimization is performed over a minimal set of unknown parameters, in particular, only one pose unknown (6 DOF) is considered for the location of the calibration grid for each stereo pair. This insures global rigidity of the structure going from left view to right view. In this way the uncertainties on the intrinsic parameters (especially that of the focal values) for both cameras it becomes smaller.

After this operation, the spatial configuration of the two cameras and the calibration planes may be displayed in a form of a 3D plot, like shown in fig. 4.

In figure 5 is reported the vision test rig: the two telecameras, the checkerboards and the robot.

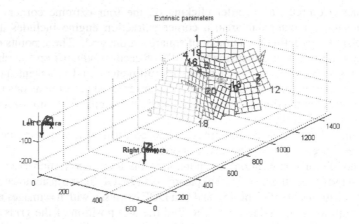

Fig. 4. Calibration planes

2.3 The Path Planning Software

A software was developed that allows to choose the end-effector trajectory points. By means of this software, it is possible to select "objective" points, for which the robot must journey, e "obstacle" points, that must be avoided.

The software recognizes the positions of such points in the work space, using a developed camera model [1,2,3].

The procedure starts from a couple of images (taken from two different cameras, fig. 5); the operator selects (with the cursor) a point on the first image of the couple and this will fix a point in a plane. Subsequently, on the second image appears a green line, that represents the straight line that links the focus of the first camera to that point. Now the operator can fix the real position (in the work space) of that point by clicking on this green line.

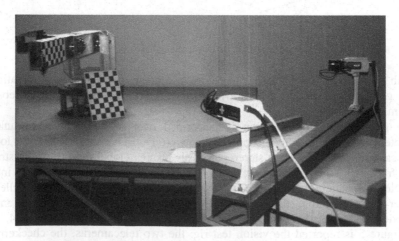

Fig. 5. The stereoscopic vision system

In figure 6 the couple of images is reported; on the left is reported the first image and on the right the second one; on the second image is also reported a white solid thick line that is the line that links the focus of the first camera to the point selected on the image on the left.

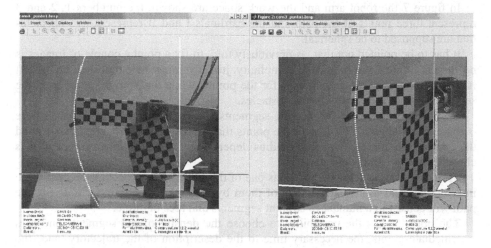

Fig. 6. Point assigning by the couple of images

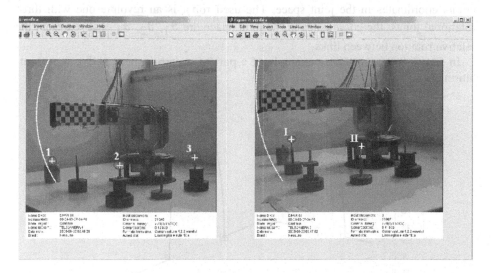

Fig. 7. Path assigning

This procedure gives the coordinates of the selected point in the frame of the working space (world frame). Once a point has been assigned in the work space, by means of inverse kinematics it is possible to compute the joint coordinates of the robot when the robot's end-effector is in that position.

Finally the procedure permits to assign a point either as belonging to the path, or as representing an obstacle; in this last case, the path will be computed in order to avoid that point.

In figure 7 the robot arm and the work space are shown; the numbers 1, 2 and 3 represent three points of the path and the cardinals I and II represent two obstacles that are supposed to be spherical.

It has to be pointed out that, as previously told, to fix a point a couple of images is needed; in figure 7, for the sake of simplicity, just two images are reposted: on the left is the first image of the couple used for the points, while on the right is reported the second image of the couple for the obstacles.

The path is made up by straight segments that link the selected points (those belonging to the path). To each of the points that represents an obstacle, is associated the center of a sphere, the sphere radius depends by obstacle dimensions and it is chosen when the procedure starts.

If one of straight segment intersects one of this sphere, the procedure records these intersections and joints each couple of them by means of an arc of a circle. So, the path will consist in a number of straight segments and arcs of circle.

The operator has the possibility to choose the density of the segments and arcs intermediate points, the necessary time to the description of the trajectory, and the obstacles dimensions. For every feature of analyzed trajectory, it is necessary to carry out cinematic inversion, by means of which it is possible to calculate the trajectory points coordinates in the joint space. The used robot is an revolute one with three rotational joints; the coordinates in the joint space are ϑ_1, ϑ_2, ϑ_3, that represent the relative rotation between links.

In figure 8 is reported an example of a part of a path in perspective represent-tation.

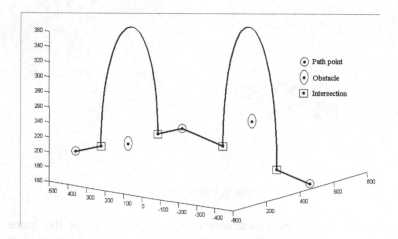

Fig. 8. Example of path in perspective wiew

In figure 9 the robot arm and an example of path are shown. In the same figure the points and the obstacles are, also, clearly visible. The points are marked with the same meanings used in the previous figure.

Fig. 9. Example of path in the work space

3 Conclusions

A technique that uses a vision system in path planning, has been proposed and tested at the Laboratory of Robot Mechanics of the D.I.M.E. This technique permits to plan the robot end-effector path starting from two images of the work space, recorded with a vision system, that is previously calibrated. The customer must only choose, with the mouse on the monitor, the points that belong to the path or represent an obstacle; and the procedure computes the robot end-effector path.

The procedure is divided in two steps: the first step supplies to find the cartesian coordinates of the points that belongs to geometric path and of those points that represent an obstacle; the second step carries out cinematic inversion to calculate the points coordinates in the joint space. Once time information are fixed, it will be also possible to calculate velocities and accelerations that each joint must have in order to describe the planned trajectory.

Future developments of studied vision-planning system, are acknowledgment of the objects in the work space, acknowledgment of surfaces and volumes, and its equations. This last aspect demands the contemporary use of more cameras, mainly in the cases of objects that have cavity. Ulterior developments will concur the improvement of obstacles acknowledgment modalities, and more "fluid" trajectory planning by means of a real-time control with vision system.

References

[1] Niola, V., Rossi, C.: A method for the trajectories recording of a robot arm: early results. In: Proc. 9th WSEAS International Conference on Computers, Athens (July 11-16, 2005)

[2] Niola, V., Rossi, C.: Video acquisition of a robot arm trajectories in the work space. WSEAS Transactions on Computers 4(7), 830–836 (2005)

[3] Niola, V., Rossi, C., Savino, S.: Modelling and Calibration of a Camera for Trajectories Recording. In: Proc. 5th WSEAS Int. Conf. on Signal Processing, Robotics and Automation, Madrid (February 15-17, 2006)

[4] Fusiello, A.: Visione Computazionale: appunti delle lezioni - Informatic Department, University of Verona (March 3, 2005)

[5] Sharma, R., Hutchinson, S.: Motion perceptibility and its application to active vision-based servo control. Technical Report UIUC-BI AI RCV-94-05, The Beckman Institute, Università dell'Illinois (1994)

[6] Sharma, R.: Active vision for visual servoing: a review. In: IEEE Workshop on Visual Servoing: Achivement, Application and Open Problems, Maggio (1994)

[7] Sharma, R., Hutchinson, S.: Optimizing hand/eye configuration for visual-servo system. In: IEEE International Confeence on Robotics and Automation, pp. 172–177 (1995)

[8] Mei, C.: Camera Calibration Toolbox for Matlab, http://www.vision.caltech.edu/bouguetj/calib_doc

[9] Niola, V., Rossi, C., Savino, S.: Modelling and calibration of a camera for robot trajectories recording. In: Proc. 5th WSEAS Int. Conf. on Signal Processing, Robotics and Automation, Madrid (February 15-17, 2006)

[10] Niola, V., Rossi, C., Savino, S.: Perspective Transform and Vision System for Robot Trajectories Recording. In: Proc. 5th WSEAS Int. Conf. on Signal Processing, Robotics and Automation, Madrid (February 15-17, 2006)

[11] Sharma, R., Hutchinson, S.: On the observability of robot motion under active camera control. In: Proc. IEEE International Conference on Robotics and Automation, pp. 162–167 (May 1999)

[12] Feddema, J.T., George Lee, C.S., Mitchell, O.R.: Weighted selection of image features for resolved rate visual feedback control. IEEE Trans. Robot. Automat. 7, 31–47 (1991)

[13] Brancati, R., Rossi, C., Savino, S.: A Method for Trajectory Planning in the Joint Space. In: Proc. of 14th International Workshop on Robotics in Alpe-Adria-Danube Region, Bucharest, Romania, pp. 81–85 (May 26-28, 2005)

Tracking Trajectories with a Robotic Manipulator with Singularities

Luis Gracia and Josep Tornero

Department of Systems Engineering and Control, Technical University of Valencia,
Camino de Vera s/n, P.O. Box: 22012, Valencia, Spain
{luigraca,jtornero}@isa.upv.es

Abstract. This research presents a trajectory control for non-redundant serial-link manipulators that is valid for trajectories with ordinary singularities of codimension one and non-ordinary singularities of any codimension. Firstly, it is presented a unified view of tracking algorithms for trajectories with ordinary singularities. Afterwards, several singularity classifications are indicated and illustrated. Then, it is developed a procedure to solve the indeterminate motion of non-ordinary singularities, which is applied to several cases. Finally, the proposed trajectory control is presented and simulated for the 2R manipulator case.

Keywords: Singularity classification, adjoint Jacobian, trajectory control.

1 Introduction

Nowadays, robotic manipulators are widely used in many areas, such as manufacturing, surgery, research, etc. Their control involves the inverse kinematics problem, which may be singular for specific configurations, what causes unacceptably large joint velocities. Singularities often coincide with a workspace boundary but can occur inside the workspace limits. If singular configurations are simply avoided the manipulator's workspace is reduced, certain types of operations are impossible (e.g. full-arm extension using straight-line motion), and the motion-planning process is complicated. However, works on the singularity problem indicate that with proper time scaling [1] or path reparameterization [2]-[5] it is possible to follow any path near and at a singularity, without incurring large joint velocities. Therefore, the aim of this research is to provide a unified view of the singularity problem and to develop a trajectory control valid not only for ordinary singularities, but also for non-ordinary singularities.

The paper is organized as follows. Section 2 presents the classical singularity characterization for robotic manipulators and the assumptions that will be considered for the rest of the paper. Section 3 presents and discusses several techniques that have been developed for damping the joint velocities around and at singular configurations. Next, section 4 presents a unified view of recent singularity classifications and shows illustrative examples. Furthermore, section 5 develops a method to solve the inverse kinematics of non-ordinary singularities, which is illustrated with several cases. Meanwhile, section 6 presents the proposed trajectory control, which is validated in simulation for a trajectory with ordinary and non-ordinary singularities. Finally, section 7 points out the more outstanding contributions of this research.

F. Mele et al. (Eds.): BVAI 2007, LNCS 4729, pp. 595–605, 2007.
© Springer-Verlag Berlin Heidelberg 2007

2 Classical Singularity Characterization for Robotic Manipulators

For a *non-redundant serial-link manipulator*, the relation between configuration $\mathbf{q}$ and end-effector position and orientation $\mathbf{p}$ is highly nonlinear and expressed as:

$$\mathbf{p} = \mathbf{f}(\mathbf{q}), \tag{1}$$

where $\mathbf{f}$ is called the *kinematic function*. The first order kinematics results:

$$\dot{\mathbf{p}} = \frac{d\mathbf{f}(\mathbf{q})}{d\mathbf{q}} \, \dot{\mathbf{q}} = \mathbf{J} \, \dot{\mathbf{q}}, \tag{2}$$

where $\mathbf{J}$ is called the Jacobian matrix or simply *Jacobian*. The inverse of the *Jacobian* is used to compute the joint velocities that produce the desired end-effector motion:

$$\dot{\mathbf{q}} = \mathbf{J}^{-1} \, \dot{\mathbf{p}}. \tag{3}$$

Nevertheless, the joint velocities result infinite when the *Jacobian* is singular (i.e. $|\mathbf{J}|=0$), what happens for the so called non-regular or *singular configurations*.

Similarly, if it is considered a *redundant serial-link manipulator* the singularity, when computing the active joint velocities with the pseudo-inverse of the *Jacobian*, arises when the *Jacobian* loses its full rank. (A simple example of a *redundant robot* is a four-bar mechanism with four active planar revolute joints, i.e. a 4R manipulator, where the two linear and one angular positions of the end-effector are considered.)

The *wrist partitioning method* separates the inverse kinematics problem of industrial manipulators in two problems and singularities are separated into singularities in the motion of the wrist center and wrist singularities. In order to overcome wrist-subassembly singularities, spherical wrists with redundant degrees of freedom have been developed. The redundant degrees of freedom can be determined with pseudo-inverse [6] (i.e. minimum norm of the joint velocities), constraint functions [7], etc.

On the other hand, there are relatively few papers [4] that analyze singularities of parallel-link manipulators, which are less popularized. Their kinematics is given by:

$$\mathbf{f}_{plm}(\mathbf{p},\mathbf{q}) = 0 \quad \rightarrow \quad \frac{d\mathbf{f}_{plm}}{d\mathbf{p}} \, \dot{\mathbf{p}} + \frac{d\mathbf{f}_{plm}}{d\mathbf{q}} \, \dot{\mathbf{q}} = \mathbf{J}_p \dot{\mathbf{p}} + \mathbf{J}_q \dot{\mathbf{q}} = 0 \tag{4}$$

where not only the inverse ($\mathbf{J}_q$) but also the forward ($\mathbf{J}_p$) kinematics may be singular.

2.1 Robotic Manipulator Assumptions for This Research

For the rest of the work it is be assumed a non-redundant (square *Jacobian*) serial-link manipulator since they are more common in practice, although it would be possible to extend the subsequent developments to parallel-link manipulators like in [4].

Moreover it will be considered *codimension one singularities* (i.e. $\mathbf{J}$ has a maximum rank deficiency of one), since singularities with a higher order codimension are not very common in practice. However with a recursive *singular-value-decomposition* (SVD) the codimension d problem is reduced to codimension one [5], although the computational time is increased.

3 Limiting the Joint Velocities Around and at Singularities

3.1 Damped Least Square (DLS) Method

One way to prevent large values of joint velocities around and at singular configurations is to introduce a damping factor into the inverse calculation of $\mathbf{J}$, at the expense of deviating from the desired path. It would also be possible to place bounds to joint accelerations, although it requires a proper trajectory planner [8] in order to avoid path deviations. The DLS method is relevant to damp joint velocities and minimizes:

$$I = \| \dot{\mathbf{p}} - \mathbf{J}(\mathbf{q})\dot{\mathbf{q}} \|^2 + \lambda \| \dot{\mathbf{q}} \|^2 , \tag{5}$$

where index I is formulated similarly to an optimum control problem and λ is the damping factor to be determined. There are several problems associated with the DLS method. A constant λ would introduce an algorithmic error, also away form a singular point. This error is introduced in terms of both direction and magnitude. On the other hand, the value of λ is not straightforward, e.g. it can be determined as a function of the smallest singular value of $\mathbf{J}$ [9], although SVD has a high computational cost.

3.2 Adjoint Jacobian Method

Since it is not possible to invert $\mathbf{J}$ at a singularity, there are several *Jacobian*-based methods that use another form of $\mathbf{J}$ in its place. For example, [10] uses $\mathbf{J}^T$ in place of $\mathbf{J}^{-1}$, while other approaches [11] use the *adjoint Jacobian*:

$$\dot{\mathbf{q}} = b \cdot \mathrm{adj}(\mathbf{J}) \, \dot{\mathbf{p}} , \tag{6}$$

where b is the *motion parameter*, which specifies the magnitude of the motion.

Note that (6) *decouples* de direction and the magnitude of the motion. In particular, there is no trajectory error if $b = |\mathbf{J}|^{-1}$ (not possible at singularities), i.e. (6) is equivalent to (3), otherwise there is *only* magnitude error (i.e. no path deviation).

Moreover, it is possible to design the motion parameter in order to achieve a *global time* although around and at singularities the motion magnitude must be limited.

3.3 The Null Space Approach

From the previous subsection, it is apparent that with appropriate path timing exact path tracking is generally possible at singularities. If the path is parameterized by a scalar s, this entails making $\dot{s}$ (and usually higher derivatives) zero at the singular point. The idea is equivalent to finding a *reparameterization* $\eta = f(s)$ such that the path's inverse kinematic solution $\mathbf{q}(s)$ is smooth with respect to η. This reparameterization always exists at singularities for non-redundant robots if $\mathbf{J}$ has a rank deficiency of 1 and the path's tangent has a component in the singular direction [12].

If $\mathbf{J}$ is square and has a rank deficiency of 1, then the manipulator's motion can be controlled within the (one-dimensional) null space of $\mathbf{J}$ [3]. The whole procedure is:

$$\mathbf{p} = \mathbf{g}(s) \rightarrow \dot{\mathbf{p}} = \mathbf{J} \, \dot{\mathbf{q}} \rightarrow \mathbf{S}(s) \, \dot{s} = \mathbf{J} \, \dot{\mathbf{q}} \rightarrow (\mathbf{J} \ \ -\mathbf{S}) \begin{pmatrix} \dot{\mathbf{q}} \\ \dot{s} \end{pmatrix} = \mathbf{0} \rightarrow \begin{pmatrix} \dot{\mathbf{q}} \\ \dot{s} \end{pmatrix} = \begin{pmatrix} \mathrm{adj}(\mathbf{J}) \ \mathbf{S} \\ |\mathbf{J}| \end{pmatrix} \eta , \tag{7}$$

where the new parameter η is equivalent to $b \cdot \dot{s}$ in (6). In fact, this approach is equivalent to the *adjoint Jacobian* method: the direction and magnitude of the motion are decoupled; no direction error is introduced; a subsequent time analysis based on parameter η must be considered in order to achieve the desired global time. If the parameter η is constant and determined from the initial kinetic energy (i.e. with an initial nonzero differential motion) it is obtained a differential motion called *natural* [5].

4 Classifications of Singular Configurations

The classical singularity characterization, presented in section 2, does not take into account the approaching/departure to/from the singular configuration. This is important because, if the singular configuration is crossed in a certain direction, the so called *non-degenerate direction*, it is possible to apply the joint velocities that produce a desired end-effector motion. Meanwhile, for all the rest (*degenerate*) *directions* the end-effector velocity at the singular configuration must be null, i.e. $\dot{s} = 0$.

Next, we present several singularity classifications of based on this idea.

4.1 Singularity Classification Based on the Null Space Approach

According to (7), there are two types of singular configurations ($|J|=0$) depending if $\mathrm{adj}(J)\cdot S$ is the null vector.

Type A (Sefl-motion) or Ordinary Singularity: The end-effector motion is in a degenerate direction S since $\mathrm{adj}(J)\cdot S$ is not the null vector and it is obtained a so called *self-motion*, because there is no end-effector motion ($\dot{s} = 0$) but the joint velocities are not zero ($\dot{q} \neq 0$). The self-motion represents a *differential motion* and can be seen as a redundant manipulator. It is an *instantaneously self-motion* if the end-effector motion is zero *only* instantaneously or a *continuously self-motion* otherwise. Usually, the instantaneously self-motion has several possible *branches* at the ordinary singularity.

Type B or Non-ordinary Singularity: The end-effector motion is in the non-degenerate direction S since $\mathrm{adj}(J)\cdot S$ is the null vector and it is obtained an indeterminate motion (0/0) with (3) or immobility ($\dot{q} = 0$, $\dot{s} = 0$) with (6) or (7). The non-ordinary singularity represents a *non-differential motion* and requires high order derivatives in order to solve the indeterminate motion.

A similar classification to this one is presented in [4] for parallel-link manipulators.

Characterization Based on Matrix Ranks: An alternative and simple method, that avoids the computation of the null space of (7), can be applied in order to characterize singularities: they are non-ordinary if $\mathrm{rank}(J)=\mathrm{rank}([J\ -S])$ and ordinary otherwise.

4.2 Singularity Classification by *Kieffer*

Kieffer made in his research a singularity classification (e.g. see [12]) that is complementary to the previous one.

Turning Point: It is an ordinary singularity of the instantaneously self-motion type ($\dot{s} = 0$, $\ddot{s} \neq 0$) and it often coincides with the workspace boundary.

Osculation Point: It is a ordinary singularity of the continuously self-motion type ($\dot{s} = 0$, $\ddot{s} = 0$) that requires a pause (null acceleration) in the end-effector motion.

Bifurcation Point: It is a non-ordinary singularity that complicates the mathematics by offering, through the use of higher order derivatives to solve the indeterminate motion, multiple solutions or *branches*. They do not require null end-effector motion.

Isolated Point: It is a non-ordinary singularity that requires the same mathematics analysis of bifurcations but that has no real solution or *branch*.

4.3 Escaping from Singularities

Next we discuss the way of escaping from singularities.

Instantaneously Self-motion or Turning Point: Using the adjoint *Jacobian* method (6) or the null space approach (7) the singularity is automatically escaped. The magnitude of b or η establishes the *escaping velocity* and its sign the *escaping branch*.

Continuously Self-motion or Osculation Point: Using (6) or (7) the singularity can not be escaped until it is achieved, through the self-motion, the non-degenerated direction (adj($\mathbf{J}$)·$\mathbf{S}$=0) and the singularity changes to a non-ordinary singularity.

Bifurcation Point: Once the indeterminate motion is solved, through the use of higher order derivatives, one *branch* must be selected and the singularity is escaped.

Isolated Point: It is not possible to escape from the singularity.

4.4 Singularity Examples with the Classical Two Bar Mechanism

All the previous types of singularities are illustrated in Fig. 1 for the classical two bar mechanism with two planar revolute joints, i.e. a 2R manipulator, where the two linear positions of the end-effector are considered.

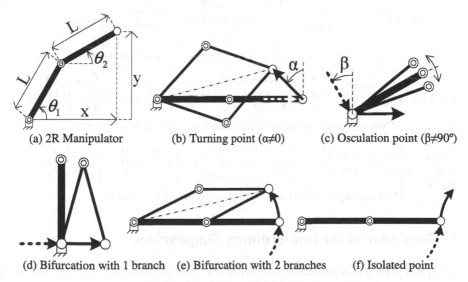

(a) 2R Manipulator   (b) Turning point ($\alpha\neq0$)   (c) Osculation point ($\beta\neq90°$)

(d) Bifurcation with 1 branch   (e) Bifurcation with 2 branches   (f) Isolated point

Fig. 1. Graphical examples of singularity for the 2R manipulator

All the singularities of Fig. 1 will be mathematically justified. The kinematic function (1) and the first order kinematics (2) for this 2R manipulator (Fig. 1 (a)) are {(8), (9)}, meanwhile singularity occurs when both bars are parallel (10).

$$\mathbf{p} = \mathbf{f}(\mathbf{q}) \rightarrow \begin{pmatrix} x \\ y \end{pmatrix} = L \begin{pmatrix} \cos(\theta_1) + \cos(\theta_2) \\ \sin(\theta_1) + \sin(\theta_2) \end{pmatrix} \tag{8}$$

$$\dot{\mathbf{p}} = \mathbf{J}\,\dot{\mathbf{q}} \rightarrow \begin{pmatrix} \dot{x} \\ \dot{y} \end{pmatrix} = L \begin{pmatrix} -\sin(\theta_1) & -\sin(\theta_2) \\ \cos(\theta_1) & +\cos(\theta_2) \end{pmatrix} \begin{pmatrix} \dot{\theta}_1 \\ \dot{\theta}_2 \end{pmatrix} \tag{9}$$

$$|\mathbf{J}| = 0 \rightarrow L^2 \sin(\theta_2 - \theta_1) = 0 \rightarrow \theta_2 = \theta_1 \text{ or } \theta_2 = \theta_1 + 180°. \tag{10}$$

Next, it is indicated the trajectory parameterization and subsequent singularity characterization for each case of Fig. 1:

Fig. 1 (b) →
$$\begin{cases} \begin{pmatrix} \dot{x} \\ \dot{y} \end{pmatrix} = \begin{pmatrix} -\sin(\alpha) \\ \cos(\alpha) \end{pmatrix} \dot{s} \rightarrow \begin{pmatrix} \dot{\theta}_1 \\ \dot{\theta}_2 \\ \dot{s} \end{pmatrix} = \begin{pmatrix} \sin(\theta_2 - \alpha) \\ \sin(\alpha - \theta_1) \\ L\sin(\theta_2 - \theta_1) \end{pmatrix} \eta \\[2ex] \begin{pmatrix} \theta_{1\,sing} \\ \theta_{2\,sing} \end{pmatrix} = \begin{pmatrix} 0 \\ 0 \end{pmatrix} \rightarrow \begin{pmatrix} \dot{\theta}_{1\,sing} \\ \dot{\theta}_{2\,sing} \\ \dot{s}_{sing} \end{pmatrix} = \begin{pmatrix} -\sin(\alpha) \\ \sin(\alpha) \\ 0 \end{pmatrix} \eta_{sing} \rightarrow \begin{array}{l} \text{Ordinary} \\ \text{singularity } (\alpha \neq 0) \end{array} \\[2ex] \ddot{s} = L\sin(\theta_2 - \theta_1)\dot{\eta} + L\cos(\theta_2 - \theta_1)\eta(\dot{\theta}_2 - \dot{\theta}_1) \\ \ddot{s}_{sing} = 2\,L\sin(\alpha)\eta_{sing}^2 \rightarrow \ddot{s}_{sing} \neq 0 \rightarrow \text{Instantaneously self-motion} \end{cases} \tag{11}$$

Fig. 1 (c) →
$$\begin{cases} \begin{pmatrix} \dot{x} \\ \dot{y} \end{pmatrix} = \begin{pmatrix} 1 \\ 0 \end{pmatrix} \dot{s} \rightarrow \begin{pmatrix} \dot{\theta}_1 \\ \dot{\theta}_2 \\ \dot{s} \end{pmatrix} = \begin{pmatrix} \cos(\theta_2) \\ -\cos(\theta_1) \\ L\sin(\theta_2 - \theta_1) \end{pmatrix} \eta \\[2ex] \begin{pmatrix} \theta_{1\,sing} \\ \theta_{2\,sing} \end{pmatrix} = \begin{pmatrix} \beta \\ \pi + \beta \end{pmatrix} \rightarrow \begin{pmatrix} \dot{\theta}_{1\,sing} \\ \dot{\theta}_{2\,sing} \\ \dot{s}_{sing} \end{pmatrix} = -\begin{pmatrix} \cos(\beta) \\ \cos(\beta) \\ 0 \end{pmatrix} \eta \rightarrow \begin{array}{l} \text{Ordinary} \\ \text{singularity } (\beta \neq 90°) \end{array} \\[2ex] \ddot{s}_{sing} = -L\eta_{sing}(\dot{\theta}_{2\,sing} - \dot{\theta}_{1\,sing}) = 0 \rightarrow \text{Continuously self-motion} \end{cases} \tag{12}$$

Fig. 1 (d) →
$$\begin{cases} \begin{pmatrix} \dot{x} \\ \dot{y} \end{pmatrix} = \begin{pmatrix} 1 \\ 0 \end{pmatrix} \dot{s} \rightarrow \begin{pmatrix} \dot{\theta}_1 \\ \dot{\theta}_2 \\ \dot{s} \end{pmatrix} = \begin{pmatrix} \cos(\theta_2) \\ -\cos(\theta_1) \\ L\sin(\theta_2 - \theta_1) \end{pmatrix} \eta \rightarrow \begin{pmatrix} \theta_{1\,sing} \\ \theta_{2\,sing} \end{pmatrix} = \begin{pmatrix} \pi/2 \\ -\pi/2 \end{pmatrix} \rightarrow \begin{pmatrix} \dot{\theta}_{1\,sing} \\ \dot{\theta}_{2\,sing} \\ \dot{s}_{sing} \end{pmatrix} = \begin{pmatrix} 0 \\ 0 \\ 0 \end{pmatrix} \eta_{sin} \\ \text{Non-ordinary singularity (indterminate motion solved in section 5)} \end{cases} \tag{13}$$

Fig.1(e) and Fig.1(f) →
$$\begin{cases} \begin{pmatrix} \dot{x} \\ \dot{y} \end{pmatrix} = L\begin{pmatrix} -\sin(s) \\ \cos(s) \end{pmatrix} \dot{s} \rightarrow \begin{pmatrix} \dot{\theta}_1 \\ \dot{\theta}_2 \\ \dot{s} \end{pmatrix} = \begin{pmatrix} \sin(\theta_2 - s) \\ \sin(s - \theta_1) \\ L\sin(\theta_2 - \theta_1) \end{pmatrix} \eta \rightarrow \begin{pmatrix} \theta_{1\,sing} \\ \theta_{2\,sing} \\ s_{sing} \end{pmatrix} = \begin{pmatrix} 0 \\ 0 \\ 0 \end{pmatrix} \rightarrow \begin{pmatrix} \dot{\theta}_{1\,sing} \\ \dot{\theta}_{2\,sing} \\ \dot{s}_{sing} \end{pmatrix} = \begin{pmatrix} 0 \\ 0 \\ 0 \end{pmatrix} \eta_{sir} \\ \text{Non-ordinary singularity (indterminate motion solved in section 5).} \end{cases} \tag{14}$$

5 Resolution of the Non-ordinary Singularities

In [5] it is presented a procedure in order to solve the indeterminate motion *only in the vecinity* of non-ordinary singularities based on SVD (high computational cost).

The indeterminate form of (6) implies that the linear equations of the first order kinematics (2) are not independent, and hence there are infinite solutions. Nevertheless, not all those solutions are valid because, since the non-ordinary singularity represents a non-differential motion, the second order kinematics (i.e. the curvature of the path) must be guaranteed. Next, it will be shown a procedure to solve the indeterminate motion that separates the differential part of the motion (i.e. the linear and integrable equations) from the non-differential part of the motion (i.e. the non-linear and non-integrable equations). The method is valid for non-ordinary singularities of any codimension. The differential part of the motion is given by the independent equations of (2). On the other hand, the time derivative of (2) is:

$$\mathbf{J}\,\ddot{\mathbf{q}} + \frac{d\mathbf{J}}{dt}\dot{\mathbf{q}} = \ddot{\mathbf{p}} = \mathbf{S}\,\ddot{s} + \frac{d\mathbf{S}}{dt}\dot{s} \rightarrow \mathbf{J}\,\ddot{\mathbf{q}} = \mathbf{S}\,\ddot{s} + \frac{d\mathbf{S}}{dt}\dot{s} - \frac{d\mathbf{J}}{dt}\dot{\mathbf{q}}. \tag{15}$$

Therefore, the second hand of (15) must lie in the column space of $\mathbf{J}$, that is:

$$\mathbf{h}^{\mathrm{T}}\mathbf{J} = 0 \rightarrow \mathbf{J}^{\mathrm{T}}\mathbf{h} = 0 \rightarrow \mathbf{h}^{\mathrm{T}}\left(\mathbf{S}\,\ddot{s} + \frac{d\mathbf{S}}{dt}\dot{s} - \frac{d\mathbf{J}}{dt}\dot{\mathbf{q}}\right) = 0, \tag{16}$$

where $\mathbf{h}$ are the orthogonal vectors to $\mathbf{J}$, which number is equal to the rank deficiency of $\mathbf{J}$, that can be computed from the null space of $\mathbf{J}^{\mathrm{T}}$. Then, the non-differential part of the motion is given by the non-linear scalar equations of (16), which may require numerical computation, that can give none, one or multiple real solutions (branches).

Note that (16) does not involve the unknown joint accelerations, instead it only involves the unknown joint velocities like (2). As a practical application of the previous theory it will be solved the indeterminate motions of Fig. 1 (d), (e) and (f):

$$\text{Fig. 1 (d)} \rightarrow \begin{cases} \mathbf{J}_{\text{sing}} = L\begin{pmatrix} -1 & 1 \\ 0 & 0 \end{pmatrix} \rightarrow \mathbf{h}_{\text{sing}} = \begin{pmatrix} 0 \\ 1 \end{pmatrix} \\ (2) \rightarrow L(-\dot{\theta}_{1\,\text{sing}} + \dot{\theta}_{2\,\text{sing}}) = -\dot{s}_{\text{sing}} \\ (16) \rightarrow \dot{\theta}_{1\,\text{sing}}^2 - \dot{\theta}_{2\,\text{sing}}^2 = 0 \end{cases} \rightarrow \dot{\theta}_{1\,\text{sing}} = -\dot{\theta}_{2\,\text{sing}} = L\,\dot{s}_{\text{sing}}/2 \tag{17}$$

$$\text{Fig. 1 (e)} \rightarrow \begin{cases} \mathbf{J}_{\text{sing}} = L\begin{pmatrix} 0 & 0 \\ 1 & 1 \end{pmatrix} \rightarrow \mathbf{h}_{\text{sing}} = \begin{pmatrix} 1 \\ 0 \end{pmatrix} \\ (2) \rightarrow L(\dot{\theta}_{1\,\text{sing}} + \dot{\theta}_{2\,\text{sing}}) = \dot{s}_{\text{sing}} \\ (16) \rightarrow L^2(\dot{\theta}_{1\,\text{sing}}^2 + \dot{\theta}_{2\,\text{sing}}^2) - \dot{s}_{\text{sing}}^2 = 0 \end{cases} \rightarrow \begin{cases} \dot{\theta}_{1\,\text{sing}} = L\,\dot{s}_{\text{sing}} \text{ and } \dot{\theta}_{2\,\text{sing}} = 0 \text{ or} \\ \dot{\theta}_{2\,\text{sing}} = L\,\dot{s}_{\text{sing}} \text{ and } \dot{\theta}_{1\,\text{sing}} = 0 \end{cases} \tag{18}$$

$$\text{Fig. 1 (f)} \rightarrow \begin{cases} \mathbf{J}_{\text{sing}} = L\begin{pmatrix} 0 & 0 \\ 1 & 1 \end{pmatrix} \rightarrow \mathbf{h}_{\text{sing}} = \begin{pmatrix} 1 \\ 0 \end{pmatrix} \\ (2) \rightarrow L(\dot{\theta}_{1\,\text{sing}} + \dot{\theta}_{2\,\text{sing}}) = \dot{s}_{\text{sing}} \\ (16) \rightarrow L^2(\dot{\theta}_{1\,\text{sing}}^2 + \dot{\theta}_{2\,\text{sing}}^2) + \dot{s}_{\text{sing}}^2 = 0 \end{cases} \rightarrow \begin{array}{l} \text{There are no real} \\ \text{values for } (\dot{\theta}_{1\,\text{sing}}, \dot{\theta}_{2\,\text{sing}}). \end{array} \tag{19}$$

6 Trajectory Control

The desired joint velocities will be given by the classical *trajectory control*, i.e. a derivative feedforward plus a proportional feedback (given by the real joint positions):

$$\mathbf{J}\,\dot{\mathbf{q}}_{\text{ref}} = \mathbf{S}\,\dot{s} + \mathbf{K}_{\text{p}}(\mathbf{g}(s) - \mathbf{f}(\mathbf{q}_{\text{real}})) \rightarrow \mathbf{J}\,\dot{\mathbf{q}}_{\text{ref}} = \mathbf{M} \tag{20}$$

$$\dot{\mathbf{q}}_{\text{ref}} = \text{adj}(\mathbf{J})(\mathbf{S}\,\dot{s} + \mathbf{K}_{\text{p}}(\mathbf{g}(s) - \mathbf{f}(\mathbf{q}_{\text{real}})))/|\mathbf{J}| \rightarrow \dot{\mathbf{q}}_{\text{ref}} = \mathbf{N}/|\mathbf{J}|, \tag{21}$$

where the error of the end-effector position is corrected with gain matrix $\mathbf{K}_{\text{p}}$.

In order to compute the desired joint velocities it is proposed the algorithm:

$$\text{if } (|\mathbf{J}| > \varepsilon_1) \text{ then } \dot{\mathbf{q}}_{ref} = \mathbf{N}/|\mathbf{J}| \tag{22}$$

$$\text{if } (|\mathbf{J}| > \varepsilon_1 \text{ and } \exists |\dot{q}_{ref\,i}| > \dot{q}_{max}) \text{ or } (|\mathbf{J}| < \varepsilon_1 \text{ and } \|\mathbf{N}\|_\infty > \varepsilon_2)$$
$$\text{then } \dot{\mathbf{q}}_{ref} = \mathbf{N}\,(\dot{q}_{max}/\|\mathbf{N}\|_\infty)\,\text{sign}(|\mathbf{J}|) \tag{23}$$

$$\text{if } (|\mathbf{J}| < \varepsilon_1 \text{ and } \|\mathbf{N}\|_\infty < \varepsilon_2) \text{ then } \textit{The indetermminate motion must be solved}, \tag{24}$$

where (22) is for regular configurations; (23) is a kind of *saturation* for high-gain regular configurations and ordinary singularities; and (24) is for non-ordinary singularities. Note that ordinary and non-ordinary singularities are *numerically* characterized through ε_1 and ε_2, which values highly depend on the used numerical precision.

In order to solve the indeterminate motion of (24), it is *set to zero* the maximal set of equations of (20) that guarantee that the *new expression* of (20) has the same number of singular values of matrix $[\mathbf{J}\,-\mathbf{M}]$ close to zero. The non-differential part of the motion is obtained from the differential part of motion similarly to (16):

$$\mathbf{J}\,\ddot{\mathbf{q}}_{ref} = \mathbf{S}\,\ddot{s} + \frac{d\mathbf{S}}{ds}\dot{s}^2 + \mathbf{K}_p(\mathbf{S}\,\dot{s} - \mathbf{J}\,\dot{\mathbf{q}}_{real}) - \frac{d\mathbf{J}}{dt}\dot{\mathbf{q}}_{ref} \tag{25}$$

$$\mathbf{h}^T\mathbf{J} = 0 \rightarrow \mathbf{J}^T\mathbf{h} = 0 \rightarrow \mathbf{h}^T\left(\mathbf{S}\,\ddot{s} + \frac{d\mathbf{S}}{ds}\dot{s}^2 + \mathbf{K}_p(\mathbf{S}\,\dot{s} - \mathbf{J}\,\dot{\mathbf{q}}_{real}) - \frac{d\mathbf{J}}{dt}\dot{\mathbf{q}}_{ref}\right) = 0, \tag{26}$$

where the desired joint velocities $\dot{\mathbf{q}}_{ref}$ are obtained (they may require numerical computation) from the desired motion $(\ddot{s}, \dot{s})$, the current joint velocities $\dot{\mathbf{q}}_{real}$, the current desired point on the path s and the current configuration $\mathbf{q}_{real}$.

Another *trajectory control* can be used to correct the error of the joint positions and the resulting joint velocity vector would be used by the low-level dynamic control.

Note that the proposed algorithm *corrects the error* of end-effector position not only in the path's perpendicular directions, like [3], but *also in the path's tangent directions*. This is important because it allows to retrieve the target on the path when the joint velocities have been saturated, e.g. around and at an ordinary singularity.

Moreover, the proposed algorithm is *valid* not only for ordinary singularities but *also for non-ordinary singularities*. For example, with the trajectory control of [3], based on the null space approach, it is not possible to cross a non-ordinary singularity, since the motion stops completely.

Also note that, since it has been solved the indeterminate motion at non-ordinary singularities, it is not necessary to design complex control laws like [5], which is based on the second order kinematics of the null space approach (subsection 3.3).

6.1 Application Example of the Trajectory Control

To illustrate the applications of the proposed trajectory control it will be considered the 2R manipulator of Fig. 1 (a) again. The tracking trajectory will be the straight line from $(x_{right}, y_{right})=(2L, 0)$ to $(x_{left}, y_{left})=(-2L, 0)$ and vice versa, i.e. from $\theta_1 = \theta_2 = 0$ to

$\theta_1 = \theta_2 = \pi$ and vice versa. Note that this trajectory has three singular points: two ordinary singularities (instantaneously self-motion or turning points) at the trajectory end-points; and another singularity at the center of the first revolute joint. This third singularity can be ordinary (continuously self-motion or osculation point, see Fig.1 (c)) or non-ordinary (bifurcation with one branch, see Fig.1 (d)). Two initial configurations are considered (see Fig. 2 (a) and (b), where the thick dashed line means the desired initial motion from the desired initial point on the trajectory). The values used in the simulation are $\{\varepsilon_1 = 10^{-6}, \varepsilon_2 = 10^{-3}, L = 1 \text{ m}, \dot{\theta}_{1\max} = \dot{\theta}_{2\max} = 1 \text{ rad/s}, \dot{s} = \pm 0.5 \text{ m/s}, \mathbf{K}_p = [2,0;0,2]\}$ and the two bar dynamics has been neglected, i.e. $\dot{\mathbf{q}}_{real} = \dot{\mathbf{q}}_{ref}$.

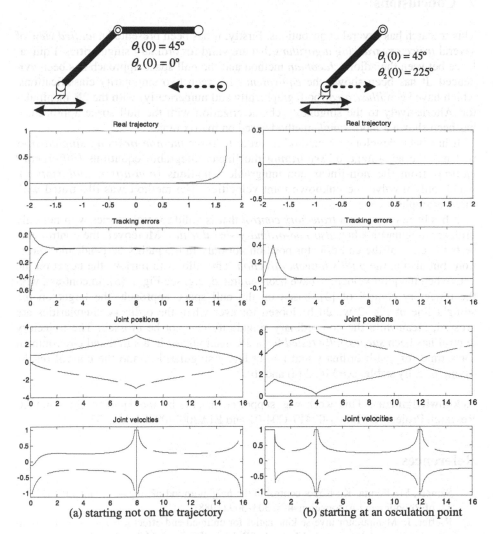

Fig. 2. Trajectory control for the 2R manipulator

It is shown in Fig. 2 (a) and (b) the real trajectory and the tracking errors for each initial configuration. In particular for the first case (starting not on the trajectory) it is obtained an asymptotical convergence to the trajectory, and small tracking errors are present at the ordinary singularities due to the joint velocities saturation. For the second case (starting at an osculation point on the trajectory) the tracking error is linearly increased until the joint positions reach the non-degenerate direction, through maximal joint velocities, and then the tracking errors converge asymptotically to zero. There are small tracking errors at ordinary singularities again.

7 Conclusions

This research has several contributions. Firstly, it has been presented a *unified view* of several *trajectory tracking algorithms* that are valid for ordinary singularities. Equivalence between the adjoint *Jacobian* method and the null space approach has been evidenced. It has been shown the *equivalence* between two singularity classifications, which have been *illustrated* (both graphically and numerically) with the 2R manipulator. Alternatively to the singularity characterization with the null space approach, it has been shown a more *simple* method based on matrix ranks.

It has been developed a method in order to *solve the non-ordinary singularities* that has the advantage of *separating* the linear integrable equations (*differential motion*) from the non-linear non-integrable equations (*non-differential motion*), which only involve the unknown joint velocities. The method was illustrated with three examples.

It has been proposed a *trajectory control* that is valid for trajectories with not only ordinary singularities but *also non-ordinary singularities*. Moreover, the control corrects the error of the end-effector position not only in the path's perpendicular directions but also in the *path's tangent direction*. This allows to retrieve the target on the path when the joint velocities have been saturated, e.g. see Fig. 2 (b). In contrast, with the trajectory control of [3], based on the null space approach, the target on the straight line of Fig. 2 would be loosed for ever when the ordinary singularities are crossed, meanwhile the non-ordinary singularity can not be crossed. The trajectory control has been *successfully tested* for a 2R manipulator in a simulated environment for a trajectory with ordinary and non-ordinary singularities, and the control results asymptotically stable, see Fig. 2 (a) and (b).

Acknowledgments. This work was supported in part by the Spanish Government: Research Projects DPI2004-07417-C04-01 and BIA2005-09377-C03-02.

References

1. Sampei, M., Furuta, K.: Robot control in the neighborhood of singular points. IEEE Journal of Robotics and Automation 4(3), 303–309 (1988)
2. Kieffer, J.: Manipulator inverse kinematics for untimed end-effector trajectories with ordinary singularities. International Journal of Robotics Research 11(3), 225–237 (1992)
3. Nenchev, D.N.: Tracking Manipulator trajectories with ordinary singularities: a null space-based approach. The Int. Journal of Robotics Research 14(4), 399–404 (1995)

4. Nenchev, D.N., Uchiyama, M.: Singularity-consistent path planning and motion control through instantaneous self-motion singularities of parallel-link manipulators. Journal of Robotic Systems 14(1), 27–36 (1997)
5. Nenchev, D.N., Tsumaki, Y., Uchiyama, M.: Singularity-consistent parameterization of robot motion and control. The Int. J. of Robotics Research 19(2), 159–182 (2000)
6. Liegeois, A.: Automatic supervisory control of the configuration and behavior of multi-body mechanisms. IEEE Trans. on Systems, Man and Cybernetics SMC-7, 868–871 (1977)
7. Stanisic, M.M., Pennock, G.R.: A non-degenerate kinematic solution of a seven-jointed robot manipulator. The Int. J. of Robotics Research 4(2), 10–20 (1985)
8. Lloyd, J.E., Hayward, V.: Singularity-robust trajectory generation. The International Journal of Robotics Research 20(1), 38–56 (2001)
9. Maciejewski, A.A., Klein, C.A.: Numerical filtering for the operation of robotic manipulators through kinematically singular configurations. J. of Rob. Syst. 5, 527–552 (1988)
10. Chiacchio, P., Chiaverini, S., Sciavicco, L., Siciliano, B.: Closed-loop inverse kinematics schemes for constrained reundant manipulators with task space augmentation and task priority strategy. Int. Journal of Robotic Research 10(4), 410–425 (1991)
11. Tsumaki, Y., Nenchev, D.N.: Jacobian adjoint matrix based approach to teleoperation. In: Int. Symp. On Microsystems, Intelligent Materials and Robots, Sendai, Japan, pp. 532–535 (1995)
12. Kieffer, J.: Differential analysis of bifurcations and isolated singularities for robots and mechanisms. IEEE Transactions on Robotics and Automation 10(1), 1–10 (1994)

Motion Planning for Wheeled Mobile Robots Based on Singularity Criteria

Luis Gracia and Josep Tornero

Department of Systems Engineering and Control, Technical University of Valencia,
Camino de Vera s/n, P.O. Box: 22012, Valencia, Spain
{luigraca,jtornero}@isa.upv.es

Abstract. This research presents a motion planning for wheeled mobile robots based on a cost index that assesses the nearness to singularity of forward and inverse kinematic models. The cost index can be used straightforward for many planning techniques (tree graphs, roadmaps, etc.) in order to choose one path among several possible collision-free paths. This path would avoid not only slip and impossible control actions but also high amplification of wheel velocities' error and high values for wheel velocities. To illustrate the applications of the proposed approach it is considered an industrial forklift that is equivalent to the tricycle WMR and several results are shown in a simulated environment.

Keywords: Kinematics singularity, forward and inverse kinematics, cost index.

1 Introduction

Wheeled Mobile Robots (WMR) have been widely studied in the past fifteen years. Due to kinematic constraints, WMR are not integrable (non-holonomic). Therefore, standard techniques developed for robot manipulators are not directly applicable. In particular, the motion planning of WMR is still a relevant issue. Examples of motion planning for WMR are available in the literature [1]-[4]. On the other hand, the singularity of WMR kinematics must be avoided since it implies slip or impossible control actions [5]. In the same way, in the vicinity of singularities there is high amplification of active joints' error or high values for active joints. Therefore, the aim of the present research is to develop a motion planning for WMR based on singularity criteria.

The paper is organized as follows. Section 2 presents the kinematic modeling and singularity of WMR considering four types of wheels: *fixed*, centered orientable (hereinafter *orientable*), *castor* and *Swedish*. Next, section 3 discusses the possibilities for motion planning and develops a *cost index* based on singularity criteria. To illustrate the applications of the proposed motion planning it is considered an industrial forklift (equivalent to the tricycle WMR) and several simulation results are shown. Finally, section 4 points out the more outstanding contributions of this research.

2 Kinematic Modeling and Singularity of Wheeled Mobile Robots

Firstly it will be introduced some terminology. Assuming horizontal movement, the position of the WMR body is completely specified by 3 scalar variables (e.g. x, y, θ), referred to in [6] as WMR posture, $\mathbf{p}$ in vector form. Its first-order time derivative is

F. Mele et al. (Eds.): BVAI 2007, LNCS 4729, pp. 606–615, 2007.
© Springer-Verlag Berlin Heidelberg 2007

called WMR velocity vector $\dot{\mathbf{p}}$ and separately (v_x, v_y, ω) WMR velocities [7]. Similarly, for each wheel, wheel velocity vector and wheel velocities are defined.

2.1 Kinematic Models of the Four Common Types Wheels

The kinematic modeling of a wheel is used as a previous stage for modeling the whole WMR [5]-[8]. Here, the four common wheels will be considered: *fixed*, *orientable*, *castor* and *Swedish*. As it is easy to obtain their equations using a vector approach, e.g. see [5] among many other possibilities, the detailed development will be omitted.

The matrix equation of the off-centered orientable wheel or *castor* wheel is:

$$
\mathbf{v}_{\text{slip } i} = \begin{pmatrix} \cos(\beta_i + \delta_i) & \sin(\beta_i + \delta_i) & l_i \sin(\beta_i + \delta_i - \alpha_i) - d_i \cos\delta_i & -d_i \cos\delta_i & 0 \\ -\sin(\beta_i + \delta_i) & \cos(\beta_i + \delta_i) & l_i \cos(\beta_i + \delta_i - \alpha_i) + d_i \sin\delta_i & d_i \sin\delta_i & r_i \end{pmatrix} \begin{pmatrix} \dot{\mathbf{p}} \\ \dot{\beta}_i \\ \dot{\varphi}_i \end{pmatrix},
\tag{1}
$$

where it has been used the parameters of Fig. 1 (a) and the variables of Table 1.

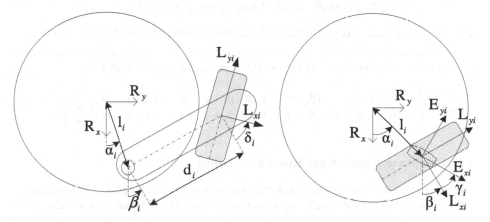

Fig. 1. *Castor* wheel parameters: l_i, d_i, α_i, β_i, δ_i *Swedish* wheel parameters: l_i, α_i, β_i, γ_i

Table 1. Frames, variables and constants

Symbol	Description
R	Frame attached to the robot body with the Z-axis perpendicular to the floor surface
$\bar{\text{R}}$	Frame attached to the floor and instantaneously coincident with the robot frame R. This frame allows to avoid the dependency on a global stationary frame [7]
(L_i, E_i)	Frames attached to the wheel i and to the roller of the *Swedish* wheel i, with the X-axes coincident with their rotation axle
$\dot{\mathbf{p}}$	WMR velocity vector in coordinate frame $\bar{\text{R}}$, equivalent to $(^{\bar{R}}v_{Rx} \ ^{\bar{R}}v_{Ry} \ ^{\bar{R}}\omega_R)^{\text{T}}$ or $(v_x \ v_y \ \omega)^{\text{T}}$
$\mathbf{v}_{\text{slip } i}$	Sliding velocity vector of the wheel in coordinate frame L_i (E_i for *Swedish* wheels)
$(\dot{\beta}_i, \dot{\varphi}_i)$	Angular velocity of the steering link and rotation velocity of the wheel in L_{xi}-axis
$\dot{\varphi}_{ri}$	Rotation velocity of the rollers in E_{xi}-axis (it is usually a free wheel velocity)
(r_i, r_{ri})	Wheel equivalent radius and roller radius

Fig. 2. *Swedish* wheel (also called *Mecanum, Ilon* or *universal*) with rollers at 45°

The equation of the *orientable* wheel can be obtained from (1) with $d_i = \delta_i = 0$:

$$\mathbf{v}_{\text{slip }i} = \begin{pmatrix} \cos\beta_i & \sin\beta_i & 1_i \sin(\beta_i - \alpha_i) & 0 \\ -\sin\beta_i & \cos\beta_i & 1_i \cos(\beta_i - \alpha_i) & r_i \end{pmatrix} \begin{pmatrix} \dot{\mathbf{p}} \\ \dot{\varphi}_i \end{pmatrix}. \tag{2}$$

The previous equation is also valid for *fixed* wheels, where the angle β_i is constant.

The matrix equation of the *Swedish* wheel (see Fig. 2) is (3) where it has been used the parameters of Fig. 1 (b) and the variables and constants of Table 1.

$$\mathbf{v}_{\text{slip }i} = \begin{pmatrix} \cos(\beta_i + \gamma_i) & \sin(\beta_i + \gamma_i) & 1_i \sin(\beta_i + \gamma_i - \alpha_i) & r_i \sin\gamma_i & 0 \\ -\sin(\beta_i + \gamma_i) & \cos(\beta_i + \gamma_i) & 1_i \cos(\beta_i + \gamma_i - \alpha_i) & r_i \cos\gamma_i & r_{ri} \end{pmatrix} \begin{pmatrix} \dot{\mathbf{p}} \\ \dot{\varphi}_i \\ \dot{\varphi}_{ri} \end{pmatrix} \tag{3}$$

2.2 Composite Equation and Kinematic Models

Once the type of WMR wheels and their equations are established, a compound kinematic equation for the WMR may be defined. Using (1), (2), and (3) it results:

$$\mathbf{v}_{\text{slip}} = \begin{pmatrix} \mathbf{v}_{\text{slip }1} \\ \vdots \\ \mathbf{v}_{\text{slip }N} \end{pmatrix} = \begin{pmatrix} \mathbf{A}_{p1} & \mathbf{A}_{w1} & \cdots & 0 \\ \vdots & \vdots & \ddots & \vdots \\ \mathbf{A}_{pN} & 0 & \cdots & \mathbf{A}_{wN} \end{pmatrix} \begin{pmatrix} \dot{\mathbf{p}} \\ \dot{\mathbf{q}}_{w1} \\ \vdots \\ \dot{\mathbf{q}}_{wN} \end{pmatrix} = \begin{pmatrix} \mathbf{A}_p & \mathbf{A}_w \end{pmatrix} \begin{pmatrix} \dot{\mathbf{p}} \\ \dot{\mathbf{q}}_w \end{pmatrix} = \mathbf{A} \, \dot{\mathbf{q}} \,, \tag{4}$$

where N is the no. of wheels; $\mathbf{v}_{\text{slip}}$ is the composite sliding velocity vector; $\dot{\mathbf{q}}_{wi}$ is a vector with all the wheel velocities of wheel i; $\dot{\mathbf{q}}_w$ is the composite vector of all the wheel velocities; $\dot{\mathbf{q}}$ is the vector of all the velocities; $\{\mathbf{A}_{pi}, \mathbf{A}_{wi}\}$ are the multiplying matrices obtained from (1), (2), and (3); $\{\mathbf{A}_{pi}, \mathbf{A}_{wi}\}$ are the composite multiplying matrices; and $\mathbf{A}$ is the WMR kinematic matrix.

Under the *no-slip condition*, the kinematic solution for velocity vector $\dot{\mathbf{q}}$ results:

$$\mathbf{A} \cdot \dot{\mathbf{q}} = 0 \tag{5}$$

$$\dot{\mathbf{q}} \in \mathcal{N}(\mathbf{A}) \rightarrow \dot{\mathbf{q}} = \mathbf{B} \cdot \boldsymbol{\eta}, \tag{6}$$

where matrix $\mathbf{B}$ forms a basis of $\mathcal{N}(\mathbf{A})$, η is an m-dimensional vector representing WMR mobility, and m is the WMR mobility degree given by the nullity of $\mathbf{A}$:

$$m = \dim(\eta) = \dim(\mathcal{N}(\mathbf{A})) = \dim(\dot{\mathbf{q}}) - \text{rank}(\mathbf{A}) = k - g . \tag{7}$$

In order to use variables with physical meaning, the mobility vector η should be replaced with a set of freely *assigned* velocities. Depending on whether wheel velocities or WMR velocities are chosen, a forward or inverse kinematic model is obtained. If a mix of both types of velocities is chosen a mixed solution is achieved.

In order to check if an m-set of velocities $\dot{\mathbf{q}}_a$ can be assigned, it must be verified that the determinant of the submatrix they define in (5) is non zero, that is:

$$\begin{pmatrix} \dot{\mathbf{q}}_{na} \\ \dot{\mathbf{q}}_a \end{pmatrix} = \begin{pmatrix} \mathbf{B}_{na} \\ \mathbf{B}_a \end{pmatrix} \cdot \eta \tag{8}$$

$$\text{if } |\mathbf{B}_a| \neq 0 \rightarrow \dot{\mathbf{q}}_{na} = \mathbf{B}_{na} \cdot \mathbf{B}_a^{-1} \cdot \dot{\mathbf{q}}_a , \tag{9}$$

where $\dot{\mathbf{q}}_{na}$ are the remaining non-assigned velocities of $\dot{\mathbf{q}}$.

Alternatively to the previous procedure, based on the null space concept, it is possible to apply another method based on separating the m assigned velocities in (5):

$$\mathbf{A}_{na} \, \dot{\mathbf{q}}_{na} = -\mathbf{A}_a \, \dot{\mathbf{q}}_a . \tag{10}$$

To check if an m-set of velocities could be assigned $\dot{\mathbf{q}}_a$, it must be verified that matrix $\mathbf{A}_{na}$ is, in general, of full rank g:

$$\text{rank}(\mathbf{A}_{na}) = \text{rank}(\mathbf{A}) = g . \tag{11}$$

Therefore, the singularity of a kinematic model is given by $|\mathbf{B}_a| = 0$ in (9) or alternatively when matrix $\mathbf{A}_{na}$ in (10) loses its full rank g. In [5] it is characterized the singularity of WMR with a generic geometric approach.

It is important to remark that, in order to obtain a correct singularity result with $|\mathbf{B}_a| = 0$ in (9) all the elements of matrix $\mathbf{B}$ must be always definite (i.e. non infinite).

Taken into account that the elements of matrix $\mathbf{A}$ are always definite, the previous is achieved using a free-division row reduction (*Gauss-Jordan* elimination) for computing the null space of $\mathbf{A}$. Using that approach, it is obtained for (5) an expression similar to the reduced row echelon form and (8) is particularized:

$$\begin{pmatrix} a_1 & 0 & 0 \\ 0 & \ddots & 0 \\ 0 & 0 & a_g \end{pmatrix} \mathbf{H} \begin{pmatrix} \dot{\mathbf{q}}_{na} \\ \dot{\mathbf{q}}_a \end{pmatrix} = \mathbf{0} \rightarrow \dot{\mathbf{q}} = \begin{pmatrix} \dot{\mathbf{q}}_{na} \\ \dot{\mathbf{q}}_a \end{pmatrix} = \begin{pmatrix} \begin{pmatrix} \prod_{i=2}^{g} a_i & 0 & 0 \\ 0 & \ddots & 0 \\ 0 & 0 & \prod_{i=1}^{g-1} a_i \end{pmatrix} \mathbf{H} \\ -\left(\prod_{i=1}^{g} a_i\right) \mathbf{I} \end{pmatrix} \eta = \mathbf{B} \, \eta' \tag{12}$$

where $\mathbf{I}$ is the identity matrix, the coefficients a_i are always definite and must be nonnull, the elements of matrix $\mathbf{H}$ are always definite, and all the elements of $\mathbf{B}$ are always definite, as required.

On the other hand, in [9] it is considered a kinematic solution with redundant information (dim($\dot{q}_a$)>m) applying weighted left pseudoinverse to (10):

$$\dot{q}_{na} = -\left(A_{na}^T \left(\sqrt{\mu_{na}}\right)^T \sqrt{\mu_{na}} \, A_{na}\right)^{-1} A_{na}^T \left(\sqrt{\mu_{na}}\right)^T \sqrt{\mu_a} \, A_a \, \dot{q}_a \,. \tag{13}$$

where $\left(\sqrt{\mu_{na}}, \sqrt{\mu_a}\right)$ are the pre-multiplying weight matrices in (10) and, again, singularity arises when matrix A_{na} loses its full rank or equivalently when $\left|A_{na}^T \, A_{na}\right| = 0$.

2.3 Practical Use of Kinematics Singularity

When singularity arises for an m-set of assigned velocities there are two approaches:

- *Loss of degrees of mobility:* in order to avoid incompatibility the assigned velocities are coordinated properly, what implies a loss of degrees of mobility.
- *Kinematics Incompatibility:* no type of coordination for the assigned velocities is considered, so the kinematic incompatibility is not solved. If the assigned velocities are wheel velocities (forward kinematics), slip (due to the incompatibility, not because of accelerations) is inevitable. If they are WMR velocities (inverse kinematics), impossible (infinite) control action values are obtained.

In the same way, the singularity of a redundant forward kinematics (13) would produce an infinite error in the estimation of the WMR velocity vector.

Therefore, it is obtained the following criterion: *singularity* (i.e. mobility degree loss, slip, impossible control actions, or infinite error in the estimation) *has to be avoided.* Moreover, *nearness to singularity is neither desirable* since it implies: high amplification of wheel velocities' error (redundant and non-redundant forward kinematics) or high values for wheel velocities (non-redundant inverse kinematics).

If the singularity depends on the steering angles of *orientable* or *castor* wheels the previous criterion is a *planning criterion*, i.e. the upper level planner (path generator) has to develop paths not close to singularities, otherwise it becomes *design criterion*.

3 Motion Planning for Wheeled Mobile Robots

3.1 Introduction

Given a starting and ending configuration of a given WMR, a motion planning problem consists of automatically computing a collision-free path. This gives rise to the famous *piano mover problem*, i.e. any solution appears as a path in the admissible (i.e. collision-free) *configuration space*. Many papers have proposed general, exact, approximate, efficient ... methods in order to represent and explore this admissible configuration space: e.g. cellular decomposition, polygon representation, etc. (see [1] for a synthesis of these approaches). One classical approach is based on *tree graphs* whose leafs are the WMR posture and whose branches are the paths from one posture to another. Then, the planner checks, during the construction of the tree graph, if the goal has been achieved.

In order to avoid the high computational cost of the tree-graph method, it was developed the *roadmap* technique that builds a graph whose nodes are collision-free configurations and whose edges denote the presence of collision-free paths between two configurations. The roadmaps tend to capture both the coverage and connectivity of the configuration space and replace the concept of deterministic completeness by the concept of probabilistic completeness.

However, numerous classical methods work only when the WMR is holonomic and not when there is some *non-holonomic constraint* between its configuration parameters. In order to overcome this, in [2] it is developed a planner that firstly generates a collision-free path ignoring the non-holonomic constraints and afterwards the path is transformed into one that is feasible with respect to these constraints.

On the other hand, other planners are *specific for one task*, e.g. in [3] it is presented a planner for parallel parking based on a geometric characterization for collision avoidance. Moreover, other types of approaches do not *explicitly* generate collision-free paths; instead, they integrate the WMR motion planning with the WMR control using tools like *fuzzy*, neural networks, reactive architecture, etc. For example, in [4] it is used artificial potential fields: the WMR is attracted by the objective configuration and repelled by the obstacles.

Furthermore, if it is associated a time value to each point of the path it becomes a trajectory; otherwise, it is usually used a forward constant velocity across the path.

3.2 Cost Index Based on Kinematics Singularity

Here it is introduced a *cost index* based on kinematics singularity that is useful for many types of planners (based on tree graphs, roadmaps, etc.), since it allows to choose the path with minimum cost index among several possible collision-free paths.

In the cost index it will be weighted the nearness to singularity of forward and inverse kinematics. This will allow avoiding singularity and nearness to singularity, i.e. high amplification of the WMR velocities' error or high values for wheel velocities.

Similarly to robotic manipulators, the singularity of *inverse kinematic models* can be deal with a null velocity on the path at the singularity point, which is equivalent to a loss of degrees of mobility. It implies to stop the WMR in order to reorientate it and/or its wheels, as it is pointed out in [10] for the five types of WMR classified according to [6]. This may be appropriate when there is not much space available (e.g. for parking maneuvers) but not in a general case, since it involves an important waste of time. Therefore, this option will not be considered here.

The nearness to singularity of *forward kinematic models* produces high amplification of the WMR velocities' error, what implies a tracking error if the assigned wheel velocities are actuated wheel velocities or an estimation error if they are sensed wheel velocities. Both types of forward models will be considered in the cost index.

Therefore, it is proposed the following *cost index*:

$$J = \sum_{i=1}^{N} \left(\frac{1}{f_1\left(\left|\mathbf{B}_a\right|_{\mathrm{inv}\,i}\right)} + \frac{f_2(N-i+1)}{f_3\left(\left|\mathbf{B}_a\right|_{\mathrm{fwd\,act}\,i}\right)} + \frac{f_4(N-i+1)}{f_5\left(\left|\mathbf{A}_{na}^{T}\,\mathbf{A}_{na}\right|_{\mathrm{fwd\,sensed}\,i}\right)} + f_6\left(\dot{\boldsymbol{\beta}}_{o\,i}\right) \right) + f_7(D), \quad (14)$$

where N is the number of branches/edges of the path in the tree-graph/roadmap; f_i is a generic non-linear function; $|\mathbf{B}_a|_{\mathrm{inv}\,i}$ is the singularity of the inverse kinematic model; $|\mathbf{B}_a|_{\mathrm{fwd\,act}\,i}$ is de singularity of the forward models with actuated wheel velocities as assigned; $\left|\mathbf{A}_{na}^{T}\,\mathbf{A}_{na}\right|_{\mathrm{fwd\,sensed}\,i}$ is de singularity of the forward model with redundant sensed wheel velocities; $\dot{\boldsymbol{\beta}}_{oi}$ is the steering velocity vector of all the *orientable* wheels; and D is the length or distance of the collision-free path.

Note that, the singularity of forward models has been multiplied by $f_j\,(N-i+1)$ since the tracking/estimation error of the initial branches/edges is more important because it is propagated across the whole path. However, in order to limit the uncertainty of the estimation other global or local position sensors are required.

Note also that, it has been introduced the steering velocities of the *orientable* wheels because they are not present in the velocity vector $\dot{\mathbf{q}}$, see (2).

3.3 Motion Planning for an Industrial Forklift

The cost index of the previous subsection will be particularized to the case of the industrial forklift of Fig. 3, which is equivalent to the tricycle WMR, where the origin of R (tracking point) has been located at the middle point of the *fixed* wheels. The traction of this industrial forklift is given by both *fixed* wheels, which are *properly coordinated* through a differential mechanism depending on the steering angle of the *orientable* wheel. Moreover, this WMR has three encoders measuring the rotation of both *fixed* wheels and the steering angle of the *orientable* wheel.

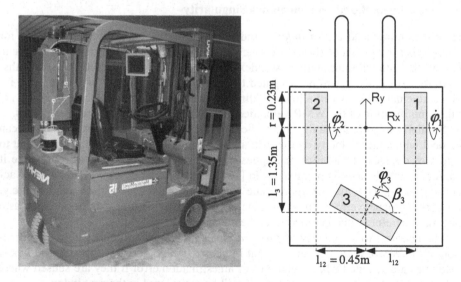

Fig. 3. Industrial forklift Nichiyu FBT15 series 65 and equivalent tricycle representation

The composite equation (4) of this WMR results:

$$\mathbf{v}_{slip} = \begin{pmatrix} \mathbf{v}_{slip\,1} \\ \mathbf{v}_{slip\,2} \\ \mathbf{v}_{slip\,3} \end{pmatrix} = \left(\begin{array}{ccc|ccc} 1 & 0 & 0 & 0 & 0 & 0 \\ 0 & 1 & l_{12} & r & 0 & 0 \\ 1 & 0 & 0 & 0 & 0 & 0 \\ 0 & 1 & -l_{12} & 0 & r & 0 \\ \cos\beta_3 & \sin\beta_3 & l_3\cos\beta_3 & 0 & 0 & 0 \\ -\sin\beta_3 & \cos\beta_3 & -l_3\sin\beta_3 & 0 & 0 & r \end{array} \right) \begin{pmatrix} {}^{\bar{R}}\dot{\mathbf{p}} \\ \dot{\varphi}_1 \\ \dot{\varphi}_2 \\ \dot{\varphi}_3 \end{pmatrix}. \qquad (15)$$

Under the no-slip condition, a kinematic solution (12) is:

$$\begin{pmatrix} \dot{\mathbf{p}} \\ \dot{\varphi}_1 \\ \dot{\varphi}_2 \\ \dot{\varphi}_3 \end{pmatrix} = \begin{pmatrix} 0 \\ -l_3\cos\beta_3 \\ \sin\beta_3 \\ (L\sin\beta_3 - l_3\cos\beta_3)/r \\ (L\sin\beta_3 + l_3\cos\beta_3)/r \\ l_3/r \end{pmatrix} \eta \cdot \tag{16}$$

For the redundant forward kinematics, (10) is particularized to:

$$\begin{pmatrix} 1 & 0 & 0 \\ 0 & 1 & l_{12} \\ 0 & 1 & -l_{12} \\ \cos\beta_3 & \sin\beta_3 & l_3\cos\beta_3 \end{pmatrix} \dot{\mathbf{p}} = - \begin{pmatrix} 0 & 0 \\ r & 0 \\ 0 & r \\ 0 & 0 \end{pmatrix} \begin{pmatrix} \dot{\varphi}_1 \\ \dot{\varphi}_2 \end{pmatrix} \rightarrow \mathbf{A}_{nap} \dot{\mathbf{p}} = - \begin{pmatrix} 0 & 0 \\ r & 0 \\ 0 & r \\ 0 & 0 \end{pmatrix} \begin{pmatrix} \dot{\varphi}_1 \\ \dot{\varphi}_2 \end{pmatrix}. \tag{17}$$

where it has been considered together the first and third equation of (15), and the last equation (used only to compute $\dot{\varphi}_3$) has been obviated.

Therefore, the kinematics singularity is given by:

$$\eta = v_y \rightarrow \left| \mathbf{B}_a \right|_{inv} = -l_3\cos\beta_3 = 0 \rightarrow \beta_3 = \pm 90°$$

$$\eta = \dot{\varphi}_1 \rightarrow \left| \mathbf{B}_a \right|_{fwd\,act1} = (l_{12}\sin\beta_3 - l_3\cos\beta_3)/r = 0 \rightarrow \beta_3 = \begin{cases} \text{atan}(l_3/l_{12}) \\ \text{atan}(l_3/l_{12}) + 180° \end{cases}$$

$$\eta = \dot{\varphi}_2 \rightarrow \left| \mathbf{B}_a \right|_{fwd\,act2} = (l_{12}\sin\beta_3 + l_3\cos\beta_3)/r = 0 \rightarrow \beta_3 = \begin{cases} -\text{atan}(l_3/l_{12}) \\ -\text{atan}(l_3/l_{12}) + 180' \end{cases} \tag{18}$$

$$\dot{\mathbf{q}}_a = (\dot{\varphi}_1, \dot{\varphi}_2) \rightarrow \left| \mathbf{A}_{nap}^T \mathbf{A}_{nap} \right|_{fwd\,sensed} = 0 \rightarrow \text{No solution, never singular.}$$

The cost index (14) will be particularized to:

$$J = \sum_{i=1}^{N} \left(\frac{K_1}{\left| \mathbf{B}_a \right|_{inv\,i}^2} + \frac{K_2(N-i+1)}{\max\left(\left| \mathbf{B}_a \right|_{fwd\,act1\,i}^2, M \right)} + \frac{K_3(N-i+1)}{\max\left(\left| \mathbf{B}_a \right|_{fwd\,act2\,i}^2, M \right)} + \frac{K_4(N-i+1)}{\left| \mathbf{A}_{nap}^T \mathbf{A}_{nap} \right|_{fwd\,sensed\,i}^2} \right) + \\ + \sum_{i=1}^{N} \left(K_5 \left(\dot{\beta}_{3\,i} \right)^2 \right) + D, \tag{19}$$

where K_j is the weight of each term in the cost index and M is a kind of singularity saturation in order to not reduce in excess the WMR maneuverability.

Note that the industrial forklift has one degree of mobility ($m = 1$), i.e. one instantaneous degree of freedom, that allows to specify a forward tracking velocity v_y. It has another non-instantaneous degree of freedom through the angle β_3 of the *orientable* wheel that allows turning. Therefore, this WMR can track 2-dimensional paths.

In order to obtain simulation results, it will be considered the *tree graph technique* together with the previous cost index. It will be used a constant forward velocity on the path, e.g. $v_y = 1$ m/s, and the following motion equations between *leaves*/samples:

$$x_{k+1} = x_k + (v_y/\omega)(\sin(\theta_k + \omega T) - \sin\theta_k)$$
$$y_{k+1} = y_k - (v_y/\omega)(\cos(\theta_k + \omega T) - \cos\theta_k) \qquad \theta_{k+1} = \theta_k + \omega T, \tag{20}$$

where T is the sample time, and it has been considered a constant forward motion v_y and a constant turning motion ω between samples.

If the WMR angular velocity ω is null, it must be used the following equations:

$$x_{k+1} = x_k + v_y T \cos\theta_k \qquad y_{k+1} = y_k + v_y T \sin\theta_k \qquad \theta_{k+1} = \theta_k. \tag{21}$$

Note that the distance D of each collision-free path results $v_y \cdot T \cdot N$.

For the construction of the tree graph it will be considered three possible steering velocities for the *orientable* wheel: $\{-\dot\beta_{3\ max}, 0, \dot\beta_{3\ max}\}$. During the construction of the tree graph it will be verified if the goal has been achieved within a tolerance.

The parameters used for the simulations results of Fig. 4 are: $v_y = 1$ m/s, T = 0.5 s, N = 22, $\dot\beta_{3\ max} = 0.4$ rad/s, M = 0.01, $K_1 = K_5 = 18$, $K_2 = K_3 = K_4 = 3$; and it has been considered two rectangular obstacles that represent two warehouse shelves. The goal WMR posture **p** in the first example of Fig. 4 is (5, 0, any): the continuous thick line is the path with minimum cost index; the dashed thick line is the path with minimum distance; the continuous thin lines are *some* (a sample) of the collision-free paths.

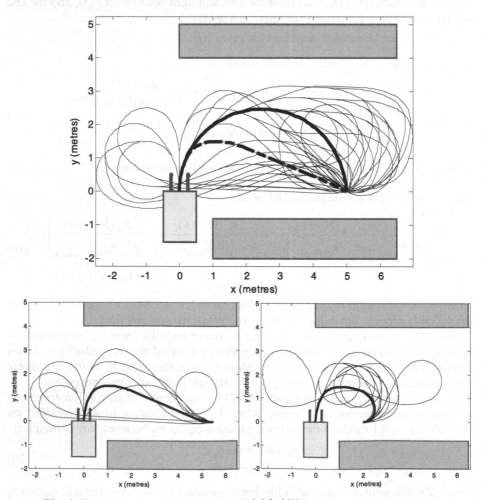

Fig. 4. Simulation examples for the industrial forklift in a warehouse environment

Meanwhile, the goal WMR posture **p** for the second and third example of Fig. 4 is (5.5, 0, 0) and (2, 0, π) respectively. Again, the continuous thick line is the path with minimum cost index and the continuous thin lines are some of the collision-free paths.

4 Conclusions

In a previous work [5] the authors had characterized the singularity of WMR kinematics. In this paper it has been shown how to use WMR singularity or nearness to WMR singularity for motion planning. In particular, it has been proposed a cost index that assesses the nearness to singularity of forward and inverse kinematic models.

This cost index can be used straightforward for many planning techniques (tree graphs, roadmaps, etc.) in order to choose one path among several possible collision-free paths. Therefore, the chosen path would avoid not only slip and impossible control actions (i.e. the singularity of forward and inverse kinematic models) but also high amplification of wheel velocities' error and high values for wheel velocities (i.e. the nearness to the singularity of forward and inverse kinematic models).

To illustrate the applications of the proposed approach it has been considered an industrial forklift that is equivalent to the tricycle WMR. Finally, several results have been shown for this WMR in a simulated environment.

It is suggested as further work to integrate the presented motion planning with other classical techniques like artificial potential fields, fuzzy planners, etc.

Acknowledgments. This work was supported in part by the Spanish Government: Research Projects DPI2004-07417-C04-01 and BIA2005-09377-C03-02.

References

1. Latombe, J.-C.: Robot Motion Planning, ch. 7, Kluwer Academic Publishers, Dordrecht (1991)
2. Laumond, J.-P., Jacobs, P.E., Taïx, M., Murray, M.: A motion planner for nonholonomic mobile robots. IEEE Trans. on Robotics and Automation 10(5), 577–593 (1994)
3. Gracia, L., Tornero, J.: Geometric parallel parking planner for car-like vehicles. In: Industrial Simulation Conference, Valencia, Spain, pp. 357–361 (2003)
4. Borenstein, J., Koren, Y.: Real-time obstacle avoidance for fast mobile robots. IEEE Transactions on Systems Man and Cybernetics 19, 1179–1187 (1989)
5. Gracia, L., Tornero, J.: Kinematic modeling and singularity of wheeled mobile robots. Advanced Robotics 21(7), 793–816 (2007)
6. Campion, G., Bastin, G., D'Andrea-Novel, B.: Structural properties and classification of kinematic and dynamic models of wheeled mobile robots. IEEE Transactions on Robotics and Automation 12(1), 47–61 (1996)
7. Muir, P.F., Neuman, C.P.: Kinematic modeling of wheeled mobile robots. Journal of Robotic Systems 4(2), 281–329 (1987)
8. Alexander, J.C., Maddocks, J.H.: On the kinematics of wheeled mobile robots. The International Journal of Robotics Research 8(5), 15–27 (1989)
9. Gracia, L., Tornero, J.: Kinematic modeling of wheeled mobile robots with slip. Advanced Robotics 21(11), 1253–1279 (2007)
10. Gracia, L., Tornero, J.: Kinematic control of wheeled mobile robots. Latin American Applied Research 37(4) (2007)

Author Index

Lecture Notes in Computer Science

Sublibrary 6: Image Processing, Computer Vision, Pattern Recognition, and Graphics

Vol. 4170: J. Ponce, M. Hebert, C. Schmid, A. Zisserman (Eds.), Toward Category-Level Object Recognition. XI, 618 pages. 2006.

Vol. 4153: N. Zheng, X. Jiang, X. Lan (Eds.), Advances in Machine Vision, Image Processing, and Pattern Analysis. XIII, 506 pages. 2006.

Vol. 4142: A. Campilho, M. Kamel (Eds.), Image Analysis and Recognition, Part II. XXVII, 923 pages. 2006.

Vol. 4141: A. Campilho, M. Kamel (Eds.), Image Analysis and Recognition, Part I. XXVIII, 939 pages. 2006.

Vol. 4122: R. Stiefelhagen, J.S. Garofolo (Eds.), Multimodal Technologies for Perception of Humans. XII, 360 pages. 2007.

Vol. 4109: D.-Y. Yeung, J.T. Kwok, A. Fred, F. Roli, D. de Ridder (Eds.), Structural, Syntactic, and Statistical Pattern Recognition. XXI, 939 pages. 2006.

Vol. 4091: G.-Z. Yang, T. Jiang, D. Shen, L. Gu, J. Yang (Eds.), Medical Imaging and Augmented Reality. XIII, 399 pages. 2006.

Vol. 4073: A. Butz, B. Fisher, A. Krüger, P. Olivier (Eds.), Smart Graphics. XI, 263 pages. 2006.

Vol. 4069: F.J. Perales, R.B. Fisher (Eds.), Articulated Motion and Deformable Objects. XV, 526 pages. 2006.

Vol. 4057: J.P.W. Pluim, B. Likar, F.A. Gerritsen (Eds.), Biomedical Image Registration. XII, 324 pages. 2006.

Vol. 4046: S.M. Astley, M. Brady, C. Rose, R. Zwiggelaar (Eds.), Digital Mammography. XVI, 654 pages. 2006.

Vol. 4040: R. Reulke, U. Eckardt, B. Flach, U. Knauer, K. Polthier (Eds.), Combinatorial Image Analysis. XII, 482 pages. 2006.

Vol. 4035: T. Nishita, Q. Peng, H.-P. Seidel (Eds.), Advances in Computer Graphics. XX, 771 pages. 2006.

Vol. 3979: T.S. Huang, N. Sebe, M.S. Lew, V. Pavlović, M. Kölsch, A. Galata, B. Kisačanin (Eds.), Computer Vision in Human-Computer Interaction. XII, 121 pages. 2006.

Vol. 3954: A. Leonardis, H. Bischof, A. Pinz (Eds.), Computer Vision – ECCV 2006, Part IV. XVII, 613 pages. 2006.

Vol. 3953: A. Leonardis, H. Bischof, A. Pinz (Eds.), Computer Vision – ECCV 2006, Part III. XVII, 649 pages. 2006.

Vol. 3952: A. Leonardis, H. Bischof, A. Pinz (Eds.), Computer Vision – ECCV 2006, Part II. XVII, 661 pages. 2006.

Vol. 3951: A. Leonardis, H. Bischof, A. Pinz (Eds.), Computer Vision – ECCV 2006, Part I. XXXV, 639 pages. 2006.

Vol. 3948: H.I. Christensen, H.-H. Nagel (Eds.), Cognitive Vision Systems. VIII, 367 pages. 2006.

Vol. 3926: W. Liu, J. Lladós (Eds.), Graphics Recognition. XII, 428 pages. 2006.

Vol. 3872: H. Bunke, A.L. Spitz (Eds.), Document Analysis Systems VII. XIII, 630 pages. 2006.

Vol. 3852: P.J. Narayanan, S.K. Nayar, H.-Y. Shum (Eds.), Computer Vision – ACCV 2006, Part II. XXXI, 977 pages. 2006.

Vol. 3851: P.J. Narayanan, S.K. Nayar, H.-Y. Shum (Eds.), Computer Vision – ACCV 2006, Part I. XXXI, 973 pages. 2006.

Vol. 3832: D. Zhang, A.K. Jain (Eds.), Advances in Biometrics. XX, 796 pages. 2005.

Vol. 3736: S. Bres, R. Laurini (Eds.), Visual Information and Information Systems. XI, 291 pages. 2006.

Vol. 3667: W.J. MacLean (Ed.), Spatial Coherence for Visual Motion Analysis. IX, 141 pages. 2006.

Vol. 3417: B. Jähne, R. Mester, E. Barth, H. Scharr (Eds.), Complex Motion. X, 235 pages. 2007.

Vol. 2396: T.M. Caelli, A. Amin, R.P.W. Duin, M.S. Kamel, D. de Ridder (Eds.), Structural, Syntactic, and Statistical Pattern Recognition. XVI, 863 pages. 2002.

Vol. 1679: C. Taylor, A. Colchester (Eds.), Medical Image Computing and Computer-Assisted Intervention – MICCAI'99. XXI, 1240 pages. 1999.